KEYS TO THE ARCANA

This remarkable twelfth-century Qur'anic commentary by Muḥammad b. ʿAbd al-Karīm al-Shahrastānī is preserved in a single manuscript in Tehran and marks the achievement of a lifelong, arduous quest for knowledge. The introduction and opening chapter of this virtually unknown work are presented here in a bilingual edition with an introduction and contextual notes by Dr Toby Mayer. In *Keys to the Arcana*, Shahrastānī breaks down the text of the Qur'an and analyses it from a linguistic point of view, with reference to the history of Qur'anic interpretation. The author's aim is to use an elaborate set of complementary concepts – the 'keys' of the work's title – to unearth the esoteric meanings of the Qur'anic verses. Dr. Mayer's meticulous translation of Shahrastānī's Introduction and Commentary on *Sūrat al-Fātiḥa*, supplemented by the Arabic text, allows access to this unique work for the first time.

TOBY MAYER is a Research Associate at The Institute of Ismaili Studies, London, where he teaches courses on Sufism and Tafsīr. After completing his undergraduate degree in Indian Studies at the University of Cambridge, he went on to study Medieval Arabic thought at the University of Oxford, where he did his doctoral thesis on Ibn Sīnā's *Book of Allusions* (*Kitāb al-Ishārāt*). In conjunction with Professor Wilferd Madelung, he has published a critical edition and translation of Shahrastānī's *Kitāb Muṣāraʿat al-falāsifa*, entitled *Struggling with the Philosopher: A Refutation of Avicenna's Metaphysics* (2001). Dr. Mayer has previously held a lectureship in Islamic philosophy and mysticism at the School of Oriental and African Studies (SOAS), University of London.

The Institute of Ismaili Studies

Qur'anic Studies Series, 6

Series editor, Omar Alí-de-Unzaga

Previously published titles:

Suha Taji-Farouki, editor,
Modern Muslim Intellectuals and the Qur'an
(2004)

Abdullah Saeed, editor,
Approaches to the Qur'an in Contemporary Indonesia
(2005)

Annabel Keeler
Sufi Hermeneutics: The Qur'an Commentary of Rashīd al-Dīn Maybudī
(2006)

Fahmida Suleman, editor,
Word of God, Art of Man: The Qur'an and its Creative Expressions
(2007)

Feras Hamza and Sajjad Rizvi, editors, with Farhana Mayer,
An Anthology of Qur'anic Commentaries,
Volume I: On the Nature of the Divine
(2008)

Keys to the Arcana

Shahrastānī's esoteric commentary on the Qur'an

A translation of the commentary on *Sūrat al-Fātiḥa* from Muḥammad b. ʿAbd al-Karīm al-Shahrastānī's ***Mafātīḥ al-asrār wa maṣābīḥ al-abrār***

BY

TOBY MAYER

With the Arabic text reproduced from the edition by M. A. Adharshab

UNIVERSITY PRESS

in association with

THE INSTITUTE OF ISMAILI STUDIES

LONDON

OXFORD
UNIVERSITY PRESS

Great Clarendon Street, Oxford OX2 6DP
Oxford University Press is a department of the University of Oxford.
It furthers the University's objective of excellence in research, scholarship,
and education by publishing worldwide in
Oxford New York
Auckland Cape Town Dar es Salaam Hong Kong Karachi
Kuala Lumpur Madrid Melbourne Mexico City Nairobi
New Delhi Shanghai Taipei Toronto

With offices in

Argentina Austria Brazil Chile Czech Republic France Greece
Guatemala Hungary Italy Japan Poland Portugal Singapore
South Korea Switzerland Thailand Turkey Ukraine Vietnam

Oxford is a registered trade mark of Oxford University Press
in the UK and in certain other countries

Published in the United States
by Oxford University Press Inc., New York

First published 2009

British Library Cataloguing in Publication Data
Data available

Library of Congress Cataloging in Publication Data
Data available

Arabic verse, *Sūrat al-Fātiḥa*:
Typography by Tom Milo using Win Soft Tasmeem
Typeset by John Saunders Design & Production
Printed in Great Britain
on acid-free paper by
MPG Books Group

ISBN 978-0-19-953365-7

1 3 5 7 9 10 8 6 4 2

The Institute of Ismaili Studies

The Institute of Ismaili Studies was established in 1977 with the objectives of promoting scholarship and learning on Islam, in historical as well as contemporary contexts, and fostering better understanding of Islam's relationship with other societies and faiths.

The Institute's programmes encourage a perspective which is not confined to the theological and religious heritage of Islam, but seeks to explore the relationship of religious ideas to broader dimensions of society and culture. The programmes thus *encourage* an interdisciplinary approach to Islamic history and thought. Particular attention is given to the issues of modernity that arise as Muslims seek to relate their heritage to the contemporary situation.

Within the Islamic tradition, the Institute promotes research on those areas which have, to date, received relatively little attention from scholars. These include the intellectual and literary expressions of Shiʿism in general and Ismailism in particular.

The Institute's objectives are realised through concrete programmes and activities organised by various departments of the Institute, at times in collaboration with other institutions of learning. These programmes and activities are informed by the full range of cultures in which Islam is practised today. From the Middle East, South and Central Asia, and Africa to the industrialised societies in the West, they consider the variety of contexts which shape the ideals, beliefs and practices of the faith.

In facilitating the *Qur'anic Studies Series* and other publications, the Institute's sole purpose is to encourage original research and analysis of relevant issues, which often leads to diverse views and interpretations. While every effort is made to ensure that the publications are of a high academic standard, the opinions expressed in these publications must be understood as belonging to their authors alone.

QUR'ANIC STUDIES SERIES

THE QUR'AN has been an inexhaustible source of intellectual and spiritual reflection in Islamic history, giving rise to ever-proliferating commentaries and interpretations. Many of these have remained a realm for specialists due to their scholarly demands. Others, more widely read, remain untranslated from the primary language of their composition. This series aims to make some of these materials from a broad chronological range – the formative centuries of Islam to the present day – available to a wider readership through translation and publication in English, accompanied where necessary by introductory or explanatory materials. The series will also include contextual-analytical and survey studies of these primary materials.

Throughout this series and others like it which may appear in the future, the aim is to allow the materials to speak for themselves. Not surprisingly, in the Muslim world where its scriptural sources continue to command passionate interest and commitment, the Qur'an has been subject to contending, often antithetical ideas and interpretations. This series takes no sides in these debates. The aim rather is to place on record the rich diversity and plurality of approaches and opinions which have appealed to the Qur'an throughout history (and even more so today). The breadth of this range, however partisan or controversial individual presentations within it may be, is instructive in itself. While there is always room in such matters for personal preferences, commitment to particular traditions of belief, and scholarly evaluations, much is to be gained by a simple appreciation, not always evident today, of the enormous wealth of intellectual effort that has been devoted to the Qur'an from the earliest times. It is hoped that through this objective, this series will prove of use to scholars and students in Qur'anic Studies as well as other allied and relevant fields.

Contents

Tables and diagram

Note on transliteration, diagram and abbreviations

Standard conventions for transliterating Arabic have been used in the English part of the text, as they are found for instance in the *International Journal of Middle Eastern Studies*. This system represents Arabic expressions as they would be if read aloud. Hence, for example, *tāʾ marbūṭa* is only represented as *-at* when the relevant word is in the construct state, otherwise as *-a*. Technical terms and citations in transliteration have been italicised. More common terms such as Qurʾān, ḥadīth, Ismāʿīlī, Sunnī, Shīʿī, Ṣūfī, although fully transliterated, have not been italicised. A transliteration and translation of the *Sūrat al-Fātiḥa* has been inserted just before the exegesis of the Exordium, to provide the reader with an easy reference for the numerous citations from this chapter. The verses have not been numbered, since the numeration of the verses constitutes a key point in Shahrastānī's discussion.

The Exordium diagram

The diagram on p. 186 rendering the schematic representation of the arcana of the Exordium, is based directly on folio 44A, of Ms 8086/B78, the unicum manuscript held at the library of the National Consultative Assembly, Tehran.

Abbreviations

EI[1] *Encyclopaedia of Islam*, 1st edition (Leiden, 1913–1934).
EI[2] *Encyclopaedia of Islam*, 2nd edition (Leiden, 1960–2002).
EIr *Encyclopaedia Iranica*, ed. Ehsan Yarshater (London and New York, 1985).

Foreword

One of the more exciting developments in Islamic Studies over the past few decades has resulted in a radically new assessment of the theological outlook and personality of the celebrated author of the *Book of Religions and Sects (Kitāb al-Milal wa'l-niḥal)*, Muḥammad b. ʿAbd al-Karīm al-Shahrastānī (d. 548/1153). Shahrastānī's unconventional approach to the variety of religious and philosophical traditions had already provoked certain questions among his contemporaries, to be sure, and some indeed suspected him of secret sympathies for the 'people of the fortresses', i.e. the Nizārī Ismāʿīlīs. But his reputation as a mainstream Sunnī thinker of the Ashʿarī school had been firmly established by respected biographers such as Ibn Khallikān and Tāj al-Dīn al-Subkī, and remained for a long time unchallenged in modern scholarship as well. Especially Shahrastānī's major theological treatise, the *Nihāyat al-aqdām fī ʿilm al-kalām*, seemed to confirm this perception in the eyes of most students of Islamic thought. However, the question of his secret Ismāʿīlī affinities was again put on the table in 1956, when Sayyid M. R. Jalālī-Nāʾīnī drew attention, for the first time, to the work whose first part appears in the present volume in a revised edition[1] along with a fully annotated translation and a thoughtful introduction by Toby Mayer, the *Mafātīḥ al-asrār wa maṣābīḥ al-abrār*.

Although Jalālī-Nāʾīnī described the *Mafātīḥ al-asrār* only very briefly as a major commentary on the first two chapters of the Qurʾān, preserved in a Tehran unicum of 'nearly 1000 pages',[2] he nevertheless pointed to its importance as one among Shahrastānī's later works, and, in effect, boldly ventured at that time that it might indeed reveal those Ismāʿīlī beliefs which, he suggested, the theologian had earlier been compelled to hide behind an 'Ashʿarī mask', due to his position at the court of the Saljūq Sultan Sanjar (d. 552/1157).[3] Jalālī-Nāʾīnī himself seems to have somewhat modified his position later, apparently now preferring to adopt Shahrastānī among the Shīʿa more generally,[4] and his original suggestion remained without echo until M. T. Dānish-pazhūh, adducing evidence from a number of other angles, came forward with a colourful portrait of 'the grand dāʿī from Shahrastāna'.[5] In the West, the Ismāʿīlī thesis received strong support for the first time in 1974. In a seminal lecture delivered to the 7th Congress of Arabic and Islamic Studies held in Göttingen, W. Madelung, focussing on Shahrastānī's *Kitāb al-Muṣāraʿa*, sharply argued in favour of an Ismāʿīlī rather than an Ashʿarī inspiration of this famous anti-philosophical treatise.[6] But the first in-depth study of the *Mafātīḥ al-asrār* was undertaken only in the eighties of the past century. Having thoroughly analysed the Arabic text for a period of ten years (1983-93) with his students at the École Pratique des Hautes Études in Paris, G. Monnot concluded unequivocally that the full expression of Shahrastānī's thought is to be sought in this Qurʾānic commentary, and that it propounds evidently a Nizārī Ismāʿīlī doctrine.[7]

Yet another reaction from the traditional camp was still to come. Apart from a simple attempt to dismiss the *Mafātīḥ al-asrār* as spurious,[8] mention must be made here of the lengthy discussion of the 'Ismāʿīlī hypothesis' by D. Gimaret in his introduction to what is unquestionably now the most authoritative European translation of the *Kitāb al-Milal wa'l-niḥal*.[9] Reiterating against Madelung (and his close colleague Monnot, without naming him) the traditional view that the *Nihāyat al-aqdām* should be seen as nothing less than a systematic defence (rather than an exposition of the limits) of Ashʿarism, Gimaret nevertheless recognised the great theologian's originality, adduced himself much of the evidence that speaks against a one-sidedly Sunnī presentation of his overall thought, and frankly admitted that 'it is undeniable that certain aspects of Shahrastānī's personal doctrine as expressed in the *Muṣāraʿa*, the *Majlis*,[10] and indeed the *Milal* itself, manifestly evoke major themes of Ismāʿīlism'.[11] Oddly enough, he did not include the *Mafātīḥ al-asrār* into his consideration on the grounds that the text was not available to him.

All the more, the present publication of the first volume of the *Mafātīḥ* both in Arabic and in English fills an obvious gap, and it is my privilege to welcome it here. Toby Mayer's introduction discusses the relevant issues with great perception, and it is a pleasure to follow his subtle argument step by step. As Mayer shows in detail, the *Mafātīḥ* not only reflects Shahrastānī's vast learning in the traditional Qurʾānic sciences, but also his reception of Shīʿī and Ṣūfī hermeneutics as transmitted from the 'family of the Prophet', as well as being evidence of a profoundly original religious thought based on specifically Nizārī Ismāʿīlī key concepts. The authenticity of the text seems beyond question given that numerous parallels with

Shahrastānī's other works have been identified, including an explicit cross-reference on folio 170B of the manuscript to his discussion of the two prototypes of opposing views, the 'Sabians' and the 'Ḥanīfs', in the *Kitāb al-Milal.*

As Mayer also suggests, the anonymous teacher in Qur'ānic arcana, to whom Shahrastānī alludes in the autobiographical part, presenting him in the role of the no less mysterious 'servant of God' of Q. 18:65, or Khiḍr, may well have been no one else than Ḥasan-i Ṣabbāḥ himself. A word may be added here on the initiatory role of Khiḍr in Muslim traditions. While this role of the 'eternal saint' has hardly been studied in Ismā'īlism,[12] it is, of course, profoundly rooted in Ṣūfism, and plays as such a prominent part in the Ṣūfī hermeneutics of Rashīd al-Dīn Maybudī.[13] It would seem, therefore, that Maybudī's *Kashf al-asrār* should also be considered among Shahrastānī's sources, particularly in view of the fact that both Qur'ānic commentaries share a common formal structure in so far as they both deal systematically with the exoteric meaning of every piece before going into the arcana. In any case, as Toby Mayer points out, the influence of the Ṣūfī milieu in which Shahrastānī moved as a student, should probably not be underestimated. One may also venture that it was thanks to the interest of an influential Shāfi'ī Ṣūfī family, the Banū Ḥamūya from Juwayn, that the *Mafātīḥ* has been preserved in the first place; for the only extant manuscript was copied in 667/1269 from the autograph for Ṣadr al-Dīn Ibrāhīm al-Ḥamū'ī (644/1247-722/1322), the learned Shaykh under whose guidance the Īlkhān Ghāzān Khān converted to Islam in 694/1295. His father, Sa'd al-Dīn al-Ḥamū'ī (d. *c.* 650/1232), was known for Shī'ī-esoteric leanings,[14] and their common ancestor, Abū'l-Ḥasan 'Alī b. Muḥammad b. Ḥamūya (d. 539/1144 in Nīshāpūr), was evidently a personal acquaintance of Shahrastānī himself.[15] Interestingly, the father of Abū'l-Ḥasan 'Alī and eponym of the family, Muḥammad b. Ḥamūya (d. 530/1135), was also known as a 'disciple of Khiḍr'![16]

Hermann Landolt

NOTES

1 *Editio princeps* by M. 'A. Ādharshab, vol. 1, Tehran, 1418/1997.

2 In fact, 434 folios. See the facsimile edition published in two volumes by the Iranian Centre for the Publication of Manuscripts, Tehran, 1368 Sh./1409/1989.

3 See Jalālī-Nā'īnī's edition of Afḍal al-Dīn Ṣadr Turka al-Iṣfahānī's *Tanqīḥ al-adilla wa'l-'ilal fī tarjamat Kitāb al-Milal wa'l-niḥal*, 2nd edn. Tehran, 1335 Sh./1956, introduction, pp. 13–14.

4 Jalālī-Nā'īnī, *Sharḥ-i ḥāl wa āthār-i Ḥujjat al-Ḥaqq Abū'l-Fatḥ Muḥammad b. 'Abd al-Karīm b. Aḥmad Shahrastānī*. Tehran, 1343 Sh./1964; idem, *Du Maktūb*. Tehran, 1369 Sh./1990, introduction, p. 9.

5 Dānish-pazhūh, Muḥammad Tāqī. 'Dā'ī al-Du'āt Tāj al-Dīn-i Shahrastāna', in *Nāma-yi āstān-i Quds*, vol. 8. 1347 Sh./1968.

6 Now published as *Struggling with the Philosopher*, ed. and tr. Wilferd Madelung and Toby Mayer, London, 2001. The same scholar also summarised his conclusions on a more general basis. See W. Madelung, 'Aspects of Ismā'īlī Theology: The Prophetic Chain and the God Beyond Being', in S. H. Nasr, ed. *Ismā'īlī Contributions to Islamic Culture*, Tehran, 1977, pp. 53–65.

7 Detailed summaries of G. Monnot's analyses were progressively published as 'Islam: Exégèse coranique' in *Annuaire de l'École Pratique des Hautes Études*, vols. 92 (1983–84) – 101 (1992-93). See also Monnot's article on Shahrastānī in *EI*[2], vol. ix, p. 214.

8 A.K. Kazi and J.G. Flynn, trs., *Muslim Sects and Divisions: The Section on Muslim Sects in Kitāb al-Milal wa'l-Niḥal*. London, Boston, Melbourne and Henley, 1984.

9 D. Gimaret and G. Monnot, trs., *Livre des religions et des sects*, vol. 1, Leuven, 1986; vol. 2, trs. J. Jolivet and G. Monnot, Leuven, 1993. My review of vol. 1 in *Bulletin critique des annales islamologiques* 24 (1988), pp. 63–65.

10 For a French translation of the *Majlis* (including the Persian text in the revised edition of Jalālī-Nā'īnī in *Du Maktūb*) see D. Steigerwald, *Majlis: Discours sur l'Ordre et la création*, Saint-Nicolas, 1998.

11 *Livre*, introduction, pp. 52–63, esp. 57f.

12 Note that the Fāṭimids are 'the Khiḍr of this period' (*Khiḍr-i dawr*) for Nāṣir-i Khusraw (*Dīwān* ed. Mujtabā Mīnuvī and Mahdī Muḥaqqiq, p. 68; cf. p. 246).

13 See A. Keeler, *Sufi Hermeneutics: The Qur'an Commentary of Rashīd al-Dīn Maybudī*, London, 2006.

14 See *EI*[2], vol. viii, p. 703.

15 See 'Alī b. Zayd al-Bayhaqī, *Tatimmat Ṣiwān al-hikma*, Lahore 1351/1932, p. 138, text also reproduced by Jalālī-Nā'īnī in *Du Maktūb*, introduction p. 36.

16 See J. Spencer Trimingham, *The Sufi Orders in Islam*, Oxford 1971, pp. 261f.

I

Translator's introduction

Context of the commentary

More than one context presents itself for Shahrastānī's accomplishment in his Qur'ān commentary, the first volume of which is presented here translated into English, based on Dr Muḥammad ʿAlī Ādharshab's *editio princeps.*[1] The work belongs to the great thinker's last years and, to judge from his own words, amounted for him to the achievement of an arduous quest. Expressed in the broadest terms, the latter's circumstances were the Seljuq period's counterpoints of exoteric and esoteric science, vying revelationist and philosophical epistemologies, and lastly Sunnism and different forms of Shīʿism (some revolutionary). These all find unexpected resolution in Shahrastānī's less known and chronologically later works, which are only now getting scholarly attention. But among these, the Qur'ān commentary – holding pride of place in any Muslim thinker's *oeuvre* through the prestige and foundationality of the divine Word within the tradition – is a witness of distinct value. It enshrines at its core a worldview sufficiently radical for some to have consigned it to pseudepigraphical status,[2] and for its very survival to have slenderly rested on a unicum manuscript held at the library of the National Consultative Assembly in Tehran.[3] Yet this precious – sadly incomplete – text preserves a superlative example of anagogic interpretation within Islamic culture.

While penetrating the *sensus anagogicus* of the Qur'ān in many ways represented the climax of our author's intellectual journey, to map the latter is hard through his own secrecy. The path may be tentatively reconstructed combining the limited materials available: references by contemporaries and in later *rijālī* works,[4] key evidence from the corpus of Naṣīr al-Dīn al-Ṭūsī (d. 672/1274) a century later, and finally, the striking but all too dark allusions by Shahrastānī himself to his own development. Abū'l-Fatḥ Muḥammad b. Abī'l-Qāsim ʿAbd al-Karīm b. Abī Bakr Aḥmad al-Shahrastānī, known as 'the most learned' (*al-afḍal*), 'proof of the Truth' (*ḥujjat al-Ḥaqq*) and 'the crown of religion' (*tāj al-dīn*), was most likely born in the year 479/1086 in the township of Shahrastāna (to be identified with the settlement near Nasā or Darreh Gaz close to the Iran-Turkmenistan border, not the towns of that name in Fārs and near Iṣfahān).[5] It was here that he would have received his earliest education, as well as in Gurgānj, the town of Khwārazm on the River Oxus/Jayḥūn.

At some point in his youth Shahrastānī left 'in quest of knowledge' (*fī ṭalab al-ʿilm*), journeying 140 miles south east to Ṭūs – famously linked with his epoch-making older contemporary Abū Ḥāmid Muḥammad al-Ghazālī (d. 505/1111). This first rite of passage – seemingly the real inception of Shahrastānī's intellectual quest – saw him attach himself to a figure who had actually been Ghazālī's fellow student, Abū'l-Muẓaffar Aḥmad b. Muḥammad b. al-Muẓaffar al-Khawāfī (d. 500/1106), chief justice (*walī al-qaḍā*) in Ṭūs and its surrounding districts. No common lawyer, Khawāfī is described as having been the 'foremost in speculation (*anẓar*) among his contemporaries and the most expert of them in the methods of disputation and jurisprudence [...]'.[6] He had studied, in his youth, under such famous figures as Abū Ibrāhīm al-Ḍarīr and al-Juwaynī, known as the '*imām al-ḥaramayn'* (d. 478/1085), who compared him with his other chief students in the famous statement reported by Subkī: 'Khawāfī's strong point is verification, Ghazālī's is speculation, and Kiyā's is explanation.'[7] Shahrastānī's thorough grounding in the Shāfiʿī rite is doubtless rooted in his early connection with this impressive legist.

Shahrastānī's search extended as he traveled to one of the world's original university towns, Nīshāpūr, which, in the 5th and 6th centuries AH, was a lure for scholars and intellectuals in eastern Islam, as well as having long been a forum for the mystical movement. Shahrastānī now studied under the greatest living pedagogues, no doubt benefiting from Nīshāpūr's new Niẓāmiyya college and making full use of its library.[8] It is probable that he here began to make his mark as a scholar and it has been argued that by the time he left Nīshāpūr, Shahrastānī was already operating as a teacher, not just a student.[9] Prominent among his teacher-mentors at this time is the name of Abū Naṣr ʿAbd al-Raḥīm b. ʿAbd al-Karīm b. Hawāzin al-Qushayrī (d. 514/1120), a scholar of wide fame and learning, skilled in jurisprudence, *uṣūl*, Ashʿarī theology, mathematics, rhetoric and belles-lettres. Though well known in his generation in his own right,[10] Abū Naṣr was in fact none other than the son of the celebrated Ashʿarī scholar, Ṣūfī theorist and mystical exegete, Abū'l-Qāsim al-Qushayrī (d. 465/1074).

A seeming trait of Shahrastānī's biography is that despite the mystical zeitgeist and the impingement of Ṣūfī influences throughout his milieu, the Ṣūfī strain of Islamic esoterism leaves no trace on his reputation or extant writings. Another example of a teacher with striking Ṣūfī connections is Abū'l-Ḥasan ʿAlī b. Aḥmad b. Muḥammad al-Aḥzam al-Madīnī (d. 494/1101) known as 'the caller to prayer' (*al-mu'adhdhin*), who appears to have supplied the young Shahrastānī's groundwork in Prophetic Tradition. Madīnī had himself supposedly been instructed in his youth by the great scholar of mysticism, Abū ʿAbd al-Raḥmān Muḥammad b. al-Ḥusayn al-Sulamī (d. 412/1021).[11] However, the most significant case of Shahrastānī's debt to a contemporary scholar chronicled as a Ṣūfī (e.g. by Subkī), may well be that of Abū'l-Qāsim Salmān al-Anṣārī (d. 512/ 1118).

Ṣūfī cynosures had taught the youthful Anṣārī, notably the aforementioned Abū'l-Qāsim al-Qushayrī as well as Abū Saʿīd b. Abī'l-Khayr (d. 440/1049). Though cited as among Anṣārī's teachers in *uṣūl* and Tradition, mysticism too was surely in their bequest to him, for he is commended by Fārisī for his sanctity, as '[...] the imam, the pious, godfearing ascetic, at one time the beloved of his age. His house was the house of righteousness, Ṣūfism and *askesis*. He was amongst those who were peerless in the science of principles (*uṣūl*) and scriptural exegesis [...]'.[12] Subkī's account also conveys an evocative picture of this intensely spiritual character:

> [Anṣārī's] gnosis was half spoken (*fawqa lisānihi*) and his meaning was greater than his outward [words]. He was in possession of seniority in Ṣūfism and the mystical path, modest in his eating. He earned his livelihood by making paper, and he never mixed [with people], nor did he enter sociably into any worldly eating-house. He would be seated in the great library of the Niẓāmiyya at Nīshāpūr, applying himself to his religion. He was stricken at the end of his life with weakness in his eyesight, and a cavity got going in his ear.[13]

Moreover, this shy, godly figure seems to have shared a supernatural aura with others from the mystical cadre, given Subkī's transmission of the following (on the authority of Abū Naṣr ʿAbd al-Raḥmān b. Muḥammad al-Khāṭibī):

> I heard Maḥmūd b. Abī Tawba, the vizier, say: 'I proceeded to the door of Abū'l-Qāsim al-Anṣārī and lo! the door was closed and he was having a conversation with someone, so I stood for an hour and the door was opened – and no one but he was in the house! So I said "With whom were you having

a conversation?" and he said "One of the spirits (*jinn*) was here to whom I was speaking [...]".'[14]

This last quotation is, inter alia, evidence that Anṣārī was of sufficient eminence to be visited by the highest state-functionaries such as the vizier, and keep them waiting.

Anṣārī's slight recorded legacy is in the disciplines of the religious mainstream, as a traditionist, scriptural exegete and Ashʿarī theologian.[15] But Shahrastānī signals that he truly marked a crux in his search, confiding to him a way into the arcanal reaches of the revealed text. In particular, though he regails this teacher as 'the defender of the sunna', he also states that Anṣārī was versed in a hermeneutic of the Qur'ān issuing from the Prophet's lineage, initiating Shahrastānī into these dimensions: '[...] he would inform me about the [different] readings of the noble words from the People of the Prophet's House and their friends (may God be pleased with them), in line with buried arcana and firm principles in the science of the Qur'ān'.[16] The innuendo here is startling. The 'buried arcana and firm principles in the science of the Qur'ān' (*asrār dafīna wa uṣūl matīna fī ʿilm al-Qur'ān*) seem an allusion to the lattice of complementarities by which Shahrastānī penetrates the *sensus anagogicus* and which is discussed in detail below. These are none other than the arcana (*asrār*) referred to in the title of his commentary. The added detail that Anṣārī conferred these hermeneutical keys to his disciple as a legacy from the Prophet's line and its 'friends' (*awliyā'*) hints strongly that he is Shahrastānī's original contact with the heritage of Ismāʿīlī thought. For there are remarkable grounds for arguing that the roots of Shahrastānī's hermeneutical system for the arcana lie in the latter. The conclusion seems to be that Anṣārī's reputation for Ṣūfism hid other, unchronicled influences, handed in turn to our own author. Perhaps Anṣārī's interlocutor overheard (potentially so disastrously) by the Seljuq vizier, was in fact anything but a *jinn*.

Rather than the finale, Anṣārī was the verge of the real breakthrough in Shahrastānī's quest – now pursued apace on the basis of Anṣārī's leads. In the autobiographical passage from the beginning of the *Mafātīḥ al-asrār* (henceforth *Mafātīḥ*) in which Shahrastānī speaks of Anṣārī with his imam-based interpretation, he goes onto allude to another, greater figure in his inner formation. This anonym seems to have been Shahrastānī's most decisive mentor, significantly likened by him to the unearthly figure of God's 'virtuous servant' (generally identified with the immortal sage *al-Khaḍir*, 'the Green One') encountered by Moses in Q. 18:65–82:

> So I searched for 'the truthful' as passionate lovers might search. And I found one of the virtuous servants of God, just like Moses (peace be upon him) with his young man: 'Then the two of them found one of Our servants whom We bestowed as a mercy from Us, and We taught him knowledge from Our presence' (Q. 18:65). So I learnt from him the ways of the creation (*khalq*) and of the Command (*amr*), the degrees of contrariety (*taḍādd*) and hierarchy (*tarattub*), the twin aspects of generality (*ʿumūm*) and specificity (*khuṣūṣ*), and the two rulings of the accomplished (*mafrūgh*) and the inchoative (*musta'naf*). I thus had my fill of this single dish, not the dishes which are the foods of error and the starting points of the ignorant. I quenched my thirst from the fountain of submission with a cup whose blend was from Tasnīm [...].[17]

This passage, with its allusion and pathos, points to the climax of our author's intellectual journey – the achievement of his quest. Everything points to a teacher of crowning importance, bearing prime responsibility for Shahrastānī's esoteric hermeneutic and higher theology. Significantly, the Qur'ānic passage cited is often found as a prooftext for the prerogatives of an esoteric dimension in Islam, be it Ṣūfī or Shīʿī. The stark asymmetry of exoteric and esoteric norms is implied in the Qur'ānic tale as it unfolds: the archetypal wisdom-mouthpiece will shock Moses with his bizarre behaviour and end by summarily dismissing the great prophet for failing to keep faith with him, with the words: 'This is the parting (*firāq*) between you and me' (Q. 18:78). The initiator's anonymity in Shahrastānī's account obviously implies the need for circumspection, as expected for a sectarian figurehead of this kind. Moreover, as will emerge, at least three of the hermeneutical complementarities which Shahrastānī drew (presumably in more depth than from Anṣārī earlier) from this 'virtuous servant of God' smack of contemporary Ismāʿīlī doctrine and form part of the total argument for our author's own Ismāʿīlī links.[18] It follows that behind the mystagogue's intentionally blurred image may lie a living authority in Ismāʿīlī teaching, a learned *dāʿī* – a henchman, perhaps, of the inceptor of Nizārī Ismāʿīlism, al-Ḥasan b. al-Ṣabbāḥ (d. 518/1124), or even the man himself?

Dates for this contact are of course an enigma. Ādharshab speculates however, that even while at Nīshāpūr Shahrastānī was inwardly on a trajectory tangential to the Ashʿarī and Shāfiʿī establishment which he publicly fostered. He suggests that through frustration with the latter he returned to Khwārazm, and there used his newfound rhetorical skills to preach, galling peers with his idiosyncracy.[19] A barbed comment by Khwārazmī lends itself to this interpretation: 'And there had been disputes and talks between us and he used to go to excesses in supporting the teaching of the philosophers and defending them. And I was present many times at sessions of his preaching and the expression "God said" and "God's Messenger did not say" was not in them, nor responding to legal questions.'[20] This indeed suggests that Shahrastānī was giving freer rein to his personal intellectual and spiritual interests.

Shahrastānī set out for the Ḥijāz on the Greater Pilgrimage (*ḥajj*) in the year 510/1116, probably aged about thirty years old. He then opted to live in the caliphal capital Baghdad for three years (511/1117–514/1120) during which time he was involved at the principal Niẓāmiyya college, inter alia convening further sessions of preaching from which he gained wide popularity, though an elitist mentality may mean that Khwārazmī is slyly belittling him in alluding to this. It yet hints that the fresh approach for which Shahrastānī stood touched a nerve in the populace.[21] Whatever the case, Khwārazmī also snubs him more openly by alleging nepotism in his appointment at the Baghdad Niẓāmiyya – through his friendship with Asʿad al-Mayhanī, a figure of prominence at the college who had been close to him back in Khurāsān.[22] Khwārazmī's illfeeling, whether from pious suspicion or rivalry, is sensed in these references to Shahrastānī.

Perhaps again not easily fitting the establishment's mold, by 514/1120 our author felt driven to head back east for Merv, the so-called *Shāhjān*, most famous of the towns of Khurāsān and chosen by the Seljuq sultan Sanjar as his capital. Free again to operate as a private scholar, Shahrastānī now set to work on the cycle of books on which his posthumous reputation rests, no doubt making full use of Merv's great library. Above all, as a major centre of the Seljuq government, the city gave hope of solid backing for Shahrastānī's projects. He was in fact successful in gaining the support of at least two powerful regional figures: Abū Tawba Naṣīr al-Dīn Maḥmūd b. al-Muẓaffar al-Marwazī, Seljuq vizier from 521/1127 to 526/1131, and also Tāj al-Maʿālī Majd al-Dīn Abū'l-Qāsim ʿAlī b. Jaʿfar b. Ḥusayn, Quddāma al-Mūsawī, syndic (*naqīb*) of the ʿAlids in Tirmidh and generally recognised as the headman in Khurāsān. Both these figures were well-known as patrons of scholars and promoters of learning in Khurāsān and through them Shahrastānī even succeeded in approaching the court of the Seljuq ruler himself, Sanjar, presently becoming 'close to the mighty throne of the Sultan and his confidant'.[23]

In these meridian years Shahrastānī would draft his famous study in comparative religion and philosophy, *al-Milal wa'l-niḥal* (The Religions and Sects; henceforth *Milal*), for the vizier Naṣīr al-Dīn,[24] next his major study of Kalām theology, *Nihāyat al-aqdām fī 'ilm al-kalām* (The Furthest Steps in Theology; henceforth *Nihāya*),[25] and finally his *Muṣāra'at al-falāsifa* (Wrestling with the Philosophers; henceforth *Muṣāra'a*),[26] dedicated to the 'Alid syndic Tāj al-Ma'ālī. All three works fit Shahrastānī's role as a leading authority on dogmatics in the Seljuq religious scene: respectively, a universal heresiography, a plenary treatment of Ash'ari orthodoxy, and a refutation of Avicennism on behalf of scriptural norms. But the message of these books is not stereotypical and scrutiny shows their deeper contiguity with the unusual teachings of the *Mafātīḥ*, as may emerge from the following.

The architecture of the *Milal* uses two great spans: the first being 'on the exposition of the adherents of religions and religious denominations (*milal*) consisting in the Muslims and People of Scripture and in whoever has the like of the scripture of the Muslims';[27] and the second, 'a commentary on the people of opinions and sects (*niḥal*) who are ranged against the adherents of religions in the manner of contrariety (*taḍādd*) as we mentioned, their reliance being on the sound primordial predisposition, perfect intellect and pure mind'.[28] The prior overarching section deals with recognized scriptural traditions and an elaborate account of Islamic groups is naturally included in it, along with Jewish, Christian and Mazdean doctrines; the second section instead covers supposedly non-scriptural belief systems, comprising treatments of the Hellenistic philosophers, 'eternalists' (*dahriyya*), pseudo-Sabaeans of Ḥarrān, image-worshippers and so-called Brahmins. In this manner, the differential of the two spanning sections of the book is clearly presented in terms of the principle of contrariety. Moreover, the organisation of the material *within* these sections explicitly builds on the leitmotif of both hierarchy[29] and contrariety (*al-tarattub wa'l-taḍādd*). And again, in each chapter and subsection the account moves systematically from the general level (*'umūm*) to the specific (*khuṣūṣ*).

These characteristic contours of the *Milal* are very noteworthy since the couples hierarchy/contrariety and generality/specificity are conceptual talismans with wide and profound applications throughout Shahrastānī's thought, especially in his discussion of scriptural arcana, to which they are vital keys. The weaving of his doxography on the loom of these complementarities is fully consistent with these deeper aspects of his thought, with their arguably Ismāʿīlī stimulus. Amongst various other features of the *Milal* which are similarly noteworthy, mention might also be made here of the richness of data which was clearly available to the author concerning Ismāʿīlism, particularly the 'new mission' (*daʿwa jadīda*) of al-Ḥasan b. al-Ṣabbāḥ;[30] and the long section of over thirty-five pages, considered 'one of the most important things in this book', in which the Ḥanīfs defend the 'true faith' against the pseudo-Sabaeans. Monnot has pointed out that this theological dialogue may well emerge from the celebrated debate between the 'free-thinking' philosopher Abū Bakr al-Rāzī (d. 311/923) and the major Ismāʿīlī thinker and missionary Abū Ḥātim al-Rāzī (d. 322/933), as presented in the latter's *Aʿlām al-nubuwwa*.[31] According to Monnot then, Shahrastānī's Ḥanīfs ultimately represent Ismāʿīlī teaching.[32] It will emerge that, in other works, our author indeed refers to his Ismāʿīlī 'higher theology' in these very terms.[33] The most recent discovery in this unsuspected Ismāʿīlī dimension of our author's best known work is that, in key respects, it is indebted to an earlier Iranian-Khurāsānian tradition of Ismāʿīlī heresiography, enshrined in Abū Ḥātim al-Rāzī's *Kitāb al-Zīna* and in particular Abū Tammām's *Kitāb al-Shajara*. (On this, see Gaiser, 'Satan's Seven Specious Arguments'.)

Comparable idiosyncracies of the *Nihāya*, for their part, are the more striking given its prima facie aim of rehearsing Ashʿarī teachings. It opens with the strongly universalistic ruling that the doctrine espoused by the elite 'people of truth in all religious communities' (*madhhab ahl al-ḥaqq min ahl al-milal kullihā*) affirms the existence of a Creator and that 'God was and there was naught with Him' (*kāna'llāhu wa lam yakun maʿahu shay'*).[34] A similar judgement comes at the start of the second chapter in regard to the teaching that the inception of whatsoever exists is through God – again acknowledged by these 'people of truth'. The term is numinous and the referent designedly enigmatic.[35] Steigerwald notes that the grouping can hardly simply be equated with the Ashʿarīs (to whom Shahrastānī generally refers in the text as 'our colleagues', *aṣḥābunā*). Yet neither can his *ahl al-*

ḥaqq simply be a code for the Ismāʿīlīs (which, in any case, would surely be too bold in the context of this Ashʿarī treatise) since he clearly acknowledges the presence of the *ahl al-ḥaqq* both in Islam (*min ahl al-islām*) and in other faiths (*min ahl al-milal*).[36] The safest identification of the *ahl al-ḥaqq* of Islam in our author's mind is probably simply with the final arbiters of truth within the religion. Given his overall views, this means the Prophet, his Household and its adherents, in which case the *ahl al-ḥaqq* in other faiths are apparently to be interpreted as pre-Islamic prophets, imams and *their* adherents. The terminology may thus hint at Ismāʿīlī teaching after all, Shahrastānī's underlying concept being of the perennity of the core truths and religious structures of Ismāʿīlism – as assumed in many relevant sources, from the Ikhwān al-Ṣafāʾ with their notion of an 'eternal wisdom' (*al-ḥikma al-khālida*) to the *Asās al-taʾwīl* of al-Qāḍī Nuʿmān, with its central concept of the timeless mission of the true faith (*daʿwat al-ḥaqq*), or the *Ithbāt al-imāma* of Aḥmad al-Naysābūrī, which details the repetition of the religious hierarchy for each great prophet and indeed employs the expression *ahl al-ḥaqīqa*. Minimally speaking, the ecumenical undercurrents here in Shahrastānī's text chime with positions in his late works with their arguable Ismāʿīlī trend, for example, his subtly inclusive interpretation of Islam's abrogation of earlier faiths in the *Mafātīḥ* itself, discussed below.

Whatever the case, the author's comparativist impulse remains very much in evidence in the *Nihāya*. Shahrastānī establishes the teachings of his Ashʿarī colleagues on a series of twenty theses (*qawāʿid*, sing. *qāʿida*) in careful distinction from those of the Muʿtazila, philosophers, 'eternalists' (*dahriyya*), extremist Shīʿa (*ghulāt*), and even pseudo-Sabaeans and 'Brahmins'. Though these schools are obviously foils for the text's Ashʿarism, the latter is not servile. In some details Shahrastānī explicitly criticises the school and takes things in a new direction. Ādharshab notes that while Shahrastānī's teaching in the work is basically 'in line with the Ashʿarī school [...] from time to time he may oppose this school (*qad yukhālifu hādhā'l-madhhab aḥyānan*)'.[37] Steigerwald claims that he gives *creatio ex nihilo* a different interpretation from Ashʿarism and develops a concept of primordial instauration (*ibdāʿ*) in its place, adopted from the 'ancient sages'.[38] Moreover, in her view, his concept of the necessity of imamate is much closer to Shīʿism than to Ashʿarism, despite the fact that Shahrastānī is here formally critical of Shīʿism.[39]

A noteworthy divergence to which Guillaume drew attention in his edition and abridged paraphrase of the *Nihāya*, is the discussion of divine aid (*tawfīq*) and abandonment (*khidhlān*) in human moral agency.[40] Shahrastānī criticises *both* the Ashʿarī and Muʿtazilī positions here, the first being allegedly guilty of 'extremism' (*ghulūw*) and the second of 'shortfall' (*taqṣīr*). For the Ashʿarīs take both aid and abandonment as God's direct compulsion of specific individuals, respectively to obey and disobey Him. The Muʿtazilīs instead take aid to be God's general bequest of guidance to humanity as a whole via intellect, revelation and divine law, and they basically deny that abandonment (in the sense of causing human wrongdoing) is conceivable for God. Ashʿarism's 'extremism' here clearly lies in attributing to God the agency of sin and Muʿtazilism's 'shortfall' lies in stinting God's omnipotence.

Shahrastānī's own answer to the antinomy typically draws subtle consequences from his beloved distinction of generality (*ʿumūm*) and specificity (*khuṣūṣ*). A general kind of divine aid must be carefully marked out from a specific one, and the presence of the general is compatible with the absence of the specific.[41] For Shahrastānī, general aid is constituted by the universal bequest to humanity of reason and thereby the basic theological truths which flow from it, and then prophetic guidance. But qua specific, aid may be absent for a given individual: 'Man's adult independence and mature intelligence need great support from *tawfīq*. This is where men stumble (*mazillat al-aqdām*) [...] *Khidhlān* means that God does leave [the individual] to trust in himself and his own resources.'[42] So when aid is withdrawn at the individual level, God's 'abandonment' is indeed in evidence.

In sum, by using his generality/specificity complementarity, Shahrastānī manages to acknowledge God's justice like the Muʿtazilīs, since He never withholds aid absolutely, *and* to acknowledge God's omnipotence like the Ashʿarīs, since He indeed figures in individual wrongdoing through engaging in *khidhlān*. However, the vital point here is simply that Shahrastānī is clearly *not* immured in the Ashʿarī viewpoint, even in this, his most Ashʿarī work. More especially, the generality/specificity *distinguo* – to be explored at greater length below – is a major element in the lattice of complementarities for decoding the Qur'ān's arcana in the *Mafātīḥ*, and to recall, it features prominently in the teachings derived by Shahrastānī from his initiating 'virtuous servant' of God.

Next, the *Muṣāraʿa* too wields the generality/specificity principle,[43] as well as other elements from his complementarities.[44] Despite its notional analogy with Ghazālī's *Tahāfut al-falāsifa* (The Incoherence of the Philosophers; henceforth, *Tahāfut*),[45] Shahrastānī's own critique of Avicennism is arguably fraught with the enigmatic servant's teachings and belongs among the works most evidential of the author's Ismāʿīlī links. Thus his completed treatment of five philosophical 'issues' (*masā'il*, sing. *mas'ala*)[46] within the *Muṣāraʿa* generally breaks down into three further sub-sections: the first, made up of quotations from Ibn Sīnā; the second, made up of Shahrastānī's criticism of these on the basis of alleged internal inconsistency and *ilzām* (i.e. bringing out absurdities from Ibn Sīnā's premises); and the third, made up of what Ibn Sīnā *should* have said. It is this last sub-section, entitled 'the correct choice' (*al-mukhtār al-ḥaqq*) which is particularly valuable for re-constructing the deeper Shahrastānian cosmological and metaphysical system. The keynote of the latter is found to be an extreme transcendentalism in keeping with contemporary Ismāʿīlī thought.

Scrutiny in fact reveals a submerged unity within these sections, so that the *ilzām*, then Shahrastānī's remedy of Ibn Sīnā's absurdity-entailing premises and then his preferred solution to the issue in question, are profoundly concordant. Hence, most of the *ilzām* arguments turn Ibn Sīnā's own principle of divine simplicity against him; Shahrastānī's remedy is to treat as equivocal the predicates which threaten to compound divinity; finally, the transcendentalised sense retained by him for the predicate as applied to God, is crucial in his 'correct choice' of solution to the given issue. In more detail: if a general concept such as 'intellect' (*ʿaql*), 'oneness' (*waḥda*), 'substantiality' (*jawhariyya*) or 'being' (*wujūd*) were equally applied to God and creatures, it would make God a *compositum*. For such a concept would amount to a kind of genus and insofar as it is found both in God and in others, God would unavoidably comprise the genus in question *and* a differentia. In this way, composition is implied in the very idea of the so-called 'Necessary Being' (*wājib al-wujūd*), the core of Ibn Sīnā's thought. For, claims Shahrastānī, 'being' is a pseudo-genus which would then be present in the divine identity together with the differentia 'necessary'. His most uncompromising remedy for this impasse is to limit 'being' to a level beneath God, who in Himself is 'exalted and sanctified above His glory falling within the hierarchy of existents (*taqaddasa wa taʿālā ʿan an yakūna jalāluhu taḥta'l-tartīb fi'l-mawjūdāt*)'.[47] This is a patently Neoplatonic, in fact Plotinian, turn of thought, unusual in Islam but wholly characteristic of contemporary Ismāʿīlism.[48]

The concord of the subsections comes out in the following. From a slightly different angle to that just presented, Shahrastānī urges denying any idea of God which has a counterpart (*qasīm*), giving as prooftext Q. 2:22: 'Do not knowingly set up rivals (*andād*) for God.'[49] For divine composition would again follow, with God demarcated from the said counterpart within a shared genus, by combining the latter and a differentia. Shahrastānī metaphorises this as a law court: 'Contraries are litigants and variant things are legal appellants, and their judge is not numbered amongst either of His two appellants, the two litigants before Him.'[50] Yet he stresses the paradox that the Qur'ān itself enjoins using divine predicates with formal counterparts: 'And to God belong the most beautiful names, so call upon Him with them. And spurn those who deviate in respect of His names – they will be punished for what they used to do' (Q. 7:180).[51] By citing this last verse and Q. 2:22 in juxtaposition, Shahrastānī celebrates the paradox, whose solution, we learn, is to take such terms as *equivocal* rather than univocal (or even the middle option, as analogical).

This is an unusual and extreme solution, atomising the meaning of the word, giving it discrete senses, and setting the word's 'divine' sense outside human understanding. Yet we discover that Shahrastānī keeps a single crucial sense for these divine equivoques. If God is described as X and X has a counterpart –X, then, according to Shahrastānī, X here means God's being the *cause* of both X and –X. In regard to the predicate 'truth', for example, God is truth in the sense that He makes the truth true and He makes the false false; likewise God is 'living' in the sense that He causes life and death in others.[52] For Shahrastānī, inter-related opposites and paired contraries point to an absolutely independent, i.e. non-paired, agent, both to bring them about in existence and to relate them (*jāmiʿ ghanī ʿalā'l-iṭlāq*). Crucially, this then becomes the key to Shahrastānī's own preferred solutions to questions addressed by Ibn Sīnā, for instance his (admittedly enigmatic) argument for God. While Shahrastānī maintains that God in Himself is strictly indemonstrable, or rather that He is 'too well known for His existence to be proved by anything',[53] he nevertheless holds that there is an argument for the necessity of God's existence from the presence of necessity and its counterpart in the world.[54] The same reasoning follows in arguing for God's inconceivably elevated unity, which Shahrastānī holds to be the ultimate source of relative instances of unity *and* multiplicity in the world:

> 'Oneness' is applied to God (Exalted is He) and to existents purely equivocally (*bi'l-ishtirāk al-maḥḍ*). He is one *unlike* the [relative] 'ones' mentioned – one such that the two opposites, unity and multiplicity, both emanate from Him, one in the sense that He brings things that are 'one' into existence. He was unique in unicity, then He made it overflow on His creation. Unity and existence belong to Him without an opposite opposing Him or a rival comparing with Him, 'And do not knowingly set up rivals for God! (Q. 2:22).'[55]

In sum, the homology of the *Muṣāraʿa* and the *Mafātīḥ* lies in the former's use of certain of the servant's complementarities and its intensely transcendentalist theology, presumably Ismāʿīlī in basis. This last is demonstrably the mainstay of the whole exercise from issue to issue.[56] It may be noted that the *Muṣāraʿa* euphemises this atypical higher theology as 'the Ḥanīfī revelation' (*al-sharʿ al-ḥanīfī*).[57] Texts show that Ismāʿīlism was exactly self-styled thus at the time.[58] Moreover, Naṣīr al-Dīn al-Ṭūsī independently confirms that the counter-Avicennan theology of the *Muṣāraʿa* was indeed Ismāʿīlī. As part of his agenda of defending Avicennism, he formulated a reply to the *Muṣāraʿa*, called *Maṣāriʿ al-muṣāriʿ* (Wrestlings with the Wrestler), in which he identified its core teaching – that God must be raised beyond all degrees and contraries – as the teaching of the Nizārī Ismāʿīlīs (*madhhab al-taʿlīmiyyīn*).[59] The point is telling, because an insider's. Ṭūsī had himself been an active affiliate and had authorised (if not actually himself written) a thorough account of the Nizārī system in his *Rawḍat al-Taslīm* (Paradise of Submission). In his separate Nizārī Ismāʿīlī confession, he tells of the process of his entry to the community, explaining that his father directed him to a local philosopher, Kamāl al-Dīn Muḥammad Ḥāsib, who would intimate that 'the truth [may be found] among people who are, in the eyes of the group that you know, the most contemptible people'. That is, the then much feared Nizārīs. Ṭūsī's Ismāʿīlī-inclined father, we learn, was educated by a maternal uncle described as an actual student-attendant of our own Shahrastānī. And astonishingly, Ṭūsī refers to the latter at this point as Chief Missionary (*dāʿī al-duʿāt*) – a high rank indeed in the *daʿwa* hierarchy.[60]

In this we spy the full, stressful complex of Shahrastānī's allegiances. It is not that he was a figurehead in one realm, a nonentity in the other. Rather, he operated as a figurehead in both: in public, a doctor of Ashʿarī orthodoxy, a veteran of the *madāris niẓāmiyya*, a Seljuq courtier and confidant of the sultan; but, it would seem, in secret, a leading missionary and authority in Ismāʿīlism, considered the prime political and religious threat by the Seljuqs themselves throughout the period. Negotiating this split may have been torment. Certainly, contemporary references show that our author failed to escape suspicion. Samʿānī (d. 562/1166) says in his *Taḥbīr* that Shahrastānī 'was suspected of heresy (*ilḥād*) and inclining to [the heretics]; he was extreme in Shīʿism'.[61] Subkī (quoting Dhahabī, quoting Samʿānī again) says more specifically that Shahrastānī 'was suspected of inclining to the people of the mountain fortresses, meaning the Ismāʿīlīs, their missionary activity, and defending their calamities'.[62] Perhaps expectedly, Subkī immediately tries to salvage his fellow Ashʿarī's reputation against the allegation: 'I don't know whence Ibn al-Samʿānī had that, for Abū'l-Fatḥ's works indicate the very opposite!' Shahrastānī was simply too big a name, too fine a contributor to the Shāfiʿī-Ashʿarī heritage to be lightly surrendered to such a claim.

But suspicions like Samʿānī's must have volatised our author's situation. Indeed, court vicissitudes sank both his patrons. Firstly, Sultan Sanjar in 526/1132 took against his vizier Naṣīr al-Dīn, prompting Shahrastānī to excise the old introduction to the *Milal* which praised him as sponsor. Another introduction was discreetly inserted. Presently Shahrastānī's new patron, the ʿAlid syndic Tāj al-Maʿālī, was in turn to fall foul of Sanjar – arrested and imprisoned on his orders on the grounds of informers' allegations.[63] Finally, Sanjar himself met his nemesis in the form of the pagan Ghuzz federation of the Qarā Khiṭāy, who defeated him at Qaṭwān near Samarqand in 536/1141. While the great Seljuq ignominiously took flight to Tirmidh and then Balkh, his old rival the Khwārazm-Shāh seized the opportunity to ransack his capital Merv. It seems likely that the collapse of Sanjar's state and of the sustentative environment of the court at Merv irreparably damaged Shahrastānī's situation. The odd truncation of the *Muṣāraʿa*, which ends after five issues instead of the scheduled seven, is probably explained by the said events. At any rate, Shahrastānī hints at some such cataclysm in the following words:

> When I brought the discussion on this issue to this point, and wanted to start on the sixth and seventh issues, I was diverted from their exposition by something the heaviness of which distressed me, and the burden of which weighed heavily on me, consisting in the trials of the time and the blows of misfortune (*fitan al-zamān wa ṭawāriq al-ḥidthān*). And to God complaints are addressed and upon Him is reliance in adversity and prosperity![64]

It thus seems that Shahrastānī abandoned Merv around 536/1141, taking final refuge in his birthplace Shahrastāna. By now probably nearing his sixties, he lived on in relative isolation for the last decade of his life. The composition of the *Mafātīḥ* is known to have begun a little way into this period, in 538/1143.[65] Shahrastānī was to die ten years later in 548/1153. Ādharshab poignantly notes that a recent report by one of the councils for surveying the Iranian-Soviet (now Iran-Turkmenistan) borders states that in the ruins of the old town of Shahrastāna a grave was found which locals simply refer to as 'Mullā Muḥammad's grave'.[66] Whatever the value of this, there is significance in the geographical circularity of Shahrastānī's biography, its return to its beginning. For he himself, as already quoted, presents his intellectual biography as a consuming quest. And according to one eminent modern mythographer, heroic quests do generally include these returns to beginnings. As though bearing out Shahrastānī's own charged sense of his intellectual search, it turns out that the basic rites of passage of such pilgrimages each feature in his biography: the 'nuclear unit of the monomyth' comprising separation, initiation and return.[67]

It is in the hitherto neglected works post-dating his rite of return and final seclusion that Shahrastānī's deeper views truly emerge. In this, our Qur'ān commentary is twinned conceptually and also probably chronologically, with the *Majlis* (Preaching Session; henceforth *Majlis*)[68] – a Persian witness to his higher thought rescued from oblivion by Nā'īnī, and more recently studied and rendered into French by Steigerwald.[69] The latter's rich analysis should be consulted for a fuller understanding of this text and its vital link with the *Mafātīḥ*. Suffice to say here that the *Majlis* amounts to a bright sidelight on the conceptual system at work in Shahrastānī's penetration of Qur'ānic arcana. The treatise's sermonic form should not mislead the reader, for the theological, cosmological and hermeneutical world of the *Mafātīḥ* is also on show here, but in brief. Complementarities from the list presented below are eloquently framed and explored, including revelation/hermeneutics (*tanzīl*/*ta'wīl*, literally 'sending down' and 'taking back up'), creation/the Command (*āfarīnish*/*farmān*), and the accomplished/the inchoative (*mafrūgh*/*musta'naf*).

Such are, moreover, already in use in the *Majlis*, not only as core aspects of a great, self-consistent philosophical system, but to unfold the Word's *anagōgē*. Notably, Shahrastānī is occupied for the whole last part of the work by an elaboration of that topos of Muslim esoterism, the Moses-Khaḍir encounter (Q. 18:65 ff).[70] To anticipate here the following section: Shahrastānī's interpretation takes Khaḍir, whose actions outrage the conventional law, as representing the dimension of the accomplished, while Moses represents that of the inchoative. The specifically Ismāʿīlī complexion of this would of course stand on the question of the pedigree of these concepts, as discussed below. But the Ismāʿīlism of other elements in the *Majlis* is transparent. For instance, the messianic figure called the *qāʾim* who will sift those worthy of Paradise from the rest is identified in line with Ismāʿīlī traditions as none other than ʿAlī b. Abī Ṭālib.[71] A cyclical understanding of the development of the Prophet is adopted in the text, of likely Ismāʿīlī provenance.[72] Perhaps most notable of all, Shahrastānī evaluates the different theological movements of Islam in the light of the story of Satan's refusal to prostrate before Adam.[73] Adam is significantly presented here as the original 'mediator of the Command' (*mutawassiṭ-i amr*), that is, the functional archetype of the imam in Shīʿism. It is vital in this connection that Shahrastānī claims that the group he himself espouses is alone in its true commitment to what God and His Messenger said.[74] The definitely Ismāʿīlī thrust of the discussion in fact only comes out by matching it with the equivalent portion of the *Mafātīḥ*, i.e. the arcana of Q. 2:34 where this story is first referred to. All becomes explicit here in Shahrastānī's comments:

> [...] Just as Iblīs did not acknowledge the present, living, current imam, the commonalty are the same as that, while the expectant Shīʿa only acknowledge the awaited, hidden imam. And God has blessed servants on earth who do not get ahead of Him in speaking and they act on His Command, servants who are the purified servants of God, over whom Satan has no authority [...].

In this explosive statement, our author explicitly criticises both the Sunnī masses (*al-ʿāmma*) and the 'expectant', i.e. Twelver, Shīʿa (*al-shīʿa al-muntaẓira*) for refusing, like Iblīs, to acknowledge the pontifex right in their midst, who is referred to as 'the present, living, current imam' (*al-imām al-ḥāḍir al-ḥayy al-qāʾim*) – a concept which it would seem wayward to account for as other than Ismāʿīlī.[75]

Shahrastānī goes on to equate the said purified servants' speech with God's, their hand with God's, allegiance to them with allegiance to Him and war on them with war on Him. He then says:

> Whoever loves them has loved God, whoever submits to them has submitted to God, whoever prostrates to them has prostrated to God, whoever turns

towards them has turned towards God and whoever places confidence in them has placed confidence in God. 'So what is it with these people who don't even understand a statement'[76] and they talk on about how the prostration to Adam took place and what its interpretation was?! They do not grasp that prostration to Adam was prostration to God – rather, that so long as prostration to God is not combined with prostration to Adam, it is *not* prostration to God, just as, so long as the formula 'no god but God' is not combined with the formula 'Muḥammad is God's messenger', it is *not* the formula of testification and of sincerity![77]

The Qurʾān commentary

Basic issues

The present translation and study of Shahrastānī's *Mafātīḥ* is part of a bigger attempt in modern scholarship to retrieve this unusual text from the very brink of oblivion. Aside from the work of Ādharshab, vital preliminary research has already been done by Monnot who, in 'Islam: exégèse coranique' has translated many significant passages into French and provided a detailed synopsis of Shahrastānī's text. For a summary of Monnot's contribution, readers are referred to Steigerwald, *La Pensée*, pp. 70–72. Most recently, Steigerwald has also included a valuable discussion of the text in her article 'Ismāʿīlī Taʾwīl'.

The unicum of the *Mafātīḥ* contains (1) twelve introductory chapters, (2) the commentary on the Exordium (*al-Fātiḥa,* Q. 1), and (3) the commentary on the chapter of the Cow (*Sūrat al-Baqara,* Q. 2). (1) and (2) are presented in this volume, respectively providing a full exposition, and a good sample, of Shahrastānī's hermeneutics. Early in the introduction he says that his work is to be a verse by verse commentary, claiming that through this and the twelve introductory chapters, 'all other commentaries have become redundant!'[78] Shahrastānī's *Mafātīḥ* is indeed conscientiously inclusive in framework and combines detailed discussion of concerns such as variant readings, lexicography, semantics and tradition-based exegesis, with intensive discussion of the arcanal dimensions of each verse. Systematic study of verses under such headings is hardly unique to Shahrastānī, whose models are probably to be sought among works of Shīʿī exegesis representative of the post-Būyid Muʿtazilī turn.[79] In its involved linguistic and exoteric aspect, the *Mafātīḥ* should be viewed as strictly a 'commentator's commentary' in its author's intention – aimed at the specialist, not the beginner. It shows off the ripe state of the Qurʾānic sciences in Shahrastānī's time, coordinating a wealth of received material on the scripture, derived from respected *ḥadīth* compendia (particularly Bukhārī), also from exegetical works like Ṭabarī's *Jāmiʿ al-bayān*, through to numerous, more obscure sources like Ibn Fāris's linguistic studies.

Though the arcana are naturally the most intellectually striking dimension of the overall project, they should not be casually isolated from the content of these earlier rubrics. It is not just that they build *technically* on the foregoing material. A deeper issue is also implicit, which might equally be presented in terms of 'etiquette' (*adab*) or epistemology. For our author, the Qurʾān is the sacred text par excellence. A process of self-humbling is therefore called for in its would-be student, the proper inward configuration needed for ascent to its higher meanings. The subtleties of these levels of meaning are only reached via the intellectual catharsis enshrined in the disciplines of the earlier rubrics.

Cumulatively, the arcana induce a liminal sense of the Qurʾān's deeper intelligibility. Verse by verse a scheme of higher concepts, noumenal yet profoundly consistent, sharpens into focus: a *philosophy* of the scripture. This scheme, ostensibly Ismāʿīlī in basis, has intrinsic interest as a major example of a sapiential (i.e. *ḥikma*-based) approach to the Qurʾān. And this seems to have been how the author's actual contemporaries classed it in their reactions. Bayhaqī notably writes:

> [Shahrastānī] was composing a Qurʾān commentary, interpreting the verses according to the canons of the law and wisdom (*ḥikma*), and other things too. So I said to him, 'This is to give up what is right! The Qurʾān is not to be commented on except by the reports of the pious ancestors consisting of the companions and their successors. Wisdom [i.e. philosophy] is something quite separate from the exegesis of the Qurʾān and its hermeneutic – especially so if its hermeneutic is already recorded. One may not combine the law and wisdom better than the imam Ghazālī did (may God have mercy on him)!' Shahrastānī was consumed by anger because of that [...].[80]

So Bayhaqī's attention, as ours, is mainly drawn by the aspect of the commentary stressed even in its title: *Keys to the Arcana*. Greatest interest inevitably lies in this anagogic aspect rather than in Shahrastānī's richly informative but otherwise derivative discussion of the literal. Yet a vital point is that Shahrastānī asserts comparably high credentials, the same authoritative transmission, for his insights on the arcana and the tools by which he unlocks them, as he does for the other side of his commentary. He proudly holds his hermeneutic to be guaranteed by the same levels of prophetic authority and religious sanction which Bayhaqī associates with transmitted commentary (*tafsīr bi'l-ma'thūr*). And it is this, not prickliness over Ghazālī's repute, which may really explain his aggrieved reaction to Bayhaqī's judgement of his efforts, mentioned in the above passage. Shahrastānī in fact expresses horror at all personal, opinion-based interpretation of divine writ and takes pride in avoiding it. For example: 'I seek refuge with God, the All-Hearing, the Omniscient, from speaking about [Qur'ānic verses] on the basis of a personal opinion and independent reasoning, rather than an authoritative report and chain of transmission, and [I seek refuge with God from] investigating their arcana and their meanings randomly and extravagantly [...].'[81] In another typical statement in which our author is discussing the arcana of the *basmala*,[82] he says: 'Who is it who has the ability to comprehend these arcana without guidance from the people of the Qur'ān, who are the people of God and His elect (peace be upon them) or has the audacity to bring them up in books without permission and authorization from them?' He goes on to pray:

> I take refuge with God, the Hearer, the Knower, from the stoned Satan, so that there may not occur in my thought, neither flow from my pen that by which I would take up my seat in hellfire. May God (Mighty and Majestic) grant refuge from hellfire and its blazing, and may He protect us from swerving and slipping up in the hermeneutic of the verses of the Qur'ān and their exegesis![83]

Scorn for individualistic subjectivity in interpretation explains Shahrastānī's recourse to those known as 'the people of the Qur'ān' (*ahl al-Qur'ān*) in hermeneutics. Such expressions here mean the Prophet's lineage or its representatives.[84] A strong Shī'ī element is thus at work in this aspect of Shahrastānī's commentary, such that in all matters anagogic he ascribes what he says to the imams' authority. Aside from the heightened aura with which this invests his daring teachings in this field, this ascription also follows from his views on the canonisation of the Qur'ān. In Chapter 2 of his introduction, having gone over the standard account of the historical events leading up to the *textus receptus*,[85] Shahrastānī quickly takes a controversial turn, albeit basing himself on traditional reports.

He begins by mentioning the case of Q. 33:23,[86] a verse at first missing from the ʿUthmānic text as it was being assembled, but recovered for it by Zayd b. Thābit from Khuzayma b. Thābit.[87] Shahrastānī stresses that the verse refers inter alia to ʿAlī b. Abī Ṭālib.[88] Does the chronicled case of this verse's first omission hint at a wider picture of resistance to preserving revelations on the Prophet's Household?[89] This is essentially the older Shīʿī claim, that just as the Bible's transmission had involved (according to prevalent Muslim teaching) a suppressive conspiracy (*kitmān*), so had the Qurʾān's.[90] Shahrastānī goes on to refer to other generally acknowledged cases of material dropped from the Muslim scripture.[91]

No less bold is his look at the credentials of the two main agents of the ʿUthmānic project. While Saʿīd b. al-Āṣ was esteemed as a linguist, he had not recited to nor *been* recited to by the Prophet.[92] On these grounds, Ubayy b. Kaʿb (for whom the Prophet is said to have gone through the whole Qurʾān, and whose recitation was followed by many early Muslims) stood against the project.[93] For his part, Zayd b. Thābit was known as 'the scribe of the revelation'. Yet even he was criticised by the nonpareil authority on the Qurʾān, Ibn Masʿūd, when he gave notice that he had already acquired 70 chapters of revelation from the Prophet in person when Zayd 'with his sidelocks'[94] was still amusing himself with other children. The Prophet had indeed backed Ibn Masʿūd's recitation as a facsimile of the revelation as sent down.[95] On these grounds, Shahrastānī says that Ibn Masʿūd, like Ubayy b. Kaʿb, resisted ʿUthmān's codification and protested his destruction of rival versions, dubbing him 'the codex burner'. The gist of a report is given that the Caliph finally acted against his outspoken critic, dispatching a slave who knocked Ibn Masʿūd down, so killing him.[96] Shahrastānī goes on to cite great early authorities like Ibn ʿAbbās himself and ʿĀʾisha, that the ʿUthmānic text contained orthographical errors and solecisms (*alḥān*) originating with its transcribers.[97]

Matching these criticisms is Shahrastānī's support for the reality of a codex of ʿAlī b. Abī Ṭālib. Through a series of reports he outlines how, after the Prophet's death, ʿAlī set about a definitive version of the Qurʾān, not even enrobing till he had seen the task through.[98] The text's fidelity in sequence etc. rested on the Prophet's direction in his lifetime.[99] Aside from its virtually apographal status, it contained ʿAlī's own commentary, focused mainly on parallel verses (or perhaps equivocations) – such details presumably adding to the plausibility of its existence.[100] Our author also argues its existence rationally: that the Prophet should not have charged someone with the central task of collecting the Qurʾān (none being better placed for this than ʿAlī) is incredible.[101] At any rate, the product was reportedly rather bigger than the extant version, a tradition stating that it was 'a camel load' in quantity.[102]

The tale's denouement has ʿAlī and his slave Qanbar convey this load to the Prophet's mosque, only to be rebuffed by all present. His duty done, ʿAlī swears henceforth to hide the text: 'By God! You will never see it again.'[103] The scenario's improbability is offset by the precedent of Aaron, to whom ʿAlī is openly likened in well-known traditions.[104] Shahrastānī thus brackets ʿAlī's situation with Aaron's at the time of the Torah's revelation to Moses at Sinai. For, as both the Bible and Qurʾān tell, Aaron had to bow to a similar rebellion in the famous event of the golden calf, acquitting himself to his brother Moses, in the Qurʾānic account, with the statement 'the people reckoned me as weak and nearly killed me' (Q. 7:150) and by stressing his motive of preserving unity: 'I feared lest you would say "You have caused a division among the Israelites and [so] disrespected what I said."' (Q. 20:94)[105] But the real thrust of this parallel only comes out when Shahrastānī ventures that though the Torah in its prevalent form is subject, according to the Qurʾān, to human meddling (*taḥrīf*), the original tablets etched by God Himself remain in a copy with the Jewish high priesthood, Aaron's descendents (*ʿinda'l-khāṣṣati min awlādi Hārūn*). Clearly, the imamate descending from ʿAlī and the Prophet is taken to be the precise Islamic counterpart of the Aaronides. We infer that Shahrastānī takes it that the ʿAlid codex is likewise the verbatim divine Word protected in Islam's own 'high priesthood'.[106]

That the latter's main function is indeed to safeguard the Qurʾān is argued through a number of prooftexts, notably 'the tradition of the two precious things' (*ḥadīth al-thaqalayn*). Found in both Shīʿī and Sunnī sources, the Prophet here bequeaths the Muslims 'two precious things: God's Scripture and my immediate family'. He next promises that 'as long as you hold fast to them both, you will never go astray. The two will not be sundered till they reach me at the Pool [of Paradise]'.[107] For Shahrastānī, this tradition is the true significance of Q. 15:19: 'We it is who sent down the

Remembrance, and We are the protector thereof.' Against a widespread view, this verse is *not* taken by him as a pledge that the 'Uthmanic Vulgate is beyond taint. It instead means that 'though the Qur'ān is neglected with one people, it is protected and shielded with another people',[108] the Prophet having assured his followers that the Qur'ān would *never* be separated from his elect descendents in the *ḥadīth al-thaqalayn*. And though 'Alī's oath that 'you will never see it again' makes open access to his codex impossible, access of a kind is indeed feasible through the imamate's teachings.

Vitally, if unexpectedly, Shahrastānī combines all this with basic reverence for the 'Uthmānic text, which he declares to enshrine God's Word.[109] He quotes 'Alī's own ban on derogating 'Uthmān and his codification, and he mentions how he and other imams set an example of respect by personally transcribing it.[110] Shahrastānī also draws attention to how the Qur'ān honours the Torah and the Gospel, simpliciter, as divinely revealed, despite the intractable questions of authenticity applying to them.[111] Light is shed on this outwardly contradictory stance when Shahrastānī refers to both pre-Qur'ānic scriptures as having multiple transmissions. The case of the Torah with its massoretic and supposed Aaronic transmission has already been mentioned. The Gospel instead comes down in four primary lines through Matthew, Mark, Luke and John – these in fact being likened by Shahrastānī to exegesis in which lie quotations of God's Word.[112] Notwithstanding their involved transmission, the Qur'ān inculcates awe for these scriptures. That Shahrastānī here envisages a parallel with the Muslim scripture seems inescapable. His teaching amounts to a theory of binary transmission for the Qur'ān. His 'meta-Qur'ān' is made present through two channels, neither of which suffices per se. For while the 'Uthmānic text has the said problems in transcription, the 'Alid codex is only *implicit* in the imams' teachings and may never be seen openly. But together, the two channels do allow a uniquely authentic encounter with God's Word – an achievement precisely claimed for the *Mafātīḥ* in view of its careful blend of both transmissive lines.

So, despite this theory's obvious controversy, irreverence for the 'Uthmānic text does not follow from it. The 'Uthmānic text remains sacred as a portal to the noumenon of the Word.[113] The real upshot of Shahrastānī's theory seems instead to be just to reinforce his reliance on the imamate in the arcana. Yet, in view of this, it may be surprising how little he frames his analysis of particular verses in terms of the explicit sayings of the imams. While he clearly takes it that his basic hermeneutical keys derive from the imamate, its link with the details of his analysis of this or that verse's *anagōgē* seems only *implied.* In one major statement, he even claims the imams' authority in a more mystical than conventional sense. In launching his discussion of the *basmala*'s arcana he says:

> [...] since I am specified by the transmitted prayer 'O God, benefit us by that which You teach us, and teach us that by which You benefit us, by the truth of the chosen ones amongst Your servants', *I found in myself* [translator's emphasis] the faculty of being guided to the word of prophecy and I understood the language of the divine message, so I was thereby rightly guided to the arcana of words in the glorious Qur'ān without my doing exegesis of the Qur'ān by [mere] personal opinion.[114]

Here the derivation of Shahrastānī's hermeneutic from the Prophet's line seems metaphysical rather than historical. In fact, it means the author's *spiritual* effacement in the imams – as he says, he is singled out by the prayer which requests that God teach through the 'chosen ones amongst God's servants'. Through this inner relationship Shahrastānī explicitly says that he finds *within himself* the ability to do hermeneutics, which is, a priori, no longer mere individual opinion. It appears that such a claim springs from the idea, present in certain Ismāʿīlī teachings, of the true disciple's inward configuration (*tamaththul*) of the imam.[115]

Main hermeneutical concepts

As alluded to earlier, apropos of the virtuous servant of God in Shahrastānī's quest, Ismāʿīlism is the likely source for the hermeneutic talismans had from him – the 'keys' of the work's title. These are formed of the said complementarities, the full list of which covers creation/the Command, hierarchy/contrariety, the accomplished/the inchoative, and also, better known antonyms from Qur'ānic exegesis such as generality/specificity, the abrogating/the abrogated, the clear/the ambiguous, and revelation/hermeneutics.[116] Through applying these, either singly or in coordination, to each verse, the arcanal aspect of the Qur'ān opens.

Firstly, creation (*khalq*) and the Command (*amr*) are seen as the two great orders of reality issuing from God. The Command, identified with the Qur'ānic *esto*, '*kun*' ('be!'), is the very means by which the things of creation enter existence, a prerequisite, then, for the entire created realm.[117] It bears close comparison with the concept of the Logos in John 1: 1–3, without which 'was not anything made that was made'. It is vital that Shahrastānī extends his identification of the Command to encompass the entire Qur'ān, and the religious law in principle rooted in the latter (i.e., precisely, divine *commandments*). Hence he takes the scripture to have a literal cosmogonic role, and with this as premise, he develops a radically non-figurative kind of esoteric hermeneutic, far, say, from the *sensus allegoricus* of the Quadriga in Christian scholasticism. Shahrastānī is instead led to theorise on the Qur'ān's occult significance at the level of its very words, particles and letters. In these ingenious interpretations (of which cases will come, in sketching the Exordium commentary below), outer reality is viewed as unfolding *through* the Qur'ān's details and deep structures; the impact is not the other way around. In sum, our author's positive identification of the Qur'ān with the creational blueprint brings about an ingenious sensitivity to its literal aspect: the location of certain verses between others, the use of a *kāf* here or a *nūn* there, the very shape of this or that Arabic letter.

The correspondence (the term is used here in a consciously Swedenborgian way) between the two great orders of reality is thus profound; they interrelate unfathomably. In line with this, in one passage Shahrastānī equates creation and the Command with the 'scales' referred to in many Qur'ānic verses.[118] He gives prooftexts for the mutual implication of creation and the Command, for example: the very formula 'Be [= Command] and it is [= creation]' (e.g. Q. 16:40); also: '[...] He created humanity [= creation]. He taught it speech [= Command]' (Q. 55:1–4); again 'A goodly word [= Command] is as a goodly tree [= creation]' (Q. 14:24).[119] In such dicta, either the Command reference or the creation reference precedes. This spurs Shahrastānī deeper into the symbolism of the scales, concluding that 'when what is weighed consists in things pertaining to the Command and the religious law, its scales are the creation and creational things; and when what is weighed consists in creational things, its scales consist in things pertaining to the Command'.[120] In other words, to fathom a thing from one dimension, it is counterpoised with its equivalent in the other, as the load in one scale-pan of a balance is only gauged by placing its equal in the twin. The deep mutuality of revelation and reason, of religion and philosophy, and of the spiritual and physical order, thus rests for Shahrastānī on the Qur'ānic topos of the scales. So foundational is the complementarity of creation/the Command to our thinker that he often elaborates the others through subdividision with it. It is noteworthy in this connection that the relevant complementarity was central to Ismāʿīlī thought, much of whose theological concern focused on the Command-Logos. This hypostasis was daringly assimilated by Ismāʿīlī philosophers of the time with the *deus revelatus*, the very demiurge.[121]

Next, hierarchy (*tarattub*) and contrariety (*taḍādd*) are seemingly drawn from Ismāʿīlī theory too.[122] The first of these great principles is an ultimate 'vertical' differential while the second is an ultimate 'horizontal' one. Their role, in simple form, in the internal organisation of the *Milal* was remarked above. But, given Shahrastānī's mentioned habit of schematic elaboration, here in the *Mafātīḥ* he further splits contrariety between creation and the Command, and even says that contrarieties *within* creation and the Command can be in two distinct ways. Thus, within creation there may be contrariety between an existent and a non-existent, and also between one existent and another; and within the Command there may be contrariety between faith and unbelief, and also between one faith and another faith. The Qur'ān, for Shahrastānī, is marked by its constant expression of the contrariety principle: 'There is no verse in regard to the believers but another verse follows it in regard to the unbelievers, and there is no quality of good without one of the qualities of evil being mentioned after it.'[123] He even claims that 'were you to examine the words of the Qur'ān you would find this contrariety in every word, except what God wills'.[124] The scripture's title, *al-Furqān* ('the Criterion', from the verbal root *faraqa*, 'to discriminate'), is said by our exegete to voice this trait. On the other hand, the title *al-Qur'ān*, derived through a semantic etymology from *qarina*, 'to join' (rather than its standard, historical derivation from *qara'a*, 'to recite'),[125] is said to voice the scripture's correlative trait of 'gathering together the things hierarchically ordered within it (*mutarattibāt fīhi*)'. Both characteristics are alluded to in one breath in Q. 17:106: 'And it is a Qur'ān that We have divided up (*faraqnā-hu*) [...].'

Given the Qur'ān's cosmic function, hermeneutics and metaphysics merge. Thus hierarchism in holy scripture matches that in existence itself. Shahrastānī quotes a prophetic tradition confirming that there is no existence at all without hierarchy: 'Human beings continue to prosper as long as they are different. When they become equal they are destroyed.'[126] He goes on to point out hierarchies in different species of being – between one angel and another, one prophet and another and one human being and another.[127] One human will thus be a teacher of knowledge, and another, a disciple (in view of hierarchy); and where one will be a disciple, another will be a mere 'dungfly' (in view of contrariety)![128] Ismāʿīlī teachings doubtless leave their stamp here, notably the principle of authoritative instruction (*taʿlīm*) with its teacher-disciple (*ʿālim-mutaʿallim*) relationship, also the stark juxtaposition of initiates and the rest, and the general mirroring of cosmic and human hierarchies, the latter expressed par excellence in the levels of the *ḥudūd al-dīn*.

Shahrastānī harnesses this hierarchism in unexpected ways. It emerges, for example, as his own 'rational' grounds for the Qurʾān's inimitability. For if humanity ranks above other species through its faculty of speech and reason (both covered by the word *nuṭq*), this faculty being inimitable for whatever ranks below humanity, then prophets rank above humans through the *perfection* of that faculty, this perfection being likewise inimitable for whatever ranks below prophets.[129] Moreover, given that *nuṭq* covers speech *and* reason, not only the Qurʾān's inimitability qua speech follows from this line of thought but also qua reason, i.e. in its intellectual/ethical content. On these grounds, our author, perhaps surprisingly, stands against claiming the rhetorical superlativity of this or that part of the Qurʾān.[130] For, he says, such implies having a standard *beyond* it, in using which the text is evaluated. Rather, through hierarchy in *nuṭq* the whole scripture should be viewed as a priori inimitable.[131] In this, Shahrastānī, at a stroke, shelves proofs for inimitability based on analyses of the Qurʾān's rhetorical perfection as also on the supernatural information supposedly within it.[132] In place of the pseudo-aposteriority of such proofs, his own has radical apriority.

For its part, the complementarity of the accomplished (*mafrūgh*) and the inchoative (*mustaʾnaf*) is also argued to have a likely Ismāʿīlī source.[133] However, in chapter ten of his introduction, Shahrastānī simply draws them from a prophetic tradition which he quotes in full. It may be noted, nevertheless, that this full version of the tradition seems absent from the respected Sunnī compendia, and this may be because the context, as our author provides it, is a clash between the great Abū Bakr and ʿUmar.[134] The

Prophet is upset to hear them get heated discussing predestination, as he gathers from them on intervening. He tells them to think in terms of a mighty angel whose constitution is half fire, half ice. The fire in it is not allowed to melt the ice and the ice in it is not allowed to extinguish the fire. The great angel praises God without cease for maintaining its paradoxical nature in existence. But 'Umar finally puts the question bluntly to the Prophet: are the lives of us humans as yet unfolding (*anif*), i.e. inchoative (*musta'naf*), or are they instead already accomplished (*mafrūgh*), with contents quite determined? The Prophet concedes that they are accomplished. But nevertheless we must also act: 'Act! And each is eased towards what he has been created for', says the Prophet.

This then, for Shahrastānī, is the original authority for the terms,[135] of which (by some lapsus calami?) he takes the symbol of the inchoative to be the angel's ice and that of the accomplished to be its fire, while it seems more natural that the solid element, ice, stands for the accomplished and the mobile element, fire, stands for the inchoative. (Perhaps what was in his mind is that ice is as yet in a state of latency, and is resolved through the action of fire, hence the equation of ice with the inchoative and fire with the accomplished). But such details should not divert us from the genius of the Prophet's explanation. The symbol of the paradoxical angel effects the necessary transition from the natural viewpoint in which the antinomy remains intractable, to a viewpoint in which the logically 'impossible' combination of the terms is taken positively, as perpetual testimony to the Supreme Being's power.[136]

Shahrastānī has both exegetical and theological uses for the complementarity. In theology, extreme positions like that of the necessitarian Jabriyya, who unqualifiedly denied free will, and the libertarian Qadariyya, who unqualifiedly affirmed it, are held to follow from ignorance of the complementarity. From the Jabriyya's fixation with the dimension of the accomplished arises their negligence (*tafrīṭ*) in claiming that God commands sinners what they are unable to fulfil – a teaching which fosters laxism. On the other hand, from the Qadariyya's fixation on the dimension of the inchoative arises their exaggeration (*ifrāṭ*) in denying that human actions depend on God – a teaching which stints God's omnipotence. The key is to acknowledge the coexistence of the two dimensions, in step with the Prophet: '[...] his statement [to 'Umar] "act!" is an allusion to the judgement of the inchoative and "each is eased towards what he has been created for" is an allusion to the judgement of the accomplished'.[137] All this echoes Shahrastānī's aforementioned discussion of aid and abandonment in the *Nihāya*, in which context however, he relied on another complementarity – that of generality/specificity – to solve the clash between necessitarians and libertarians.

The exegetical use of the inchoative/accomplished complementarity has to do with reconciling Qur'ānic verses, the prime exegetical task of *tarjīḥ*. Some, for instance, urge Muḥammad to reprove and guide unbelievers, as Q. 20:44: 'Speak to him a gentle word, perhaps he will pay heed or be god-fearing.' Others instead say that such efforts are vain, as Q. 2:6: 'It is all the same for them if you warn them or do not warn them. They will not believe.' But as Shahrastānī sees it: for him who does not understand the two judgements [the inchoative and accomplished], combining the verses of those who defy admonition with the verses of the command to admonish, is hard. 'And that is the secret of secrets!'[138] That is, revelations urging guidance refer to the inchoative and verses repudiating it refer to the accomplished. Again, Shahrastānī puts this complementarity with creation/the Command, to yield a more involved picture. The accomplished and the inchoative in the Command (qua Qur'ān) are the two kinds of verse just mentioned, necessitarian ones and those of commandment or admonition, respectively. Next, the accomplished and the inchoative in creation are the two great classes of being: spiritual ones above space-time and material ones within space-time.[139]

The next complementarity, generality (*'umūm*) and specificity (*khuṣūṣ*), is standard in Qur'ān interpretation, without necessary derivation from Ismā'īlism. Yet even here some read Ismā'īlī influence.[140] Whatever the case, Shahrastānī's handling seems subtler than normal in legal exegesis (not least in his own Shāfi'ī school), where the pair are used to weigh the force of different injunctions and again, to reconcile revelations.[141] But for Shahrastānī further degrees enter: general, specific, and *individual*. As he says: 'There is no general expression in the Qur'ān without specification having entered it, and there is no specification without individualisation having joined it.'[142] The past trend, he says, has been to overlook the last of these registers, i.e. individualisation (*tashkhīṣ*).

Shahrastānī brings out even more shades of meaning, using Qur'ānic verses. 'Humanity' (*nās*), for instance, covers the whole human species in a verse like Q. 2:21: 'O humanity (*ayyuhā'l-nās*)! Worship your Lord.' But such commands are not binding on the level of total generality, given that Islamic law grants that children and the mad are not legally answerable, though they of course fall within humanity. A higher degree of specificity is understood from a verse like Q. 2:199: 'Then hasten to where humanity (*nās*) hastens.' Referring to the rites at 'Arafāt in the Greater Pilgrimage, this in fact tells those answerable to imitate a more specific group, whom Shahrastānī calls the 'rightly-guided guides' (*al-hudāt al-mahdiyūn*). These are, nonetheless, called 'humanity' in the said verse. Finally 'humanity' is also found in the Qur'ān at the individual level since traditional commentaries state that *nās* in the following verse (Q. 4:54) means none other than the Prophet himself: '[...] or are they jealous of humanity (*nās*) because of what God gave them in His bounty?'[143]

In this look at *nās* in the Qur'ān, Shahrastānī takes the stock *distinguo* into no less than *four* degrees: general, relatively specific, more specific, and finally, individual. A like dilation is found in the case of 'mercy' (*raḥma*) in the Qur'ān. Three degrees of it are yielded from a single verse, namely Q. 7:156–7, in which they unfold in precise sequence: '[1] My mercy encompasses everything, and [2] I will stipulate it for those who are God-conscious and give the poor-due and who believe in Our signs, [moreover for] [3] those who follow the Messenger, the unlettered prophet.' In this, the most universal register of the concept comes first: 'My mercy encompasses everything.' It is next relatively specified as for the godly, but not limited in time or tradition: 'I will stipulate it for those who are God-conscious and give the poor-due and who believe in Our signs.' Lastly it is mentioned, in a yet sharper register, as for the godly of Islam: '[...] those who follow the Messenger, the unlettered prophet'. And beyond this, Shahrastānī draws attention to a wholly individual sense for 'mercy' in the Qur'ān, given that a verse like Q. 21:107 uses 'mercy' for the Prophet alone: 'We only sent you as a mercy for the worlds (*raḥmatan li'l-'ālamīn*).'

Shahrastānī's look at the otherwise standard exegetical pair, the abrogating (*nāsikh*) and abrogated (*mansūkh*), holds surprises despite its brevity. Abrogation is the main tool for the task – already mentioned several times – of reconciling verses and weighing divine injunctions. Prima facie contradiction is resolved on grounds of chronology, the earlier Qur'ānic ruling taken to be abrogated, the later, abrogating.[144] But it turns out that Shahrastānī's concern here is not just one Qur'ānic verse's relation with another but the Qur'ān's relation as a whole with earlier scriptures. That is, he covers not just intra-textual abrogation but also inter-textual abrogation. A startling, ecumenical side to his thought comes into view, perhaps to be expected for the author of the *Milal* with its global interest in beliefs.

In fact, the unmistakable thrust of his discussion is to *deny* abrogation in the recognisable sense. Our author moots three definitions: abrogation might be taken as the annulment of an established injunction (*rafʿ al-ḥukm al-thābit*); it might be the expiry of the time allotted to the injunction (*intihāʾ muddat al-ḥukm*); or finally, it might be viewed as a process of perfection (*takmīl*, alternatively 'supplementation').[145] In the following discussion, Shahrastānī favours the third. That any revelation becomes redundant is ill sounding to him – it cannot be what abrogation means. He even states categorically: 'Never hold the opinion that one divine system (*sharīʿa min al-sharāʾiʿ*) is negated by another or that its injunctions are annulled and others laid down.'[146] Instead, for Shahrastānī, each successive *sharīʿa* is supplementary (*mukammila*) to what preceded it in an unfolding process from Adam till the Resurrection.[147]

Despite appearances, Shahrastānī does not compromise Islam's axiomatic superiority in this. He proposes that it is the final and noblest (*ashraf*) of *sharīʿa*s.[148] But his subtler sense of the true status of this *sharīʿa* comes out in the following three models. Our author starts with a case from creational data (*khalqiyyāt*) – that of foetal development, as celebrated in, for example, Q. 23:12–14. He says: 'Were the sperm, amongst *khalqiyyāt*, negated or annulled, it would not attain the second stage, nor the third, but it would reach the limit of its perfection and would not become another form of perfection, with the fulfilment of its identity.'[149] That is, the biological process is mainly seen in terms of continuity, with earlier stages persisting within the growing organism. Next, Shahrastānī moves on to data linked to the Command-Logos (*amriyyāt*) and explicitly brings in the case of revealed systems or *sharīʿa*s. He here draws an exact parallel with the continuum of foetal development, using close phraseology: 'Were the first *sharīʿa* negated or annulled, it would not attain the second [stage] and the third, but it would reach the limit of completion and would not become a form of perfection, with the consolidation of its identity.'[150] Finally Shahrastānī comes to the case of intra-textual abrogation, the chain of abrogated and abrogating rulings within the Qurʾān. The Qurʾān, he says, contains two aspects. Only one is in fact liable to processes of abrogation, namely, that aspect consisting of the juristic branches (*furūʿ*). Yet God, he still stresses, only abolishes for some perfection (*li-kamālin*) in which [the abrogated] has culminated.'[151] The other aspect of the Qur'ān is, by contrast, wholly changeless, amounting to the 'principles of religion' (*uṣūl al-diyāna*) and the 'Mother of the Scripture' (*Umm al-Kitāb*). Shahrastānī likens this to the essence in relation to the form (*al-dhāt li'l-ṣūra*) and the foundation in relation to the house (*al-asās li'l-bayt*).[152]

In each case above, Shahrastānī seems to accent continuity over change. The harshest case is, in fact, abrogation within the Qur'ān, where the changeable aspect is, in passing, cast in terms of pure abolition (*maḥw*). But there is still the general stress on continuity in the *Umm al-Kitāb*, the changeless core of the scripture.[153] At any rate, when Shahrastānī delves further into abrogation within the Qur'ān (i.e., in the juristic branches) it is, after all, given a twist which practically denies that rulings expire – a negation then, of abrogation as widely understood. He thus takes up the supposed abrogation of the 'verse of acquittal' by the 'verse of the sword'. The first is Q. 109:6: 'To you your religion and to me my religion.' The second is represented by Q. 2:216: 'Fighting is prescribed for you' and Q. 9:14: 'Fight them, God will punish them at your hands.' Our thinker stands against the view that the charge to fight simply *overturns* the charge to leave alone 'the religions of the unbelievers'. For him, the verse of acquittal represents the ne plus ultra in self-acquittal through verbal declaration, unsurpassable as the credal affirmation of monotheism. It is simply that once this affirmation is in place it must be complemented by acquittal through action, namely, the affirmation of monotheism militarily.[154] Both self-acquittals stand in their own right, though the second assumes the first. And crucially, this non-eliminative concept of abrogation extends for Shahrastānī to *all* cases of abrogation within the Qur'ān: 'Likewise every verse of the Qur'ān which is said to be abrogated by another verse, the abrogating verse is found to be set up by the abrogated, not annulling it, nor negating it (*lā rāfiʿa wa lā mubṭila*).'[155] The rigour of the legislation in this example disabuses us of the idea that Shahrastānī's generous concept of abrogation blunts the earnestness of his faith. Yet the clear thrust of each of his models of abrogation is that, whatever the right of the abrogating form to assert itself, its role is to confirm, not eliminate. In terms of inter-faith relations – of utmost concern – implicit in our thinker's concept seems to be the Islamic state's upkeep of earlier faith communities as official 'custodial peoples' (*ahl al-dhimma*). On their payment of the protection tax (*jizya*) the state was in fact bound actively to defend them and their places of worship from attack. Is this not a vital upshot of Shahrastānī's talk of the later *sharīʿa* subsuming but not eliminating the earlier? There are again possible Ismāʿīlī stimuli for elements of his concept here.[156]

Next, Shahrastānī notes that the clear/ambiguous complementarity stands out since the Qur'ān itself states that its verses are split in line with it, notably in Q. 3:7: '[God] it is who sent down to you the scripture consisting in clear verses (*muḥkamāt*) – they are the essence [literally, mother] of the scripture – and other ambiguous ones (*mutashābihāt*)[...].' Though views vary on how to define these categories, Shahrastānī rules that the 'people of realisation' amongst the learned simply define the clear verses through the aforementioned dimension of the *accomplished* and the ambiguous verses through the *inchoative*.[157] He next observes that hermeneutics (*ta'wīl*) – the problematic task of interpretation, as against mere exegesis (*tafsīr*) – focuses on the text's ambiguous or inchoative part. Shahrastānī seems to draw this from the next part of the same verse (Q. 3:7): 'As for those in whose hearts is deviation, they follow what is ambiguous of it, seeking dissension and seeking its hermeneutic (*ta'wīl*).' Hermeneutics, centring on the ambiguous, is here barred to the plain believer and is made the imamate's preserve. Though unstated by Shahrastānī, this privilege follows from the rest of this famous verse, for it goes on to state that the Qur'ān's hermeneutic is only known by God Himself and by 'the firm-rooted in knowledge', i.e. the imams.[158]

In sum, this hinted background means that while the accomplished side of the Qur'ān is open to Sunnī exegesis, its inchoative side is only open to the imams. The practical upshot of this only comes out when Shahrastānī, as before, further splits the clear/ambiguous between creation and the Command to get a more elaborate final scheme. Firstly, there are the clear verses, some of which correspond with the accomplished aspect of creation (i.e. events already fulfilled through divine predestination, *qadar*) and others of which correspond with the accomplished aspect of the Command (i.e. already known legal injunctions).[159] All such verses, as clear, fall within the scope of conventional exegesis. But secondly, there are the ambiguous verses, some of which correspond with the inchoative aspect of creation (i.e. forthcoming events through the divine decree, *qaḍā'*) and others of which correspond with the inchoative aspect of the Command (i.e. legal injunctions which, though rooted in scripture, are only subsequently actualised).[160] It may be taken, then, that for Shahrastānī, all in these last categories, comprising Qur'ānic prophecies about the future as well as later legal applications rooted in its verses, falls *beyond* the reach of conventional exegesis and rests on the hermeneutic of the imams. If this brief, allusive and complex discussion has been decoded rightly, it shows that Shahrastānī's dependence on the imamate reaches even to the legal side of his religion, albeit that in the light of his Shāfiʿī links this presumably stayed just a theoretical implication of his teaching.

Reference is made at points of the commentary to the imamate's prime, indeed divine, role. In the doxology, Shahrastānī even speaks of the role of the imams as mirroring that of the angels. Angels are the means of 'sending down' (*tanzīl*) revelation, the first part of the process. The imams and their scholar-adherents (*al-ʿulamāʾ al-ṣādiqa*) are then the means of 'taking back up' (*taʾwīl*, 'hermeneutics', literally translated) the revelation, the second but no less important part of the revelatory process.[161] Both in tandem bring about the full cycle of revelation, from God to God, and both in fact exercise a *divine* function, as enshrined in Q. 15:9: 'We send down the Remembrance and We are its protector.' That is, God is the true agent of the descent of the scripture to earth through the angels and He is also the true protector of its ultimate meanings through the imams. Shahrastānī even speaks of the imams (and their scholar-adherents) in terms that the Qur'ān reserves for angels, as ranged in ranks 'accompanying [the believer] on all sides' (Q. 13:11: *muʿaqqibāt min bayni yadayhi wa min khalfihi*), thus stressing the deep kinship of the two orders of divine functionary.[162]

The Exordium commentary

The above lattice of complementarities is used to the full in opening the Qur'ān's arcanal dimension. Each verse, to repeat, is explored in depth under slightly shifting headings such as lexicography (*lugha*), linguistic coinage (*waḍʿ*), etymology (*ishtiqāq*), grammar (*naḥw*), harmonious order (*naẓm*), exegesis (*tafsīr*), semantics (*maʿānī*) and, finally, arcana (*asrār al-āyāt*). Data under the earlier headings are often assumed in this last, which is therefore the true fruit of the overall project. Interest is also concentrated in the arcana because of their Ismāʿīlī trend. Their content will thus be the focus in the following.

A prime case of how Shahrastānī's commentary finds fulfilment in the arcana is in the question of whether the *basmala*-formula should be taken as integral to the Exordium, or not, and simply be seen as a division-marker. This is arguably the problematic to the whole Exordium commentary. From the beginning, some took the consecrative formula to lie outside the text of the chapter itself or indeed *any* of the scripture's chapters.[163] But the partisans of this view had to deal with the clear definition of the Exordium as sevenfold, from its identification in prophetic traditions with the mysterious Seven Doubled Ones (or Seven Repeated Ones, *sabʿun min al-mathānī*) of Q. 15:87: 'We have given you [Muḥammad] Seven Doubled Ones and the mighty Qur'ān.' In this identification, the said 'doubling' is taken to refer to the repetition of the Exordium in each cycle (*rakʿa*) of Islam's formal prayer (*ṣalāt*). But the main point is that the identification of the Exordium as the *Seven* Doubled Ones implied its division into seven verses – straightforward enough if the *basmala* was included as verse one, harder if it was not. So the authorities who took the *basmala* as outside the text had to work out a *new* verse division to make seven verses out of the six left. They did this by treating the words '[...] those whom You have graciously favoured' (*anʿamta ʿalayhim*) in verse seven as the end of a new verse six, with the rest of that verse as the new seventh.[164]

Shahrastānī argues against this from tradition, reason, and, finally, from what transpires in the arcana. Of the first kind of proof is a prophetic tradition that any affair begun *without* the consecrative formula is 'emasculated' (*abtar*).[165] Religious consensus also holds that there are four pauses in the Exordium's recitation, and *anʿamta ʿalayhim* is not one of them – going against the adjustment made by those who exclude the *basmala* from the numbered verses. On the other hand, a proof from reason centres on the phonological harmony (*insiyāq*) of the verse endings. For this clearly involves the vowel *-ī* followed by a final consonant whose vowel remains unpronounced, thereby generating the following perfect sevenfold series: *-ḥīm*, *-mīn*, *-ḥīm*, *-dīn*, *-ʿīn*, *-qīm*, and *-līn*.[166] The phrase *anʿamta ʿalayhim* breaks this pattern.

Valid though such proofs are, for Shahrastānī it is only through the arcana that deeper certainty is reached. His exploration of the arcana thus uncovers an unforeseen division of the Exordium into precisely seven elements. But this sevenfold pattern differs from the one simply involving its number of verses. In this new interpretation, the doubling referred to in the Exordium's Qur'ānic title is not to do with the repetition of its verses in prayer-cycles; rather, it involves a set of profound conceptual doublings, echoes or perhaps 'reprises' (*mardūdāt*) which run through the whole chapter. The vital point is that these *mardūdāt* – explored in detail in the arcana – *only* reach the perfect aggregate of seven if the *basmala*-formula is seen as within the chapter. For our thinker then, this upshot of the arcana is the real proof that the formula is part of it. Needless to say, most of the *mardūdāt* involve unearthing the function of the hermeneutic complementarities within the Exordium's verses. The complementarities readily fit Shahrastānī's needs here.

Setting aside the unfolding of the seven doublings for now, Shahrastānī's first section on arcana is dedicated to God's name, *Allāh.* These teachings on the arcana of God's *nomen proprium* are credited to a group called 'the magnifiers of God's names' (*al-muʿaẓẓimūn li-asmāʾiʾllāh*).[167] While such authorities spurn the claim that the name is derivative (*mushtaqq*), Shahrastānī does, under 'linguistic coinage', air theories to the contrary. He gives thought-provoking etymologies for the name '*Allāh*' from *waliha*, 'to become mad with love' (the idea being that such madness befalls God's worshippers) and also from *lāha*, 'to hide oneself' (implying God's absolute transcendence of creation).[168] Another prominent view, attributed here to al-Ḥasan al-Jurjānī, is that the name comes from the verb *aliha*, 'to seek protection'. This produces the word *ilāh* (god), signifying that 'refuge is taken in Him' (*yūlahu ilayhi*) on the analogy of *imām* (leader), which signifies that the individual in question 'is followed as example' (*yuʾtammu bihi*). The Arabic definite article, *al-* was then supposedly added to this earliest form of the word as an honorific, yielding *al-ilāh*, 'the god'. But through frequent use the *a* of *al-* and the *i* of *ilāh* coalesced, leaving the name in its familiar form: *Allāh.*[169]

But, as just mentioned, Shahrastānī himself denies that the divine *nomen proprium* is just some accident of linguistic history: 'How', he protests, '*could* there be an etymology for it?'[170] In the arcana he instead gives a set of interpretations which show the deep theological sense of the word's form. As he puts it: '[...] the letters, which are the basis of the word, point to what it is obligatory to know and is made known to be obligatory'.[171] Perhaps the most gripping of these interpretations takes the pronoun *Huwa* (He) as its starting point. The pronoun is implied by the final *h* of the word *Allāh* which, fully vowelled in the nominative, would be *Allāhu*. *Huwa* would then be yielded from the final *hu* by adding the consonantal 'consort' (*qarīna*) of *u* namely *w*. Shahrastānī says that this seed of the divine name stands for a first reification of the godhead, acknowledging its 'thingness' (*shay'iyya*). More particularly, it refers to God's majesty (*jalāl*) or utter transcendence, given that it acknowledges, by implication, that *only* God's 'He-ness' (*huwiyya*) or quoddity (the fact *that* He is) is known, not His identity (*māhiyya*) or quiddity (*what* He is), which stays wholly outside understanding.

Next, the *l*, central to the name as a whole, is added to this basic *hu* and great meaning is again found in this. In Arabic, the prepositional form *li-* signifies that what adjoins it has the status of possession (or perhaps, responsibility). Shahrastānī renders it with the stock grammatical term, the '*lām* affirming possession' (*lām al-tamlīk*). Prefixed to the pronoun *-hu* to make *lahu* (i.e. 'His', or perhaps 'due to Him'), it acknowledges that everything other than God is His possession (*milk*) and dominion (*mulk*). This then is held by our author to refer to the great complement of God's attribute of majesty or transcendence, namely, His 'bounty' or 'creative largesse' (*ikrām*) – a complementarity rooted in Q. 55:26–7: 'All that is in the world will pass away and your Lord's face (or 'self') alone will endure in its majesty and bounty (*dhū'l-jalāli wa'l-ikrām*).' The impact of these twin attributes of majesty and bounty is later spelt out in Shahrastānī's statement: 'He is veiled from them through His majesty, so they may not perceive Him, and He manifests Himself to them through His bounty, so they may not deny Him.'[172] So it is that these two affirmations – one through the final *h* and one through the medial *l* of the name – capture the paradox that God is at once incomprehensible *and* undeniable, or as Shahrastānī puts it: 'Insofar as He is He (*Huwa*) He is ungraspable and insofar as all belongs to Him (or is due to Him, *la-hu*) He is undeniable.' Lastly the *a* is prefixed to the *l* to give *al-*, the Arabic definite article. For Shahrastānī, the true meaning of grammatical definition (*taʿrīf*, literally 'making known') in regard to God is to get across that He is indeed *better* known (*aʿraf*) than all else.

So it is that through this ingenious understanding, the divine *nomen proprium* voices synthetically the *deus absconditus* and the *deus revelatus*. For it enshrines in its extrema the paradox that God is both wholly hidden (i.e. through-*hu*) *and* unhidden (i.e. through *al-*). Moreover, through its median (i.e. *l*), the name shows precisely in *what* way the hiddenness does not contradict the apparentness. Before moving on, it may be noted that the direction of this analysis moves from the *h* of reification, through the *l* affirming possession, to the *a* of grammatical definition. This inverts the sequence of phonemes in the natural, verbal articulation of the name. Thus the unfolding of the inward meanings of the name by Shahrastānī is in a chiastic or mirror relation with its outward letters. The relation of inward signficance with outward form often involves such inversions.

A prime role of the Qur'ān in Shahrastānī's thought is to express God for the benefit of creation. This is, in fact, an act of self-giving amounting to a substantive manifestation, particularly in the case of the divine names in the text. Shahrastānī thus shifts from the milder stance that the divine names tell us about God, to the stance that God is actually offered to His creation through them. He here makes use of the old Ṣūfī distinction of God's disclosure through something else (*taʿrīf*) and His self-disclosure (*taʿarruf*): 'Wherever you find in the Qur'ān a verbal expression for whatever is linked to one of the divine names, it is for the sake of disclosing [God], every disclosure (*taʿrīf*) being [God's own] *self-disclosure* (*taʿarruf*) to something, and every self-disclosure being an epiphany (*tajallī*) of His [...].'[173] Jaʿfar al-Ṣādiq's words are quoted here to carry the point: 'God manifests Himself (*tajallā*) to His servants through His scripture.'[174] These grounds yield a strangely positivistic scriptural mysticism in which sense and reference merge and divine names in the text are credited with an objective cosmological function.

Such premises change the very concept of hermeneutics. As said earlier in presenting Shahrastānī's identification of the Qur'ān with the Command, the penetration of the Qur'ān's higher meanings is seen here *ipso facto* as an encounter with the world's transcendental roots. God's *nomen proprium* is a good case of such reasoning. For Shahrastānī, the constituent letters of the divine name (i.e. the *alif, lām, lām, hā'*) are the root cause of created existence in a literal sense; he even terms them the 'four foundations' (*al-mabādi' al-arbaʿa*).[175] He traces the germinal form of tridimensional space, the so-called 'primary body', to the different characteristics of the Arabic letters in question. The height of this body follows from the vertical extension of the *alif*, its breadth from the horizontal extension of the *lām*, and its depth from the cavity (so to speak) of the *hā'*.[176] While literally causal for our author, these correspondences surely also function to sacralise the whole spatial domain. The divine name is in effect iconised in the very structure of space. Again, an Ismāʿīlī background is at hand for all this. It appears, for example, to have been a doctrine in the circle of the renegade Fāṭimid *dāʿī* al-Ḥasan b. Ḥaydara al-Akhram (d. 408/1018).[177]

Shahrastānī links the great names of God found in a chain in the *basmala*, that is, *Allāh*, *al-Raḥmān*, *al-Raḥīm*, with primary divine functions. The sequential attributes of *ilāhiyya*, *raḥmāniyya* and *raḥīmiyya*, he explains, are responsible for existentiating, maintaining, and rewarding creatures.[178] He also speaks of each as sustaining one of the three 'worlds': respectively that of creation, the Command, and the future *eschaton* (or the 'world of merit').[179] Qurʾānic texts are given for these correspondences. The link of *ilāhiyya* with creation follows from Q. 48:87: 'If you ask them who created them, they will surely say *Allāh*.' That of *raḥmāniyya* with the Command follows by a more associative kind of thinking, from Q. 25:60: 'What is *al-Raḥmān*? Are we to prostrate to whatever you command us?' Finally, that of *raḥīmiyya* with the eschatological realities of reward and merit follows from Q. 33:43: 'He is compassionate (*raḥīm*) towards the believers.'[180] It is important here that the mode of mercy (*raḥma*) manifest in the name *Raḥmān* is not the same as the mode in the name *Raḥīm*. The former name is more intensive in its grammatical form, so that the analogous form *ghaḍbān*, from *ghaḍiba* 'to be angry', means not just 'angry' but '*consumed by* anger', 'furious'. The epithet *Raḥmān*, 'infinitely merciful', is kept in the Qurʾān for God alone and is even treated as close to the divine *nomen proprium* itself in its exclusivity: 'Pray to *Allāh* or pray to *al-Raḥmān*.' (Q. 17:110.) The case of the name *Raḥīm* is quite different, for it applies to God *and* creature, so the Qurʾān describes the Prophet by it, as in Q. 9:128: 'For the believers [the Prophet] is full of pity, compassionate (*raḥīm*).'

Shahrastānī's teaching on *Raḥmān* and *Raḥīm* goes back to a very early tradition on Q. 7:156, as already quoted in the context of the general/specific complementarity: 'My mercy encompasses everything and I will stipulate it for those who are God-conscious [...].' In an interpretation on the authority of such great exegetes of the first period as Ibn ʿAbbās, Muqātil b. Sulaymān and Saʿīd b. Jubayr, the verse refers (as mentioned above) to both a universal, indiscriminate mode of mercy and a particular, discriminate one. In line with the verse, the first of these modes covers all existents whatsoever, while the second is held back for the God-conscious believers alone. This splitting of mercies would have a long history and would get detailed treatment in the thought of the great Ibn al-ʿArabī (d. 638/1240) who sharply marks off what he calls the 'mercy of gratuitous gift' (*raḥmat al-imtinān*) which is to do with the intensive name *Raḥmān*, from the 'mercy of obligation' (*raḥmat al-wujūb*) which is to do with the name *Raḥīm*.[181] Be that as it may, in his discussion Shahrastānī captures the symmetry between the two epithets in a potently chiastic formula: *Raḥmān* is exclusive in predicability (used only of God) but inclusive in operation (extending to all existents) while *Raḥīm* is inclusive in predicability (used of God and creature) but exclusive in operation (extending only to believers). In Shahrastānī's own tighter phraseology: '*Raḥmān* is specific as a name (*khāṣṣ al-ism*) but general in meaning (*ʿāmm al-maʿnā*) and *Raḥīm* is general as a name (*ʿāmm al-ism*) but specific in meaning (*khāṣṣ al-maʿnā*).'[182]

The question of the seven doublings finally enters here, for Shahrastānī says that the two mercies of the *basmala* are one of the said sevenfold set. They are, in fact, the *second* of the doublings, the first being the entire *basmala*-formula of verse one, and the entire *ḥamdala*-formula of verse two (i.e. 'Praise belongs to God, the Lord of the worlds'). The two formulae go naturally together, for even outside the Qurʾānic context the *basmala* is the consecrative formula with which the believer's activities begin, whereas the *ḥamdala* is the thanksgiving formula with which the believer's activities end, or in Shahrastānī's words, the two verses are 'sequential in verbal expression (*lafẓ*) and concordant in meaning (*maʿnā*) [...] "in the name of God" is at beginnings and "praise belongs to God" is at completions'.[183] This per se is evidence that the *basmala* must be within the Exordium. As Shahrastānī says, the evocation of praise and gratitude to God in the *ḥamdala* logically follows the evocation of God's grace and mercy in the *basmala*, so the *ḥamdala* assumes the presence of the *basmala*.

Shahrastānī offers an arcanum from the *ḥamdala* which, though brief, shows well how arcana build on earlier headings. Under the lexicography (*lugha*) of verse two he has said that the word *ḥamd* (praise) in Arabic could have two distinct senses: either eulogy or thanks. *Ḥamd* means eulogy if it responds to a noble quality in the praised and it means thanks if it responds to some grace from the praised. Next, God is fundamentally attributed with both majesty and bounty, as expressed in Q. 55:27 where He is 'possessor of majesty and bounty (*dhūʾl-jalāli waʾl-ikrām*)'. With impressive consistency, Shahrastānī now proposes in the arcana that *ḥamd* in the *ḥamdala* has both its senses at once: eulogy in view of God's inherent majesty and thanks in view of His inherent bounty.[184]

The third doubling comes in verses two and four, the twin titles of God: 'the Lord of the worlds' (*Rabb al-ʿālamīn*) and 'the Ruler of the Day of Judgement' (*Mālik yawm al-dīn*). On etymology Shahrastānī cites the *Maqāyīs* of Aḥmad b. Fāris (d. 395/1004) for the view that the first of these means 'the educator of creatures'. This follows by deriving *rabb* from *rabā*, 'to grow' (hence, form II, *rabbā* = 'to make grow', 'to educate') and through interpreting *ʿālamīn* as each genus of creation.[185] It matters to Shahrastānī that the epithet 'Lord of the worlds' relates specifically to creation and this world, while 'Ruler of the Day of Judgement' relates to the Command and the next world (as implied by texts like Q. 82:19: '[...] *the Command that day is God's*'). Creation concerns the corporeal while the Command concerns the spiritual, in other words, God's realm of omnipotence (*jabarūt*) as distinct from His realm of sovereignty (*malakūt*) respectively. A passage follows which presents the subtle dependence of created beings on those of the world of the Command, an intensity of relation which Shahrastānī strips of the clumsy analogy of physical proximity:

> [...] there is no existent amongst the existents of the world which He has created out of something or which He has originated *ex nihilo*, without there being an angel from His realm of sovereignty which directs it, and a Word (or Logos) which is its active agent determining it – even the rain drop from the sky falls accompanied by an angel and the mote of dust from the earth rises upwards accompanied by an angel. The two worlds are not adjacent to one another in the manner of bodies, nor do they combine intimately in the manner of bodies with shape and form. Rather they are distinct in significance and in reality [...].[186]

Shahrastānī finds the fourth doubling in verse three of the Exordium, where God is mysteriously acknowledged *again* as 'the Infinitely Merciful, the Compassionate'. Here revert the two mercies already discussed under the *basmala* in verse one. Yet nothing in the Qur'ān should be seen as random or pleonastic – for Shahrastānī these mercies certainly have some new significance. He finds this in their very placing in the Exordium's structure, whose every detail he takes as meaningful, indeed, as deeply related to the greater order of reality. These mercies, in brief, are located between 'Lord of the worlds' in verse two and 'Ruler of the Day of Judgement' in verse four. Now, these epithets were said above to relate respectively to the dimensions of creation and the Command. So

Shahrastānī proposes that the mercies in the context of verse three are evoked in a fresh sense, insofar as they here have a mediatory function, interlinking these two great dimensions.[187]

The next doubling, the fifth, is found in the two declarations of verse five: 'It is You we worship and it is You we ask for help.' Shahrastānī's complementarities, notably generality/specificity and the Command/creation, have already served in the arcana. The one now used as the key to this verse's arcanum is the inchoative/accomplished. For unspoken in the phrase 'It is You we worship' is not just the undertaking of God's commandment but also the acknowledgement that the human agent acts freely in response to it, for merit or demerit. For our author then, this first declaration of verse five negates unqualified necessitarianism, and is rooted in the dimension of the inchoative. But balancing this is the second declaration, 'it is You we ask for help', which acknowledges the human agent's dependence on divine aid and which therefore negates unqualified libertarianism, as rooted in the dimension of the accomplished.[188]

A good case of the mentioned 'positivism' of the mysticism of the *Mafātīḥ*, follows here when we are told of two definitive influxes of divine light. The creature undergoes one influx on its projection into existence (*ījād*) by God, and another in its heart on its self-submission (*taslīm*) to God. Now Shahrastānī states enigmatically that the Arabic letters *kāf* and *nūn* trigger both. For *kāf* and *nūn* in the form of the divine creative fiat *kun* ('Be!', as mentioned in Q. 16:40 etc.) trigger the first influx of the creature's history. Next, the cardiac light of submission too is triggered through contact with the same letters, but how? We learn that this is because the declarations of verse five of the Exordium *ipso facto* enact the creature's self-abandonment to God. Accordingly, the details of the Arabic of these declarations must be weighed: *iyyāka naʿbudu wa iyyāka nastaʿīn*. Shahrastānī notes that the second person singular pronominal suffix *-ka* ('you', as in 'it is You'), technically known as 'the "k" of addressing' (*kāf al-khiṭāb*), grammatically betokens direct confrontation with, or witnessing of (*mushāhada*), the addressee. The latter is implied to be actually present to the speaker. Next, the inflexion of the first person plural of the imperfect *na-* ('we', as in 'we worship' and 'we ask for help') betokens the speaker's capacity in carrying through the action of the verb. The *kāf* and the *nūn* of verse five thus fulfil the criteria for reception of the cardiac light: respectively, acknowledgement of the divine object and free self-submission thereto.[189] Thus, both influxes indeed equally come about by the letters *kāf* and *nūn* according to this letter mysticism, which contrasts with the numerological variety. For its part, the topos of the cardiac 'light of *taslīm*' can doubtless be traced to texts such as Q. 39:22 which asks whether 'one whose breast God has opened to Islam so that he has a light from his Lord' is not better than 'those whose hearts are hardened against God's remembrance'. That said, Shahrastānī seems briefly to shift in this talk of self-submission as an inner 'photic' experience, to the experiential terms more usual of Ṣūfism.

According to Shahrastānī, the Exordium pivots on verse five. For its earlier verses have to do with positive declaration (*taʿrīf*) i.e. the declaration of truths about God, while its later verses have to do with 'entrustment' (*taklīf*) i.e. the worshipper's entrustment of needs to God. This follows from the famous tradition, one of the 'divine sayings' (*aḥadīth qudsiyya*): 'I divide the formal prayer between Me and My worshipper into two halves [...]'.[190] Our exegete claims to find a subtle pattern in verse five which reflects its pivotal status: at a deep level it looks back to and retraces the verse with which the chapter began – the *basmala*. The two verses thus bracket the Exordium's first half. Shahrastānī here shows that buried in verse five is the same set of three divine names found at the start: 'In the name of God (*Allāh*), the Infinitely Merciful (*al-Raḥmān*), the Compassionate (*al-Raḥīm*).' His premise is that the request for help in 'It is You we ask for help' is in in fact twofold: for God's help simpliciter, and for God's help qua guidance. When this consideration is skilfully coupled with pertinent verses from the Qur'ān, his proof emerges: verse five points (1) to *Allāh* in the statement 'It is You whom we worship', because the name *Allāh* primarily bespeaks the deservingness of being worshipped. It points (2) to *al-Raḥmān* in the request for help simpliciter in the statement 'It is You we ask for help', because the name *Raḥmān* bespeaks the deservingness of being asked for help, as for instance shown by Q. 21:112: 'Our Lord is *al-Raḥmān*, the one sought for help (*mustaʿān*).' Lastly, it points (3) to *al-Raḥīm* in the request for help qua guidance, again in the statement 'It is You we ask for help', because the name *Raḥīm* bespeaks the deservingness of being asked for guidance, as for instance shown by Q. 7:52: '[The scripture is] a guidance and a mercy (*hudan wa raḥma*) for a people who believe.'

The unfolding of the arcana of the rest of the chapter, verses six and seven, is complex and makes wide use of the complementarities. The real key however seems to be hierarchy/contrariety. Hierarchy in the first instance underlies the plea in verse six, 'Guide us on the straight path' and the statement in verse seven, 'The path of those You have graciously favoured'. In Shahrastānī's view, the former plea pertains to the guidance-seekers, and the 'graciously favoured' in the latter statement refers to the guides stationed above them.[191] Bringing in other complementarities, our author says that the seekers belong to the inchoative while the guides (in the final analysis, the imamate) belong to the accomplished.[192] On the other hand, contrariety is at work between these two groups and the two mentioned in the rest of verse seven: 'Not those against whom is Your wrath nor those who go astray'. These are the precise infernal analogue of the same two ranks – described by our author as a disparity (*tafāwut*) rather than a hierarchy (*tarattub*).[193] So the 'guides' are in contrariety with those subject to divine anger ('those against whom is Your wrath'), while the 'seekers' are in contrariety with 'those who go astray'. These two pairs – the guides and the guided, and their infernal opposites – are the sixth and seventh of Shahrastānī's doublings. The sevenfold chain thus ends and with it not only the divulgence of the supposed true sense of the Exordium's Qur'ānic epithet, the Seven Doubled Ones, but also the real proof that the *basmala* is an inseparable part of the chapter, since the formula yields the first two doublings of the series, which runs, in sum, as follows:

(1) The *basmala* and the *ḥamdala* (verses one and two).
(2) The two modes of mercy represented by the names *al-Raḥmān* and *al-Raḥīm* in the *basmala* (verse one).
(3) 'The Lord of the worlds' = creation (verse two), 'the Ruler of the Day of Judgement' = the Command (verse four).
(4) The mediatory forms of the *basmala*'s two modes of mercy (verse three), interconnecting between creation and the Command, as represented by verse two and verse four.
(5) The two affirmations (verse five): 'It is You we worship' = inchoative; 'it is You we ask for help' = accomplished.
(6) 'Guide us on the straight path, the path of those You have graciously favoured' = hierarchy of guided and guides, respectively (verses six and seven).
(7) 'Not (of) those against whom is Your wrath, nor those who go astray' = infernal guides and guided respectively, in contrariety with (6) (verse seven).

To conclude: Excluding (1), this series emerges through the complementarities or 'keys' which Shahrastānī took himself to have inherited (albeit via Anṣārī and the 'virtuous servant') from the imamate. It is through the latter that his hermeneutical keys have their supposed authority and prophetic aura. That said, the minutiae of the arcana seem to emerge by a secondary process, worked out by the author's initiators or by himself as an independent hermeneut. It may be that to prove in detail the Ismāʿīlī roots of this methodology for entering the awesome terra incognita of the Qur'ān's interior is to miss the obvious point. We are confronted, in all this, by the liminal awareness of a great structure of higher-order concepts underlying the text of the scripture. This mysterious system is, arguably, at one with the coordinated body of teachings which Shahrastānī puts to use in other contexts, notably the philosophical context of the *Muṣāraʿa*, where he uses it to challenge the supposed impostures of Avicennan metaphysics. In the *Muṣāraʿa*, Shahrastānī explicitly attributes his counter-Avicennan philosophy to the prophets – it is a *ḥanīf* revelation, a prophetic kind of philosophical thought.[194] The 'philosophical' system of revelation discovered in the Qur'ānic arcana is then the obverse of this revealed system of philosophy evinced in the *Muṣāraʿa*. With this Janus-faced, fundamentally noumenal body of teachings, we finally and decisively penetrate to the core of Shahrastānī's identity and worldview – the Shahrastānian 'truth'. And it is surely here that the Ismāʿīlī stimulus of his thought most shows through: a concept of truth in which the religious and the philosophical wholly unite, a complete mergence of both 'wisdoms' (*jāmiʿ al-ḥikmatayn*).

Note on the Arabic text

As already mentioned, this translation is based on the first volume of Ādharshab's edition. The annotation has partly drawn on references provided in the latter, some of which (e.g. references to certain *rijāl* works) have proved hard to verify, but which have been retained for their potential value to researchers. The Arabic of Ādharshab's edition has also been provided here for consultation and coordination with the text of the translation. All annotation is, however, confined to the translation, including information on any emendations to the Arabic text. The system followed in noting these emendations is that the text as corrected (and translated) is placed *before* the colon, and as uncorrected, *after* the colon. Depending on the case, these emendations will be Ādharshab's corrections of the original manuscript or my corrections of Ādharshab's edition; the latter is always marked with the initials MA. Apart from these noted emendations, Ādharshab's text has been modified only a little in its punctuation and the arrangement of some paragraphs, in order to bring it in line with the English translation. Qur'ānic quotations are in floriated brackets and are vowelled more fully than in Ādharshab's text.

Some words are called for, regarding the manuscript used for Ādharshab's edition, the unicum, MS no. 8086/B78, from the Library of the Iranian National Consultative Assembly, Tehran.[195] The manuscript contains 434 folios, i.e. 868 pages of 25 lines each, 34 cm long and 13.5 cm wide. The first part of this is taken up with Shahrastānī's introductory chapters, ending at folio 27A, and the second part is his commentary on the Exordium, ending at folio 45A – together comprising the contents of the present volume. Part one of Shahrastānī's commentary on Q. 2, the Cow, ends at folio 240B. Part two then begins with Q. 2:124 ('And when his Lord tried Abraham with certain words [...]') and ends at the completion of Q. 2.

The commentary is written in black ink on Syrian paper with rubrics in red, and on the cover the full title given is:

> The Book of the Keys to the Arcana and the Lanterns of the Godly in the Exegesis of the Qur'ān, the composition of the imam, the researcher, the crown of the community and the faith, Muḥammad b. ʿAbd al-Karīm al-Shahrastānī – may God water his garden with the showers of forgiveness and cause him to take his place in the highest of paradises!

Beneath this title is the following statement:

> ʿUbayd Allāh, the one confidant in His grace, Ibrāhīm b. Muḥammad b. al-Mu'ayyad Abū'l-Majāmiʿ al-Ḥamawī al-Juwaynī[196] had it transcribed for himself (*istansakhahu li-nafsihi*), may God protect him, guide him and grant him success in achieving what takes him forward to His satisfaction, and may He forgive him and his predecessors, and forgive him his lapses and excesses, and may He set in order the affairs of his two abodes [i.e. this world and the next] through His grace, and may He forgive through His longed for bounty the sins which he sent ahead of him, by the truth of Muḥammad and his pure chosen family, may God bless him and his family as long as night is quiet and day is bright! The writing of these lines was completed on 4th Shaʿbān 667 AH [=1268 CE].

Another inscription is found at the end of the commentary on Q. 2, which says: 'The transcription of the book is completed, praise be to God and how excellent is His aid, at the conclusion of God's month of al-Aṣamm [= 'the deaf one', an epithet of the month of Rajab] Rajab, 667 AH. O God, forgive its transcriber Muḥammad b. Muḥammad al-Zanjī!' The latter inscription strongly suggests that the commentary as it came into the hands of the scribe in question, was not longer than the content of the Tehran manuscript, since it clearly states 'The transcription of the book is completed [...]' and not 'The transcription of the *second part* is completed [...]'.

Important information on the history of the commentary's composition is found in a number of references in the manuscript. For example: 'The beginning of this composition occurred in the months [*sic.*] of the year 538 AH [=1143 CE].' Following it is found the statement: 'We are transcribing it from the handwriting of the author [himself].' In the margin of folio 241A is found the statement by Shahrastānī:

> This is the beginning of volume two of the Qur'ān commentary. O God, benefit us by that which You teach us, and teach us that by which You benefit us, by the truth of the Chosen One (upon him be peace). The volume was finished in Muḥarram of the year 540 AH [1145 CE]. May God endow it with good and may He seal it with bliss!

After it there is another statement: 'A transcript of the original in the handwriting of the author.' Finally, on the last page of the manuscript is the following statement by the scribe: 'This manuscript was transcribed from the original which is in the handwriting of the author, the imam, the knower of the arcana of the Qur'ān, crown of the faith al-Shahrastānī, may God cover him in His grace. The original was in two volumes, and this narration [...].' The part of the page containing the remainder is truncated, including, it would seem, the date of the completion of the second volume of the commentary by Shahrastānī. This last statement incidentally implies again that this was the full extent of the work in the scribe's possession.

ACKNOWLEDGEMENTS

It is hard to list all the friends and colleagues owed thanks in this unwieldy project. I am indebted for many details hidden within the overall process – whether a suggested translation of some strange expression, tracing an obscure ḥadīth, sharing a valuable bibliographical reference, or some unsuspected resonance in wider Ismāʿīlī thought. In this regard I would particularly like to thank Feras Hamza, Muhammad Reza Jozi, Abdeali Qutbuddin, Mustafa Shah, and also Omar Alí-de-Unzaga. His and Fahmida Suleman's practical support and contribution to the form of the book have been vital. Others have tussled with my text in more gruelling depth. In this category, I give thanks to Hamid Haji, who read through my original 'first approach' translation; and especially to Farhana Mayer, for editing the book. I am additionally grateful to Maha Sharba for keying in the Arabic, to Hasan Al-Khoee for his work checking it and to Eleanor Kilroy for setting it. I finally mention that my entrée to the secret and enthralling realms of Shahrastānī's higher thought was through working on his *Kitāb al-Muṣāraʿa* with Wilferd Madelung, for which I am thankful.

NOTES

1 M. A. Ādharshab (ed.), *Tafsīr al-Shahrastānī*, vol. 1. Note that Ādharshab's complete edition has been published by Mirās-i Maktūb in the course of 2008 in two volumes. The first of these two new volumes includes the material of the earlier 1997 volume (which is the one used for my translation), comprising the commentary to the end of the Exordium as well as the commentary on Q. 2 up to verse 123. The second volume covers the commentary on Q. 2:124–286. Since the complete edition has not been referred to in my translation it is not entered in the bibliography.

2 See the introduction by the translators (Kazi and Flynn) in Shahrastānī, *Muslim Sects and Divisions*, p. 1 and pp. 3–4. Here the coincidence in the opening of the doxology of *Kitāb al-Milal* and *Mafātīḥ al-asrār*, is dismissed as evidence: 'It is more probable that the *tafsīr* is the work of some unknown author who attributed it to Shahrastānī, and cited the opening of the *Milal* in an attempt to show that it was by the same author'. Op. cit., p. 4.

3 Iranian National Consultative Assembly, MS 8086/B78. In 1989, this was published by Markaz-i Intishār-i Nusakh-i Khaṭṭī, Tehran, in a facsimile in two volumes, as Shahrastānī's *Mafātīḥ al-asrār*.

4 The biographical sources on Shahrastānī go back to three scholars contemporary to him. (1) Abū Muḥammad Maḥmūd b. Muḥammad b. ʿAbbās b. Arslān al-Khwārazmī (d. 568/1172) in his *Tārīkh-i Khwārazm*. This work is not extant but is

quoted in Yāqūt al-Ḥamawī, *Muʿjam al-buldān* (Beirut, 1374–76/1955–57), vol. 3, pp. 376–77. (2) Abū Saʿd ʿAbd al-Karīm b. Muḥammad al-Samʿānī (d. 562/1167) in his *Dhayl taʾrīkh Baghdād*. Again, this is not extant but is quoted in Subkī, *Ṭabaqāt al-shāfiʿiyya al-kubrā*, vol. 6, p. 128 ff. Shahrastānī is also mentioned in Samʿānī, *al-Taḥbīr fīʾl-muʿjam al-kabīr*, vol. 2, pp. 160–61. (3) Ẓahīr al-Dīn Abūʾl-Ḥasan ʿAlī b. Zayd al-Bayhaqī (d. 565/1170) in his *Taʾrīkh ḥukamāʾ al-islām*, p. 143. All the later references to him by Dhahabī, Ibn al-ʿImād, Abūʾl-Fidāʾ, Ibn Khallikān, Ibn Ḥajar, Ṣafadī and others, go back to these earliest sources.

5 479/1086 is the date given by Shahrastānī himself (as quoted from Ibn al-Samʿānī by Ibn Khallikān). The date 469/1076–7 is given by Ibn al-Samʿānī, *Taḥbīr*, vol. 2, p. 163. Others give the date 467/1074. For the various honorifics (*alqāb*) quoted here, see Ādharshab, ed., *Tafsīr al-Shahrastānī*, p. 47.

6 ʿAbd al-Ghāfir b. Ismāʿīl al-Fārisī, *Taʾrīkh Naysābūr* (part 1 of *al-Muntakhab min al-Siyāq*, Qum, 1403), p. 270. Fārisī was Abūʾl-Qāsim al-Qushayrī's grandson, knew Ghazālī and was his first biographer.

7 Subkī, *Ṭabaqāt al-shāfiʿiyya* (Cairo, 1324/1906), vol. 4, p. 102.

8 The library is referred to in numerous sources, e.g. as the *khizānat al-kutub* in Bākharzī, *Dumyat al-qaṣr*, pp. 179, 414.

9 As argued by Ādharshab in the introduction to his edition: Ādharshab, ed., *Tafsīr al-Shahrastānī*, p. 59. Ādharshab claims that it is inconceivable that a mere student from the Niẓāmiyya of Nīshāpūr might accede to the prestigious chair of preacher at the Niẓāmiyya of Baghdad, as Shahrastānī shortly did.

10 As well as in Nīshāpūr, Abū Naṣr al-Qushayrī is known to have resided temporarily in Baghdad, where even figures from the caliphal court attended his lectures at the Niẓāmiyya. In his last year in the city he became the focus of such controversy that brawls took place, resulting in one of the sons of Niẓām al-Mulk being assaulted and wounded. Niẓām al-Mulk was provoked by these events respectfully to send Qushayrī back to Nīshāpūr. Subkī, *Ṭabaqāt al-shāfiʿiyya* (Cairo, 1383/1964), vol. 4, p. 249; Ibn Kathīr, *al-Bidāya waʾl-nihāya*, vol. 12, p. 187.

11 Sulamī is best known for his compendium of Ṣūfī Qurʾān commentary, *Ḥaqāʾiq al-tafsīr*, and his hagiographical work *Ṭabaqāt al-ṣūfiyya*. Abū Zakariyyā al-Muzakkī and Abūʾl-Qāsim al-Sarrāj are also mentioned as Madīnī's teachers. Ādharshab, *Tafsīr al-Shahrastānī*, p. 51; also Samʿānī, *al-Ansāb*, folio 517A.

12 Fārisī, *Taʾrīkh Naysābūr*, biography no. 797, p. 386.

13 Subkī, *Ṭabaqāt al-shāfiʿiyya*, vol. 7, p. 96–99. The report is on the authority of ʿAbd al-Ghāfir.

14 Ibid.

15 As well as mentioning Anṣārī's skill in exegesis, Subkī says that he produced a commentary on the famous Ashʿarī treatise, *al-Irshād ilā qawāṭiʿ al-adilla fī uṣūl al-iʿtiqād* by Juwaynī, and also a commentary on the *Kitāb al-Ghunya* (i.e. *al-Ghunya fī uṣūl al-dīn*, an Ashʿarī treatise, drawing on Juwaynī's *Irshād*, by ʿAbd al-Raḥmān b. Maʾmūn al-Mutawallī). A manuscript of Anṣārī's *Sharḥ al-Irshād* is available in the Garrett Collection at Princeton University Library, MS 3023. Subkī, moreover, states that Anṣārī had studied under Juwaynī and that he transmitted prophetic traditions from a list of authorities including Abūʾl-Ḥusayn b. Makkī, ʿAbd al-Ghāfir b. Muḥammad al-Fārisī (not to be confused with ʿAbd al-Ghāfir b. Ismāʿīl, see note 6), the female scholar Karīma al-Marwaziyya, Abū Ṣāliḥ al-Muʾadhdhin, and also, as mentioned, Faḍl Allāh b. Aḥmad al-Mayhanī (Abū Saʿīd b. Abīʾl-Khayr) and

Abū'l-Qāsim al-Qushayrī. The latter seems to have been a particular influence, for after suspending his studies with him at Nīshāpūr to visit the Ḥijāz and go via Baghdad to Syria (where he associated with the shaykhs of the region and visited the various shrines), Anṣārī returned to Nīshāpūr and resumed acquiring *uṣūl* under Qushayrī. Ibid.

16 See English text, p. 65; Arabic text, p. 3.

17 See English text, p. 65; Arabic text, p. 3. *Tasnīm* = a wellspring in Paradise.

18 The relevant complementarities are creation/the Command, contrariety/hierarchy, and the accomplished/the inchoative.

19 Ādharshab, ed., *Tafsīr al-Shahrastānī*, pp. 48–49, note 6.

20 Yāqūt al-Ḥamawī, *Muʿjam al-buldān*, vol. 3, p. 377.

21 According to Ādharshab '[...] people at that time were eager to hear something new, and had found it with al-Shahrastānī'. Ādharshab, ed., *Tafsīr al-Shahrastānī*, p. 49, note 1.

22 Yāqūt al-Ḥamawī, *Muʿjam al-buldān*, vol. 3, p. 377.

23 Bayhaqī, *Ta'rīkh ḥukamā' al-islām*, p. 140.

24 According to its first introduction, the *Milal* was first completed in 521/1127.

25 A tentative dating of the *Nihāya* to the mid-1130s seems in order (following Steigerwald, *La pensée*, p. 297). Not only does this text refer often to the *Milal*, thus surely coming later, but Steigerwald suggests that the *Nihāya* was motivated to dispel doubts about Shahrastānī's Sunnī orthodoxy arising from the *Milal*, which, for some tastes, was a disturbingly free treatment of religious and philosophical belief (ibid., p. 64). Note that most scholars prefer the vowelling *Nihāyat al-aqdām fī ʿilm al-kalām* (The Furthest Steps in the Science of Kalām) in contrast to Guillaume's vowelling *Nihāyat al-iqdām fī ʿilm al-kalām* (The Limit of Daring in Theology). See, for example, Paul Kraus, 'Les "controverses" de Fakhr al-Dīn Rāzī', p. 207, note 6; and Steigerwald, *La pensée*, p. 63. The vocalisation *aqdām* is in fact supported by several other instances of the same phrase in Shahrastānī's works.

26 The *Muṣāraʿa* certainly post-dates the *Milal*, since it refers to it. Madelung and Mayer, *Struggling with the Philosopher*, p. 19 (English) and p. 2 (Arabic). Madelung argues *a terminus ad quem* of 536/1141 for the *Muṣāraʿa*. Ibid., pp. 12–13.

27 Shahrastānī, *Milal*, vol. 1, p. 33. The section in question is objected to by some modern Shīʿī clergy because of the allegedly inaccurate way Shahrastānī discusses the beliefs of Shīʿī groups. e.g. al-Shaykh ʿAbbās al-Qummī, *al-Kunā wa'l-alqāb*, vol. 2, p. 374.

28 Shahrastānī, *Milal*, vol. 2, p. 6.

29 It has been proposed that the use of hierarchy implies some notion of evolution through the series, in the understanding of Godhead. Steigerwald, *La pensée*, p. 60.

30 e.g. Shahrastānī quotes al-Ḥasan b. al-Ṣabbāḥ's *al-Fuṣūl al-arbaʿa* in its entirety in *Milal*, vol. 1, pp. 160–162.

31 Rāzī, *Aʿlām al-nubuwwa*, pp. 3–9 (= chapter 1, *fī mā jarā baynī wa bayna'l-mulḥid*). For the dialogue as rendered by our own author, see Shahrastānī, *Milal*, vol. 2, pp. 9–45.

32 Shahrastānī, *Livre des Religions et des sectes*, p. 12.

33 Against this identification, Michot has argued that the Sabaeans in Shahrastānī's debate are symbols of a contemporary popularised Avicennism and the Ḥanīfs are simply symbols of Islamic philosophical orthodoxy. Michot, 'L'Avicennisation de la sunna, du Ṣabeisme au Leurre de la Ḥanīfiyya', pp. 113–120. It is to be noted,

however, that a rather older theory than Monnot's again roots Shahrastānī's Sabaean-Ḥanīf dialogue in the Ismāʿīlī heritage. This is the theory incepted by Massignon that the dialogue was again lifted by Shahrastānī straight from al-Ḥasan b. al-Ṣabbāḥ. The theory was repeated by Hodgson, and supported more recently by Landolt. Massignon, *Essai sur les Origines*, p. 58; Hodgson, *The Order of Assassins*, pp. 332–3; Landolt's introduction to Ṭūsī, *Paradise of Submission*, p. 9.

34 Bukhārī, LIX, 1.

35 Rendering the expression as 'theists' is surely too bland. e.g. Guillaume, *Summa Philosophiae*, p. 25 (English), p. 54 (Arabic).

36 'A plusieurs reprises dans le *Nihāya*, Shahrastānī utilise l'expression les "hommes de la vérité" (*ahl al-ḥaqq*) d'une manière énigmatique. S'il s'agit des Ashʿarites, pourquoi ne l'exprime-t-il pas clairement, puisqu'il les mentionne à plusieurs reprises dans son oeuvre?' Steigerwald, *La pensée*, p. 64. For the distinction made by Shahrastānī between the *ahl al-ḥaqq* of Islam (*min ahl al-islām*) and those of other religions (*min ahl al-milal*), see e.g., Guillaume, *Summa Philosophiae*, p. 54 (Arabic).

37 Ādharshab, ed., *Tafsīr al-Shahrastānī*, p. 54.

38 Steigerwald, *La pensée*, p. 65.

39 Idem.

40 Guillaume, *Summa Philosophiae*, p. xii.

41 On logical grounds, specific aid may not be taken here as a subset of general aid, but must be a distinct set. The two are separate kinds of aid, otherwise it would be impossible for general aid to be present but specific aid to be absent.

42 Guillaume, *Summa Philosophiae*, p. 132 (English paraphrase), p. 413 (Arabic).

43 Madelung and Mayer, *Struggling with the Philosopher*, pp. 57–58 (English), pp. 63–64 (Arabic).

44 Hierarchy is in particular invoked at various points, for example in the argument that God's knowledge transcends universals and particulars, and in the argument for prophecy (and the imamate). Madelung and Mayer, *Struggling with the Philosopher*, pp. 72–73 (English), pp. 89–91 (Arabic) and pp. 97–98 (English), pp. 130–132 (Arabic).

45 Ghazālī's *Tahāfut al-falāsifa* is in reality only the best-known case of a set of critiques of (mainly Avicennan) philosophy, of which Shahrastānī's is one. Others are Ibn al-Malāhimī's *Tuhfat al-mutakallimīn*, Fakhr al-Dīn al-Rāzī's *Sharḥ al-ishārāt*, al-Farīd al-Ghaylānī's *Ḥudūth al-ʿālam*, and later Shihāb al-Dīn ʿUmar al-Suhrawardī's *Rashf al-naṣā'iḥ*.

46 The issues covered are: (i) Ibn Sīnā's diaeresis of being; (ii) his concept of God as the Necessary Being and his proof of God on that basis; (iii) his argument for God's unicity; (iv) his teaching that the objects of God's knowledge are universals; and (v) his teaching of the eternity of the world.

47 Madelung and Mayer, *Struggling with the Philosopher*, p. 32 (English) and p. 22 (Arabic).

48 See e.g., Walker, *Ḥamīd al-Dīn al-Kirmānī*, p. 83 ff.

49 Madelung and Mayer, *op. cit.*,. pp. 43, 57 (English), pp. 42, 62 (Arabic).

50 Ibid., p. 43 (English), p. 41 (Arabic).

51 Ibid., p. 43 (English), p. 42 (Arabic).

52 'He is the living in the sense that He causes to live and He causes to die'. Ibid., p. 43 (English), p. 41 (Arabic).

53 That God is too well-known to be demonstrated is justified by Shahrastānī through a series of Qur'ānic verses (Q.40:12, Q.39:45 and Q.17:46) indicating that the prophets summon to monotheism, not to theism which is *ex consensu gentium*. Ibid., p.56 (English), p. 61 (Arabic).

54 'He is necessary in His existence in the sense that He necessitates the existence of other than Him, and annihilates [...]'. Ibid., p. 43 (English), p. 41 (Arabic).

55 Ibid., pp. 56–57 (English), p. 62 (Arabic).

56 Other cases of this transcendentalism in the work are as follows: God's wholesale elevation is used by Shahrastānī against Ibn Sīnā's theory that God's direct causation is only of one, first, effect topping a vast cosmic hierarchy. Shahrastānī holds that God is not just to be viewed as the top of the cosmic order, but as wholly beyond it. Then given that all things within the hierarchy are equally contingent in existence, all depend on God's direct causation, irrespective of whether they are high or low in degree. Ibid., p. 58 (English), pp. 64–5 (Arabic). Next, against Ibn Sīnā's teaching that God's knowledge is confined to universals, Shahrastānī elevates God's knowledge beyond either universals or particulars. Unconfined by these counterparts, God is in a single immediate relation with both universals and particulars. Ibid., p. 73 (English), pp. 90–1 (Arabic). Finally, against Ibn Sīnā's doctrine of the eternity of the world, Shahrastānī claims that for all the philosopher's attempts to elevate God, he grossly fails, even likening him to the notorious contemporary anthropomorphists, the Karrāmiyya. For Ibn Sīnā famously reasons that the inception of the world at a point in time inflicts change upon the 'unitary essence' of God. According to Shahrastānī, this taints God with temporality in a manner objectively parallel with the Karrāmiyya's tainting of God with spatiality when they reasoned that the inception of the world in part of *space* inflicts change on God. Shahrastānī's God is instead beyond either time or space, which are strictly conterminable with the created world itself. His God is an utterly transcendent Creator in confrontation with His entire cosmic artifact which is intrinsically structured by limitations of time and space. Shahrastānī here rehearses a set of ingenious arguments which show that it is as absurd to treat time as infinite as it is to treat space as infinite – his own development of arguments dating from Philoponus (d. circa 575 CE). The finitude of time devolves on the nature of time, just as that of space devolves on its nature. Ibn Sīnā thus has no more right to impute deficiency to God for not making the world extend limitlessly back in time than he does for His not making it extend limitlessly out in space. Ibid., p. 80 (English), pp. 101–2 (Arabic).

57 Ibid., p. 91 (English), p. 119 (Arabic).

58 For example 'Umāra al-Yamanī and al-Mu'ayyad fī'l-Dīn al-Shīrāzī both refer to Ismā'īlism in these terms, calling the reigning imam the 'Protector of the Ḥanīf faith' (*'iṣmat al-dīn al-ḥanīf*). See Smoor, "Umāra's odes describing the Imām', p. 559.

59 Ṭūsī, *Maṣāri' al-muṣāri'*, pp. 87–8.

60 Ṭūsī, *Contemplation and Action*, pp. 26–7 (English), p. 3 (Persian).

61 Sam'ānī, *Taḥbīr*, p. 161.

62 Subkī, *Ṭabaqāt al-shāfi'iyya*, pp. 128–130.

63 Nā'īnī's introduction to Hāshimī (tr.), *Tawḍīḥ al-milal*, p. 27.

64 Madelung and Mayer, *Struggling with the Philosopher*, p. 91 (English), p. 120 (Arabic).

65 The date is given in the work itself. Iranian National Consultative Assembly MS 8086/B78, folio 241A.

66 Ādharshab, ed., *Tafsīr al-Shahrastānī*, p. 50, note 3.

67 Campbell, *The Hero with a Thousand Faces*, p. 30, p. 245, etc.

68 It has been tentatively dated to circa 538/1145. Steigerwald, *La pensée*, p. 297.

69 Nā'īnī first included the *Majlis* as an appendix to his edition of the Persian translation of the *Milal* by Iṣfahānī, *Tanqīḥ al-Adilla*. It was then republished in Nā'īnī's *Sharḥ-i ḥāl*. Steigerwald's text, published with her French translation, is based on Nā'īnī's later (1369 Sh./1990) edition which combines the manuscript he originally employed in his earlier effort (no. 593 from the Library of the National Consultative Assembly in Tehran) with one from Istanbul (= treatise 25 of manuscript number 2023 of the Baghdādī Wahbī collection). Shahrastānī, *Majlis*, p. 25.

70 Ibid., p.100–109.

71 Ibid., p. 94.

72 Steigerwald, *La pensée*, p. 69.

73 Shahrastānī, *Majlis*, pp. 97–99.

74 Ibid., p. 99.

75 See Monnot, 'Islam: exégèse coranique', in *Annuaire de l'École Pratique des Hautes Études*, tome 95 (1986–7), pp. 255–6; Steigerwald, 'Al-Shahrastānī's Contribution to Medieval Islamic Thought', p. 265; Ādharshab, ed., *Tafsīr al-Shahrastānī*, p. 71.

76 The expression 'so what is it with these people who don't even understand a statement' is from Q. 4:78.

77 MS 8086/B78, folio 122A.

78 See English text, p. 66; Arabic text, p. 4.

79 e.g. Tabarsī, *Majma' al-bayān*. See Bar-Asher, *Scripture and Exegesis in Early Imāmī Shī'ism*, p. 80.

80 Bayhaqī, *Ta'rīkh ḥukamā' al-islām*, p. 143.

81 See English text, p. 66; Arabic text, p. 4.

82 i.e. The opening formula 'In the Name of God, the Infinitely Merciful, the Compassionate (*Bi'smi'llāh al-Raḥmān al-Raḥīm*).'

83 See English text, p. 153; Arabic text, p. 91.

84 In calling the imams 'the people of the Qur'ān' the implicit reference may be 'the tradition of the two precious things' (*ḥadīth al-thaqalayn*), discussed below in the text.

85 The start of this account is the affair of Yamāma when many knowledgeable in the Qur'ān died defeating the counter-Muslim prophet Musaylima and the Ḥanīfa tribe. For the safety of the text (so far, largely oral), the Caliph Abū Bakr bade Zayd b. Thābit collect together the fragments on which it had been recorded (shoulder blades, leaves etc.). The resulting parchments were given on Abū Bakr's death to 'Umar's daughter Ḥafṣa, widow of the Prophet; then bound into a single codex by the incoming Caliph, 'Umar. Next, a more public effort was made under 'Uthmān's caliphate through a concern to stop quarrelling between the Muslims of Syria and Iraq. Zayd b. Thābit was again appointed, as well as Sa'īd b. al-'Āṣ, 'Abd Allāh b. al-Zubayr and 'Abd al-Raḥmān b. al-Ḥārith (also Abān b. Sa'īd?). This team assembled a codex afresh from the available fragments and people's memories, and the resulting text was supposedly found to tally perfectly with the earlier Ḥafṣa codex. The Caliph then established this prototype in Medina and sent versions of the same

to Mecca, Kufa, Basra, Damascus and Yemen. See English text, p. 68ff.; Arabic text, p. 7ff.

86 See English text, p. 69; Arabic text, p. 8.

87 Bukhārī, *Faḍā'il al-Qur'ān*, 3; Bukhārī, *Maghāzī*, 17; Tirmidhī, *Tafsīr Sūra* 9, 19.

88 Q. 33:23 may be translated as follows: 'Amongst the faithful are men who fulfil what they pledge themselves to God to do. For amongst them is he who fulfils his promise and amongst them is he who bides his time. And they are quite unchanging.' In connection with this verse it is recorded that 'Abd Allāh b. al-Ḥārith b. 'Abd al-Muṭṭalib, Ḥamza and Ja'far b. Abī Ṭālib are covered by the words 'he who fulfils his promise', while 'Alī b. Abī Ṭālib is referred to as 'he who bides his time'. The reference is to the martyrdom of the individuals mentioned – 'Alī's as yet being in the future at the time the verse was revealed.

89 See English text, p. 69; Arabic text, p. 8.

90 See Amir-Moezzi, *The Divine Guide in Early Shi'ism*, p. 79 ff.

91 Shahrastānī gives seventy names of hypocrites, said to be originally recorded in Q. 9:64; and also the 'verse of lapidation' (*āyat al-rajm*) said to be found originally in Q. 33. This last has 73 verses in the *textus receptus*, but originally had 286 or even 300 verses according to Ubayy b. Ka'b. See English text, p. 71; Arabic text, pp. 9–10.

92 See English text, p. 70; Arabic text, p. 9.

93 See English text, p. 70; Arabic text, p. 9.

94 This refers to the fact that Zayd b. Thābit had originally studied in a Jewish context in Medina. See Lecker, *Jews and Arabs in Pre- and Early Islamic Arabia*, pp. 259–271.

95 See English text, p. 70; Arabic text, pp. 8–9.

96 Ibn al-Athīr, *Usd al-ghāba*, vol. 3, p. 384; Ibn Abī'l-Ḥadīd, *Sharḥ Nahj al-balāgha*, vol. 3, p. 41. See English text, p. 70; Arabic text, p. 9.

97 See English text, p. 73; Arabic text, p. 11.

98 See English text, p.73; Arabic text, p. 12.

99 See English text, p. 73; Arabic text, p. 12.

100 Parallels or equivocations = *mā ya'tariḍu min al-kalāmayn al-maqṣūdayn*. See English text, p. 73; Arabic text, p. 12.

101 See English text, p. 74; Arabic text, pp. 12–13.

102 See English text, p. 74; Arabic text, p. 12.

103 See English text, p. 74; Arabic text, p. 12.

104 A list of such traditions is provided in Mūsawī, *Murāja'āt*, pp. 150–153.

105 Quoted by Shahrastānī, see English text, p. 74; Arabic text, p. 12.

106 For a discussion, including numerous references to textual authorities, of the supposed Qur'ānic recension of 'Alī, the *Kitāb 'Alī*, and the *Muṣḥaf Fāṭima*, see Modarresi, *Tradition and Survival*, vol. 1, p. 2 ff, and p. 17 ff.

107 The tradition is found in different forms in the *Ṣaḥīḥ* compendia. See Hindī, *Kanz al-'ummāl*, vol. 1, p. 44, ḥadīth 874. Quoted by Shahrastānī, see English text, pp. 74–5; Arabic text, p. 13.

108 See English text, p. 75; Arabic text, p. 13.

109 See English text, p. 76; Arabic text, p. 14.

110 See English text, pp. 72, 75; Arabic text, pp. 11, 13.

111 See English text, pp. 75, 76; Arabic text, p. 14.

112 See English text, p. 76; Arabic text, p. 14.

113 Its sacredness is confirmed in a final declaration in Shahrastānī's discussion that

'The Qur'ān in our midst is the Word of God between the two covers, protected by God's protection from change, solecism and error'. Ādharshab presents this as evidence of Shahrastānī's basic conformity over the *textus receptus*, but the statement must also be fitted with the controversies raised earlier by our author. It would in fact appear from the remainder of the passage that he is really referring here to the 'meta-Qur'ān', accessed by combining the textus receptus with the hermeneutic of the imams. For, as he explains, the scripture is protected because 'its [true] scribe does not doze, and its [true] intoner does not utter solecisms', i.e., presumably, ʿAlī b. Abī Ṭālib. Shahrastānī goes on: 'It has a people who intone it with its true intonation, and know it with both its esoteric interpretation and its sending down', i.e., the imams. Ādharshab, *Tafsīr al-Shahrastānī*, p. 122–3, note 5. Also see English text, p. 76; Arabic text, p. 14.

114 See English text, p. 153; Arabic text, pp. 90–1.

115 See, e.g., Ṭūsī, *Contemplation and Action*, pp. 45–46 (English) and p. 16 (Persian).

116 I do not discuss these here in the precise order in which Shahrastānī presents them.

117 e.g. Q. 16:40: 'Our statement to something when We will it is simply that We say to it "Be!" (*kun*) and it is (*fa-yakūn*).' The whole idea of God's existentiating command in fact has likely roots in the Hexaemeron of Genesis 1. Here God's creative activity on successive 'days' is framed in exactly the same terms – namely, His address 'let there be X', followed by 'and there was X'; e.g. 'And God said (*yomer*, from *amar*, which can also mean 'to command', esp. late), 'Let there be light' (*yehī or*), and there was light (*wayhī or*).' Gen. 1:3.

118 e.g. Q. 55:7–9: 'He has raised heaven and established the scales (*mīzān*), lest you transgress the scales. So establish weighing with equity and stint not the scales!' See English text, p. 118; Arabic text, p. 60.

119 See English text, p. 118; Arabic text, pp. 59–60.

120 See English text, p. 118; Arabic text, p. 60.

121 Both Dānish-pazhūh and Steigerwald trace Shahrastānī's use of the pair to Ismāʿīlī influence. Dānish-pazhūh, 'Dāʿī al-Duʿāt Tāj al-Dīn-i Shahrastāna', p. 82; Steigerwald, *La pensée*, p. 131. The concern with the Command-Logos is typically reflected in the thought of Sijistānī (d. circa 361/971) in turn indebted to that of Nasafī (d. 330/942). But its roots lie deeper still, in early Ismāʿīlī teachings on the feminine demiurgic principle called Kūnī, traced by some scholars to the Gnostic schools of late antiquity such as the Valentinians and Ophites. See Heinz Halm, 'The Cosmology of the Pre-Fatimid Ismāʿīliyya', in Daftary, *Medieval Ismaʿili History and Thought*, pp. 75–83.

122 Dānish-pazhūh, op. cit., p. 82. Also see Monnot, 'Opposition et hiérarchie dans la pensée d'al-Shahrastânî'.

123 See English text, p.116; Arabic text, pp. 57–8.

124 See English text, p.116; Arabic text, pp. 57–8.

125 On the distinction of semantic and historical etymologies, see Bronkhorst, 'Etymology and Magic'.

126 Dārimī, *Muqaddima*, 32.

127 Shahrastānī bases hierarchy, in each of these, on quotations from the Qur'ān: for angels, Q. 37:164; for prophets, Q. 17:55; for scholars, Q. 58:11; and for human agents in general, Q. 6:132.

128 See English text, p. 117; Arabic text, p. 59.

129 See English text, p. 120ff.; Arabic text, pp. 61–2.
130 See English text, p. 121; Arabic text, p. 62.
131 See English text, p. 121; Arabic text, p. 62.
132 See Boullata, 'The Rhetorical Interpretation of the Qur'ān: *i'jāz* and Related Topics'.
133 Dānish-pazhūh, 'Dā'ī al-Du'āt', p. 82. For the occurrence of the terms in a definitely Ismā'īlī (albeit later) context, see Ṭūsī, *Contemplation and Action*, p. 46 (English) and pp. 16–17 (Persian).
134 Only the last part of the tradition, in which 'Umar consults the Prophet, is generally transmitted; e.g., Ṭabarī, *Jāmi' al-bayān*, vol. 7, p. 70 (on Q. 11:106). The image of a great angel combining fire and ice in its make-up is, however, found in a number of sources, such as al-Shaykh al-Ṣadūq, *Kitāb al-Tawḥīd*, p. 280 and *Tafsīr Furāt al-Kūfī* on Q. 7:46. However, the ḥadīth in the elaborate form transmitted by Shahrastānī as a basis for the terms *mafrūgh* and *musta'naf*, has proved impossible to trace in any earlier source.
135 The terminology, however, could also be traced to the Qur'ān. Q. 55:31 = *mafrūgh*; Q. 47:16 = *musta'naf*.
136 The symbolism chimes with Jewish traditions in which heaven (*shamayim*) is said, via a 'semantic' etymology, to be an angel miraculously combining fire (*'esh*) and water (*mayim*). See Freedman (tr.), Midrash Rabbah: Genesis, vol. 1, pp. 32–33. Other Jewish traditions speak of angels in general as made from fire and water, with God harmonising the opposing elements. See Talmud Yerushalmi, tractate on Rosh Ha-Shanah, ii, 58a.
137 See English text, p. 114; Arabic text, p. 56.
138 See English text, pp. 115–16; Arabic text, p.57.
139 See English text, p. 115; Arabic text, p. 56.
140 Dānish-pazhūh, op. cit., p. 82.
141 See e.g. Khadduri, *al-Shāfi'ī's Risāla*, p. 96 ff. In the simplest application of the distinction, the verse established as general prevails over the verse established as specific.
142 See English text, p. 109; Arabic text, p. 50.
143 See English text, p. 109; Arabic text, p. 51.
144 Khadduri, *al-Shāfi'ī's Risāla*, p. 123 ff.
145 See English text, pp. 111–12; Arabic text, p. 53.
146 See English text, p. 112; Arabic text, p. 53.
147 Shahrastānī may even hint here at a cyclical concept of time and religious history, for he adds that the Resurrection will in turn prove to be 'another genesis' (*al-nash'at al-ukhrā*), a term deriving from Q. 53:47. While the phrase need not connote cyclicity in that context, Shahrastānī's use of it must be placed with other allusions in his commentary, notably, his praising God in the doxology for concluding prophecy with the 'Chosen One' Muḥammad, 'conclusion in the sense of utmost degree and perfection, not conclusion in the sense of abatement and passing away'. See English text, p. 63; Arabic text, p. 1. Q. 33:44 is implicitly referred to here, where Muḥammad is called the 'Seal of the Prophets' (*khātim al-nabiyīn*). Shahrastānī seems to interpret this title as an affirmation of the perfection (*kamāl*) of prophethood through Muḥammad, and pointedly denies that it refers to the passing away (*zawāl*) of prophethood through him. Minimally, this leaves matters open for the future advent of the expected figure known as the

qā'im. On the Ismā'īlī concept of the 'great cycle' (*al-kawr al-a'ẓam*), see Daftary, *The Ismā'īlīs: Their History and Doctrines*, pp. 140, 295, 297.

148 See English text, pp. 63, 112; Arabic text, pp. 1, 54.

149 See English text, p. 112; Arabic text, p. 53.

150 See English text, p. 112; Arabic text, p. 53–4.

151 See English text, p.112; Arabic text, p. 54.

152 See English text, p. 112; Arabic text, p. 54.

153 Juxtaposing abolition of verses with the 'Mother of the Scripture' rests on Q. 13:39: 'God abolishes (*yamḥū*) and establishes what He wills, and with Him is the Mother of the Scripture (*Umm al-Kitāb*).'

154 See English text, p. 113; Arabic text, p.54.

155 See English text, p. 113; Arabic text, p. 54.

156 See for example the model of foetal development in al-Mu'ayyad fī'l-Dīn (d. 471/1078): Shīrāzī, *al-Majālis al-Mu'ayyadiyya, Majlis* 182, pp. 516–519.

157 See English text, p. 111; Arabic text, p.52.

158 Note though that the imams' inclusion with God here depends on the punctuation espoused by Shī'ism and supported by great early authorites like Mujāhid b. Jabr al-Makhzūmī, but is ruled out by the standard punctuation of the *textus receptus*. See e.g. Ṭabarī, *Jāmi' al-bayān* on Q. 3:7.

159 In Shahrastānī's words 'the known prior ruling', *al-ḥukm al-sābiq al-ma'lūm*. See English text, p. 111; Arabic text, p. 52.

160 In Shahrastānī's words 'the delayed incepted ruling', *'al-ḥukm al-muta'akhkhir al-mashrū'*. See English text, p.111; Arabic text, p.53.

161 See English text, p. 64; Arabic text, p. 2.

162 See English text, p.64; Arabic text, p. 2.

163 In excluding the formula from the body of the Exordium, such authorities were doubtless partly motivated by its duplicating Q. 1:3 in meaning: 'The Infinitely Merciful, the Compassionate.'

164 The view has been revived in certain more recent editions and translations of the Qur'ān such as Muhammad Ali (tr.), *The Holy Qur'ān*, p.3.

165 Suyūṭī, *al-Durr al-manthūr*, vol. 1, p. 10. See English text, pp. 154–5; Arabic text, p. 92.

166 These constitute the last syllable of the final word of each verse: *al-raḥīm, al-'ālamīn, al-raḥīm, al-dīn, nasta'īn, al-mustaqīm*, and *al-ḍāllīn*.

167 See English text, p. 144; Arabic text, p. 82.

168 See English text, pp. 147, 149; Arabic text, pp. 85, 86.

169 See English text, pp. 147–8; Arabic text, p. 85.

170 Shahrastānī's point is, presumably, that the name is mysteriously at one with the One named, such that everything derives from it, while it is without derivation.

171 Note that the Arabic might also be translated as 'the letters which are the basis of the word refer to what one must have gnosis of [...]' etc. See English text, p. 145; Arabic text, p. 83.

172 See English text, p. 159; Arabic text, p. 96.

173 See English text, p. 157; Arabic text, p. 94.

174 See English text, p. 157; Arabic text, p. 93.

175 See English text, p. 145; Arabic text, p. 83.

176 See English text, p. 146; Arabic text, p. 84.

177 From Ibn al-Akhram's doctrines in the end arose the Druze. Hence the letter

mysticism in question was condemned in Fāṭimī teaching as typifying his deviation, and deemed crudely anthropomorphic. See Kirmānī, *Majmūʿat rasāʾil al-Kirmānī*, pp. 134–137, especially p. 139.

178 See English text, pp. 153, 156; Arabic text, pp. 90, 93.

179 See English text, p. 156; Arabic text, p. 93.

180 See English text, p. 156; Arabic text, p. 93.

181 This is explored, for example, in the chapter on Zakariyyā in Ibn al-ʿArabī's *Fuṣūṣ al-ḥikam*. See Izutsu, *Sufism and Taoism*, p. 116 ff.

182 See English text, pp. 150–1; Arabic text, p. 88.

183 See English text, p. 155; Arabic text, p. 92.

184 See English text, p. 159; Arabic text, p. 96.

185 See English text, pp. 160–1; Arabic text, pp. 96–7.

186 See English text, p. 168; Arabic text, p. 104.

187 See English text, p. 164; Arabic text, p. 100. Presumably each mercy retains its distinct scope within this new interlinking role, the *raḥma raḥmāniyya* being undiscriminating and the *raḥma raḥīmiyya* being discriminating.

188 See English text, p. 172; Arabic text, p. 107.

189 See English text, pp. 172–3; Arabic text, p. 107.

190 Muslim, *Ṣalāt*, 38; Abū Dawūd, *Ṣalāt*, 132; Ṭabarī, *Jāmiʿ al-bayān*, vol. 1, p. 66.

191 See English text, p. 178; Arabic text, pp. 112–13.

192 See English text, p. 179; Arabic text, p. 113.

193 See English text, p. 185; Arabic text, p. 119. It seems that the infernal classes are a disparity, not a hierarchy, because in them the leaders rank below the led.

194 Madelung and Mayer, *Struggling with the Philosopher*, e.g., pp. 56, 71, 89, 91.

195 On the facsimile, see note 3.

196 This is evidently the Ṣūfī traditionist, Shaykh al-Islām Shams al-Dīn Abū Isḥāq Ibrāhīm Ṣadr al-Dīn Muḥammad b. al-Muʾayyad Abī Bakr b. Abī ʿAbd Allāh Muḥammad b. Ḥamūya b. Muḥammad al-Juwaynī al-Khurāsānī (644–722/1246–1322), the author of *Pearls of the Two Necklaces* (*Farāʾid al-simṭayn*) and student of Naṣīr al-Dīn al-Ṭūsī.

II

Keys to the Arcana and Lanterns of the Godly in the Exegesis of the Qur'an

[Shahrastānī's preface]

In the name of God, the Infinitely Merciful, the Compassionate, and from Him we seek help.

Praise be to God, the praise of those who give thanks because of the totality of His praiseworthy acts, all of them, for the totality of His favours, all of them – blessed, good, plentiful praise, as befits Him. May God bless Muḥammad the Chosen One, the Prophet of Mercy, the Seal of the Prophets, and bless his good, pure family, an eternal blessing, purifying it till Doomsday, as He blessed Abraham and the family of Abraham – verily He is Praiseworthy, Glorious!

Praise be to God, who blessed His creatures by dispatching prophets and messengers, by corroborating them through sending down scriptures and by indicating the routes of the paths to follow – a blessing whose event is magnificent and whose benefit is universal. By His injunctions He put straight the movements of the children of Adam and by His revealed laws He protected the world order; He made them the sources of His ordinance, the wellsprings of His instruction, the places of the epiphany of His Command and the mines of His secret. Thus He (Exalted is He) said: 'O Children of Adam! When Messengers from among you come to you, who narrate Our signs, then whoever refrains from evil and amends – no fear will come upon them, nor will they sorrow.'[1]

Praise be to God, who blessed the last community with the Chosen One, Muḥammad (may God bless him and his family), instead of past communities and bygone centuries – a blessing most universal in benefit and one most magnificent as an event.[2] For He made his religion the most perfect of religions and nations, made his revealed law the most important of revealed laws and sects, and He appointed him the leader of the community, the chief of the good and the key to blessing. He concluded prophecy with him – conclusion in the sense of utmost degree and perfection, not conclusion in the sense of abatement and passing away.[3] He singled him out with the mighty scripture which 'falsehood does not approach from before or
behind.'[4] So He said (Mighty is the One Who speaks): 'God has blessed the 2
believers, insofar as He sent a Messenger from amongst themselves, who recites His signs to them, purifies them and teaches them the scripture and

wisdom, even though they were earlier in manifest error.'[5] He called the scripture *Qur'ān*, gathering together the things ordered hierarchically within it,[6] and *Furqān* ('criterion', 'distinction'), distinguishing between contraries. For He said (mighty is the recollection of Him): 'It is a Qur'ān which We divided up (*faraqnāhu*) so that you might recite it to men at intervals, and We send it down in steps.'[7]

He assigned the scripture to be conveyed by Muḥammad's pure offspring and to be transmitted by his righteous radiant companions 'who recite it as it ought to be recited' and study it as it ought to be studied. For the Qur'ān is his legacy[8] and they are his heirs, and they are one of the 'two precious things'.[9] Through them is the 'meeting of the two oceans',[10] belonging to them is the 'distance of the two bows'[11] and with them is knowledge of the two universes and the two worlds.

Just as the angels (peace be upon them) accompany [the Qur'ān] on all sides in its sending down, likewise the guiding imams and truthful scholars accompany it on all sides in its exegesis and hermeneutic: 'We send down the Remembrance and We are its protector'.[12] Thus the sending down of the Remembrance is by way of the accompanying angels and the protection of the Remembrance is by the scholars who know the sending down of it and the hermeneutic of it, what is clear of it and what is ambiguous of it, what is abrogating of it and what is abrogated of it, the general of it and the particular of it, the summary of it and the detailed of it, the absolute of it and the circumscribed of it, the explicit of it and the concealed of it, the literal of it and the esoteric of it, and they judge it by God's judgement consisting in what is accomplished of it and what is inchoative of it, the decree of it and the ordinance of it, the commands of it and the checks of it, the obligations of it and the interdictions of it, the licit of it and the illicit of it, the punishments of it and the injunctions of it, by truth and certainty, not by opinion and guesswork: 'They are those whom God guides and they are those who possess minds.'[13] For the Qur'ān is 'a guidance for mankind'[14] in general and 'a guidance and a mercy for a people who believe'[15] in particular, and a guidance and remembrance for the Prophet (may God bless him and his family) and for his people, which is more particular than both the first and the second: 'Verily, it is a remembrance for you [sing.] and for your [sing.] people.'[16]

The companions (may God be pleased with them) were in agreement that the knowledge of the Qur'ān was specific to the people of the Prophet's

house (upon them be peace), since they used to ask ʿAlī b. Abī Ṭālib (may
God be pleased with him):[17] 'Have you, the people of the house, been
singled out over us by anything other than the Qur'ān?' And he used to say: 3
'No, by Him who splits the grain and absolves the soul! Apart from by what
is in this scabbard of my sword! [...] (to the end of the saying).'[18]

Thus the exception of the Qur'ān, by way of this specification, points to the companions' consensus that the Qur'ān and the understanding of it, [i.e.] its sending down and its hermeneutic, is specific to the People of the House.[19] The scholar of the community, ʿAbd Allāh b. ʿAbbās (may God be pleased with him) has been the origin of the exegesis of all the commentators, and the Messenger of God (may God bless him and his family) sent for him in order to say, 'O God! Instruct him in religion and teach him hermeneutics'.[20] So he became the pupil of ʿAlī (may God be pleased with him) so that *he* instructed him in religion and taught him hermeneutics.[21]

In my youth, I used to hear Qur'ān commentary from my shaykhs, simply 'auditing',[22] so that I was vouchsafed attainment and I made notes on it according to my teacher, the defender of the sunna, Abū'l-Qāsim Salmān, the son of Nāṣir al-Anṣārī (may God be pleased with them both), learning as he spoke. Then he would inform me about the different readings of the noble words from the People of the House and their friends (may God be pleased with them), in line with buried secrets and firm root-principles in the science of the Qur'ān. The One who was on the right side of the valley in the blessed field called me from the goodly tree:[23] 'O you who believe! Be conscious of God and be with the truthful.'[24]

So I searched for 'the truthful' as passionate lovers might search. And I found one of God's virtuous slaves, just as Moses (peace be upon him) searched with his young man: 'Then the two of them found one of Our slaves whom We bestowed as a mercy from Us, and We taught him knowledge from Our presence.'[25] I learnt from him the ways of creation and of the Command, the degrees of contrariety and hierarchy, the twin aspects of generality and specificity, and the two principles of the accomplished and the inchoative. I thus satisfied myself with this single bellyfull, not those which are the foods of error and the starting points of the ignorant.[26] I quenched my thirst from the fountain of submission with a cup whose blend was from Tasnīm.[27] I was guided to the language of the Qur'ān: its harmony, its order, its eloquence, its concision, its linguistic purity, and its skilfulness. It is ranked above the ranks of the speech of the Arabs as the speech of the Arabs is ranked above the other languages of men, as the tongue of man is ranked above the tongue of birds and the voices of mute beasts. And each rank is inimitable for what is beneath it amongst ranks.

4 Then I turned my gaze from the outward expression to the meaning, and I found it to be an ocean whose wonders never cease and whose marvels are inexhaustible – an ocean whose bottom is deep and whose depth is vast, an ocean of holy words reinforced by seven oceans, an ocean full of pearls and the diver is single and an ocean full of divers and the pearl is single! So I began considering whether to dive in by swimming, the hand being cut off and the shore far away, or whether to search for a boat, the usurper having taken it by force or the prescient person having punched a hole in it. So He urged me, He whose urging is a sound judgement and obedience to whom is a duty for you, to 'the meeting of the two seas' though you spend a long time.[28] For *there* is the confluence of the two rivers, the fountainhead of life and the fish which took its course in the ocean as in a tunnel.[29] Thus I found a learned scholar and I followed him so that he would teach me what he had been taught by way of guidance. And [again, like Moses] I noticed a fire and found guidance at the fire. So I transcribed recitation, grammar, language, commentary and Qur'ānic semantics from their exponents, as they quoted it in books, by pure authentic transcription, without taking any liberty therein by adding or subtracting, except in elaborating what was summary or abridging what was prolix. I commented on each verse using what I heard about it consisting in arcana, and I examined them carefully through the allusions of the godly, and I prefaced the investigation of them with sections on the science of the Qur'ān which are the 'Keys of the Criterion', expounding twelve chapters by way of which other commentaries have become redundant. I called the commentary 'The Keys to the Arcana and the Lanterns of the Godly'. And I seek refuge with God, the All-Hearing, the Omniscient, from speaking about them on the basis of a personal opinion and independent reasoning rather than an authoritative report and chain of transmission, and I seek refuge with God from investigating their arcana and their meanings randomly and extravagantly, rather than paying heed to the scales of truth, 'setting up the weight by justice',[30] affirming the truth and declaring erroneous opinion[31] to be false. Indeed, He is[32] the best of refuges and the noblest of shelters!

Keys to the Criterion
(Mafatīḥ al-furqān)

Shahrastānī's introduction to his hermeneutical methodology

Chapter 1
On the beginnings and endings of the descent of the Qur'ān,[33] 6
and the sequence[34] *of its descent*

It is transmitted on the authority of ʿAbd Allāh b. ʿAbbās[35] (may God's good pleasure be upon him) that he said: 'The first of what God sent down was "Recite! In the name of your Lord" upto "He taught man what he knew not".'[36] And in the transmission of Mujāhid:[37] 'The first of what descended of the Qur'ān was "Recite!" and "Nūn. By the Pen".'[38]

It is transmitted on the authority of Jābir b. ʿAbd Allāh[39] (may God be pleased with him): 'The first thing which descended of the Qur'ān was "O Thou Enwrapped."'[40] In the *Kāfī* of al-Kulaynī,[41] it is transmitted on the authority of al-Ṣādiq Abū ʿAbd Allāh Jaʿfar the son of Muḥammad[42] (peace be upon them both), that he said: 'The first of what God (Exalted is He) sent down to His Messenger (may God bless him and his family) was "In the name of God, the Infinitely Merciful, the Compassionate. Recite! In the name of your Lord",'[43] and in some of the transmissions: 'The first of what God (Exalted is He) sent down was the chapter of the Exordium.'[44]

On the authority of ʿUthmān b. ʿAffān[45] (may God's good pleasure be upon him) the chapter of Immunity[46] was the last of what descended of the Qur'ān.[47] [It is transmitted] on the authority of al-Barāʾ b. ʿĀzib[48] that he said: 'The last verse to descend was "They will ask you for a pronouncement. Say: God has pronounced for you concerning [inheritance from] those who leave no direct heir."'[49] [It is transmitted] on the authority of Ibn Shihāb[50] that he said: 'The last of the Qur'ān in time, at Mecca,[51] was the verse of usury and the verse of debt.'[52] [It is transmitted] on the authority of ʿAṭāʾ b. Abī Rabāḥ[53] and Ibn ʿAbbās: 'The last verse to descend was "And be mindful of a day in which you are returned to God."'[54] Ibn ʿAbbās said: 'God's Messenger lingered on for seven nights after this verse.[55] He appeared in public on Saturday and passed away on Monday'.[56] [It is transmitted] on the authority of al-Ṣādiq Jaʿfar b. Muḥammad (peace be upon him), that he said: 'The last chapter to descend was "When God's victory and triumph come."'[57]

[It is transmitted] on the authority of Ibn ʿAbbās: 'The Qur'ān was sent down as a single whole to the lowest heaven during the Night of Power[58]

(and in one report: 'The Qur'ān descended as a single whole in the month
of Ramaḍān to the "Frequented House"');[59] then it descended piecemeal
over twenty years,' and he recited: 'It is a Qur'ān which We divided up so
that you might recite it to men at intervals, and We send it down in steps.'[60]
[It is transmitted] on the authority of Wāthila b. al-Asqaʿ:[61] 'The scriptures
of Abraham (peace be upon him) descended in the first night of the month
of Ramaḍān; the Torah descended to Moses (peace be upon him) on the
sixth of the month of Ramaḍān; the Psalms descended to David (peace be
7 upon him)[62] on the twelfth of the month of Ramaḍān; the Gospel
descended to Jesus (peace be upon him) on the eighteenth of the month of
Ramaḍān; and God sent down the Qur'ān to Muḥammad on the twenty-
fourth of the month of Ramaḍān.'[63] [It is transmitted] on the authority of
al-Ṣādiq: 'Everything has a springtime, and the springtime of the Qur'ān is
the month of Ramaḍān.'[64]

The transmitters disagree on the sequence of the descent of the chapters of the Qur'ān, for example, Muqātil b. Sulaymān[65] on the basis of his authorities, Muqātil also on the authority of the Commander of the Faithful, ʿAlī[66] (may God be pleased with him), al-Kalbī[67] on the authority of Ibn ʿAbbās, Ibn Wāqid[68] by his chain of transmission, and what is related on the authority of the portion [*sic.*] of al-Ṣādiq's codex. There is not much difference between his codex and the codex of Ibn Wāqid, over the order and sequence of the chapters, except in regard to a number of chapters which have been mentioned. And he who has knowledge of them has set them out in charts, which I pass on in such a way as to take no liberty in regard to them. That will come after discussing the collection of the Qur'ān, if God (Exalted is He) wills.

Chapter 2
On the manner of the collection of the Qur'ān

When the Muslims finished with the affair of al-Yamāma,[69] the slaughter of men and the reciters of the Qur'ān being intense there, Abū Bakr[70] (may God's good pleasure be upon him) ordered Zayd b. Thābit[71] to collect together the Qur'ān. So he set about transcribing it, gathering it from pieces of vellum, shoulder blades, palm leaves and the breasts of men. Thus nothing came to pass in his days except writing it down on scattered parch-

ments. Then when the affair reached ʿUmar[72] (may God's good pleasure be
upon him) he ordered that it be written down in a single codex, and it
became a single manuscript. And the parchments of Abū Bakr (may God be
pleased with him) were with him for a long time until he died; then they
were transferred[73] to [ʿUmar's] daughter Ḥafṣa.[74] Then when ʿUthmān
(may God's good pleasure be upon him) took over the caliphate, the Syrians
and the Iraqis differed in the matter of the Qurʾān, and each community
had codices contradicting those of its fellow community. The situation
reached the point that one of them accused the other of unbelief. Hudhayfa 8
b. al-Yamān[75] reported this to ʿUthmān b. ʿAffān (may God's good pleasure
be upon him) and said: 'Get a grip on this nation before they disagree with
one another as the Jews and Christians disagreed with one another!'[76] So
ʿUthmān sent someone to Ḥafṣa asking her 'Send us the codex for us to
transcribe'. So she sent it to him.[77] Then ʿUthmān summoned Zayd b.
Thābit and Abān b. Saʿīd,[78] and ordered them both to collect together the
Qurʾān. So they collected it together and collated it with ʿUmar's copy, and
lo and behold! they were one and the same.

In one transmission, ʿUthmān ordered Zayd b. Thābit, ʿAbd Allāh b. al-Zubayr,[79] Saʿīd b. al-ʿĀṣ[80] and ʿAbd al-Raḥmān b.[81] al-Ḥārith b. Hishām[82] – so they transcribed it into codices. And he said to the band of three Qurashīs: 'If you and Zayd b. Thābit disagree on something of the Qurʾān, write it down in the dialect of the Quraysh, for indeed it was in their language that it descended'.[83] So they acted thus, till when the codices were transcribed, ʿUthmān returned to Ḥafṣa her codex, and he sent a manuscript of the codex to each region. Then Zayd b. Thābit said: 'A verse has been lost from the chapter of the Confederates[84] when the codex was transcribed, which I used to hear God's Messenger (may God bless him and his family) recite. I found it with Khuzayma b. Thābit [al-Anṣārī]:[85] "Amongst the faithful are men who fulfil what they pledge themselves to God to do. For amongst them is he who fulfils his promise and amongst them is he who bides his time, and they are quite unchanging".[86] So I added it in its proper place.' This is an authentic tradition which al-Bukhārī transmitted in *al-Jāmiʿ al-Ṣaḥīḥ* on the authority of Mūsā b. Ismāʿīl on the authority of Ibrāhīm [b. Saʿd].[87]

Some of the people of learning said: How many verses like it did they lose consisting in what referred to the virtues of the People of the [Prophet's] House (peace be upon them)! Since the verse in question[88] descended in regard to four individuals who made a covenant with God (Exalted is He) to surrender the spirit in the path of God:[89] ʿAbd Allāh b. al-Ḥārith b. ʿAbd al-Muṭṭalib, Ḥamza b. ʿAbd al-Muṭṭalib and Jaʿfar b. Abī Ṭālib[90] (may God be pleased with them), who fulfilled their promise when ʿAbd Allāh was martyred at the Battle of Badr, Ḥamza at the Battle of Uḥud and Jaʿfar al-Ṭayyār[91] at the Battle of Muʾta. *And the one who 'bided his time' was ʿĀlī b. Abī Ṭālib* (may God be pleased with him).

Shubāba transmitted on the authority of Isrāʾīl on the authority of Abū
Isḥāq on the authority of Muṣʿab b. Saʿd, that he said: 'When the disagreement of men over the Qurʾān grew great, some of them using the recitation
9 of ʿAbd Allāh b. Masʿūd,[92] since the Prophet (may God bless him and his
family) said "Who wishes to recite the Qurʾān freshly, just as it was sent down, let him use the recitation of Ibn Umm ʿAbd!"[93] and some using the recitation of Ubayy b. Kaʿb,[94] since the Prophet (may God bless him and his family) recited the whole Qurʾān to him, and some using the recitation of Sālim the client of Ḥudhayfa – then ʿUthmān brought together the companions of God's Messenger (may God bless him and his family) and he said: "I have decided to write down codices according to the reading of Zayd b. Thābit, then I will send them out to the garrison towns." They replied: "What an excellent thing you have decided on!" He said: "So which man is the best at Arabic?" They replied: "Saʿīd b. al-ʿĀṣ!" He said: "And which man is the best at writing?" They replied: "Zayd b. Thābit is the scribe of the revelation!" He said: "Then let Saʿīd dictate and let Zayd write".[95] Then he wrote the codices and sent them to the garrison towns.' [Muṣʿab b. Saʿd] said: 'And I saw men saying "By God, ʿUthmān is excellent! By God, ʿUthmān is excellent!"'[96]

Ubayy b. Kaʿb had opposed him and refused him his codex, and he used to say: 'Saʿīd b. al-ʿĀṣ is merely the best of men at Arabic and he never recited to the Messenger of God any chapter of the Qurʾān nor did the Prophet recite any chapter to him.' ʿAbd Allāh b. Masʿūd also opposed him and disapproved of him in his work with the codices, since he burnt them. Ibn Masʿūd used to call ʿUthmān 'the codex burner' for a time so that the long and the short of it was that ʿUthmān ordered a slave of his, so he took it upon himself. The slave threw Ibn Masʿūd to the ground crushing his chest and he died from that. And it was through Ibn Masʿūd's opposition. So now the codices of the two of them[97] have been abandoned. Consensus has come about on what ʿUthmān put together and he did not have much leeway in the process of collecting since the collecters were Zayd b. Thābit and Saʿīd b. al-ʿĀṣ. They transcribed what was in Ḥafṣa's hand from[98] the collection of Abū Bakr and ʿUmar – except certain additions which they found in the hands of men and which Abū Bakr and ʿUmar had left out (may God's good pleasure be upon them both). Then ʿUthmān (may God be pleased with him) ordered that one of the manuscripts amongst them be placed in the mosque of Medina and they called it 'the Prototype' (*imām*). He dispatched a manuscript to Mecca, a manuscript to Kufa, a manuscript to Basra, a manuscript to Damascus and a manuscript to Yemen.[99] They agreed to say: There is no Qur'ān except what the Prototype contains.

Zirr[100] b. Ḥubaysh transmitted on the authority of Ubayy b. Kaʿb that he said to him: 'What number do you give to the verses of the chapter of the Confederates?'[101] He said: 'I replied, "Seventy-three or seventy-two". He said, "Is that all?" I replied, "That's all!" He said, "By God! It used to be equal to the chapter of the Cow[102] and it used to contain the verse of lapidation."' Zirr said: 'I said, "O Abū'l-Mundhir, and what is the verse of lapidation?" Ubayy said, "When the married man and the married woman commit adultery, stone them both utterly as an exemplary punishment from God. And God is Mighty, Wise!"'[103]

Likewise Saʿīd b. al-Musayyib [al-Makhzūmī][104] transmitted that ʿUmar b. al-Khaṭṭāb (may God be pleased with him) said within a long narrative, 'Do not forget the verse of lapidation, for it has been sent down and we recited it: "Stone the married man and the married woman utterly when they commit adultery, as an exemplary punishment from God. And God is Mighty, Wise!" Were it not said that ʿUmar adds to God's book, I would have written it in with my own hand.'[105]

ʿAṭā' transmitted on the authority of Ibn ʿAbbās (may God be pleased with him) in regard to His statement (Exalted is He) 'The hypocrites are alarmed that a chapter is sent down to them which informs them of what is in their hearts',[106] that there were the names in this chapter of seventy persons from amongst the hypocrites, individually, with both their names and the names of their fathers. Then[107] it was abrogated out of sympathy for their children. And in it was 'Remember what is recited in your houses consisting in the signs of God [and the sunna].'[108]

It has been transmitted on the authority of ʿAbd Allāh b. Masʿūd that he did not transcribe the last two chapters (*al-muʿawwadhatayn*) in the codex[109] and it is transmitted on the authority of Ubayy b. Kaʿb that he transcribed the standing prayer (*qunūt*) in the codex as two chapters.[110] Likewise it is transmitted on the authority of ʿAbd Allāh b. Masʿūd that he did not write the Exordium[111] of the Scripture in his codex. He was asked: 'Why did you not write down the Exordium (*al-Fātiḥa*) of the Scripture?' He replied: 'If I wrote it at the start of the chapter of the Cow[112] then I would write it at the beginning of every chapter, in the opinion thereby that just as it is the opening (*fātiḥa*) of the Scripture, it is the opening for every chapter.'

It is transmitted on the authority of Abū'l-ʿĀliya[113] and Mujāhid that they both said: 'The chapter of the Confederates[114] was three hundred verses, all of which were lost. Amongst them was His statement, "O God! Punish the unbelievers, and cast terror into their hearts, and make their statements at odds". And much perished from it at the Battle of Musaylima[115] – though the licit and illicit did not perish from it.'

And the statement of ʿUmar b. al-Khaṭṭāb (may God be pleased with him): 'I fear that if the slaughter of the reciters is as intense as it was at the Battle of Musaylima, something may perish from the Qurʾān.'

11 Suwayd b. ʿAlqama transmitted [a narrative] and said: 'I heard ʿAlī b. Abī Ṭālib (may God honour him) say: "O people! Beware of excess in the matter of ʿUthmān and your calling him 'the codex burner'. For by God, he only burned them on the authority of notables from amongst the companions of God's Messenger (may God bless him and his family)." ʿUthmān gathered us together and asked, "What do you say in regard to this recitation over which people disagree? One man meets with another and says 'my Qurʾān is better than your Qurʾān'. This will lead to unbelief!" So we said "So what is your opinion?" He replied: "I am decided upon uniting people over a single codex, for if you are in disagreement today, those who come after you will be fiercer in disagreement." We said: "How excellent is what you have decided!" So he sent someone to Zayd b. Thābit and Saʿīd b. al-ʿĀṣ and said: "One of the two of them will write and the other will dictate".[116] And the two disagreed in nothing save a single letter in the chapter of the Cow.[117] One of them said *al-tābūt*[118] and the other said *al-tābūh*.'[119]

ʿAbd Allāh b. Masʿūd said: 'I withdraw from the codices. I have taken from the mouth of the Prophet seventy chapters when Zayd b. Thābit, "he of the sidelocks",[120] was still playing with the boys!'[121]

It was said: ʿUthmān only chose him because he was the scribe of the revelation and knew about writing in Arabic and Persian.

It was transmitted that when ʿUthmān looked at the codex which was written and completed, he said: 'I see a solecism in it, but the Arabs will render it correctly with their tongues.'

And what is transmitted on the authority of Ibn ʿAbbās, that he recited 'Do not those who believe perceive [...]';[122] and it was said to him 'Do not those who believe *know* [...]'. He said: 'I am of the opinion that the scribe wrote it while he was dozing.'

ʿĀ'isha used to say about some of the readings: 'They are an error of the scribe.'[123] What then do you imagine of the companions – that they saw solecism and error in the codex *without* amending it, and they just said "the Arabs will render it correctly with their tongues"? Variations in readings are [in fact] countless and innumerable, some of them occurring in the transcription and others occurring in the pronunciation – and how can the consensus [of the companions] remain unimpaired despite this difference, notwithstanding the fact that what is between the two covers is the Word of God?

Leave all this aside! How did they not seek[124] the collection of ʿAlī b. Abī
Ṭālib?[125] Was he not better at writing than Zayd b. Thābit? Was he not 12
better at Arabic than Saʿīd b. al-ʿĀṣ? Was he not closer to God's Messenger (may God bless him and his family) than the whole community? Instead, they all neglected his collection, took it as redundant, paid no attention to it and made it fall into utter oblivion! After finishing preparing God's Messenger (may God bless him and his family), washing him, shrouding him, praying over him and burying him, ʿAlī (peace be upon him) swore an oath that he would not don an outer garment except for congregational prayer, until he collected the Qurʾān, since he was strictly charged to do that. So he collected it as it was sent down, without alteration, distortion, addition or subtraction. And the Prophet (may God bless him and his family) had indicated the places of the sequence, position, the placing earlier or later.

Abū Ḥātim said: "Alī placed each verse beside what was similar to it.'

It is transmitted on the authority of Muḥammad b. Sīrīn[126] that there were many who wanted it and said: 'Were we to encounter that compilation, we would encounter much knowledge in it.'[127]

It has been said that ʿAlī's codex contained the text as well as exegetical interpolation, and whatever he came across consisting in two intended expressions[128] he would write down in the horizontal margin and the side notes. It is reported that when he finished collecting it, he and his slave Qanbar brought it out to the people. They were in the mosque whence they carried it together and left it, and it is said that it was a camel-load. And he said to them: 'This is God's Scripture, as He sent it down to Muḥammad, which I have collected together between the two covers.' Thereupon they said: 'Away with your codex! We have no need for it!' So he said: 'By God! You will never see it again. My duty was only to inform you when I had collected it.' So he returned to his house, saying 'O my Lord! Verily my people view this Qur'ān as redundant',[129] and he left them as they were, just as Aaron (peace be upon him) left the people of his brother Moses after the evidence went against them. And he gave an excuse to his brother with his statement 'I was afraid you would say "You make division amongst the children of Israel and were not attentive to what I said",'[130] and with his statement 'O son of my mother! The people reckoned me as weak and nearly killed me. Do not let enemies rejoice at my misfortune, nor count me with sinners!'[131]

Would you then say, brother, if you were even-handed with me, that the
Prophet (may God bless him and his family) was inspired with the like of
this Qur'ān and would leave it scattered on shoulder blades, parchments,
13 the fronds of trees and in the breasts of men, and give no indication of him
who was to be entrusted with it, knowing that the like of that scattered thing, were it not collected together, would disappear, neglected, and people would become divided over it, after it was precisely sent down as a means for uniting people, and for their following what it contained? And He (Exalted is He) has said: 'Follow what is sent down to you from your Lord and do not follow friends other than Him. Little do you reflect.'[132] Or else, he did indicate and give an order and explained the manner of the sequence consisting in placing earlier and placing later? Then who is it who undertook that on the basis of the procedure of direct stipulation and indication [if not 'Alī]?

It is well-known how those who undertook to collect it delved into it without consulting the People of the House (peace be upon them) on a reading (*ḥarf*), after their agreeing that the Qur'ān was particular to them and that they were one of the 'two precious things' in the statement of the Prophet (may God bless him and his family), 'I leave amongst you two precious things: God's Scripture and my immediate family (in one report, "the People of my House"). As long as you hold fast to them both, you will never go astray. The two will not be sundered till they reach me at the Pool of Paradise.'[133]

To be sure, by God, the Qur'ān is protected, on account of His statement (Exalted is He): 'We it is who sent down the Remembrance, and We are the protector thereof.'[134] He protected it in the protection of the People of the House, for 'the two will never be sundered'. For the word does not cease to reach them, on account of His statement (Exalted is He): 'We have caused the word to reach them.'[135] The union of the 'two precious things' will not be sundered, on account of His statement: 'The collection of it and the recitation of it are incumbent upon Us.'[136] So though its transcription is neglected with one people, it is protected and shielded, praise be to God, with another people: 'Nay, it is a glorious Qur'ān on a Guarded Tablet!'[137]

No condemnation is conveyed on the authority of ʿAlī (peace be upon him) of what the companions collected (may God's good pleasure be upon them), unlike what ʿUthmān said, 'I see a solecism in it and the Arabs will render it correctly', nor like what Ibn ʿAbbās said, 'The scribe wrote it while he was dozing'. Rather, he used to recite from the codex and write it in his own hand from the Prototype. Similarly, the imams from his posterity (peace be upon them) intoned the scripture just as he intoned it and taught their children likewise.[138]

And God (Exalted is He) is too noble and glorious to leave His noble and glorious scripture in possession of a solecism such that the Arabs would render it correctly. 'Nay! But He has noble servants. They do not speak until He has spoken. And they act by His command.'[139]

It is not thought far-fetched that His revealed scripture has two versions 14
which do not differ in the manner of contrariety, and both of them are the 'Word of God' (Mighty and Majestic). Did He not write the Torah with His own hand – as the report mentions[140] – and on the basis of that there is a special version on tablets, it being in the possession of the elite amongst the descendents of Aaron (peace be upon him)? Despite the fact that the Jews 'displaced the words from their places',[141] the Torah did not depart from the noble status of 'God's Word', and you recite from the Qur'ān how He magnified it and reported that it is 'a guidance and a light by which the prophets pass judgement'.[142]

Likewise, the Gospel is 'God's scripture' – and it has four versions which four men amongst the apostles collected, there being innumerable differences between them. So they are not in their totality the 'Word of God'

(Exalted is He) in the sense of revelation. Rather, they are like a portion of the Qur'ān from the commentators' exegesis, set forth by John, Mark, Luke and Matthew, and *within* them are sections which are revelation from God (Exalted is He). Yet despite that, God (Exalted is He) mentioned them in the Qur'ān in the manner of respect and magnification. He said: 'and confirming what was before it of the Gospel [*sic.*].'[143]

So the Qur'ān which is in our midst is the Word of God between the two covers, protected by God's protection from change, alteration, solecism and error – for the scribe of it is not dozing, and the intoner of it is no solecist! It has a people who intone it with its true intonation, and know it in both its hermeneutic and its sending down.[144] They dismiss the doubt of the doubters and the claim of those who allege falsification: 'And those firm-rooted in knowledge say: "We believe in it. All is from our Lord." And only those possessed of minds take heed.'[145]

Chapter 3
On the difference between reporters over the order of the descent of the chapters of the Qur'ān, like Muqātil from his authorities, Muqātil on the authority of ʿAlī, al-Kalbī on the authority of Ibn ʿAbbās, Ibn Wāqid by his chain of transmission, and Jaʿfar b. Muḥammad al-Ṣādiq

The foremost and first in excellence among the companions and successors (may God be pleased with them) differed over the order of the descent of the chapters of the Qur'ān and the order of their transcription in codices.

The next foremost found codices in the Ḥijāz, Iraq and Syria, differing in chapters, verses and words. So they abandoned them and agreed to return to the codex which was 'the Prototype', containing a little variation in transcription. For example, His statement (Exalted is He) 'and they say God has taken a son'[146] was written in the codices of the people of Syria without the 'and', but was written in the Medinan codices with the 'and'.[147] Similarly, 'and Abraham bequethed it (*awṣā bihā*)'[148] was written in them with an initial *alif*, but in others than them without an *alif* (= *waṣṣā*). And it was written in them 'Be quick in the race!'[149] without 'and',[150] and it is written in them, 'Verily God is the Independent, the Praiseworthy'[151] but in other than them 'He is the Independent'.[152] Again, for example, 'with rivers flowing beneath them',[153] without 'from'.[154] And again, for example, 'and the Psalms',[155] and 'with the Psalms'.[156]

It has been said that when the codex was submitted to Ubayy b. Kaʿb, he changed three letters. In it was 'it had not grown old (*lam yatasanna*)', however, he transcribed it 'it had not gone mouldy (*lam yatasannah*)'.[157] In it was 'so give respite (*imhil*) to the unbelievers', however, he transcribed it *mahhil*.[158] And in it was 'There is no change for the creation of God (*li-khalqi'llāh*)'[159] with two *lāms*, so he struck out one of the two *lāms*.

Amongst what is encountered in the orthography of the Qur'ān, contrary to what is customary,[160] is: 'On the day it comes (*yawma ya'ti*)';[161] 'what we were seeking (*mā kunnā nabghi*)';[162] 'we will summon (*sa-nadʿu*)';[163] and 'he summons man (*yadʿu'l-insān*)'.[164] And 'what is it with these (*mā li hā'ulā'i*)?';[165] 'what a book this is (*mā li hādha'l-kitāb*)!';[166] 'what kind of Messenger is this (*mā li hādha'l-rasūl*)?';[167] 'what is the matter with those who disbelieve (*mā li'lladhīna kafarū*)?'[168] are four places in the Qur'ān in which the *lām* is written in isolation.[169]

Likewise, 'the council (*al-malā'*)' is written in some of them with the *wāw*
and the *alif*;[170] and likewise 'from the tidings of the ones sent (*min nabā'i'l-*
mursalīn)'[171] is written in some of them with a *yā'* after the *hamza*;[172] and
'from behind a veil (*min warā'i ḥijāb*)'[173] with a *yā'* after the *hamza*;[174]
'from the prompting of my soul (*min tilqā'i nafsī*)';[175] 'We have made it 16
with might (*bi-ayydin*) and verily We [...]'.[176]

In the chapter of the Ant (Q. 27) is 'or I will certainly slaughter him (*aw la-aadhbaḥannahu*)'[177] with a superfluous *alif*, and in Repentance (Q. 9) is 'and they would have scurried (*wa la-aawḍaʿū*)',[178] and in the Family of ʿImrān (Q. 3) is 'we would follow you (*wa la-attabaʿnākum*)'.[179]

It was said about them and the like of them: 'Some of them are in accordance with the dialect of Quraysh[180] and their writing, and some of them are in accordance with the dialect of Hudhayl[181] and Ḥārith b. Kaʿb.'[182] Perhaps the scribe was combining the customs of the tribes, as an embellishment for the codex through the orthography. It is comparable with the *imāla*, *ghunna*, *idghām*, *tafkhīm* and *tarqīq* current on some tongues.[183]

It has been said, concerning the meaning of the statement of the Prophet 'The Qur'ān was sent down according to seven readings (*aḥruf*)',[184] that they are the forms in which words are capable of occuring and they are what the seven reciters differed over, consisting in *imāla*, *ishmām*,[185] and *idghām*. It is said that it is attributable to the difference of the seven languages extending from God (Exalted is He) upon creatures. Since the tongue of every people flows according to what it is accustomed to and shrinks from the uncustomary, God therefore facilitated for them the recitation of the Qurʾān out of mercy and compassion. And it has also been said that [this ḥadīth] refers to seven hidden dimensions (*abṭun*) of esoteric interpretation, since [the Prophet] said that every verse amongst them has an outer and an inner aspect and called them 'letters' (*ḥurūf*), in that the *ḥarf* of everything is its limit, and its extremity by which it is limited.[186] So the *ḥurūf* of meanings are their limits at which they end, and these *ḥurūf* are the vessels of meanings and arcana – without the externals being abandoned – and it finally winds up at what is ineffable and what expression and speech are not created for. And we will mention that, God willing!

Then, the order of the descent of the Qurʾān, on the authority of the revelation itself, was chapter by chapter and verse by verse. It is what none understands save the elite of the scholars who are in possession of authentic reports and clear prooftexts. As for the chapters, they have been transmitted [here] as to how they descended on the basis of the difference of reports, whether they are Meccan or Medinan, and how they were transcribed in the five codices. We have seen them brought together in tables according to the differences in them between the reporters. So we have transmitted them as we found them, and there is no responsibility on the one who transmits! And we appended to them the citation of the long chapters, the Doubled Ones (*al-mathānī*)[187] and the short divided (*al-mufaṣṣal al-qiṣār*).

17 The transcript is from men who are trustworthy and from books which are respected, beside which doubts do not hover. Perhaps you will not find them recorded in other commentaries, for they are devoid of the likes of them, not because the exegetes were without understanding of them and reliance on them, but due to the small amount of benefit in them and the large amount of grave matters bound up with them. I have cited them in their tables as I found them, and God knows best what is right in regard to them. And I desire the good!

[In the following tables, the number in the first column refers to the order of descent. The numbers in brackets refer to the numeration of the sūras in the standard codex.]

The order of the descent of the Qurʾān

No.	Muqātil from his authorities	Muqātil from the Commander of the Faithful (may God honour him)	Ibn ʿAbbās (may God be pleased with him)	Ibn Wāqid	al-Ṣādiq (may God be pleased with him)
1	Iqraʾ (96)	Iqraʾ (96)	Iqraʾ (96)	Iqraʾ (96)	Iqraʾ (96)
2	Nūn (68)	Nūn (68)	Nūn (68)	Nūn (68)	Nūn (68)
3	Wa'l-Ḍuḥā (93)	al-Muzammil (73)	Wa'l-Ḍuḥā (93)	al-Muzammil (73)	al-Muzammil (73)
4	al-Muzammil (73)	al-Muddaththir (74)	al-Muzammil (73)	al-Muddaththir (74)	al-Muddaththir (74)
5	al-Muddaththir (74)	Tabbat (111)	al-Muddaththir (74)	Tabbat (111)	Tabbat (111)
6	Tabbat (111)	Kuwwirat (81)	al-Fātiḥa (1)	Kuwwirat (81)	Kuwwirat (81)
7	Kuwwirat (81)	al-Aʿlā (87)	Tabbat (111)	al-Aʿlā (87)	al-Aʿlā (87)
8	al-Aʿlā (87)	Wa'l-Layl (92)	Kuwwirat (81)	Wa'l-Layl (92)	Wa'l-Layl (92)
9	Wa'l-Layl (92)	Wa'l-Fajr (89)	al-Aʿlā (87)	Wa'l-Fajr (89)	Wa'l-Fajr (89)
10	Wa'l-Fajr (89)	Wa'l-Ḍuḥā (93)	Wa'l-Layl (92)	Wa'l-Ḍuḥā (93)	Wa'l-Ḍuḥā (93)
11	A-lam Nashraḥ (94)	A-lam Nashraḥ (94)	Wa'l-Fajr (89)	A-lam Nashraḥ (94)	A-lam Nashraḥ(94)
12	al-Raḥmān (55)	Wa'l-ʿAṣr (102)	A-lam Nashraḥ (94)	Wa'l-ʿAṣr (103)	Wa'l-ʿAṣr (103)
13	al-Kawthar (108)	al-Kawthar (108)	al-Raḥmān (55)	Wa'l-ʿĀdiyāt (100)	Wa'l-ʿĀdiyāt (100)
14	al-Takāthur (102)	al-Dīn (107)	Wa'l-ʿAṣr (103)	al-Kawthar (108)	al-Kawthar (108)
15	al-Dīn (107)	al-Kāfirūn (109)	al-Kawthar (108)	al-Takāthur (102)	al-Takāthur (102)
16	al-Fīl (105)	al-Fīl (105)	al-Takāthur (102)	al-Dīn (107)	al-Dīn (107)
17	al-Kāfirūn (109)	al-Ikhlāṣ (112)	al-Dīn (107)	al-Kāfirūn (109)	al-Kāfirūn (109)
18	al-Ikhlāṣ (112)	al-Takāthur (102)	al-Fīl (105)	al-Fīl (105)	al-Fīl (105)[188]
19	Wa'l-Najm (53)	Wa'l-Najm (53)	al-Kāfirūn (109)	al-ʿAlaq (96)	al-Falaq (113)
20	al-Aʿmā (80)	al-Aʿmā (80)	al-Ikhlāṣ (112)	al-Nās (114)	al-Nās (114)
21	Wa'l-Shams (91)	Quraysh (106)	Wa'l-Najm (53)	al-Ikhlāṣ (112)	al-Ikhlāṣ (112)
22	al-Burūj (85)	al-Qāriʿa (101)	al-Aʿmā (80)	Wa'l-Najm (53)	Wa'l-Najm (53)
23	al-Tīn (95)	al-Qiyāma (75)	al-Qadar (97)	al-Aʿmā (80)	al-Aʿmā (80)
24	Quraysh (106)	al-Humaza (104)	Wa'l-Shams (91)	al-Qadar (97)	al-Qadar (97)

No.	Muqātil from his authorities	Muqātil from the Commander of the Faithful (may God honour him)	Ibn ʿAbbās (may God be pleased with him)	Ibn Wāqid	al-Ṣādiq (may God be pleased with him)
25	al-Qāriʿa (101)	al-Murasalāt (77)	al-Burūj (85)	Wa'l-Shams (91)	Wa'l-Shams (91)
26	al-Qiyāma (75)	Qāf (50)	Wa'l-Tīn (95)	al-Burūj (85)	al-Burūj (85)
27	al-Humaza (104)	al-Ṭāriq (86)	Quraysh (106)	Wa'l-Tīn (95)	Wa'l-Tīn (95)
28	Wa'l-Mursalāt (77)	al-Qamar (54)	al-Qāriʿa (101)	Quraysh (106)	Quraysh (106)
29	Qāf (50)	Ṣād (38)	al-Qiyāma (75)	al-Qāriʿa (101)	al-Qāriʿa (101)
30	al-Balad (90)	al-Jinn (72)	al-Humaza (104)	al-Qiyāma (75)	al-Qiyāma (75)
31	al-Ṭāriq (86)	Yā Sīn (36)	Wa'l-Mursalāt (77)	al-Humaza (104)	al-Humaza (104)
32	al-Qamar (54)	al-Furqān (25)	Qāf (50)	Wa'l-Mursalāt (77)	Wa'l-Mursalāt (77)
33	Ṣād (38)	al-Malā'ika (35)	al-Balad (90)	Qāf (50)	Qāf (50)
34	al-Aʿrāf (7)	Maryam (19)	al-Ṭāriq (86)	al-Balad (90)	al-Balad (90)
35	al-Jinn (72)	Ṭā Hā' (20)	al-Qamar (54)	al-Ṭāriq (86)	al-Ṭāriq (86)
36	Yā Sīn (36)	al-Wāqiʿa (56)	Ṣād (38)	al-Qamar (54)	al-Qamar (54)
37	al-Furqān (25)	al-Shuʿarā' (26)	al-Aʿrāf (7)	Ṣād (38)	Ṣād (38)
38	al-Malā'ika (35)	al-Naml (27)	al-Jinn (72)	al-Aʿrāf (7)	al-Aʿrāf (7)
39	Maryam (19)	al-Qaṣaṣ (28)	Yā Sīn (36)	al-Jinn (72)	al-Jinn (72)
40	Ṭā Hā'(20)	Hūd (11)	al-Furqān (25)	Yā Sīn (36)	Yā Sīn (36)
41	al-Shuʿarā' (26)	Yūsuf (12)	al-Malā'ika (35)	al-Furqān (25)	al-Furqān (25)
42	al-Naml (27)	al-Ḥajj (22)	Maryam (19)	al-Malā'ika (35)	al-Malā'ika (35)
43	al-Qaṣaṣ (28)	al-Anʿām (6)	Ṭā Hā' (20)	Maryam (19)	Maryam (19)
44	Banū Isrā'īl (17)	Wa'l-Ṣāffāt (37)	al-Shuʿarā' (26)	Ṭā Hā' (20)	Ṭā Hā' (20)
45	Yūnus (10)	Luqmān (31)	al-Naml (27)	al-Wāqiʿa (56)	al-Wāqiʿa (56)
46	Hūd (11)	Saba' (34)	al-Qaṣaṣ (28)	al-Shuʿarā' (26)	al-Shuʿarā' (26)
47	Yūsuf (12)	al-Rūm (30)	Banū Isrā'īl (17)	al-Naml (27)	al-Naml (27)
48	al-Ḥijr (15)	al-Qadar (97)	Yūnus (10)	al-Shuʿarā' (26)	al-Qaṣaṣ (28)
49	al-Anʿām (6)	Wa'l-Shams (91)	Hūd (11)	Banū Isrā'īl (17)	Banū Isrā'īl (17)

50	Wa'l-Ṣāffāt (37)	al-Burūj (85)	Yūsuf (12)	Yūnus (10)	Yūnus (10)
51	Luqmān (31)	al-Tīn (95)	al-Ḥijr (15)	Hūd (11)	Hūd (11)
52	Saba' (34)	al-Mu'min (20)	al-An'ām (6)	Yūsuf (12)	Yūsuf (12)
53	Alif Lām Mīm al-Sajda (32)	Ḥā' Mīm al-Sajda (41)	Wa'l-Ṣāffāt (37)	al-Ḥijr (15)	al-Ḥijr (15)
54	Ḥā' Mīm al-Mu'min (40)	al-Dukhān (44)	Luqmān (31)	al-An'ām (6)	al-An'ām (6)
55	Ḥā' Mīm al-Sajda (41)	Ḥā' Mīm 'Ayn Sīn Qāf (42)	Saba' (34)	Wa'l-Ṣāffāt (37)	Wa'l-Ṣāffāt (37)
56	Ḥā' Mīm 'Ayn Sīn Qāf (42)	al-Jāthiya (45)	al-Zumar (39)	Luqmān (31)	Luqmān (31)
57	al-Zukhruf (43)	al-Aḥqāf (46)	al-Mu'min (40)	Saba' (34)	Saba' (34)
58	al-Dukhān (44)	al-Kahf (18)	Ḥā' Mīm al-Sajda (41)	al-Zumar (39)	al-Zumar (39)
59	al-Jāthiya (45)	Alif Lām Mīm al-Sajda (32)	Ḥā' Mīm 'Ayn Sīn Qāf (42)	al-Mu'min (40)	al-Mu'min (40)
60	al-Aḥqāf (46)	al-Anbiyā' (21)	al-Zukhruf (43)	Ḥā' Mīm al-Sajda (41)	Ḥā' Mīm al-Sajda (41)
61	Wa'l-Dhāriyāt (51)	al-Naḥl (16)	al-Dukhān (44)	Ḥā' Mīm 'Ayn Sīn Qāf (42)	Ḥā' Mīm 'Ayn Sīn Qāf (42)
62	al-Ghāshiya (88)	Nūḥ (71)	al-Jāthiya (45)	al-Zukhruf (43)	al-Zukhruf (43)
63	al-Kahf (18)	Ibrāhīm (14)	al-Aḥqāf (46)	al-Dukhān (44)	al-Dukhān (44)
64	al-Naḥl (16)	al-Ṭūr (52)	Wa'l-Dhāriyāt (61)	al-Jāthiya (45)	al-Jāthiya (45)
65	Nūḥ (71)	al-Mulk (67)	al-Ghāshiya (88)	al-Aḥqāf (46)	al-Aḥqāf (46)
66	Ibrāhīm (14)	al-Ḥāqqa (69)	al-Kahf (18)	Wa'l-Dhāriyāt (51)	Wa'l-Dhāriyāt (51)
67	al-Anbiyā' (21)	al-Ma'ārij (70)	al-Naḥl (16)	al-Ghāshiya (88)	al-Ghāshiya (88)
68	al-Mu'min (40)	al-Naba' (78)	Nūḥ (71)	al-Kahf (18)	al-Kahf (18)
69	al-Ra'd (13)	Wa'l-Nāzi'āt (79)	Ibrāhīm (14)	al-Naḥl (16)	al-Naḥl (16)
70	al-Ṭūr (52)	Wa'l-Dhāriyāt (51)	al-Anbiyā' (21)	Nūḥ (71)	Nūḥ (71)
71	al-Mulk (67)	Inshaqqat (84)	al-Mu'minūn (23)	Ibrāhīm (14)	Ibrāhīm (14)
72	al-Ḥāqqa (69)	Infaṭarat (82)	al-Ra'd (13)	al-Anbiyā' (21)	al-Anbiyā' (21)
73	al-Ma'ārij (70)	al-Zumar (39)	al-Ṭūr (52)	al-Mu'minūn (23)	al-Mu'minūn (23)
74	al-Naba' (78)	al-'Ankabūt (29)	al-Mulk (67)	Alif Lām Mīm al-Sajda (32)	Alif Lām Mīm al-Sajda (32)
75	Wa'l-Nāzi'āt (79)	Yūnus (10)	al-Ḥāqqa (69)	al-Ṭūr (52)	al-Ṭūr (52)
76	Infaṭarat (82)	al-Ḥijr (15)	al-Ma'ārij (70)	al-Mulk (67)	al-Mulk (67)
77	Inshaqqat (84)	al-Mu'minūn (23)	al-Naba' (78)	al-Ḥāqqa (69)	al-Ḥāqqa (69)
78	al-Rūm (30)	al-Muṭaffifūn (83)	al-Nāzi'āt (79)	al-Ma'ārij (70)	al-Ma'ārij (70)
79	al-'Ankabūt (29)	al-Anfāl (8)	Infaṭarat (82)	al-Naba' (78)	al-Naba' (78)

No.	Muqātil from his authorities	Muqātil from the Commander of the Faithful (may God honour him)	Ibn ʿAbbās (may God be pleased with him)	Ibn Wāqid	al-Ṣādiq (may God be pleased with him)
80	al-Insān (76)	al-Baqara (2)	Inshaqqat (84)	al-Nāziʿāt (79)	al-Nāziʿāt (79)
81	al-Zumar (39)	Āl ʿImrān (3)	al-Rūm (30)	Infaṭarat (82)	Infaṭarat (82)
82	al-Wāqiʿa (56)	al-Nisāʾ (4)	al-ʿAnkabūt (29)	Inshaqqat (84)	Inshaqqat (84)
83	al-Muṭaffifūn (83)	al-Māʾida (5)	al-Muṭaffifūn (83)	al-Rūm (30)	al-Rūm(30)
84	al-Fātiḥa (1)	al-Aḥzāb (33)	al-Baqara (2)	al-ʿAnkabūt (29)	al-ʿAnkabūt (29)
85	al-Baqara (2)	al-Mumtaḥina (60)	al-Anfāl (8)	al-Muṭaffifūn (83)	al-Muṭaffifūn (83)
86	al-Anfāl (8)	al-Ḥadīd (57)	Āl ʿImrān (3)	al-Baqara (2)	al-Baqara (2) [189]
87	Āl ʿImrān (3)	Sūrat Muḥammad (47)	al-Ḥashr (59)	al-Anfāl (8)	al-Anfāl (8)
88	al-Ḥashr (59)	al-Raʿd (13)	al-Aḥzāb (33)	Āl ʿImrān (3)	Āl ʿImrān (3)
89	al-Aḥzāb (33)	al-Raḥmān (55)	al-Nūr (24)	al-Aḥzāb (33)	al-Aḥzāb (33)
90	al-Nūr (24)	al-Insān (76)	al-Mumtaḥina (60)	al-Mumtaḥina (60)	al-Mumtaḥina (60)
91	al-Ṣamad (112)	al-Ṭalāq (65)	al-Fatḥ (48)	al-Nisāʾ (4)	al-Nisāʾ (4)
92	al-Fatḥ (48)	Lam Yakun (98)	al-Nisāʾ (4)	Idhā Zulzilat (99)	Idhā Zulzilat (99)
93	al-Nisāʾ (4)	al-Shams (91)	Idhā Zulzilat (99)	al-Ḥadīd (57)	al-Ḥadīd (57)
94	Idhā Zulzilat (99)	Idhā Zulzilat (99)	al-Ḥajj (22)	Sūrat Muḥammad (47)	Sūrat Muḥammad (47)
95	Wa'l-ʿAṣr (103)	al-Naṣr (110)	al-Ḥadīd (57)	al-Raʿd (13)	al-Raʿd (13)
96	al-Ḥajj (22)	al-Nūr (24)	Sūrat Muḥammad (47)	al-Raḥmān (55)	al-Raḥmān (55)
97	al-Ḥadīd (57)	al-Munāfiqūn (63)	al-Insān (76)	al-Insān (76)	al-Insān (76)
98	Sūrat Muḥammad (47)	al-Mujādala (58)	al-Ṭalāq (65)	al-Ṭalāq (65)	al-Ṭalāq (65)
99	al-Ṭalāq (65)	al-Ḥujurāt (49)	Lam Yakun (98)	Lam Yakun (98)	Lam Yakun (98)
100	al-Qadar (97)	Limā Tuḥarrimu (66)	al-Jumuʿa (62)	al-Ḥashr (59)	al-Ḥashr (59)
101	Lam Yakun (98)	al-Jumuʿa (62)	Alif Lām Mīm al-Sajda (32)	al-Naṣr (110)	al-Naṣr (110)
102	al-Jumuʿa (62)	al-Ṣaff (61)	al-Munāfiqūn (63)	al-Nūr (24)	al-Nūr (24)
103	al-Munāfiqūn (63)	al-Tawba (9)	al-Mujādala (58)	al-Ḥajj (22)	al-Ḥajj (22)
104	al-Mujādala (58)	al-Falaq (113)	al-Ḥujurāt (49)	al-Munāfiqūn (63)	al-Munāfiqūn (63)

105	al-Ḥujurāt (49)	al-Nās (114)	Limā Tuḥarrimu (66)	al-Mujādala (58)	al-Mujādala (58)
106	Limā Tuḥarrimu (66)	al-Fatḥ (48)	al-Taghābun (64)	al-Ḥujurāt (49)	al-Ḥujurāt (49)
107	al-Taghābun (64)	al-Qāriʿa (101)	al-Ṣaff (61)	Limā Tuḥarrimu (66)	Limā Tuḥarrimu (66)
108	al-Ṣaff (61)	Wa'l-ʿĀdiyāt (100)	al-Mā'ida (5)	al-Ṣaff (61)	al-Ṣaff (61)
109	al-Mā'ida (5)	al-Aʿrāf (7)	al-Tawba (9)	al-Jumuʿa (62)	al-Jumuʿa (62)
110	al-Tawba (9)	Banū Isrā'īl (17)	al-Naṣr (110)	al-Taghābun (64)	al-Taghābun (64)
111	al-Naṣr (110)	al-Ghāshiya (88)	al-Wāqiʿa (56)	al-Fatḥ (48)	al-Fatḥ (48)
112	Wa'l-ʿĀdiyāt (100)		Wa'l-ʿĀdiyāt (100)	al-Tawba (9)	al-Tawba (9)
113	al-Falaq (113)		al-Falaq (113)	al-Mā'ida (5)	al-Mā'ida (5)
114	al-Nās (114)		al-Nās (114)		
		Al-Mā'ida, al-Zukhruf, al-Taghābun and al-Balad are omitted from it.		Al-Fātiḥa is omitted from it, there being no difference between [Ibn Wāqid and al-Ṣādiq] except over this chapter.	He does not mention al-Fātiḥa. He says: 'It and al- Baqara are in a single quire and the total is [ ] letters.[190] And *al-muʿawwadhatān* [i.e. al-Falaq and al-Nās] are on the margin.'

Mention of the sequence of chapters in the codices

No.	Codex of the Commander of the Faithful ʿUthmān (may God be pleased with him)	ʿAbd Allāh b. Masʿūd[191]	Ubayy b. Kaʿb[192]	The transmission of Muḥammad b. Khālid al-Barqī[193]	From: The History of Ibn Wāḍiḥ[194]
1	al-Fātiḥa (1)	al-Fātiḥa (1)	al-Fātiḥa (1)	Umm al-Kitāb (1)	al-Fātiḥa (1)
2	al-Baqara (2)	al-Baqara (2)	al-Baqara (2)	al-Baqara (2)	al-Baqara (2)
3	Āl ʿImrān (3)	al-Nisāʾ (4)	al-Nisāʾ (4)	Maryam (19)	Yūsuf (12)
4	al-Nisāʾ (4)	Āl ʿImrān (3)	Āl ʿImrān (3)	al-Zukhruf (43)	al-ʿAnkabūt (29)
5	al-Māʾida (5)	al-Aʿrāf (7)	al-Anʿām (6)	al-Dukhān (44)	al-Rūm (30)
6	al-Anʿām (6)	al-Anʿām (6)	al-Aʿrāf (7)	al-Jāthiya (45)	Luqmān (31)
7	al-Aʿrāf (7)	al-Māʾida (5)	al-Māʾida (5)	al-Aḥqāf (46)	Alif Lām Mīm al-Sajda (32)
8	al-Anfāl (8)	Yūnus (10)	Yūnus (10)	Sūrat Muḥammad (47)	Ḥāʾ Mīm al-Sajda (41)
9	al-Tawba (9)	al-Tawba (9)	al-Anfāl (8)	al-Fatḥ (48)	Waʾl-Dhāriyāt (51)
10	Yūnus (10)	al-Naḥl (16)	al-Tawba (9)	al-Fajr (89)	al-Insān (76)
11	Hūd (11)	Hūd (11)	Hūd (11)	al-Balad (90)	Waʾl-Nāziʿāt (79)
12	Yūsuf (12)	Yūsuf (12)	Maryam (19)	al-Shams (91)	Kuwwirat (81)
13	al-Raʿd (13)	al-Kahf (18)	al-Shuʿarāʾ (26)	Waʾl-Layl (92)	Infaṭarat (82)
14	Ibrāhīm (14)	Banū Isrāʾīl (17)	al-Ḥajj (22)	Waʾl-Ḍuḥā (93)	Inshaqqat (84)
15	al-Ḥijr (15)	al-Anbiyāʾ (21)	Yūsuf (12)	A-lam Nashraḥ (94)	al-Aʿlā (87)
16	al-Naḥl (16)	Ṭā Hāʾ (20)	al-Kahf (18)	Waʾl-Tīn (95)	Iqraʾ (96)
17	Banū Isrāʾīl (17)	al-Muʾminūn (23)	al-Naḥl (16)	Iqraʾ (96)	Lam Yakun (98)
18	al-Kahf (18)	al-Shuʿarāʾ (26)	al-Zukhruf (43)	Āl ʿImrān (3)	Āl ʿImrān (3)
19	Maryam (19)	Waʾl-Ṣāffāt (37)	Banū Isrāʾīl (37)	Waʾl-Ṣāffāt (37)	Hūd (11)
20	Ṭā Hāʾ (20)	al-Aḥzāb (33)	al-Zumar (39)	Ṣād (38)	al-Ḥijr (15)
21	al-Anbiyāʾ (21)	al-Ḥajj (22)	Ṭā Hāʾ (20)	al-Zumar (39)	al-Ḥajj (22)
22	al-Ḥajj (22)	al-Qaṣaṣ (28)	al-Anbiyāʾ (21)	al-Dukhān (44)	al-Aʿrāf (7)
23	al-Muʾminūn (23)	al-Naḥl (27)	al-Qaṣaṣ (28)	Ḥāʾ Mīm al-Sajda (41)	al-Dukhān (44)
24	al-Nūr (24)	al-Nūr (24)	al-Muʾminūn (23)	Ḥāʾ Mīm ʿAyn Sīn Qāf (42)	al-Raḥmān (55)

25	al-Furqān (25)	al-Anfāl (8)	Saba᾿ (34)	al-Ḥujurāt (49)	al-Ḥāqqa (69)
26	al-Shuʿarā᾿ (26)	Maryam (19)	al-ʿAnkabūt (29)	Qāf (50)	al-Maʿārij (70)
27	al-Naml (27)	al-ʿAnkabūt (29)	al-Furqān (25)	Wa'l-Dhāriyāt (51)	al-Aʿmā (80)
28	al-Qaṣaṣ (28)	al-Rūm (30)	al-Mu᾿min (40)	Wa'l-Ṭūr (52)	Wa'l-Shams (91)
29	al-ʿAnkabūt (29)	Yā Sīn (36)	al-Raʿd (13)	ʿAyn Mīm Yatasā᾿alūn (78)	al-Qadar (97)
30	al-Rūm (30)	al-Furqān (25)	al-Qaṣaṣ (28)	Wa'l-Nāziʿāt (79)	Zulzilat (99)
31	Luqmān (31)	al-Ḥijr (15)	al-Naml (27)	ʿAbasa (80)	al-Humaza (104)
32	Alif Lām Mīm al-Sajda (32)	al-Raʿd (13)	al-Ṣāffāt (37)	Innā Anzalnāhu (97)	al-Fīl (105)
33	al-Aḥzāb (33)	Saba᾿ (34)	Ṣād (38)	A-lam Yakun (98)	Yūnus (10)
34	Saba᾿ (34)	al-Malā᾿ika (35)	Yā Sīn (36)	al-Nisā᾿ (4)	al-Nisā᾿ (4)
35	al-Malā᾿ika (35)	Ibrāhīm (14)	al-Ḥijr (15)	al-Rūm (30)	al-Naḥl (16)
36	Yā Sīn (36)	Ṣād (38)	Ḥā᾿ Mīm ʿAyn Sīn Qāf (42)	Luqmān (31)	al-Mu᾿minūn (23)
37	al-Ṣāffāt (37)	Sūrat Muḥammad (47)	al-Rūm (30)	Alif Lām Mīm al-Sajda (41)	Yā Sīn (36)
38	Ṣād (38)	Luqmān (31)	al-Zukhruf (43)	al-Aḥzāb (33)	Ḥā᾿ Mīm ʿAyn Sīn Qāf (42)
39	al-Zumar (39)	al-Zumar (39)	Ḥā᾿ Mīm al-Sajda (41)	al-Saba᾿ (34)	al-Wāqiʿa (56)
40	al-Mu᾿min (40)	al-Mu᾿min (40)	Ibrāhīm (14)	al-Malā᾿ika (35)	al-Malā᾿ika (35)
41	Ḥā᾿ Mīm al-Sajda (41)	al-Zukhruf (43)	al-Malā᾿ika (35)	Yā Sīn (36)	al-Muddaththir (74)
42	Ḥā᾿ Mīm ʿAyn Sīn Qāf (42)	al-Sajda (32)	al-Fatḥ (48)	Wa'l-Najm (53)	al-Dīn (107)
43	al-Zukhruf (43)	Ḥā᾿ Mīm ʿAyn Sīn Qāf (42)	Sūrat Muḥammad (47)	al-Qamar (54)	Tabbat (111)
44	al-Dukhān (44)	al-Aḥqāf (46)	al-Ḥadīd (57)	al-Ḥāqqa (69)	al-Ikhlāṣ (112)
45	al-Jāthiya (45)	al-Jāthiya (45)	Nūḥ (71)	al-Maʿārij (70)	al-Naṣr (110)
46	al-Aḥqāf (46)	al-Dukhān (44)	al-Aḥqāf (46)	Nūḥ (71)	al-Qāriʿa (101)
47	Sūrat Muḥammad (47)	al-Fatḥ (48)	Qāf (50)	al-Jinn (72)	al-Burūj (85)
48	al-Fatḥ (48)	al-Ḥadīd (57)	al-Dukhān (44)	al-Aʿlā (87)	al-Tīn (95)
49	al-Ḥujurāt (49)	al-Ḥashr (59)	Luqmān (31)	al-Ghāshiya (88)	al-Naḥl (16)
50	Qāf (50)	Alif Lām Mīm al-Sajda (32)	al-Jāthiya (45)	al-Mā᾿ida (5)	al-Mā᾿ida (5)
51	al-Dhāriyāt (51)	Qāf (50)	al-Mujādala (58)	al-Furqān (25)	Yūnus (10)
52	al-Ṭūr (52)	al-Ṭalāq (65)	al-Mulk (67)	al-Shuʿarā᾿ (26)	al-Raʿd (13)
53	Wa'l-Najm (53)	al-Ḥujurāt (49)	Alif Lām Mīm al-Sajda (32)	al-Naml (27)	Maryam (19)
54	al-Qamar (54)	al-Mulk (67)	al-Raḥmān (55)	al-Qaṣaṣ (28)	al-Shuʿarā᾿ (26)

No.	Codex of the Commander of the Faithful ʿUthmān (may God be pleased with him)	ʿAbd Allāh b. Masʿūd	Ubayy b. Kaʿb	The transmission of Muḥammad b. Khālid al-Barqī	From: The History of Ibn Wāḍiḥ
55	al-Raḥmān (55)	al-Taghābun (64)	al-Wāqiʿa (56)	al-ʿAnkabūt (29)	al-Zukhruf (43)
56	al-Wāqiʿa (56)	al-Munāfiqūn (63)	al-Jinn (72)	al-Raḥmān (55)	al-Ḥujurāt (49)
57	al-Ḥadīd (57)	al-Jumuʿa (62)	al-Najm (53)	al-Wāqiʿa (56)	Qāf (50)
58	al-Mujādala (58)	al-Ṣaff (61)	al-Maʿārij (70)	al-Ṭalāq (65)	al-Qamar (54)
59	al-Ḥashr (59)	al-Jinn (72)	al-Muzammil (73)	Limā Tuḥarrimu (66)	al-Mumtaḥina (60)
60	al-Mumtaḥina (60)	Nūḥ (71)	al-Muddaththir (74)	al-Mulk (67)	al-Ṭalāq (65)
61	al-Ṣaff (61)	al-Mujādala (58)	al-Qamar (54)	Nūn (68)	al-Balad (90)
62	al-Jumuʿa (62)	al-Mumtaḥina (60)	al-Ṭūr (52)	al-Insān (76)	A-lam Nashraḥ (94)
63	al-Munāfiqūn (63)	Limā Tuḥarrimu (66)	Wa'l-Dhāriyāt (51)	Wa'l-Mursalāt (77)	al-ʿĀdiyāt (100)
64	al-Taghābun (64)	al-Raḥmān (55)	Nūn (68)	Idhā Zulzilat (99)	al-Kawthar (108)
65	al-Ṭalāq (65)	al-Najm (53)	al-Ḥāqqa (69)	al-ʿĀdiyāt (100)	al-Kāfirūn (109)
66	Limā Tuḥarrimu (66)	al-Dhāriyāt (51)	al-Ḥashr (59)	al-Anʿām (6)	al-Anʿām (6)
67	al-Mulk (67)	al-Ṭūr (52)	al-Mumtaḥina (60)	Ṭā Hā' (20)	Banū Isrā'īl (17)
68	Nūn (68)	al-Qamar (54)	Wa'l-Mursalāt (77)	al-Anbiyā' (21)	al-Anbiyā' (21)
69	al-Ḥāqqa (69)	al-Ḥāqqa (69)	al-Nisā' (4)	al-Ḥajj (22)	al-Furqān (25)
70	al-Maʿārij (70)	al-Wāqiʿa (56)	al-Insān (76)	al-Mu'minūn (23)	al-Qaṣaṣ (28)
71	Nūḥ (71)	Nūn (68)	al-Qiyāma (75)	al-Nūr (24)	al-Mu'min (40)
72	al-Jinn (72)	Wa'l-Nāziʿāt (79)	Kuwwirat (81)	al-Ḥadīd (57)	al-Mujādala (58)
73	al-Muzammil (73)	al-Maʿārij (70)	Wa'l-Nāziʿāt (79)	al-Mujādala (58)	al-Ḥashr (59)
74	al-Muddaththir (74)	al-Muddaththir (74)	al-Ṭalāq (65)	al-Ḥashr (59)	al-Jumuʿa (62)
75	al-Qiyāma (75)	al-Muzammil (73)	al-Taghābun (64)	al-Mumtaḥina (60)	al-Munāfiqūn (63)
76	al-Insān (76)	al-Muṭaffifūn (83)	al-Aʿmā (80)	al-Qāriʿa (101)	Nūn (68)
77	Wa'l-Mursalāt (77)	al-Aʿmā (80)	al-Muṭaffifūn (83)	Alhākum (102)	al-Jinn (72)
78	al-Naba' (78)	al-Insān (76)	Inshaqqat (84)	Wa'l-ʿAṣr (103)	Wa'l-Mursalāt (77)
79	Wa'l-Nāziʿāt (79)	al-Qiyāma (75)	al-Tīn (95)	al-Humaza (104)	al-Ḍuḥā (93)
80	al-Aʿmā (80)	Wa'l-Mursalāt (77)	Iqra' (96)	al-Fīl (105)	Nūḥ (71)

81	Kuwwirat (81)	al-Nabaʾ (78)	al-Ḥujurāt (49)	Quraysh (106)	al-Takāthur (102)
82	Infaṭarat (82)	Kuwwirat (81)	al-Munāfiqūn (63)	al-Aʿrāf (7)	al-Aʿrāf (7)
83	al-Muṭaffifūn (83)	Infaṭarat (82)	al-Jumuʿa (62)	Ibrāhīm (14)	Ibrāhīm (14)
84	Inshaqqat (84)	al-Ghāshiya (88)	Limā Tuḥarrimu (66)	al-Ḥijr (15)	al-Kahf (18)
85	al-Burūj (85)	al-Aʿlā (87)	al-Fajr (89)	al-Naḥl (16)	al-Nūr (24)
86	al-Ṭāriq (86)	Wa'l-Layl (92)	al-Balad (90)	Banū Isrāʾīl (17)	Ṣād (38)
87	al-Aʿlā (87)	Wa'l-Fajr (89)	Wa'l-Layl (92)	al-Kahf (18)	al-Zumar (39)
88	al-Ghāshiya (88)	al-Burūj (85)	Infaṭarat (82)	al-Ṣaff (61)	al-Jāthiya (45)
89	Wa'l-Fajr (89)	Inshaqqat (84)	Wa'l-Shams (91)	al-Jumuʿa (62)	Sūrat Muḥammad (47)
90	al-Balad (90)	Iqraʾ (96)	al-Burūj (85)	al-Munāfiqūn (63)	al-Ḥadīd (57)
91	Wa'l-Shams (91)	al-Balad (90)	al-Ṭāriq (86)	al-Taghābun (64)	al-Muzammil (73)
92	Wa'l-Layl (92)	Wa'l-Ḍuḥā (93)	al-Aʿlā (87)	al-Muzammil (73)	al-Qiyāma (75)
93	Wa'l-Ḍuḥā (93)	al-Ṭāriq (86)	al-Ghāshiya (88)	Kuwwirat (81)	al-Nabaʾ (78)
94	A-lam Nashraḥ (94)	Wa'l-ʿĀdiyāt (100)	al-Ṣaff (61)	A-Raʾayta (107)	al-Ghāshiya (88)
95	Wa'l-Tīn (95)	al-Dīn (107)	Lam Yakun (98)	al-Kawthar (108)	Wa'l-Fajr (89)
96	Iqraʾ (96)	al-Qāriʿa (101)	Wa'l-Ḍuḥā (93)	al-Kāfirūn (109)	Wa'l-Layl (92)
97	al-Qadar (97)	Lam Yakun (98)	A-lam Nashraḥ (94)	al-Naṣr (110)	al-Naṣr (110)
98	Lam Yakun (98)	Wa'l-Shams (91)	al-Qāriʿa (101)	al-Anfāl (8)	al-Anfāl (8)
99	Idhā Zulzilat (99)	Wa'l-Tīn (95)	al-Takāthur (102)	al-Tawba (9)	al-Tawba (9)
100	Wa'l-ʿĀdiyāt (100)	al-Humaza (104)	Wa'l-ʿAṣr (103)	Yūnus (10)	Ṭā Hāʾ (20)
101	al-Qāriʿa (101)	al-Layl (92)	al-Humaza (104)	Hūd (11)	Sabaʾ (34)
102	al-Takāthur (102)	Quraysh (106)	Idhā Zulzilat (99)	Yūsuf (12)	al-Malāʾika (35)
103	al-ʿAṣr (103)	al-Takāthur (102)	Wa'l-ʿĀdiyāt (100)	al-Raʿd (13)	al-Ṣāffāt (37)
104	al-Humaza (104)	al-Qadar (97)	al-Fīl (105)	al-Muddaththir (74)	al-Aḥqāf (46)
105	al-Fīl (105)	Idhā Zulzilat (99)	al-Qadar (97)	al-Qiyāma (75)	al-Fatḥ (48)
106	Quraysh (106)	Wa'l-ʿAṣr (103)	al-Kāfirūn (109)	Infaṭarat (82)	al-Ṭūr (52)
107	al-Dīn (107)	al-Naṣr (110)	al-Naṣr (110)	al-Muṭaffifūn (83)	al-Najm (53)
108	al-Kawthar (108)	al-Kawthar (108)	Tabbat (111)	Inshaqqat (84)	al-Ṣaff (61)
109	al-Kāfirūn (109)	al-Kāfirūn (109)	Quraysh (106)	al-Burūj (85)	al-Taghābun (64)
110	al-Naṣr (110)	Tabbat (111)	al-Dīn (107)	al-Ṭāriq (86)	al-Ṭalāq (65)
111	Tabbat (111)	al-Ikhlāṣ (112)	al-Kawthar (108)	Tabbat (111)	Limā Tuḥarrimu (66)
112	al-Ikhlāṣ (112)		al-Ikhlāṣ (112)	al-Ikhlāṣ (112)	al-Muṭaffifūn (83)

30 'In the name of God, the Infinitely Merciful, the Compassionate. O God, we seek Your help, we extol You for good, and we repudiate (*nakhlaʿu*) and leave whoever disobeys You.'

'In the name of God, the Infinitely Merciful, the Compassionate. O God, it is You we worship and You to whom we pray and prostrate, You we hurry to and are quick to serve (*naḥfidu*). We fear Your punishment and we hope for Your mercy – truly Your punishment overtakes the unbelievers!'[195]

From the Book of Sufficiency on the Chapters of the Qurʾān, on the authority of Abū ʿAbd Allāh al-Ḥusayn b. Aḥmad al-Rāzī:[196]

The Long Seven[197] are: the Cow (Q. 2), the Family of ʿImrān (Q. 3), Women (Q. 4), the Table (Q. 5), Cattle (Q. 6), the Heights (Q. 7), and the seventh of them is the Spoils (Q. 8) and Repentance (Q. 9).[198] The Doubled (*mathānī*) Seven are the seven chapters the first of which is the chapter of Jonah and the last of which is the Bee: (thus) Jonah (Q. 10), Hūd (Q. 11), Joseph (Q. 12), Thunder (Q. 13), Abraham (Q. 14), the Rocky Tract (Q. 15) and the Bee (Q. 16). It is as though the Long Seven are the starting points in the mighty Qurʾān and the Doubled Seven are the ones which follow them in length and in meanings.

It is also said that the Doubled Seven are the Exordium of the Scripture because it is doubled up in every formal prayer and because the doubled ones *in regard to meaning* are within it and inside it, as will follow.[199]

The Seven Hundreds: the first of them is the chapter of the Tribe of Israel and the last of them is the chapter of the Believers. Thus: the Tribe of Israel (Q. 17), the Cave (Q. 18), Mary (Q. 19), *Ṭā Hāʾ* (Q. 20), the Prophets (Q. 21), the Pilgrimage (Q. 22), the Believers (Q. 23).[200]

They are called the Hundreds because each chapter of them is a hundred verses or approximately that, and they follow the Doubled Ones.

The Elaborated [part] (*mufaṣṣal* = 'divided up')[201] is so called because [the sūras in it] are short chapters due to the closeness of the division of one chapter from another, as is obvious. It is also said it is called Elaborated (*mufaṣṣal*) due to what is in [the sūras] by way of elucidation and detailing. And the former is more correct, since the Elaborated is not greater in elucidation and detailing than the other part.

From The Book of the Select in Readings, on the authority of Abū Bakr Muḥammad b. Mūsā al-Ṣaydalānī:[202] 31

The Long Seven are seven chapters: the Cow (Q. 2), the Family of ʿImrān (Q. 3), Women (Q. 4), the Heights (Q. 7), Cattle (Q. 6), the Table (Q. 5), Jonah (Q. 10). Abū ʿUbayda said: 'The Spoils is amongst the Doubled Ones, and it is amongst the first of what descended at Medina; and Jonah (Q. 10) descended at Mecca.' The Hundreds are eleven[203] chapters: Immunity (Q. 9), the Bee (Q. 16), Hud (Q. 11), Joseph (Q. 12), the Cave (Q. 18), the Tribe of Israel (Q. 17), the Prophets (Q. 21), *Ṭā Hā'* (Q. 20), *Qad Aflaḥa* (Q. 23), the Poets (Q. 26), Those Who Set in Ranks (Q. 37).

The Doubled Ones are twenty chapters: the Confederates (Q. 33), Pilgrimage (Q. 22), the Ant (Q. 27), the Story (Q. 28), Light (Q. 24), the Spoils (Q. 8), Mary (Q. 19), the Spider (Q. 29), Rome (Q. 30), *Yā Sīn* (Q. 36), the Rocky Tract (Q. 15), Thunder (Q. 13), the Criterion (Q. 25), Sheba (Q. 34), the Angels (Q. 35), Abraham (Q. 14), *Ṣād* (Q. 38), the chapter of Muḥammad (Q. 47), Luqmān (Q. 31), the Crowds (Q. 45).

The *Ḥā' Mīms* are seven chapters: the Believer (Q. 40), the Ornaments (Q. 43), *Ḥā' Mīm* the Prostration (Q. 41), *Ḥā' Mīm ʿAyn Sīn Qāf* (Q. 42),[204] Smoke (Q. 44), the Dunes (Q. 46), Bowing the Knee (Q. 45).

The Examined Ones (*mumtaḥina*) are fourteen[205] chapters: Victory (Q. 48), Iron (Q. 57), the Gathering (Q. 59), *Alif Lām Mīm* the Prostration (Q. 32), *Qāf* (Q. 50), Divorce (Q. 65), the Private Apartments (Q. 49), Blessed (Q. 67), Mutual Cheating (Q. 64), the Hypocrites (Q. 63), the Ranks (Q. 61), the Jinn (Q. 72), Noah (Q. 71), Disputation (Q. 58).

The Elaborated is what is in the chapters – forty-nine chapters – which he has enumerated.

In the Book of Sufficiency [the following] is quoted, on the authority of the Messenger of God: 'I was given the Long Seven in place of the Torah, I was given the Hundreds in place of the Gospel, I was given the Doubled Ones in place of the Psalms, and I surpassed by way of the Elaborated.'[206]

On the authority of Saʿīd b. Jubayr[207] in regard to God's statement (Exalted is He) 'We have bestowed on you seven of the Doubled Ones',[208] is that he said: They are the Long Seven: the Cow (Q. 2), the Family of ʿImrān (Q. 3), Women (Q. 4), the Table (Q. 5), Cattle (Q. 6), the Heights (Q. 7), and Jonah (Q. 10) becomes the seventh.[209]

The like of that is reported on the authority of Yaḥyā b. al-Ḥārith al-

Dīnārī, who adds: The Spoils (Q.8) and *Immunity* (Q.9) are not counted among the Long Seven.

Chapter 4
32 *On readings (qirāʾāt)*

Know that after the collection of the codex by the companions (may God be pleased with them) and after the consensus on it, different readings are ascribed to them. The emigrants, helpers, and successors to them in excellence, according to their degrees and their ranks in knowledge, used to recite the Qurʾān in sundry ways consisting in one or other dialect (but they did not differ much, such that the *meaning* differed) – till the knowledge of the readings ended up with a community of the learned who devoted themselves exclusively to them and set about pinning them down, so they became thereby models from whom people acquired knowledge and by whom they were guided in regard to the readings.

They are ten individuals,[210] seven of whom are the famous ones to whom is recourse in knowledge about readings and upon whom is dependence in their understanding of them. Three of them are those whom people have chosen, and they added them to the other seven in their reading and excellence. So these ten individuals are the readers of the three garrison towns: [those from] the Ḥijāz, [those from] Iraq, and [those from] Syria. We mention their names, their genealogies, and who obtained knowledge from them or traced any report back to them.

The Ḥijāzīs
being the inhabitants of Mecca and Medina

From Mecca:

[1.] Ibn Kathīr:
Abū Muḥammad [or] Abū Maʿbad [or] Abū ʿAbbād, ʿAbd Allāh b. Kathīr al-Dārimī al-Kinānī, the client of ʿAmr b. ʿAlqama [al-Kinānī]. He died in Mecca in the year 120[/738].[211] Well-known transmissions on his authority:

al-Qawwās: This was Abūʾl-Ḥasan Aḥmad b. ʿAwn al-Nabbāl [ʻthe bowman'], he being also known as al-Qawwās [ʻthe bowmaker'].[212] He went through the Qurʾān in the presence of[213] Wahb b. Wāḍiḥ,[214] and he went through it in the presence of Ismāʿīl b. ʿAbd Allāh al-Qusṭ.[215] He said: 'I went through the Qur'ān in the presence of Shibl b. ʿAbbād[216] and Maʿrūf b. Mushkān[217] who went through it in the presence of Ibn Kathīr'.

al-Barqī: Abū'l-Ḥasan Aḥmad b. Muḥammad b. ʿAbd Allāh b. Abī Bizza al- 33
Barqī,[218] he having gone through the Qur'ān in the presence of ʿIkrima b. Sulaymān,[219] and ʿIkrima having gone through it in the presence of Shibl and al-Qusṭ, who both went through it in the presence of Ibn Kathīr; and by way of Abū ʿAmr Muḥammad b. ʿAbd al-Raḥmān al-Barqī al-Makkī, nicknamed Qunbul,[220] from al-Qawwās; and by way of Abū Bakr Muḥammad b. Mūsā al-Hāshimī from Qunbul.

Ibn Fulayḥ: Abū Isḥāq ʿAbd al-Wahhāb b. Fulayḥ al-Makkī[221] went through the Qur'ān in the presence of Da'ūd b. Shibl. Da'ūd went through it in the presence of his father and of al-Qusṭ, who went through it in the presence of Ibn Kathīr by his chain. He transmitted from Ibn Kathīr also by way of Abū ʿAbd al-Raḥmān al-Laythī [= Nāfiʿ] from Abū Badra by his chain from Ibn Kathīr.

Ibn Kathīr went through the Qur'ān in the presence of Mujāhid b. Jabr[222] and Dirbās, the client of Ibn ʿAbbās, who went through it in the presence of Ibn ʿAbbās, and Ibn ʿAbbās went through it in the presence of Ubayy b. Kaʿb, and Ubayy went through it in the presence of the Messenger of God.

From Medina:

[2.] Nāfiʿ:[223]
Abū Ruwaym [or] Abū'l-Ḥusayn [or] Abū ʿAbd al-Raḥmān Nāfiʿ b. ʿAbd al-Raḥmān b. Abī Nuʿaym, the client of Jaʿwana b. Shaʿūb al-Laythī, whose origin was from Iṣfahān; he died in Medina in the year 177 [/792–3], and it is also said: 166 [/781–2]. Transmissions mentioned from him:

Qālūn:[224] He was Abū Mūsā ʿĪsā b. Mīnā Qālūn by way of Abū'l-Nashīṭ Muḥammad b. Hārūn al-Marwazī from Qālūn, from Nāfiʿ.

Warsh:[225] Abū'l-Qāsim, ʿUthmān b. Saʿīd, nicknamed 'Warsh', Abū ʿAmr, Abū Saʿīd, by way of Abū'l-Azhar, ʿAbd al-Ṣamad b. ʿAbd al-Raḥmān al-ʿAtīqī from Warsh, from Nāfiʿ.

34 *al-Madanī*:[226] Abū Bishr Ismāʿīl b. Jaʿfar al-Madanī, by way of Abū'l-Zaʿrā' ʿAbd al-Raḥmān b. ʿAbdūs,[227] from Abū ʿUmar Ḥafṣ b. ʿUmar al-Azdī,[228] from Abū Bishr, from Nāfiʿ. They went through the Qur'ān collectively to Nāfiʿ.

Nāfiʿ said: 'In Medina I came across models who are imitated. So I looked at what two of them agreed upon and adopted it; and I looked at what one of them was alone in and rejected it – till I put together this reading of mine.'

The Iraqis

(being) the people of Basra and Kufa

From Basra:

[3.] Abū ʿAmr:
Abū ʿAmr b. al-ʿAlā' b. ʿAmmār b. ʿAbd Allāh b. al-Ḥuṣayn b. al-Ḥārith b. Julhum b. Khuzāʿa b. Māzin b. Mālik b. ʿAmr b. Tamīm, and it is said his name was ʿArabān, also Zabbān, also Yaḥyā, also ʿUyayna,[229] and it is said his filionymic agnomen was his name. He was pious, religious and learned in the Qur'ān and lexicography. He died in Kufa at the house of Muḥammad b. Sulaymān in the year 154 [/771], when he was 86. It is said that he had gold teeth. Well-known transmissions on his authority:

al-Yazīdī: Abū ʿAmr b. Yaḥyā Mubārak al-Yazīdī,[230] by way of al-Sūsī[231] and Abū ʿUmar al-Dawrī, who both went through the Qur'ān in the presence of al-Yazīdī, and he went through it in the presence of Abū ʿAmr [b. al-ʿAlā'] and Abū ʿAmr went through it in the presence of Saʿīd b. Jubayr and Mujāhid b. Jabr[232] and others, who both went through it in the presence of Ibn ʿAbbās, and Ibn ʿAbbās went through it in the presence of Ubayy b. Kaʿb.

Shujāʿ:[233] Abū Nuʿaym Shujāʿ b. Abī Naṣr al-Balkhī,[234] by way of Abū Jaʿfar Muḥammad b. Ghālib[235] who went through it in the presence of Shujāʿ, and Shujāʿ went through it in the presence of Abū ʿAmr by his chain.

35 From Kufa:

[4.] ʿĀṣim:[236]
This was Abū Bakr ʿĀṣim b. Abi'l-Najūd al-Kūfī, he being the client[237] of

Banū Ḥanīfa b. Mālik. It is said that the name of Abū'l-Najūd was Bahdala,[238] and it is said that it was the name of his mother. He died in the year 128 [/746]. Transmissions mentioned from him:

Ibn ʿAyyāsh:[239] Abū Bakr b. ʿAyyāsh b. Sālim al-Asadī al-Ḥannāṭ, by way of Abū Yūsuf Yaʿqūb b. Khalaf al-Aʿshā[240] and Yaḥyā b. Ādam al-Kūfī,[241] both of them from Abū Bakr by the transmission of al-Shumūnī[242] from al-Aʿshā, from Abū Bakr from ʿĀṣim, and the transmission of Shuʿayb b. Ayyūb[243] from Yaḥyā from Abū Bakr from ʿĀṣim.

Ḥafṣ:[244] Abū ʿAmr Ḥafṣ b. Sulaymān b. Mughīra al-Bazzāz al-Asadī, by way of ʿAmr[245] and ʿUbayd[246] the sons of al-Ṣabbāḥ, from Ḥafṣ by the transmission of Abū'l-Ḥasan Rawʿān b. Aḥmad al-Daqqāq[247] from ʿAmr and Ḥafṣ from ʿĀṣim. And the transmission of Abū Luʿyān Aḥmad b. Sahl b. Fīrūz[248] from ʿUbayd from Ḥafṣ from ʿĀṣim, and Āṣim went through the Qur'ān in the presence of Zirr b. Ḥubaysh,[249] and Zirr went through it in the presence of ʿAbd Allāh b. Masʿūd, and ʿĀṣim also went through it in the presence of Abū ʿAbd al-Raḥmān al-Sulamī,[250] and al-Sulamī went through it in the presence of the Commander of the Faithful, ʿAlī b. Abī Ṭālib (may God be pleased with him).

[5.] Ḥamza:

Abū ʿUmāra Ḥamza b. Ḥabīb b. ʿUmāra al-Zayyāt,[251] the client of the Banū ʿIjl, from the sons of Aktham b. Ṣayfī. He was pious and religious, and he used to transport oil from Iraq to Ḥulwān[252] and transport walnuts and cheese from Ḥulwān to Kūfa. He died at Ḥulwān in 156 [/773]. Well-known transmissions on his authority:

Abū Muḥammad [or] Abū ʿĪsā Sulaym[253] b. ʿĪsā,[254] by way of Abū Muḥammad Khalaf b. Hishām al-Bazzāz,[255] and Khallād b. Khālid al-Aḥwal,[256] who both went through the Qur'ān in the presence of Sulaym.
Sulaym went through the Qur'ān in the presence of Ḥamza ten times, and 36
Ḥamza went through it in the presence of ʿAbd al-Raḥmān b. Abī Laylā[257] and Sulaymān[258] b. Mihrān al-Aʿmash.[259] And Abū ʿAmr Ḥafṣ b.[260] ʿUmar al-Dawrī from Sulaym[261] from Ḥamza. So what was by way of [Ibn Abī] Laylā went back to ʿAlī b. Abī Ṭālib, and what was by way of al-Aʿmash was from ʿAbd Allāh b. Masʿūd.

[6.] al-Kisāʾī:
Abū'l-Ḥasan ʿAlī b. Ḥamza[262] was among those learned in Arabic and lexicography. He and Muḥammad b. al-Ḥasan al-Faqīh and al-Aḥnaf and Ibrāhīm al-Mawṣilī died on the same day, and Hārūn al-Rashīd commanded his son al-Ma'mūn to pray over them in one of the villages of Rayy called al-Zanbūya in the year 189 [/805], and it is also said: 181 [/797], and also 182 [/798]. Known transmissions on his authority:

Abū ʿUmar Ḥafṣ b. ʿUmar al-Dawrī and Abu'l-Ḥārith[263] Layth b. Khālid[264] both went through the Qur'ān in the presence of al-Kisāʾī and *he* went through it in the presence of Ḥamza four times. Al-Kisāʾī used to choose recitations and came across authorities in Kufa who were reciters and jurists; he relied, in regard to what he chose, on readings which go back to the Prophet (may God bless him and his family), and on readings transmitted from ʿAlī b. Abī Ṭālib, al-Ḥasan b. ʿAlī and Ibn ʿAbbās. He recited one reading against Ibn Masʿūd's recitation, namely, His statement (Exalted is He), '[…] and that God does not let slip the reward of the believers', which in the codex of ʿAbd Allāh b. Masʿūd is '*and* God does not let slip the reward of the believers'.[265]

The Syrians

[7.] Ibn ʿĀmir:[266]
Abū ʿImrān or Abū ʿUthmān or Abū Hushaym ʿAbd Allāh b. ʿĀmir al-Yaḥṣubī,[267] who died in Damascus in the year 118 [/736]. Transmissions mentioned from him:

Ibn Dhakwān: Abū ʿAmr ʿAbd Allāh b. Muḥammad b. Dhakwān,[268] and it is also said: ʿAbd Allāh b. Aḥmad b. Bashīr b. Dhakwān, the reciter of the people of Damascus. Abū ʿAbd Allāh b. Mūsā b. Sharīk al-Akhfash al-
37 Dimashqī went through the Qur'ān in the presence of Ibn Dhakwān.[269]

Hishām: Abū'l-Walīd Hishām b. ʿAmmār al-Dimashqī.[270] They both went through the Qur'ān in the presence of Ayyūb b. Tamīm al-Nakhaʿī al-Qārī ['the reciter'],[271] and Ayyūb went through it in the presence of Yaḥyā b. al-Ḥārith al-Dhamārī,[272] and Yaḥyā went through it in the presence of Ibn ʿĀmir. Abū ʿAmr b. Aḥmad b. Yūsuf al-Taghlabī,[273] one of the transmitters of Ibn ʿĀmir, also went through the Qur'ān in the presence of Ayyūb.

Ibn Dhakwān said: Ibn ʿĀmir went through the Qurʾān in the presence of a man, and that man went through it in the presence of ʿUthmān b. ʿAffān. Al-Akhfash said: Ibn Dhakwān did not name for us the man in whose presence Ibn ʿĀmir went through the Qurʾān, but Hishām named him for us, for he said, 'It was al-Mughīra b. Abī Shihāb al-Makhzūmī,[274] in whose presence Ibn ʿĀmir went through the Qurʾān, and al-Mughīra went through the Qurʾān in the presence of ʿUthmān, without anyone between them, and ʿUthmān went through it in the presence of the Prophet'.

So these seven are those on whose authority the famous readings are transmitted. As for the three others whom people chose and admitted to their ranks in their knowledge of readings – the first of them is:

[8. Ibn al-Qaʿqāʿ:]

Abū Jaʿfar Yazīd b. al-Qaʿqāʿ al-Madanī,[275] the client of ʿAbd Allāh b. ʿAbbās b. Abī Rabīʿa al-Makhzūmī. He was the teacher of Nāfiʿ and he used to recite the Qurʾān in the Prophet's Mosque (may God bless him and his family). He was killed at al-Ḥarra, and [the Battle of] al-Ḥarra took place at the end of sixty-three years after the arrival of the Prophet (may God bless him and his family) in Medina.[276] They do not count him among the seven because he used to recite anomalous (*shādhdha*) and unusual (*gharība*) readings.

His two transmitters: ʿĪsā b. Wardān al-Ḥudhāʾ[277] and Sulaymān b. Muslim al-Jammāz.[278] Sulaymān said: 'Abū Jaʿfar informed me that he learnt recitation from his patron ʿAbd Allāh b. ʿAbbās, and from Abū Hurayra.'[279] We have already mentioned the chain of transmission of Ibn ʿAbbās.

[9. Yaʿqūb b. Isḥāq:]

The second [of the three further readers], namely, Abū Muḥammad Yaʿqūb
b. Isḥāq b. Zayd b. ʿAbd Allāh al-Ḥaḍramī[280] al-Baṣrī, died on Sunday in 38
the year 85 [/704]. He opted in recitation for a sound choice from outside of
the tradition. He ran through the recitations in the presence of Sallām b.
Sulaymān,[281] and Sallām went through the Qurʾān in the presence of ʿĀṣim
by his chain of transmission.

His two transmitters: Abū ʿAbd Allāh Muḥammad b. al-Mutawakkil al-Luʾluʾī, known as Ruways,[282] and Rawḥ b. ʿAbd al-Muʾmin al-Muqriʾ,[283] by way of Muḥammad b. [Wahb b.] Yaḥyā b. al-ʿAlāʾ al-Thaqafī[284] from Rawḥ from Yaʿqūb. Likewise, Muḥammad b. al-Jahm b. Hārūn[285] transmitted from al-Walīd b. Ḥassān al-Thawrī[286] from Yaʿqūb.

[10. Khalaf b. Hishām:]

The third: Abū Muḥammad Khalaf b. Hishām b. Ṭālib b. Ghurāb al-Bazzār al-Kūfī.[287] He was a leader in Prophetic Tradition and the Qurʾān, and knowledgeable about the kinds of readings. He died in the year 229 [/843-4]. It is transmitted from him by way of Abū Isḥāq Ibrāhīm al-Marwazī,[288] the brother of Abū'l-ʿAbbās, Khalaf's copyist, that he said: 'I went through the Qurʾān in the presence of Khalaf, and Khalaf went through it in the presence of Sulaym, and Sulaym went through it in the presence of Ḥamza al-Zayyāt.' And we have already mentioned Ḥamza's chain of transmission.

So one may rest content with this sum for the chains of the ten reciters and their names, and also the chain of their transmitters – to whom is recourse in the science of recitation.

Next: let no one opine that the recitations attributed to these reciters are their inventions. Rather, they are their *preferences*, consisting in what they heard from their forebears, one generation after another, till it reaches back to the Prophet (may God bless him and his family). So the recitations of the people of Kufa, Basra and the districts of Iraq reach back to the Commander of the Faithful, ʿAlī (may God be pleased with him) and ʿAbd Allāh b. Masʿūd; and the recitations of the people of the Ḥijāz and Tihāma and its districts reach back to ʿUthmān b. ʿAffān, Ubayy b. Kaʿb and Zayd b. Thābit (God's good pleasure be upon them); and the recitations of the people of Syria and its districts reach back to ʿUthmān b. ʿAffān (may God be pleased with him). And the origin for the recitation of these people is from the recitation of the Prophet (may God bless him and his family). For it is not
39 for anyone amongst the companions and the successors, and anyone else, to
recite with a reading which consists in his own invention, without precedent, just as it is not for anyone amongst them to do exegesis of the Qurʾān by his personal opinion.

The Prophet has said (may God bless him and his family): 'Whoever does exegesis of the Qurʾān on the basis of his personal opinion – even if he gets it right, he has erred, and if he errs, let him take his place in hellfire!'[289]

It has been said 'There is nothing further from men's intellects than the exegesis of the Qurʾān';[290] except for men to whom God gives understanding in regard to the Qur'ān, men who are the 'pegs of the earth', the safety of its inhabitants, the inheritors of the prophets, one of the 'two precious things', the best of the two universes and the two worlds. They are the folk of God, His elect, His party and [the depositories of] His secret, the mines of His wisdom, and the rulers of His creation.[291]

We ask God (Exalted is He), to make us their adherents, those who hear and obey them, who pursue and strive for their approval, are thought well of by them, and stick to their guardianship forever and ever Amen – O Lord of the Worlds!

Chapter 5
On what is desirable and undesirable for the reciter of the Qur'ān in regard to 'seeking refuge [with God]' (istiʿādha)

Among the things desirable for the reciter is to cleave to the well-known recitations handed down from the companions, the successors, and the recognised reciters, and not to overstep them at all for something from his own inventions or deviations taken from the recitations of people with affectations, even though such recitations sustain the meanings and are right in the outward forms of inflection.

It is also desirable for him to choose[292] from them the purest of them in expression, the most inclusive in meaning, the finest in poetic order and harmony, and the best in language and clarity of Arabic; not the ill-seeming and barbarous which none amongst the luminaries of the reciters knows, let alone lay people - like the *ʿanʿana* of the tribe of Tamīm or the *kaskasa* of the tribe of Rabīʿa,[293] and whatever else amongst the rarities of transmissions. So he does not change the *ḥamza* [= '] into an *ʿayn* [= ʿ] in His statement (Exalted is He): 'Maybe God will give (*'an ya'tī*) victory',[294] such that
he recites *ʿan ya'tī* – this being the *ʿanʿana* of Tamīm. Nor does he make 40
the *kāf* of the feminine [= *ki*] a *sīn* [= *s*] in His statement (Exalted is He): 'Your Lord has made a stream beneath you (*qad jaʿala rabbuki taḥtaki sariyyā*),'[295] so he recites *qad jaʿala rabbusi taḥtasi sariyyā* – this being the *kaskasa* of Rabīʿa. Likewise, he should not recite with anomalies from recitations the methods of which are unsound, hence whose transmission is not passed on; unless he just wants to study them for learning, without adhering to them in recitation. Instead, he must stick to the clear and well-

known recitations, the reliable and approved transmissions, the middle course in chanting (*tartīl*) and the minimum in lowering and raising the voice. He should not recite it quickly as poetry is recited, nor read it hastily like the sneezing of a little goat,[296] nor declaim it laboriously such that the skin of the listener crawls and his heart recoils from it, nor lower his voice such that he hides its recitation from someone close to him. But let him comply with the optimum in things, namely their middling aspects, similar to what God commanded and forbade His Prophet (may God bless him and give him peace): 'Neither declaim the prayer, nor speak it in a low tone, but seek a middle course between.'[297] It is transmitted on his authority (peace be upon him) that he passed by Abū Bakr when he was lowering his voice, so he said: 'Raise your voice a little', and he passed by 'Umar when he was declaiming, so he said: 'Lower your voice a little.' It is transmitted on the authority of Sa'īd b. Jubayr that he said: 'Recite the Qur'ān illuminating by it, and do not pronounce it in a guttural way.'

It is desirable for the reciter when he pronounces the Qur'ān not to go out of his way in pronunciation such that he crosses over the line of exaggerating and overdoing it – as is reported of Ḥamza al-Zayyāt,[298] although Ḥamza did not himself adopt it, rather he used to do that with any student whose understanding was yet small and whose tongue was too light, to acquaint him, by conveying it in the pronunciation, with the quantity which was its proper limit.

Full, formal pronunciation[299] is that he geminates the geminated, pronounces without gemination the ungeminated, lengthens the lengthened, shortens the shortened, pronounces without a vowel the unvowelled, pronounces with a vowel the vowelled, pronounces with a glottal stop (*hamza*) what has a glottal stop, interrupts the interrupted, connects up the connected, and expresses the letters from their places of articulation clearly, without mixing them with others. So he geminates the geminated in such a way as to remove it from pronounciation without gemination, he pronounces with a vowel the vowelled in such a way as to remove it from the vowelless, he pronounces without a vowel the vowelless in such a way as to remove it from the vowelled; he is never ever seen to exaggerate or overdo,
41 such that his articulation with a vowel becomes gemination or his articulation without a vowel becomes a pause and a quiescence. He shortens the shortened in such a way as to remove it from the lengthened, he lengthens the lengthened in such a way as to remove it from the shortened – not that

the single beat be like the two beats or three. And he pronounces with a glottal stop what has a glottal stop, with a delicate pronunciation which removes it from what is without a glottal stop, not that he *lean* on it so he geminates it – given that articulating the glottal stop without gemination is even allowed in the whole Qur'ān, unless it is an initial glottal stop, for articulating it without gemination is impossible since articulating it without gemination would be close to the vowelless, and beginning with the vowelless is impossible.

As for what the moderns invented, calling it the 'recitation of the poetic measure'[300] – it consists in affectation, deviation and unsoundness and it is not transmitted from the Arabs, in whose language the Qur'ān was sent down. God's Messenger has said: 'Recite the Qur'ān in the tones and voices of the Arabs.'[301]

It is desirable that he intone the Qur'ān melodiously.[302] So he pauses at the absolute, recommended and suitable pauses so as to distinguish one meaning from another through the termination and inception [of syntactic units]; and in intoning he takes note of nasalisation (*ghunna*) in its places amongst the weak letters before which is nunnation (*tanwīn*), for that embellishes the voice. He takes note of velarisation (*tafkhīm*) in the name '*Allāh*' when there is a final 'u' or 'a' in front of it; and he takes note of 'thinning' (*tarqīq*) in it when there is a final 'i' in front of it.[303] He indicates the strongest letter in the word and so he brings out the weakest clearly from its point of articulation. He indicates the instances of '*mā*' as negation in the Qur'ān by indicating negation [in his tone of voice], and the instances of '*mā*' as affirmation, by indicating affirmation.[304] When he brings a story to an end he pauses, so he makes clear the beginning of the next story and the statement which is after it, and when he reaches a passage of admonition, he is admonished and repeats it, when he reaches a passage of acknowledgement of God's favours he acknowledges them and brings them to mind, and when he reaches a passage of marveling, he marvels and meditates: 'Those [whom We gave the Scripture] intone it as it should be intoned. They have faith in it.'[305]

As for the 'seeking refuge' at the start of the recitation – it is emphatically recommended for him. God (Exalted is He) said: 'When you recite the Qur'ān, seek refuge in God.'[306] The inhabitants of Basra and Ibn Kathīr recited: 'I seek refuge in God from the stoned Satan'; in a transmission of Qunbul on the authority of Ibn Kathīr: 'I seek refuge in God the Mighty,

the All-Hearing'; in a transmission of Ḥafs on the authority of ʿĀṣim: 'I seek
refuge in God the Mighty, the All-Hearing, the All-Knowing'; on the
42 authority of Nāfiʿ, Ibn ʿĀmir and al-Kisāʾī: 'I seek refuge in God from the
stoned Satan, verily God is the All-Hearing, the All-Knowing'; and on the
authority of Ḥamza: 'We seek refuge in God, the All-Hearing, the All-
Knowing, from the stoned Satan.'[307]

In a saying of Ibn Masʿūd, he said: 'I went through the Qurʾān in the presence of the Messenger of God (may God bless him and give him peace) and I commenced [the recitation] by saying: "I seek refuge in God, the All-Hearing, the All-Knowing", but then he said to me, "'I seek refuge in God *from the stoned Satan*', since I sat before Gabriel (peace be upon him) and I said: 'I seek refuge in the All-Hearing, the All-Knowing', and Gabriel said to me: 'I seek refuge in God *from the stoned Satan.*' Gabriel said: 'I took it from Michael thus, and Michael [took it thus] from Isrāfīl and Isrāfīl took it thus from the Guarded Tablet'."[308] And this corresponds with what is in God's Scripture: 'When you recite the Qurʾān, seek refuge in God *from the stoned Satan.*'[309]

In one of the reports: Whosoever says three times when he wakes up: 'I seek refuge with God, the All-Hearing, the All-Knowing from the stoned Satan', and he recites three verses from the end of the Chapter of the Gathering,[310] God entrusts him to seven thousand angels who pray over him till it becomes evening, and if he dies on that day he dies a martyr.[311] On the authority of [Jaʿfar] al-Ṣādiq (peace be upon him) is that he used to seek refuge from Satan, after setting out, saying: 'I seek refuge in God, the All-Hearing, the All-Knowing, from the stoned Satan.'

Amongst the things desirable for the reciter of the Qurʾān is that he be ritually pure, hence the man in a state of major ritual impurity and the menstruating woman may not recite the Qurʾān. There is no [absolute] objection to someone in a state of minor ritual impurity reciting, but it is better that he be ritually pure, facing the direction of Mecca, reciting it in the manner of glorification and reverently, in the most plaintive voice, in the most serene moment and mood, and with the most attentive heart and mind. His skin will tremble from it when he comes to a verse of punishment and retribution, and his skin will grow supple from it when he comes to a verse of mercy and grace. God (Exalted is He) listens to everyone who recites the Qurʾān in a beautiful voice.[312]

Chapter 6

On the number of chapters, verses, words and letters of the Qur'ān, according to what they disagreed and agreed upon 43

The number of chapters in the Qur'ān, on the basis of how 'Uthmān's codex is found, also being transmitted on the authority of 'Alī (may God be pleased with him), is 114;[313] on the basis of what is found in the codex of 'Abd Allāh b. Mas'ūd, in that he did not count the last two chapters,[314] and he counted the Dawn's Glory and Have We not Expanded[315] as a single chapter, is 111;[316] on the basis of what is found in the codex of Ubayy b. Ka'b, in that he counted the standing prayer[317] as two chapters, 116;[318] and on the basis of the statement of whoever counts the Spoils and Immunity[319] as a single chapter, 113.[320]

Its verses in the numbering of the Kufans, being the numbering which al-Kisā'ī transmitted on the authority of Ḥamza and Ḥamza traced it back to 'Alī b. Abī Ṭālib (may God be pleased with him), are 6,236; in the reckoning of the Basrans, being the numbering which their codices followed, 6,204; in the numbering of the former Medinan, on the authority of al-Ḥusayn b. 'Alī and 'Abd Allāh b. 'Umar, 6,217; in the numbering of the latter Medinan, on the authority of Abū Ja'far, Shayba and Ismā'īl, 6,214; in the numbering of the Meccans, 6,219; and in the numbering of the inhabitants of Syria, 6,226.

Its words are 77,439, and it is also said: 77,436. Its letters are 323,514, and it is said 322,617, and it is said 325,188, and it is also said: 321,675.[321] It has been said that the cause of disparity in the number of letters and words is that certain of them counted each geminated letter as *two* letters, so that for him its letters came to be more than the letters of whoever counted it as a single letter. And certain of them, for example, counted[322] '*fī khalq*'[323] as two words so he would count *fī* as a word and *khalq* as a word, so the number of its words became greater than the number of whoever counted them [*fī khalq*] as a single word.

In a manuscript conveyed on the authority of one of the later enumerators, namely, 'Abd Allāh b. 'Abd al-'Azīz: 44

The number of verses in the Qur'ān is 6,246, the words in them are 77,436, and letters in them are 325,211. The number of what is in the Qur'ān by way of *alif* is 48,955,[324] *bā'* is 1,255,[325] *tā'* is 15,199,[326] *thā'* is 1,255,[327] *jīm* is 3,273,[328] *ḥā'* is 3,993,[329] *khā'* is 2,416,[330] *dāl* is 2,412,[331] *dhāl* is 4,642,[332] *rā'* is 11,793,[333] *zā'* is 1,455,[334] *sīn* is 4,991,[335] *shīn* is 2,243,[336] *ṣād* is 2,581,[337] *ḍād* is 2,657,[338] *ṭā'* is 1,274,[339] *ẓā'* is 842,[340] *'ayn* is 9,525,[341] *ghayn* is 2,258,[342] *fā'* is 8,477,[343] *qāf* is 6,813,[344] *kāf* is 15,344,[345] *lām* is 33,422,[346] *mīm* is 26,134,[347] *nūn* is 26,464,[348] *wāw* is 24,436,[349] *hā'* is 17,575,[350] and *yā'* is 24,919.[351] They reckoned the verses of the chapter of the Exordium as 7, its words as 28 (it is also said 29), its letters as 144, and its complete words as 12. Beneath every number is an arcanum, and 'above everyone possessing knowledge is a knower'![352]

Chapter 7
On the enumeration of the exegetes amongst the companions and others, and the enumeration of the commentaries compiled, also the works on Qur'ānic semantics and their authors

Those who discussed the exegesis of the Qur'ān amongst the companions, were: the Commander of the Faithful, 'Alī;[353] 'Abd Allāh b. 'Abbās;[354] 'Abd Allāh b. Mas'ūd;[355] Ubayy b. Ka'b;[356] Sa'īd b. al-Musayyib;[357] 'Umar b. al-Khaṭṭāb;[358] and Mu'ādh b. Jabal,[359] (may God be pleased with them).[360]

Amongst those who transmit on their authority, and the compilers of exegesis, were: 'Alī b. Abī Ṭalḥa al-Wālibī,[361] on the authority of Ibn 'Abbās; 'Aṭīya b. Sa'd al-'Awfī,[362] on the authority of Ibn 'Abbās, who has has a
45 Qur'ān commentary; 'Ikrima,[363] the client of Ibn 'Abbās, on the authority of Ibn 'Abbās, who has a Qur'ān commentary; al-Ḍaḥḥāk b. Muzāḥim al-Hilālī,[364] on the authority of Ibn 'Abbās, who has a Qur'ān commentary; Mujāhid b. Jabr and Sa'īd b. Jubayr,[365] on the authority of Ibn 'Abbās; al-Kalbī, Muḥammad b. al-Sā'ib,[366] on the authority of Abū Ṣāliḥ Bādhān, the client of Umm Hānī', on the authority of Ibn 'Abbās, who has a Qur'ān commentary; 'Aṭā' b. Abī Rabāḥ;[367] 'Aṭā' b. Abī Muslim al-Khurāsānī;[368] 'Aṭā' b. Dīnār;[369] Abū Bakr Muḥammad b. Muslim b. Shihāb al-Zuhrī;[370] Abū Sa'īd b. Abī'l-Ḥasan al-Baṣrī,[371] who has a Qur'ān commentary; Qatāda b. Di'āma al-Sadūsī,[372] who has a Qur'ān commentary; Abū'l-'Āliya al-Riyāḥī,[373] who has a Qur'ān commentary; Muqātil b. Ḥayyān,[374] who has a Qur'ān commentary; Muqātil b. Sulaymān,[375] who has a Qur'ān commentary; al-Ḥasan b. Wāqid al-Wāqidī,[376] who has a Qur'ān commentary;

Ismāʿīl b. ʿAbd al-Raḥmān[377] al-Suddī,[378] who has a Qurʾān commentary; ʿAbd Allāh b. Abī Jaʿfar al-Rāzī,[379] who has a Qurʾān commentary; Muḥammad b. Jurayj,[380] who has a Qurʾān commentary; Sufyān b. Saʿīd al-Thawrī,[381] who has a Qurʾān commentary; Sufyān b. ʿUyayna,[382] who has a Qurʾān commentary; Wakīʿ b. al-Jarrāḥ,[383] who has a Qurʾān commentary; Hushaym b. Bashīr,[384] who has a Qurʾān commentary; Shibl b. ʿAbbād al-Makkī,[385] who has a Qurʾān commentary; Warqāʾ b. ʿUmar,[386] who has a Qurʾān commentary; Zayd b. Aslam,[387] who has a Qurʾān commentary; Rawḥ b. ʿUbāda al-Qaysī,[388] who has a Qurʾān commentary; Muḥammad b. Yūsuf al-Firyābī,[389] who has a Qurʾān commentary; Qubayṣa b. ʿUqba al-Suwāʾī,[390] who has a Qurʾān commentary; Abū ʿAbd Allāh Mūsā b. Masʿūd al-Nahdī,[391] who has a Qurʾān commentary; Saʿīd b. Manṣūr,[392] who has a Qurʾān commentary; ʿAbd Allāh b. Wahb al-Fihrī,[393] who has a Qurʾān commentary; ʿAbd al-Ḥamīd b. Ḥumayd,[394] who has a Qurʾān commentary; Muḥammad b. Ayyūb,[395] who has a Qurʾān commentary; Abū Bakr[396] al-Aṣamm,[397] who has a Qurʾān commentary; Abū Saʿīd ʿAbd Allāh b. Saʿīd al-Ashajj,[398] who has a Qurʾān commentary; Abū Ḥamza al-Thumālī,[399] who has a Qurʾān commentary; al-Musayyib b. Sharīk,[400] who has a Qurʾān commentary; ʿAbd Allāh b. Ḥāmid,[401] who has a Qurʾān commentary; Abū Bakr b. ʿAbdūs,[402] who has a Qurʾān commentary; Abū ʿAmr Aḥmad b. Muḥammad al-Furātī [*sic.*],[403] who has a Qurʾān commentary; Abū Bakr b. Fūrak,[404] who has a Qurʾān commentary; Abūʾl-Qāsim b. Ḥabīb,[405] who has a Qurʾān commentary; Abū ʿAlī ʿAbd al-Wahhāb Liḥyāʾī [*sic.*],[406] who has a Qurʾān commentary; al-Qāḍī ʿAbd al-Jabbār,[407] who has a Qurʾān commentary; Muḥammad b. ʿUthmān,[408] who has a Qurʾān commentary; Abūʾl-Ḥasan Muḥammad b. al-Qāsim al-Faqīh;[409] Abū Isḥāq Aḥmad b. Muḥammad[410] al-Thaʿlabī,[411] who has a Qurʾān commentary;[412] Abū Bakr
ʿAbd Allāh b. Muḥammad al-Naqqāsh,[413] who has a work containing the 46
Qurʾān commentary of Gabriel, the Qurʾān commentary of the Prophet, and the Qurʾān commentary of the companions; [and] ʿAlī b. Muḥammad al-Wāḥidī.[414]

And there is a Qurʿān commentary in accordance with every school amongst the schools of the scholastic theologians, which the proponent of the doctrine composed on the basis of his school. So the Muʿtazila have Qurʾān commentaries, the Ashʿariyya have Qurʾān commentaries, the Karrāmiyya have Qurʾān commentaries, the Khawārij have Qurʾān commentaries, and the Shīʿa have Qurʾān commentaries.

Writers on Qur'ānic semantics

Abū Zakariyyā' Yaḥya b. Ziyād al-Farrā';[415] Abū Isḥāq Ibrāhīm b. al-Sarī al-Zajjāj;[416] 'Alī b. Ḥamza al-Kisā'ī;[417] Abū 'Ubayd al-Qāsim b. Sallām;[418] Abū'l-Ḥasan Sa'īd b. Mas'ada al-Akhfash;[419] Abū 'Ubayda Ma'mar b. al-Muthannā al-Tamīmī;[420] Abū 'Alī al-Ḥasan b. Yaḥyā b. Naṣr al-Jurjānī,[421] author of 'The Harmonious Order'; al-Mu'arraj b. 'Amr b. Abī Fāyid (*sic*) al-Sudūsī;[422] al-Naḍr b. Shumayl;[423] 'Obscure Language in the Qur'ān' by 'Abd Allāh b. Muslim b. Qutayba al-Dīnawarī al-Qutaybī;[424] 'The Obscurity' of Quṭrub Abū 'Alī Muḥammad b. al-Mustanīr,[425] Abū Bakr Muḥammad b. al-Qaffāl al-Shāshī,[426] Abū Muslim Muḥammad b. Baḥr,[427] and the likes of them reckoned amongst the authorities in semantics. Some composed works on Qur'ānic exegesis, but they are reckoned amongst the authorities in semantics, not among the exegetes proper.

So we will expound in the notes [marked] with the *hamza*-symbol [*sic.*],[428] lexicography, grammar, readings, exegesis and scriptural semantics. Then we will make allusion to the arcana which are the lanterns of the godly, and we have titled the book as that. We ask God (Exalted is He) to preserve us from exegesis based on personal opinion, the seduction of the ego and the whisperings of Satan, and that He guide us on His straight path, the path of those whom He favoured amongst the prophets, the truthful ones, the martyrs and the righteous – and how excellent are they as friends! If I say 'the people of the Qur'ān say', or 'the masters of the arcana [say]', or 'he to whom I trace back some word, consisting in the significance of a verse' – I do not thereby intend *myself*. God forbid! I simply mean the veracious ones of the people of the Prophet's house, for they are the ones familiar with the arcana, and they consist in the elect and the elite.

Chapter 8

47 ## *On the meaning of* tafsīr (*exegesis*) *and* ta'wīl (*hermeneutics*)

The lexicographers say: *Tafsīr* is the second form *maṣdar* of the verb *fasara* which means to make something apparent and to explain it. It is said: 'I disclosed (*fasartu*)[429] the thing', 'I am disclosing (*afsiru*), (with the vowel 'i'), with a disclosure (*fasr*)' – if I make it evident. Then if it is intense in difficulty it is said: 'he commented (*fassara*)[430] on it with a commentary (*tafsīr*)'.

Some of them said: It is not farfetched that the idea of disclosure (*fasr*) goes back to the idea of unveiling (*sifr*). It is said: 'The lady unveiled (*safarat*)', when she bared her face. Then *safara* and *fasara* would fall under the category of the metathetic, like *jadhaba*[431] and *jabadha*.[432] Next, *tafsīr* (commentary) is simply what the outer form of the expression, in respect of lexicography, indicates, so Arabic is glossed (*tufassaru*, 'commented on') by Arabic or by Persian. Likewise, Persian is glossed by Arabic – and both these things are called *tafsīr*.

The foundation of commentary (*tafsīr*) is two things: The first of them is what the expression indicates on the basis of the lexicography held in common by the lexicographers; the second is what learning through aural instruction (*sam*ʿ) supplies,[433] be it either [through] the report or the prophetic tradition. Thus the expression is open to interpretation, and, despite its openness, an authoritative prooftext exists for it, in which case, one must relate the expression to a tradition. Sometimes the expression is equivocal, so its proper signification is determined through aural instruction, and sometimes it is general, so that it is *particularised* through aural instruction. Amongst the things encumbent on the individual independently working out the commentary, is that he be learned about the different significations of the language, knowledgeable about the difference of positions of the commentators and reporters on it. For, many of the expressions of the revelation indicate some meaning, and the turning of that meaning to one signification among others or to one individual among others has been mentioned in the reports – such as, 'By those who tear out with violence',[434] and like, 'By the ones that scatter',[435] 'By those who range themselves in ranks',[436] [and] 'By the charging mares'.[437] For the expression simply indicates thereby the idea of 'tearing out', 'scattering', 'ranging in a rank', and 'charging', and then aural instruction has arrived at the interpretation of that, at one time as 'angels', and at another time as 'warriors'. So it is necessary to leave the meaning to aural instruction, it being impossible to proceed arbitrarily by opinion or by analogical reasoning. The [following] statement of the Prophet (may God bless him and his family) is linked to this: 'Whoever comments on the Qur'ān by his own opinion, let him take his place in hellfire!'[438]

Next, the commentators are well-known by their names which we have 48
mentioned, so what is transmitted from *them*, via an authentic transmission, is said to be 'Qur'ānic exegesis' (*tafsīr*).

As for *ta'wīl* (hermeneutics), the lexicographers say that it is from *awl*, which means 'returning'. It is said, 'the thing went back (*āla*)/ goes back (*ya'ūlu*),' when it returns, it being the *exegesis* of what the thing goes back to. On these grounds the term 'exegesis' is more general than 'hermeneutics', for all hermeneutics is exegesis, while all exegesis is not hermeneutics.

Most scholars arrive at the difference between the two expressions in two different ways. Some of them say: Exegesis is ranged against the expressions and hermeneutics is ranged against the *meanings*. It is said, 'he did an exegesis of the Qur'ān', if he elucidated what is incomprehensible among its expressions, and 'he did a hermeneutic of it (*awwalahu*)', if he elucidated what is unintelligible among its meanings. [For example] God (Exalted is He) said: 'That is the scripture wherein is no doubt.'[439] The exegesis of this is, 'wherein is no dubiety'; and the hermeneutic of this is 'they may not doubt it' – for it is a predication with the sense of prohibition.

Some say: The word 'exegesis' is applied to elucidating the meanings of the Qur'ān, the meanings of prophetic reports and poems. The word 'hermeneutics' is applied to what pertains to [practical] religion. Thus the various hermeneutical interpretations become root-principles for the various legal rites; and exegesis is not like that.

Some of them say: exegesis is knowledge of the occasioning causes of the descent of the chapters and verses – their background stories – and the relation of the generalities amongst them to specific nations and individuals. For example, [regarding] His statement (Exalted is He): 'And if two groups of believers fall to fighting',[440] they say: they are the Aws and the Khazraj.[441] Also, His statement: 'Do you not see those who exchange God's blessing for unbelief?'[442] They say: they are the Banū Umayya and the Banū Makhzūm. Again, [regarding] His statement: 'Say to those who stay back, amongst the desert Arabs',[443] it is said: they are the Banū Ḥanīfa. Such things are only determined through auditing.[444]

They say: Hermeneutics depends on the comprehension of the intellect. Al-Ḥusayn b. al-Faḍl al-Bajalī[445] said: Hermeneutics is turning the verse to a meaning which the expression conveys, consistent with what is before and after the verse.

It is said: Hermeneutics is inquiring into the intention of the speaker of the word, and what its meaning goes back to (*ya'ūlu*).

It is said the sciences of the Qur'ān subdivide into comprehending its outward expressions and comprehending its meanings. Comprehending

the expressions divides into four subdivisions: (1) the knowledge of breaks 49
and starting-points, being the knowledge of pauses and inceptions;[446] (2) the knowledge of the difference of readings; (3) the knowledge of lexicographical exegesis; and (4) the knowledge of the vowelling. As for comprehending the meanings, there are three subdivisions: (1) the knowledge of the descent of revelation and its occasioning causes, and that is up to the specialists in Prophetic Tradition; (2) the knowledge of that on which there is difference of opinion, consisting in the ambiguous verses (*mutashābihāt*), by way of what pertains to the root-principles of the religion, and that is up to the people of speculative reason and intellect; and (3) the knowledge of what pertains to revealed laws and rulings, and that is upto the people of juristic inference (*ijtihād*) and analogical reasoning. On this basis, nothing of the Qur'ān depends on aural instruction or Prophetic Tradition except the occasioning causes of the descent of the revelation, alone. And the remainder have commented on the Qur'ān by their opinion, either by speculative reason in the case of the root-principles or by juristic inference in the case of the branches.[447]

If anyone pondered the verses of the Qur'ān he would not find amongst them a single verse in which a report and religious authority (*tawqīf*) was dispensable; otherwise the exegesis and hermeneutic of it would be according to mere personal opinion and estimation.

Since those who make a distinction between exegesis and hermeneutics do not mention the subdivisions of exegesis and the subdivisions of hermeneutics, the distinction of the two is unproven by their explanation, for sometimes two subdivisions of them are not antonymous, so the distinction of the two is inauthentic. [Thus] some of them have posited 'sending down' (*tanzīl*)[448] and 'hermeneutics' (*ta'wīl*, literally 'taking back') as antonyms, some of them have posited 'the literal' (*ẓāhir*)[449] and 'hermeneutics' as antonyms, some of them have posited 'the literal' and 'the esoteric' (*bāṭin*)[450] as antonyms, and 'exegesis' (*tafsīr*) and 'hermeneutics' as antonyms. The two terms may coincide in meaning, so exegesis is a hermeneutic and hermeneutics is an exegesis, the literal is esoteric and the esoteric is literal!

The two terms may also differ in meaning, such that exegesis would be unlike hermeneutics, for instance, His statement (Exalted is He): 'Do they only wait for God to come to them in the shadows of the clouds?'[451] Let us mention here the subdivisions of hermeneutics (*ta'wīl*) after verifying its meaning. What has been said about it is that it is derived from *awl*, i.e. 'returning'. That is correct, and the commonalty are in accord with it. It has also been said about it that it is derived from *al-awwal* 'the beginning'/'the first', the antonym of 'the last'. Thus one of the great ones of the imams (may God be pleased with them) said: '*Ta'wīl* (hermeneutics) is returning something to its beginning (*awwaluhu*), just as *ta'khīr* (drawing out) is pushing it through to its end (*ākhiruhu*).' This is a powerful pronouncement whose style is that of prophetic pronouncements. Since the final end of everything is its beginning, it is said of it that it is the *ta'wīl* ('taking to the beginning') of it, it being derived from *awl*, which means 'returning'.

50 Next, hermeneutics as mentioned in the Qur'ān [itself] has more than one subdivision. Amongst them is (1) the hermeneutic of the vision, in the sense of dream interpretation: 'This is the hermeneutic (*ta'wīl*) of my dream from before'.[452] Amongst them is (2) the hermeneutic of events: 'He will teach you about the hermeneutic (*ta'wīl*) of events'.[453] Amongst them is (3) the hermeneutic of actions: 'That is the hermeneutic (*ta'wīl*) of what you were incapable of bearing patiently.'[454] Amongst them is (4) the return to the consequence and final end (*ma'āl*): 'Are they but waiting for the final fulfilment (*ta'wīl*) of it?'[455] Amongst them is (5) referring to God and the Messenger: 'And if you are at odds in something, refer it back to God and the Messenger, if you believe in God and the Last Day. That is better and more excellent as a reference (*ta'wīl*)';[456] and, 'I will inform you of its hermeneutic (*ta'wīlahu*), so send me [to Joseph]!'[457] And amongst them is (6) the hermeneutic of the ambiguous verses: 'As for those in whose hearts is a swerving – they go after what is ambiguous in it, seeking dissension and seeking its hermeneutic (*ta'wīl*)'.[458]

In the Qur'ān are rulings of the 'accomplished' (*al-mafrūgh*), rulings of the 'inchoative' (*al-musta'naf*), mutually opposed rulings on the basis of contrariety, and rulings differing in superiority on the basis of hierarchy.[459] So viewing the 'inchoative' is the literal, the sending down [of the Qur'ān], and exegesis; and viewing the principle of the 'accomplished' is the esoteric, hermeneutics, the meaning and the inner reality. 'And those firm-rooted in knowledge say "we believe in it, all is from our Lord." And only those possessed of minds pay heed!'[460]

Chapter 9

On generality and specificity, the clear and the ambiguous, the abrogating and the abrogated

Generality and specificity do not devolve on expressions qua letters and sounds, but qua referring to their meanings by usage or convention, in minds and actual individuals. Generality and specificity are thus in minds and individuals, generality being more appropriate to minds and specificity being more appropriate to individuals.

There is (1) no general expression in the Qur'ān without specification having entered it, and there is (2) no specification without individualisation (*tashkhīṣ*) having joined it. As for (1) specifying generalities, it is like His statement (Exalted is He): 'O Mankind (*nās*)! Worship your Lord',[461] it
being something addressed in general to the whole of mankind and 51
whomever is predicated by the term 'humanity'. Next, its legal enforcement on the basis of its generality is impossible, since the deranged individual and the youngster are human beings, yet what is addressed does *not* extend to them. Thus it is necessary to make the general expression specific to whoever has a mature intelligence, the deranged individual not being intelligent, and the youngster not being mature.

As for (2) individualising specificities, it consists in something which many of the learned have neglected. For 'mankind' (*nās*) has [just] been specified as those who are legally obligated, yet ['mankind'] may [also] be individualised as a specified grouping: 'Then hasten from where mankind (*al-nās*) hastens',[462] the legal obligation to hasten being upon specified human beings, while 'from where mankind hastens' is [a reference to] a community *other* than the ones [simply] legally obligated, namely, the rightly guided guides. And specified amongst the latter is even a single individual who is [spoken of as] 'mankind' (*nās*): 'Or are they jealous of mankind (*nās*) because of what God gave them in His bounty?'[463] It is stated in exegesis that [*nās* in this last citation] is Muḥammad (may God bless him and his family), and that is the individualising of the specific, its relation to individuals being analogous to the relation of specificity to generality.

In the same vein is His statement (Exalted is He): 'My mercy encompasses everything',[464] that being general without any generality above it. Next, He specified the mercy for a certain people, so He said: 'I will stipulate it for those who are God-conscious and give the poor-due and those who believe in Our signs'.[465] Next, He specified it [further] for a community, for He said: 'Those who follow the Messenger, the unlettered prophet'.[466] Next, He individualised it with a specific person who is a 'mercy': 'We only sent you [Muḥammad] as a mercy for the worlds'.[467] In the same vein is His statement (Exalted is He): 'We believe in the Lord of the worlds',[468] which is an allusion to the generality of [God's] lordship for all worlds. Then after it He said 'the Lord of Moses and of Aaron',[469] that being the specification of the lordship for the two individuals.

Just as the lordship is generalised and specified, likewise servanthood is generalised and specified in His statement 'there is nothing in the heavens and the earth but it comes to the Infinitely Merciful as a servant',[470] which is a generality in servanthood; and in His statement 'the servants of the Infinitely Merciful',[471] that being a specificity in servanthood; and [it is further specified] in His statement 'a spring from which God's servants drink',[472] which is the individualisation of that specific thing. So, in line with the two aspects of lordship and servanthood there is a specificity and a gen-
52 erality, equally whether the lordship is with reference to the creation or the servanthood is in a genitive relation with the Lord (Exalted is He).

One of the learned used to claim knowledge of exegesis, so the Commander of the Faithful, ʿAlī (may God be pleased with him) said: 'Who is the God of both the believer and the unbeliever?' He replied: 'God.' ʿAlī said: 'You spoke the truth.' Then he said to him: 'Who is the protector of the believer and the unbeliever?' The man replied: 'God.' ʿAlī said: 'You lie; "that is because God is the protector of those who believe, and that the unbelievers have no protector."'[473] Thus ʿAlī tested him through generality and specificity, and since he was unaware of that, he silenced him in argument and let him know that he had no knowledge of the Qur'ān. Allusions to the arcana of generality and specificity will follow in my exegesis. The manner in which good and evil relate to predestination is the same as the relation of generality and specificity – and that is the hidden science and the buried arcanum which only those who know understand.

As for the clear and the ambiguous, know that the primary division for verses in the Qur'ān is the division of the clear and the ambiguous. God (Exalted is He) said: 'He it is who sent down to you the scripture consisting in clear verses – they are the mother of the scripture – and other ambiguous ones'.[474] The commentators differed about which the clear ones are and which the ambiguous ones are, as follows in [my] exegesis.

It is amazing that in their case, both the clear and the ambiguous verses have ended up consisting of *ambiguous* verses, since the exegesis of them does not prove to be based on certainty! Next, *hermeneutics* only extends to the ambiguous amongst them, not to the clear, since He said: 'As for those in whose hearts is deviation, they follow what is ambiguous of it, seeking dissension and seeking its hermeneutic'.[475] What the people of realisation amongst the learned (may God multiply them) accept, is that the verses have been subdivided into verses pertaining to creation and verses pertaining to the 'Command'. Next the creation verses subdivide: into clear, 'accomplished' (*mafrūgh*) verses which do not change and do not alter, and they in themselves are perfect, containing no omission, holy, without any lack; and into ambiguous, 'inchoative' (*musta'naf*) verses which alteration and change do reach, and they are incomplete, *heading for* perfection. Like that the Command verses subdivide into the clear 'accomplished' ones and into the ambiguous 'inchoative' ones. So everything concerned with the rulings of the accomplished divine destiny (*qadar*), and the known prior
ruling, consists in the clear ones; and everything concerned with the rulings 53
of the inchoative divine decree (*qaḍār'*), as well as the delayed, already incepted (*mashrū'*), ruling, consists in the ambiguous ones.[476]

The clear may be mentioned in the Qur'ān in opposition to the elaborated (*mufaṣṣal*), as He (Exalted is He) said: '*Alif, Lām, Rā'*. A scripture whose verses are made clear and are elaborated',[477] that is, 'made clear' through being sent down (*tanzīl*) and 'elaborated' through hermeneutics (*ta'wīl*). So the elaboration is in contrast to the clarification. It has also been said that the clear ones are those to which abrogation does not extend at all, they being the ten verses at the end of the chapter of Cattle and in the chapter of *Subḥān*.[478] It has also been said that the clear ones are all the verses of the Qur'ān and the ambiguous ones are the letters which are at the beginnings of the chapters, which are called 'the openings of the chapters'.

It is said that the ambiguous ones are those which announce divine comparability, which the Creator's transcendence (Exalted is He) rids them of,[479] and the clear ones are those which announce divine unicity and holiness.[480]

As for the abrogating and the abrogated, it has been said about the definition of abrogation that it is the annulment of the established ruling, and it is said that it is the termination of the period of the ruling. It has also been said that it is a completion, in the sense that the objectives of the rulings –

when they reach their culmination and attain their aim – have been completed by other rulings which have objectives nobler and more complete than the earlier ones. Just like that is our statement about created things, such as the 'abrogation' of the sperm drop by the clot and the clot by the foetus, till the seventh stage, which is 'another creature'.[481]

The revealed laws began from Adam (peace be upon him) and end with the Resurrection,[482] which is 'another genesis'.[483] Every revealed law abrogates what was before it, that is, it brings it to completion in what comes after it, consisting in *another* perfection. God (Exalted is He) said: 'We abrogate no verse, nor cause it to be forgotten, without Us bringing what is better than it, or equivalent to it'.[484] So understand this subtle point and never hold the opinion that one revealed law is negated by another revealed law or that its injunctions are annulled and others are laid down. For were the sperm drop, amongst creaturely things, negated or annulled, it would not attain the second stage, nor the third, but it would reach the limit of its perfection and would not become another form of perfection, with the fulfillment[485] of its identity. Likewise, were the first revealed law negated or
54 annulled, it would not attain the second and the third, but it would reach its limit of completion and it would not become a form of perfection, with the consolidation of its identity. Likewise, the final revealed law, which is the noblest of revealed laws, has included rulings which do not change, being the root-principles of the religion, occupying the same position as the foundation for the house and the essence for the form. They are the clear ones among the verses, which are 'the mother of the scripture'.[486] And it has [also] included rulings which *do* change and they are the 'branches' of the religion, occupying the same position as the branches for the tree and the forms for the essence, and they are the ambiguous ones among the verses, which 'God erases and establishes as He wills'.[487] He only erases for a perfection it has resulted in, and He only establishes for a new beginning which is heading towards some perfection.

Thus setting up[488] the call to monotheism is in regard to speech, since it results in a perfection by which the truth is utterly distinguished from the false, and discrimination is wholly freed from the troop (sic),[489] so that He says in the chapter of Freeing,[490] concerning the religions of the unbelievers: 'To you your religion, and to me my religion'.[491] [Next] He started the call to monotheism in regard to *action*, with the sword – for the proponent of the truth to be distinguished from the proponent of the false, 'so that God might purify those who believe and bring the unbelievers to nothing'.[492] So *some* people had the view that the verse of acquittal, 'To you your religion and to me my religion', is abrogated by the verse of the sword, 'Fighting is prescribed for you',[493] [and] 'Fight them, God will punish them at your hands'.[494] They do not understand that His statement, 'To you your religion and to me my religion', is a limit in acquittal through speech and setting up[495] monotheism by tongue and creed, and it is only totally perfected when the beginning of acquittal through action is established and setting up monotheism by the sword and dispatching lives (*izhāq*). Likewise, [in the case of] every verse of the Qur'ān which is said to be abrogated by another verse, the abrogating verse is found to be set up by the abrogated, not annulling it, nor negating it. 'God erases and establishes what He wills, and with Him is the mother of the scripture.'[496]

Chapter 10

*On the two principles of the accomplished (***mafrūgh***) and the inchoative (***musta'naf***), and the two sides of contrariety (***taḍādd***) and hierarchy (***tarattub***), according to the two foundations of the creation (***khalq***) and the Command (***amr***)* 55

Know that the expression 'the accomplished and the inchoative' is simply obtained from the two shaykhs, 'the two 'Umars', Abū Bakr and 'Umar (may God's good pleasure be upon them), inasmuch as they spoke about divine predestination (*qadar*) and their voices were raised so that their voices reached the Prophet (may God bless him and his family), he being in his private apartment. So he came out to them, and his two cheeks were like a pomegranate cut into two halves, and he said (upon him and his family be peace): 'What are you doing?' They said: 'We are speaking about divine predestination (*qadar*).' So he said: 'Do you not speak of an angel which God (Exalted is He) has created half of fire and half of ice, and the fire does not melt the ice and the ice does not extinguish the fire? Its glorification is "Blessed be He who combines fire and ice!"' Then 'Umar went up to him so that he was sitting right in front of him and he said: 'O Messenger of God, are we involved in a matter commencing (*mubtada'*) or are we involved in a matter already accomplished (*mafrūgh*)?' – and in one transmission he said 'Is the matter under way?'[497] He (upon him be peace) replied: 'We are involved in a matter already accomplished.' Then 'Umar said: 'If the matter is already accomplished, what is action for then?' and he replied (upon him and his family be peace): 'O 'Umar, act! And each is eased (*muyassar*) to whatever he is created for.'[498]

Thus the expression 'the accomplished' and 'the inchoative' is taken from that session. Some people have the doctrine that all judgements are accomplished, predetermined in eternity, and human beings are compelled under the currents of divine predestinations, powerless to hold back from whatever He advances them to and unable to advance to whatever He holds them back from, so that they arrive at the extreme of negligence (*tafrīṭ*) in denying human capacity and affirming that God commands people to do what cannot be done.

Other people have the doctrine that all judgements are inchoative, determined by the choice of the human being. All those commanded [i.e. responsible human beings] have free will in regard to the currents of divine commandment, through which there is benefit or harm, and they incept faith and unbelief, so that [these people] arrive at the extreme of exaggeration (*ifrāṭ*) in affirming creaturely independence and denying the need for divine assistance in all acts.

56 The two doctrines are traceable back to the two sides of exaggeration and negligence. The origin of the two is the disagreement of the two shaykhs in regard to the two principles. If only they had understood that the correct teaching on it was a *tertium quid*, neither necessitarianism (*jabr*) nor delegation (*tafwīḍ*), and that the accomplished and the inchoative were after the pattern of an angel half of which was of fire and half of which was of ice, fire being comparable to the accomplished and ice being comparable to the inchoative. Just as the fire does not melt the ice nor the ice extinguish the fire, likewise the principle of the accomplished does not invalidate the principle of the inchoative, and the principle of the inchoative does not invalidate the principle of the accomplished. Therefore the Prophet (God bless him and his family) transferred the thinking of [Abu Bakr and 'Umar] to that angel, and when they came back to him to set the argument straight after this judgement, 'If the matter is already accomplished, what is action for then?', he replied, 'Act! And each is eased to whatever he is created for.' Thus he ruled in favour of *both* principles. For his statement 'act!' is an allusion to the principle of the inchoative and 'each is eased to whatever he is created for' is an allusion to the principle of the accomplished.

And you – when you regard things pertaining to the creation you find them in line with two subdivisions. One of them is existents *actually* occurring, complete in essence, transcending matter, time and space, such as the holy ones amongst the angels and the 'ones brought near' amongst the spiritual beings. The second is existents *potentially* occurring, heading for perfection, created from matter, and in a time and a place. Likewise, when you regard things pertaining to the Command, you find them in line with two subdivisions. One of them is accomplished rulings, which have become perfect, and perfect words which have been completed. As He (Exalted is He) says: 'Perfected is the Word[499] of your Lord in truth and justice, there is none who alters His words.'[500] The second is inchoative rulings which are heading for perfection and completion. Thus, on the part of the principle of the accomplished it is said, 'The pen [of destiny] flowed as it is', and it is said, 'Your Lord has finished with (*faragha*) the matter of creation, character, livelihood and the time of death'.[501] And the report is quite right: 'The happy person is whoever is happy in their mother's womb and the unhappy person is whoever is unhappy in their mother's womb.'[502] The verses of 'closing up',[503] 'sealing'[504] and 'shutting'[505] all refer to it, and the verses on giving up on the faith of the unbelievers are predicated on it: 'It is all the same for them if you warn them or do not warn them. They will not believe';[506] 'It is all the same if you summon them or you stay silent';[507] 'Perhaps you torment yourself with grief over their footsteps if they do not believe in this discourse',[508] etc. 57

Consisting in the principle of the inchoative is [the statement], 'The pen of divine commandment flowed as it will be'; the preacher's directing free men to do good, to believe in the truth and to speak what is true; and the determination of reward for deeds, the good of them and the evil of them, the faith[-based] of them and the unbelief [-based] of them, the obedience of them and the disobedience of them. The verses of divine commandment, instruction, admonition and warning refer to it, and the verses of examination, temptation, of giving hope and of encouragement are predicated on it, such as His statement(s) (Exalted is He): 'stand and warn';[509] 'and warn them';[510] 'so that you may warn a people';[511] 'that you may warn by it and as a reminder for those who believe';[512] 'speak to him a gentle word, perhaps he will pay heed[513] or be godfearing';[514] 'so remind, for a reminder is useful – he who is godfearing will pay heed',[515] etc.

Combining the verses of those who come out against admonition and the verses of the command to admonish is hard for whoever does not understand the two principles. And that is the secret of secrets!

As for contrariety and hierarchy in the verses of the Qur'ān, it is based on the innate disposition of creatures, consisting in good people and evil people, friends and enemies [of God], believers and unbelievers, saints and sinners. There is no story which does not contain the mention of the two groups and the verdict on the two opposing parties. [Ja'far] al-Ṣādiq (peace be upon him) has said: 'Half of the Qur'ān concerns us and half of it concerns our enemy – and what concerns our enemy concerns us too.'[516] As long as the fight exists between the truth and the false, and the partisan of the truth and the partisan of the false, and so long as the Judge of judges makes a judgement between the two, the messengers and the prophets (peace be upon them) being mediators in this judgement, the mention of this contrariety continues on the tongue of prophecy and is written on the scrolls of the message, till He separates them on the Day of Separation in regard to what they differed over.

Just as you find, amongst existents, contrariety between two contradictories in *two* different ways, such as between an existent and a non-existent thing, or such as between one existent and another existent, likewise you find amongst things pertaining to the Command, contrariety between two contradictories in *two* different ways, such as between faith and unbelief, or such as between one faith and another faith, one Islam and another Islam, and one religion and another religion – so that were you to examine
58 the words of the Qur'ān you would find this contrariety in relation to every word, except what God wills. There is no verse in regard to the believers but another verse follows it in regard to the unbelievers, and there is no quality of good without one of the qualities of evil being mentioned after it; and like that is the hierarchy and the disparity between one individual and another individual, and one act and another act. Then how are the two parties associated in one ruling and how are the two distinct in another ruling, the verdict of the religious law being based on the focal point (*mawḍi'*) of association, and the verdict of the Resurrection being based on the focal point of distinction? Well, it will simply become obvious to you from the scales of the true and the false, for the two are associated in the ruling of 'existence' and the two are distinct in the fact that the truth is true and the false is false. Like that is veracity and lying, for the two of them are associated in hearing and distinct in seeing. And like that is good and evil,

for the two of them are associated in form and distinct in meaning. Each match (*mithāl*)[517] has an explanation to be sought out via its appropriate 'focal point'.

Contrariety between things is not restricted to the contrariety of motion and rest, combination and separation, heat and cold, wetness and dryness, blackness and whiteness, sweetness and bitterness, and gentleness and roughness, nor is it restricted to the like of knowledge and ignorance, power and incapacity, longing and aversion, speech and silence, blindness and seeing, and deafness and hearing, nor is it confined to the like of life and death, animate and inanimate beings, angels and demons. Instead *most* contrariety in the glorious Qur'ān and on the tongue of the prophets (upon them be peace) is contrariety between like and like, such as one command and another, one word and another, one intellect and another, one soul and another, one nature and another, one innate disposition and another, and so on, consisting in things *similar* to one another in respect of outward form, shape and name, but *dissimilar* in respect of meaning, through their substance and inner reality; and for every match (*mithāl*) and likeness (*mathal*) there is a parable and a text in the Qur'ān and traditions – and that will emerge in their appropriate places.

As for hierarchy and disparity between words and between the possessors of ranks and degrees – it too is known from the verses. All created beings also acknowledge that by their innate nature and of necessity. So the angels say, 'There is not one of us but has his known position',[518] and they acknowledge Adam's superiority (peace be upon him), against the one who said, 59
'Will You place on [Earth] one who will make mischief in it?',[519] since he informed them about their names, after their statement, 'Glory be to You! We have no knowledge except what You taught us.'[520] Likewise are the prophets (peace be upon them): 'We have favoured some of the prophets over others.'[521] Likewise are the scholars (*'ulamā'*), after them: '[God will raise those who believe among you] and those who have been given knowledge, in ranks.'[522] Likewise are those who act, after them: 'To all are ranks, through what they did.'[523] Likewise are human beings in general, for [one is] a scholar and [another is] a student, that being hierarchy. And the rest of humanity are dungflies without good in them, that being contrariety!

In the traditions is: 'Human beings continue to prosper as long as they are different, and when they become equal they are destroyed.'[524] So equality is simply due to darkness, the darkness of non-existence; and hierarchy and disparity are simply due to light, the light of existence. God (Exalted is He) said: 'We have built heaven with might, and it is We who make its extent, and the earth We have laid out – how gracious is the One who spreads it! And all things We have created in pairs. Perhaps you may consider.'[525]

This is the innate nature, and what is other than that is a departure from innate nature. So were you to search for contrariety and hierarchy in creation and the things pertaining to creation, you would find them both in accordance with this principle, and were you to search for them in the Command and things pertaining to the Command, you would find them both in accordance with the like of that, in a completely identical way.

As for the foundation of the creation and the Command in the science of the Qur'ān – it is the basis upon which are built all the principles of the accomplished and the inchoative, contrariety and hierarchy, the origin and the return. It is the scale by which the judgements of the worlds are weighed: one of its scale-pans is the creation and what falls under it, and the second is the Command and what falls under it. God (Exalted is He) said: 'We have raised heaven and set up the scales.'[526]

He (Exalted is He) said: 'God it is who sent down the scripture through the truth and the scales'.[527] Whoever has an iota of intellect knows that the scales of the 'two precious things' are neither associated with the sky nor associated with the scripture. Instead, the scales placed in association with the 'raised heaven' are like the Command in association with creation, and like the 'goodly word' in association with the 'goodly tree',[528] and like the
60 statement 'no god but God' in association with the statement 'Muḥammad is God's Messenger'. Likewise, the scales placed in association with the 'sending down of the scripture with the truth' are like the association of 'The All-Merciful. He taught the Qur'ān. He created man. He taught him the explanation'.[529] So that when what is weighed consists in things pertaining to the Command and pertaining to the religious law, its scales are the creation and things pertaining to creation; and when what is weighed consists in things pertaining to creation, its scales consist in things pertaining to the Command.[530] The one(s) addressed by His statement 'Establish weighing with equity and stint not the scales',[531] are a specified people who establish equity. In their hand are the scales of equity for the Day of Resurrection: 'We set down equitable scales for the Day of Resurrection, so no soul is wronged in anything. Though it is of the weight of a mustard seed, We bring it, and We are sufficient as reckoners.'[532]

Chapter 11

*On the miraculous inimitability of the Qur'ān in terms of harmonious order (*nazm*), linguistic purity (*faṣāḥa*), concision (*jazāla*), eloquence (*balāgha*) and guidance (*hidāya*)*

Harmonious order (*naẓm*)

Its perfection and its nobility have been borne in mind in the symmetry of its letters, and the congruity of their points of articulation, so *ḥā'* and *'ayn*, *qāf* and *ghayn*, *ḍād* and *ṭā'* and other [such consonants] whose pronunciation would weigh heavily on the tongue, are not arranged together. Thus everything that is in the Qur'ān consisting of ordered letters, is words in line with a symmetry and harmony (*tanāṣuf*) the like of which is not found in the speech of the Arabs or any other language.

Its perfection and its nobility have been borne in mind in the construction of the words on the basis of a symmetry between the threefold [in radical letters], the fourfold, the fivefold and the sixfold, and on the basis of the coupling together of two expressions which are close together in letters and analogous in meaning.

Like that is the ordering of one verse with another verse, for the nobility in them is the harmony of the meanings and the congruence of the phrases and structures (*mabānī*), and the symmetry of the opening parts and the closing parts, the beginnings and the ends.

All nobility in the harmonious ordering of the *letters*, one of them with 61
another, is only in the bare expression, not the meaning. All nobility in the ordering of the *verses*, one of them with another, is only in the bare meaning, not the expression. The nobility in the ordering of the [individual] *words*, some of them with others, is, however, from both points of view: the expression *and* the meaning.

[Linguistic purity (*faṣāḥa*)]

It is realised from two points of view. One of them is the plain enunciation (*ifṣāḥ*) of the verbal expression from its points of articulation with correctness and clarity. The second is the plain enunciation of the meaning free from confusion with other than it, by the expression corresponding with it, declaring the reality of it, and equivalent to it in its generality and specificity. Then linguistic purity might be in respect of a solitary expression and it might be in respect of two expressions or more. It might declare a single thing by various expressions, one of which being more suggestive of what is meant and more explicit about what is in mind, so that expression is called the most linguistically pure (*afṣaḥ*) of the expressions.

[Stylistic concision (*jazāla*)]

It might be from two points of view. The first of them is in respect of simple expressions – and it is selecting the threefold over the fourfold and fivefold, except in what necessity produces. The second is in respect of compound expressions – and it is that the meaning be brought about by the shortest phrase and the most succinct expression, so that it breaks the neck and strikes the joint!

[Eloquence (*balāgha*)]

Most of it is in regard to the meaning. It is that whatever is formed in the mind, consisting in the meaning, is pure (*faṣīḥ*), apposite, powerful, expressed by the most apposite of phrases in suggestiveness, the most pure of them in lucidity, and the most concise of them in expression. It is something well known and indisputable that man is distinguished from the animal and the angel by speech (*nuṭq*), received from another and rendered to another. For, [on the one hand], no animal has the ability to receive what is in the mind of another by the medium of speech, or to render it to another in that way. [On the other hand], no angel has the ability to receive and render except by way of activity and passivity; and understanding and
62 giving to understand amongst them goes on in a manner without speech or verbal expression. Thus, man is singled out by speech which is his essential superiority (1) over what transcends him, consisting in the angels, and (2) over what is beneath him, consisting in the animals. [Next], since *nuṭq* is general to two meanings: the first of them is thinking and discerning, and the second is the *declaration* of what is thought and discerned. Furthermore, 'speakers' (*nāṭiqūn*) are according to a hierarchy and an inequality in regard to [the two meanings of *nuṭq*] as a whole. [So this hierarchy] culminates in ascension to the rank of independence from discursive thinking in the category of 'discerning', such that the unseen becomes for him openly seen and what arises for someone else through discursive thinking arises for him through innate nature. It is the same in the category of 'declaration', so that all of his speech becomes revelation and what arises

for someone else through authoritative instruction, arises for him through intuition. Thus his speech is distinguished as a whole, in these two ways, from the speech of other speakers, in perfection and nobility; and just as speech comes to be the inimitable miracle of man over the animal, likewise that *perfection* in respect of it comes to be the inimitable miracle of the prophet over man. As the kinds of inimitability in the basis of speech vary, though its genus is inimitable (for Arabic is inimitable and Persian is inimitable), likewise the kinds of inimitability in the *perfection* of speech vary, though its species is inimitable (for linguistic purity is inimitable and eloquence is inimitable, likewise harmonious order and concision, and likewise maxims, similitudes, exhortations and reproofs). Then what is more appropriate is that it be said: the Qur'ān in its totality is miraculously inimitable in its phraseology and its meaning, and Arabs are incapable of contradicting it. 'Say: were men and *jinn*[533] to combine to bring the like of this Qur'ān, they would not bring the like of it, though one of them helped the other.'[534]

Whoever takes it upon himself to search for the most pure of its words and verses has belittled the Qur'ān, since he selects words restricted in number from it. He has underestimated the perfection of linguistic purity for it and implied that the rest is not up to the splendor of that perfection. What he understands – perhaps what he *believes*[535] – to be linguistically pure is other than what he declares bad as rejected. Whoever occupies himself with criticism must have some speech superior to what is criticised, so that the criticism by him holds true.

The wellspoken amongst the Arabs placed the Qur'ān outside the genus of human speech. For sometimes they described it as 'patent magic' and at
other times they attributed it to God (Exalted is He). Likewise the *jinn* when 63
they overheard it, said: 'Truly we have heard a marvelous recitation, directing the way to guidance.'[536] Thus they described it in regard to the verbal expression as 'the marvel', and they described it in regard to the meaning as 'direction' and 'guidance', bringing the diction and the meaning together within the perfection. Since perfection in the sound is that it be understood speech, and perfection in speech is that it give information about guidance: 'Do they not see that it does not speak to them, nor guide them to some way?' For, since the voice of the calf is stripped of the two perfections, it is a 'lowing'.[537] So whoever takes into account the linguistic purity, concision, harmonious order, and eloquence in respect of the verbal expression

[alone], has acknowledged the first perfection, not the second perfection; and whoever takes into account the direction, guidance, the notification of truths and the legal ordinance [all] in respect of the meaning *together with* the first perfection, has exhausted the limit of eloquence (*balāgh*) and inimitable perfection. 'Say: Then bring a scripture from God's presence which gives better guidance than [the Torah and the Qur'ān].'[538]

Seldom do we find in the Qur'ān the mention of nobility and perfection in it, without it also alluding to direction, the Spirit, mercy, warning, and reminding. God (Exalted is He) said: '[...] the month of Ramaḍān in which the Qur'ān was sent down as a guidance for human beings and clear proofs for that guidance, and the criterion'.[539] He said: 'Thus do We inspire you with a Spirit through Our Command.'[540] He said: 'We have brought them a scripture which We spell out according to knowledge, a guidance and a mercy for a people who believe.'[541] He said: 'So that you may warn thereby, and as a reminder for the believers'.[542] And He said: 'and warn[543] thereby those who are God-fearing'.[544]

So just as we considered the side of the verbal expression, so that we understood its eloquence as transcending all other kinds of eloquence, it is necessary for us to consider the side of the meaning, so that we understand its guidance as transcending all other kinds of guidance.

Just as the Prophet is simply distinguished from the ordinary human being in that it is revealed to him that there is no god but God, and this claim of his is itself miraculously inimitable since no one challenged him in that claim (although some denier rejected him, yet a denier is not the same as a challenger), likewise the Qur'ān is simply distinguished from the rest of speech in that it *comprises* that monotheism and the negation of God's 'rivals', for no one objects to it in respect of this special feature (although some rejecter denied it, yet a rejecter is not the same as an objector).

So the Prophet and the Qur'ān vindicate one another in bearing witness, with the mutual vindication of the truth and the *exponent* of the truth – for the exponent of the truth is recognised through the truth with a summary recognition, and the truth is recognised through the exponent of the truth
64 with a detailed recognition. Likewise, the Prophet's veracity is recognised through the Qur'ān and the Qur'ān's veracity is recognised through the Prophet, for the two vindicate one another and testify to one another, so the Prophet testifies to the Qur'ān and the Qur'ān testifies to the Prophet – the blessings of God be upon him and his family!

Chapter 12
On the prerequisites for exegesis of the Qur'ān

God (Exalted is He) said: 'And We sent down to you the Remembrance (*dhikr*) for you to explain to human beings what is sent down to them.'[545] The Address thus indicates by its explicit stipulation and its express wording, that it stands in need of an explainer, since He did not say 'for *it to be explained* to human beings' – for not everyone who understands the language is permitted to comment on the Qur'ān. For the Arabs used to know about their language, but He did not rest content with their understanding of the Arabic language, so He said 'for *you* [singular] to explain to human beings what is sent down to them, and perhaps they will meditate'.[546]

Upon my life, the exegete must have a sound, first class knowledge of language, grammar and comprehension of the methods of [the Arabs'] figures of speech and the manners of their idioms, especially if he is a non-Arab. Next, he must follow the statements of the exegetes amongst the companions and successors, and take them from respected transmitters. Next, he has to audit traditions and investigate the dispositions of the traditionists, especially [in the case of] whichever of them pertain to the exegesis of the Qur'ān, so that he only takes them from the *sunan* and *ṣaḥīḥ* works[547] relied upon by such specialists in prophetic traditions. So that all he comments on amongst the words and verses is based on an authentic transmission, and an authentic report and account, not that he exercises independence in regard to it, by way of mere opinion. The Prophet (may God bless him and his family) has said: 'Whoever does exegesis of the Qur'ān on the basis of his own opinion, even if he is right, he has erred, and if he errs let him take his place in hellfire!'[548]

Amongst the exegetes is he who says: The words of the Qur'ān are in [certain] divisions. One of them is what can only be commented on through the explicit text of a report or hearing a tradition, such as the explanation of obscure verses, and supplying the detail (*tafṣīl*) for summary verses – like His statement (Exalted is He): 'Establish the formal prayer (*ṣalāt*) and pay the poor-due (*zakāt*).'[549] For only informal supplication (*du'ā'*) is understood, on the basis of lexicography, from the expression 65
ṣalāt, and only 'purification' and 'increase'[550] from the expression *zakāt*. That is prior to the consensus that they be turned away from their original

lexical significance to their significance in the religious law. So relating the expression to the specific 'pillars [of Islam]' is only subsequent to the explanation of what is mentioned synoptically by the Lawgiver, and that is only brought about after auditing traditions. In that vein are the oaths mentioned at the beginnings of the chapters, such as: 'By those who range themselves in ranks';[551] 'By the ones that scatter';[552] 'By the charging mares'[553] etc. One may neither relate them merely to the meanings referred to by the expression, nor may one relate them to the angels or to human individuals described by them *except* by an explicit text and a teaching. In that vein are the letters at the beginning of the chapters, [explained merely] according to the doctrine of whoever it is that comments on them – for it is only permissible to comment on them by way of a report or tradition. Like that are the occasioning causes of the descent of the verses (*asbāb al-nuzūl*), specifying general verses, generalising specific verses, relating summary verses (*mujmalāt*) to delimited verses, and directing homonymous expressions to one of the possible significations – all of that is only established through authentic traditions.

As for what it is possible to comment on, it is the externals of the scripture and its explicit texts, and whatever the verbal expression exclusively allows. So if the exegete applied his mind and thought about it he would know that he had not violated the meaning of the expression linguistically and he had not really contradicted sense perception and reason. But that is not the case with exegesis of the Qur'ān through personal opinion and analogical reason (*qiyās*)!

Like that is the hermeneutic of whatever outwardly suggests anthropomorphism (*tashbīh*) or nihilistic abstraction (*ta'ṭīl*), or necessitarianism (*jabr*) or libertarianism (*qadar*). For that is [indeed] permissible through the exercise of intellect and linguistic analogy since it is definitely known that anthropomorphism and nihilistic abstraction is false and relating the words of the Qur'ān to something false is impermissible, so in consequence there is no escape from an interpretation [in these cases]. And its criterion is that one not deviate from what is demanded by the [Arabic] language and usage in respect of it, and one does not lean towards any doctrine or teaching, and partisanship for it, but one heads down the main street, sticks to the middle, steers clear of the little back streets, does not rely on servile imitation of forefathers, is thoroughly versed in the methods of educating children, and does not say, 'We found our forefathers following a certain

religion and we guide ourselves by their footsteps,'[554] or 'We found our
forefathers following a certain religion and *we follow* in their footsteps.'[555] 66

Bearing these criteria in mind in doing the exegesis and interpretation of the ambiguous verses is very hard. Most exegetes barely fulfil that, for you will find all commentaries based on the doctrines deemed lawful [by the authors], so the libertarian does exegesis of the verses on divine predestination in line with what is consistent with his doctrine, the Ashʿarite in line with what is consistent with his doctrine, and the anthropomorphist holds fast to the literal and says: 'The literal is with me and hermeneutics is subject to opinion. I will not relinquish the literal aspect of the verbal expression for something subject to opinion. My aim is to say: I will not turn aside from the literal nor depend on interpretation.' The exponent of nihilistic abstraction instead abandons the literal, interpreting away liturgical practices in their entirety for men, and the restrictions upon them, religion being [reduced to] the recognition of *that man* [i.e., the imam]. Al-Ṣādiq, Jaʿfar b. Muḥammad (peace be upon him) washed his hands of them.[556] [On the other hand] amongst those who suspend judgement (*wāqifa*)[557] is one who says: 'I suspend judgement (*aqifu*) and I entrust the knowledge of it to God, so I say everything is from God's presence, and that is the way of safety.' It is just as one of the pious forbears said concerning the divine 'session on the Throne': 'The session is known and its manner is unknown. Faith in it is an obligation and inquiring into it is an innovation.'[558]

This confusion only befell them because they did not come to knowledge from its proper gateway and they did not cling to the lower end of its ropes, so the gate slammed shut against them, the ropes were severed for them and the roads of doctrines (*madhāhib*) led them on as confused people going astray: 'That is because they denied Our signs[559] and were heedless of them,'[560] God's signs being His friends (*awliyā'*),[561] as He (Exalted is He) said: 'We made Mary's son and his mother a sign.'[562] He had also said (Mighty is He who speaks): 'If they referred it to the Messenger and to the possessors of the Command amongst them, those able to think out the matter amongst them would surely have known it,'[563] and not everyone 'able to think out' is correct – otherwise the use of 'amongst them' *twice* would be futile.

Recall the report from the Prophet (God bless him and his family): "Alī is of me and I am of 'Alī';[564] and he said, when the chapter of Immunity (Q. 9) came down: 'A man amongst you will let you know about it.'[565]

On the authority of ʿAbd Allāh b. Masʿūd (may God be pleased with him) is: 'The Qur'ān was sent down according to seven readings,[566] and there is no reading but it has an exoteric and an esoteric side, and ʿAlī has the knowledge of both the exoteric and the esoteric side of it.'[567]

ʿAlī has said (may God be pleased with him): 'By God! No verse came down but I have known what it was sent down about and where it was sent
67 down. Truly my Lord bestowed on me an intelligent heart and an inquiring tongue.'[568]

It is transmitted that Sudayr al-Ṣayrafī questioned Jaʿfar b. Muḥammad al-Ṣādiq (peace be upon him), saying: 'May I be your ransom! Your partisans have differed about you, and they kept on differing till some of them said: "The Imam is spoken to in his ear."[569] Others said: "It is revealed to him." Others said: "It is thrown into his heart". Others said: "He is shown in his dream." And others said: "He gives his verdict simply by way of the books of his forefathers." So which of their responses should I adopt, may God make me your ransom!' [Jaʿfar] said: 'Don't adopt anything of what they say, Sudayr. We are God's proof and His trustees over His creation. What we consider permitted is from the scripture of God and what we consider forbidden is from it too.'[570]

It is transmitted that al-Fayḍ[571] b. al-Mukhtār came [to see] Jaʿfar b. Muḥammad (peace be upon him), and he said: 'May I be your ransom! What is this divergence among your partisans? For sometimes I sit in their circle in Kufa and I almost fall into doubt. So I go back to al-Mufaḍḍal[572] and I find what I depend on with *him*'. So Abū ʿAbd Allāh said: 'For sure! Men are seduced into lying about us until it is as if God (Mighty and Majestic) imposes it upon them and desires nothing else from them. Truly, I relate some prophetic tradition to one of them and he will not leave my presence without presenting it according to *other* than its proper interpretation.'[573]

It had been written to him that a people amongst his partisans said: 'Formal prayer is a man, fasting is a man, the poor-due is a man and the Greater Pilgrimage is a man. So whoever recognises that man has prayed, fasted, paid the poor-due and gone on the Greater Pilgrimage. They likewise interpret things forbidden by religion as certain individuals.'[574] So [Jaʿfar] said: 'Whoever professes God in this way which you have asked about is a polytheist[575] in my opinion – patent in polytheism! And know that these people are a people who hear what they do not attend to the reality of and what they do not understand the proper bounds of, for they set down the

bounds of these things by comparison with their opinions and the limitation of their minds, and they do not set them down according to the bounds of what they are commanded – giving the lie to and calumniating God and His Messenger, and being brazen on behalf of sins. God (Exalted is He) does not send any prophet who summons to some kind of recognition without the latter also involving an element of obedience, and God (Mighty and Majestic) only accepts [righteous] activity on the part of the worshippers through the obligations which He imposes on them, subsequent to their recognition of the one who brings them from His presence. So the beginning of that is the recognition of the One whom he summons to, namely 68
God, other than whom there is no god, His unity, the confession of His lordship, the recognition of the Messenger who gives an account of Him and the acceptance of what he brings. Next, the recognition of the imams after the messengers, obedience to whom is a duty in every age and time for its people. Next, acting on the basis of what God (Mighty and Majestic) imposed on His worshippers, consisting in acts of obedience outwardly and inwardly, and avoiding what God (Mighty and Majestic) forbade them – forbidding outwardly and inwardly.[576] And He only forbade the outward by the inward and the inward by the outward, both together, and the root and the branch are comparable with that.'[577]

It is transmitted on the authority of ʿAlī (may God be pleased with him) that the Qurʾān was mentioned, and he said: 'Its outward aspect is obligatory action and its inward aspect is hidden and veiled knowledge'.[578]

On the authority of Jaʿfar b. Muḥammad (peace be upon him) is that a man questioned him saying: 'Those who resist us[579] say about His statement (Exalted is He), "So ask the people of remembrance, if you do not know",[580] that the "remembrance" is the Torah and the "people of remembrance" are the learned amongst the Jews.' So Jaʿfar said: 'By God, in consequence [the Jews] would summon us to their religion! Rather, by God, we [the imams] are the people of remembrance to whom God (Exalted is He) commands that questioning be referred.'[581] Like that, it is conveyed on the authority of ʿAlī (may God be pleased with him) that he said: 'We [the imams] are the people of remembrance.'[582]

It is transmitted that Abū Dharr al-Ghifārī (may God be pleased with him) observed the Greater Pilgrimage (*al-mawsim*) after the decease of God's Messenger, and when people crowded around in the rite of circumambulation he stood at the door of the Kaʿba and grasped the ring of the door and called out, 'O people!', three times, so they gathered round and listened. Then he said: 'Whoever recognises me has recognised me, and whoever does not recognise me – I am Abū Dharr al-Ghifārī! I will report to you what I heard from the Messenger of God. I heard him say when I was present, "Verily, I leave amongst you two precious things: God's Scripture, and my offspring. And they will not be sundered until they come to me at the Pool, just like these two," and he brought together the two index fingers of his hands, joining them and making them equal. "I do not say 'like *these* two'" joining the middle finger and the index finger of his right hand, "since one of them is longer than the other. Truly, the analogy for the two of them in regard to you is Noah's ark. Whoever climbs aboard it is saved and whoever abandons it drowns."'[583]

ʿAlī has said (may God be pleased with him): 'Consult me before you lose
69 me, for no one is more knowledgeable about what is on the two Tablets than I am.'[584] And he said: 'Were a cushion folded for me and I were to sit on it, I would give judgement for the people of the Torah by their Torah, and for the people of the Gospel by their Gospel, and for the people of the Qurʾān by their Qurʾān.'[585] And he said (peace be upon him): 'There is no verse but it has four senses:[586] an exoteric and an esoteric, a boundary and a point of ascent (*maṭlaʿ*). The exoteric pertains to the recitation; the esoteric pertains to the understanding; the boundary is the rulings on the licit and the forbidden; and the point of ascent is what God wants from the worshipper through the verse.'

Jaʿfar b. Muḥammad (peace be upon him) said: 'God's Scripture is on the basis of four things: outward expression, allusion, subtleties and realities.'[587]

ʿAbd Allāh b. Masʿūd said: 'The Qurʾān was sent down according to seven readings (*aḥruf*). Every verse amongst them has an exoteric and an esoteric aspect, and every reading (*ḥarf*) amongst them has a boundary and a point of ascent.'[588]

The exegesis of the Exordium
(*Tafsīr* Sūrat al-Fātiḥa)

بِسْمِ ٱللَّهِ ٱلرَّحْمَٰنِ ٱلرَّحِيمِ

ٱلْحَمْدُ لِلَّهِ رَبِّ ٱلْعَٰلَمِينَ

ٱلرَّحْمَٰنِ ٱلرَّحِيمِ

مَٰلِكِ يَوْمِ ٱلدِّينِ

إِيَّاكَ نَعْبُدُ وَإِيَّاكَ نَسْتَعِينُ

ٱهْدِنَا ٱلصِّرَٰطَ ٱلْمُسْتَقِيمَ

صِرَٰطَ ٱلَّذِينَ أَنْعَمْتَ عَلَيْهِمْ

غَيْرِ ٱلْمَغْضُوبِ عَلَيْهِمْ وَلَا ٱلضَّآلِّينَ

Sūrat al-Fatīḥa
The chapter of the Exordium

Bi'smi'llāh al-Raḥman al-Rāḥīm
In the name of God, the Infinitely Merciful, the Compassionate

al-ḥamdu li'llāh Rabbi'l-ʿālamīn
Praise belongs to God the Lord of the Worlds

al-Raḥman al-Rāḥīm
the Infinitely Merciful, the Compassionate

Māliki yawmi'l-dīn
the Ruler of the Day of Judgement

iyyāka naʿbudu wa iyyāka nastaʿīn
it is You we worship and it is You we ask for help

ihdinā'l-ṣirāt al-mustaqīm
guide us on the straight path

ṣirāt alladhīna anʿamta ʿalayhim
the path of those whom You have graciously favoured

ghayr al-maghḍubi ʿalayhim wa lā'l-dāllīn
not those against whom is wrath, nor those who go astray.

Mention of the excellences of the chapter of the Exordium 72

In the name of God, the Infinitely Merciful, the Compassionate

Imam Abū ʿAbd Allāh Muḥammad b. Ismāʿīl al-Bukhārī mentioned in *al-Jāmiʿ al-ṣaḥīḥ*, by his chain of transmission on the authority of Abū Saʿīd b. al-Muʿallā [who] said:

> I was praying in the mosque and the Prophet called me, but I did not respond to him. Then I said: 'O Messenger of God, I was praying!' He said: 'Did God (Mighty and Majestic) not say "Respond to God and to the Messenger when he calls you to that which vivifies you"?'[589] Then he said to me: 'For sure, let me teach you a chapter which is the mightiest of the chapters in the Qurʾān, before you leave the mosque.' Then he took hold of my hand, and when he wanted to leave I said: 'Didn't you say, O Messenger of God, "For sure, let me teach you a chapter which is the mightiest of the chapters of the Qurʾān"?' He said: '"Praise belongs to God, the Lord of the Worlds [...]" is the Seven Doubled Ones and the Mighty Qurʾān is what I was given!'[590]

Ubayy b. Kaʿb reported on the authority of the Prophet that he said:

> 'Shall I not teach you a chapter the like of which was not sent down in the Torah, nor in the Gospel, nor in the Psalms, nor in the *Furqān*?' I said: 'For sure, Messenger of God!' He said: 'What do you recite in the formal prayer when you stand for it?' I said: 'The Exordium of the Scripture.' Then he said: 'That is it! And it is the Seven Doubled Ones of which God (Mighty and Majestic) said: "We have bestowed on you Seven of the Doubled Ones and the Mighty Qurʾān."'[591]

On the authority of Abū Hurayra (may God be pleased with him), on the authority of the Prophet, [who] said: '"Praise belongs to God, the Lord of the Worlds [...]" is seven verses – of which "In the name of God, the Infinitely Merciful, the Compassionate" is one (verse) – which are the Seven Doubled Ones, and which are the Mother of the Qurʾān and are the Exordium of the Scripture.'[592]

ʿAbd Khayr reported on the authority of ʿAlī, Saʿīd b. Jubayr [reported]
on the authority of Ibn ʿAbbās (may God be pleased with him), and al-Rabīʿ 73
b. Anas on the authority of Abūʾl-ʿĀliya, that they said in regard to His

statement 'We have bestowed on you seven of the Doubled Ones':[593] 'It is the Exordium of the Scripture.' They are on the authority of Abū Hurayra, on the authority of the Prophet [who] said:

> God (Mighty and Majestic) said: 'I divide the formal prayer[594] between Me and My worshipper into two halves, so half of it belongs to him. My worshipper says, when he commences the formal prayer, "In the name of God, the Infinitely Merciful, the Compassionate", thus My worshipper mentions Me. Then he says: "Praise belongs to God, the Lord of the worlds", so I say: "My worshipper has praised Me." Then he says: "The Infinitely Merciful, the Compassionate", so I say: "My worshipper has lauded Me." Then he says: "Master of the Day of Judgement", so I say: "My worshipper has glorified Me." Then he says: "It is You we worship and it is You we ask for help." So this verse is between Me and My worshipper, in two halves. The rest of the chapter belongs to My worshipper, and for My worshipper is whatever he requests.'[595]

On the authority of Abū Saʿīd al-Khudrī, he said:

> We alighted at a place and a slave girl came up to us and said: 'Our men are absent,[596] and the chief of the tribe has been bitten by a snake! Is there any wizard amongst the people?' A man stood up and said: 'Yes!' and we used not to accuse him of any spell-casting (*ruqya*) and did not think of him as being proficient in it. So he went and cast his spell on him and thirty sheep were ordered for him – and I believe that he said 'and he gave us milk to drink'.[597] [Abū Saʿīd] said: When he came back we said: 'We never thought of you as being proficient in spell-casting!' [The man] said: 'Neither *was* I proficient in it! I cast a spell on him simply using the Exordium of the Scripture.' [Abū Saʿīd] said: So when we arrived at Medina, I said: 'Don't speak about it at all till I come to God's Messenger and I mention that to him.' So I came to him and I mentioned that to him and he said: 'What was it that showed you that [the Exordium] is a spell?! Distribute [the sheep you got in reward] and assign me a share with you.'[598]

Mention of the names of the chapter of the Exordium

The chapter is called: the Exordium of the Scripture; the Mother of the Scripture; and also the Seven Doubled Ones.[599] The people of exegesis say: It is called the Exordium (*al-fātiḥa* = the opening) of the Scripture, simply

because the Qur'ān and the formal prayer open with it; and it is called the Mother (*umm*) of the Qur'ān, because it leads (*ta'ummu*) the Qur'ān and is at the head of it, or else because it is the foundation of the Qur'ān, the 'mother' of something being its foundation, and since the Exordium con- 74
tains ideas which are the foundations of the scripture it is called the Mother of the Qur'ān. They also say: It is called the Seven Doubled Ones (*mathānī*) simply because it is seven verses which descended twice – once at Mecca and once at Medina. Or else, because it is doubled in the formal prayer, in recitation, and the reiterated [terms] within it are doubled, such as 'the Infinitely Merciful, the Compassionate', 'it is You [...]' and 'it is You [...]', and 'the path [...]' and 'the path [...]'. It is said it is called *mathānī* because it was made an exception of (*istuthniyat*) for this community, for it did not emerge for any community except for this community. Abū Muʿādh said: 'I doubled up (*thanaytu*) property for you in the sense that I made an exception (*istathnaytu*)'. Saʿīd b. Jubayr transmitted on the authority of Ibn ʿAbbās that he said: 'He made an exception of it (*istathnāhā*, i.e. He held it back) for this community, till He made it emerge for them'. And it was said: The Doubled Ones are the Qur'ān [as a whole], since stories, reports, commanding and forbidding are repeated in it, and similitudes and exhortations are reiterated in it. It is said 'the fold of the thing (*thinyu'l-shay'*) is its side' and 'his doubled up ones (*mathānī*) are his garments (*maʿāṭif*)'.[600] In the chapter [of the Exordium] there are 'doubled ones', 'folded garments' and 'couples' among the expressions and words, as will come [to be seen] presently, through the arcana of the verses.

Mention of the descent of the chapter of the Exordium

The majority of the people of exegesis said that it descended at Mecca, and this is the statement of ʿAlī, Qatāda and al-Wāqidī, the transmission of Abū Ṣāliḥ on the authority of Ibn ʿAbbās, and the statement of Ubayy b. Kaʿb. The consensus of the community indicates that, in line with the fact that the chapter of the Rocky Tract[601] is Meccan and within it is His statement (Exalted is He) 'We *have* bestowed on you seven of the Doubled Ones'.[602] Abū Maysira said: The first of what Gabriel had the Prophet recite (may God bless them both) was the chapter of the Exordium of the Scripture.[603] Some said: It descended at Medina; that being the transmission of Manṣūr on the authority of Mujāhid, and the statement of al-Zuhrī, Muqātil, ʿAṭāʾ al-Khurāsānī and others. What is most appropriate is that there be a combination of the two transmissions so it is said: It descended twice, once at Mecca and once at Medina.[604]

75 Mention of the number of its verses and the formula *bi'smi'llāh* ('In the name of God')

Abū Saʿīd al-Maqburī[605] transmitted from Abū Hurayra (may God be pleased with him) on the authority of the Prophet, that he said: '"Praise belongs to God, the Lord of the Worlds [...]" is seven verses, one of which is "In the name of God, the Infinitely Merciful, the Compassionate."'[606] Ibn Abī Mulayka transmitted on the authority of Umm Salama who said: 'The Messenger of God used to say "In the name of God, the Infinitely Merciful, the Compassionate. Praise belongs to God, the Lord of the Worlds" to its end. He split it up verse by verse and reckoned it to be seven verses. He counted "In the name of God, the Infinitely Merciful, the Compassionate" as a verse, but did not count "*ʿalayhim*" [as the end of one].'[607]

Abū Rawq transmitted on the authority of al-Ḍaḥḥāk, on the authority of Ibn ʿAbbās (may God be pleased with him) who said: 'The first of what Gabriel sent down on Muḥammad (the blessings of God upon them both) [is that] he said: "O Muḥammad! Take refuge in the One who hears, the One who knows, from the stoned Satan." Then he said: "Say: 'In the name of God, the Infinitely Merciful, the Compassionate'."'

In the tradition of Abū Isḥāq al-Sabīʿī[608] on the authority of ʿAmr b. Sharḥabīl: 'God's Messenger confided in Khadīja at the outset of the revelation and said: "I've become scared that something has attacked me!" So she said: "What is it?" He said: "When I secluded myself, I heard the summoning [of something]. So I ran away." Then she informed Abū Bakr and Abū Bakr rushed him to Waraqa b. Nawfal and he told him the story. So Waraqa said to him: "When he comes to you, hold your ground with him!" Then Gabriel came to [the Prophet] and said to him: "Say: In the name of God, the Infinitely Merciful, the Compassionate. Praise belongs to God, the Lord of the Worlds."'[609]

Some say: The first of what descended was the beginning of the chapter

'Recite, in the name of your Lord',[610] then after that the 'Mother of the Qur'ān' descended.

Sa'īd b. Jubayr transmitted on the authority of Ibn 'Abbās: 'And We have bestowed on you seven of the Doubled Ones',[611] he said, '[this means] the Exordium of the Scripture', then he said: '"In the name of God, the Infinitely Merciful, the Compassionate" is the seventh verse.'

The community agreed that the Exordium is seven verses, except that they disagreed on whether the 'In the name of God' formula is the first verse of them, or 'whom You have graciously favoured' is [the end of] the sixth.

The scholars of Medina, Basra and Kufa, like Mālik b. Anas, al-Awzā'ī, 76
and Abū Ḥanīfa and his associates, said: It [the formula]is not one of the
verses of the Exordium, nor of any chapter except in the case of the chapter
of the Ants.[612] It is only a divider between one chapter and another which
thereby begins auspiciously and blessedly with the name of God, Mighty
and Majestic.

The scholars of the Ḥijāz and others like al-Shāfi'ī, Sufyān al-Thawrī and 'Abd Allāh b. al-Mubārak (may God be pleased with them)[613] said that it is the first verse of the Exordium[614] of the Scripture for sure, and most of them were in accord with the view that it is an [integral] verse of every chapter except Repentance.[615] However, the enumerators had reckoned it as a verse of the Exordium but did *not* reckon it as a verse of every chapter, due to what was transmitted on the authority of the Prophet, that he said: 'In the Qur'ān is a chapter which disputes in defense of her Lord, and it is thirty verses, namely, the chapter of Dominion.'[616] They said: It is thirty verses *minus* the 'In the name of God [...]' formula.

Muslim b. al-Ḥajjāj mentioned in his *Ṣaḥīḥ*, by his chain of transmission, on the authority of the Prophet, that he said: 'A chapter has been sent down to me which, of its nature, is such and such, and (the chapter) is: "In the name of God, the Infinitely Merciful, the Compassionate. Verily, We have bestowed abundance upon you" (to the end of the verse).'[617]

It is transmitted on the authority of 'Alī b. Abī Ṭālib (may God be pleased with him) that when he began the chapter in the formal prayer, he used to recite 'In the name of God, the Infinitely Merciful, the Compassionate'. And it is transmitted that he used to proclaim it aloud in the Exordium even at the noon and mid-afternoon prayer.[618]

Ibn Burayda transmitted on the authority of his father who said: 'God's Messenger said: "Shall I not tell you a verse which has not come down to anyone other than me, since Solomon?" I said: "Certainly!" He said: "With what thing do you open the Qur'ān when you begin the formal prayer?" I said: "With 'In the name of God, the Infinitely Merciful, the Compassionate'." He said "That's it!"'[619]

Jābir b. ʿAbd Allāh transmitted on the authority of God's Messenger that he said to him: 'What do you say when you stand up for the formal prayer?' He said: 'I say "Praise belongs to God, the Lord of the Worlds."' [The Prophet] said: 'Say "In the name of God, the Infinitely Merciful, the Compassionate."'[620]

On the authority of Abū Hurayra (may God be pleased with him) is that a man began the formal prayer with 'Praise belongs to God', so the Messenger of God (may God bless him and give him peace) said: 'Fellow!
77 Don't you know that "In the name of God, the Infinitely Merciful, the Compassionate" is part of [the chapter] "Praise [...]"?[621] Thus whoever omits it has omitted a verse of "Praise [...]"!'[622]

Like him, Ṭalḥa b. ʿUbayd Allāh said that God's Messenger said: 'Whoever omits "In the name of God, the Infinitely Merciful, the Compassionate" has omitted a verse of God's Scripture.'[623]

ʿAlī b. al-Ḥusayn b. Shaqīq said: 'I heard ʿAbd Allāh son of al-Mubārak (may God be pleased with them both) say: "Whoever neglects to recite the 'In the name of God' formula has omitted one hundred and thirteen[624] verses of the Qur'ān."'[625]

On the authority of Saʿīd b. Jubayr, on the authority of Ibn ʿAbbās (may God be pleased with him), [who] said: 'God's Messenger (may God bless him and his family) did not know the end[626] of a chapter till "In the name of God, the Infinitely Merciful, the Compassionate" came down to him.'[627]

On the authority of ʿAbd Allāh b. Masʿūd who said: 'We did not know the division between the chapters until "In the name of God, the Infinitely Merciful, the Compassionate" came down.'[628]

Saʿīd b. Jubayr and Ibn ʿAbbās pronounced the 'In the name of God [...]' formula aloud in every cycle of the formal prayer.

Al-Azraq b. Qays said: 'I did the formal prayer with Ibn al-Zubayr and he recited "In the name of God, the Infinitely Merciful, the Compassionate"; and he said "Not those against whom is wrath nor those who go astray", then he said "In the name of God, the Infinitely Merciful, the Compassionate".'

The people of the two sanctuaries[629] make a division between every two chapters with 'In the name of God, the Infinitely Merciful, the Compassionate'. On the authority of al-Ḥasan b. Mujāhid, on the authority of the people of Medina: 'We did not used to pronounce aloud the "I take refuge with God [...]" formula nor did we completely say it under our breath, but we did used to recite [aloud] "In the name of God, the Infinitely Merciful, the Compassionate" at the beginning of the Exordium, the beginning of the chapter of the Cow,[630] between two chapters, and when we began any portion of a chapter.' And ʿĀṣim used to agree with the people of Medina.

As for the people of Basra, and Ḥamza, they joined the end of one chapter to the chapter which followed it and they left out the 'In the name of God [...]' formula – it being a transmission of al-Farrāʾ on the authority of al-Kisāʾī – *except* at the beginning of the Exordium of the Scripture, when they pronounced it aloud. The *prima facie* sense of the practice of al-Kisāʾī is that he used to make a division between two chapters with the 'In the name of God [...]' formula, and likewise when he began a portion of a chapter. On the authority of Abū ʿAmr is the like of that and nothing has come on the authority of Ibn ʿĀmir in regard to that matter.

Khalaf [b. Hishām] said: 'We used to recite in the presence of Sulaym 78
[b. ʿĪsā], so we said the "I take refuge with God [...]" formula and the "In the name of God [...]" formula under our breath in the whole of the Qurʾān.' He said, '*He* [in turn] used to recite likewise in the presence of Ḥamza [al-Zayyāt].'

On the authority of Saʿīd b. Jubayr is that the companions did not know the ending of a chapter till 'In the name of God, the Infinitely Merciful, the Compassionate' descended. When it descended they knew that the chapter had ended and another chapter had descended.[631]

On the authority of al-Ṣādiq (upon him be peace): 'Whoever prays with "In the name of God, the Infinitely Merciful, the Compassionate" is closer to the mightiest name of God than the iris of the eye is to the white of it.'[632] On his authority in the commentary of al-ʿAyyāshī:[633] '"In the name of God, the Infinitely Merciful, the Compassionate" is the greatest, mightiest name of God.'[634] And on his authority in the book of al-Kulaynī, he said: 'O Mufaḍḍal![635] Defend yourself against all people[636] with "In the name of God, the Infinitely Merciful, the Compassionate" and with "Say, He is God, One [...]".[637] Recite them to your right[638] and your left, in front of you and behind you, above you and beneath you. When you enter the presence of a tyrannical ruler recite them[639] three times whenever you look at him, counting with your left hand. Then[640] do not separate yourself from them [i.e. keep doing this] till you leave his presence.'[641]

On the authority of Jābir b. ʿAbd Allāh who said: 'God's Messenger said: "How do you recite when you stand in the formal prayer?" I [Jābir] said: "I say 'Praise belongs to God, the Lord of the Worlds'." He said: "Say: 'In the name of God, the Infinitely Merciful, the Compassionate. Praise belongs to God, the Lord of the Worlds'."'[642]

In the authentic compendium of traditions of the people of the Prophet's house (peace be upon them) is that God's Messenger and the imams from his progeny (peace be upon them) used to recite aloud 'In the name of God [...]' in whichever of the formal prayers are recited aloud, at the beginning of the Exordium of the Scripture and at the beginning of the chapters in every cycle of prayer; and they would recite it under their breath in whichever chapters [*sic*] were recited under the breath. They said: 'We children of Fāṭima concur in that.'[643]

On the authority of al-Ṣādiq (peace be upon him): 'Dissimulation is my religion and the religion of my forefathers, except in three things: drinking alcoholic beverages, wiping socks,[644] and omitting to say "In the name of God, the Infinitely Merciful, the Compassionate"[645] aloud.'[646] On the authority of Saʿīd b. Jubayr is that he used to do likewise, starting with [the formula] *and* finishing off with it.

It is transmitted that Muʿāwiya b. Abī Sufyān arrived at Medina and led
79 the people in a formal prayer in which he was reciting aloud, and he recited the Exordium of the Scripture omitting the formula 'In the name of God [...]'. When he concluded his prayer the emigrants and helpers in the mosque called out to him on every side, 'Muʿāwiya, have you robbed the prayer or just forgotten?!' So he led them in another prayer, reciting the 'In the name of God [...]' formula for the chapter which was *after* it, i.e. at the end of the Exordium not at the beginning of it![647]

In some reports is that 'In the name of God, the Infinitely Merciful, the Compassionate' is a verse of the Qurʾān which Satan stole.[648]

Thus, whoever says that it is a verse of every chapter and was sent down with it, judges that were it merely a division between one chapter and another it would have been written between the two chapters of the Spoils and Repentance, and were it merely for commencing every chapter, it would also be written at the beginning of the chapter of Repentance. Moreover, were it [in this way] for seizing as booty[649] it would have been written in another colour than black, like the chapter names and verse numbers, and not in the manner in which the verses are [themselves] written. So it is known [for sure] that it is sent down in every chapter and it is proven with certainty that it is [an integral] part of the Exordium through the profusion of reports and by what we will mention presently at the time of discussing the arcana.

The exegesis of the verse of the *tasmiya* formula, His statement, Exalted is He: *Bi'smi'llāh al-Raḥmān al-Raḥīm* ('In the name of God, the Infinitely Merciful, the Compassionate')

The [word] 'In' (*bi-*)

Lexicography

The people of exegesis discuss the 'in' of 'In the name of God [...]': What is the purpose of starting with it, why is it written long, and why is the *alif* dropped from it?[650] They say: It involves an ellipsis and an abridgement, so the implication of it is '*I start off the recitation* in the name of God' or 'I started [...]' or '*they* started the recitation' or 'I began', and the context makes it clear that you are beginning, so mentioning it can be dispensed with. The ellipsis might be after the formula, the implication of it being 'In God's name I start off the recitation' – that being the statement of Tha'lab. The sense is similar in the case of anything[651] people start doing, such as standing, sitting, eating and drinking.[652] The predicate in the ellipsis is sometimes stated explicitly, as when He (Mighty and Majestic) says: 'In the name of God is [the Ark's] moving and resting';[653] and He said: 'Recite in the name of your Lord'.[654] So there is a proof in that, of the fact that the predicate has been elided whenever it is *not* mentioned, whether before (the 80
formula) or after it. And the meaning of it is: 'I begin[655] this affair "In the name of God", seeking auspiciousness and asking for blessing.'

Grammar

The grammarians from amongst the Basrans term [*bā'*] the 'letter of connection'. As it might be said 'I wrote with (*bi-*) the pen', 'I cut with (*bi-*) the knife'. The meaning of it is that the *bā'* connects verbs to nouns. It is a preposition.

Exegesis

The statement of someone 'I start this in the name of God' has two significations. The first of them is that its meaning is: 'I start it in the name of God asking for blessing thereby, looking for auspiciousness through mentioning it, seeking success for the request, facilitating good, aiming for excellence of the outcome.' It is as if one said: 'I start it with the mention of Him, asking for blessing through His name, so that the affair reaches completion and is not curtailed.'

The second signification is that its meaning is: 'By *God* I start off and by God I accomplish what I am resolved upon', 'the name' being a pleonasm (*ṣila*) according to this signification. The lexicographers have endorsed this interpretation, so it might be said: 'I do this for your face (*li-wajhika*)',[656] 'Were it not for your placing (*makānuka*) I would not abide here',[657] and 'were it not for the shadow (*ẓill*) of X striking me'[658] etc. 'Face', 'placing' and 'shadow' are pleonastic augments in speaking, to show respect. This is the assertion of Abū 'Ubayda, and he adduces as evidence the statement of Labīd:

> For the year – then the word 'peace upon you both!'
> And whoever weeps for a whole year[659] has made his plaint!

That is: 'Then "peace upon you both".'[660]

It is said in line with this signification that 'the name' is included in it simply for there to be a distinction between swearing an oath and asking for auspiciousness.[661]

If we say that 'the name' is a pleonasm, then it means the One *named*, and [on the other hand] according to the first signification it would have the sense of 'naming'. It could also mean 'the One named' through the ellipsis of a verb, the sense being: 'With God's strength, power and facilitation I begin.'

81 **Orthography**

As for the lengthening of the *bā'*, it has been made comparable to the *alif* [in length] because of two things. The first of them is that they only wanted to start God's Speech and His Scripture with a visually emphatic and lengthened letter. The second is that since they dropped the *alif* from the formula, they gave back the length of the *alif* to the *bā'* – only omitting the *alif* from [the orthography of] *ism* due to the frequency of its use, abbreviating. And when suchlike is not in frequent use, they *do* register the *alif* in it. It is also said that the *bā'* is lengthened simply so that it not be confused with the *sīn*.

[The expression] *al-ism* ('the name')

Etymology

There are two statements on the etymology of *ism*. The first of them (it being the statement of the Basrans) is that it is from *samuw* ['height'] and the meaning of it is that it rises above (*yasmu ʿalā*) the meaning and it manifests the meaning. The diminutive of *ism* is *sumay*. The second is that it is from *sima*, which means 'sign' (*ʿalāma*), since it descends upon (*ʿalā*) the thing named. The first assertion is more correct, since were [*ism*] derived from *wasm*,[662] then *wusaym* would be said in the diminutive of it, as they say *waʿd* and *wuʿayd*,[663] and *waṣl* and *wuṣayl*.[664]

Abū Saʿīd al-Khudrī transmitted on the authority of the Prophet: Jesus the son of Mary (peace be upon them both) was handed by his mother to the teacher, and the teacher said to him: 'Say: In the name of God (*bi'smi'llāh*)!' Jesus said to him: 'And what is *ism*?' (i.e. and what is *bā'*, *sīn*, *mīm*?). He said: 'I don't know.' Jesus (peace be upon him) said: 'The *bā'* is the glory (*bahā'*) of God, the *sīn* is His sublimity (*sanā*), and the *mīm* is His dominion (*mulk*).'[665]

The statement about the arcana of the letters and their meanings is simply that it is[666] a safekeeping of the prophets and bosom friends [of God] (peace be upon them), and the intellects of others are incapable of understanding them.

Statement on the name *Allāh* and its exegesis

A group of the scholars of Basra and others said: The origin of the word is *ilāh* (god); then the *lām* was introduced[667] and the *alif* was pronounced as 'a' [instead of 'i'] to give emphasis and glorification. Thus it became *al-'alāh*. Next the original *hamza* (='a) was omitted by way of abbreviation due to its frequent repetition in speech, so it became *al-lāh*. Then one of the *lāms* was assimilated to the other and they said '*Allāh*'. This is one of the two state- 82
ments of Sībawayhi.[668] Abū'l-ʿAbbās Aḥmad b. Yaḥyā narrated it on the authority of al-Khalīl.

The scholars of Kufa said: Its origin is *lāh*, then the *alif* and the *lām* were added to the word so they said '*Allāh*'. This is the choice of al-Mubarrad and al-Zajjāj, and both statements are mentioned by Sībawayhi.[669]

Abū Naṣr Ismāʿīl b. Ḥammād al-Jawharī,[670] the author of the book *al-Ṣiḥāḥ*, said: The root of the word is *ilāh*, on [the pattern of] *fiʿāl* in the sense of the passive participle, since He is 'made God' in the sense of 'is worshipped' – like our saying [of someone], *imām* (leader) in the sense of the passive participle, since his example is followed (*mu'tamm bihi*). And he said: It is derived from their saying 'He worshipped (*alaha*, with 'a') with a worshipping (*ilāhatan*)', i.e. he served with a serving. From this is the statement of Ibn ʿAbbās: 'and flout you and your worshipping (*ilāhatuka*)',[671] meaning 'your service'. He said: Sībawayhi said it was feasible that its origin was *lāh*[672] into which the [initial] *alif* and the [first] *lām* were introduced, so it would be analogous to a proper name like *al*-ʿAbbās and *al*-Ḥasan, except that it is different from proper names insofar as it is an attribute.[673]

Arcana

Those who magnify God's names say: Though you consider the name *Allāh* to be amongst proper names and you do *not* hold the doctrine that it is etymologically derivative – and how [could there be] an etymology for it! – [nevertheless] do not fail to give attention to an arcanum in the composition of its letters and that the root of the word and its construction is from the *alif*, the *lām* and the *hā'*. It has been said in respect of language: the *alif* is for grammatical definition (*taʿrīf*), the *lām* is to affirm possession (*tamlīk*), and the *hā'* is for reification (*shay'iyya*).[674] It was said in respect of wisdom: nothing is grasped of the majesty of God (Exalted is He) except His quoddity (*huwiyya*)[675] alone, for He is He; amongst the [established] supplications is: 'O He (*Huwa*) who is He.' The root of [*Huwa*] is the *hā'* alone (*h*), except that if it is vowelled with the strongest of the vowels – that being the pronunciation of the final consonant with 'u' (= *rafʿ*) – it is vowelled together with its [consonantal] 'consort', namely *wāw*. Next the *lām* for affirming possession is joined to the *hā'* so that everything comes to belong to Him (*lahu*) as a creation and a command, a possession (*milk*) and a dominion (*mulk*).[676] For insofar as He is He (*hu*), He is ungraspable, while insofar as everything belongs to Him (*lahu*), He is undeniable. The former is His majesty and the latter is His bounty.

Next, to the *lām* was joined the *alif* by way of grammatical definition (*taʿrīf*), though He is better known (*aʿraf*) than anything,[677] more evident than every outward thing *and* more hidden than every inward thing. As ʿAlī said (may God be pleased with him): 'God (Exalted is He) is too mighty to

be seen yet too evident to be hidden!'[678] Thus the letters which are the basis 83
of the word ['*Allāh*'] point to what it is obligatory to know and is made known to be obligatory.[679] No letter of any of the names of existents points to any part or attribute of the thing named except this highest name. For each letter of it points out something special and, taken as a whole, they point to the entirety of gnosis!

There is no crossing-point for the intellects of men of intellect except these ideas, and whoever crosses beyond it arrives at the maelstrom of perplexity and only withdraws again from it with grief! Due to that, since some people cross beyond the word *Huwa* ('He'), they join it with *mā Huwa* ('what is He?'), thus they seek a [divine] quiddity (*māhiyya*). Next they cross over to quantity, so they say 'how much is He?' Next they cross further to quality, so they say 'how is He?' So they arrive at polytheism,[680] dualism, Trinitarianism, anthropomorphism and nihilistic abstraction, and they stray from the right way.

The prophets (upon them be peace), set up instruction in the like of the meanings of the names in the chapter of Sincerity,[681] insofar as He incepted pure monotheism through '*Huwa*' and He added to it '*Allāh*', 'the One (*al-Aḥad*)', 'the Absolute (*al-Ṣamad*)'.[682] So the Name *Allāh* bestows[683] the idea of His divine status through the negation of quiddity; 'the One' bestows the idea of pure monotheism through the negation of quantity; and 'the Absolute' bestows the idea of exaltation through the negation of quality. And [as for] everything joined to *Huwa* ('He') consisting of 'what?' (*mā*), 'how much?' (*kam*) and 'how?' (*kayf*) – He transcends that; and [as for] everything joined to the *hā'* (*h*) of '*Allāh*', by way of the *lām* of dominion and possession, and the *alif* of the Command (*al-amr*) and the Logos – He is [really] described by that!

It is extraordinary that the *lām* in the orthography is repeated and the *alif* of pronunciation[684] is repeated, the name not going beyond the four letters in respect of the tongue and the pen.

It has been said that from the four letters are inferred the four foundations which are the root-principles of existents, beings having arisen through them. It is as if those foundations arose through these transcendent letters, and the existents [in turn] arose through those intelligible foundations, so the cause of the existence of existents is His name (Exalted is He), *Allāh*, and nothing but Him is named thereby.

In line with the four letters is the hierarchy of four levels in His statement

84 (Exalted is He): 'Praise the name of your Lord, the Most High, who creates and makes regular, and who determines, then guides.'[685] The relation of 'making regular' with 'creating' is like that of 'guiding' with 'determining'. Wherever there is a creating, a making regular follows it, for symmetry to arise; and wherever there is a determining, He follows it up with a guiding, for perfection to arise. Thus creating arises through the *alif* of the Command (*al-amr*), making regular arises through the first *lām*, determining arises through the second *lām*, and guiding (*hidāya*) arises through the final *hā'*. It is the highest name, the glorification, praise and magnification of which is obligatory. It is the first word (*ism*) with which the pen flowed. [For it says] in a report: 'The first of what God (Exalted is He) wrote with the pen is "Verily, I am *Allāh*, there is no God but I."'

It is what is written on the side of the Throne. From its three letters arises the primary body, having height like the *alif* (ا), breadth like the *lām* (ل), and depth like the *hā'* (ه). From these three letters is the composition of the statement of the testimony of faith: *lā ilāha illā'llāh* ('no god but God').

The coining [of the word '*Allāh*']

Some of the learned said: This noun is not derivative. The Creator (Exalted is He) possesses it uniquely, it being analogous in its character to proper names, none sharing it with Him. He said (Exalted is He): 'Do you know any namesake (*samiyy*) of Him?'[686] That is: do you know anyone called *Allāh* other than Him? This teaching is narrated on the authority of al-Khalīl b. Aḥmad and Ibn Kaysān, and it is the choice of Abū Bakr al-Qaffāl al-Shāshī. It is a noun coined for the sake of glorification, the custom of the [pagan] Arabs being to call whatever they glorified '*ilāh*' (god) and they used to call the idols which they used to worship '*āliha*' (gods).

Likewise is the custom of the Persians. They call the one who is glorified amongst their kings by the word which is the translation of the word *al-ilāh* (the deity), saying *khudāwand* (Lord) and *khudāygān*, for this word refers to any referent attributed by the attributes of majesty and glory. It is His proper name (majestic is the praise of Him), [a statement about God] being incepted by mentioning it – *then* it is followed by the mentioning of His attributes. So it is said: *Allāh* is Powerful, Knowledgeable. *Allāh* is Creator, Giver of the Command.

85 Al-Mufaḍḍal said: The names which are attributes are exclusively etymologically derivative, as *al-Raḥmān* (the Infinitely Merciful) [and] *al-*

Raḥīm (the Compassionate) are from *raḥima* ('he had mercy');[687] *al-ʿAzīz* (the Mighty) is from *ʿazza* ('he was strong'), and the like of these. As it is said: from *al-ilāh* (the deity) is *alaha, ya'lahu* ('he worshipped, he worships') and *ta'allaha, yata'allahu* ('he became a god, he becomes a god'). [Al-Mufaḍḍal] said: And by way of the proof that [the name *Allāh*] is not etymologically derived from any verb is that it is not put in the dual and it is not pluralised, while *al-ilāh* ('the god') is pluralised as *al-āliha*. So it is proven that ['*Allāh*'] is a proper name for the One who is worshipped. Some who espoused this idea said: The formula of the testimony of faith comprises a negation and an affirmation. If what is affirmed and made subject to exception shared with what is negated in its inferred sense, then the distinction between the two of them would not hold true, and it would be equivalent to your saying 'There is no Zayd except Zayd'.

The majority said: It is derivative. Then they differed as to its etymology. Al-Naḍr b. Shumayl said: It is from *ta'alluh* (devotion), and it is said 'he worshipped with a worshipping' (*alaha ilāhatan*) i.e. 'he adored with an adoring'. Thus He is termed *ilāh* (deity) since only the adoration of Him is correct. Mujāhid said: *Allāh* is He whom everything worships (*ya'lahu*), i.e. adores. Muqātil b. Sulaymān transmitted on the authority of al-Ḍaḥḥāk, on the authority of Ibn ʿAbbās, regarding His word '*Allāh*'; he said: He means Himself, in that He is 'the worshipped one' and there is no worshipped one other than Him. Al-Aʿshā said: 'We urged the goddess (*al-ilāha*) to return.'[688] The 'goddess' here is the sun which they called *ilāha* for the sake of glorification. Ru'ba[689] said: '[The women] gave glorification and uttered the ritual phrase "we belong to God and we are returning to God!" in view of my devotion (*ta'alluhī*).'[690]

Ta'alluh is devoutness and piety. Some said that this name is derived etymologically from [the word *waliha* in the phrase] 'Those who worship Him *became mad with love* (= *waliha*).' They 'became infatuated' (*tawallahū*), i.e. their hearts were fixated with Him, they took refuge in Him and they regarded succor and help from Him with longing. So they said '*alaha/ya'lahu alahan*', 'he was/is confounded [with] a confounding', i.e. he was perplexed. Its root is *walaha, yawlahu*, 'he became/becomes mad' with passionate love (*walah*); and *alihtu*, 'I have become agitated' on account of[691] X, i.e. 'my anguish increased for him', [which is in form] just like *walihtu* ('I went mad').

Al-Ḥasan b. Yaḥyā al-Jurjānī[692] said: The root of '*Allāh*' is *ilāh* (deity) and *ilāh* is a noun coined through their saying 'the man sought protection (*aliha*) from X', when he sought refuge from something which befell him, so [X] granted him sanctuary (*ālaha*), i.e. [X] protected him and gave him safety. So He is called *ilāh* (deity) because *yūlahu ilayhi* ('refuge is taken in Him'), just like the *imām* (leader), who is *yu'tammu bihi* ('followed as an example'). Then they wanted to give Him emphasis through grammatical definition which is the *alif* and the *lām*,[693] in that they assigned this name to Him especially, not to any other. So they said *al-ilāh* (the deity). Then the two *hamzas*[694] combined in a word of which their use was frequent, so they elided the radical *hamza* [= the initial 'i' of *ilāh*] and they said '*Allāh*', on the grounds that there is some indication of [the radical *hamza*] in what is left behind.

86 **Exegesis**

Abū Ṣāliḥ and al-Ḍaḥḥāk transmitted on the authority of Ibn ʿAbbās (may God be pleased with him) who said: He is the one they take refuge in (*ya'lahūna ilayhi*)[695] and His statement 'Is there any deity (*ilāh*) besides *Allāh*?'[696] means 'Is refuge taken in other than Him in important matters?' Al-Mubarrad said: ['*Allāh*'] is from their saying *alihtu ilayhi* meaning 'I dwelt'.

The poet said:

> I dwelt in it (*alihtu ilayhā*), mishaps being copious.[697]

And someone said:

> I stayed in it (*alihtu ilayhā*), riding camels being halted.

Thus it is feasible that the meaning is 'I took refuge in Him' and 'I had recourse to Him', and it is feasible [also] that it is 'I dwelt in Him'. A poet says:

> She hid (*lāhat*) and was not known that day by any bird of prey,
> If only she came out so we saw her!

i.e. she concealed herself.

Another said:

> My Lord hid Himself (*lāha*) from created beings without exception,
> The Creator of the world who is not seen but sees *us*

i.e. He conceals Himself from created things.

Semantics

Abū ʿAmr b. al-ʿAlāʾ said:[698] He is the one I take refuge in (*alihtu*) in regard to something when I am bewildered in regard to it – so He is called *ilāh* (deity) because intellects are bewildered in regard to His tremendousness. It is said: The meaning [of ʻ*Allāh*ʼ] is ʻthe Highʼ, from their saying ʻHe hid Himself (*lāha*), given He is so highʼ, hence the sun is called *ilāha* (goddess). It is said: Its meaning is ʻthe one deserving of the attributes of majesty.ʼ And it is said: Its meaning is ʻthe One capable of *creatio ex nihilo* (*ikhtirāʿ*).ʼ
Shahr b. Ḥawshab said:[699] Its meaning is ʻthe Creator of everythingʼ. 87
Likewise, it is transmitted on the authority of the forebears among the imams, in regard to the meaning of *lā ilāha illāʾllāh* (ʻno god but Godʼ), that it means ʻno creator but Godʼ.

Statement on the name[s] *al-Raḥmān al-Raḥīm* (ʻthe Infinitely Merciful, the Compassionateʼ) and their exegesis

Lexicography

The learned scholars of the community said: They are two words etymologically derived from *raḥma* (mercy), placed together for intensification, combined for emphasis and repeated with two different expressions, though they both correspond in meaning. That is more beautiful than their repeating it with a single expression, as when they say ʻ*jādd mujidd*ʼ (ʻearnest and diligentʼ) and ʻ*ḥaṭūm muḥaṭṭim*ʼ (ʻshattering and crashingʼ). God (Exalted is He) said: ʻVerily it is an evil abode and placeʼ.[700] ʿAdī b. Zayd said: ʻHe found her word to be a lie and a severance.ʼ[701]

The reality of the meaning in regard to this repetition is that He possesses vast mercy, whose mercy is uninterrupted and whose grace on His servants is incessant. So it is as if He said: ʻIn the name of God, whose mercy is uninterrupted and who has graces after graces.ʼ Whoever holds this opinion says: they are two names placed together for intensification, like *nadmān* and *nadīm* (ʻruefulʼ and ʻconfidantʼ), and *lahfān* and *lahīf* (ʻsorrowfulʼ and ʻsorryʼ). The meaning of both of them [*raḥmān* and *raḥīm*] is ʻpossessor of mercyʼ. This is the assertion of Abū ʿAmr b. al-ʿAlāʾ, Abūʾl-Haytham and Quṭrub.

Amongst the learned scholars are those who distinguish between the two names. One group says ʻ*al-Raḥmān*ʼ is stronger in intensification than ʻ*al-Raḥīm*ʼ since it is based on [the paradigm] *faʿlān*, and it only applies on grounds of the intensification of the verb, like *ghaḍbān* (furious) for someone filled[702] with anger (*ghaḍab*), and *sakrān* (drunkard) for someone whom intoxication (*sukr*) overwhelms.

Exegesis and semantics

Abū 'Ubayda said: *Al-Raḥmān* is 'the possessor of mercy' and *al-Raḥīm* is 'the Merciful'. Ibn 'Abbās said in the transmission of 'Aṭā': *Al-Raḥmān* is 'the kind', 'the very tender', the One Merciful (*al-Raḥīm*) to His friends and to the people who are obedient to Him. He also said in one transmission: *Al-Raḥmān* is 'the loving' and *al-Raḥīm* is 'the very tender', and they are two loving (*rafīqān*) names. And he said in the transmission of Abū Ṣāliḥ: Two loving names, one of which is more delicate (*araqq*) than the other. Al-Ḥusayn b. al-Faḍl said: Perhaps [Ibn 'Abbās] said 'two loving names, one of which is more loving (*arfaq*) than the other'. It is transmitted on his authority that he said: *Al-Raḥmān* (the Infinitely Merciful) is the one tender
88 towards the pious man *and* the dissolute man in providing for them, and in the heavens and the earth there is no *Raḥmān* other than Him. And *al-Raḥīm* (the Compassionate) is for the believers in particular. It is also transmitted on his authority that he said: *Al-Raḥmān* is for the whole of His creation and *al-Raḥīm* is for the believers in particular. Sa'īd b. Jubayr said: He is *al-Raḥmān* because He is inclusive of the believer *and* the unbeliever in [giving] mercy. God (Exalted is He) says: 'My mercy encompasses everything.'[703] And *al-Raḥīm* is the one who specifies the believers for mercy. He says (Exalted is He): 'I will stipulate [mercy] for those who are God-conscious.'[704] This is also the statement of Muqātil.

Manṣūr transmitted on the authority of Mujāhid that he said: *Al-Raḥmān* is for the people of the herebelow, *al-Raḥīm* is for the people of the hereafter. [The following invocation] comes in a report: 'O *Raḥmān* of the herebelow, O *Raḥīm* of the hereafter!'[705] Whoever espoused this doctrine said: '*Al-Raḥmān* is specific as a name but general in meaning, and *al-Raḥīm* is general as a name but specific in meaning.' The meaning of that is that no one may be called the name *al-Raḥmān* other than God (Exalted is He), while it is general in meaning insofar as He is tender towards all His creatures in providing for them and deflecting distress from them, that only being the case through the intensification of [the action of] the verb. [Next, the significance of] our statement that *al-Raḥīm* is general as an expression but specific in meaning, is that *other* than God (Exalted is He) might be called by this name, as He (Exalted is He) says 'unto the believers [the Prophet] is full of pity, compassionate (*raḥīm*)',[706] and He said in the description of [the Prophet's] companions '[...] compassionate (*ruḥamā'*) among themselves',[707] while He [also] said '[God] is Compassionate (*Raḥīm*) towards the believers' –[708] *al-Raḥīm* [as a divine name] applying specifically to the believers.

Amongst the scholars are those who espouse the idea that *al-Raḥīm* is more intensive than *al-Raḥmān* insofar as His mercy is in fact specified for the believers. God (Exalted is He) said: 'Say: Who has forbidden the beauty of God which He has produced for His servants, and the goodly things by way of provision? Say: They are for those who are believers within the life of the herebelow, theirs alone on the Day of Resurrection!'[709] He (Exalted is He) said, as a quotation of Abraham (upon him be peace): '"[My Lord] provide fruits for whomever amongst [this city's] people believes in God and the Last Day." [God] said:[710] "And whoever disbelieves – I indulge him a little, then I force him into the punishment of hellfire."'[711]

We have reported on the authority of a group of exegetes that *al-Raḥīm* is specific to the believers, it being the assertion of Wakīʿ b. al-Jarrāḥ.[712] It is transmitted on the authority of Thaʿlab and it is transmitted on the authority of ʿIkrima[713] that he said: '*Al-Raḥmān* (the Infinitely Merciful) is with a single mercy and *al-Raḥīm* (the Compassionate) is with a hundred mercies.' He simply took this from [the Prophet's] statement (may God 89
bless him and his family): 'God[714] (Exalted is He) has a hundred mercies and sends one of them down to earth and divides it between His creatures. In regard to it they are tender towards one another and are loving towards one another. And He holds back ninety-nine for Himself to give mercy thereby to His servants on the Day of Resurrection!'[715]

Amongst the scholars are those who say: He only combines the two words *al-Raḥmān al-Raḥīm*, insofar as *al-Raḥmān* is a name which the languages of the people of both scriptures share – they used to say '*Raḥmānan*'. The polytheists of Mecca used to reject this name, as He reports about them, for He says (Exalted is He): 'When it is said to them "prostrate to *al-Raḥmān*" they say "What is *al-Raḥmān*?"'[716] And He says: 'And they disbelieve in *al-Raḥmān*.'[717] [Yet] they used to acknowledge *al-Raḥīm*, so He combines the two of them. Another group say: '*Al-Raḥmān* is Hebrew, and because of this the Arabs denied it. He combined the two names for that reason.' This is incorrect, for the Qur'ān was only sent down in the language of the Arabs, and other than their language is not in it. *Al-Raḥmān* has been found in the speech of the Arabs, like *al-lahfān* ('the very sad'), *al-ghaḍbān* ('the furious') and *al-nadmān* ('the rueful'). Al-Shanfarā said:

Has not this lass beaten her racing camel?
Has not my Lord *al-Raḥmān* severed (*qaṭaʿa*) her right hand?[718]

The Arabs used to say: 'There is no *Raḥmān* save the *Raḥmān* of the Yamāma tribe!', meaning 'of Musaylima, the Liar', so God (Exalted is He) said: 'And they disbelieve in *al-Raḥmān*'.[719] Next, mercy (*raḥma*) is in two senses. The first of them is the *will* to give grace, and the second is the grace itself. So when it is said 'He is eternally *Raḥīm* and *Raḥmān*', its meaning is the superabundance of graces, and when it is said 'May God mercy (*raḥima*) X', its meaning is 'May God give grace to him'. He (Exalted is He) has said: 'Is it they who apportion the mercy (*raḥma*) of your Lord?'[720] i.e. the grace of your Lord. *Al-Raḥmān* is He who assumes responsibility for His servants[721] with sufficiency, provision and safekeeping. For the initial establishing of [His creatures] is through His mercy, as is their perpetuation. And *al-Raḥīm* is He who assumes responsibility for His *righteous* servants, through attentiveness, loving-kindness and bounty. For the initial establishing of *them* [too] is through His mercy, as is their perpetuation. And it could be said: 'O *Raḥmān* of the herebelow and the hereafter, and O *Raḥīm* of the two of them!'[722]

90 Mercy (*raḥma*) in lexicography comes down to tenderheartedness, solicitude, softness and gentleness, and the opposite of it is boorishness and hardheartedness. The *perfection* of [mercy] is action in regard to – [i.e.] forgiving, pardoning, being gracious and being bountiful – [so it] is applied to the Creator (Exalted is He) not regarding the first sense but regarding the second sense.[723] It is analogous to the hermeneutic of whatever is mentioned amongst the attributes ascribed to God (Mighty and Majestic), such as 'reviving', 'satisfaction', 'displeasure', 'anger', 'sorrow', 'joy', 'longing', 'laughter', and whatever is comparable with that.

Ibn al-Mubārak[724] said: *Al-Raḥmān* is He who when asked bestows and when not asked is angered. He chanted:

God is angered if you neglect to ask Him
But the little son of Adam is angered when you ask him!

It has been said: The name *Allāh* refers to the fact that He (Exalted is He) is the refuge of creatures who are in need of Him for establishing their existence; the name *al-Raḥmān* refers to the fact that He (Exalted is He) is the sanctuary of creatures who are in need of Him for perpetuating their existence; and the name *al-Raḥīm* refers to the fact that He (Exalted is He) is the place of asylum for the elect amongst His servants who take refuge in Him in hardships, and they put their trust in Him in all situations. The harmonious order of the three names will follow, in discussing the arcana.

Statement on the arcana of the order of the words in the formula *Bi'smi'llāh al-Raḥmān al-Raḥīm* ('In the name of God, the Infinitely Merciful, the Compassionate')

The exegetes talk about the meanings of the words and terms on the basis of lexicography and transmitted tradition; they do not discuss their arcana in regard to harmonious order and sequence, and on account of what [particular] idea the verse of the formula 'In the name of God [...]' is allotted *these* names and not other names, what is the arcanum involved in putting the name of *Allāh* in front of the name *al-Raḥmān* and of putting the name *al-Raḥmān* in front of the name *al-Raḥīm*. Who is it who has the ability to comprehend these arcana without guidance from the people of the Qur'ān, who are the people of God and His elect (peace be upon them), or [who] has the audacity to bring them up in books without permission and authorisation from them? However, since I am specified by the transmitted
prayer 'O God, benefit us by that which You teach us, and teach us that by 91
which You benefit us, by the truth of the chosen ones amongst Your servants', I found in myself the faculty of being guided to the word of prophecy and I understood the language of the divine message, so I was thereby rightly guided to the arcana of words in the glorious Qur'ān without my doing exegesis of the Qur'ān by my personal opinion. I take refuge with God, the Hearer, the Knower, from the stoned Satan, so that there may not occur in my thought, neither flow from my pen that by which I would take my place in hellfire.[725] May God (Mighty and Majestic) grant refuge from hellfire and its blazing, and may He protect us from swerving and slipping up in the hermeneutic of the verses of the Qur'ān and their exegesis!

The people of the Qur'ān said: '*Bi'smi'llāh al-Raḥmān al-Raḥīm*' is a verse sent down like the rest of the verses. It is definitely part of the Exordium, it is the first verse with which the Primordial Pen (*al-qalam al-*

awwal) flowed, the first verse with which Gabriel came down to the Chosen One, Muḥammad (God's blessings upon them both), in the chapter: 'Recite, in the name of your Lord',[726] or 'O you who are enwrapped!'[727] or the Exordium[728] (according to the variation in transmitted reports), the first verse which [the Prophet] taught Khadīja and the People of his House (peace be upon them) and the first verse which he recited in the formal prayer and uttered aloud. The proof of that is the authentic reports which we have transmitted and the mighty arcana which we are presently occupied with mentioning. The community have agreed by consensus on the fact that the Exordium is seven verses and most of [the community have agreed] on the fact that it is the Seven Doubled Ones. Whoever said that (the 'In the name of God' formula) is *not* part of the Exordium and have considered [the words] 'on whom You have bestowed grace' (*an'amta 'alayhim*) as the end of the sixth verse,[729] consider you then the verse endings: how they find their phonological harmonisation (*insiyāq*) with respect to the verbal expression. You will be in no doubt that they consist in a *kasra* ('i'), then after it a vowelless *yā'* (= y), and after it a pause [i.e. a consonant whose vowel is not pronounced due to the rules of recitation], namely: *-ḥīm* [in *al-Raḥīm*], *-mīn* [in *'ālamīn*], *dīn* [in *mālik yawm al-dīn*], *-'īn* [in *nasta'īn*], *-qīm* [in *mustaqīm*], and *-līn* [in *ḍāllīn*]. So were you to say '*an'amta 'alayhim*[730] is the end of a verse', you have eliminated the successive phonological harmony at the end of the verses and you have introduced among them what does not correspond with them as a verbal expression. On the other hand, pausing on *'alayhim* is incorrect, for the pauses in the Exordium, by the consensus of the reciters, are four – and they do not allow for the pause on *'alayhim*. Thus the disparity in phonological harmony and the impermissibility of pausing *both* prove the fact that *'alayhim* is not the end of the sixth verse. These consist in indications which cause mere opinion to be overcome and which show the way to certainty. As for certainty [itself] in regard to [the 'In the name of God' formula] – it is only hunted down by way of [the verses'] meanings.

92 The people of the Qur'ān who recite it with its true recitation, said: Affairs which have any significance have a beginning, a middle, and a completion – and everything without a beginning has no completion and everything without a completion has no beginning. At all beginnings is recited 'In the name of God [...]'. The Prophet (may God bless him and give him

peace) said: 'Every affair having significance which is not begun with "In the name of God" is emasculated (*abtar*)!'[731] And at all completions is recited 'Praise belongs to God', [for] He (Exalted is He) said: 'The closure of their prayer is "Praise belongs to God, the Lord of the Worlds".'[732]

Beginnings are driven forward to completions by both the general and the specific mercy within [the 'In the name of God ...' formula], to the middle parts.[733] Next, the general infinite mercifulness flanks 'In the name of God', it being at beginnings; and the specific compassionateness flanks 'Praise belongs to God, the Lord of the Worlds', it being at completions. Generality with beginnings is more fitting and specificity with completions is more proper. So were 'In the name of God, the Infinitely Merciful, the Compassionate' not a verse of the Exordium, the Exordium would not be complete, instead it would be an emasculated chapter. Yet it is indeed amongst 'affairs having significance' (and *what* a significance!) and having a completion (and what a completion!).[734]

What is transmitted – 'Every affair having significance which is not begun with the praise of God is emasculated (*abtar*)'[735] – is an *in*authentic report, praise being recited at the culmination of receiving grace, just as the name *Allāh* is recited over that *through which* is the grace. Do not all undertakings and works begin with 'In the name of God [...]' and end with 'Praise belongs to God'?

Another arcanum in regard to the Doubled Ones which will be [fully] explained to you at the [very] end of the exegesis on the chapter [of the Exordium] is that the Doubled Ones are in the Exordium itself and that they are seven reprises [*mardūdāt* = echoes] of ideas – verbally and semantically.

The first Doubled One amongst them is 'In the name of God' (*bi'smi'llāh*) and 'Praise belongs to God' (*al-ḥamdu li'llāh*). The two of them are sequential in regard to verbal expression, and in regard to the meaning – as we explained – they are concordant. For 'In the name of God' is at beginnings and 'Praise belongs to God' is at completions.

The second Doubled One is two mercies which are between beginnings and completions: a general mercy inclusive of all existents, without any distinction between one existent and another, that being because He is generous (*jawād*); and a specific mercy which specifies *some* existents in line with
the distinction between one existent and another, that being because He is 93
noble-hearted (*karīm*). For were there not the generality of His mercy, the

beginnings would not get under way, orientated towards the completions; and were there not the specificity of His mercy, the completions would not be consonant with the beginnings. God (Exalted is He) said: 'My mercy encompasses everything',[736] (this) being an allusion to the generality of mercy for creatures, both the godly amongst them and the sinful amongst them. And He said: 'I will stipulate it for those who are God-conscious and give the poor-due and those who believe in Our signs',[737] (this) being an allusion to the specificity of mercy for the godly and not the sinful amongst them, and for the believer amongst them, not the unbeliever amongst them. You have understood the principle of generality and specificity in the introductions to the science of the Qur'ān.[738] So the general and the specific in consequence, are another Doubled One. The rest of the Doubled Ones will follow presently, God willing.

Another arcanum is that 'the worlds' may be enumerated in the sequence of their relation with the Creator (Exalted is He) as three: the world of creation, the world of the Command, and the world of merit (*thawāb*). Next, the three worlds are determined in line with the three [divine] names. Thus, godhead (*ilāhiyya*) bestows the idea of creation. God (Exalted is He) says: 'If you ask them who created them, they will surely say "God (*Allāh*)".'[739] The infinite mercifulness (*raḥmāniyya*) bestows the idea of the Command. God (Exalted is He) says: 'When it is said to them "Prostrate to the Infinitely Merciful (*al-Raḥmān*)", they say "What is *al-Raḥmān*? Are we to prostrate to whatever you command us?"'[740] So they do not deny the name *Allāh*, since they do not dispute with [the Prophet] in regard to [the idea of] creation, [but] they do deny the name *al-Raḥmān*, since they dispute with him in regard to the Command: 'they say [...] "Are we to prostrate to whatever you command us?" And it increases them in aversion.'[741] [Finally] the compassionateness (*raḥīmiyyah*) bestows the idea of merit. God (Exalted is He) said: 'He is compassionate towards the believers. Their greeting on the day they will meet Him is "Peace!" and He has made ready for them a bountiful reward.'[742]

Then the first is a creation and origination *ex nihilo*, next is a commissioning and command, and next is a reward and merit. Like that is the hierarchy in the three names: the first is *Allāh*, the second is *al-Raḥmān*, and the third is *al-Raḥīm*. And unless the bestowal of grace precedes, gratitude would be unnecessary, thus the mention of grace and mercy precedes, and praise and gratitude follows on from it.[743] This is a proof that the 'In the name of God [...]' formula is part of the chapter for sure and separating the two of them is in no way permitted.

Another arcanum is that 'God (Exalted is He) manifests Himself to His servants through His scripture' [which] is amongst the words of al-Ṣādiq, Jaʿfar b. Muḥammad (may God's good pleasure and peace be upon them both). And just as He manifests Himself through His scripture, He manifests Himself through His exalted names to those who are singled out, consisting in His friends, such that the godhead (*ilāhiyya*) in self-manifestation
(*tajallī*) is to *one* of His saints, the infinite mercifulness (*raḥmāniyya*) is to 94
another, and the compassionateness (*raḥīmiyya*) is to another – and all three may be combined for another. Wherever you find in the Qur'ān a verbal expression for whatever is linked to one of [these] divine names, it is for the sake of disclosing [God] (*taʿrīf*), every disclosing being [God's own] *self*-disclosure (*taʿarruf*) to something, and every self-disclosure being an epiphany of His (*tajallin lahu*) – and the epiphany might be general and it might be specific.

His statement (Exalted is He) that 'Your Lord is God (*Allāh*), who created the heavens and the earth'[744] is a general self-disclosure; and His statement (Exalted is He), 'My protector is God (*Allāh*), who sent down the Scripture, He befriends the righteous'[745] is a particular self-disclosure. So the epiphany occurs through these three names to the three worlds so that they come into being and exist, and [also] to the three individuals, i.e. the prophets, the truthful ones and the martyrs, such that they subsist through them, they are in the right on the basis of them, and they take refuge in them. As for the harmonious order of the words and the letters in respect of the verbal expression, the hierarchy of one of them after another, the patent inimitability from the point of view of the balance of the anterior and posterior elements,[746] and the wisdom in the numbers of the words (why they are four) and the numbers of the letters (why they are nineteen) – 'this is not our nest, so let us go our way!'[747] since it is amongst the sciences particular to the prophets and the friends of God (upon them be peace). However, we are given to understand that if we consider the verses with *their* guidance, we see the harmonious order comprising hidden meanings, and if we regard the words with *their* hinting, we see the harmonious order as comprising buried arcana, and we turn our gaze from them to the letters, understanding that they too are not without other arcana, and that they equate – in respect of number – with their analogues amongst existents. [We also understand] that since they were the first of what was written by the Primordial Pen upon the Guarded Tablet, they are the very foundations of existents. From the light of every letter amongst them arises an existent in the higher and lower worlds. They are that which unlocks the unseen and the keys of the heavens and the earth and they are the celestial letters and the intelligible end-points which none knows save He, blessed be God, the Lord of the Worlds!

95 Statement on the exegesis of: *Al-ḥamdu li'llāh* ('praise belongs to God')

Exegesis and lexicography

Some of the exegetes said: It is the beginning of a eulogy and a praising with which God (Exalted is He) extols Himself as a magnification of His majesty, and as an instruction for His worshippers so that when they praise Him they say 'Praise belongs to God'. Some of them said: It involves the ellipsis of a verb, so its meaning is '*Say*: "Praise belongs to God".' For the outward expression of it is the predicate of a nominal sentence,[748] while the *meaning* of it is an imperative. This is the statement of al-Kisāʾī and it is transmitted on the authority of Ibn ʿAbbās likewise. It is said: The ellipted statement at the beginning of the chapter is detatched from 'Praise belongs to God'.

As for the *alif* and the *lām* in it[749] – [it is] due to the universal inclusion of the genus [of 'praise'],[750] and it may be due to familiar acquaintance.[751] The *lām* in His statement '*li'llāh*',[752] stands for the genitive and so it could be for declaring possession, in line with the fact that He is the possessor of praise. It could also be for distinction and entitlement, like it is said: 'The gate belongs to the house.'

Next, 'praise' (*ḥamd*) has two meanings. The first of them is 'thanks' and the second is 'eulogy' and 'laudation'. So, if it is in return for gracious favour, its meaning is 'thanks' and if it is for an excellent quality and a virtue, it is in the sense of 'eulogy'. It is said 'I praise X for his gracious favour' (i.e. I thank him), and 'I praise X for his heroism' (i.e. I eulogise him).

In the book of al-Khalīl is:[753] Praise (*ḥamd*), being fine eulogy, is the antonym of derision (*hijāʾ*), and laudation (*madḥ*) is the antonym of blaming (*dhamm*). Al-Akhfash said:[754] The praise of God is the eulogising of Him and thanks for His gracious favours. It is said, 'X purchases praise with his property', i.e. [he purchases] laudation. And it is said to a man, 'Never praise someone so you put him to the test!' i.e. never laud him.

He (Exalted is He) said: 'Say: Praise belongs to God, Who has not taken any son',[755] i.e. eulogy[756] is God's due because of that. In the Prophetic Tradition is: 'Nothing is more dear to God than praise, and because of that He eulogises *Himself*, so He says "Praise belongs to God".'[757] In the formal prayer we say: 'O Our Lord! To You belongs praise, as worthy of eulogy and glory.'[758] Thus 'praise' (*ḥamd*) conveys the idea of 'thanks' (*shukr*) as a whole, while 'thanks' does *not* convey the idea of 'praise' as a whole.[759] So 'praise' (*ḥamd*) is a noun applied in common to the genus 'eulogy' (*thanāʾ*)[760] and 'thanks' (*shukr*) in response to some gracious favour as well as for other than that.

Ibn ʿAbbās said in the transmission of ʿAṭāʾ, Abū Ṣāliḥ, al-Ḍaḥḥāk, and 96
Yūsuf b. Mihrān, it being the statement of Muqātil also: The meaning of 'Praise belongs to God' is 'Thanks is God's due', in that He works for His creatures, thus they praise Him, and He is gracious to them so they thank Him.

Al-Ḥakam transmits on the authority of al-Suddī, who said: The first part of this chapter is 'Praise belongs to God', and it is a eulogy for God; the middle part of it is sincerity (*ikhlāṣ*); and the last part of it is requesting God. Al-Ḥasan said: 'Praise' is in the sense of eulogy.

Grammar

The portion of grammar in respect of it is that '*al-ḥamd*' is [nominative, hence is] pronounced with a final 'u' [= *al-ḥamdu*] because of coming at the beginning; and '*Allāh*' is pronounced with the vowel 'i' because of the governing *lām* with 'i' [= *li'llāhi*].

Arcana

The people of the Qurʾān said that God (Exalted is He) has majesty and bounty.[761] So through His majesty He is entitled to eulogy and through His bounty He is entitled to thanks. The *alif* and the *lām* (= *al-*) are due to the universal inclusion of the genus 'eulogy' and the genus 'thanks' as [properly] belonging to God, Who is 'possessor of majesty and bounty'.[762] He is veiled from them through His majesty, so they may not perceive Him, and He manifests Himself to them through His bounty, so they may not deny Him.

His statement (Mighty and Majestic): *Rabbi'l-ʿālamīn* ('the Lord of the Worlds')

Harmonious order [and vowelling]

Since He mentioned thanks, He mentioned after it what necessitates praise and thanks, so He said: 'The Lord of the Worlds', this being the reason for the order between it and what is before it. *Rabb* ('Lord') is vowelled with 'i' because it is an attribution belonging to God,[763] and *al-ʿālamīn* ('of the Worlds') instead is with 'i' because of the genitive.

Lexicography

Rabb (lord) has two meanings. The first of them is: Someone 'lorded' (*rabba*) something if he instructed (*rabbā*) it, improved it, and perfected it. He 'lorded' (*rabba*) his estate if he took care of it. Al-Aṣmāʿī said this. The second is: Someone 'lorded' something if he possessed it, so he is its 'lord' (*rabb*), i.e. its possessor (*mālik*). Al-Jawharī said: 'I lorded (*rababtu*) the people' means 'I governed them, and I was placed over them'. He said: It is from *rubūbiyya* (lordship). And X 'lorded' his son, he lords him with a lording (*yarubbuhu rabban*) and he raised him (*rabbabahu*)[764] in the sense
97 that he instructed him,[765] *al-marbūb* ('the lorded') being in the sense of *al-murabbā* ('the one instructed', 'raised', or 'educated').[766]

Others said: 'I educated (*rabbaytu*) the lad, I educated him with an education (*tarbiyatan*)', when you put his affairs in order and took care of him; *rabbabtuhu tarbiyatan* ('I educated him an educating') being similar to that.[767]

It is said 'X lorded (*rabba*) in a place' and *arabba* i.e. 'he lived[768] in it', so he is the 'inhabitant' (*rābb*) and the 'dweller' (*muribb*). *Al-Rabb* ('the Lord') is amongst the names of God (Exalted is He), and expresses all of these meanings. For He is the One who educates (*murabbī*), the Creator, the Master, the Ruler, and the One who concerns Himself with [His creatures'] affairs. 'The lord' is not predicated of anyone whatsoever, unless he is in a possessive relation with something. It is said 'the lord *of the slave*' and 'the lord *of the house*'. The designation of the master who is obeyed as '*rabb*' (lord), has been mentioned in the language of the Arabs. Al-Aʿshā said:

> We destroyed one day the lord (*rabb*) of Kinda and his son,
> And the lord (*rabb*) of Maʿadd – between a deep valley and a cypress tree.[769]

In the story of Ḥunayn when the companions of God's Messenger were put to flight, a man said: 'Now sorcery has come to nought!' Ṣafwān b. Umayya said 'Get you to your grave![770] A lord (*rabb*) of Quraysh is more dear to me than a lord of Hawāzin!'[771]

As for the exegesis of *al-ʿālamūn* ('the worlds') – it is the plural of *ʿālam* (world). There is no collective singular for *al-ʿālam* in its expression, like *al-rahṭ* (group), *al-jaysh* (army), *al-qawm* (people) and the like. Its etymological derivation is in two ways. The first of them is that it is from *ʿilm* (knowledge), so it is the noun for what is perceived and is known. The second is that it is from *al-ʿalam* (sign) and *al-ʿalāma* (emblem), meaning 'indication'. So ['the worlds'] are an indication of the Creator.[772]

The first way is the statement of al-Farrāʾ, Abū ʿUbayda, Abū Muʿādh al-Naḥwī,[773] al-Naḍr b. Shumayl and Abū'l-Haytham. Al-Naḍr said: It is a noun for the numerous plurality. Abū Muʿādh al-Naḥwī said: It is humanity.[774] Abū'l-Haytham said: It is the noun for *jinn* and men. Al-Farrāʾ and Abū ʿUbayda said: It is a noun for what is endowed with intellect,[775] they being four: angels, men, jinn and demons.

The second way is the statement of Ibn Fāris, the author of *al-Mujmal*. He said: [The worlds (*al-ʿālamūn*) are] each genus of the creation, for each is, in itself, a guidepost (*maʿlam*) and a sign (*ʿalam*).[776] He mentioned this in the *Kitāb al-Maqāyīs*. He said: And one group said the world is termed 98
ʿālam because of their being treated collectively [within it], so He is 'the Lord of the Worlds (*ʿālamīn*)', meaning 'the Lord of created beings as a whole'.

Al-Jawharī said in *al-Ṣiḥāḥ*: *Al-ʿālam* is creation and the plural is *ʿawālim*, and *al-ʿālamūn* (the worlds) are the kinds of created being.[777]

Exegesis

What the exegetes say goes back to these two same ways. Al-Rabīʿ b. Anas transmitted on the authority of Shahr b. Ḥawshab, on the authority of Ubayy b. Kaʿb who said: The worlds are the angels, they being eighteen thousand angels within the bounds of the herebelow. With every angel are helpers, whose number none knows save God, and over and above them is an earth white as marble, the breadth of which is a forty day journey of the sun – and none knows its length save God – full of angels. He said: They are spiritual beings and they are 'the worlds' whose upper limit is the Bearers of the Throne.

Ibn ʿAbbās said in the transmission of Saʿīd b. Jubayr, ʿIkrima, and ʿAṭiyya, in regard to His statement 'the Lord of the Worlds': They are jinn and human beings.[778]

Abū ʿAmr b. al-ʿAlāʾ said: 'They are the spiritual beings', this being the transmission of al-Kalbī on the authority of Ibn ʿAbbās. Qatāda, Mujāhid and al-Ḥasan said in one of the two transmissions: 'The worlds are the totality of created beings', this being the statement of Abū Rawq and al-Ḍaḥḥāk, and the transmission of ʿAṭāʾ and al-Ḍaḥḥāk on the authority of Ibn ʿAbbās, and the choice of Abū Isḥāq and Abū ʿUbayd. They justified themselves using His statement (Exalted is He): 'Pharaoh said "What is the Lord of the Worlds?" [Moses] said "The Lord of the heavens and the earth, and what is between the two!"'[779] This is the more accurate, since it is the exegesis of Moses [himself] (upon him be peace).

ʿAmr transmitted on the authority of al-Ḥasan: He means thereby the world at every moment, since there is a [new] world for every moment. This is [also] the choice of al-Qaffāl, for he said: What is intended by 'the worlds' here is the ranks of created beings, and what every moment of theirs combines together, consisting of human beings and jinn, whoever is past of them,[780] whoever is yet to come, and whoever [now] exists – till the Day of Resurrection. Al-ʿAjjāj said:[781] 'The Khindif tribe is the crown of this world',[782] only meaning [by 'world'] whichever human beings there were in their epoch.

99 Ibn ʿAbbās said: 'The Lord of the Worlds' is the master of what He created and its God.[783] Saʿīd b. al-Musayyib said: God (Exalted is He) has a thousand 'worlds',[784] six hundred in the ocean and four hundred on dry land.[785] Al-Ḍaḥḥāk said: Amongst them are three hundred and sixty 'worlds'[786] barefoot and naked, not knowing who their Creator is, and forty wearing garments. Wahb b. Munabbih said: God (Exalted is He) has eighteen thousand worlds, and the earth (*al-dunyā*) is just one one of them. Abū'l-ʿĀliya said: Jinn and human beings are one of the 'worlds'. Abū Saʿīd al-Khudrī said: God (Mighty and Majestic) has forty thousand worlds. The earth (*al-dunyā*) is just one of them. Muqātil b. Ḥayyān said: God (Exalted is He) has eighty thousand worlds, forty thousand in the ocean and forty thousand on dry land. Kaʿb said: No one may number the worlds except God (Mighty and Majestic).

Arcana

The people of the Qur'ān, the people of God and His elect, said: Neither neglect the generalities (*'umūmāt*) of the Qur'ān nor its specificities (*khuṣūṣāt*), for in everything which is in a genitive relation with the Lord (Exalted is He) as an act, a statement, a creation or a command, there is a specificity and a generality. In the case of each of the names of God (Exalted is He) which is in a possessive relation with everything in His creation in general, there is also a specificity of possessive relation with one of His creation. Acquaint yourselves with the arcanum in His statement (Exalted is He), as a quotation of Pharaoh's sorcerers: 'We believe in the Lord of the Worlds, the Lord of Moses and Aaron',[787] and in His statement (Exalted is He): 'My mercy encompasses everything, and I will stipulate it for those who are God-conscious' [upto the end of] the verse.[788] So the possessive relation of lordship with 'the worlds' in their entirety,[789] is conditional upon its possessive relation with a specific people, or with a specific individual, such that the whole world is contained within him and belongs to him and *is* him!

Next, the procedure for juxtaposing (*al-naẓar bayna*) 'Praise belongs to God' and 'the Lord of the Worlds, the Infinitely Merciful, the Compassionate, the Ruler of the Day of Judgement', is that since He (Exalted is He) mentioned 'praise' in the sense of eulogy (*thanā'*) and thanks (*shukr*) to God, He mentioned after it that for which He merits eulogy and thanks, consisting in the education of the 'worlds',[790] the mercy upon them both generally and specifically, and also kingship (*mulk*) of the Day of Judgement, [in the sense of it being] His property (*milk*) and His dominion (*mulk*).

Just as '*bismi'llāh al-Raḥmān al-Raḥīm*' ('In the name of God, the Infinitely Merciful, the Compassionate') and '*al-ḥamdu li'llāhi Rabbi'l-'ālamīn*' ('Praise belongs to God, the Lord of the Worlds') correspond with one another in pronunciation, and complement each other in regard to
beginnings and completions, inceptions and outcomes, the two of them 100
being the first Doubled One; and between the two of them are two mercies joining beginnings to completions: a general mercy and a special mercy, they being the second Doubled One; likewise '*Rabbi'l-'ālamīn*' ('the Lord of the Worlds') and '*māliki yawmi'l-dīn*' ('Ruler of the Day of Judgement') correspond with one another in pronunciation and complement each other in beginning and completion, the creation and the Command, dominion

and property,[791] the corporeal and the spiritual, the current life and the afterlife, the two of them being the third Doubled One. And between the two of them are two [other] mercies,[792] joining beginnings to completions, combining the creation and the Command, acting freely in regard to God's dominion and property, overmastering the corporeal and the spiritual, expressing the current life and the afterlife, the two of them being the fourth Doubled One.

To Him belongs praise in the current life *and* the afterlife! For [on the one hand] the two mercies in the formula 'In the name of God [...]' are affirmed for the beginnings of things and their completions, outstripping the sources to reach manifest phenomena. And [on the other hand] the two mercies in regard to the laudation, coming between 'the Lord of the Worlds' and 'Ruler of the Day of Judgement', are affirmed for the creation and the Command, outstripping corporeal things to reach spiritual things, forming a link between the herebelow and the hereafter, and the two of them convey another idea – different from the idea in the formula 'In the name of God [...]'. This is the utility in their repetition.

His statement (Majestic and Mighty): *Māliki yawmi'l-dīn* ('the Ruler of the Day of Judgement')

[Vowelling]

A group of the Qur'ān reciters recited with the *alif*,[793] saying: This is the recitation of the Prophet (may God bless him and his family), and of the rightly-guiding Caliphs, of Ṭalḥa and Zubayr, of Saʿd, ʿAbd al-Raḥmān b. ʿAwf, Ibn Masʿūd, Ibn ʿAbbās, Muʿādh, Ubayy b. Kaʿb, Abū Dharr, Anas, and Abū Hurayra, and amongst the successors and *their* followers a large group [recited like this], and ʿĀṣim, ʿĪsā b. ʿUmar, al-Kisāʾī, Khalaf, al-Ḥasan, Yaʿqūb, Abū ʿUbayda, and al-Akhfash. [Next] a group recited it without the *alif* and [with] the 'i' of the *lām* and the 'i' of the *kāf*,[794] in line with the *nomen adjectivum*, that being the recitation of the Prophet (may God bless him and his family), ʿUthmān, ʿAlī, Zayd b. Thābit, Ibn ʿUmar, Shayba, Nāfiʿ, Mujāhid, Ibn Kathīr, Ibn Muḥayṣin,[795] Ḥumayd, Yaḥyā b. Waththāb, Ḥamza, Abū ʿAmr and Ibn ʿĀmir. Umm Salama transmitted on the authority of the Messenger of God likewise (may God bless him and his family).

It is also recited '*Mālika yawmi'l-dīn*' and '*malika*', with the pronuncia- 101
tion of the *kāf* with final 'a' in line with the vocative, that being the recitation of A'mash and 'Aṭiyya b. Qays. It has also been recited with the pronunciation of the *kāf* with final 'u' in line with the nominative.

Lexicography

As for the difference between *mālik* and *malik* – it is said that there is *no* difference between the two, they being two expressions like *fārih* and *farih* (lively), *fākih* and *fakih* (humorous) and the like of them. Abū 'Ubayda, al-Akhfash, al-Aṣma'ī, Abū Ḥātim and Abū'l-Haytham said: *Mālik* is more extensive and expressive in laudation. It is said 'God is the *mālik* (= ruler) of everything';[796] and it is not said 'the *malik* (= king) of everything', it only being said 'the *Malik* of humanity', 'the *Malik* of the Day of Judgement'. One is not a *mālik* (ruler) of something without exercising power over it, while one might be the *malik* (king) of something without exercising power over it, as it might be said 'the king of the Arabs and the Persians'.[797]

It has also been said: *Mālik* is more expressive in the laudation of the Creator than *malik*, and *malik* is more expressive in the laudation of created beings than *mālik*, since a creature might be a *mālik* (ruler, possessor) though it is not a *malik* (king). Abū 'Ubayd said: 'What I chose is "*maliki yawmi'l-dīn*", because the chain of transmission for it back to the Prophet was firmer, and those who are the reciters of this amongst the learned class are more numerous.' He (Exalted is He) has said: 'So exalted be God, the True King (*al-Malik al-Ḥaqq*)',[798] 'the Very Holy King (*al-Malik al-Quddūs*)',[799] 'Dominion (*al-mulk*) on that day belongs to God'[800] – *mulk* being the verbal noun of *malik*, none other. And *mulk* holds for the *mālik* (ruler) *and* the *malik* (king). Then they are both linguistically pure and correct terms, and the meaning of them both is 'the Lord' (*al-Rabb*). It is said he exercised/exercises power (*malaka/yamliku*) over the thing as his property (*milk*) so he is a *mālik* (ruler),[801] and he exercised/exercises power (*malaka/yamliku*) over it as his dominion (*mulk*) so he is a *malik* (king).

Exegesis

There are two significations in what I will explain about it. The first of them is that its meaning is power; and the second is that it consists in binding and tying. Al-Mufaḍḍal said: Whoever recites with the *alif* (= '*Mālik*') – the meaning of it is 'the One with power on the Day of Judgement' by way of

possession and dominion (*al-milka wa'l-mulk*); and whoever recites '*Malik*' – the meaning of it is that His is the high authority on the Day of Judgement. [Then] in line with the second signification, the *mālik* of something is whoever binds it to himself; and the *malik* (king) of a people is whoever occupies himself[802] with them and controls their affair, and from this is [the expression] 'I kneaded (*malaktu*) the dough'. So whoever recites '*Mālik*', Abū'l-ʿAbbās says, the meaning of it is 'the One Who rules soundly (*bi'l-iḥkām*) over the Day of Judgment', i.e. He exercises jurisdiction on the
102 Day of Judgement and He presides over its execution. And whoever recites '*Malik*' – its meaning is that He is the king (*malik*) on this day which is the Day of Reckoning and of Requittal, on account of His statement 'Dominion (*al-mulk*) on that day belongs to God',[803] in line with the meaning that no authority continues for anyone, over anyone he has mastery of, in the way that is the case in the herebelow, nor does anyone intercede for anyone except by His permission, nor is anyone capable of passing judgement or giving a verdict between creatures on [that day] except God. The figure of speech in this possessive construction is like someone's statement 'X is the prince of this country', i.e. he is the prince *in* (*fī*) this country – and the implication is He is the King on the Day of Judgement.

It is said: In His statement (Exalted is He) 'the Lord of the Worlds' there is an allusion to the dominion of the herebelow and what it contains, and in His statement 'the King of the Day of Judgement' there is an allusion to the fact that He is King in the hereafter. So for this reason the Day of Judgement is characterised by [being a] possession (*milk*) and dominion (*mulk*). What is intended by 'the Day' is the time at which reckoning and requital takes place. The 'Day of Judgement' is the Day of Resurrection. God (Exalted is He) says: 'They will roast in it on the Day of Judgement (*al-dīn*)',[804] *dīn* being reckoning and requital. God (Exalted is He) says: 'Verily, the Judgement (*dīn*) will surely take place',[805] and He says 'That is the right judgement (*al-dīn al-qayyim*)',[806] i.e. sound reckoning. In the proverb is 'As you judge (*tadīnu*), you are judged (*tudānu*)',[807] i.e. just as you do, you are repaid, and as you repay, you are repaid. Khālid b. Nawfal said:[808]

Understand and be certain that your domain is transient
And understand that as you judge (*tadīnu*), so you are judged (*tudānu*).

Qatāda said: It means a day when God passes judgement (*yadīnu*) on creatures for their acts. Abū Rawq transmitted on the authority of al-

Ḍaḥḥāk, on the authority of Ibn ʿAbbās (may God be pleased with him), who said: On that day, no one is capable of jurisdiction (*ḥukm*) as is their prerogative (*milk*) in the herebelow. He said: The Day of Judgement is the day of reckoning for created beings and it is the Day of Resurrection. He will pass judgement on them for their acts. And this is the statement of ʿAṭāʾ on the authority of Ibn ʿAbbās (may God be pleased with him) and the statement of Saʿīd b. Jubayr and al-Ḥasan, and the choice of Abū ʿUbayd. Ibn ʿAbbās, al-Suddī and Muqātil said: The meaning [of 'Master of the Day of Judgement'] is 'the Judge of the Day of Reckoning'. Mujāhid said the like of that.

Al-Kalbī said on the authority of Ibn ʿAbbās: *Dīn* is giving a verdict and jurisdiction.[809] God (Exalted is He) said: 'Do not let tender-heartedness for them seize you in [executing] the judgement of God (*dīn Allāh*)',[810] i.e. in
regard to God's jurisdiction. God (Exalted is He) said: '[Joseph] could not 103
take his brother in the king's *dīn*',[811] i.e. in his jurisdiction. It is said of the [divine] Judge (*al-Ḥākim*), [that He is] '*Dayyān*'.[812] The meaning is: none is capable of jurisdiction and giving a verdict on that day, other than Him.

Semantics

Al-Farrāʾ said: It is said 'tribe X rendered homage (*dāna*) to Y', i.e. they obeyed him; and 'I subjugated/subjugate (*dintu/adīnu*) the people', i.e. 'I conquered them, so they rendered homage (*dānū*)', i.e. they obeyed and were humble towards him. 'The *dīn* belongs to God',[813] is simply from this. The *dīn* of a man is his character, his action, his obedience and his customary behaviour. Al-Quraẓī said:[814] Ruler on a day on which nothing is of use except '*dīn*', i.e. obedience, action, and compliance.

Arcana

The people of the Qurʾān, by whom its verses are mastered and by whom they are explained in detail, said: To God (Exalted is He) belong the creation and the Command,[815] and His are the origination and the return, and His are possession and dominion. 'King' (*malik*) is a name taking in all the attributes of majesty and perfection, implying the idea of commanding, of exercising judgement, and giving a verdict; and since '*dīn*' is a word taking in [the idea of] obedience, acting on His command, compliance with His judgement and submission to His verdict, the word '*al-Malik*' is put in a possessive relation with '*yawm al-dīn*'.

God (Exalted is He) said: 'What is it that would make you grasp what the Day of Judgement is? Again, what is it that would make you grasp what the Day of Judgement is? A day when no soul will be able to do anything for another soul and the Command that day is God's!'[816] He also said: 'True dominion (*mulk*) that day belongs to the Infinitely Merciful.'[817] Thus the name 'the Lord of the Worlds' conveys the idea of creation, and the name 'King of the Day of Judgement' conveys the idea of the Command. So all things which pertain to creation are His realm of omnipotence (*jabarūt*), they being more appropriate to bodies; and all things pertaining to the Command are His realm of sovereignty (*malakūt*), they being more appropriate to spirits. Thus all things pertaining to creation are His dominion (*mulk*)[818] and all things pertaining to the Command are His possession (*milk*).

Al-Ṣādiq Abū ʿAbd Allāh Jaʿfar, b. Muḥammad [al-Bāqir] (God's good pleasure and peace be upon them both) said: The spirits are His possession (*milk*) and the bodies are His dominion (*mulk*). So He causes His possession to occupy His dominion, and He has stipulations for *them* while *they* have a promise on His part. Thus if they fulfil His stipulations, He fulfils His promise to them.

He said (peace be upon him): God (Exalted is He) founded His religion after the model of His creation, so that one might infer His religion from His creation, and His uniqueness[819] from His religion.

104 For there is no existent in the world which He has either created out of something or which He has originated *ex nihilo*, without there being an angel from His realm of sovereignty which directs it, and a Word which is its active agent determining it – even the rain drop from the sky falls accompanied by an angel and the mote of dust from the earth rises upwards accompanied by an angel. The two worlds are not adjacent to one another in the manner of material bodies, nor do they combine intimately in the manner of bodies with shape and form. Rather, the two are distinct in idea and in reality. In the same way that a generality and a specificity are applied to the noun 'the Lord' and its possessive relation with 'the worlds', it is entailed that a generality and a specificity similarly apply to the noun 'the Ruler' and its possessive relation with 'the Day of Judgement'.

Just as every specificity, deriving from a generality, reaches a terminus in some determinate individual amongst the things pertaining to creation, likewise every specificity, deriving from a generality, reaches a terminus in some determinate individual amongst the things pertaining to the Command. And just as the Lord (Exalted is He) manifests Himself through the name of lordship [= *Rabb*] to a determinate individual or to two individuals ('the Lord, *Rabb*, of Moses and Aaron')[820] and He manifests Himself by the name of divinity [= *ilāh*] to specific individuals or to a determinate individual ('we worship your god, *ilāh*, and the god of your fathers Abraham, Ishmael and Isaac, as one god'),[821] the uniqueness [of God] being confirmed by this specification and grammatical definition, likewise, the Lord (Exalted is He) manifests Himself through the name of rulership [= *Mālik*] and of kingship [= *Malik*] to a determinate individual or specific individuals. So He said [in general]: 'I take refuge with the Lord of humanity, the King of humanity, the God of humanity';[822] and they are also specified human beings: 'Or do they envy human beings for what God has given them of His bounty?'[823]

Abū Jaʿfar Muḥammad, son of ʿAlī al-Bāqir (God's good pleasure and peace be upon them both) said: 'We [the imams] are human beings and our partisans are the likenesses of human beings, and the rest of humanity are apes!'[824]

God (Mighty and Majestic) has said: 'Then surge down from the place whence humanity surges down.'[825]

The Prophet said: 'Humanity is twofold: the one who knows and the one who learns – and the rest of humanity are dungflies with no good in them!'[826]

In the whole Qur'ān there is no name of God (Exalted is He) put in a possessive relation with specific individuals amongst humanity, apart from these three names: Allāh, the Lord (*Rabb*), and the King (*Malik*). And just as they are in a possessive relation with created beings in general, they are in a possessive relation with human beings specifically.

It has been mentioned in reports that David (peace be upon him) asked 105
God (Mighty and Majestic) that it might be said 'O god of David!' as it is said 'O god of Abraham, Ishmael and Isaac!' Yet [God] did not rule in favour of that. So were there not some hidden arcanum in that, by way of loving-kindness and magnanimity, He would not have differentiated between one person and another in regard to it.

Next, just as He (Exalted is He) manifested Himself through the name of lordship [= *Rabb*] to the descendents gathered from amongst the children of Adam, for He said 'Am I not your Lord [*Rabb*]?'[827] and they confessed, saying 'For sure!' either by the mute language of their state or by the language of the spoken word, likewise He (Exalted is He) manifests Himself through the name of kingship[828] [= *Malik*] to the assembled universe on the Day of Judgement in the hereafter, for He says 'Whose is dominion (*al-mulk*) today?' till they confess, saying 'God's, the One, the Omnipotent!'[829] either by the mute language of their state or by the language of the spoken word.

His statement, Majestic and Mighty: *Iyyāka naʿbudu wa iyyāka nastaʿīn* ('It is You we worship and it is You we ask for help')

Lexicography and grammar

The lexicographers say *iyyā* is a singular pronoun the termination of which changes just as the terminations of [other] pronouns change, and it is a particle of specification. Al-Akhfash said: The *kāf* in [*iyyā-ka*] is not a noun. It is simply for indicating the second person, with the same position as the *kāf* of *dhālika* and the *hā'* and the *yā'* in *iyyāhu* and *iyyāya*.[830] This is the choice of Abū ʿAlī al-Fasawī,[831] who said: It is a noun in a genitive construction with the second person [pronoun], and the *kāf* [= *ka*] is in place of the vowelling with final 'i', through the genitive relation of '*iyyā*' with it. And the totality of it is in place of the vowelling with final 'a',[832] by way of the occurrence of [the action of] the verb to Him – namely, 'worshipping' and 'seeking help'.

The author of The Harmonious Order said: The meaning of '*iyyāka*' is specification. You say *iyyāka aqūlu* ('I'm saying *to you*'), i.e. the statement is specifically for you. Its meaning is: 'I single You out for worship and I single You out for taking refuge in.'

Al-Zajjāj said: *ʿIbāda* (worship) in lexicography is obedience with bowing down. It is said 'a passable (*muʿabbad*) road', i.e. a well-worn one which passers-by have trampled down, so it became the shiny beaten track.

106 Exegesis and semantics

Ibn ʿAbbās said: 'It is You we worship' is [in meaning] 'We declare Your unity, we fear You and we hope for You,[833] O our Lord – and none other'. 'It is You we ask for help' [i.e.] for us to be obedient, and for all our affairs.[834]

This is the transmission of Abū Rawq and al-Ḍaḥḥāk on his authority. He said in another transmission: '(You) we worship' is [in meaning] 'we declare Your unity', and '(You) we ask for help' is 'in order to worship You'.

Mujāhid said: 'We ask for help' is [in meaning] 'we seek the vouchsafement of attaining the execution of worship.' Al-Akhfash said: The worshipper is the monotheist exerting himself.

The authorities in semantics (*ahl al-maʿānī*) said: [The meaning is] 'we bow down to You and we humble ourselves in obedience and glorification, and we ask You for power and to vouchsafe the attainment of this worship and for persevering in it'. *Istiʿāna* (asking for help) is seeking for assistance and for facilitation.[835] It is said '*istaʿantuhu*' ('I asked him for help') and '*istaʿantu bihi*' ('I sought help from him'). Muḥammad b. Jarīr [al-Ṭabarī] said: Its meaning is: '"It is You we worship", none other than You, "and it is You we ask for help" – i.e. we ask for assistance – none other than You.'[836] It is said: He repeated '*iyyāka*' ('it is You') so that it would be more indicative of sincerity and exclusive distinction, just as He (Mighty and Majestic) said, as a quotation of Moses (peace be upon him): 'That we may praise You very much (*kay nusabbiḥaka kathīran*) and remember You very much (*nadhkuraka kathīran*).'[837]

It is said: He simply placed 'worshipping' ahead of 'asking for help' so that it would be more indicative of humility, and the *wāw* ('and') implies association and combining, so the meaning is: '"It is You we ask for help" *in the execution of the worship of You*.' It is also said: '"and it is You we ask for help" for the like of (such) worship in the inchoative (*musta'naf*), and for persevering and enduring in it.'

Arcana [and harmonious order]

The manner of the order between what comes before the two expressions and the two expressions themselves is that just as the Lord (Exalted is He) taught us how to invoke Him with the most exalted names, and He explained to us how to praise Him with the greatest praises, He followed that by mentioning sincerity in worship and seeking help, how to single Him out through declaring divine unity, praise, eulogy, glorification, obedience, and unreserved acceptence (*taslīm*), and how to single Him out through seeking help through Him and asking for the vouchsafement of attainment from Him. For the preceding names suggest the eulogy of Him, gratitude to Him, the worship of Him and seeking help from Him. They are

107 the names of majesty and bounty, mercy, gracious favour, possession (*milk*) and dominion (*mulk*) in the two abodes, and power and omnipotence in the two mansions.[838]

The two phrases are in correspondence and balance with one another in verbal expression and in meaning, they being the fifth Doubled One amongst the seven Doubled Ones. The first expression indicates the acceptance of divine commandment, the acknowledgement of human capacity to act and of acquisition,[839] and implicit in it is the negation of unqualified necessitarianism (*al-jabr al-maḥḍ*). The second expression indicates the reality of predetermination, the seeking of assistance and facilitation, and implicit in it is the negation of unqualified libertarianism (*al-qadar al-maḥḍ*). The principle of 'the commencing' and of the inchoative (*musta'naf*) is involved in the worship and the carrying out thereof, while the principle of the accomplished (*mafrūgh*) and of predestination is involved in seeking help and the need for it.

'Seeking help' might be placed *before* 'worshipping', that being so in the standing supplication (*qunūt*) and the supererogatory supplication (*du'ā*): 'O God, we ask You for help', [coming] firstly, and 'O God, it is You we worship', secondly.[840] And 'worshipping' might [also] be placed *before* 'seeking help', that being in the act of worship and the formal prayer (*ṣalāt*): 'It is You we worship and it is You we ask for help.' [This is] because supplication is turning one's attention to need and the seeking of a response, and worship is turning one's attention to humble adoration and making every effort in obedience. Next, just as He alluded by the first '*iyyāka*' to the fact that worship is for Him (Exalted is He) and is specifically His, for there is nothing worshipped apart from Him, likewise He alluded by the second '*iyyāka*' to the fact that seeking assistance and the vouchsafement of attainment is from Him, for there is no recourse apart from Him.

The whole of the chapter from its beginning upto 'it is You we worship', are items of identification, and the whole of it from ('it is You we worship') upto the end of the chapter are entrustments.[841] In the famous report is: 'I divide the formal prayer between Me and my worshipper into two halves.' In regard to that, when the worshipper says 'It is You we worship and it is You we ask for help', the Lord (Exalted is He) says: 'This is between Me and My worshipper' [upto the end of] the report in its entirety.[842]

Some of the people of allusion said: The *kāf* and the *nūn* are interconnected in the two words. The *kāf*[843] entails direct witnessing (*mushāhada*) since it is a second person pronoun which only belongs to someone present,[844] and the *nūn*[845] entails [our] exertion (*mujāhada*),[846] since it is a verbatim quotation from someone with capacity and power. Just as beings receive light by contact with the *kāf* and the *nūn* upon origination and existentiation,[847] likewise hearts receive light by contact with the *kāf* and the *nūn* upon obedience and unreserved acceptance (*taslīm*).

Some of them said: The name *Allāh* gives the idea of the deservingness of worship. God (Exalted is He) said: 'Worship *Allāh*.'[848] The name *al-* 108
Raḥmān (the All Merciful) gives the idea of the deservingness of being sought for help. God (Exalted is He) said: 'Our Lord is *al-Raḥmān*, the One Sought for help.'[849] The name *al-Raḥīm* (the Compassionate) gives the idea of the deservingness of [being sought for] guidance. God (Exalted is He) said: '[...] a guidance and an act of compassion (*raḥma*) for a people who believe.'[850] So, just as the beginning of the identification [section] is by these three names, likewise the beginning of the entrustment [section] is by these three *ideas*. And God knows best!

His statement, Majestic and Mighty: *Ihdinā'l-ṣirāṭ al-mustaqīm* ('Guide us on the straight path')

Lexicography

The lexicographers said: 'I guided (*hadaytu*) X on the road with a guiding (*hidāya*)', 'I guided him in religion with guidance (*hudan*) and a guiding (*hidāya*)'; 'the guide' (*hādī*) is the one on the right course who points out the road. *Hādī* is the neck, it being called that because it is ahead of the body. The 'heads' (*hawādī*) of horses and and wild animals are the ones which lead the way. Moreover, everything ahead is called *hādī*, even if it is not ahead for pointing out [which way to go] – thus the neck is called *hādī*. *Ihtadā* ('he was guided') is the eighth form from *hudā*. From it is His statement (Exalted is He): 'If they believed in the like of what you believed, they would have been guided (*ihtadaw*)'[851] i.e. they would have recognised their correct course. *Hadaytu la-ka* ('I acted as a guide for you') has the meaning 'I made clear to you'. From it is His statement (Exalted is He): 'Does it not guide them (*yahdi la-hum*)?'[852] i.e. does it not become clear to them? Also His statement (Exalted is He): 'As for Thamūd, We guided them',[853] i.e. We made clear to them.

Some people say: the origin of *hidāya* (guiding) is *iḥāla* (conveying). It is said: 'I conveyed (*hadaytu*) the bride to the house of her husband with a conveying (*hady*)'; 'I conducted (*ahdaytu*) her with a conducting (*ihdā'*)'; 'I presented (*ahdaytu*) a gift (*hadiyya*)'; 'I am giving (*uhdī*) it with a giving (*ihdā'*)'; *hadiyya* is a verbal noun too, and from it is *hadī* [= present, offering].

In the Prophetic Tradition is that the Prophet (may God bless him and his family) came out during his illness in the course of which he died, 'being supported (*yuhādī*) between two men', i.e. he was propped up by them because of his weakness and his staggering along. The [action of] the verb from it extends to two objects, it extending to the second simply through one of the two prepositions, *ilā* (to) and *li-* (to). And the preposition might be ellipted, so it is said *hadaytuhu'l-ṭarīq* ('I guided him to the way'), this being idiomatically purer. It is also said *hadaytu hadya fulān* ('I led along X's course'), if you followed his behaviour.

Al-Mufaḍḍal b. Salama said:[854] His statement 'Guide us' means 'increase us
109 in guidance and direction, and may our hearts not swerve from it after You have guided us to it.' Others said: Guiding, in the Qur'ān, is in line with two significations. [The first is] guiding by summoning and announcing. [This is] like His statement (Exalted is He): 'Does it not guide them?'[855] and His statement: 'Verily, you [Muḥammad] guide unto a straight path.'[856] He said in the description of Satan, 'It is decreed for him that whoever turns to him in friendship he will lead astray and he will guide him to the punishment of the inferno',[857] i.e. he will summon him. The second signification is guiding by vouchsafing attainment and by [actually] establishing,[858] like His statement (Exalted is He) 'He leads astray whom He wills and He guides whom He wills',[859] and like His statement 'God summons to the abode of peace and guides whom He wills',[860] and His statement 'If God willed, He would have guided humanity as a whole',[861] and His statement 'You [Muḥammad] will not be able to guide everyone whom you love, but God guides whomever He wills'[862] – so what is denied for [the Prophet] is guidance by vouchsafing attainment and by the [actual] creation of faith, and what is affirmed for him is guidance by summoning and announcing. So His statement 'Guide us on the straight path' means 'vouchsafe attainment, inspire us, direct us and establish us'. Some of the scholastic theologians said: Its meaning is 'make us travel the path to Paradise and make us approach it', like His statement (Exalted is He) 'He will guide them and improve their condition'.[863]

Exegesis and semantics

They continued to fret over the exegesis of 'Guide us' simply due to an obscurity in it from two points of view. The first of them is that a request can only be for something that the one requesting lacks, and whatever is already present is not sought through requesting. The second is that requesting is only when what is requested is not given; when God (Exalted is He) removes deficiencies by setting up guidelines in regard to actions, He has guided them and freed them from any need to request [guidance]. As for the first, they have replied to it that its meaning is '*confirm* us on Your straight path', and as for the second, they have replied to it in one of two ways: either as vouchsafing attainment and the creation of guidance (that being the way of the Ashʿariyya) or as guidance to the way to Paradise (that being the way of the Muʿtazila). If they comprehended the generalities and specificities of the Qurʾān in its clear and its ambiguous verses they would not proceed haphazardly in its shadows![864] We will come back to this, God willing.

The exegetes say: The 'straight path' is the clear and even road which has no crookedness in it, nor curving, and there is no disagreement in it in word or deed,[865] nor is there any inconsistency in it in regard to negation and affirmation. Next, some of them said it is God's Scripture – that being the claim of ʿAlī, ʿAbd Allāh b. Masʿūd, and Abū'l-ʿĀliya. Jābir b. ʿAbd Allāh, 110
al-Kalbī, Muqātil and ʿAṭāʾ said on the authority of Ibn ʿAbbās: It is Islam. Saʿīd b. Jubayr and al-Suddī said: It is the way to Paradise. ʿĀṣim al-Aḥwal transmitted on the authority of Abū'l-ʿĀliya al-Riyāḥī, that it is the way of God's Messenger and his Companions after him, Abū Bakr and ʿUmar (may God be pleased with them both). ʿĀṣim said: 'We mentioned that to al-Ḥasan, and he said "Abū'l-ʿĀliya has spoken the truth."' Muḥammad b. al-Ḥanafiyya said: It is God's religion other than which He will not accept.

Semantics

Al-Qaffāl said:[866] The meaning is requesting God (Exalted is He) to guide them and direct them to the way in which there are no deviations, nor disagreement, nor inconsistency like the inconsistency in the circumstances of the folk of the two scriptures[867] and the disagreement in the banner of the polytheists. The likening of truth to a path is in regard to the fact that the truth is like a clear, well-trodden road over which are raised signposts and a lighthouse, and it conducts the person adhering to it to the place he is striving for. The truth is just like that – its signposts are clear and its indications are obvious to the one who contemplates them, and it conducts its adherent to correctness and the attainment of reward.

Next He explained 'the straight path', saying (Mighty is the One who speaks): 'The path of those whom You have graciously favoured (*ṣirāṭ alladhīna anʿamta ʿalayhim*).'

[His statement, Mighty and Majestic:] *Ṣirāṭ alladhīna anʿamta ʿalayhim* ('The path of those whom You have graciously favoured')

Exegesis

It means: [the path of those] on whom You have bestowed the vouchsafement of attainment, guidance and correctness in word and deed – they being the prophets and the saints (peace be upon them). They are the ones mentioned in His statement (Exalted is He): 'Whoever obeys God and the Messenger is with those whom God has graciously favoured, consisting in the prophets, the truthful ones, the martyrs and the righteous.'[868] This is the transmission of ʿAṭāʾ and Abū Rawq on the authority of al-Ḍaḥḥāk, on the authority of Ibn ʿAbbās (may God be pleased with him).[869]

Ibn ʿAbbās also said: They are the people of Moses and Jesus (peace be upon them both), prior to their distortion of their scriptures. ʿAbd al-Raḥmān b. Zayd said: They are the Prophet and the believers. ʿIkrima said: '[…] whom You have graciously favoured' with evidences for faith and
111 uprightness. Ubayy b. Kaʿb, al-Wāqidī and al-Ḥasan b. al-Faḍl said the like of that [too]. Muḥammad b. Jarīr [al-Ṭabarī] said: '[…] whom You have graciously favoured' through guidance to the true path, and to whom You have vouchsafed the attainment of proper conduct.

Lexicography and semantics

Niʿma, with the vowelling of the *nūn* with an 'i', is that which God graciously favours the worshipper with, consisting in worldly comforts and religious insights (*maʿārif*). With the vowelling of the *nūn* with an 'a' [= *naʿma*], it is comfortable living and luxury of life. [For example, it is said:] 'He has lived/lives (*naʿima/yanʿamu*)[870] with a luxury of life (*naʿma*), so he is soft (*nāʿim*)'; and 'I graciously favoured him (*anʿamtu ʿalayhi*)[871] with an [act of] favouring (*inʿāman*) and a gracious favour (*niʿma*).'

The religious scholars differed over the reality of *niʿma*, be it in revelation or reason. Some people said: It is unqualified pleasure. Others said: It is pleasure free from the blemishes of any detriment in the present and the future, and in line with this doctrine, God (Exalted is He) has no gracious favour at all upon the unbeliever – neither religious nor worldly, and that which they enjoy is a deception and a lure to destruction. ʿAlī b. al-Ḥusayn al-Wāqidī said: '[…] whom You have graciously favoured' with gratitude for prosperity and with patience in adversity, and this is specific to the believers.

Some of the people of learning said: The 'straight path' is what God mentioned from the beginning of the chapter upto its end, consisting in the mention of the divine names and praises, sincerity in worship and seeking help, asking for guidance on the path of the prophets and saints, and taking refuge from the way of 'those against whom is wrath and those who go astray'.

[Arcana]

Those whom God graciously favoured with guidance said: Just as God (Exalted is He) explained to us how we should praise Him and worship Him, how we should seek His help and place our confidence in Him, likewise He taught us how to make a request in need, which needs are most important and which requests are most perfect. Since guidance is the most important thing of all for the worshipper and the most general of needs in both religion and the world, the hereafter and the present life,[872] He connected this most important and general thing to worship and seeking help. That [then] is the manner of harmonious order (*naẓm*) between the previous verse and the subjoined verse.

Another arcanum is that praises and eulogies for perfection have preceded. Whoever begs out of some need must preface a eulogy and praise to 112
the one needed, just as the one who mentions a praise and eulogy for someone worthy of praise must submit some need to him, so that it becomes clear that the one praised is the end-point of the quest for [fulfilment of] needs and what is with him is the obtainment of desires, and that one is without need through him, while he is indispensable, and that he is longed for, not loathed. So He connected the most important of needs and the most universal of requirements, to the most complete of praises and the most perfect of glorifications.

As for the arcanum in 'Guide us on the straight path' – how He connected 'the path' to 'guide us' notwithstanding the fact that guidance (*hidāya*) already conveys the idea of 'the path' (and it was [seemingly] necessary to rest content with mentioning guidance), and likewise 'the path' conveys the idea of straightness and He has [apparently superfluously] qualified it with it, and He made the 'straight path' characteristic of a specific people, they being those whom He graciously favoured consisting in the prophets, and He [apparently superfluously] confirmed that by the negation of the way of the adversaries who go astray and who lead astray – [the arcanum is] that within guidance occur both contrariety and hierarchy.

As for contrariety, it is like what is mentioned in His statement[873] (Exalted is He): 'He will guide them to the punishment of the inferno.'[874] So He has affirmed [the idea of] guiding unto punishment, just as He affirmed [the idea of] guiding unto reward, that being contrariety. As for hierarchy, it is like what is mentioned in His statement (Exalted is He): 'Does he who guides to the truth have more right to be followed, or he who does not guide – unless [the latter himself in turn] be guided?'[875] So He has affirmed a guide and a guided, that being hierarchy. His statement 'Guide us on the straight path' is to negate the former contrary and His statement 'the path of those You have graciously favoured' is to affirm the latter hierarchy.

Another arcanum: 'Guide us' is asking for guidance and it is unqualified, and His statement 'on the straight path' is a specification of that unqualified idea. His statement 'the path of those whom You have graciously favoured' is an individualisation of that specific idea. [Finally] His statement 'not those upon whom is wrath nor those who go astray' is a [further] resolution (*talkhīṣ*) of that individualised idea so that no taint of indiscrimination is left in the request.

Another arcanum is that the one who seeks guidance must have some guide who assists him in his search. The guide in reality is God (Mighty and Majestic); however, He attaches His guidance to a specific people by whom He has explained the path, thus He said 'The path of those whom You have
113 graciously favoured'[876] – so that you may understand that in the world there is a people whom God has graciously favoured with guidance and a people to whom God has vouchsafed the attainment of *seeking* guidance. Thus the first of the two is knowledgeable and the second is instructed. The first of the two is guiding and the second is guided, the two of them being paired – so they turn out to be the sixth Doubled One amongst the seven Doubled Ones.

Another arcanum is that the seeker of guidance is one commencing, so his is the principle of the commencing and the inchoative (*musta'naf*). And the guide of the seeker is at an end, so his is the principle of the perfect and the accomplished (*mafrūgh*). Thus the principle of the two realities (*kawnayn*) comes out clearly in the reference to the two parties, and the existence of the two principles proves true. [Another arcanum] is that the world is not devoid of those whom God graciously favours with guidance, they being the 'accomplished ones' (*mafrūghūn*), the perfect attainers, just as it is not devoid of those to whom God vouchsafes the attainment of seeking guidance, they being the ones commencing, heading for perfection.

Another arcanum is that generality and specificity occur in guidance the same as they occur in all expressions and ideas. God (Mighty and Majestic) has a general guidance penetrating all existents in proportion to their circumstances and their natures – and *specifically* in animals, for every animal is specified by being guided to whatever is beneficial for its existence and its survival, by seeking the protection of the species of it and the individual of it – that being through nature and innate predisposition, not through instruction and thinking. *More* specific than that is the guidance of humanity, for it is specified by being guided to whatever is beneficial for its existence and its survival, by seeking the protection of the species of it and the individual of it *and* seeking the benefit[877] of other than its own species – that indeed being through instruction and thinking. More specific *still* than that is the guidance of the prophets and saints (peace be upon them), for they are specified by being guided to whatever is beneficial for their existence and their survival by seeking the protection of the species of them and the individual of them and seeking the benefit of other than their species amongst humanity, both in their present way of life and in their life to come – that being through revelation and inspiration. Then just as humanity comes to be king over the species of animals through the special guidance it has, likewise the prophet[878] (peace be upon him) comes to be king over the classes of humanity through the guidance specific to him. And just as the movements of the human being come to be the inimitable miracles of the animal (I mean the human being's movements pertaining to thought, speech and action) likewise the movements of the prophets (peace be upon them) come to be the inimitable miracles of the human being (I mean their movements pertaining to the innate predisposition, to revelation and 114
character) – for they are those whom God (Mighty and Majestic) graciously

favours with heavenly, holy guidance, and their path is the path of God, their religion is the faith of God, and their law is the law of God, so whoever emulates them is guided to the straight path and whoever is hostile towards them is the one who falls down into the very midst of Hell.[879]

If you have understood the degrees of generality and specificity in guidance, you know the place at which the feet slip up of those who go astray in regard to it. Those amongst the libertarians who said that God (Exalted is He) might guide the believer and the unbeliever by raising up signs and proofs, and that the one guided aright is just he who considers [these signs] and learns, while the one who goes astray is just he who resists [these signs] and is haughty, relating to it His statement (Exalted is He) 'As for Thamūd, We guided them, yet they prefered blindness over guidance'[880] – they have gone astray since they judged [the matter] on the basis of the generality of guidance not the specificity. Those amongst the necessitarians who said that God (Exalted is He) has guided the believer but not the unbeliever by vouchsafing attainment and the creation of faith, so whoever is rightly guided is so by the guidance of God and whoever goes astray does so by God's leading astray, relating to it His statement (Mighty and Majestic) 'Whomever God guides, he is guided aright, and whomever God leads astray, they are the losers'[881] – they have gone astray since they judged [the matter] on the basis of the specificity of guidance not the generality.[882]

How far are the two quarrelling parties from understanding the arcana of the Qur'ān in regard to generality and specificity, contrariety and hierarchy, the accomplished and the inchoative, affirming both the realities (*kawnayn*) and confirming both principles! 'Do they not ponder the Qur'ān, or are there locks upon their hearts?'[883]

Another arcanum: bringing out the meanings through expressions and words is a matter of confidence, that being exegesis (*tafsīr*). However, individualising the words and meanings through individuals and specific persons is a difficult matter, that being hermeneutics (*ta'wīl*). Just as the mercy of God (Mighty and Majestic) is individualised through an individual who is the Prophet (may God bless him and his family) in his person and as an individual, on the evidence of His statement (Exalted is He) 'We only sent you as a mercy to the worlds',[884] likewise the gracious favour of God (Mighty and Majestic) is individualised through his person (peace be upon him and his family) on the evidence of His statement 'They acknowledge God's gracious favour, then they deny it'.[885] So mercy and gracious

favour are found in the revelation in an unqualified sense (*'alā'l-iṭlāq*), the
two of them generally comprehending [all] existents with the generality of
existence itself, kindness being present in their very existence and perpetuation, and in the repulsion of injuries from them. Next, the two of them are
in *hermeneutics*[886] in a personalised sense, the two of them specifying an 115
individual or two individuals with the specificity of subtlety and intimacy in
the [particular] *modes* of existence of the two people, the perpetuation of
their species and the repulsion of injuries from the two of them.

Moreover, just as praise (*ḥamd*) and dominion (*mulk*) are two terms for eulogy and glory, in lexicography and in the revelation, likewise they are terms for two individualised people, in semantics and in esoteric hermeneutics. So 'the mercy of God' is a certain man, and 'the gracious favour of God' is one individual *par excellence.* 'Praise belongs to God'[887] is His praise-giver in every circumstance, and 'dominion belongs to God'[888] is a dominion mighty in artfulness![889] In the Qur'ān is 'to Him belongs the dominion and to Him belongs the praise'[890] and in it is 'to Him belongs the praise and to Him belongs the dominion'.[891] The *lām* might be the *lām* of possession and it might be the *lām* of specification.[892] In the same way 'the path' (*al-ṣirāṭ*) in the revelation is a straight road (*ṭarīq mustaqīm*), while in esoteric hermeneutics it is a righteous individual (*shakhṣ mustaqīm*).

His statement, Mighty and Majestic: *Ghayr al-maghḍūbi 'alayhim wa lā'l-ḍāllīn* ('Not those against whom is wrath, nor those who go astray')

Grammar [and recitation]

The grammarians said: In regard to the vowelling of '*ghayr*' with 'i' there are four possible aspects. The first of them is because it is an appositive for '*alladhīna*'. The second is because it is a qualification *of* '*alladhīna*'. The third is because it is an appositive or an adjective for the pronominal suffix in ''*alayhim*'. And the fourth is that it is with the intention of repeating '*al-ṣirāṭ*'.

The allocation of [these] assertions

Al-Farrā' said: '*Alladhīna*' is a definite noun and definite nouns are not attributed by indefinite nouns nor indefinite nouns by definite nouns, except that '*alladhīna*' is not a *determinate* definite noun like 'Zayd' and ''Amr', but is instead comparable to inclusive indefinite nouns, [so it is] like 'the man' and 'the camel'. Then, since '*ghayr*'[893] is [also] put in a genitive relation with something unknown amongst nouns [i.e. in the phrase *al-maghḍūbi 'alayhim*], which is similar to a term which is an indeterminate definite noun, in that case it can be qualified by it, as it is said 'The path of the one who goes straight, not the unjust (*ghayr al-jā'ir*)'. Were it a determinate and circumscribed noun, like ''Abd Allāh' or 'Zayd', it could not be qualified by an indefinite noun.

Abū 'Alī said: Were you to say '*ghayr*' is vowelled with final 'i' in apposition to '*alladhīna*' – it is correct. The difference between an appositive and an adjective, in the statement of Sībawayhi, is that the appositive has the
116 implication of the repetition of the governing word (*'āmil*), through the evidence for the permissibility of the preposition's repetition explicitly, such as His statement (Exalted is He) 'The leaders of those who were arrogant amongst his people said to those (*li'lladhīna*) who were weak – *to those* (*li-man*) who had faith amongst them [...]';[894] and as for the adjective, it does *not* imply the repetition of the governing word.

As for inflecting the pronominal suffix of ''*alayhim*' with 'i', either as an appositive or as an adjective – it is like the inflection of '*alladhīna*' with ['i'].

As for the fourth aspect – namely, that it is with the intention of repeating '*al-ṣirāṭ*' ('the path') – its implication is: the path of other than those against whom is wrath. Abū Bakr al-Sarrāj said:[895] '*Ghayr*', with what is in a genitive construction with it, is a definite noun, and it is the adjective describing those graciously favoured with faith. And whoever is graciously favoured is not an object of wrath.

Al-Khalīl transmitted on the authority of Ibn Kathīr: '*Ghayr al-maghḍūbi 'alayhim*' is vowelled with final 'a',[896] and it has two aspects. The first of them is [that it is] the circumstantial expression for '*alladhīna*' or the *hā'* and the *mīm* (= *hum*) of ''*alayhim*', i.e. 'not those against whom is wrath' (*lā maghḍūban 'alayhim*). The second is: [that it expresses an] exception, and its implication is: 'except (*illā*) those against whom is wrath'.

It is transmitted on the authority of 'Umar and 'Alī that they both recited '*wa ghayra'l-ḍāllīn*' ('and not those who go astray').

As for the restoration of '*lā*' in the recitation of the commonalty, in His statement '*wa lā'l-ḍāllīn*' ('nor those who go astray'), Abū 'Ubayda said: It is amongst the pleonastic letters (*ḥurūf al-zawā'id*) for perfecting speech, mentioning which is deemed to be beautiful, the meaning being [arrived at through] their elimination. [This is] just as al-ʿAjjāj said: 'Into a fountain – not (*lā*) of nymphs! – did he enter, and he knew not'[897] i.e. into a fountain of nymphs. So in consequence, its meaning is '*and* those who go astray', like His statement (Exalted is He) 'Not equal are the living and not (*wa lā*) the dead'.[898]

Al-Farrāʾ said: The meaning of '*ghayr*' here is the same one as '*lā*', it being like your saying 'X is not (*ghayr*) virtuous and not (*lā*) decent'. Al-Zajjāj said: '*Lā*' may be in apposition to '*ghayr*', simply because '*ghayr*' implies the idea of negation, so it is in the sense[899] of 'not (*ghayr*) those against whom is wrath and not (*ghayr*) those who go astray'. Al-Mubarrad said likewise. And the author of The Harmonious Order said: '*Lā*' is added simply as an emphasis of the negation and to show that those who go astray are other than those against whom is wrath. If '*al-ḍāllīn*' ('those who go astray') were in apposition to it without the mention of '*lā*', it is conceivable that 'and those who go astray' be in itself a descriptive qualification of 'those against whom is wrath'.

Exegesis 117

As for exegesis, ʿAdī b. Ḥātim transmitted on the authority of the Prophet that he said 'nor those against whom is wrath' refers to the Jews, [and] 'nor those who go astray' refers to the Christians, this being the statement of Ibn ʿAbbās, Ibn Masʿūd, Mujāhid, al-Kalbī, al-Suddī and Muqātil. The confirmation of that is His statement (Exalted is He) about the Jews: 'whom God has cursed and *been wrathful against* (*wa ghaḍiba ʿalayhi*)',[900] and His statement about the Christians: 'Do not follow the passions of a people who have gone astray (*qad ḍallū*) earlier.'[901]

Al-Ḍaḥḥāk transmitted on the authority of Ibn ʿAbbās (may God be pleased with him), that he used to say: 'O God! Inspire us with Your true religion, it being "No god but God, He alone, without associate", so that You are not wrathful against us as You were wrathful against the Jews, nor make us go astray as You made the Christians go astray so that You punish us as You punished them.'

Al-Farrā' said: It is not denied that the Jews go astray and the Christians are subject to wrath, as indeed are the polytheists. And yet each party amongst them is singled out by a term which has been supplied with the definite article [*al-ḍāllūn, al-maghḍūb ʿalayhim*]. Similarly, 'those who go astray' are *all* of them polytheistic, yet the term polytheism [with the definite article, *al-shirk*] is specific to whoever has no scripture.

Semantics

It has been said in exegesis: wrath from God (Exalted is He) is mentioned in two senses. The first of them is the desire for giving punishment. The second is punishment itself. It is said that he against whom is wrath is whoever it is whose return to 'the straight path' is not expected, while 'those who go astray' are those for whom all hope is not lost. For whomever God is wrathful against and curses, His knowledge of him has preceded, that he is an unbeliever who will die in his [state of] unbelief, and [on the other hand] whoever goes astray from the road, perhaps he will be guided aright after going astray.

The meaning in regard to His statement 'not those against whom is wrath' (*'ghayr al-maghḍūbi 'alayhim'*), is: 'not those against whom You have become wrathful' (*ghayr alladhīna ghaḍibta 'alayhim*).

Al-Akhfash said: Every verb which governs its object transitively through a preposition, its plural and dual is [expressed] in the pronoun attached to the preposition, like your statement *al-ma'khūdhu minhu/minhum/minhā* ('the one taken possession of/the ones taken possession of') and *al-*
118 *mamrūru bihi/bihimā/bihim* ('the one passed by/the two passed by/the ones passed by'). For the sign of the plural, the dual, masculine gender and feminine gender, is subjoined to the *ends* of words, upon their completion.

Lexicography

Ḍalāl in lexicography means 'disappearing' (*ghaybūba*). It might be said 'the water went astray (*ḍalla*) in the milk' when it disappeared, and 'the unbeliever went astray' when he disappeared from the [right] path, and he swerved from the goal of the way. 'Going astray' (*ḍalāl*) is ruination (*halāk*), and it comes down to 'disappearing'. 'Going astray' is predicated hyperbolically of [desperate] love, and that also comes down to 'disappearing'. To this may be traced His statement (Exalted is He): 'You are in your old straying (*ḍalāl*).'[902]

Arcana

Those granted knowledge and faith, and informed about the arcana of the Qur'ān, say that humanity is twofold: the one who knows and the one instructed; the guide and the seeker. The rest of humanity are dungflies, and they also are twofold: one ranged against the one who knows and guides, as an opponent, and one ranged against the one instructed and seeking, as an opponent. So 'those against whom is wrath' are the adversaries of those who know consisting in the prophets and saints (peace be upon them). And 'those who go astray' are the adversaries of the ones instructed [and] the seekers consisting in the believers, in order that the two categories on the side of the false correspond with the two categories on the side of the true. So the two are paired – and that is the seventh Doubled One.

Another arcanum is that since the prophets and the saints (peace be upon them) are those who know by innate predisposition and they have the status of ones 'accomplished' (*al-mafrūgh 'anhum*) since they have attained to the supreme limit and to perfection, and for that reason He explained the Path through them,[903] and He caused the gracious favour of guidance to emanate upon them – likewise those who dispute with them through contrariety have the status of 'the ones against whom is wrath' by being cursed, ones 'accomplished' through the completion of being led astray, ones despaired of in regard to direction and guidance.

Just as the ones instructed are commensurate with the beginning and have the status of the inchoative and the commenced, likewise those who are ranged against them through contrariety, consisting of those who go astray, do not have the status of those against whom God is wrathful, nor is He finished with them (*farigha 'anhum*) by the completion of their going
astray, and despair for them in respect of direction and guidance would be 119
incorrect. Rather, they are commensurate with the possibility of departing from going astray, towards guidance and faith. Thus the two groups are ranged against each other as 'accomplished' and 'inchoative', and the two categories are at odds in truth and falsehood, gracious favour and wrath, guidance and going astray. And although hierarchy (*tarattub*) is more appropriate to the side of the truth, still, *disparity* (*tafāwut*) on the side of the false is comparable with hierarchy on the side of the truth.

'We have given you seven Doubled Ones' (Q. 15:87): The summary of what we mentioned about the arcana:

Doubled One (1)

In the name **of God** | **the Infinitely Merciful** | **the Compassionate**
(At beginnings= the perfect consecrating words) | the generality of mercy | the specificity of mercy

(In the middles)
Doubled One (2)

'My mercy encompasses everything'+ | 'I will stipulate it for those who are God-conscious'

Praise belongs to God
(At completions= the best individuating words)

the Infinitely Merciful of the herebelow | the Compassionate of the Hereafter

Outward gracious favour | Inward gracious favour

Doubled One(3)

Lord of the Worlds | **the Infinitely Merciful** | **the Compassionate**
the creation the herebelow
the beginning | the mercy of creation | the mercy of reward
the return | and the Command | and merit

Doubled One (4)

Ruler of the Day of Judgement
the Command the hereafter

Doubled One (5)

It is You whom we worship
The duty of legal obligation

No necessitarianism…
=the principle of the inchoative, on the basis of capacity.
'[Act] and no dereliction of duty!'

And it is You we ask for help
Asking for the vouchsafing of attainment

…and no delegation
=the principle of the accomplished, on the basis of seeking aid and being insignificant, and
'each is eased to what he has been created for'

Doubled One (6)

Hierarchy

Guide us on the straight path
Seeking guidance

The one headed for perfection
(=the instructed)

The path of those You have graciously favoured
Guiding the seeker

The 'accomplished' perfected one
(=the knower)

Contrariety

Disparity

Not those against whom is wrath
The one who leads astray

Nor those who go astray*
The one led astray

Doubled One (7)

+ MA *wasiʿat* : _.
* This final part of the schema is absent from the extant MS, and has been reconstructed.

Amongst the arcana of the Exordium is the discussion of the numbers of verses, words and letters, and the calculation of the number of them to a set figure. You understand that the Exordium is a single chapter, that it is subdivided into two halves as was mentioned: 'I divide the formal prayer[904] between Me and My worshipper.' And you have understood that the first half is a giving of information and the second half is an entrustment.[905] 121

Next, it is divided into thirds, so a third is the praises of God (Exalted is He) especially, a third is the needs of the servant especially, and a third is between the two of them. As He said (Mighty and Majestic) in regard to 'It is You we worship and it is You we ask for help': 'This is between Me and My servant.'

Next, it is divided into quarters, they being the four pauses in it: [after] '*al-Raḥīm*' ('the Compassionate'), '*al-dīn*' ('of judgement'), '*nastaʿīn*' ('we ask for help'), [and] '*al-ḍāllīn*' ('those who go astray'). [It is also divided into four] in regard to meaning: the 'In the name of God [...]' formula, the praising, the worshipping, and the guidance.

Next, it is divided into fifths, they being the names, praises, worship, the need for the vouchsafing of attainment, and the seeking of guidance.

Next, it is divided into sixths, they being the names at the beginnings and praises at the completions, the effusion of mercy upon the two worlds of the creation and the Command, the establishment of obedience in the twin conditions of human capacity and seeking help, turning towards the saints of God and disavowal of the enemies of God.

Next, it is divided into sevenths, they being the seven verses proportionate in their beginnings and breaks, they also being the seven Doubled Ones balanced in their verbal expressions and meanings.

Next, the complete words [of the Exordium], from every one of which is understood a complete meaning, are twelve words. Next, the simple words of it are twenty-eight words. Next, its letters, if they are calculated in line with the sequence of the orthography, are one hundred and forty two; and if they are calculated in line with the sequence of the oral articulation, they are one hundred and forty-four, and it consists in the multiplication of twelve by twelve.

Who is it that understands the arcana of these numbers and [the Exordium's] composition from numerable data;[906] and [understands] that the oneness in it corresponds with the oneness of the Command; that the two in it corresponds with the two worlds, the two worlds of the creation

and the Command, the corporeal and the spiritual; that the three in it cor-
122 responds with the first principles, the Command, the Pen, and the Tablet; that the four in it corresponds with whatever is four; that the five in it corresponds with whatever is five; and likewise the six, the seven, the twelve and the twenty-eight, so that it is established that the entire cosmos is within it, it being the keys of the unseen, the means for unlocking the heavens and the earth, the opener (*fātiḥa*) of every perfection and the seal of every pronouncement – opened with laudation and sealed with supplication – and it is the cure for every illness?

[It is said] in a report on the authority of the Prophet: 'Anything which [the chapter of] Praise will not cure, nothing will cure!'[907] And [it is said] on the authority of ʿAbd Allāh b. ʿAbbās that [he said]: "Alī (may God be pleased with him) began to comment with me on the Exordium from the time of the first third of the night. Thus we reached morning and he was not yet done with the commentary on the *bāʾ* of "*bi'smi'llāh*"!'

On the authority of some of the learned scholars is that everything which is mentioned in the revealed scriptures is mentioned in the Qurʾān, and everything which is mentioned in the Qurʾān is mentioned in the Exordium, and everything which is mentioned in the Exordium is mentioned in 'In the name of God, the Infinitely Merciful, the Compassionate' (*bi'smi'llāh al-Raḥmān al-Raḥīm*), and everything which is mentioned in that, is mentioned in the *bāʾ* of *bi'smi'llāh.* Do not be surprised at that, nor at their assertion that the judgements of the holy law are all mentioned in the formula 'no god but God'. You well know that the limbs of the human being are all hidden in the sperm drop of it, and that the elements of the tree are all concealed in the kernel of it, while only the eye of the attainers amongst human beings may actually see them!

Notes to the translation

Shahrastānī's preface

1 Q. 7:35.
2 There is a parallelism between the earlier praise of God for bestowing prophets on humanity in general and this praise of God for bestowing the Prophet Muḥammad on 'the last community', the Muslims, in particular. Shahrastānī describes this second bestowal with nearly equivalent expressions, but in the second case in the elative and reversed, the whole thus being a chiasmus.
3 This refers to Q. 33:40, which speaks of Muḥammad as *khātim al-nabīyīn*, the seal, i.e. conclusion, of the prophets. On the possible significance of Shahrastānī's interpretation of this Qur'ānic epithet in terms of Muḥammad constituting the perfection (*kamāl*), but not the passing away (*zawāl*), of prophecy, see my introduction, p. 57.
4 Q. 41:42.
5 Q. 3:164.
6 'Qur'ān' is sometimes derived from the root *q-r-n*, 'to join together', rather than *q-r-'*, 'to recite'.
7 Q. 17:106.
8 MA *Tirkatuhu* : *yazkīhi*. Ādharshab (*Tafsīr al-Shahrastānī*, p.104, note 4) prefers *tirka* ('legacy') because he takes this to refer to the so-called *ḥadīth al-thaqalayn*: '*anā tārikun fī-kum thaqalayn* [...]'. (See next note). For the phrase '[...] who recite it as it ought to be recited' in the previous sentence of the text, see Q. 2:121.
9 The expression is taken from the *ḥadīth al-thaqalayn* according to which the Prophet said he was leaving behind him (*tārik*) two precious (sometimes rendered 'weighty') things (*thaqalān*), namely, the Qur'ān and his own descendants. Muslim, *Faḍā'il al-ṣaḥāba*, 36, 37. See below, note 133.
10 Q. 18:60. See also Q. 55:19–20.
11 Q. 53:9.
12 Q. 15:9. The Remembrance (*al-Dhikr*) is here a title for the Qur'ān. The reference to angels accompanying the Qur'ān on all sides uses expressions drawn from Q. 13:11.
13 Q. 39:18.
14 Q. 2:185.
15 Q. 16:64.
16 Q. 43:44.
17 'Alī b. Abī Ṭālib b. 'Abd al-Muṭṭalib al-Hāshimī al-Qurashī, Abū'l-Ḥasan, known as 'the Commander of the Faithful' (*Amīr al-Mu'minīn*) (d. 40/661). A figure of monumental importance in Islamic history and spirituality, and, for Shī'ī Muslims, second only to the Prophet himself. Extraordinary for his courage, saintliness and learning, he was the cousin and adopted son of the Prophet who raised him from the age of five; married the Prophet's daughter Fāṭima; counted as the fourth of the 'righteous caliphs', he was martyred by a Khārijite rebel after a troubled period of leadership. The first imam of Shī'ī Islam. 'Asqalānī, *al-Iṣāba*, vol. 2, pp. 501–503, biography 5690; Ibn al-Athīr, *Usd al-ghāba*, vol. 4, pp. 91–125, biography 3783;

concerning his position in Qur'ānic exegesis see Abū Nu'aym al-Iṣfahānī, *Ḥilyat al-awliyā'*, vol. 1, pp. 61–87; see Ibn al-Athīr, *al-Kāmil fī'l-ta'rīkh*, on the events of the year 40; Ibn al-Jawzī, *Ṣifat al-ṣafwa*, vol. 1, pp. 119–144; *EI*[2], vol. 1, pp. 381–386 (L. Veccia Vaglieri).

18 According to some traditions, 'Alī kept certain materials linked to the Qur'ān in a scabbard – sometimes presented in maximal terms as comprising the true codex of the Qur'ān and its commentary. See e.g. Ibn Ḥanbal, *Musnad*, vol. 2, p. 121, ḥadīth 782. For the tradition cited here by Shahrastānī, consult the variety of transmitted materials in 'Abd al-Muṭṭalib, *Ṣaḥīfat 'Alī b. Abī Ṭālib 'an rasūl Allāh*. Also see below, note 127.

19 The companions have asked specifically whether the *exception* to equality between them and the People of the House lies in anything other than the latter's special relationship with the Qur'ān.

20 Ibn al-Athīr, *Usd al-ghāba*, vol. 2, p. 43.

21 Ibn Ziyād al-Naqqāsh quotes Ibn 'Abbās in his commentary: 'It is magnificent that I studied exegesis under 'Alī b. Abī Ṭālib!' (*jalla mā ta'allamtu min al-tafsīr min 'Alī b. Abī Ṭālib*). Ḥusaynī, *Sa'd al-su'ūd*, p. 285.

22 *Samā'an mujarradan*. This is one of the main modes of study or of textual transmission in the Muslim tradition: listening in a group, perhaps taking notes. Of greater authority is when the student recites a text in the presence of (*qara'a 'alā*) the teacher, who occasionally intervenes with corrections. A degree even more authoritative is also sometimes distinguished, in which the student goes through a thorough critical review (*'araḍa*) of the text with the teacher. *EI*[2], vol. 8, pp. 1019–1020 (R. Sellheim).

23 See Q. 28:30.

24 Q. 9:119.

25 Q. 8:65.

26 Compare the prophetic tradition: *al-mu'minu ya'kulu fī mi'an wāḥidin wa'l-kāfiru ya'kulu fī sab'ati am'ā'*. Bukhārī, *Aṭ'ima*, 12; Muslim, *Ashriba*, 182–186; Tirmidhī, *Aṭ'ima*, 20; Ibn Māja, *Aṭ'ima*, 3.

27 See Q. 83:27.

28 See Q. 18:60. The reference throughout is to Moses' quest for the waters of immortality, as described in the Qur'ān here, a quest Shahrastānī likens to his own study of the scripture.

29 Compare Q. 18:61.

30 See Q. 55:9.

31 MA *al-ra'y al-fā'il : al-ra'y al-qā'il*.

32 MA *innahu : lahu*.

Chapter 1
On the beginnings and endings of the descent of the Qur'ān and the sequence of its descent

33 i.e. the revelation of the Qur'ān.

34 MA *wilā' : mudda*.

35 'Abd Allāh b. 'Abbās b. 'Abd al-Muṭṭalib al-Qurashī al-Hāshimī (d. 68/686–7). A noted companion of the Prophet from Mecca; considered to be the very 'father of Qur'ānic exegesis'; known as '*al-ḥibr*' ('the Doctor') and viewed as the greatest

scholar of the first generation of Muslims, narrating some 1600 ḥadīths from the Prophet. He gave classes for the Muslim public on different subjects according to the days of the week: exegesis, law, the Prophet's military expeditions, history, poetry. Accompanied the Muslim armies on their expeditions to Egypt (18/639–21/642), Ifrīqiyā (27/647), Jurjān and Ṭabaristān (30/650) and later, Constantinople (between 54/674 and 60/680); commanded a wing of the army of ʿAlī b. Abī Ṭālib at the Battle of the Camel (36/656) and the Battle of Ṣiffīn (37/657); after serving ʿAlī as his official representative at Basra, Ibn ʿAbbās appears to have fallen out with him after the Battle of Nahrawān (38/658). ʿAsqalānī, *al-Iṣāba*, vol. 2, pp. 322–326, biography 4781; Ibn al-Jawzī, *Ṣifat al-ṣafwa*, vol. 1, p. 314; Iṣfahānī, *Ḥilyat al-awliyā'*, vol. 1, pp. 314–329; Ibn al-Athīr, *Usd al-ghāba*, vol. 3, pp. 290–296, biography 3035; Ibn al-Jazarī, *Ghāyat al-nihāya*, vol. 1, pp. 425–426; *EI*[2], vol. 1, pp. 40–41 (L.Veccia Vaglieri).

36 Q. 96:1–5. For the report from Ibn ʿAbbās, see Suyūṭī, *Itqān*, vol. 1, p. 24.

37 Mujāhid b. Jabr al-Makkī, Abū'l-Ḥajjāj (d. 104/722). The client of al-Sā'ib b. al-Sā'ib al-Makhzūmī, Mujāhid was a famed reciter and major exegete from the generation of the successors (*tābiʿūn*). He studied with many companions (transmitting on the authority of ʿAbd Allāh b. ʿAbbās, ʿĀ'isha, Umm Salama, Umm Hānī, Juwayriyya bt. al-Ḥārith, Jābir b. ʿAbd Allāh, ʿUmar b. al-Khaṭṭāb, Saʿīd b. Jubayr and ʿAbd al-Raḥmān b. Abī Laylā) but is mainly seen as the disciple of Ibn ʿAbbās. In one report he thrice went over the Qur'ān with Ibn ʿAbbās, stopping at each verse and checking its reference and historical context (*sabab al-nuzūl*) with him. Shibl b. ʿAbbād al-Makkī (see note 216) transmitted his Qur'ānic exegesis and though Mujāhid was proclaimed the most learned exegete of his generation, his material supposedly partly derived from Jewish and Christian sources, causing some purists to reject his contribution. Famous for his quest to acquaint himself directly with the marvels (*ʿajā'ib*) referred to in scripture, for instance visiting the ruins of Babel in relation to the figures of Hārūt and Mārūt (see Q. 2:102). Dā'ūdī, *Ṭabaqāt al-mufassirīn*, vol. 2, pp. 305–308; Dhahabī, *Tadhkirat al-ḥuffāẓ*, vol. 1, p. 92; ʿAsqalānī, *Tahdhīb al-tahdhīb*, vol. 10, p.42; Iṣfahānī, *Ḥilyat al-awliyā'*, vol. 3, p. 279; Ibn al-Jazarī, *Ghāyat al-nihāya*, vol. 2, p. 41; Ibn Saʿd, *Ṭabaqāt*, ed. H. Sachau *et al.*, vol. 5, p. 467.

38 Q. 68:1. For the report from Mujāhid, see Suyūṭī, *Itqān*, vol. 1, p. 24.

39 Jābir b. ʿAbd Allāh b. ʿAmr al-Khazrajī (d. 78/697). A Medinan companion of the Prophet who took part in all the early battles of Islam except Badr; transmitted as many as 1,540 ḥadīth included in Bukhārī, Muslim and other compendia. Qāḍī ʿIyāḍ, *Shifā'*, vol. 1, p. 154; Mizzī, *Tahdhīb al-kamāl*, vol. 3, pp. 291–299.

40 Q. 74:1. For the report from Jābir, see Zarkashī, *Burhān fī ʿulūm al-Qur'ān*, vol. 1, p. 207.

41 Abū Jaʿfar Muḥammad b. Yaʿqūb al-Kulaynī (d. 328/939). The great Twelver Shīʿī scholar; compiled his monumental study of Shīʿī traditions, the *Kāfī* (comprising *al-uṣūl min al-kāfī* and *al-furūʿ min al-kāfī*) over a twenty-year period. *EI*[2], vol. 5, pp. 362–363 (W. Madelung).

42 Abū ʿAbd Allāh Jaʿfar b. Muḥammad al-Ṣādiq (d. 148/765). The sixth imam of Twelver Shīʿism and the fifth of Ismāʿīlī Shīʿism; after ʿAlī b. Abī Ṭālib (see note 17), the most renowned imam for piety and knowledge; his students also included numerous prominent figures of Sunnism, notably Abū Ḥanīfa (founder of the Ḥanafī legal rite) and Mālik b. Anas (founder of the Mālikī legal rite), who trans-

mitted many prophetic traditions from him. *EI*², vol. 2, pp. 374–375 (M.G.S. Hodgson).

43 Q. 96:1. See Ibn Bābūya al-Qummī, *ʿUyun akhbār al-riḍā*, vol. 2, p. 6.

44 Q. 1. Zamakhsharī, *Kashshāf*, vol. 4, p. 775.

45 ʿUthmān b. ʿAffān b. Abī'l-ʿĀṣ b. Umayya al-Qurashī (d. 35/656). Amongst the very greatest companions of the Prophet and from the Meccan aristocracy he married two of the Prophet's daughters and went on to become the third 'righteous caliph' of Islam. Famously mild-tempered, he is sometimes criticised for the nepotistic promotion, during his caliphate, of his fellow clan the Umayyads. He was murdered by a group led by Muḥammad b. Abī Bakr, brother of the Prophet's wife ʿĀʾisha and the son of the first Caliph. *EI*², vol. 10, pp. 946–949 (G. Levi Della Vida-[R.G. Khoury]).

46 *Barāʾa*. More commonly known as 'Repentance' (*al-Tawba*), Q. 9.

47 Suyūṭī, *Itqān*, vol. 1, p. 27.

48 Al-Barāʾ b. ʿĀzib b. al-Ḥārith al-Awsī al-Anṣārī (d. circa 72/691–2). A partisan of ʿAlī amongst the companions.

49 Q. 4:176. For the report from al-Barāʾ b. ʿĀzib, see Suyūṭī, *Itqān*, vol. 1, p. 27.

50 Muḥammad b. Muslim al-Zuhrī (d.124/741). The celebrated traditionist.

51 *Al-ʿUrsh* was a name for Mecca.

52 Q. 2:278 and Q. 2:282, respectively. For the report from Ibn Shihāb, see Suyūṭī, *Itqān*, vol. 1, pp. 27–28.

53 ʿAṭāʾ b. Abī Rabāḥ (d. 115/733). A great Meccan jurist of the early period. 'Master' (*sayyid*) of the successors, he transmitted materials from highly respected authorities. Abū Ḥanīfa studied under him and said 'I have not seen the like of him'. Ibn al-Jazarī, *Ghāyat al-nihāya*, vol. 1, p. 513; Dhahabī, *Mīzān al-iʿtidāl*, vol. 3, p. 70; Subkī, *Ṭabaqāt al-shāfiʿiyya al-kubrā*, vol. 5, p. 467.

54 Q. 2:281. For the report from ʿAṭā b. Abī Rabāḥ and Ibn ʿAbbās, see Suyūṭī, *Itqān*, vol. 1, p. 27. On Ibn ʿAbbās, see note 35.

55 The figure of seven nights is according to Muqātil (see note 65); the figure nine is also recorded in several sources.

56 Suyūṭī, *Itqān*, vol. 1, p. 27 (with a slight difference in wording).

57 Q. 110. For the tradition from Jaʿfar al-Ṣādiq, see Ibn Bābūya, *ʿUyūn al-akhbār al-riḍā*, vol. 2, p. 6.

58 The Night of Power (*Laylat al-Qadr*) is the night in CE 610, commemorated towards the end of each Ramaḍān, when the Qurʾān is understood to have descended to the Prophet when he secluded himself for prayer in the cave of Ḥirāʾ. See Q. 97.

59 *Al-Bayt al-maʿmūr*. Either the Kaʿba itself at Mecca, or according to some interpretations, the Kaʿba's celestial archetype. The expression is used at Q. 52:4.

60 Q. 17:106. For the report from Ibn ʿAbbās, see Suyūṭī, *Itqān*, vol. 1, p. 41.

61 Abū Shidād Wāthila b. ʿAbd Allāh (also: b. ʿAbd al-ʿUzzā) b. al-Asqaʿ (d. 83/702, alternatively 85/704). A companion of the Prophet often mentioned by Shahrastānī in his commentary. One in a group of poor ultra-pious believers known as the *Ahl al-Ṣuffa* (see *EI*², vol. 1, pp. 266–267, W. Montgomery Watt). He is said to have served the Prophet for three years; later settled in Basra; witnessed the conquest of Damascus (14/635), settling in a village nearby; last of the companions to die in Damascus, aged 98 or even (according to some sources) 105; narrated 76 ḥadīth. Ibn al-Jazarī, *Ghāyat al-nihāya*, vol. 2, p. 358.

62 *ʿalayhi ʾl-salām* : _ MA.
63 Suyūṭī, *Iṭqān*, vol. 1, p. 42.
64 Majlisī, *Biḥār al-anwār*, vol. 89, p. 213. Also see Kulaynī, *Uṣūl*, *Bāb al-nawādir*, ḥadīth 10.
65 Muqātil b. Sulaymān b. Kathīr al-Azdī al-Khurāsānī, Abūʾl-Ḥasan al-Balkhī (d. 150/767). Sometimes called Ibn Dawāl Dūz. Counted as one of the companions of the imams al-Bāqir and Jaʿfar al-Ṣādiq. A great early authority in Qurʾānic exegesis. From Balkh; at different times resident in Merv, Baghdad, and Basra. His exegetical contribution is neglected due to supposed inaccuracies in his handling of chains of transmission (*isnād*) and also his tendency to attribute much exegetical material to the 'People of the Book', i.e. Jews and Christians. Thus Dāʾūdī in *Tabaqāt al-mufassirīn* says: 'They called him a liar, parted company with him, and he was accused of theological corporealism (*tajsīm*) by the seventh generation.' Transmitted material from Mujāhid, ʿAṭāʾ b. Abī Rabbāḥ, Abū Isḥāq al-Sabīʿī, al-Ḍaḥḥāk b. Muzāhim al-Hilālī, Muḥammad b. Muslim b. Shihāb al-Zuhrī and others. Al-Shāfiʿī is reported as saying 'All men depend on three people: Muqātil b. Sulaymān in Qurʿānic exegesis, on Zuhayr b. Abī Sulmā in poetry, and on Abū Ḥanīfa in theology'. Numerous works are attributed to him: *Naẓāʾir al-Qurʾān* (Correspondences in the Qurʾān), *al-Tafsīr al-kabīr* (The Great Commentary), *al-Nāsikh waʾl-mansūkh* (The Abrogating and the Abrogated), *Tafsīr al-khamsamiʾa āya* (The Commentary on One Hundred and Fifty Verses), *al-Qirāʾāt* (Readings), *Mutashābih al-Qurʾān* (The Ambiguous in the Qurʾān), *Nawādir al-tafsīr* (Rarities of the Qurʾān), *al-Wujūh waʾl-naẓāʾir* (Significations and Correspondences), *al-Jawābāt fīʾl-Qurʾān* (Responses in the Qurʾān), *al-Radd ʿalāʾl-qadariyya* (Refutation of the Libertarians), *al-Aqsām waʾl-lughāt* (Oaths and Idioms), *al-Taqdīm waʾl-taʾkhīr* (Placing Earlier and Later), *al-Āyāt al-mutashābihāt* (The Ambiguous Verses). Shahrastānī presently transmits the order of the sequence of the descent of the chapters of the Qurʾān from Muqātil, on the basis of his authorities, and also from him on the authority of ʿAlī (see text, p. 79). Dāʾūdī, *Ṭabaqāt al-mufassirīn*, vol. 2, p. 330. Also see: ʿAsqalānī, *Tahdhīb al-tahdhīb*, vol. 10, p. 379; Nawawī, *Tahdhīb al-asmāʾ waʾl-lughāt*, vol. 2, p. 111; Dodge, *Fihrist of al-Nadīm*, pp. 75, 80, 82, 444; Dhahabī, *Mīzān al-iʿtidāl*, vol. 4, p. 173; Ibn Khallikān, *Wafayāt al-aʿyān*, vol. 3, p. 342; Ahmad b. ʿAlī al-Baghdādī, *Taʾrīkh Baghdād*, vol. 13, p. 160; Ṭūsī, *Ikhtiyār maʿrifat al-rijāl*, p. 390, no. 733; EI^2, vol. 7, pp. 508–509 (M. Plessner-[A.Rippin]).
66 See note 17.
67 Abūʾl-Naḍr Muḥammad b. al-Sāʾib al-Kalbī al-Kūfī (d. 146/763) An expert genealogist and early Shīʿī exegete from Kufa; of wide-ranging interests such as history, other religions, philology and poetry – all employed in his unextant commentary on the Qurʾān, supposedly the longest ever produced. His list of works includes *Tafsīr al-āy alladhī nazala fi qawmin bi-aʿyānihim* (Commentary on the Sign Which Came Down Among a People in Themselves), and also *Nāsikh al-Qurʾān wa mansūkhuhu* (The Abrogating and the Abrogated of the Qurʾān). He transmitted on the authority of al-Shaʿbī and a group of others. Dhahabī, *ʿIbar*, vol. 1, p.106. Dāʾūdī, *Ṭabaqāt al-mufassirīn*, vol. 2, pp. 144–145; Ibn al-ʿImād al-Ḥanbalī, *Shadharāt al-dhahab*, vol. 1, p. 217; Dodge, *Fihrist of al-Nadīm*, pp. 75, 205–206, 239; Dhahabī, *Mīzān al-iʿtidāl*, vol. 3, p. 556; Ṣafadī, *al-Wāfī biʾl-wafayāt*, vol. 3, p. 83; Ibn Khallikān, *Wafayāt al-aʿyān*, vol. 3, p. 436.

68 This appears to be al-Ḥasan b. Wāqid al-Qurashī al-Marwazī (d. 157/775 or 159/777), although he is elsewhere referred to by Shahrastānī as al-Ḥasan b. Wāqid al-Wāqidī. See note 376.

Chapter 2
On the manner of the collection of the Qur'ān

69 The reference is to the Battle of 'Aqrabā (12/633), fought after the Prophet's death between the Muslims and the Banū Ḥanīfa tribe (from the region known as al-Yamāma) united under their 'prophet' Musaylima. Though the Muslims were victorious, many in their ranks were killed. *EI*[2], vol. 7, pp. 664–5 (W. Montgomery Watt).

70 'Abd Allāh b. 'Āmir, Abū Bakr al-Ṣiddīq (d. 13/634). A figure of monumental importance in early Islam. Originally a merchant, known to be an expert genealogist, he became the Prophet's very close friend, even accompanying him in his escape from Mecca to Medina in CE 622. The father of the Prophet's wife 'Ā'isha; on his death he became the first 'righteous caliph' of Islam. *EI*[2], vol. 1, pp. 109–111 (W Montgomery Watt).

71 Zayd b. Thābit b. al-Ḍaḥḥāk al-Khazrajī (d. 45/665). One of the great companions of the Prophet. When the Caliph 'Umar (see next note) used to leave Medina he would appoint Zayd as his representative. Described (by Abū Hurayra) as 'the scholar of this community'. Ibn al-Jazarī, *Ghāyat al-nihāya*, vol. 1, p. 296; *EI*[2], vol. 11, p. 476 (M. Lecker).

72 i.e. When 'Umar assumed power. 'Umar b. al-Khaṭṭāb b. Nufayl al-Qurashī al-'Adawī, Abū Ḥafṣ (d. 23/644). A figure in the first rank of importance in early Islam and a close companion of the Prophet, with a famously fiery personality; after an initial phase of hostility towards the new faith, his conversion amounted to a turning point in Islam's fortunes; father of the Prophet's wife Ḥafṣa (see note 74), he became the second 'righteous caliph' of Islam and presided over the early phase of the Islamic conquests. Ibn al-Athīr, *Usd al-ghāba*, vol. 3, p. 19; 'Asqalānī, *al-Iṣāba*, biography 4781; Ibn al-Jawzī, *Ṣifat al-ṣafwa*, vol. 1, p. 101; Iṣfahānī, *Ḥilyat al-awliyā'*, vol. 1, p. 38; *EI*[2], vol. 10, pp. 819–821 (G. Levi Della Vida-[M. Bonner]).

73 MA *ḥattā māta thumma 'nṭaqalat : fa-qāma.*

74 Ḥafṣa bt. 'Umar b. al-Khaṭṭāb (d. 45/665). After losing her first husband, Khunays b. Ḥudhāfa, at the Battle of Badr, she married the Prophet in 3/625. Stories suggest her strong emotional bond with her co-wife 'Ā'isha. She was credited with knowledge of reading and writing. *EI*[2], vol. 3, pp. 63–65 (L. Veccia-Vaglieri).

75 Ḥudhayfa b. al-Yamān al-'Absī (d. 36/657). A companion of the Prophet, he participated in the Islamic conquests of the Sassanian empire during the caliphate of 'Umar and is said to have been privy to a secret from the Prophet concerning the 'hypocrites' (*munāfiqūn*). He was appointed governor by 'Umar over al-Madā'in (i.e. Ctesiphon); 225 traditions are attributed to him in the works on Prophetic Tradition. Ibn al-Jazarī, *Ghāyat al-nihāya*, vol. 1, p. 203; Mizzī, *Tahdhīb al-kamāl*, vol. 4, pp. 191–200.

76 Compare Ṭabarī, *Jāmi' al-bayān*, vol. 1, p. 26. Here, the conflict of Syrians and Iraqis is presented as having been specifically witnessed by Ḥudhayfa during his military campaign in the Armenian steppes.

77 Having made use of Ḥafṣa's codex, 'Uthmān's committee returned it to her, it being considered to be her private property. After her death Marwān b. al-Ḥakam (d. 65/685) confiscated and destroyed the codex. Balādhurī, *Ansāb al-ashrāf*, vol. 1, p. 427. Also see Suyūṭī, *Itqān*, vol. 1, p. 61.

78 Abān b. Sa'īd b. al-'Āṣ b. Umayya al-Qurashī (d. 13/634). A Meccan noble. After early opposition to Islam he converted in 7/630. In 9/632 he was sent by the Prophet on a mission to Baḥrayn; according to the sources he was responsible for dictating the revelations gathered in 'Uthmān's codex to Zayd b. Thābit, by 'Uthmān's command (other accounts state however that this was Sa'īd b. al-'Āṣ, for example, see English text p. 69; Arabic text, p. 8).

79 'Abd Allāh b. al-Zubayr b. al-'Awwām (d. 73/692). The well-known anti-caliph, son of Asmā', the daughter of Abū Bakr and sister of 'Ā'isha. He was closely related to the Prophet on both sides and is said to have personally killed the exarch Gregory on the Muslim expedition against the Byzantines in Ifrīqiyā in 267/647. He commanded the infantry on 'Ā'isha's side against 'Alī at the Battle of the Camel (35/656). Said to have been the originator of the advice at the arbitration at Dūmat al-Jandal to bribe 'Amr b. al-'Āṣ, he refused to take the oath to Yazīd as Mu'āwiya's heir-presumptive, taking refuge at Mecca. After al-Ḥusayn's martyrdom at Karbalā', Ibn al-Zubayr began to take action against the Umayyads in his own cause, putting himself forward as *amīr al-mu'minīn* (the 'Commander of the Faithful'). He was besieged in Mecca by al-Ḥajjāj in 72/692, defeated and killed. *EI*[2], vol. 1, pp. 54–55 (H.A.R. Gibb).

80 Sa'īd b. al-'Āṣ b. Sa'īd b. al-'Āṣ b. Umayya al-Qurashī (d. 59/678). His Umayyad father was killed fighting on the pagan side at the Battle of Badr (2/624). Sa'īd, however, quickly won prestige as a Muslim, for eloquence, learning and largesse, at the head of an aristocratic group. Especially favoured by the Caliph 'Uthmān, he became unpopular as governor of Kufa after his appointment in 29/649. Though supporting 'Ā'isha, he declined to take part in the Battle of the Camel (35/656). He was appointed by Mu'āwiya as governor of Medina in 49/669 till 54/674. *EI*[2], vol. 8, p. 853 (C.E. Bosworth).

81 MA *ibn* : _.

82 'Abd al-Raḥmān b. al-Ḥārith b. Hishām b. al-Mughīra al-Qurashī al-Makhzūmī (d. 43/663). One of the successors from the Qurayshite nobility, he was considered to be a 'trustworthy' (*thiqa*) transmitter. He was raised in 'Umar's family, 'Umar having married his mother on the death of 'Abd al-Raḥmān's father. He died during Mu'āwiya's reign in Medina. Ibn al-Athīr, *Usd al-ghāba*, vol. 3, p. 432.

83 Ibn Abī Dā'ūd al-Sijistānī, *Kitāb al-Maṣāḥif*, edited and translated by Arthur Jeffery as *Materials for the History of the Text of the Qur'ān*, p. 19; also Suyūṭī, *Iṭqān*, vol. 1, p. 61; Ṭabarī, *Jāmi' al-bayān*, vol. 1, pp. 20–21.

84 Q. 33.

85 Khuzayma b. Thābit b. al-Fākih b. Tha'laba al-Anṣārī al-Khaṭmī (d. 37/657). Medinan companion of the Prophet from the aristocracy of Aws before Islam and among their foremost heroes. He carried the standard of the Banū Khaṭma (a sub-tribe of Aws, one of the clans of the Anṣār in Medina) at the conquest of Mecca and was killed at Ṣiffīn fighting for 'Alī. 38 prophetic traditions were transmitted by him in Muslim, Bukhārī and others. Mizzī, *Tahdhīb al-kamāl*, vol. 5, pp. 455–456.

86 Q. 33:23.

87 Bukhārī, *Faḍā'il al-Qur'ān*, 3; Bukhārī, *Maghāzī*, 17; also Tirmidhī, *Tafsīr Sūra* 9, 19.

88 i.e. Q. 33:23.

89 i.e. to be martyred.

90 Jaʿfar b. Abī Ṭālib (8/629). The cousin of the Prophet and elder brother of ʿAlī. One of the emigrants to Ethiopia, he was later martyred at the battle of Muʾta. Called *al-Ṭayyār* ('the Flyer') after the Prophet dreamed of him in the wake of the battle with bloody wings in a throng of angels – evoking the fact that both hands had been cut off in the lead-up to his death. *EI*², vol. 2, p. 372 (L. Veccia Vaglieri).

91 See the previous note for an explanation of this name.

92 Abū ʿAbd al-Raḥmān ʿAbd Allāh b. Masʿūd b. Ghāfil b. Ḥabīb b. Shamkh al-Hudhalī (d. 32/652). Famous companion of the Prophet, Qurʾān-reader and transmitter of exegetical material; humble in origin; in some accounts, one of the first to embrace Islam (Sakhāwī, *al-Kawākib al-durriyya*, vol. 1, p. 333, claims that he was third, after Khadīja bt. Khuwaylid and ʿAlī b. Abī Ṭālib); received the Qurʾān directly from the Prophet and is said to have been the first to recite it publicly in Mecca; one of the emigrants to Ethiopia; present at the Battle of Badr and of Uḥud; after the Prophet's death, took part at the decisive Battle of Yarmūk (13/636); during the caliphate of ʿUmar, was given important administrative and diplomatic functions; settled in Kufa in 21/642, where he enjoyed great respect; finally clashed with the authority of the Caliph ʿUthmān b. ʿAffān and fell from grace. Iṣfahānī, *Ḥilyat al-awliyāʾ*, vol. 1, p. 124; Ibn al-Jawzī, *Ṣifat al-ṣafwa*, vol. 1, p. 154; Mizzī, *Tahdhīb al-kamāl*, vol. 10, p. 532; *EI*², vol. 3, pp. 873–875 (J.-C. Vadet).

93 Ibn Umm ʿAbd, i.e. Ibn Masʿūd. For the tradition, see Iṣfahānī, *Ḥilyat al-awliyāʾ*, vol. 1, p. 124; also *Muqaddimat al-mabānī*, in Arthur Jeffery, *Two Muqaddimas*, p. 93.

94 Ubayy b. Kaʿb b. Qays b. ʿUbayd, Abū Mundhir al-Anṣārī al-Madanī (d. 21/642 or 29/649 or 34/654). A companion of the Prophet and member of the Anṣār; originally from amongst the Jewish Banūʾl-Najjār and one of their rabbis. Secretary to the Prophet in Medina and one of the foremost Qurʾān reciters, he was even known as *Sayyid al-Qurrāʾ*. As the Prophet's secretary he is said to have memorized passages of the Qurʾān at the time of their revelation, reciting them over to the Prophet 'for guidance and instruction'; he possessed his own alternative recension of the Qurʾān which was declared defective by ʿUmar b. al-Khaṭṭāb. Iṣfahānī, *Ḥilyat al-awliyāʾ*, vol. 1, p. 250; Ibn al-Athīr, *Usd al-ghāba*, vol. 1, p. 61; Ibn al-Jawzī, *Ṣifat al-ṣafwa*, vol. 1, p. 189; ʿAsqalānī, *al-Iṣāba*, vol. 1, p 31; Ibn Saʿd, *Ṭabaqāt* (Cairo, 1377/1957), vol. 3, pp. 498–502; *EI*², vol. 2, pp. 764–765 (A. Rippin). See also Bukhārī, *Faḍāʾil al-Qurʾān*, *bāb* 8 (= *al-qurrāʾ min aṣḥāb rasūl Allāh*), passim.

95 Sijistānī, *Kitāb al-Maṣāḥif*, p. 24.

96 On the subject of people's approval of ʿUthmān, see Sijistānī, *Kitāb al-Maṣāḥif*, p. 12.

97 MA *fa-muṣḥafāhumā* : *fa-muṣḥafuhumā*.

98 MA *min* : _.

99 On the variation in number of the manuscripts sent by ʿUthmān to the provinces, see Suyūṭī, *Itqān*, vol. 1, p. 62.

100 *Zirr b. Ḥubaysh* : *Zarri b. Ḥubaysh* MA. Zirr b. Ḥubaysh b. Ḥabasha (or Ḥubāsha), Abū Maryam al-Asadī al-Kūfī (d. 82/701). By reputation, an outstanding authority; did critical review of recitation in the presence of ʿAbd Allāh b. Masʿūd, ʿUthmān and ʿAlī; then ʿĀṣim and others did critical review of recitation in his presence. Ibn al-Jazarī, *Ghāyat al-nihāya*, vol. 1, p. 294; also Dodge, *Fihrist of al-Nadīm*, p. 64.

101 Q. 33.
102 Q. 2, which contains 286 verses.
103 *Muqaddimat al-mabānī* in Jeffery, *Two Muqaddimas*, pp. 82–83.
104 Saʿīd b. al-Musayyib b. Ḥazn b. Abī Wahb al-Makhzūmī al-Qurashī Abū Muḥammad (d. 94/712–13). Known as *Sayyid al-Tābiʿīn* (Master of the successors). His biography is in Ibn Saʿd, *Ṭabaqāt*, vol. 5, p. 88; Ibn al-Jawzī, *Ṣifat al-ṣafwa*, vol. 2, p. 44; Iṣfahānī, *Ḥilyat al-awliyā'*, vol. 2, p. 161; Ibn al-Jazarī, *Ghāyat al-nihāya*, vol. 1, p. 308; Mizzī, *Tahdhīb al-kamāl*, vol. 7, pp. 297–304.
105 Jeffery, *Two Muqaddimas*, p. 79.
106 Q. 9:64.
107 MA *thumma* : _.
108 Compare Kulaynī, *Uṣūl*, vol. 4, pp. 440–441 (= *kitāb faḍl al-Qur'ān, bāb al-nawādir*, ḥadīth 16).
109 Suyūṭī, *Itqān*, vol. 1, p. 67.
110 Idem.
111 *Sūrat al-Fātiḥa*, Q. 1.
112 i.e. Q. 2.
113 Rufayʿ b. Mihrān Abū'l-ʿĀliya al-Riyāḥī (d. 90/708–9 or 96/714). A distinguished Medinan exegete and transmitter of the Qur'ān and of prophetic traditions in the first generation of successors (*tābiʿūn*). Ibn al-Jazarī, *Ghāyat al-nihāya*, vol. 1, pp. 284–285; Mizzī, *Tahdhīb al-kamāl*, vol. 6, pp. 220–223.
114 Q. 33.
115 i.e. the Battle of ʿAqrabā (12/633).
116 Sijistānī, *Kitāb al-Maṣāḥif*, p. 22 (with a slight difference in wording).
117 Q. 2.
118 = The Ark of the Covenant.
119 Q. 2:248. Compare Ṭabarī, *Jāmiʿ al-bayān*, vol. 1, p. 26.
120 The epithet refers to Zayd's education among the Jewish tribes of the *sāfila* in Medina, or even perhaps to his Jewish origins. See 'Zayd b. Thābit, "A Jew with Two Sidelocks": Judaism and Literacy in Pre-Islamic Medina (Yathrib)' in Michael Lecker, *Jews and Arabs in Pre- and Early Islamic Arabia*, pp. 259–272.
121 Jeffery, *Two Muqaddimas*, p. 95; Sijistānī, *Kitāb al-Maṣāḥif*, p. 15; Majlisī, *Biḥār al-anwār*, vol. 89, p. 73; also Iṣfahānī, *Ḥilyat al-awliyā'*, vol. 1, p. 125.
122 Q. 13:31.
123 Jeffery, *Two Muqaddimas*, p. 105; also compare Ṭabarī, *Jāmiʿ al-bayān*, vol. 6, p. 26–27.
124 MA *lam yaṭlubū* : *lā ṭalabū*.
125 On the entire notion of the codex of ʿAlī, see Modarressi, *Tradition and Survival*, vol. 1, p. 4 ff.
126 Muḥammad b. Sīrīn Abū Bakr b. Abī ʿAmra al-Baṣrī (d. 110/728). The client of Anas b. Mālik. Considered the leading religious authority of Basra in his generation, besides al-Ḥasan al-Baṣrī. Material is transmitted on his authority concerning the *ḥurūf* of the Qur'ān. Ibn al-Jazarī, *Ghāyat al-nihāya*, vol. 2, pp. 151–152; Mizzī, *Tahdhīb al-kamāl*, vol. 16, pp. 345–350.
127 Compare: Suyūṭī, *Itqān*, vol. 1, p. 59. For a fuller discussion of the codex of ʿAlī, see Modarressi, *Tradition and Survival*, vol. 1, p. 4 ff.
128 The sense seems to be two *differently* meant instances of a single expression, i.e. an equivocation. If it is instead two *similarly* meant instances of an expression,

this may refer to the same feature described above by Abū Ḥātim when he says "Alī placed each verse beside what was similar to it'.

129 Q. 25:30.

130 Q. 20:94.

131 Q. 7:150. Compare the information in this paragraph with Kulaynī, *Uṣūl*, vol. 4, pp. 443–444 (= *kitāb faḍl al-Qurʾān, bāb al-nawādir*, ḥadīth 23); also al-Ṣaffār al-Qummī, *Baṣāʾir al-darajāt*, section 4, p. 193, ḥadīth 3.

132 Q. 7:3.

133 The sources of this tradition in the *Ṣaḥīḥ* and *Musnad* books may be consulted in Khūʾī, *al-Bayān fī tafsīr al-Qurʾān*, p. 499. For this version of the *ḥadīth al-thaqalayn* see al-Ḥākim al-Naysābūrī, *al-Mustadrak ʿalāʾl-ṣaḥīḥayn*, vol. 3, p. 148. Also see Tirmidhī, *Manāqib*, 31.

134 Q. 15:9.

135 Q. 28:51.

136 Q. 75:17.

137 Q. 85:22.

138 On the subject of the position of the imams on the ʿUthmānic codex, see Majlisī, *Biḥār al-anwār*, vol. 89, p. 74.

139 Q. 21:27.

140 Abū Dāʾūd, *Sunna*, 16; Ibn Māja, *Muqaddima*, 10.

141 Compare Q. 4:46.

142 Q. 5:44.

143 Compare Q. 3:50 and Q. 3:3.

144 *Taʾwīl* (esoteric hermeneutic) complements *tanzīl* (sending down/revelation). *Taʾwīl* lexically suggests 'taking up', as *tanzīl* refers to the journey in the opposite direction. See Shahrastānī's discussion in chapter 8.

145 Q. 3:7.

Chapter 3
On the difference between reporters over the order of the descent of the chapters of the Qurʾān [...]

146 Q. 2:116.

147 Jeffery, *Two Muqaddimas*, p. 118.

148 Q. 2:132.

149 Q. 3:133.

150 Jeffery, *Two Muqaddimas*, pp. 117–118.

151 Q. 57:24.

152 Jeffery, *Two Muqaddimas*, p. 118.

153 e.g. Q. 9:100.

154 i.e. 'With rivers flowing from beneath them'.

155 Q. 3:184.

156 Jeffery, *Two Muqaddimas*, p. 118.

157 Q. 2:259.

158 Q. 86:17.

159 Q. 30:30. It seems unclear which of the various *lām*s in the Arabic was at first mistakenly doubled: *lā tabdīla li-khalqiʾllāh*.

160 In all the cases now mentioned some consonant is omitted.
161 Q. 11:105. See *Muqaddimat al-mabānī*, in Jeffery, *Two Muqaddimas*, p. 151.
162 Q. 18:64. See *Muqaddimat al-mabānī*, in Jeffery, *Two Muqaddimas*, p. 152; also Dānī, *al-Maqnaʿ fī maʿrifa marsūm maṣāḥif ahl al-amṣār*, p. 33 and p. 108.
163 Q. 96:18. See *Muqaddimat al-mabānī*, in Jeffery, *Two Muqaddimas*, p. 37 and p. 108.
164 Q. 17:11. See *Muqaddimat al-mabānī*, in Jeffery, *Two Muqaddimas*, p. 37 and p. 108.
165 Q. 4:87.
166 Q. 18:49.
167 Q. 25:7.
168 Q. 70:36.
169 i.e. being one of the so-called 'inseparable prepositions', it would have been normal to have the orthography in which *li-* combines with the following word. e.g. *mā li-lladhīna kafarū*. See the chapter '*dhikr al-maqṭūʿ wa'l-mawṣūl*' in Dānī, *Maqnaʿ*, p. 75.
170 i.e. *al-malā'u*. It is written with *wāw* and *alif*, e.g. at Q. 23:24, and it is written without them, e.g. at Q. 7:60. See Sijistānī, *Kitāb al-Maṣāḥif*, p. 110.
171 Q. 6:34. Sijistānī, *Kitāb al-Maṣāḥif*, p. 107.
172 i.e. with *yā'* as the carrier of the *hamza*. See Sijistānī, *Kitāb al-Maṣāḥif*, p. 113.
173 Q. 42:51.
174 i.e. with *yā'* as the carrier of the *hamza*.
175 Q. 10:15. *Tilqā'i* is generally written here with *yā'* as the carrier of the *hamza*. See Sijistānī, *Kitāb al-Maṣāḥif*, p. 108.
176 Q. 51:47. The second *yā'* is superfluous. See Sijistānī, *Kitāb al-Maṣāḥif*, p. 113.
177 Q. 27:21. One would expect *aw la-adhbaḥannahu*. Note that the manuscript as reproduced by Ādharshab gives an incorrect reference for the quoted expression, as follows. *al-naml : al-naḥl* MA.
178 Q. 9:47. One would expect *wa la-awḍaʿū*. See Dānī, *Maqnaʿ*, p. 94.
179 Q. 3:167. One would expect *wa la-ttabaʿnākum*. See Zarkashī, *al-Burhān fī ʿulūm al-Qur'ān*, vol. 1, p. 380 ff.
180 The tribe of the Prophet, from Mecca and its vicinity.
181 Hudhayl were the tribe of Northern Arab descent which from early times occupied the lands east and west of Mecca, extending into the mountains in the direction of Ṭā'if. According to Ibn al-Kalbī, the tribe was the first to introduce idolatry amongst Ismāʿīl's descendents. Consult Ibn al-Kalbī, *Kitāb al-Asnām*.
182 Ḥārith b. Kaʿb, also known as the Balḥārith, were the tribe belonging to the Yemeni group who inhabited the district of Najrān, south of Mecca (sections also lived in Raydat al-Ṣayʿal in Ḥaḍramawt and in al-Falaja near Damascus). Some of the tribe professed Christianity, and the Melkite delegation sent from Najrān to the Prophet, circa 8/630, consisted in Balḥārith tribesmen. See Ibn Hishām, *Sīra*, p. 401 and pp. 958–962.
183 These are all conventions embellishing Qur'ān recitation. They are, respectively, the 'slanting' pronunciation of *ā* in Arabic, nasalisation, assimilation of the first of two consonants to the second, emphasis on a consonant (alternatively: 'velarisation'), and lengthening (literally: 'thinning') of *a* (*fatḥa*).
184 Ibn Ḥanbal, *Musnad*, 2, 332; Abū Dā'ūd, *Witr*, 22; also Ibn Ḥanbal, *Musnad*, 2, 440 (with slight difference in wording). See Zarkashī, *Burhān*, vol. 1, p. 211.

185 *Ishmām* is the pronunciation of *i* towards *u*, and *u* towards *i*.

186 *Ḥarf* means both 'letter' and 'edge'. For the prophetic tradition on the existence of the outer and inner dimensions, see Suyūṭī, *Itqān*, vol. 2, pp. 184–185.

187 In this context, the *mathānī* are those chapters of the Qur'ān which are shorter than the longest chapter and than those containing 100 verses, but which are longer than those in the portion called *al-mufaṣṣal*. See Lane, *Arabic-English Lexicon*, vol. 1, p. 360.

188 In the margin of the manuscript at this point is the statement: 'God's Messenger (may God bless him and give him peace) said, "Recite *al-Fīl* and *Quraysh* not separating them", and it is likewise transmitted in regard to *al-Ḍuḥā* and *A-lam nashrāḥ*.'

189 The manuscript has the following here in the margin: 'Upto this point is Meccan, and they differed over the end of the scripture [*sic*]. Ibn ʿAbbās said, "It consists in *al-ʿAnkabūt*"; and on Mujāhid's authority it is "*al-Muṭaffifūn*".'

190 There is a lacuna here in the manuscript as follows: *wa'l-jumla [ ] ḥarfan.* A number has evidently been omitted.

191 See note 92.

192 See note 94.

193 Abū ʿAbd Allāh Muḥammad b. Khālid b. ʿAbd al-Raḥmān b. Muḥammad b. ʿAlī al-Barqī al-Qummī. Amongst the foremost Shīʿī ḥadīth scholars and authorities on reports (*akhbār*). One of the companions of Imam Mūsā al-Kāẓim (d. 183/799) and Imam ʿAlī b. Mūsā al-Riḍā (d. 203/817), he survived until the days of Imam Muḥammad al-Taqī (d. 220/835). Often confused with his famous son Abū Jaʿfar Aḥmad al-Barqī (d. 274/887) whose *Kitāb al-Maḥāsin* seems to have grown out of an earlier version by the elder Barqī. Ṣadr, *Ta'sīs al-shīʿa li-ʿulūm al-islām*, p. 259 and p. 330. Ṭūsī, *Fihrist*, p. 148. Also see 'al-Barqī', *EI* [2], Supplement, pp. 127–128 (Ch. Pellat).

194 Aḥmad b. Abī Yaʿqūb b. Wāḍiḥ, known as 'al-Yaʿqūbī' (d. 278/892). His grandfather was among the clients of al-Manṣūr (d. 158/775), the ʿAbbāsid emperor who founded Baghdad. He travelled widely in the lands of Islam, both east and west. Shīʿī in religion, his *History* includes data omitted by other historians.

195 These two short prayers, written in the manuscript (folio 11B) at an angle after the lists, are known as the *Sūrat al-Ḥafd* and *Sūrat al-Khalʿ* which Ubayy b. Kaʿb placed in his codex (i.e. the *Qunūt* prayer – as mentioned on p. 72). It is noteworthy that we appear to have here the most ancient complete text of the two sūras.

196 Ādharshab (*Tafsīr al-Shahrastānī*, p. 140, note 1) suggests that this is the well-known 'Book of Sufficiency' (*Kitāb al-Istighnā'*), or 'The Sufficiency in the Science of the Qur'ān' (*al-Istighnā' fī ʿilm al-Qur'ān*), by Muḥammad b. Aḥmad al-Muqri' al-Naḥwī (d. 388/998), [GAL, S1, p. 597 has: Shams al-Dīn Muḥammad b. Aḥmad Abū ʿAbd Allāh al-Muqri' al-Anbārī]. He composed the *Istighnā'* in 20 volumes and put it together over a twelve-year period. Ḥajjī Khalīfa, *Kashf al-ẓunūn*, vol. 1, p. 79 and p. 441.

197 The chapters in question are called the Long Seven (*al-sabʿ al-ṭuwal*) because they are the longest chapters of the Qur'ān. See Ṭabarsī, *Majmaʿ al-bayān*, vol. 1, p. 14.

198 Amongst the chapters of the Qur'ān, the chapter of Repentance uniquely lacks the opening formula: 'In the name of God, the Infinitely Merciful, the Compassionate'. Thus it is sometimes run together with the previous chapter, the Spoils.

199 This last interpretation proves to be that of Shahrastānī himself, as explored by him in the 'arcana of the verses'.

200 Ṭabarsī, *Majmaʿ al-bayān*, vol. 1, p. 14.

201 MA *al-mufaṣṣal* : *al-sabʿ al-mufaṣṣal.*

202 This appears to be Abū Bakr Muḥammad b. Mūsā al-Wāsiṭī from Farghāna (d. 331/942 in Merv). The work quoted by Shahrastānī is seemingly not extant.

203 MA *iḥdā ʿashara* : *aḥad ʿashar.*

204 Q. 42.

205 MA *arbaʿ ʿashara* : *arbaʿ ʿashar.*

206 Suyūṭī, *Itqān*, vol. 1, p. 58; Ṭabarsī, *Majmaʿ al-bayān*, vol. 1, p. 14; Majlisī, *Biḥār al-anwār*, vol. 89, p. 27.

207 Saʿīd b. Jubayr b. Hishām al-Asadī, Abū ʿAbd Allāh (d. 175/791). A jurist famed for piety. Ibn ʿAbbās is reported as saying 'O People of Kufa! You inquire of me while Saʿīd b. Jubayr is amongst you?' Saʿīd rebelled with Ibn al-Ashʿath against al-Ḥajjāj and was killed in consequence. Dāʾūdī, *Ṭabaqāt al-mufassirīn*, vol. 2, pp. 181–182; Dhahabī, *Tadhkirat al-ḥuffāẓ*, vol. 1, p. 11; Iṣfahānī, *Ḥilyat al-awliyāʾ*, vol. 4, p. 272; Ibn al-ʿImād al-Ḥanbalī, *Shadharāt al-dhahab*, vol. 1, p. 108; Ibn al-Jazarī, *Ghāyat al-nihāya*, vol. 1, p. 305; Ibn Khallikān, *Wafayāt al-aʿyān*, vol. 2, p.112.

208 Q. 15:87.

209 It is also claimed that the term Doubled Ones in Q. 15:87 refers to the chapter of Praise (*al-Ḥamd*), i.e. the Exordium, Q. 1. Ṭabarsī, *Majmaʿ al-bayān*, vol. 1, p. 14.

Chapter 4
On readings (qirāʾāt)

210 In the margin of the manuscript (12B) are the following ten names: Ibn Kathīr, Nāfiʿ, Abū ʿAmr, ʿĀṣim, Ibn ʿĀmir, Ḥamza, Kisāʾī, Ibn al-Qaʿqāʿ, Yaʿqūb b. Isḥāq, Khalaf b. Hishām.

211 ʿAbd Allāh b. Kathīr b. Zādhān b. Fīrūzān b. Hormuz, 'imam' Abū Maʿbad al-Makkī al-Dārī (al-Dārānī). Born in Mecca 45/665, he remained by consensus the foremost authority in readings (*qirāʾāt*) until his death. From a family of Iranian origin that had emigrated to Yemen, he was the client of ʿAmr b. ʿAlqama al-Kinānī and earned his livelihood as a perfumer (= *dārānī*). It is also said that his name was al-Dārī because he was from the tribe of Banū'l-Dār b. Hānīʾ. His recognition as a 'canonical reader' was through the Shāfiʿī scholar, Ibn Mujāhid, who was connected with Ibn Abī Bizza (Bizzī, also Bizzā) and Muḥammad b. ʿAbd al-Raḥmān ('Qunbul') – the direct pupils of Ibn Kathīr himself. See Ibn al-Jazarī, *Ghāyat al-nihāya*, vol. 1, p. 433; also Mizzī, *Tahdhīb al-kamāl*, vol. 10, p. 439.

212 Aḥmad b. Muḥammad b. ʿAlqama b. Nāfiʿ b. ʿUmar b. Ṣubḥ b. ʿAwn, Abū'l-Ḥasan al-Nabbāl al-Makkī (d. 240/854, or 245/859). In his time, the foremost authority in Mecca on recitation. Ibn al-Jazarī, *Ghāyat al-nihāya*, vol. 1, pp. 123–124.

213 On this translation, see note 22.

214 Wahb b. Wāḍiḥ, Abū'l-Qāsim al-Makkī (d. 190/806). Studied recitation with critical review under Ismāʿīl al-Qusṭ, then with Shibl b. ʿAbbād and Maʿrūf b. Mushkān. Later Aḥmad b. Muḥammad al-Qawwās and Aḥmad b. Muḥammad al-Bizzī (i.e. Ibn Abī Bizza) transmitted recitation on his authority with critical

review. The leadership of Qur'ān-reciters at Mecca fell to him. Ibn al-Jazarī, *Ghāyat al-nihāya*, vol. 2, p. 361.

215 Ismāʿīl b. ʿAbd Allāh b. Qusṭanṭīn, Abū Isḥāq al-Makhzūmī (= cliental agnomen) al-Makkī, known as al-Qusṭ (d. 170/786). Recited in the presence of Ibn Kathīr and of his two associates Shibl b. ʿAbbād and Maʿrūf b. Mushkān. Ibn al-Jazarī, *Ghāyat al-nihāya*, vol. 1, pp. 165–166; also Dodge, *Fihrist of al-Nadīm*, vol. 1, p. 64.

216 Shibl b. ʿAbbād, Abū Dā'ūd, al-Makkī (d. 148/765). Transmitted exegesis from Mujāhid b. Jabr al-Makkī. One of the most eminent associates of Ibn Kathīr; declared to have been a trustworthy and accurate reciter. Ibn al-Jazarī, *Ghāyat al-nihāya*, vol. 1, pp. 323–324; also Mizzī, *Tahdhīb al-kamāl*, vol. 8, p. 269.

217 Maʿrūf b. Mushkān, Abū'l-Walīd al-Makkī (d. 165/782). Reciter of Mecca, with Shibl. Descended from the Iranians sent in ships by the Sasanian emperor to drive the Abyssinians from Yemen, he studied recitation with critical review (*ʿaraḍa*) under Ibn Kathīr. Ibn al-Jazarī, *Ghāyat al-nihāya*, vol. 1, pp. 303–304.

218 Aḥmad b. Muḥammad b. ʿAbd Allāh b. al-Qāsim b. Nāfiʿ b. Abī Bizza, Abū'l-Ḥasan al-Bizzī al-Makkī (d. 250/864). Reciter of Mecca and the caller to prayer of the Sacred Mosque. Ibn al-Jazarī, *Ghāyat al-nihāya*, vol. 1, pp. 119–120.

219 ʿIkrima b. Sulaymān b. Kathīr, Abū'l-Qāsim al-Makkī (d. before 200/815). Studied, with critical review, under Shibl and Ismāʿīl al-Qusṭ; Aḥmad b. Muḥammad al-Bizzī studied under him with critical review. He was the leading authority in recitation for the Meccans after Shibl and his associates. Ibn al-Jazarī, *Ghāyat al-nihāya*, vol. 2, p. 515.

220 Muḥammad b. ʿAbd al-Raḥmān b. Khālid b. Muḥammad b. Saʿīd b. Jurja, Abū ʿAmr al-Makhzūmī (= cliental agnomen), nicknamed Qunbul (d. 291/903). The foremost authority of the reciters of the Ḥijāz; he studied recitation, with critical review, under Aḥmad b. Muḥammad b. ʿAwn al-Nabāl. Ibn al-Jazarī, *Ghāyat al-nihāya*, vol. 2, pp. 165–166.

221 ʿAbd al-Wahhāb b. Fulayḥ b. Riyāḥ (d. circa 250/864). Studied recitation with critical review and auditing, under Dā'ūd b. Shibl and a large number of young men (*fityān*) of Mecca and their shaykhs, amounting to 80 people. Ibn al-Jazarī, *Ghāyat al-nihāya*, vol. 1, pp. 480–481.

222 MA *Jabr* : *Jabīr*. See note 37.

223 Nāfiʿ b. ʿAbd al-Raḥmān b. Abī Naʿīm, Abū Ruwaym, also Abū Naʿīm, also Abū'l-Ḥasan, also Abū ʿAbd Allāh (d. 169/785–6, or 170/786–7, or 167/783–4, or 150/767, or 157/774), al-Laythī (= cliental agnomen) given that he was the client of Jaʿwana b. Shaʿūb al-Laythī. One of the 'seven reciters'. Originally from Iṣfahān, he was said to have been a black man, of fine appearance. Studied recitation, with critical review, under a group of successors in Medīna. Ibn al-Jazarī, *Ghāyat al-nihāya*, vol. 2, pp. 330–334; Bukhārī, *al-Ta'rīkh al-kabīr*, vol. 4, part 2, p. 87; Mizzī, *Tahdhīb al-kamāl*, vol. 19, p. 22; Dodge, *Fihrist of al-Nadīm*, pp. 63, 70, 79, 80, 81.

224 ʿĪsā b. Mīnā b. Wardān b. ʿĪsā b. ʿAbd al-Ṣamad b. ʿUmar b. ʿAbd Allāh al-Zarqī, also al-Marrī, nicknamed Qālūn (d. 220/835). Reciter and grammarian of Medīna; it is said that he was the stepson of Nāfiʿ and it was he who named him Qālūn due to the excellence of his recitation, *qālūn* being from Greek *kalos, kale, kalon*, meaning 'excellent'. Ibn al-Jazarī, *Ghāyat al-nihāya*, vol. 1, pp. 615–616; Dodge, *Fihrist of al-Nadīm*, p. 64; also Ibn Taghrībirdī, *al-Nujūm al-zāhira*, vol. 2, p. 235.

225 ʿUthmān b. Saʿīd, or alternatively Saʿīd b. ʿAbd Allāh b. ʿAmr b. Sulaymān b.

Ibrāhīm, Abū Saʿīd, and also Abū'l-Qāsim, or Abū ʿAmr, al-Qurashī (= cliental agnomen) al-Qibṭī al-Miṣrī, nicknamed 'Warsh' (d. 197/813). In his day acknowledged as the chief authority of the recognized reciters, he critically reviewed the Qur'ān with Nāfiʿ many times. Died in Egypt. Ibn al-Jazarī, *Ghāyat al-nihāya*, vol. 1, p. 502; also Ibn Taghrībirdī, *al-Nujūm al-zāhira*, vol. 2, p.155; also Ibn al-ʿImād al-Ḥanbalī, *Shadharāt al-dhahab*, vol. 1, p. 349.

226 Ismāʿīl b. Jaʿfar b. Abī Kathīr al-Anṣārī (= cliental agnomen) Abū Isḥāq or alternatively Abū Ibrāhīm (and Abū Bishr, according to Shahrastānī) al-Madanī (d. 180/796, or 177/793). He recited in the presence of Shayba b. Naṣṣāḥ (see Ibn al-Jazarī, *Ghāyat al-nihāya*, vol. 1, pp. 329–330), then in the presence of Nāfiʿ and Sulaymān b. Muslim b. Jamāz and ʿĪsā b. Wardān. Died in Baghdad. Ibn al-Jazarī, *Ghāyat al-nihāya*, vol. 1, p. 163; also Dodge, *Fihrist of al-Nadīm*, pp. 64, 81.

227 ʿAbd al-Raḥmān b. ʿAbdūs, Abū'l-Zaʿrāʾ al-Baghdādī (d. shortly after 280/893). Studied recitation, with critical review, under Abū ʿUmar al-Dawrī with numerous transmissions. Ibn al-Jazarī, *Ghāyat al-nihāya*, vol. 1, pp. 373–374.

228 Ḥafṣ b. ʿUmar b. ʿAbd al-ʿAzīz b. Ṣuhbān, Abū ʿAmr al-Dawrī al-Azdī al-Baghdādī al-Naḥwī ('the grammarian') al-Ḍarīr ('the blind man') (d. 246/860). There is confusion whether his name is Abū ʿAmr or Abū ʿUmar. Resident of Samarrā, leader in recitation and the chief authority in his period; the first person to collect recitation; recited in the presence of Ismāʿīl b. Jaʿfar on the authority of Nāfiʿ. Ibn al-Jazarī, *Ghāyat al-nihāya*, vol. 1, pp. 255–256; Dhahabī, *Mīzān al-iʿtidāl*, vol. 1, p. 265; Dodge, *Fihrist of al-Nadīm*, p. 557.

229 Ibn al-Jazarī renders the lineage of Abū ʿAmr at greater length: Zabbān b. al-ʿAlāʾ b. ʿAmmār etc. etc., with more than 20 variations occurring in his name. Ibn al-Jazarī transmits (on Qāḍī Asad al-Yazīdī's authority) that he was said to be Abū ʿAmr from Fārs, from the locale known as Kāzirūn. Ibn al-Jazarī, *Ghāyat al-nihāya*, vol. 1, pp. 288–289; also Dodge, *Fihrist of al-Nadīm*, pp. 63, 68, 70, 72–73, 78, 87, 90–93, 103, 109, 191, 231.

230 Yaḥyā b. al-Mubārak b. al-Mughīra, Abū Muḥammad al-ʿAdwī al-Baṣrī, known as al-Yazīdī (d. 202/817–18). Grammarian and reciter; resident of Baghdad; known as al-Yazīdī because of his association with Yazīd b. Manṣūr al-Ḥumayrī (the maternal uncle of the caliph al-Mahdī). The latter studied recitation, with critical review, under Abū ʿAmr al-Yazīdī, taking over the responsibility for that from him. He also studied recitation under Ḥamza al-Zayyāt (see below in text). Died in Merv. Ibn al-Jazarī, *Ghāyat al-nihāya*, vol. 2, p. 375. It seems that Shahrastānī mentions the agnomen of al-Yazīdī as 'Abū ʿAmr' while Ibn al-Jazarī mentions it in numerous contexts as 'Abū Muḥammad'.

231 Ṣāliḥ b. Ziyād b. ʿAbd Allāh b. Ismāʿīl b. Ibrāhīm b. al-Jārūd, Abū Shuʿayb al-Sūsī al-Raqqī (d. 261/874–5). Studied recitation with critical review, and auditing, under Abū Muḥammad al-Yazīdī, and was amongst his most eminent students. Ibn al-Jazarī, *Ghāyat al-nihāya*, vol. 1, pp. 332–333; also Mizzī, *Tahdhīb al-kamāl*, vol. 9, pp. 29–30.

232 MA *Saʿīd ibn Jubayr wa Mujāhid ibn Jabr : Saʿīd wa Mujāhid ibnay Jubayr*. This is an error repeated in the manuscript. It appears that the copyist abridged and wrote these names in the form mentioned, in the mistaken belief that Saʿīd and Mujāhid were brothers. Also see note 365. Saʿīd and Mujāhid are amongst those in whose presence Abū ʿAmr b. al-ʿAlāʾ recited (see above in text), as confirmed by Ibn al-Jazarī, *Ghāyat al-nihāya*, vol. 1, pp. 288–292.

233 Shujāʿ b. Abī Naṣr, Abū Nuʿaym, al-Balkhī (d. 190/806). Amongst the most eminent associates of Abū ʿAmr b. al-ʿAlāʾ. Died in Baghdad. Ibn al-Jazarī, *Ghāyat al-nihāya*, vol. 1, p. 324.

234 MA *al-Balkhī: al-Bajlī.*

235 Muḥammad b. Ghālib, Abū Jaʿfar al-Anmāṭī al-Baghdādī (d. 254/868). Studied recitation under Shujāʿ who in turn studied it under Abū ʿAmr. Ibn al-Jazarī, *Ghāyat al-nihāya*, vol. 2, pp. 226–227.

236 ʿĀṣim b. Bahdala, Abū'l-Najūd Abū Bakr al-Asadī (= cliental agnomen) al-Kūfī. Some report that Abū'l-Najūd was the name of his father, no first name for him other than that being known, while Bahdala was the name of his mother; others state that the first name of Abū'l-Najūd was in fact ʿAbd Allāh. Leadership of the reciters in Kufa devolved to him after Abū ʿAbd al-Raḥmān al-Sulamī. Numerous accounts of the date of his death are mentioned, among them: 120/738, 127/745, 128/746, 130/748. Ibn al-Jazarī, *Ghāyat al-nihāya*, vol. 1, p. 349; also Dodge, *Fihrist of al-Nadīm*, pp. 64–5, 70, 73.

237 MA *huwa mawlā : huwa fī mawlā.*

238 MA *Bahdala : Bahāla Bahdala.*

239 Also known as Shuʿba (rather than Abū Bakr) b. ʿAyyāsh b. Sālim, Abū Bakr al-Ḥannāṭ al-Asadī al-Kūfī (d. 193/809 or 194/810). Rated as an impeccable transmitter. There are thirteen variations of his first name, the most correct of which is seemingly Shuʿba. Ibn al-Jazarī, *Ghāyat al-nihāya*, vol. 1, pp. 325–326; Dodge, *Fihrist of al-Nadīm*, pp. 65, 80.

240 Ibn al-Jazarī mentions the name of his father and grandfather as follows: Yaʿqūb b. Muḥammad b. Khalīfa b. Saʿīd b. Hilāl, Abū Yūsuf al-Aʿshā ('the blind man') al-Tamīmī al-Kūfī (d. circa 200/815–16). He studied recitation, with critical review, under Abū Bakr Shuʿba, and Muḥammad b. Ḥabīb al-Shumūnī. Ibn al-Jazarī, *Ghāyat al-nihāya*, vol. 2, p. 390.

241 Yaḥyā b. Ādam b. Sulaymān b. Khālid b. Usayd Abū Zakariyyā al-Ṣilḥī (d. 203/818–819). Transmitted recitation on the authority of Abū Bakr b. ʿAyyāsh, by auditing. Ibn al-Jazarī, *Ghāyat al-nihāya*, vol. 2, pp. 363–364; Dodge, *Fihrist of al-Nadīm*, pp. 67, 78, 82, 506, 549.

242 Muḥammad b. Ḥabīb, Abū Jaʿfar al-Shumūnī al-Kūfī. Studied recitation, with critical review, under Abū Yūsuf al-Aʿshā. Ibn al-Jazarī, *Ghāyat al-nihāya*, vol. 2, pp. 114–115.

243 Shuʿayb b. Ayyūb b. Ruzayq, Abū Bakr, also known as Abū Bakr al-Ṣarīfīnī (d. 130/748 or 131/748–9). He studied recitation with critical review, and auditing, under Yaḥyā b. Ādam. Ibn al-Jazarī, *Ghāyat al-nihāya*, vol. 1, p. 327; Mizzī, *Tahdhīb al-kamāl*, vol. 8, pp. 362–363.

244 Ḥafṣ b. Sulaymān b. Mughīra, Abū ʿAmr b. Abī Dāʾūd al-Asadī al-Kūfī al-Ghaḍirī al-Bazāz, also known as Ḥufayṣ (d. 180/796). He studied recitation with critical review and dictation (*talqīn*) under ʿĀṣim, as the latter's stepson. Ibn al-Jazarī, *Ghāyat al-nihāya*, vol. 1, pp. 254–255; also al-Dhahabī, *Mīzān al-iʿtidāl*, vol. 1, p. 261.

245 ʿAmr b. al-Ṣabbāḥ b. Ṣubayḥ, Abū Ḥafṣ al-Baghdādī (d. 221/836). Skilled reciter, transmitted recitation with critical review and auditing on the authority of Ḥafṣ b. Sulaymān. Al-Dānī said that they were brothers. It has also been said that he and ʿUbayd were one and the same (see note 246). Ibn al-Jazarī, *Ghāyat al-nihāya*, vol. 1, p. 601.

246 'Ubayd b. Ṣabbāḥ b. Abī Shar' b. Ṣubayḥ, Abū Muḥammad al-Nahshalī al-Kūfī, later al-Baghdādī. Studied recitation with critical review under Ḥafṣ, who studied under 'Āṣim; Aḥmad b. Sahl al-Ashnānī and others transmitted recitation from him. Abū 'Alī al-Ahwāzī said: "Amr b. al-Ṣabbāḥ and 'Ubayd b. al-Ṣabbāḥ were not brothers'. Ḥāfiẓ Abū 'Amr said, '[...] they were brothers', while others said 'they are one and the same'. Ibn al-Jazarī, *Ghāyat al-nihāya*, vol. 1, pp. 494–496.

247 Ibn al-Jazarī mentions him with the name Ḥamdān b. Abī 'Uthmān al-Daqqāq. He says: 'he transmitted recitation with critical review on the authority of Ḥafṣ'. Ibn al-Jazarī, *Ghāyat al-nihāya*, vol. 1, p. 260.

248 Aḥmad b. Sahl b. al-Fayrūzān (not as in the manuscript, Fīrūz) (d. 307/919–920). Shaykh Abū'l-'Abbās al-Ashnānī recited in the presence of 'Ubayd b. al-Ṣabbāḥ the associate of Ḥafṣ; he recited in the presence of a group of the associates of 'Amr b. al-Ṣabbāḥ. Ibn al-Jazarī, *Ghāyat al-nihāya*, vol. 1, pp. 59–60.

249 MA *Ḥubaysh: Jubaysh*. See note 100.

250 'Abd Allāh b. Ḥabīb b. Rabī'a, Abū 'Abd al-Raḥmān al-Sulamī al-Ḍarīr (= 'the blind') (d. 73/692 or 74/693). The Kufan reciter (not to be confused with Abū 'Abd al-Raḥmān al-Sulamī, the famous Ṣūfī author of Nīshāpūr, d. 412/1021). Studied recitation under 'Alī and 'Uthmān, 'Abd Allāh b. Mas'ūd, Zayd b. Thābit and Ubayy b. Ka'b; 'Āṣim and many others studied recitation under him. Ibn al-Jazarī, *Ghāyat al-nihāya*, vol. 1, pp. 313–314.

251 Ḥamza b. Ḥabīb b. 'Umāra al-Kūfī al-Tamīmī (probably as the Banū Tamīm's client, but sometimes held to have been an actual member of the tribe) al-Zayyāt ('the oil-dealer') (d. 156/773, or 154/771, or 158/775). One of the 'seven reciters'; studied recitation, with critical review, under Sulaymān b. al-A'mash, Ḥumrān b. A'yan, Abū Isḥāq al-Sabī'ī, Ibn Abī Laylā, Ja'far b. Muḥammad al-Ṣādiq and others. Ibn al-Jazarī, *Ghāyat al-nihāya*, vol. 1, pp. 261–263; al-Dhahabī, *Mīzān al-i'tidāl*, vol. 1, p. 284; Dodge, *Fihrist of al-Nadīm*, pp. 66, 67, 69, 70, 73, 79–81, 84–85.

252 A trading post on the Iranian frontier.

253 MA *Sulaym : Salmān.*

254 Sulaym b. 'Īsā b. Sulaym b. 'Āmir b. Ghālib b. Sa'īd b. Sulaym b. Dā'ūd, Abū 'Īsā, also Abū Muḥammad al-Ḥanafī (= cliental agnomen) al-Kūfī (d. 188/804, or 189/805). He did a critical review of the Qur'ān with Ḥamza, being one of his foremost associates. Ḥafṣ b. 'Umar al-Dawrī, Khalaf b. Hishām and Khallād b. Khālid did a critical review with him. Ibn al-Jazarī, *Ghāyat al-nihāya*, vol. 1, p. 318–319; also Dodge, *Fihrist of al-Nadīm*, p. 69.

255 Khalaf b. Hishām b. Tha'lab b. Khalaf, Abū Muḥammad al-Asadī (d. 229/844). One of the ten reciters; one of those who transmitted on the authority of Sulaym, on the authority of Ḥamza. Died in Baghdad. Ibn al-Jazarī, *Ghāyat al-nihāya*, vol. 1, pp. 273–274; Dodge, *Fihrist of al-Nadīm*, p. 69, 78–81, 84, 102.

256 Khallād b. Khālid, Abū 'Īsā, also Abū 'Abd Allāh al-Shaybānī (= cliental agnomen) al-Kūfī (d. 120/738). He studied recitation, with critical review, under Sulaym. Ibn al-Jazarī, *Ghāyat al-nihāya*, vol. 1, pp. 274–275.

257 'Abd al-Raḥmān b. Abī Laylā Abū 'Īsā al-Anṣārī al-Kūfī (d. 83/702). An eminent successor. Studied recitation with critical review under 'Alī b. Abī Ṭālib; his son 'Īsā transmitted recitation on his authority. Died at the Battle of Jamājim between al-Ash'ath and al-Ḥajjāj. Ibn al-Jazarī, *Ghāyat al-nihāya*, vol. 1, pp. 376–377.

258 MA *Sulaymān : Sulaym.*

259 Sulaymān b. Mihrān al-Aʿmash, Abū Muḥammad al-Asadī al-Kāhilī (= cliental agnomen) al-Kūfī (d. 148/765). The eminent authority; he studied recitation, with critical review, under Ibrāhīm al-Nakhaʿī, Zirr b. Ḥubaysh, Zayd b. Wahb, ʿĀṣim b. Abī'l-Najūd, Mujāhid b. Jabr, Abū'l-ʿĀliya al-Riyāḥī, and others. Ibn al-Jazarī, *Ghāyat al-nihāya*, vol. 1, pp. 315–316.

260 MA *ibn : abī.*

261 MA *Sulaym : Sālim.*

262 ʿAlī b. Ḥamza b. ʿAbd Allāh b. Bahman b. Fīrūz al-Asadī (= cliental agnomen), Abū'l-Ḥasan al-Kisā'ī (d. 185/801 or 193/809). One of the descendants of Iranians from the Sawād region of Iraq; leadership of the Kufan reciters devolved to him after Ḥamza al-Zayyāt; studied recitation under Ḥamza with critical review, four times. He acted as tutor to the sons of Hārūn al-Rashīd. Ibn al-Jazarī reports the name of the village where he died as Ranbūya. Ibn al-Jazarī, *Ghāyat al-nihāya*, vol. 1, pp. 535–540; Dodge, *Fihrist of al-Nadīm*, pp. 79, 84, 112, 143, 144, 158, 191, 361, 365, 504.

263 MA *Ḥārith : Ḥarith.*

264 Al-Layth b. Khālid, Abū'l-Ḥārith al-Baghdādī (d. 240/854–5). Did critical review with Kisā'ī, being amongst his most eminent associates. Ibn al-Jazarī, *Ghāyat al-nihāya*, vol. 2, p. 34; Dodge, *Fihrist of al-Nadīm*, p. 67.

265 Q. 3:171.

266 MA *ʿĀmir : ʿIyāḍ.*

267 ʿAbd Allāh b. ʿĀmir b. Yazīd b. Tamīm b. Rabīʿa b. ʿĀmir b. ʿAbd Allāh b. ʿImrān al-Yaḥṣubī (d. 118/736). There is much variation over his filionymic agnomen, the best known version being Abū ʿImrān. The leading authority of the Syrians in recitation. He studied recitation, with critical review, under Abū'l-Dardā' and al-Mughīra b. Abī Shihāb; it is also said that he did critical review with ʿUthmān himself. He died in Damascus. Ibn al-Jazarī, *Ghāyat al-nihāya*, vol. 1, pp. 423–425.

268 Ibn al-Jazarī mentions his name in the following way: ʿAbd Allāh b. Aḥmad b. Bashīr, alternatively, Bashīr b. Dhakwān b. ʿAmr, Abū'l-Naḍr and Abū Muḥammad, al-Qurashī al-Fahrī al-Dimashqī (d. 242/856–857). He recited in the presence of a group of authorities, including Hārūn b. Mūsā al-Akhfash. Ibn al-Jazarī, *Ghāyat al-nihāya*, vol. 1, pp. 404–405.

269 Hārūn b. Mūsā b. Sharīk, Abū ʿAbd Allāh al-Taghlabī al-Akhfash al-Dimashqī (d. 292/905). The chief authority of the reciters in Damascus; studied recitation with critical review and auditing under Ibn Dhakwān. Ibn al-Jazarī, *Ghāyat al-nihāya*, vol. 2, pp. 347–348.

270 Hishām b. ʿAmmār b. Naṣīr b. Maysara, Abū'l-Walīd al-Sulamī, also al-Ẓafrī al-Dimashqī (d. 244/858 or 245/859). He studied recitation with critical review under Ayyūb b. Tamīm and others. Ibn al-Jazarī, *Ghāyat al-nihāya*, vol. 2, pp. 354–356; Dodge, *Fihrist of al-Nadīm*, p. 81.

271 Ayyūb b. Tamīm b. Sulaymān b. Ayyūb, Abū Sulaymān al-Tamīmī (not as in the manuscript, b. Tamīm al-Nakhaʿī) (d. 219/834). Recited in the presence of Yaḥyā b. al-Ḥārith al-Dhamārī, and ʿAbd Allāh b. Dhakwān recited in his presence. Ibn al-Jazarī, *Ghāyat al-nihāya*, vol. 2, p. 172; also Dodge, *Fihrist of al-Nadīm*, p. 66.

272 Yaḥyā b. Ḥārith b. ʿAmr b. Yaḥyā b. Sulaymān b. al-Ḥārith, Abū ʿAmr, also Abū ʿUmar, al-Dhamārī, later al-Dimashqī (d. 135/752–3). He met up with Wāthila b. al-Asqaʿ, transmitted on his authority and recited in his presence. Ibn al-Jazarī, *Ghāyat al-nihāya*, vol. 2, p. 367; Dodge, *Fihrist of al-Nadīm*, pp. 62, 65, 66, 80, 81.

273 Aḥmad b. Yūsuf al-Taghlabī, Abū ʿAbd Allāh al-Baghdādī (according to Ibn al-Jazarī). Transmitted recitation on the authority of Ibn Dhakwān. Ibn al-Jazarī, *Ghāyat al-nihāya*, vol. 1, pp. 152–153.

274 Al-Mughīra b. Abī Shihāb, ʿAbd Allāh b. ʿAmr b. al-Mughīra b. Rabīʿa b. ʿAmr b. Makhzūm, Abū Hāshim, al-Makhzūmī al-Shāmī (d. 91/301). Studied recitation, with critical review, under ʿUthmān b. ʿAffān; ʿAbd Allāh b. ʿĀmir studied recitation under him with critical review. Ibn al-Jazarī, *Ghāyat al-nihāya*, vol. 2, pp. 305–306.

275 Yazīd b. al-Qaʿqāʿ, Abū Jaʿfar al-Makhzūmī al-Madanī. A famous successor. It is said his name was Jandab b. Fīrūz and also simply Fīrūz. Did critical review of the Qurʾān with his patron ʿAbd Allāh b. ʿAyyāsh b. Abī Rabīʿa, ʿAbd Allāh b. ʿAbbās and Abū Hurayra; Nāfiʿ b. Abī Nuʿaym, Sulaymān b. Muslim b. Jammāz and others transmitted recitation from him. It appears that the year of his death as mentioned by Shahrastānī is at odds with that mentioned by others, e.g. Ibn al-Jazarī states that ʿAbū Jaʿfar died in Medīna in the year 130/748, and it was also said 132/749–750 or 129/746–7 or 127/744–5 or 128/745–6ʾ. Ibn al-Athīr goes to the other extreme in his *Kāmil* when he puts his death as early as 110/728. Ibn al-Jazarī, *Ghāyat al-nihāya*, vol. 2, pp. 382–384.

276 i.e. 62/681–2.

277 ʿĪsā b. Wardān, Abū'l-Ḥārith al-Madanī al-Ḥudhāʾ (d. circa 160/776–7). Did critical review with Abū Jaʿfar and Shayba; later did critical review with Nāfiʿ. Ibn al-Jazarī, *Ghāyat al-nihāya*, vol. 1, p. 616.

278 Sulaymān b. Muslim b. Jammāz, Abū'l-Rabīʿ al-Zuhrī (= cliental agnomen) al-Madanī (d. after 170/786–7). Did critical review with Abū Jaʿfar and Shayba; later did critical review with Nāfiʿ. Ibn al-Jazarī, *Ghāyat al-nihāya*, vol. 1, p. 315.

279 Abū Hurayra ʿAbd al-Raḥmān b. Sakhr al-Dawsī al-Yamanī (d. 59/679). Repeatedly cited as the authority for prophetic traditions quoted by Shahrastānī, as by others. Supposedly nicknamed due to his habit of keeping a kitten (*hurayra*) for company while herding goats for his tribe. After embracing Islam, circa 629, he depended on the Prophet's charity and became one of the ultra-pious paupers known as the *Ahl al-Ṣuffa*. Appointed governor in Baḥrayn by ʿUmar b. al-Khaṭṭāb, but was later deposed and the funds in his keeping confiscated, apparently for his leniency and pre-occupation with worship. Later, on being invited to resume his governorship, Abū Hurayra declined. Reputed for both his religiosity and keen humour, he is agreed to have been the most prolific transmitter of prophetic traditions. *EI*[2], vol. 1, p. 129 (J. Robson).

280 Yaʿqūb b. Isḥāq b. Zayd b. ʿAbd Allāh b. Abī Isḥāq, Abū Muḥammad al-Ḥaḍramī (= cliental agnomen) al-Baṣrī (d. 205/820–1). Leading authority of the people of Basra and its official reciter. Ibn al-Jazarī, *Ghāyat al-nihāya*, vol. 3, pp. 386–387; Ibn Taghrībirdī, *al-Nujūm al-zāhira*, vol. 2, p. 179; Ibn Khallikān, *Wafayāt al-aʿyān*, vol. 2, p. 406; Yāfiʿī, *Mirʾāt al-janān*, vol. 2, p. 30.

281 Sallām b. Sulaymān al-Ṭawīl, Abū'l-Mundhir al-Muznī (= cliental agnomen), al-Basrī, later al-Kūfī (d. 171/787–8). Studied recitation, with critical review, under ʿĀṣim b. Abī'l-Najūd, Abū ʿAmr b. al-ʿAlāʾ and others. Ibn al-Jazarī, *Ghāyat al-nihāya*, vol. 1, p. 309; Dodge, *Fihrist of al-Nadīm*, pp. 68, 390.

282 Muḥammad b. al-Mutawakkil, Abū ʿAbd Allāh al-Luʾluʾī al-Baṣrī, known as Ruways (d. 238/852–854). Studied recitation, with critical review, under Yaʿqūb al-Ḥaḍramī; died in Basra. Ibn al-Jazarī, *Ghāyat al-nihāya*, vol. 2, pp. 234–235; Ṣafadī, *al-Wāfī bi'l-wafayāt*, vol. 4, p. 384.

283 Rawḥ b. ʿAbd al-Muʾmin, Abūʾl-Ḥasan al-Hudhalī (= cliental agnomen) al-Baṣrī al-Naḥwī (= 'the grammarian') (d. 234/848–849 or 235/849–850). One of Ḥaḍramī's main associates, with whom he did critical review of recitation. Ibn al-Jazarī, *Ghāyat al-nihāya*, vol. 1, p. 285.

284 This is Muḥammad b. Wahb (not as in the manuscript, b. Yaḥyā) b. Yaḥyā b. al-ʿAlāʾ b. ʿAbd al-Ḥakam b. ʿUbayd b. Hilāl b. Tamīm al-Thaqafī al-Baṣrī (d. shortly after 270/883–4). Recited in the presence of Rawḥ whose company he kept, being one of his most illustrious associates. Ibn al-Jazarī, *Ghāyat al-nihāya*, vol. 2, p. 276.

285 Muḥammad b. al-Jahm b. Hārūn, Abū ʿAbd Allāh al-Samarrī al-Baghdādī, 'the scribe' (*al-kātib*) (d. 208/823–4). Transmitted readings by auditing, on the authority of Khalaf, Bazzār and Walıd b. al-Ḥassān; the associate of Yaʿqūb; died in Baghdad. Ibn al-Jazarī, *Ghāyat al-nihāya*, vol. 2, p.113.

286 al-Walīd b. Hassān al-Tawzī al-Baṣrī. Transmitted recitation with critical review on the authority of Yaʿqūb b. Isḥāq al-Ḥaḍramī; Muḥammad b. al-Jahm transmitted recitation on his authority, with critical review. Ibn al-Jazarī, *Ghāyat al-nihāya*, vol. 2, p. 359.

287 Ibn al-Jazarī mentions his surname (*nisba*) in two ways: Khalaf b. Hishām b. Thaʿlab b. Khalaf b. Thaʿlab b. Hishām b. Thaʿlab b. Dāwud b. Muqsim b. Ghālib, Abū Muḥammad al-Asadī. Or alternatively: Khalaf b. Hishām b. Ṭālib b. Ghurāb al-Bazzār al-Baghdādī. Died 229/844 in Baghdad. Ibn al-Jazarī mentions that Shahrastānī says that he was Kufan; however, he was associated with Baghdad for some time before Kufa and he attached himself to Sulaym b. ʿĪsā. Ibn al-Jazarī, *Ghāyat al-nihāya*, vol. 2, pp. 272–274; Ḥāfiẓ Abū Bakr Aḥmad b. ʿAlī al-Khaṭīb al-Baghdādī, *Taʾrīkh Baghdād*, vol. 8, p. 322; Dodge, *Fihrist of al-Nadīm*, pp. 69, 78–81, 84, 102.

288 As Ibn al-Jazarī cites him, this is: Isḥāq b. Ibrāhīm b. ʿUthmān b. ʿAbd Allāh Abū Yaʿqūb al-Marwazī, later al-Baghdādī (d. 286/899). Transmitter of the preferred reading of Khalaf on his authority. Ibn al-Jazarī, *Ghāyat al-nihāya*, vol. 1, p. 155. His brother was Aḥmad b. Ibrāhīm Abūʾl-ʿAbbās al-Warrāq, Khalaf's copyist (*warrāq*) (d. circa 270/883–4).

289 Bukhārī, *ʿIlm*, 38; Ibn Māja, *Muqaddima*, 4 and 33. It is noteworthy that Abū Dāʾūd describes a similarly worded version of this tradition as *gharīb* in status. Qurṭubī, *al-Jāmiʿ li-aḥkām al-Qurʾān*, vol. 1, p. 32.

290 A transmission of Jaʿfar al-Ṣādiq on the authority of the Prophet. Majlisī, *Biḥār al-anwār*, vol. 89, p. 100.

291 The expressions, starting with 'men to whom God gives understanding [...]' to the end of the paragraph, evidently refer to the imams.

Chapter 5
On what is desirable and undesirable for the reciter of the Qurʾān in regard to 'seeking refuge [with God]' (istiʿādha)

292 MA *yatakhayyara* : *yakhīra*.

293 See Jalāl al-Dīn al-Suyūṭī, *al-Muzhir*, vol. 1, pp. 221–222.

294 Q. 5:52.

295 Q. 19:24.

296 *Nathr al-daqal* = 'the sneezing of a little goat'. See Lane, *Arabic-English Lexicon*,

vol. 1, p. 898. Ādharshab points out that traditions presented by Majlisī (*Biḥār al-anwār*, vol. 89, p. 210) on this subject contain the phrase *nathr al-raml* (= 'scattering sand'). It is possible that *nathr al-daqal* is based on a mistranscription passed on by Shahrastānī. Ādharshab, *Tafsīr al-Shahrastānī*, p. 157, note 6.

297 Q. 17:110.

298 See note 251.

299 'Full, formal pronunciation' = *taḥqīq*. This is the articulation of the Arabic text with complete vowelling and case-endings included, which is obligatory in the case of the Qurʾān. The more informal and prevalent way of reading Arabic aloud is called *tas-hīl*.

300 'Recitation of the poetic measure' = *qirāʾat al-wazn*, apparently a form of Qurʾān recitation which tries to introduce prosodical and other considerations appropriate to the recitation of poetry.

301 Hindī, *Kanz al-ʿummāl*, vol. 1, p. 606, ḥadīth 2779.

302 *An yurattila'l-Qurʾāna tartīlan*. Evoking Q. 25:32.

303 i.e. in the former case the 'ā' in '*Allāh*' lacks *imāla*, in the latter case the 'ā' has *imāla*. For *imāla* see note 183.

304 *Mā* as an 'affirmative' particle refers to its function as a relative pronoun.

305 Q. 2:121.

306 Q. 16:98.

307 Compare Ṭabrisī, *Majmaʿ al-bayān*, vol. 1, p. 18.

308 See the various transmissions on the subject of 'seeking refuge' in Gharnāṭī, *Muqaddimat tafsīr al-muḥarrar al-wajīz fī tafsīr Kitāb Allāh al-ʿAzīz*, in Jeffery, *Two Muqaddimas*, pp. 285–87. The origin of the name Isrāfīl – the angel who tops the angelic chain of transmission here, and who is also routinely attested to in exegesis as responsible for sounding the trumpet (*ṣūr*) of Resurrection (referred to in Q. 6:73) – is obscure. The alternative spelling, *Sarāfīl* suggests the Hebrew form *Seraphiel*. This is an angel presented in Jewish texts as chief of the angelic order of Seraphim, and is mentioned, for example, in the Book of Enoch. In Islam, Isrāfīl is considered an archangel.

309 Q. 16:98.

310 Q. 59.

311 Hindī, *Kanz al-ʿummāl*, vol. 2, p. 138, ḥadīth 3491, and p. 167, ḥadīth 3597.

312 Compare: Nasāʾī, *Iftitāḥ*, 83 (and *Bāb madd al-ṣawt bi'l-qirāʾa*, passim).

Chapter 6
On the number of chapters, verses, words and letters of the Qurʾān [...]

313 Suyūṭī transmits this as 'the consensus of whoever is reliable'. Suyūṭī, *Itqān*, vol. 1, p. 66.

314 Namely, the Daybreak (*al-Falaq;* Q. 113) and Mankind (*al-Nās;* Q. 114).

315 Respectively, *al-Ḍuḥā* (Q. 93) and *al-Inshirāḥ* (Q. 94).

316 Suyūṭī states the number 112, due to Ibn Masʿūd's dropping the last two chapters, the Daybreak (*al-Falaq;* Q. 113) and Mankind (*al-Nās;* Q. 114). Suyūṭī, *Itqān*, vol. 1, p. 67.

317 The *qunūt* prayer.

318 Sometimes called *Sūrat al-Ḥafd* and *Sūrat al-Khalʿ*. Suyūṭī, *Itqān*, vol. 1, p. 66.
319 Respectively, *al-Anfāl* (Q. 8) and *Barāʾa* (Q. 9).
320 Suyūṭī, *Itqān*, vol. 1, p. 66.
321 MA _ : *wa ʿawāshiruhu ... wa khawāmisuhu.* The copyist appears to have displaced these expressions from their original location in these lists of figures, and they are omitted by Ādharshab. See the various transmissions on the numbers in Jeffery, *Two Muqaddimas*, pp. 246–247; also Zarkashī, *Burhān*, vol. 1, pp. 249–251.
322 MA *ʿadda* : *ʿidda.*
323 MA *fī khalq* _ : *fī khalq al-samāwāti.*
324 48800 according to the *Muqaddima Ibn ʿAṭiyya* (See Jeffery, *Two Muqaddimas*, p. 249); 40792 according to ʿĀmilī, *Kashkūl*, p. 192.
325 Ibn ʿAṭiya: 11201 (*sic.*); ʿĀmilī: 1140.
326 Ibn ʿAṭiya: 1199; ʿĀmilī: 1299.
327 Ibn ʿAṭiya: 1276; ʿĀmilī: 1291.
328 Ibn ʿAṭiya: 3272; ʿĀmilī: 3293.
329 Ibn ʿAṭiya: 3993; ʿĀmilī: 1179.
330 Ibn ʿAṭiya: 2416; ʿĀmilī: 2419.
331 Ibn ʿAṭiya: 5642; ʿĀmilī: 4398.
332 Ibn ʿAṭiya: 4699; ʿĀmilī: 4840.
333 Ibn ʿAṭiya: 11793; ʿĀmilī: 10903.
334 Ibn ʿAṭiya: 1570; ʿĀmilī: 9583.
335 Ibn ʿAṭiya: 5891; ʿĀmilī: 4591.
336 Ibn ʿAṭiya: 2253; ʿĀmilī: 25133 (*sic.*).
337 Ibn ʿAṭiya: 2081; ʿĀmilī: 1284.
338 Ibn ʿAṭiya: 2607; ʿĀmilī: 1200.
339 Ibn ʿAṭiya: 1274; ʿĀmilī: 840.
340 Ibn ʿAṭiya: 824; ʿĀmilī: 392.
341 Ibn ʿAṭiya: 9020; ʿĀmilī: 1020.
342 Ibn ʿAṭiya: blank; ʿĀmilī: 7499.
343 Ibn ʿAṭiya: 8497; ʿĀmilī: 2500.
344 Ibn ʿAṭiya: 6823; ʿĀmilī: 5240.
345 Ibn ʿAṭiya: 10354; ʿĀmilī: 22000.
346 Ibn ʿAṭiya: 32522; ʿĀmilī: 26591.
347 Ibn ʿAṭiya: 26135; ʿĀmilī: 20560.
348 Ibn ʿAṭiya: blank; ʿĀmilī: 2036.
349 Ibn ʿAṭiya: 25536; ʿĀmilī: 13700.
350 Ibn ʿAṭiya: 19090; ʿĀmilī: 700 (*sic.*).
351 Ibn ʿAṭiya: 25919; ʿĀmilī: 502 (*sic.*).
352 Q. 12:76.

Chapter 7
On the enumeration of the exegetes amongst the companions and others [...]

353 See note 17.
354 See note 35.
355 See note 92.

356 See note 94.
357 See note 104.
358 See note 72.
359 Muʿādh b. Jabal b. ʿAmr b. Aws al-Anṣārī al-Khazrajī, Abū ʿAbd al-Raḥmān (d. 18/639). Eminent companion. His biography is in Ibn Saʿd, *Ṭabaqāt*, vol. 3, p. 120; ʿAsqalānī, *al-Iṣāba*, biography 8039; Ibn al-Athīr, *Usd al-ghāba*, vol. 4, p. 376; Iṣfahānī, *Ḥilyat al-awliyāʾ*, vol. 1, p. 228; Ibn al-Jazarī, *Ghāyat al-nihāya*, vol. 2, p. 301; Ibn al-Jawzī, *Ṣifat al-ṣafwa*, vol. 1, p. 195.
360 MA *ʿanhum* : *ʿanhumā*.
361 ʿAlī b. Abī Ṭalḥa al-Wālibī (d. 143/760). Studied the exegesis of Ibn ʿAbbās under Mujāhid, attributing it straight back to Ibn ʿAbbās, without mentioning Mujāhid. Dhahabī, *Mīzān al-iʿtidal*, vol. 3, p. 134.
362 ʿAṭiya b. Saʿd (not as in the manuscript, Saʿīd) al-ʿAwfī. Famous successor; Sālim al-Murādī said of him: 'He used to incline to Shīʿism'. Aḥmad said: "Aṭiya used to come to al-Kalbī, studying Qurʾānic exegesis under him. He had the agnomen Abū Saʿīd.' Dhahabī, *Mīzān al-iʿtidāl*, vol. 3, pp. 79–80.
363 ʿIkrima b. ʿAbd Allāh (d. 105/723–4). The client of Ibn ʿAbbās; a famed source of learning who was relied on by Bukhārī, though Muslim eschewed him. Dhahabī, *Mīzān al-iʿtidāl*, vol. 3, p. 93; Dāʾūdī, *Ṭabaqāt al-mufassirīn*, vol. 1, p. 380; Yāqūt al-Ḥamawī, *Muʿjam al-udabāʾ*, vol. 5, p.62.
364 Al-Ḍaḥḥāk b. Muzāḥim al-Hilālī, Abūʾl-Qāsim al-Khurāsānī (d. after 100/718–9). Qurʾānic exegete from Khurāsān; ʿUbayd b. Sulaymān transmitted his Qurʾānic exegesis on his authority. Dāʾūdī, *Ṭabaqāt al-mufassirīn*, vol. 1, p. 216; Dhahabī, *Mīzān al-iʿtidāl*, vol. 2, p. 325.
365 MA *Mujāhid b. Jabr wa Saʿīd b. Jubayr* : *Mujāhid wa Saʿīd abnā Jubayr*. See note 232. For Mujāhid's biographical data, see above, note 37. For Saʿīd b. Jubayr's, see above, note 207.
366 See above, note 67.
367 See above, note 53.
368 ʿAṭāʾ b. Abī Muslim, Abū ʿUthmān, al-Khurāsānī (d. 135/752–3). His father's name was Maysara or ʿAbd Allāh; attributed to him is a work called *Tanzīl al-Qurʾān* (The Sending Down of the Qurʾān), as well as a Qurʾān commentary and a work on the abrogating and the abrogated of the Qurʾān. Dāʾūdī, *Ṭabaqāt al-mufassirīn*, vol. 1, p. 379; Ibn al-ʿImād al-Ḥanbalī, *Shadharāt al-dhahab*, vol. 1, p. 192; Dhahabī, *Mīzān al-Iʿtidāl*, vol. 3, p. 73; ʿAfīf al-Dīn al-Yāfiʿī, *Mirʾāt al-janān*, vol. 1, p. 281.
369 ʿAṭāʾ b. Dīnār al-Hudhalī (d. 126/744). From Basra. Abū Ḥātim is credited by Dhahabī as having said: "Abd al-Malik b. Marwān [the fifth Umayyad caliph] would write asking Saʿīd b. Jubayr to write down Qurʾān commentary for him, so he did that for him; then ʿAṭāʾ b. Dīnār found it and acquired it.' Dhahabī, *Mīzān al-iʿtidāl*, vol. 3, p. 70. Also see Mizzī, *Tahdhīb al-kamāl*, vol. 13, p. 43.
370 Muḥammad b. Muslim b. ʿUbayd Allāh b. ʿAbd Allāh b. Shihāb, Abū Bakr al-Zuhrī al-Madanī (d. 125/743). From the generation of successors; a transmission on his authority on the *variae lectiones* (*ḥurūf*) of the Qurʾān is mentioned; he recited in the presence of Anas b. Mālik. Ibn al-Jazarī, *Ghāyat al-nihāya*, vol. 2, pp. 262–263; Dhahabī, *Mīzān al-iʿtidāl*, vol. 4, p. 40.
371 Al-Ḥasan al-Baṣrī b. Abīʾl-Ḥasan, Abū Saʿīd (d. 110/729). The client of Zayd b. Thābit; transmitted from Zayd b. Thābit and others; an authority of great prestige,

whose circle was the claimed origin for both Ṣūfism and (Muʿtazilī) *kalām*; he is generally acknowledged in Sunnism to have been the head of the third generation of Islam; a *Kitāb al-tafsīr* (Book of Qurʾān Commentary) is attributed to him; a sizeable number transmitted on his authority. Dāʾūdī, *Ṭabaqāt al-mufassirīn*, vol. 1, p. 147; Dhahabī, *Tadhkirat al-ḥuffāẓ*, vol. 1, p. 71; Iṣfahānī, *Ḥilyat al-awliyāʾ*, vol. 2, p. 131; Ibn al-Jazarī, *Ghāyat al-nihāya*, vol. 1, p. 235; Dhahabī, *Mīzān al-iʿtidāl*, vol. 1, p. 527; Ibn Khallikān, *Wafayāt al-aʿyān*, vol. 1, p. 354.

372 Qatāda b. Diʿāma (also, Diyāma) b. ʿAzīz al-Sadūsī, al-ʿAllāma ('the Very Learned') al-Ḥāfiẓ (= knower of the Qurʾān by heart), Abūʾl-Khaṭṭāb al Baṣrī, the successor (d. 117/735 or 118/736). Blind from childhood; died in Wāsiṭ in al-Ṭāʿūn; Shaybān b. ʿAbd al-Raḥmān al-Tamīmī transmitted his Qurʾān commentary on his authority. Dāʾūdī, *Ṭabaqāt al-Mufassirīn*, vol. 2, p. 43; Ibn Kathīr, *al-Bidāya waʾl-nihāya fīʾl-taʾrīkh*, vol. 9, p. 313; Dhahabī, *Tadhkirat al-ḥuffāẓ*, vol. 1, p. 122; Ibn al-ʿImād, *Shadharāt al-dhahab*, vol. 1, p. 153; Yāqūt al-Ḥamawī, *Muʿjam al-udabāʾ*, vol. 1, p. 202; Dhahabī, *Mīzān al-iʿtidāl*, vol. 3, p. 385; Ibn Khallikān, *Wafayāt al-aʿyān*, vol. 3, p. 248; Ibn al-Athīr, *al-Lubāb fī tahdhīb al-ansāb*, vol. 1, p. 537; Nawawī, *Tahdhīb al-asmāʾ*, vol. 2, p. 57; Dodge, *Fihrist of al-Nadīm*, pp. 75, 91, 381.

373 Rafīʿ b. Mihrān, Abūʾl-ʿĀliya al-Riyāḥī (= cliental agnomen) (d. 90/709 or 91/710). He hung onto paganism and embraced Islam two years after the passing of the Prophet; transmitted on the authority of ʿAlī, Ibn Masʿūd, Ibn ʿAbbās, Ibn ʿUmar, Ubayy b. Kaʿb and others; he is one of the successors who was considered a trustworthy authority, and was known for Qurʾānic exegesis. Ibn al-Jazarī, *Ghāyat al-nihāya*, vol. 1, p. 284; Ibn Ḥajar al-ʿAsqalānī, *Tahdhīb al-tahdhīb*, vol. 3, p. 284.

374 Muqātil b. Ḥayyān al-Nabṭī (d. circa 150/767). Resided in Balkh and said to have died in India; he had the agnomen Abū Basṭām al-Khazzāz; amongst the generation of the successors of the successors; transmitted on the authority of Mujāhid, ʿUrwa and al-Ḍaḥḥāk; a Qurʾān commentary is attributed to him. Dhahabī, *Tadhkirat al-ḥuffāẓ*, vol. 1, p. 174; Dāʾūdī, *Ṭabaqāt al-mufassirīn*, vol. 2, p. 329; Dhahabī, *Mīzān al-iʿtidāl*, vol. 4, p. 171; Nawawī, *Tahdhīb al-asmāʾ waʾl-lughāt*, vol. 2, p. 110.

375 See note 65.

376 The name al-Ḥasan b. Wāqid al-Wāqidī is not encountered amongst the Qurʾānic exegetes. Ādharshab (*Tafsīr al-Shahrastānī*, pp. 166–7, note 4) believes that this is al-Ḥasan b. Wāqid al-Marwazī whom Ibn al-Nadīm mentions as one of the compilers (*muṣannifīn*) of the Qurʾān (Dodge, *Fihrist of al-Nadīm*, pp. 76, 552). It is to be noted that sources later than the *Fihrist* cite his name as 'al-Ḥusayn' instead of 'al-Ḥasan', so that we find in Dāʾūdī's *Ṭabaqāt al-mufassirīn*, for example: 'al-Ḥusayn b. Wāqid al-Qurashī al-Marwazī, the client of ʿAbd Allāh b. ʿĀmir b. Kurayz, with the filionymic Abū ʿAlī. He audited ʿAbd Allāh b. Buraydah, ʿIkrima and Maṭar b. al-Warrāq, and under him Ibn al-Mubārak and his sons ʿAlī and al-ʿAlāʾ, and ʿAlī b. al-Ḥusayn b. Shaqīq. Died 159/776 or 157/774. Authored *al-Tafsīr* (The Qurʾān Commentary), *Wujūh al-Qurʾān* (Significations of the Qurʾān), and *al-Nāsikh waʾl-mansūkh* (The Abrogating and the Abrogated).' Dāʾūdī, *Ṭabaqāt al-mufassirīn*, vol. 1, p. 160. He is likewise cited in: Ibn al-ʿImād, *Shadharāt al-dhahab*, vol. 1, p. 241; Dhahabī, *ʿIbar*, vol. 1, p. 226; Yāfiʿī, *Mirʾāt al-janān*, vol. 1, p. 334; Dhahabī, *Mīzān al-iʿtidāl*, vol. 1, p. 549; Ibn Taghrībirdī,

al-Nujūm al-zāhira, vol. 2, p. 31; Mizzī, *Tahdhīb al-kamāl*, vol. 4, p. 532. It appears that the man was sometimes called al-Wāqidī, since Ḥajjī Khalīfa at first attributes the authorship of the *Tafsīr al-Wāqidī* to Muḥammad b. ʿUmar al-Wāqidī, but then corrects this and reports from Thaʿlabī's *al-Kashf* that it is by al-Ḥusayn b. Wāqid. Ḥajjī Khalīfa, *Kashf al-ẓunūn*, vol. 1, p. 460. From the above we tentatively draw the conclusion that Shahrastānī in reality quotes from a work of al-Ḥusayn b. Wāqid on the sequence of the descent of the Qurʾān, *as though* this is from the figure called al-Ḥusayn b. Wāqid al-Wāqidī.

377 MA *ʿAbd al-Raḥmān : _.*

378 Ismāʿīl b. ʿAbd al-Raḥmān al-Suddī, Abū Muḥammad (d. 127/745). Al-Suyūṭī said: 'The model for commentaries is the commentary of Ismāʿīl al-Suddī.' He said: 'Authorities like al-Thawrī and Shuʿba transmitted on his authority.' Suyūṭī, *Itqān*, vol. 2, p. 189. Sayyid Ḥasan al-Ṣadr said: 'He was among the companions of the imam ʿAlī b. al-Ḥusayn Zayn al-ʿĀbidīn, and he cleaved to al-Ṣādiq and al-Bāqir [...] and he was the great al-Suddī.' Ṣadr, *Taʾsīs al-Shīʿa*, p. 326. Also see: Dāʾūdī, *Ṭabaqāt al-mufassirīn*, vol. 1, p. 109; Dhahabī, *Mīzān al-iʿtidāl*, vol. 1, p. 236; Ibn Taghrībirdī, *al-Nujūm al-zāhira*, vol. 1, p. 304; Ibn al-Athīr, *al-Lubāb fī tahdhīb al-ansāb*, vol. 1, p. 537.

379 ʿAbd Allāh b. Abī Jaʿfar al-Rāzī (not al-Rāziḥī, as the text of Dhahabī has it). Mentioned as a traditionist; transmitted on the authority of his father, ʿĪsā, Ayyūb b. ʿUtba, and others. Scholars were divided between those who discredited him and those who placed confidence in him. Dhahabī, *Mīzān al-iʿtidāl*, vol. 2, p. 404.

380 ʿAbd al-Malik b. ʿAbd al-ʿAzīz b. Jurayj, Abū Khālid al-Makkī (d. 150/767). Considered a trustworthy authority. Dhahabī says: 'He is subject to consensus in his trustworthiness (*thiqa*), despite his having married up to seventy women by way of temporary marriage (*mutʿa*), which was regarded as the legal mitigation (*rukhṣa*) in that regard'. Dhahabī, *Mīzān al-iʿtidāl*, vol. 2, p. 659. Dāʾūdī said: '[He was] the author of various works – *al-Tafsīr* (The Qurʾān Commentary) and others.' Dāʾūdī, *Ṭabaqāt al-mufassirīn*, vol. 1, p. 352.

381 MA *Saʿīd al-Thawrī : _ al-Thawrī*. Sufyān b. Saʿīd b. Masrūq, Abū ʿAbd Allāh al-Thawrī (from Thawr, Hamadān), also al-Kūfī (d. 161/778). A leading religious authority, theologian, jurist and traditionist, famous for asceticism and claimed by the Ṣūfis as one of their earliest representatives. Memorised the Qurʾān. Went in quest of knowledge when still a young man. His father was one of the scholars of Kufa, from whom he transmitted prophetic traditions. He was one of the first to commit the great number of prophetic traditions in his memory to writing, and is sometimes even ranked above Mālik b. Anas. He was credited with originating a defunct legal school which was strongly based on Prophetic Tradition. Author of the Qurʾān Commentary which Abū Ḥudhayfa Mūsā b. Masʿūd al-Nahdī (see below, note 391) transmitted. Died in Basra in hiding from al-Mahdī because – it is said – he always spoke the truth and was vehement in his denunciation of wrongdoing. Dāʾūdī, *Ṭabaqāt al-mufassirīn*, vol. 1, p. 186; Dhahabī, *Tadhkirat al-ḥuffāẓ*, vol. 1, p. 203; ʿAsqalānī, *Tahdhīb al-tahdhīb*, vol. 4, p. 111; Ibn al-ʿImād, *Shadharāt al-dhahab*, vol. 1, p. 250; Dhahabī, *al-ʿIbar*, vol. 1, p. 235; Dodge, *Fihrist of al-Nadīm*, pp. 52, 90, 443, 444, 456, 504, 545–546, 552; Ibn al-Athīr, *al-Lubāb*, vol. 1, p. 198; Ibn Taghrībirdī, *al-Nujūm al-zāhira*, vol. 2, p. 39; Ibn Khallikān, *Wafayāt al-aʿyān*, vol. 2, p. 127.

382 Sufyān b. ʿUyayna b. Abī ʿImrān Maymūn, Abū Muḥammad al-Hilālī al-Kūfī. A

leading religious authority and independent legist (*mujtahid*), client of Muḥammad b. Muzāḥim (= the brother of al-Ḍaḥḥāk b. Muzāḥim, see note 364). It is mentioned that he was one of Jaʿfar al-Ṣādiq's students. He audited ʿAmr b. Dīnār, al-Zuhrī and others. Dāʾūdī, *Ṭabaqāt al-mufassirīn*, vol. 1, p. 190; Dhahabī, *Tadhkirat al-ḥuffāẓ*, vol. 1, p. 262; Dodge, *Fihrist of al-Nadīm*, pp. 75, 76, 90, 331, 443–444, 547; Dhahabī, *Mīzān al-iʿtidāl*, vol. 2, p. 659. Also see: Asad Ḥaydar, *al-Imām al-Ṣādiq*, vol. 1, p. 70.

383 Wakīʿ b. al-Jarrāḥ b. Malīḥ al-Ruʾāsī, Abū Sufyān, al-Kūfī (d. 197/813). Traditionist of Iraq; author of the Qurʾān commentary which was transmitted on his authority by Muḥammad b. Ismāʿīl al-Ḥassānī. A curiosity transmitted from him is that he held the pronouncing of the *Bi'smi'llāh* formula aloud to be an innovation, as attested by Abū Saʿīd al-Ashajj (see below, note 398). Dāʾūdī, *Ṭabaqāt al-mufassirīn*, vol. 2, p. 357; Dhahabī, *Tadhkirat al-ḥuffāẓ*, vol. 1, p. 306; Iṣfahānī, *Ḥilyat al-awliyāʾ*, vol. 8, p. 368; Dhahabī, *al-ʿIbar*, vol. 1, p. 324; Dodge, *Fihrist of al-Nadīm*, pp. 76, 81, 152–153, 191, 548; Dhahabī, *Mīzān al-iʿtidāl*, vol. 4, p. 335; al-Khaṭīb al-Baghdādī, *Taʾrīkh Baghdād*, vol. 13, p. 466.

384 Hushaym b. Bashīr b. al-Qāsim b. Dīnār, Abū Muʿāwiya, b. Abī Khāzim al-Sulamī al-Wāsiṭī (d. 183/799). The author of the Qurʾān commentary transmitted by Abū Hāshim Ziyād b. Ayyūb b. Ziyād al-Baghdādī on his authority. Dāʾūdī, *Ṭabaqāt al-mufassirīn*, vol. 2, p. 352; al-Khaṭīb al-Baghdādī, *Taʾrīkh Baghdād*, vol. 14, p. 85; Dhahabī, *Tadhkirat al-ḥuffāẓ*, vol. 1, p. 248; Dhahabī, *al-ʿIbar*, vol. 1, p. 286; Dodge, *Fihrist of al-Nadīm*, pp. 76, 78, 551; Dhahabī, *Mīzān al-iʿtidāl*, vol. 4, p. 306.

385 See note 216.

386 Warqāʾ b. ʿUmar, Abū Bishr al-Yashkurī. Transmitted recitation on the authority of ʿAmr b. Dīnār and Muḥammad b. Munkadir. Ibn al-Jazarī, *Ghāyat al-nihāya*, vol. 2, p. 358.

387 Zayd b. Aslam al-ʿAdawī, al-Imam Abū ʿAbd Allāh al-ʿUmarī (= a reference to the fact that he was the client of ʿUmar b. al-Khaṭṭāb) al-Madanī (d. 136/753–4). He transmitted on the authority of his patron ʿAbd Allāh b. ʿAmr, ʿAlī b. al-Ḥusayn, Jābir b. ʿAbd Allāh and a number of others; said to have held a study circle in the Prophet's mosque in Medina. Dhahabī says: 'Zayd had a Qurʾān commentary which his son ʿAbd al-Raḥmān transmitted on his authority'. Dāʾūdī, *Ṭabaqāt al-mufassirīn*, vol. 1, p. 176; Dhahabī, *Tadhkirat al-ḥuffāẓ*, vol. 1, p. 132; Ibn al-Jazarī, *Ghāyat al-nihāya*, vol. 1, p. 296; Mizzī, *Tahdhīb al-kamāl*, vol. 6, p. 425.

388 Rawḥ b. ʿUbāda b. al-ʿAlāʾ b. Ḥassān al-Qaysī, Abū Muḥammad al-Baṣrī. Al-Khaṭīb al-Baghdādī said: 'He authored books on the customs [of the Prophet] and legal rulings and put together a Qurʾān commentary. He was trustworthy. Abū'l-Azhar Ṣāliḥ b. Dirham al-Bāhilī al-Baṣrī transmitted his Qurʾān commentary on his authority.' Al-Khaṭīb al-Baghdādī, *Taʾrīkh Baghdād*, vol. 8, p. 401; Dāʾūdī, *Ṭabaqāt al-mufassirīn*, vol. 1, p. 173; Dhahabī, *Tadhkirat al-ḥuffāẓ*, vol. 1, p. 349; Ibn al-ʿImād, *Shadharāt al-dhahab*, vol. 2, p. 13; Dhahabī, *al-ʿIbar*, vol. 1, p. 347; Dhahabī, *Mīzān al-iʿtidāl*, vol. 2, p. 58; Ibn Taghrībirdī, *al-Nujūm al-zāhira*, vol. 2, p. 179; Dodge, *Fihrist of al-Nadīm*, p. 550.

389 Muḥammad b. Yūsuf b. Wāqid b. ʿUthmān al-Ḍabbī (= cliental agnomen) al-Turkī al-Firyābī (d. 212/827). Called *al-Firyābī al-kabīr* ('the elder'). A resident of Qaysāriyya (Caesarea), the city in Syria; Bukhārī transmitted on his authority and declared: 'He was amongst the most learned of his time'. He had a book, 'The

Qur'ān Commentary', transmitted on his authority by ʿAbd Allāh b. Muḥammad b. Saʿīd b. Abī Maryam. Dā'ūdī, *Ṭabaqāt al-mufassirīn*, vol. 2, p. 292; Dhahabī, *Tadhkirat al-ḥuffāẓ*, vol. 1, p. 376; ʿAsqalānī, *Tahdhīb al-tahdhīb*, vol. 9, p. 535; Ibn al-ʿImād, *Shadharāt al-dhahab*, vol. 2, p. 28; Dhahabī, *al-ʿIbar*, vol. 1, p. 363; Dodge, *Fihrist of al-Nadīm*, p. 552; Ibn al-Athīr, *al-Lubāb*, vol. 2, p. 211; Ibn Taghrībirdī, *al-Nujūm al-zāhira*, vol. 2, p. 204; Mizzī, *Tahdhīb al-kamāl*, vol. 17, p. 360.

390 Qubayṣa b. ʿUqba al-Kūfī (d. 215/830). The associate of Sufyān al-Thawrī; Bukhārī and Ibn Ḥanbal transmitted on his authority. Dhahabī, *Mīzān al-iʿtidāl*, vol. 3, p. 384; Mizzī, *Tahdhīb al-kamāl*, vol. 15, pp. 215–218.

391 Dā'ūdī mentions him by the name Abū Ḥudhayfa Mūsā b. Masʿūd al-Nahdī. He transmitted the Qur'ān commentary of Sufyān al-Thawrī. Dā'ūdī, *Ṭabaqāt al-mufassirīn*, vol. 1, p. 186; ʿAsqalānī, *Tahdhīb al-tahdhīb*, vol. 10, p. 370; Bukhārī, *al-Ta'rīkh al-kabīr*, vol. 4, part 1, p. 295.

392 Saʿīd b. Manṣūr b. Shuʿba al-Khurāsānī. Considered trustworthy (*thiqa*); memorised the Qur'ān; author of *al-Sunan* (The Customs of the Prophet); audited Mālik and his generation; Aḥmad b. Ḥanbal praised him highly. Dhahabī, *Mīzān al-iʿtidāl*, vol. 2, p. 159.

393 ʿAbd Allāh b. Wahb b. Muslim, Abū Muḥammad al-Fihrī (not as in the manuscript, al-Qurashī) (d. 197/813). One of the leading authorities of Islam in his day; recited in the presence of Nāfiʿ. Ibn al-Jazarī, *Ghāyat al-nihāya*, vol. 1, p. 159.

394 ʿAbd al-Ḥamīd b. Ḥumayd. Credited with a Qur'ān commentary; Thaʿlabī mentions him in the *Kashf*. Ḥājjī Khalīfa, *Kashf al-Ẓanūn*, vol. 1, p. 453. Also see Mizzī, *Kamāl al-tahdhīb*, vol. 12, p. 157.

395 Muḥammad b. Ayyūb b. Yaḥyā al-Ḍurays al-Bajalī al-Rāzī (d. 294/907). Memoriser of the Qur'ān; author of *Faḍā'il al-Qur'ān* (The Excellences of the Qur'ān); died in Rayy. Dā'ūdī, *Ṭabaqāt al-mufassirīn*, vol. 2, p. 105; Dhahabī, *Tadhkirat al-ḥuffāẓ*, vol. 2, p. 643; Ibn al-ʿImād, *Shadharāt al-dhahab*, vol. 2, p. 216; Dhahabī, *ʿIbar*, vol. 2, p. 98; Ibn Taghrībirdī, *Al-Nujūm al-zāhira*, vol. 3, p. 162.

396 MA _: *ibn*.

397 Abū Bakr al-Aṣamm (d. 200/815–6). Student of Muʿammar and amongst the few Muʿtazila who inclined towards the cause of ʿAlī b. Abī Ṭālib; he has a book, *al-Tafsīr* (The Qur'ān Commentary), and other books on scholastic theology. Dodge, *Fihrist of al-Nadīm*, pp. 75, 76, 220, 358, 391, 414, 415.

398 ʿAbd Allāh b. Saʿīd b. Ḥusayn al-Kindī al-Kūfī al-Ḥāfiẓ (='memorizer of the Qur'ān by heart'), Abū Saʿīd al-Ashajj (d. 257/871). Traditionist of Kufa; author of *al-Tafsīr* (The Qur'ān Commentary), and other works; he transmitted prophetic traditions on the authority of Hushaym, Abū Bakr b. Ayyāsh and others. Dā'ūdī, *Ṭabaqāt al-mufassirīn*, vol. 1, p. 228; Dhahabī, *Tadhkirat al-ḥuffāẓ*, vol. 3, p. 501; Ibn al-ʿImād, *Shadharāt al-dhahab*, vol. 2, p. 137; Dhahabī, *al-ʿIbar*, vol. 2, p. 15; Mizzī, *Kamāl al-tahdhīb*, vol. 10, p. 179.

399 Thābit b. Dīnār, Abū Ḥamza al-Thumālī. Transmitted on the authority of ʿAlī b. al-Ḥusayn, al-Bāqir and al-Ṣādiq, surviving into the days of al-Kāẓim. He was eminent in station and high in rank. Sufyān al-Thawrī, Sharīk, Ḥafṣ b. Ghiyāth, Abū Usāma, ʿAbd al-Malik b. Abī Sulaymān, Abū Nuʿaym, Wakīʿ and ʿAbd Allāh b. Mūsā all transmitted on his authority. Tirmidhī, Ibn Māja and Nisā'ī derived prophetic traditions from him. He was the transmitter of the prayer of ʿAlī b. al-

Ḥusayn which is known as the 'Prayer of Abū Ḥamza'. Asad Ḥaydar, *al-Imām al-Ṣādiq*, vol. 1, pp. 446–447. For his biography see Dā'ūdī, *Ṭabaqāt al-mufassirīn*, vol. 1, p. 123; Ṭūsī, *al-Fihrist*, p. 14; Dodge, *Fihrist of al-Nadīm*, p. 75.

400 Al-Musayyab b. Sharīk, Abū Sa'īd al-Tamīmī al-Shaqarī al-Kūfī. Mentioned among the memorisers of the Qur'ān by heart; transmitted on the authority of al-A'mash. Aḥmad b. Ḥanbal said: 'People left out his prophetic traditions.' Dhahabī, *Mīzān al-i'tidāl*, vol. 4, p. 114.

401 It seems that this is 'Abd Allāh b. Ḥāmid b. Muḥammad, Abū Muḥammad al-Naysābūrī (d. 398/1008), the jurist and preacher. He has a biography in Dhahabī, *Ta'rīkh al-islām* (see under the events of AH 389).

402 Muḥammad b. al-Qāsim b. Ḥabīb b. 'Abdūs, Abū Bakr, known as al-Ṣaffār (d. 468/1075–6). One of the jurists of Nīshāpūr. Subkī, *Ṭabaqāt al-shāfi'iyya al-kubrā*, vol. 4, p. 194; Ibn al-'Imād, *Shadharāt al-dhahab*, vol. 3, p. 331; Dhahabī, *'Ibar*, vol. 3, p. 268; Ibn al-Jawzī, *al-Muntaẓam fī ta'rīkh al-mulūk wa'l-umam*, vol. 8, p. 299.

403 Aḥmad b. Abī Aḥmad, Abū 'Amr al-Furātī (d. 399/1009). Ascetic and preacher; his grandson, the headman of Naysābūr, Abū'l-Faḍl Aḥmad b. Muḥammad al-Furātī and others transmitted on his authority. Dhahabī, *Ta'rīkh al-islām*, events of AH 399 [/CE 1008–9].

404 'Abd Allāh b. Muḥammad b. Muḥammad b. Fūrak b. 'Aṭā' b. Mihyār, Abū Bakr al-Qabbāb al-Iṣfahānī (d. 370/980–1). The leading authority in his age, reciter and exegete of the Qur'ān. Dā'ūdī, *Ṭabaqāt al-mufassirīn*, vol. 1, p. 251; Dhahabī, *Tadhkirat al-ḥuffāẓ*, vol. 3, p. 960; Ibn al-Jazarī, *Ghāyat al-nihāya*, vol. 1, p. 454; Dhahabī, *al-'Ibar*, vol. 2, p. 356; Ibn al-Athīr, *al-Lubāb*, vol. 2, p. 238; Ibn Taghrībirdī, *al-Nujūm al-zāhira*, vol. 4, p. 139; Sam'ānī, *Ansāb*, folio 440A.

405 Abū'l-Qāsim, al-Ḥasan b. Muḥammad b. al-Ḥasan b. Ḥabīb al-Naysābūrī (d. 406/1015–6). He was an eminent Qur'ānic exegete of Khurāsān; author of the *Kitāb al-tanzīl wa tartībihi* ('Book of the Sending Down [of the Qur'ān] and its Order'). Suyūṭī, *Ṭabaqāt al-mufassirīn*, p. 32; Ibn al-'Imād, *Shadharāt al-dhahab*, vol. 3, p. 181.

406 The authority referred to is obscure. According to Ādharshab, he may be identifiable with 'Abd al-Wahhāb b. 'Aṭā' al-Khaffāf al-'Ijlī al-Baṣrī (d. 206/821–2), though note that Dā'ūdī and others mention that his agnomen is Abū Naṣr. The latter authored *al-Tafsīr* (The Qur'ān Commentary) and *al-Nāsikh wa'l-mansūkh* (The Abrogating and the Abrogated); died in Baghdad. Dā'ūdī, *Ṭabaqāt al-mufassirīn*, vol. 1, p. 363; Dhahabī, *Tadhkirat al-ḥuffāẓ*, vol. 1, p. 339; Dhahabī, *al-'Ibar*, vol. 1, p. 346; Mizzī, *Tahdhīb al-kamāl*, vol. 12, p. 149.

407 'Abd al-Jabbār b. Aḥmad b. 'Abd al-Jabbār b. Aḥmad b. al-Khalīl, the Qāḍī, Abū'l-Ḥasan al-Hamadānī al-Asadābādī (d. 415/1024). The Mu'tazilis gave him the honorific, *Qāḍī al-Quḍāt* ('Chief Judge'); he has a Qur'ān commentary and other works; died in Rayy. Dā'ūdī, *Ṭabaqāt al-mufassirīn*, vol. 1, p. 256; Baghdādī, *Ta'rīkh Baghdād*, vol. 11, p. 113; Suyūṭī, *Ṭabaqāt al-mufassirīn*, p. 16; Yāfi'ī, *Mir'āt al-janān*, vol. 3, p. 29; Dhahabī, *Mīzān al-i'tidāl*, vol. 2, p. 533; Ibn al-'Imād, *Shadharāt al-dhahab*, vol. 3, p. 642.

408 Muḥammad b. 'Uthmān is not listed amongst the Qur'ānic exegetes, but this name recurs amongst the transmitters, the most well known of them being Muḥammad b. 'Uthmān b. Abī Shayba, Abū Ja'far al-'Absi al-Kūfī al-Ḥāfiẓ (= memoriser of the Qur'ān by heart), a figure learned in prophetic traditions and

scholarly biography on whose authority al-Shāfiʿī, al-Bazzār and al-Ṭabarānī all transmitted material. Dhahabī, *Mīzān al-iʿtidāl*, vol. 3, p. 642.

409 Abū'l-Ḥasan, Muḥammad b. al-Qāsim al-Faqīh (= the jurist). Ḥajjī Khalīfa transmits on al-Thaʿlabī's authority that he recited the commentary of Abū'l-Ḥasan in his presence. Ḥajjī Khalīfa, *Kashf al-Ẓanūn*, vol. 1, p. 452.

410 MA *Abū Isḥāq Aḥmad b. Muḥammad:* _.

411 Aḥmad b. Muḥammad b. Ibrāhīm, Abū Isḥāq al-Naysābūrī al-Thaʿlabī (d. 427/1036). Said to have been unique in his age in his knowledge of Qurʾānic science; author of the great commentary known as *al-Kashf*. Al-Wāḥidī studied under him. Dāʾūdī, *Ṭabaqāt al-mufassirīn*, vol. 1, p. 65; Subkī, *Ṭabaqāt al-shāfiʿiyya al-kubrā*, vol. 4, p. 58.

412 MA *wa lahu tafsīrun* : _.

413 Abū Bakr Muḥammad b. al-Ḥasan b. Muḥammad b. Ziyād al-Naqqāsh (d. 351/962). Audited a large number of scholars in Baghdad, Basra, Mecca, Syria and Egypt; he has a Qurʾān commentary, *Shifāʾ al-ṣudūr al-muhadhdhab fī tafsīr al-Qurʾān* (The Refined Cure of Hearts in the Exegesis of the Qurʾān); Sayyid Ibn Ṭāwūs transmitted on his authority. Dhahabī, *Mīzān al-iʿtidāl*, vol. 3, p. 45; Subkī, *Ṭabaqāt al-shāfiʿiyya al-kubrā*, vol. 2, p. 148; Ibn al-Jazarī, *Ghāyat al-nihāya*, vol. 2, p. 119; Ḥusaynī, *Saʿd al-Suʿūd*, p. 285; Ibn Ḥajar al-ʿAsqalānī, *Lisān al-mīzān*, vol. 5, p. 132.

414 ʿAlī b. Aḥmad b. Muḥammad, Abū'l-Ḥasan al-Wāḥidī al-Naysābūrī (d. 468/1075–6). The Qurʾānic exegete; author of *al-Wajīz* (The Summary), *al-wasīṭ wa'l-basīṭ fī'l-tafsīr* (The Intermediary and the Simple in the Exegesis of the Qurʾān), and *Asbāb al-nuzūl* (The Occasions of the Descent [of the Qurʾān]); died in Nīshāpūr. Ibn al-Jazarī, *Ghāyat al-nihāya*, vol. 1, p. 523; Dāʾūdī, *Ṭabaqāt al-mufassirīn*, vol. 1, p. 387; Subkī, *Ṭabaqāt al-shāfiʿiyya*, vol. 5, p. 204; Suyūṭī, *Ṭabaqāt al-mufassirīn*, p. 23; Dhahabī, *ʿIbar*, vol. 3, p. 267; Ibn Khallikān, *Wafayāt al-aʿyān*, vol. 2, p. 464; Qifṭī, *Inbāh al-ruwāt*, vol. 2, p. 223; Suyūṭī, *Bughyat al-wuʿāt*, vol. 2, p. 145.

415 Yaḥyā b. Ziyād b. ʿAbd Allāh b. Marwān al-Daylamī, Abū Zakariyyā, known as al-Farrāʾ (= 'the fur dealer') (d. 207/822–3). Leading authority in Arabic; the most learned of the Kufans in grammar after Kisāʾī, under whom he studied, as well as under Yūnus; composed works on Qurʾānic semantics (*maʿānī al-Qurʾān*). Dāʾūdī, *Ṭabaqāt al-mufassirīn*, vol. 2, p. 366; Samʿānī, *al-Ansāb*, folio 420; Ibn Kathīr, *al-Bidāya wa'l-nihāya*, vol. 10, p. 261; Suyūṭī, *Bughyat al-wuʿāt*, vol. 2, p. 333; Baghdādī, *Taʾrīkh Baghdād*, vol. 14, p. 149; Dhahabī, *Tadhkirat al-ḥuffāẓ*, vol. 1, p. 372; ʿAsqalānī, *Tahdhīb al-tahdhīb*, vol. 11, p. 212; Ibn al-ʿImād, *Shadharāt al-dhahab*, vol. 2, p. 19; Ibn al-Jazarī, *Ghāyat al-nihāya*, vol. 2, p. 371; Dhahabī, *al-ʿIbar*, vol. 1, p. 354; Ibn al-Nadīm, *al-Fihrist*, p. 66; Ibn al-Athīr, *al-Lubāb*, vol. 2, p. 198; Yāfiʿī, *Mirʾāt al-janān*, vol. 2, p. 38; Yāqūt al-Ḥamawī, *Muʿjam al-udabāʾ*, vol. 7, p. 276; Ṭāshkoprizādeh, *Miftāḥ al-saʿāda*, vol. 1, p. 178; Ibn Taghrībirdī, *al-Nujūm al-zāhira*, vol. 2, p.185; Ibn Khallikān, *Wafayāt al-aʿyān*, vol. 5, p. 225.

416 Ibrāhīm b. Sirrī b. Sahl, Abū Isḥāq al-Zajjāj (d. 311/923). He has works on Qurʾānic semantics, grammar and belles-lettres; died in Baghdad. His biography is in: Dāʾūdī, *Ṭabaqāt al-mufassirīn*, vol. 1, p. 7; Qifṭī, *Inbāh al-ruwāt*, vol. 1, p. 159; Samʿānī, *al-Ansāb*, folio 172A; Ibn Kathīr, *al-Bidāya wa'l-nihāya*, vol. 11, p. 148; Suyūṭī, *Bughyat al-wuʿāt*, vol. 1, p. 411; Ibn al-ʿImād, *Shadharāt al-dhahab*,

vol. 2, p. 259; Dhahabī, *al-ʿIbar*, vol. 2, p. 148; Ibn al-Nadīm, *al-Fihrist*, p. 60; Ibn al-Athīr, *al-Lubāb*, vol. 1, p. 397; Yāfiʿī, *Mirʾāt al-janān*, vol. 2, p. 262; Yāqūt al-Ḥamawī, *Muʿjam al-udabāʾ*, vol. 1, p. 47; Ṭāshkoprīzādeh, *Miftāḥ al-saʿāda*, vol. 1, p. 163; Ibn Taghrībirdī, *al-Nujūm al-zāhira*, vol. 3, p. 208; Ibn Khallikān, *Wafayāt al-aʿyān*, vol. 1, p. 311; Ibn al-Anbārī, *Nuzhat al-alibbāʾ*, p. 244.

417 See above, note 262. Also see: Dāʾūdī, *Ṭabaqāt al-mufassirīn*, vol. 1, p. 399; Qifṭī, *Inbāh al-ruwāt*, vol. 2, p. 256; Samʿānī, *al-Ansāb*, folio 482 (recto); Suyūṭī, *Bughyat al-wuʿāt*, vol. 2, p. 162; ʿAsqalānī, *Tahdhīb al-tahdhīb*, vol. 7, p. 313; Ibn al-ʿImād, *Shadharāt al-dhahab*, vol. 1, p. 321; Ibn al-Nadīm, *al-Fihrist*, p. 19; Ibn Taghrībirdī, *al-Nujūm al-zāhira*, vol. 2, p. 130; Ibn al-Anbārī, *Nuzhat al-alibbāʾ*, p. 67; Ibn Khallikān, *Wafayāt al-aʿyān*, vol. 2, p. 457; Yāqūt al-Ḥamawī, *Muʿjam al-buldān*, vol. 1, p. 458; Khwānsārī, *Rawḍāt al-janān*, vol. 5, p. 194.

418 Al-Qāsim b. Sallām, Abū ʿUbayd al-Turkī al-Baghdādī (d. 451/1059). Native of Khurāsān; studied under Abū Zayd, Abū ʿUbayda, ʿAbd al-Malik b. Qurayb al-Aṣmaʿī, Abū Muḥammad al-Yazīdī, Ibn al-Aʿrābī, al-Kisāʾī, al-Farrāʾ and others. Composed works on the obscure language (*gharīb*) of the Qurʾān, Qurʾānic semantics, and the abrogating and abrogated. He was the leading authority of his age. His biography is in: Dāʾūdī, *Ṭabaqāt al-mufassirīn*, vol. 2, p. 32; Qifṭī, *Inbāh al-ruwāt*, vol. 3, p. 12; Ibn Kathīr, *al-Bidāya waʾl-nihāya*, vol. 10, p. 281; Suyūṭī, *Bughyat al-wuʿāt*, vol. 2, p. 253; Dhahabī, *Tadhkirat al-ḥuffāẓ*, vol. 2, p. 417; Nawawī, *Tahdhīb al-asmāʾ waʾl-lughāt*, vol. 2, p. 257; ʿAsqalānī, *Tahdhīb al-tahdhīb*, vol. 8, p. 315; Khwānsārī, *Rawḍāt al-janān*, vol. 6, p. 23; Ibn al-ʿImād, *Shadharāt al-dhahab*, vol. 2, p. 54; Ibn al-Jazarī, *Ghāyat al-nihāya*, vol. 2, p. 17; Dhahabī, *al-ʿIbar*, vol. 1, p. 392; Ibn al-Nadīm, *al-Fihrist*, p. 71; Yāfiʿī, *Mirʾāt al-janān*, vol. 2, p. 83; Yāqūt al-Ḥamawī, *Muʿjam al-udabāʾ*, vol. 6, p. 162; Dhahabī, *Mīzān al-iʿtidāl*, vol. 3, p. 371; Ibn Taghrībirdī, *al-Nujūm al-zāhira*, vol. 2, p. 241; Ibn Khallikān, *Wafayāt al-aʿyān*, vol. 3, p. 225.

419 Saʿīd b. Masʿada, Abūʾl-Ḥasan ʿal-Akhfash al-Awsaṭʾ (d. 210/825 or 215/830 or 221/836). From the people of Balkh; lived in Basra; composed works on Qurʾānic semantics, grammar and lexicography; recited lexicography in the presence of Sībawayhi, though he was older than him. Dāʾūdī, *Ṭabaqāt al-mufassirīn*, vol. 1, p. 186; Qifṭī, *Inbāh al-ruwāt*, vol. 2, p. 36; Suyūṭī, *Bughyat al-wuʿāt*, vol. 1, p. 590; Ibn al-ʿImād, *Shadharāt al-dhahab*, vol. 2, p. 36; Dodge, *Fihrist of al-Nadīm*, pp. 139, 182; Yāfiʿī, *Mirʾāt al-janān*, vol. 2, p. 61; Yāqūt al-Ḥamawī, *Muʿjam al-udabāʾ*, vol. 4, p. 242; Ibn al-Anbārī, *Nuzhat al-alibbāʾ*, p. 133; Ibn Khallikān, *Wafayāt al-aʿyān*, vol. 2, p. 122.

420 Maʿmar b. al-Muthannā al-Lughawī (ʻthe lexicographerʼ) al-Baṣrī (= cliental agnomen) al-Taymī, Abū ʿUbayda. Studied under Yūnus and Abū ʿAmr; the first person to write on the subject of *gharīb* (rare) prophetic traditions; Abū ʿUbayd al-Qāsim b. Sallām, Abū Ḥātim, al-Māzinī, al-Athram, and ʿUmar b. Shayba studied under him. Dāʾūdī, *Ṭabaqāt al-mufassirīn*, vol. 2, p. 326; Qifṭī, *Inbāh al-ruwāt*, vol. 3, p. 276; Suyūṭī, *Bughyat al-wuʿāt*, vol. 2, p. 294; Baghdādī, *Taʾrīkh Baghdād*, vol. 13, p. 252; Dhahabī, *Tadhkirat al-ḥuffāẓ*, vol. 1, p. 371; Nawawī, *Tahdhīb al-asmāʾ waʾl-lughāt*, vol. 1, p. 260; ʿAsqalānī, *Tahdhīb al-tahdhīb*, vol. 10, p. 246; Ibn al-ʿImād, *Shadharāt al-dhahab*, vol. 2, p. 24; Dhahabī, *al-ʿIbar*, vol. 1, p. 359; Ibn al-Nadīm, *al-Fihrīst*, p. 53; Yāfiʿī, *Mirʾāt al-janān*, vol. 2, p. 44; Yāqūt al-Ḥamawī, *Muʿjam al-udabāʾ*, vol. 7, p. 164; Ṭāshkoprīzādeh, *Miftāḥ al-saʿāda*, vol. 1, p. 105; Dhahabī, *Mīzān al-iʿtidāl*, vol. 4, p. 155; Ibn Taghrībirdī, *al-Nujūm*

al-zāhira, vol. 2, p. 184; Ibn al-Anbārī, *Nuzhat al-alibbā'*, p. 104; Ibn Khallikān, *Wafayāt al-a'yān*, vol. 4, p. 323; Mizzī, *Tahdhīb al-kamāl*, vol. 18, p. 275.

421 Abū 'Alī al-Ḥasan b. Yaḥyā b. Dhimr al-Jurjānī. In the course of his biography Sahmī states that 'He has a number of works, including two volumes, On the Harmonious Order (*naẓm*) of the Qur'ān[...],' Sahmī, *Ta'rīkh Jurjān*, 16/1. Shahrastānī generally quotes him as 'the author of The Harmonious Order (*al-Naẓm*) [who] said [...]'.

422 al-Mu'arraj b. 'Amr (or 'Umar) b. Munī' b. Ḥuṣayn al-Sudūsī, Abū Fayd al-Baṣrī (d. after 200/815–6). Composed works on Qur'ānic semantics and the obscure language (*gharīb*) of the Qur'ān; amongst the leading authorities in literature; he was amongst the most eminent residents of Hebron. Dā'ūdī, *Ṭabaqāt al-mufassirīn*, vol. 2, p. 340; Qifṭī, *Inbāh al-ruwāt*, vol. 3, p. 327; Suyūṭī, *Bughyat al-wu'āt*, vol. 2, p. 305; Baghdādī, *Ta'rīkh Baghdād*, vol. 13, p. 258; Dodge, *Fihrist of al-Nadīm*, pp. 76–77, 101, 104, 105; Yāqūt al-Ḥamawī, *Mu'jam al-udabā'*, vol. 7, p. 193; Ibn al-Anbārī, *Nuzhat al-alibbā'*, p. 130; Ibn Khallikān, *Wafayāt al-a'yān*, vol. 4, p. 389.

423 al-Naḍr b. Shumayl b. Kharasha (or: Kharshina), Abū'l-Ḥasan al-Māzinī al-Baṣrī al-Naḥwī ('the grammarian') al-Lughawī ('the lexicographer') al-Akhbārī ('authority on reports') (d. 204/819–20). A curiosity is that when his livelihood became impossible for him in Basra he left, heading for Khurāsān, and approximately three thousand of its inhabitants, consisting only of traditionists, grammarians, prosodists, lexicographers and authorities on reports, bade him farewell. When he reached al-Mirbad, the exit-point of Basra he said 'O people of Basra, your send-off is precious to me. Were I to find each day a *kīlja* (= a measure) of beans, I wouldn't leave you'. Yet there was no-one among them who would take that upon themselves! He died in Merv. Ibn al-Jazarī, *Ghāyat al-nihāya*, vol. 2, p. 341; Ibn al-Anbārī, *Nuzhat al-alibbā'*, vol. 2, p. 110; Yāfi'ī, *Mir'āt al-janān*, vol. 2, p. 8; Mizzī, *Tahdhīb al-kamāl*, vol. 13, p. 81; Dodge, *Fihrist of al-Nadīm*, pp. 90, 112, 190.

424 'Abd Allāh b. Muslim b. Qutayba al-Dīnawarī al-Naḥwī ('the grammarian') al-Lughawī ('the lexicographer') (d. circa 275–6/889). He was suspected of fabrication and al-Dhahabī defended him. He composed works on the vowelling of the Qur'ān, Qur'ānic semantics, the obscure language of the Qur'ān, grammar, and lexicography. Dā'ūdī, *Ṭabaqāt al-mufassirīn*, vol. 1, p. 254; Qifṭī, *Inbāh al-ruwāt*, vol. 2, p. 143; Sam'ānī, *al-Ansāb*, folio 443; Ibn Kathīr, *al-Bidāya wa'l-nihāya*, vol. 11, p. 48; Suyūṭī, *Bughyat al-wu'āt*, vol. 2, p. 63; al-Khaṭīb al-Baghdādī, *Ta'rīkh Baghdād*, vol. 10, p. 170; Dhahabī, *Tadhkirat al-ḥuffāẓ*, vol. 2, p. 631; Khwānsārī, *Rawḍāt al-janān*, vol. 5, p. 105; Ibn al-'Imād, *Shadharāt al-dhahab*, vol. 2, p. 169; Dhahabī, *al-'Ibar*, vol. 2, p. 56; Dodge, *Fihrist of al-Nadīm*, pp. 77–78, 134, 138, 170, 171, 190–191, 250, 352, 427, 491, 742; Ibn al-Athīr, *Al-Lubāb*, vol. 2, p. 242; 'Asqalānī, *Lisān al-Mīzān*, vol. 2, p. 357; Yāfi'ī, *Mir'āt al-janān*, vol. 2, p. 191; Dhahabī, *Mīzān al-i'tidāl*, vol. 2, p. 503; Ibn Taghrībirdī, *al-Nujūm al-zāhira*, vol. 3, p. 75; Ibn al-Anbārī, *Nuzhat al-alibbā'*, p. 209; Ibn Khallikān, *Wafayāt al-a'yān*, vol. 2, p. 246.

425 Muḥammad b. al-Mustanīr, Abū 'Alī al-Naḥwī ('the grammarian'), known as Quṭrub (d. 206/821–2). He kept company with Sībawayhi; studied under 'Īsā b. 'Umar; he has works on Qur'ānic semantics; Ibn al-Nadīm enumerates twenty-eight books by him. His biography is in Dā'ūdī, *Ṭabaqāt al-mufassirīn*, vol. 2, p.

254; Qifṭī, *Inbāh al-ruwāt*, vol. 3, p. 219; Ibn Kathīr, *al-Bidāya wa'l-nihāya*, vol. 10, p. 259; Suyūṭī, *Bughyat al-wuʿāt*, vol. 1, p. 242; al-Khaṭīb al-Baghdādī, *Ta'rīkh Baghdād*, vol. 3, p. 298; Ibn al-ʿImād, *Shadharāt al-dhahab*, vol. 2, p. 15; Dhahabī, *al-ʿIbar*, vol. 1, p. 35; Dodge, *Fihrist of al-Nadīm*, p. 83, 114, 190–191, 234; Ibn al-Athīr, *al-Kāmil*, vol. 6, p. 380; ʿAsqalānī, *Lisān al-mīzān*, vol. 5, p. 378; Yāfiʿī, *Mir'āt al-janān*, vol. 2, p.31; Yāqūt al-Ḥamawī, *Muʿjam al-udabā'*, vol. 7, p. 105; Ṭāshkoprizāde, *Miftāḥ al-saʿāda*, vol. 1, p.160; Ibn al-Anbārī, *Nuzhat al-alibbā'*, p. 91; Ibn Khallikān, *Wafayāt al-aʿyān*, vol. 3, p. 439.

426 Muḥammad b. ʿAlī b. Ismāʿīl, al-Imam Abū Bakr al-Shāshī al-Faqīh ('the jurist') al-Shāfiʿī, known as al-Qaffāl al-Kabīr ('the elder or great locksmith') (d. 366/976–7). He was the leading authority in his age in Transoxiana. Composed The Great Commentary (*al-Tafsīr al-Kabīr*) etc. Subkī, *Ṭabaqāt al-shāfiʿiyya al-kubrā*, vol. 3, p. 200; Suyūṭī, *Ṭabaqāt al-mufassirīn*, p. 36; Dhahabī, *al-ʿIbar*, vol. 2, p. 338; Yāfiʿī, *Mir'āt al-janān*, vol. 2, p. 381; Ibn Taghrībirdī, *al-Nujūm al-zāhira*, vol. 4, p. 111; Ibn Khallikān, *Wafayāt al-aʿyān*, vol. 3, p. 338; Ṣafadī, *al-Wāfī bi'l-wafayāt*, vol. 4, p. 112.

427 This is Abū Muslim Muḥammad b. Baḥr al-Iṣfahānī (in the original: Muslim b. Baḥr) (d. 322/934; alternatively 370/980–1). Author of a Qur'ān commentary. Abū'l-Ḥusayn b. Bābūya mentioned him in his History of Rayy: 'He was a follower of the doctrine of the Muʿtazila'. ʿAsqalānī, *Lisān al-mīzān*, vol. 5, p. 89.

428 This appears to refer to a convention in the original rubrics.

Chapter 8
On the meaning of tafsīr *(exegesis) and* ta'wīl *(hermeneutics)*

429 i.e. the 'first form' of the verb.

430 i.e. the 'second form', with the *sīn* geminated.

431 = To attract.

432 = To pull, draw.

433 Also see the technical sense of *samʿ/samāʿ* discussed above in note 22.

434 Q. 79:1.

435 Q. 51:1.

436 Q. 37:1.

437 Q. 100:1.

438 Bukhārī, *ʿIlm*, 38; Ibn Māja, *Muqaddima*, 4 and 33.

439 Q. 2:1–2.

440 Q. 49:9.

441 The two Arab tribes of Yathrib between whom there was friction until the advent of Islam, when they were subsumed within the Anṣār.

442 Q. 14:28.

443 Q. 48:16.

444 *Bi'l-samāʿ*, i.e. through transmitted instruction.

445 Al-Ḥusayn b. al-Faḍl al-Bajalī, later al-Naysābūrī, Abū ʿAlī (d. 282/895). Qur'ānic exegete and belle-lettrist. Dā'ūdī, *Ṭabaqāt al-mufassirīn*, vol. 1, p. 156.

446 i.e. the punctuation of the text.

447 'The branches' means applied law.

448 i.e. the sending down of the revelation.

449 Literally, 'the outward'.
450 Literally, 'the inward'.
451 Q. 2:210. Here, the hermeneutic would deflect the anthropomorphism of the verse, unchallenged in mere exegesis.
452 Q. 12:100. The words are Joseph's.
453 Q. 12:6.
454 Q. 18:82. MA *mā lam tasṭiʿ* : *mā lam yastaṭiʿ*.
455 Q. 7:53.
456 Q. 4:59.
457 Q. 12:45. The appropriateness of the quotation seems less clear. The point is apparently that the speaker is referring the interpretation of Pharaoh's dream *back* to the Prophet Joseph. It may be that, given Shahrastānī's use of the quotation, *ta'wīlahu* might be better rendered 'the reference for it', rather than 'its hermeneutic'.
458 Q. 3:7.
459 These varieties of 'ruling' are elaborated by Shahrastānī in chaper ten, below.
460 Q. 3:7.

Chapter 9
On generality and specificity, the clear and the ambiguous, the abrogating and the abrogated

461 Q. 2:21.
462 Q. 2:199. 'Mankind' here is taken by Shahrastānī to refer to a group narrower than the obligated Muslims in general, namely the most exemplary of them, presumably the imams.
463 Q. 4:54.
464 Q. 7:156.
465 Q. 7:156.
466 Q. 7:157.
467 Q. 21:107.
468 Q. 7:121. The words are Pharaoh's sorcerers', defeated by Moses.
469 Q. 7:122.
470 Q. 19:93.
471 Q. 25:63.
472 Q. 76:6.
473 Q. 47:11. For ʿAlī's saying, see Ibn ʿAsākir, *Ta'rīkh madīnat Dimashq*, vol. 27, p. 99; also Thaqafī, *Ghārāt*, vol. 2, pp. 736–737. Note that these references contain the name of ʿAlī's interlocutor: Ibn al-Kawwā' ʿAbd Allāh b. ʿAmr, the Shīʿī genealogist from the Banū Yashkur tribe. See Dodge, *Fihrist of al-Nadīm*, p. 195.
474 Q. 3:7. 'Mother', i.e. essence.
475 Q. 3:7.
476 See the presentation of the Command verses and the creation verses in the *Majlis*. Shahrastānī, *Majlis: Discours sur l'Ordre et la creation*, p. 80 ff.
477 Q. 11:1.
478 Respectively, Q. 6 and Q. 17. The latter is also called *Sūrat al-Isrā'* and *Sūrat Banī Isrā'īl*. It is transmitted on Ibn ʿAbbās's authority, in regard to His statement 'consisting in clear verses', [that] he said: 'In this category is "Say: Come" (Q. 6:151)

for three verses; and in this category is "Your Lord has ordained that you worship none but Him" (Q. 17:23) for three verses after it.' On the grounds of this transmission the sum total would be six verses, not ten verses. See Suyūṭī, *Itqān*, vol. 2, p. 3.

479 *yaḥuttu ʿan, i.e., yaruddu.*

480 'Which announce divine unicity and holiness', i.e. which indicate God's *transcendence.*

481 See Q. 23:12–14.

482 The text in fact says '[...] and ended (*intahat*) with the Resurrection [...]'. The perfect tense perhaps relates to a cyclical view of time.

483 Q. 53:47.

484 Q. 2:106.

485 *Istīfā'* : *istifyā'* MA.

486 i.e. the essence of the scripture. Q. 3:7.

487 Q. 13:39.

488 MA *taqrīr* : *taqdīr.*

489 'The troop', presumably, of errors. Shahrastānī is playing on words: *al-tafrīq* (discrimination) and *al-farīq* (the troop). However, Ādharshab suggests instead of *wa tabarra'a'l-tafrīqu ʿan al-farīq*: *wa tabarra'a'l-farīqu min al-furīq*, i.e. 'and one troop is freed from another'. Ādharshab, *Tafsīr al-Shahrastānī*, p. 183, note 3.

490 Usually known as the Unbelievers (*al-Kāfirūn*), Q. 109.

491 Q. 109:6.

492 Q. 3:141.

493 Q. 2:216.

494 Q. 9:14.

495 *Taqrīri* : *taqrīru* MA.

496 Q. 13:39.

Chapter 10
On the two principles of the accomplished (mafrūgh) *and the inchoative* (musta'naf) [...]

497 i.e. using the word *anif* instead of *mubtada'.*

498 Only the last portion of this tradition, is found in the 'Sound Six' Sunnī collections (*al-kutub al-sitta*) and recognised Qur'ān commentaries. See e.g. Ṭabarī, *Jāmiʿ al-bayān*, vol. 12, p. 117 (= on Q. 11:106). Compare in addition, Ibn Bābūya, *Kitāb al-Tawḥīd* (Qum, 1387), p. 280. The tradition is also discussed in Shahrastānī, *Majlis*, p. 108.

499 MA *kalima* : *kalimāt.*

500 Q. 6:115.

501 Hindī, *Kanz al-ʿummāl*, vol. 1, p. 187, ḥadīth 608, with a slight difference of wording.

502 Hindī, *Kanz al-ʿummāl*, vol. 1, p. 107, ḥadīth 491; also Ibn Bābūya al-Qummī, *Kitāb al-Tawḥīd*, p. 366.

503 e.g. Q. 2:7.

504 e.g. Q. 9:93.

505 e.g. Q. 47:24.

506 Q. 2:6.

507 Q. 7:193.

508 Q. 18:6.
509 Q. 74:2.
510 Q. 19:39; also Q. 40:18.
511 Q. 36:6.
512 Q. 7:2.
513 MA *yatadhakkaru* : *yudhakkiru.*
514 Q. 20:44.
515 Q. 87:9–10.
516 Compare Kulaynī, *Uṣūl*, vol. 4, p. 436, ḥadīth 3 and 4 (= *bāb al-nawādir, kitāb faḍl al-Qur'ān*).
517 *Mithāl* and *mathal* are used here for different kinds of couple: in the former case the coupled terms are opposed, while in the latter case they are not. I translate *mithāl* as 'match' and *mathal* as 'like' or 'likeness'.
518 Q. 37:164.
519 Q. 2:30.
520 Q. 2:32.
521 Q. 17:55.
522 Q. 58:11.
523 Q. 6:132.
524 Hindī, *Kanz al-ʿummāl*, vol. 3, p. 690, ḥadīth 8476, with a very slight difference in wording. Also compare Dārimī, *Muqaddima*, 32; and ʿAlī b. Abī Ṭālib, *Nahj al-balāgha*, p. 416.
525 Q. 51:47–9.
526 Q. 55:7.
527 Q. 42:17.
528 Q. 14:24.
529 Q. 55:1–4.
530 Shahrastānī elaborates this concept of the reciprocity of creation and the Command in his *Majlis*. e.g. Shahrastānī, *Majlis*, p. 81.
531 Q. 55:9.
532 Q. 21:47.

Chapter 11
On the miraculous inimitability of the Qur'ān [...]

533 MA *al-insu wa'l-jinn* : *al-jinnu wa'l-ins* .
534 Q. 17:88.
535 MA *iʿtaqadahu* : *intaqadahu.*
536 Q. 72:1–2.
537 MA *khuwāran* : *ḥuwāzan*. The verse quoted here (Q. 7:148) refers to the golden calf worshipped by the Israelites at Mount Sinai.
538 Q. 28:49.
539 Q. 2:185.
540 Q. 42:52.
541 Q. 7:52.
542 Q. 7:2.
543 MA *andhir* : *dhakkir.*
544 Q. 6:51.

Chapter 12
On the prerequisites for exegesis of the Qur'ān

545 Q. 16:44.
546 Idem.
547 The *ṣaḥīḥ* works cover all traditions achieving the top category of probable historicity according to the 'science of Ḥadīth'. The *sunan* works cover only legal-liturgical traditions of probable historicity. Shahrastānī presumably means the two mentioned categories to subsume all collections within the Sound Six (*al-kutub al-sitta*): (A, *ṣaḥīḥ*) *Ṣaḥīḥ al-Bukhārī*, *Ṣaḥīḥ Muslim*; (B, *sunan*) *Sunan Abī Dāwūd*, *Sunan al-Nasā'ī*, *Sunun Ibn Māja*, and *Jāmiʿ al-Tirmidhī*.
548 See above, notes 289 and 438.
549 Q. 24:56; also Q. 73:20.
550 MA *wa'l-tanmiya* : *wa'l-kammiyya* .
551 Q. 37:1.
552 Q. 51:1.
553 Q. 100:1.
554 Q. 43:22.
555 Q. 43:23. The words quoted from the verses cited here, are those of the unbelievers.
556 This doctrinal orientation, which in the name of transcendence strips the idea of God of any concrete reality, is clearly linked by Shahrastānī in practice with antinomian varieties of Shīʿism. The latter are also referred to in the text, p. 126, and hold that the believer's recognition of (*maʿrifa*, perhaps 'gnosis' of) the imam is held to be sufficient for salvation, obviating law.
557 *Wāqifa*, literally, 'those who have scruples', 'hesitaters'. The term historically refers to a variety of groups such as those who suspended judgement on the metaphysical status of the Qur'ān and those who suspended judgement on the culpability of the Muslim who sinned in ignorance. However the context implies that by the *wāqifa*, Shahrastānī means specifically scholars suspending judgement on the conflict of anthropomorphism (*tashbīh*) and nihilistic abstraction (*taʿṭīl*) in theology and exegesis. Since the hermeneutic of such scholars is equally unfounded on the imams' instruction, it also seems to be rejected by Shahrastānī in what follows.
558 The statement is famously attributed to Mālik b. Anas (d. 179/795), eponymous founder of the Mālikī legal rite. Bayhaqī, *al-Asmā' wa'l-ṣifāt*, p. 516, with a very slight difference in wording. Also see Miṣrī, *Reliance of the Traveller*, p. 854.
559 MA *bi-āyātinā* : *bi-āyāti'llāh* .
560 Q. 7:46.
561 The term *awliyā'* could also be translated as 'the saints' and in a Shīʿī context, 'the imams'. Shahrastānī seems to mean the latter.
562 Q. 23:50.
563 Q. 4:83.
564 Tirmidhī, *Manāqib*, 19. The text continues *wa lā yu'addī ʿannī illā anā aw ʿAlī* ('and none acquits me of what I owe except I or ʿAlī').
565 Compare the traditions quoted in Ṭabrisī, *Majmaʿ al-bayān*, vol. 10, p. 3.
566 *Aḥruf* could also be rendered 'letters'.
567 Iṣfahānī, *Ḥilyat al-awliyā'*, vol. 1, p. 65.

568 Iṣfahānī, *Ḥilyat al-awliyā'*, vol. 1, pp. 67–68.
569 Literally, 'The imam is scratched in his ear.'
570 Majlisī, *Biḥār al-anwār*, vol. 25, p. 261.
571 MA *Fayḍ* : *'Ayḍ*. See Majlisī, *Biḥār al-anwār*, vol. 47, p. 412.
572 i.e. al-Mufaḍḍal b. 'Umar al-Ju'fī al-Kūfī al-Ṣayrafī (? d. 145/762), a famous disciple of Ja'far al-Ṣādiq who, though initially associated with the radical orientation of Abū'l-Khaṭṭāb, was later appointed by Ja'far as his representative among his Kufan followers. He may have been a teacher of Ismā'īl b. Ja'far, the eponymous imam of Ismā'īlī Shī'ism. Ṭūsī, *Ikhtiyār ma'rifat al-rijāl*, pp. 321–329, 509 and 530–531.
573 See Majlisī, *Biḥār al-anwār*, vol. 25, p. 263; also vol. 47, p. 334.
574 This is the group associated with Abū'l-Khaṭṭāb according to the transmissions in Majlisī's *Biḥār*; however, Shahrastānī attributes this belief to the Kaysāniyya. See Shahrastānī, *Kitāb al-Milal wa'l-niḥal*, vol. 1, pp. 117–120, especially p.118.
575 MA *mushrik* : *mushtarik*.
576 See Q. 7:33.
577 Majlisī, *Biḥār al-anwār*, vol. 24, pp. 286–289.
578 Al-Qāḍī al-Nu'mān, *Da'ā'im al-Islām*, vol. 1, p. 92 (= *kitāb al-wilāya, dhikr manāzil al-a'imma*).
579 '[...] us', i.e. Muslims in general, or else the Shī'a. Alternatively, instead of *man 'anadanā*, this may be read *man 'indanā*, 'those with us [...]'.
580 Q. 16:43; also Q. 21:7.
581 Majlisī, *Biḥār al-anwār*, vol. 23, p. 172. Significantly, Shahrastānī is himself quoted as authority for the transmission of the tradition here. Also see Kulaynī, *Uṣūl*, vol. 1, p. 306 (= *kitāb al-ḥujja, bāb inna ahl al-dhikr alladhīna amara'llāhu'l-khalqa bi-su'ālihim hum al-a'imma* [*'alayhim al-salām*]), ḥadīth 7.
582 Kulaynī, *Uṣūl*, vol. 1, pp. 303–307 (= *kitāb al-ḥujja, bāb inna ahl al-dhikr* etc.), especially p. 303, ḥadīth 1. Also see al-Qāḍī al-Nu'mān, *Da'ā'im al-islām*, vol. 1, p. 59 (= *kitāb al-wilāya, dhikr wilāya min ahl bayt rasūl Allāh*).
583 See Majlisī, *Biḥār al-anwār*, vol. 23, pp. 120, 130. On the *ḥadīth al-thaqalayn*, see above, note 133.
584 For its chain of transmission, consult Majlisī's *Biḥār al-anwār*, vol. 10, pp. 117–128.
585 Al-Ṣaffār al-Qummī, *Baṣā'ir al-darajāt*, pp. 152, 154; Ibn Abī'l-Ḥadīd, *Sharḥ Nahj al-balāgha*, vol. 12, p. 197; Majlisī, *Biḥār al-anwār*, vol. 89, p. 78. Majlisī transmits on the authority of Abū Ḥāmid al-Ghazālī in his book *Bayān al-'ilm al-ladunī* that 'Alī's saying this indicates a degree not obtained through simple knowledge, instead an individual takes possession of this degree by virtue of knowledge from the divine presence (*al-'ilm al-ladunī*). Majlisī, *Biḥār al-anwār*, vol. 89, p. 103.
586 MA *ma'ānin* : *ma'ānī*.
587 Majlisī transmits it from *al-Durar al-bāhira*, with the additional statement '[...] the outward expression is for the commonalty, the allusion is for the elite, the subtleties are for the saints (*awliyā'*), and the realities are for the prophets'. Majlisī, *Biḥār al-anwār*, vol. 89, p. 103. It appears in the same form in Sulami's *Ḥaqā'iq al-tafsīr*. See Nwyia, 'Le Tafsīr Mystique', p. 188.
588 Ṭabarī, *Jāmi' al-bayān*, vol. 1, p. 12 (where the tradition is related by Ibn Mas'ūd on the Prophet's authority). Also see Suyūṭī, *Itqān*, vol. 2, pp. 184–185. Also the commentary of Ja'far al-Ṣādiq on the meaning of the transmission in 'Ayyāshī, *Kitāb al-Tafsīr*, vol. 1, p. 11.

The Exegesis of the Exordium (*Tafsīr Sūrat al-Fātiḥa*)

589 Q. 8:24.
590 Compare Bukhārī, *Tafsīr*, 1. The Prophet's implicit reference at the end is to Q. 15:87: 'We have bestowed on you Seven of the Doubled Ones and the Mighty Qur'ān.'
591 Q. 15:87. For the tradition: Tirmidhī, Nasā'ī and Naysābūrī derive it with a slightly different wording by their chain of transmission on the authority of Abū Hurayra; Mālik transmits it in the *Muwaṭṭa'* by his chain of transmission on the authority of Abū Sa'īd the client of 'Āmir b. Kurayz; Bukhārī derives it in a different form on the authority of Abū Sa'īd b. al-Mu'allā. Zamakhsharī, *Kashshāf*, vol. 1, p.19; also see Ibn Ḥajar al-'Asqalānī's gloss on it.
592 Bayhaqī, *al-Sunan al-kubrā*, vol. 2, p. 45 (= *bāb al-dalīl 'alā anna'l-basmala āya tāmma*).
593 Ibid.
594 *Qasamtu al-ṣalāta : qussimat al-ṣalātu* MA.
595 Ṭabarī gives the derivation of this prophetic tradition in his *Jāmi' al-bayān*, vol. 1, p. 86. Also see Ṭūsī, *Tibyān*, vol. 1, p. 46.
596 *Inna nafaranā ghuyyabun : inna baqaranā ghuyyabun* MA.
597 *Wa saqānā labanan : wa saqā'in* MA.
598 Compare Bukhārī, *Faḍā'il al-Qur'ān*, 9; also Bukhārī, *Tafsīr*, 1; also Bukhārī, *Ṭibb*, 33.
599 Other names for it are 'Praise [...]' (*al-Ḥamd*, from the beginning of the first verse after the *basmala*), the Perfect (*al-Wāfiya*), the Sufficient (*al-Kāfiya*), the Foundation (*al-Asās*), the Healing (*al-Shifā'*), and the Prayer (*al-Ṣalāt*). Ṭabrisī, *Majma' al-bayān*, vol. 1, p. 17; also Qurṭubī, *al-Jāmi' li-aḥkām al-Qur'ān*, vol. 1, pp. 98–114.
600 Note that the second form, *'aṭṭafa* means 'to fold', 'to double'. Thus *mi'ṭaf*, pl. *ma'āṭif*, suggests a garment which is folded or doubled in being worn, comparable perhaps with the English word 'doublet'.
601 Q. 15. The toponym, *al-Ḥijr* (literally, the Rocky Tract), is related to Ptolemy's Hegra and Pliny's Egra.
602 Q. 15:87.
603 Included in the ḥadīth of secrets bestowed on Khadīja. Suyūṭī, *al-Durr al-manthūr*, vol. 1, pp. 2–3.
604 See Ṭabrisī, *Majma' al-bayān*, vol. 1, p. 7.
605 *Maqburī : Muqrī* MA.
606 Ṭabarānī derives this in *al-Awsaṭ*, Ibn Mardawayh in his *Tafsīr*, and also Bayhaqī, on the authority of Abū Hurayra, with the addition '[...] it being the Seven Doubled Ones and the Mighty Qur'ān, and it is the Mother of the Qur'ān and the Exordium of the Scripture'. Suyūṭī, *al-Durr al-manthūr*, vol. 1, p. 3.
607 i.e. according to this report, and contrary to some reckonings, there is no verse division between 'The Path of those whom You have graciously favoured (*an'amta 'alayhim*)' and 'Not those against whom is Your wrath, nor those who go astray', all this falling within the seventh and final verse. Ibn al-Anbārī derives this tradition in *al-Maṣāḥif* on the authority of Umm Salama. Suyūṭī, *al-Durr al-manthūr*, vol. 1, pp. 3–4. Abū Dā'ūd and others transmit it. Suyūṭī, *Itqān*, vol. 1, p. 89. On Ibn Abī Mulayka, 'Abd Allāh b. 'Ubayd Allāh (d. 117/735) see Ibn al-

Jazarī, *Ghāyat al-nihāya*, vol. 1, p. 430; also Mizzī, *Tahdhīb al-kamāl*, vol. 10, pp. 310–311.

608 ʿAmr b. ʿAbd Allāh al-Hamadānī al-Kūfī al-Ḥāfiẓ (ʻMemorizer of the Qurʾānʼ), Abū Isḥāq al-Sabīʿī (d. 127/745). One of the leading figures in transmitting sayings. Dhahabī, *Tadhkirat al-ḥuffāẓ*, vol. 1, p. 114.

609 Suyūṭī, *al-Durr al-manthūr*, vol. 1, pp. 2–3; also Naysābūrī, *Asbāb al-nuzūl*, p. 11.

610 Q. 96.

611 Q. 15:87.

612 Q. 27. The formula uniquely occurs *in the body* of this chapter, as the heading of the letter from Solomon to the Queen of Sheba (Q. 27:30).

613 MA *ʿanhum* : *ʿanhumā.*

614 MA *fātiḥat al-kitāb* : *al-fātiḥat al-kitāb.*

615 Q. 9. The formula is uniquely absent from the beginning of this chapter.

616 Q. 67. For the tradition, see al-Ḥākim al-Naysābūrī, *Mustadrak*, vol. 1, p. 565; also Tirmidhī, *Faḍāʾil al-Qurʾān*, 9.

617 Q. 108. For the tradition, see Muslim, *Ṣalāt*, 14; Nasāʾī, *Iftitāḥ*, 21; Abū Dāʾūd, *Ṣalāt*, 122.

618 Recitation in the noon and mid-afternoon prayers is otherwise not aloud. According to the tradition transmitted by Ibn Abī ʿAqīl al-Yamanī: ʻThe traditions are successive (*tawātarat*) on the authority of the imams of the People of the House that there is no dissimulation in regard to speaking the formula "In the name of God [...]" aloudʼ. Majlisī, *Biḥār al-anwār*, vol. 82, pp. 74–75.

619 For the explanation of the words ʻsince Solomonʼ, see above, note 612. This prophetic tradition is derived by Abū Ḥātim, Ṭabarānī, Dāraquṭnī and Bayhaqī in their *sunan* works with a weak chain of transmission on the authority of Burayda. Suyūṭī, *al-Durr al-manthūr*, vol. 1, p. 7.

620 Dāraquṭnī and Bayhaqī derive this in ʻThe Branches of Faithʼ (*Shuʿab al-īmān*) on the authority of Jābir. Suyūṭī, *al-Durr al-manthūr*, vol. 1, p. 8.

621 See note 599.

622 Thaʿlabī derives this on the authority of Abū Hurayra, with different wording from that quoted by Shahrastānī. According to Thaʿlabīʼs transmission, the Prophet said: ʻFellow! You have disrupted the formal prayer on your own initiative. Donʼt you know that "In the name of God, the Infinitely Merciful, the Compassionate" is part of "Praise [...]"? Thus whoever omits it has omitted a verse, and whoever omits a verse has on those grounds spoiled his formal prayer.ʼ Suyūṭī, *al-Durr al-manthūr*, vol. 1, p. 7.

623 Thaʿlabī also derives this. Suyūṭī, *al-Durr al-manthūr*, vol. 1, p. 47.

624 MA *thalāth ʿashara* : *thalātha ʿashar.*

625 al-Ḥākim al-Naysābūrī transmits this. Zamakhsharī, *Kashshāf*, appendix, vol. 1, p. 1.

626 i.e. the Prophet only knew that the revelation of a given chapter was complete when the *basmala* formula came for the *next* chapter.

627 Abū Dāʾūd, Bazāz, Ṭabarānī and al-Ḥākim al-Naysābūrī derive this on the authority of Ibn ʿAbbās, as including the words ʻ[Godʼs Messenger] did not know the division (*faṣl*) of the chapterʼ, and in one version ʻ[...] the end (*khātima*) of the chapterʼ. Bazāz and Ṭabarānī have in addition: ʻ[...] so when it came down he knew that the chapter had ended and was confronting him, and another chapter had begunʼ. Suyūṭī, *al-Durr al-manthūr*, vol. 1, p. 7.

628 Bayhaqī derives this in 'The Branches of Faith' (*Shuʿab al-īmān*), and also Wāḥidī, on the authority of Ibn Masʿūd. Suyūṭī, *al-Durr al-manthūr*, vol. 1, p. 7.

629 The two sanctuaries are Mecca and Medina.

630 Q. 2.

631 Al-Ḥākim al-Naysābūrī derives this report, also declared authentic by Bayhaqī in his *Sunan*, on the authority of Ibn ʿAbbās. Suyūṭī, *al-Durr al-manthūr*, vol. 1, p. 7.

632 ʿAyyāshī transmits this via his chain of transmission on the authority of ʿAlī b. Mūsā al-Riḍā. ʿAyyāshī, *Kitāb al-Tafsīr*, vol. 1, p. 21. MA *ilā bayāḍihā* : *ilā mā fīhā*.

633 Abū'l-Naḍr Muḥammad b. Masʿūd b. Muḥammad b. al-ʿAyyāshī al-Kūfī (floruit end of the 3rd/9th century). His commentary is intermittently referred to by Shahrastānī. Descended from the Arab tribe, the Banū Tamīm, and lived in Samarqand. Shīʿī in inclination, though communally Sunnī or alternatively, originally Sunnī and fully converted to Shīʿism while young. He studied under the disciples of ʿAlī b. al-Ḥasan b. Faḍḍāl (d. 224/839) and ʿAbd Allāh b. Muḥammad al-Ṭayālisī. Credited with authoring over 200 works, mostly on law, but also on, for example, medicine, dream-interpretation and divination. All are unextant save the first half of his Qurʾān commentary which survives in an abridgement of the original with the chains of transmission omitted. See the introduction by al-ʿAllāma al-Ṭabaṭaba'ī to ʿAyyāshī, *Kitāb al-Tafsīr*, pp. ii-iii. Also Dodge, *Fihrist of al-Nadīm*, 81, 482–487; *EI*², vol. 1, pp. 794–795 (B. Lewis); *EIr*, vol. 3, pp. 163–164 (I.K. Poonawala).

634 This tradition seems absent from the extant text of ʿAyyāshī, *Kitāb al-Tafsīr*.

635 See note 572.

636 *Min al-nās kullihim* : *min al-nās* MA. Amended following Kulaynī.

637 Q. 112.

638 Other versions of this tradition have 'to your left' (*ʿan shimālika*) instead.

639 *Fa-'qraʾ-hā* : *fa-'qraʾ* MA. Amended following Kulaynī.

640 *Thumma* : _ MA. Amended following Kulaynī.

641 Kulaynī, *Uṣūl*, vol. 4, p. 431 (= *kitāb faḍl al-Qurʾān, bāb faḍl al-Qurʾān*), ḥadīth 20. On the identity of al-Mufaḍḍal, see note 572.

642 Dāraquṭnī, and Bayhaqī in *Shuʿab al-īmān*, derive this tradition on the authority of Jābir. Suyūṭī, *al-Durr al-manthūr*, vol. 1, p. 8. Majlisī, *Biḥār al-anwār*, vol. 82, p. 48. Quoted from al-Qāḍī al-Nuʿmān, *Daʿāʾim al-islām* on the authority of Jaʿfar al-Ṣādiq, on the authority of Muḥammad al-Bāqir, on the authority of Jābir.

643 Majlisī, *Biḥār al-anwār*, vol. 82, p. 81. Quoted from al-Qāḍī al-Nuʿmān, *Daʿāʾim al-islām*.

644 i.e. the legal mitigation of wiping the socks rather than the bare feet in the minor ritual ablution, which is not allowed in Shīʿī fiqh.

645 MA _ : *Bi'smi'llāh al-Raḥmān al-Raḥīm*. The formula is mistakenly given twice at this point in the manuscript.

646 Majlisī, *Biḥār al-anwār*, vol. 82, p. 81.

647 Sanʿānī, *Muṣannaf*, vol. 2, p. 92, ḥadīth 2618.

648 Bayhaqī, *al-Sunan al-kubrā*, vol. 2, p. 50 (=*bāb iftitāḥ al-qirāʾa wa'l-ṣalāt*). ʿAyyāshī also says the following: 'It is a verse of God's scripture which Satan caused them to forget'. ʿAyyāshī, *Kitāb al-Tafsīr*, vol. 1, p. 21.

649 *Sic*, i.e. dispensable, non-essential to the text.

650 The last two questions refer to aspects of the established Qurʾānic orthography of the formula.

651 MA *mā*: _.
652 As would be the case when the formula is used to consecrate some subsequent action, as is normal for a Muslim.
653 Q. 11:41.
654 Q. 96: 1.
655 *Abtadi'u* : *ahtadī* MA.
656 i.e. 'I do this for you'.
657 i.e. 'Were it not for you'.
658 i.e. 'Were it not for X [...]'.
659 MA *ḥawlan* : *qawlan*.
660 Ṭabarī said after he recited this verse: 'Thus the leader in the study of the language of the Arabs had interpreted it to the effect that [Labīd] thereby meant "[...] then 'peace upon you both'" and that the word "peace" *is* peace.' Ṭabarī, *Jāmi' al-bayān*, vol. 1, p. 52.
661 i.e. the expression *bi'llāh* would simply be an oath ('By God!'), as distinct from *bi'smi'llāh*.
662 *Wasm*, mark, cognate with *sima*.
663 *Wu'ayd* = promise.
664 *Wuṣay* = nexus. Ādharshab says here: '[Shahrastānī] should have said "as they say *'ida* and *wu'ayda*, and *ṣila* and *wuṣayla*", in order to bring out the repetition of the *wāw* in the diminutive.' Ādharshab, *Tafsīr al-Shahrastānī*, p. 213, note 2.
665 Ṭabarī transmits the mentioned tradition on the authority of Abū Sa'īd al-Khudrī with a small difference in wording, and then says: 'I fear that it is a mistake on the part of the traditionist and that he meant *bā' sīn mīm* according to the way the beginners amongst children are taught in the book of the letters of the alphabet (*ḥurūf abī jād*), and he made a mistake such that he connected it together and said *bi'sm* – since this interpretation is meaningless!' Ṭūsī, *al-Tibyān*, vol. 1, p. 53. i.e. this interpretation of the word *ism* is meaningless.
666 MA *huwa* : _.
667 i.e. the *lām* of the definite article (*lām al-ta'rīf*), *al-*.
668 Abū Bishr 'Amr b. 'Uthmān Sībawayhi (d. circa 180/796). The pioneer Arabic grammarian, of Persian descent. Author of the famous *Kitāb Sībawayhi*. *EI*[2], vol. 9, pp. 524–531 (M.S. Carter).
669 Ṭabarsī mentions the same two statements on the authority of Sībawayhi, but with greater clarity and elaboration, saying: 'Sībawayhi mentions two statements on its origin. The first of them is that it is *ilāh* on the pattern of *fi'āl*. Then the *fā'* [of the latter pattern], which is the *hamza*, was omitted and the *alif* and *lām* [*al-*] were taken as a replacement for it. The second is that its origin is *lāh*, its pattern being *fa'l*, and the *alif* and *lām* [*al-*] were subjoined to it.' Ṭabarsī, *Majma' al-bayān*, vol. 1, p. 19.
670 Abū Naṣr Ismā'īl b. Naṣr b. Ḥammād al-Fārābī al-Jawharī (d. 393/1002–1003). The celebrated Arabic lexicographer of Turkish origin. The author of *Tāj al-lugha wa ṣiḥāḥ al-'arabiyya*, commonly known as *al-Ṣiḥāḥ*. As the name of the work implies, Jawharī aimed to include in it only such items of lexicographical information as were transmitted through sound chains of authorities. *EI*[2], vol. 2, pp. 495–497 (L. Kopf).
671 Q. 7:127. Jeffery attributes this reading to Ḥasan, 'Alī and others. Jeffery, *Materials for the History of the Text of the Qur'ān*, p. 43.

672 i.e. from *lāha/yalīhu layhan* (= 'to be concealed').
673 Jawharī, *Tāj al-lugha*, vol. 6, p. 2248.
674 i.e. acknowledging that God is a 'thing'.
675 Quoddity, i.e. the fact *that* God is, as distinct from His quiddity (*māhiyya*), *what* God is.
676 This formulation involves a chiasmus, such that creation = dominion (*mulk*): Command = possession (*milk*). Al-Rāghib al-Iṣfahānī says: '*Milk* is being in possession (*tamalluk*) and in charge (*tawallī*). *Mulk* is having under control (*ḍabt*) something subject to free disposal in judgement, *milk* being as it were the genus for *mulk*, so every *mulk* is *milk* but not every *milk* is *mulk*.' Al-Rāghib al-Iṣfahānı, *al-Mufradāt fī gharīb al-Qur'ān*, vol. 2, pp. 717–719, especially p. 718 (= art. *malaka*).
677 The point depends on the fact that the meaning of *ta'rīf*, in addition to 'grammatical definition' (i.e. prefixing the definite article *al-*), is literally 'making known'.
678 Compare Kulaynī, *Furū'*, vol. 3, pp.482–483 (= *kitāb al-ṣalāt, bāb al-nawādir*), ḥadīth 1. Here the first part of the quoted statement, according to which God is 'too mighty to be seen', is said to have been given in refutation of the claim that Ubayy b. Ka'b saw God in a dream.
679 Shahrastānī's Arabic expression is again chiastic: *mā kullifa bi-ma'rifatihi wa 'urrifa bi-taklīfihi*. i.e. what is affirmed about God through the letters of the divine name is one's duty to understand and is understood to be one's duty.
680 = *Shirk*, association, i.e. of the created with the divine.
681 Q. 112.
682 MA _ : *wa'smu'llāh*. The words of the chapter of Sincerity (Q. 112) are: 'Say: He (*Huwa*) is *Allāh*, One, *Allāh*, the Absolute. He does not beget, and neither is He begotten. And there is nothing whatsoever like Him.'
683 MA *yu'ṭī* : _.
684 The expression *al-alif al-qawl* ('the *alif* of pronunciation'), is an improper genitive and it may in fact represent a lapsus calami which should read *al-alif fī'l-qawl* (the *alif* in the pronunciation), parallel to *al-lām fī'l-kitāba* (the *lām* in the orthography). i.e. the idiosyncrasy of the divine name is such that while the *lām* is written twice (rather than once and given the *tashdīd* mark as expected), the *alif* is written once but pronounced twice – the second *alif* never being written. So what is pronounced once is written twice and what is written once is pronounced twice.
685 Q. 87:1–3.
686 Q. 19:65.
687 = *Raḥima*, following the vowelling of the editor. Alternatively we might read *raḥim* (womb).
688 Maymūn b. Qays al-A'shā (d. after CE 625). Famous panegyrist from the tribe of Qays b. Tha'laba of the Bakr b. Wā'il. *EI²*, vol. 1, pp. 599–690 (W. Caskel). The entire verse is quoted on the authority of Abū 'Alī in Jawharī, *Ṣiḥāḥ*, vol. 6, p. 2224. The verse is also attributed to Mayya bt. Umm 'Utba. See Ibn Manẓūr, *Lisān al-'arab*, vol. 13, p. 468. Also see Ṭūsī, *Tibyān*, vol. 1, p. 28.
689 Ru'ba b. al-'Ajjāj al-Tamīmī (d. 145/762). The Arab poet reputed to be the greatest exponent of the *rajaz qaṣīda*. His poems addressed mainly various Umayyad caliphs and officials. Son of al-'Ajjāj – another famous poet. *EI²*, vol. 8, pp. 577–578 (W.P. Heinrichs).

690 The first hemistich of this is: 'God's is the accomplishment of the tall beauties' (*li'llāhi darru'l-ghāniyāt al-mudda*). Jawharī, *Ṣiḥāḥ*, vol. 6, p. 2224.
691 MA *'alā* : *ilā*. See Ibn Manẓūr, *Lisān al-'arab*, vol. 13, p. 469.
692 The author of The Harmonious Order (*Naẓm al-Qur'ān*). See above, note 421.
693 i.e. *al-*, the.
694 i.e. the 'a' of *al-* and the 'i' of *ilāh*.
695 See *Tafsīr Ibn 'Abbās* (margin of Suyūṭī, *al-Durr al-manthūr*), vol. 1, p. 1.
696 Q. 27:60, 61, 62, 63, 64.
697 Ibn Manẓūr, *Lisān al-'arab*, vol. 13, p. 469.
698 See above, note 229.
699 Shahr b. Ḥawshab Abū Sa'īd al-Ash'arī (d. 100/718–719). Famous successor, resident first in Damascus, then Basra. Transmitted recitation on the authority of Bayāḍ. Ibn al-Jazarī, *Ghāyat al-nihāya*, vol. 1, p. 329.
700 Q. 25:66.
701 Severence = *mann*, as in the Qur'ānic expression 'Theirs will be a reward without severence/end (*ajrun ghayru mamnūn*)' (Q. 95:6). See *Majma' al-lughat al-'arabiyya, Mu'jam alfāẓ al-Qur'ān al-Karīm*, vol. 2, p. 626. Also see Jawharī, *Ṣiḥāḥ*, appendix, vol. 2, p. 883.
702 *Al-mumtali'* : *al-mutlī'* MA.
703 Q. 7:156.
704 Idem. It seems that the entire quotation should end here and has been broken up misleadingly in Ādharshab's edition.
705 Compare: Ṭabarī, *Jāmi' al-bayān*, vol. 1, pp. 55–56; also Ṭūsī, *Tibyān*, vol. 1, p. 29. The tradition is generally attributed to Jesus Christ, transmitted on the Prophet's authority.
706 Q. 9:128.
707 Q. 48:29.
708 Q. 33:43.
709 Q. 7:32.
710 MA _ : *ta'ālā*.
711 Q. 2:126.
712 See above, note 383.
713 See above, note 219.
714 MA *li'llāh* : *Allāh*.
715 Muslim, *Tawba*, 19. Also compare Muslim, *Tawba*, 17 and Bukhārī, *Adab*, 19. Also see Ṭabarsī, *Majma' al-bayān*, vol. 1, p. 21.
716 Q. 25:60.
717 Q. 13:30.
718 Thābit ('Amr) b. Mālik al-Shanfarā, one of the most famous pre-Islamic *ṣul'ūk* (brigand) poets. Of indeterminable date but generally agreed in references to have been adopted at some point into the Banū Shabāba tribe. *EI*[2], vol. 9, pp. 301–303 (A. Arazi). Ṭabarsī also transmits this line from Shanfarā, but with *qaḍaba* instead *qaṭa'a*. Ṭabarsī, *Majma' al-bayān*, vol. 1, p. 21.
719 Q. 13:30.
720 Q. 43:32.
721 *'Ibād*, here = God's 'servants' in the widest sense, 'God's creatures'.
722 Shahrastānī has here ironically rephrased the report quoted just above, English text, p. 150; Arabic text, p. 88.

723 'The first sense', i.e. the intrinsic *will* to give grace; 'the second sense': the manifest grace itself.

724 See above, note 230.

725 The implicit reference here is to the prophetic tradition already quoted, 'Whoever does exegesis of the Qur'ān on the basis of his personal opinion – even if he gets it right, he has erred, and if he errs, let him take his place in hellfire!' Bukhārī, *'Ilm*, 38; Ibn Māja, *Muqaddima*, 4 and 33.

726 Q. 96.

727 Q. 74.

728 Q. 1.

729 i.e. rather than within the seventh verse.

730 MA *an'amta 'alayhim: lahum min 'alayhim.*

731 Some versions of this tradition have *aqṭa'* instead of *abtar*. Suyūṭī, *al-Durr al-manthūr*, vol. 1, p. 10. Also see *al-Tafsīr al-mansūb ila'l-imām al-Ḥasan al-'Askarī*, p. 10.

732 Q. 10:10. The prayer referred to is of the dwellers in Paradise.

733 The explanation of the 'middle parts' (*awsāṭ*) comes below in regard to the second 'doubled one'.

734 *Kamāl* (completion) also suggests perfection.

735 This is apparently a different version of the tradition just cited by Shahrastānī. Abū Dā'ūd, Nasā'ī and Ibn Māja all derive it on the authority of Abū Hurayra, with *aqṭa'* instead of *abtar*. Suyūṭī, *al-Durr al-manthūr*, vol. 1, p. 10.

736 Q. 7:156.

737 Idem.

738 See ch. 9, English text, p. 109; Arabic text, pp. 50–1.

739 Q. 43:87.

740 Q. 25:60.

741 Idem.

742 Q. 33:43–44.

743 Shahrastānī's point is that the praise of God in 'Praise belongs to God' comes after mentioning the mercy of God in 'In the name of God the Infinitely Merciful, the Compassionate'.

744 Q. 7:54; Q. 10:3.

745 Q. 7:196.

746 Shahrastānī's Arabic is paronomastic: inimitability = *i'jāz,* posterior elements = *a'jāz.*

747 The Arabic proverb 'This is not your nest, so go your way!' refers to someone who interferes in what is not his business. Lane, *Arabic-English Lexicon*, vol. 2, p. 2049.

748 i.e. the expression *al-ḥamdu li'llāh* (literally, 'The praise for God') is a nominal sentence to be interpreted along the lines of 'X is Y': 'The praise *is* for God'.

749 i.e. the definite article *al* in *al-ḥamdu li'llāh.*

750 i.e. praise *as such* is for God.

751 i.e. the so-called *lām al-'ahd* – the use of the definite article in Arabic 'to distinguish a noun as known to the hearer, or reader, in a particular sense'. Lane, *Arabic-English Lexicon*, vol. 2, p. 2183.

752 i.e. the prepositional particle *li* = to.

753 Al-Khalīl b. Aḥmad al-Farāhidī (d. 175/791 or 170/786 or 160/776). The famous Arab philologist of Basra, referred to intermittently by Shahrastānī. The 'Book of

al-Khalīl' mentioned by Shahrastānī here is evidently the *Kitāb al-Jumal fi'l-naḥw*. *EI*^{2}, vol. 4, pp. 962–964 (R. Sellheim).

754 This is Sa'īd b. Mas'ada 'al-Akhfash al-awsaṭ', referred to intermittently by Shahrastānī. See note 419.

755 Q. 17:111.

756 MA *al-thanā' : al-manā.*

757 Ṭabarī derives it on the authority of al-Aswad b. Sarī'. Suyūṭī, *al-Durr al-manthūr*, vol. 1, p. 12.

758 An expression to be uttered in the *i'tidāl* (straightening up) from the *rukū'* (bowing position) in the formal ritual prayer. Miṣrī, *Reliance of the Traveller*, p. 137.

759 i.e. praise is a subset of thanks, so that praise always implies thanks but thanks does not always imply praise.

760 The comma in Ādharshab's edition after *al-thanā'* is disregarded in this construal of the sentence's meaning.

761 As in Q. 55:27.

762 Idem.

763 i.e. it stands for God ('*Allāh*') and so is genitive, being in apposition to '*Allāh*', to whom 'praise belongs'.

764 One possible meaning of *rabba, yarubbu* is 'to raise', 'educate'.

765 Jawharī, *Ṣiḥāḥ*, vol. 1, p. 130; Ibn Manẓūr, *Lisān al-mīzān*, vol. 1, p. 401.

766 *Al-murabbā : al-murabbī* MA.

767 Ibn Manẓūr, *Lisān al-'arab*, vol. 2, p. 33. *Rabbaytu [...] urabbīhi : rabbat [...] urabb-tu* MA.

768 MA *aqāma : qāma.*

769 Ṭabarī, *Majma' al-bayān*, vol. 1, p. 21. In some manuscripts of the latter, this verse is rendered as *wa ahlaknā qidman* instead of *wa ahlaknā yawman* (i.e. 'We destroyed in olden times [...]' rather than 'We destroyed one day [...]'). Ṭabarī transmits it, saying, '[...] the lord of Kinda means the chief (*sayyid*) of Kinda'. Khū'ī, *Bayān*, vol. 1, p. 62. On al-A'shā, see note 688.

770 Literally, 'may dust be in your mouth'.

771 The man was Abū Sufyān. For the reply of Ṣafwān, see Zamakhsharī, *al-Kashshāf*, vol. 1, p. 10. Compare Ibn Manẓūr, *Lisān al-'arab*, vol. 1, p. 400.

772 *Al-khāliq : al-khalq* MA.

773 This is apparently Abū Muslim (also Abū 'Alī) Mu'ādh al-Naḥwī al-Harrā' (d. 188/804). From Herat, a cloth-dealer by trade; the teacher, *inter alia*, of al-Kisā'ī (not to be confused with the eminent successor). Dodge, *The Fihrist of al-Nadīm*, pp. 142–144.

774 Literally, 'The sons of Adam.'

775 *Ya'qilu : yu'qalu* MA.

776 Ibn Fāris, *Mu'jam al-maqāyīs al-lugha*, vol. 4, p. 110.

777 Jawharī, *Ṣiḥāḥ*, vol. 5, p. 1991.

778 Suyūṭī, *al-Durr al-manthūr*, vol. 1, p. 13.

779 Q. 26:23–24.

780 MA *maḍā : murtaḍā.*

781 Abū'l-Sha'thā' 'Abd Allāh b. Ru'ba, al-'Ajjāj (d. 97/715). Poet from the tribe of Tamīm who lived in Basra. Unanimously praised by the Arabic critics for the richness of his vocabulary and frequently cited by lexicographers for the same reason.

His son Ru'ba was also a famous poet (see note 689). *EI*[2], vol. 1, pp. 207–208 (Ch. Pellat).

782 Ibn Manẓūr, *al-Lisān al-ʿarab*, vol. 12, p. 420.

783 Mentioned with slightly different wording in the *Tafsīr Ibn ʿAbbās*. See the margin of Suyūṭī, *al-Durr al-manthūr*, vol. 1, p. 3.

784 i.e., presumably, types of creature.

785 Suyūṭī, *al-Durr al-manthūr*, vol. 1, p. 13.

786 Again, apparently types of creature.

787 Q. 26:47–48.

788 Q. 7:156.

789 As in the expression in question, 'The Lord of the Worlds'.

790 i.e. creatures.

791 MA *milk* : _.

792 i.e. the two mercies of Q. 1:3, where '*al-Raḥmān al-Raḥīm*' is mentioned again between these two verses, the first time being in the '*Bi'smi'llāh* [...]' formula of Q. 1:1.

793 i.e. *mālik* rather than *malik*.

794 i.e. *maliki*.

795 MA *Muḥayṣin* : *Muḥayṣ*. This is Ibn Muḥayṣin Muḥammad b. ʿAbd al-Raḥmān al-Sahmī (d. 123/740), Qur'ān reciter of the people of Mecca along with Ibn Kathīr. Numbered amongst the 'fourteen reciters'. Zarqānī, *Manāhil al-ʿirfān*, vol. 1, p. 458; also Ibn al-Jazarī, *Ghāyat al-nihāya*, vol. 2, p. 167.

796 *Mālik* could also be translated 'possessor'.

797 i.e. their titular overlord, though they might rebel.

798 Q. 20:114.

799 Q. 59:23; Q. 62:1.

800 Q. 22:56.

801 *Mālik* = active participle of *malaka*, hence, 'ruler'.

802 MA *taṣaddā* : _.

803 Q. 22:56.

804 Q. 82:15.

805 Q. 51:6.

806 Q. 30:30.

807 Zamakhsharī, *Kashshāf*, vol. 1, p. 11.

808 MA *Khālid b. Nawfal : Warqa b. Nawfal*. The correct form of the name, as given e.g. in Qurṭubī, *al-Jāmiʿ li-aḥkām al-Qur'ān*, is Khālid b. Nawfal al-Kullābī.

809 *Tafsīr Ibn ʿAbbās* in the margin of Suyūṭī, *al-Durr al-manthūr*, vol. 1, p. 4.

810 Q. 24:2.

811 Q. 12:76.

812 An intensive of the active participle *dā'in*, used for God (= 'the One who passes judgement').

813 Q. 2:193; Q. 8:39.

814 Muḥammad b. Kaʿb al-Quraẓī (d. 120/735). The eminent scholar of Medina who was descended from the famous Jewish tribe of the city, the Banū Qurayẓa. Ibn ʿAwn said of al-Quraẓī: 'I never saw one more knowledgeable in the hermeneutic of the Qur'ān than al-Quraẓī amongst the Medinan successors'. Zarqānī, *Manāhil al-ʿirfān*, vol. 1, p. 489; Dodge, *The Fihrist of al-Nadīm*, p. 142; also Ibn al-Jazarī, *Ghāyat al-nihāya*, vol. 2, p. 233.

815 Compare Q. 7:54.
816 Q. 82:17–19.
817 Q. 25:26.
818 *Mulkuhu* : *milkuhu* MA. The vowelling is determined by the quotation from Ja'far al-Ṣādiq in the following sentence.
819 *Waḥdāniyyatihi* : *wiḥdāniyyatihi* MA.
820 Q. 7:122.
821 Q. 2:133.
822 Q. 114:1–3.
823 Q. 3:54.
824 Compare Majlisī, *Biḥār al-anwār*, vol. 24, p. 95. Note how the tradition involves paronomasia: *nās-nasnās*.
825 Q. 2:199. 'Then [...]' i.e. after congregating at ʿArafāt in the sequence of rites in the Greater Pilgrimage.
826 Dārimī, *Muqaddima*, 32.
827 Q. 7:172.
828 *Al-malikiyya* : *al-mulkiyya* MA.
829 Q. 40:16.
830 MA __ : *bi-manzilati'l-kāf fī dhālik*. This phrase is seemingly mistakenly repeated by the scribe from earlier in the sentence where we had 'with the same position as the *kāf* of *dhālika*'.
831 Abū ʿAlī al-Ḥasan b. Aḥmad b. ʿAbd al-Ghaffār al-Fārisī al-Fasawī (d. 377/987). The eminent grammarian of the Basran school, possibly Muʿtazilī. He went to Baghdad, and later lived in Aleppo and Shīrāz, respectively serving at the courts of Sayf al-Dawla and ʿAḍud al-Dawla. He was the teacher of Ibn Jinnī. Dodge, *The Fihrist of al-Nadīm*, pp. 139–140; *EI*[2], vol. 2, pp. 802–803 (C Rabin).
832 i.e. the accusative.
833 MA *narjūka* : *narjū*.
834 Suyūṭī, *al-Durr al-manthūr*, vol. 1, p. 14. Also see Ṭabarī, *Jāmiʿ al-bayān*, vol. 1, p. 69, with a slightly different wording.
835 MA *al-taysīr* : *al-tafsīr*.
836 Compare Ṭabarī, *Jāmiʿ al-bayān*, vol. 1, p. 69.
837 Q. 20:33–34.
838 The two abodes/mansions refer to this world, the abode of transience (*dār al-fanā'*) and the next world, the abode of eternity (*dār al-baqā'*).
839 i.e. of merit and demerit (= *iktisāb*, an Ashʿarite technical term).
840 The punctuation is incorrect here in Ādharshab's edition. This is the sequence (i.e. in reverse) of the two expressions in one of the supplications recommended for the standing prayer at *ṣalāt al-ṣubḥ* (the dawn prayer). See e.g. Shāfiʿī, *Kitāb al-Umm*, vol. 7, p. 148.
841 *Taklīfāt*, that is, entrustments to God by the worshipper. From this point the Exordium becomes a series of requests to God by the believer.
842 See note 595.
843 i.e. the suffix *ka* in the two instances of '*iyyāka*', 'it is You [...]'.
844 In the technical terminology of Arabic grammar the second person pronominal suffix is known as the *kāf al-khiṭāb*, the '*k* of direct address'.
845 i.e. the *na-* inflection in *naʿbudu* and *nastaʿīn*, betokening the first person plural of the imperfect.

846 Shahrastānī's Arabic involves a paronomasia: *mushāhada/mujāhada.*
847 In the context of existentiation, the *kāf* and the *nūn* are to be identified with the divine imperative '*kun*' ('Be!'). See for example, Q. 3:47.
848 e.g. Q. 7:59, 65.
849 Q. 21:18.
850 Q. 7:52.
851 Q. 2:137.
852 Q. 32:26.
853 Q. 41:17.
854 Al-Mufaḍḍal b. Salama al-Ḍabbī, Abū Ṭālib (d. 291/903). The well-known belle-lettrist and Qur'ānic scholar from Kufa. Dodge, *The Fihrist of al-Nadīm*, pp. 96, 135, 137, 161, 179, 350, 742.
855 Q. 32:26.
856 Q. 42:52.
857 Q. 22:4.
858 *Bunyān* : *tibyān* MA.
859 Q. 16:93.
860 Q. 10:25.
861 Q. 13:31.
862 Q. 28:56.
863 Q. 47:5.
864 The Arabic sentence is in rhyming prose (*saj*ʿ) for rhetorical emphasis.
865 '[...] In word or deed' (*fī'l-qawli wa'l-ʿamal*) i.e. presumably, in teaching or practice.
866 See note 426.
867 i.e. the Jews and the Christians.
868 Q. 4:69.
869 Suyūṭī, *al-Durr al-manthūr*, vol. 1, p. 16.
870 = The first form of the verb.
871 = The fourth form of the verb.
872 I disregard the full-stop here in Ādharshab's edition.
873 *Qawlihi* : *qawl* MA.
874 Compare Q. 22:4.
875 Q. 10:35.
876 The sentence thus far has been formulated with a simultaneous grammatical reference. '[...] He attaches His guidance to a specific people by whom He has explained the path', might equally well be translated '[...] He puts His guidance in a genitive relation with a specific people through whom He has made "the path" grammatically definite'. In Arabic grammar the first component of a genitive compound (*iḍāfa*) is always understood to be definite, even though the definite article is absent. Thus this guidance or 'path' (*ṣirāṭ*) is specified as *the* path *of* a people graciously favoured by God, viz., presumably the prophets and imams.
877 MA *istiṣlāḥ* : *istiḥsār*.
878 The prophet in a generic sense – not just the Prophet Muḥammad.
879 Compare Q. 37:53.
880 Q. 41:17.
881 Q. 7:178.
882 This whole discussion bears close comparison with what Shahrastānī says in the

Nihāya about God's vouchsafing attainment (*tawfīq*) and the opposite, God's abandonment (*khidhlān*). See A. Guillaume, *The Summa Philosophiae*, p. xii; also p. 413 (Arabic) and p. 132 (English paraphrase). Also see the discussion in my introduction, p. 12.

883 Q. 47:24.

884 Q. 21:107.

885 Q. 16:83.

886 As earlier in the work, Shahrastānī here uses the words *tanzīl* (revelation) and *ta'wīl* (hermeneutics) with an eye on their literal sense, namely 'sending down' and 'taking back up'.

887 Q. 1:2.

888 Compare Q. 22:56.

889 In this rhetorically flavoured passage the use of rhyming prose (*saj'*) drives the Arabic.

890 Q. 64:1.

891 The sense of the expression, but not its precise form, is found in the Qur'ān, e.g. in Q. 1:2, 4. Also, Q. 17:111.

892 This refers to the prefix *li-* in expressions like the ones quoted: 'Praise belongs to God' (*al-ḥamdu li'llāh*). The *li-* 'of specification' is more emphatic than the *li-* 'of possession'. In the former case, *lahu'l-ḥamd* means that praise belongs *exclusively* to God – and 'praise', 'dominion' etc., throughout the passage are said in hermeneutics to signify a particular individual, presumably the Logos-Imam.

893 MA *ghayr* : *ism*. In line with the proper form of this quotation, we have also replaced 'the expression [*sic.*]' with 'the camel', i.e. *al-ba'īr : al-ta'bīr* MA.

894 Q. 7:75.

895 Abū Bakr Muḥammad al-Sarī b. al-Sarrāj (d. 316/928). The grammarian, lexicographer and poet who lived in Baghdad. Dodge, *The Fihrist of al-Nadīm*, pp. 109, 128, 135, 136, 139.

896 i.e. it is accusative: *ghayra'l-maghḍūbi 'alayhim*.

897 Ṭabarī says: 'Its interpretation is in the sense "Into a fountain of nymphs did he enter", i.e. into the fountain of Mecca'. Ṭabarī, *Jāmi' al-bayān*, vol. 1, p. 81. Ṭabarsī says: 'i.e. into the fountain of ruin'. Ṭabarsī, *Majma' al-bayān*, vol. 1, p. 3.

898 Q. 35:22.

899 MA _ : *wa maḥāruhu*.

900 Q. 5:60.

901 Q. 5:77.

902 Q. 12:95. Referring to what the older sons of Jacob said to him describing his great love for his son Joseph.

903 Alternatively: '[...] and for that reason He made "the path" (*ṣirāṭ*) grammatically definite through them'. See note 876.

904 *Qasamtu al-ṣalāta: qussimat al-ṣalātu* MA.

905 An entrustment, that is, of requests to God.

906 *Al-ma'dūdāt* : *al-ma'duwāt* MA.

907 'Ayyāshī, *Kitāb al-Tafsīr*, vol. 1, p. 20. Note here that 'praise' (*al-ḥamd*) may simultaneously mean the Exordium, and the praise of God in general.

Bibliography

Primary Sources

ʿAbd al-Muṭṭalib, Rifʿat Fawzī. *Ṣaḥīfat ʿAlī b. Abī Ṭālib ʿan rasūl Allāh.* Cairo, 1406/1986.

ʿAlī b. Abī Ṭālib. *Nahj al-balāgha*, ed. Ṣubḥī al-Ṣāliḥ. Beirut, 1387/1967.

Ali, Maulana Muḥammad. tr., *The Holy Qurʾān: Arabic Text, English Translation and Commentary.* Illinois and Lahore, 1393/1973.

al-ʿĀmilī, Muḥammad b. Bahāʾ al-Dīn. *al-Kashkūl.* Cairo, 1302/1885.

al-Anbārī. See Ibn al-Anbārī.

al-ʿAsqalānī. See Ibn Ḥajar.

al-ʿAyyāshī, Abūʾl-Naḍr Muḥammad b. Maṣʿūd, al-Samarqandī. *Kitāb al-Tafsīr*, ed. Hāshim al-Rasūlī al-Maḥallātī. Qum, 1380–81/1961–62.

al-Baghdādī, al-Khaṭīb al-Ḥāfiẓ Abū Bakr Aḥmad b. ʿAlī. *Taʾrīkh Baghdād aw madīnat al-salām.* Cairo, 1349/1931.

al-Bākharzī, ʿAlī b. al-Ḥasan. *Dumyat al-qaṣr wa ʿuṣrat ahl al-ʿaṣr,* ed. Muḥammad Rāghib al-Ṭabbākh. Aleppo, 1349/1930.

al-Balādhurī, Aḥmad b. Yaḥyā. *Ansāb al-ashrāf*, ed. Muḥammad Ḥamīd Allāh. Cairo, 1378–79/1959.

al-Bayhaqī, Ẓahīr al-Dīn. *Taʾrīkh ḥukamāʾ al-islām* (*Tatimmat Ṣiwān al-ḥikma*), ed. Muḥammad Kurd ʿAlī. Damascus, 1365/1946.

al-Bayhaqī, Abū Bakr Aḥmad b. al-Ḥusayn b. ʿAlī. *al-Sunan al-kubrā.* Hyderabad, 1344–57/1925–38.

____ *al-Asmāʾ waʾl-ṣifāt.* Beirut, 1405/1984.

al-Bukhārī, Abū ʿAbd Allāh Muḥammad b. Ismāʿīl al-Juʿfī. *al-Taʾrīkh al-kabīr,* known also as *Taʾrīkh al-Bukhārī.* Hyderabad, 1360/1941.

al-Dānī, Abū ʿAmr ʿUthmān b. Saʿd. *al-Maqnaʿ fī maʿrifat marsūm maṣāḥif ahl al-amṣār,* in one volume with Dānī's *Kitāb al-Naqṭ*, ed. Muḥammad Aḥmad Raḥmān. Damascus, 1359/1940.

al-Dārimī, ʿAbd Allāh b. Bahrām. *al-Sunan.* Cairo, 1398/1978.

al-Dāʾūdī, Ḥāfiẓ Muḥammad Shams al-Dīn. *Ṭabaqāt al-mufassirīn*, ed. ʿAlī Muḥammad ʿUmar. Cairo, 1392/1972.

al-Dhahabī, Shams al-Dīn Muḥammad b. Aḥmad. *al-ʿIbar fī khabar man ghabar*, ed. Ṣalāḥ al-Dīn al-Munajjid. Kuwait, 1379–80/1960.

____ *Mīzān al-iʿtidāl fī naqd al-rijāl*, ed. ʿAlī Muḥammad al-Bajāwī. Cairo, 1382/1963.

____ *Tadhkirat al-ḥuffāẓ.* Hyderabad, 1375–76/1956.

al-Fārisī, Abūʾl-Ḥasan ʿAbd al-Ghāfir b. Ismāʿīl. *Taʾrīkh Naysābūr.* Qum, 1403.

Freedman, H. tr., *Midrash Rabbah: Genesis,* 2 vols. London, 1939.

al-Gharnāṭī, ʿAbd al-Ḥaqq b. Abī Bakr b. ʿAṭiyya. *Muqaddimat tafsīr al-muḥarrar*

al-wajīz fī tafsīr Kitāb Allāh al-ʿAzīz, in Arthur Jeffery, *Two Muqaddimas*. See Jeffery, Secondary Sources Bibliography.
al-Ghazālī, Abū Ḥāmid Muḥammad, *Tahāfut al-falāsifa*, Arabic text and English tr. by Michael E. Marmura as *The Incoherence of the Philosophers*. Provo, 2000.
'Ḥājjī Khalīfa', (Kâtip Çelebi), Muṣṭafā b. ʿAbd Allāh al-Rūmī. *Kashf al-ẓunūn ʿan asāmī'l-kutub wa'l-funūn*. Beirut, 1402/1982.
al-Ḥākim al-Naysābūrī. *al-Mustadrak ʿalā'l-Ṣaḥīḥayn*. Hyderabad, 1334–42/1915–23.
al-Ḥamawī. See Yāqūt.
al-Ḥasan al-ʿAskarī (attrib.). *al-Tafsīr al-munsūb ilā'l-imam al-Ḥasan al-ʿAskarī*. Tehran, 1368/1949.
al-Ḥāshimī, Muṣṭafā Khāliqdād. *Tawḍīḥ al-Milal*. See al-Shahrastānī.
al-Hindī, ʿAlī b. Ḥusām al-Dīn al-Muttaqī. *Kanz al-ʿummāl fī sunan al-aqwāl wa'l-afʿāl*. Hyderabad, 1346/1927.
al-Ḥusaynī, Raḍī'l-Dīn ʿAlī b. Mūsā, Ibn Ṭāwūs. See Ibn Ṭāwūs.
Ibn Abī'l-Ḥadīd, ʿAbd al-Ḥamīd. *Sharḥ Nahj al-balāgha*, ed. Muḥammad Abū'l-Faḍl Ibrāhīm, 20 vols. Cairo, 1378–83/1959–63.
Ibn al-Anbārī, Kamāl al-Dīn. *Nuzhat al-alibbā' fī ṭabaqāt al-udabā'*, ed. Ibrāhīm al-Samarra'ī. Baghdad, 1378–79/1959.
Ibn ʿAsākir, ʿAlī b. al-Ḥasan. *Ta'rīkh madīnat Dimashq*, ed. Muḥibb al-Dīn ʿUmar al-ʿAmrawī, 70 vols. Beirut, 1415–19/1995–98.
Ibn al-Athīr, ʿIzz al-Dīn Abū'l-Ḥasan ʿAlī. *al-Lubāb fī tahdhīb al-ansāb*. Cairo, 1357/1938.
____ *Usd al-ghāba fī maʿrifat al-ṣaḥāba*, ed. Muḥammad Ṣābiḥ. Cairo, 1384/1964.
____ *al-Kāmil fī'l-ta'rīkh*. Beirut, 1386/1966.
Ibn Bābūya al-Qummī, 'al-Shaykh al-Ṣadūq'. *ʿUyun akhbār al-Riḍā*. Tehran, 1275/1859.
____ *Kitāb al-Tawḥīd*, ed. al-Sayyid Hāshim al-Ḥusaynī al-Ṭihrānī. Beirut, n.d.
Ibn Fāris, Aḥmad. *Muʿjam maqāyīs al-lugha*, ed. ʿAbd al-Salām Muḥammad Hārūn. Cairo, 1369/1950.
Ibn Ḥajar, al-ʿAsqalānī. *Lisān al-mīzān*. Hyderabad, 1325/1907.
____ *Tahdhīb al-tahdhīb*. Hyderabad, 1327/1909.
____ *al-Iṣāba fī tamyīz al-ṣaḥāba*. Cairo, 1359/1939.
Ibn Ḥanbal, Aḥmad. *al-Musnad*, ed. Aḥmad Muḥammad Shākir. Cairo, 1368–72/1949–53.
Ibn Hishām, ʿAbd al-Malik. *Sīra*, ed. and tr. into German by Ferdinand Wüstenfeld, *Das Leben Muhammed's nach Muhammed ibn Ishâk bearbeitet von ʿAbd el-Malik ibn Hischâm. Aus den Handschriften zu Berlin, Leipzig, Gotha und Leyden herausgegeben*. 2 vols. Göttingen, 1274–76/1858–60.
Ibn al-ʿImād, Abū'l-Falāḥ ʿAbd al-Ḥayy al-Ḥanbalī. *Shadharāt al-dhahab fī akhbār man dhahab*. Cairo, 1350/1931.
Ibn al-Jawzī, ʿAbd al-Raḥmān b. ʿAlī. *al-Muntaẓam fī ta'rīkh al-mulūk wa'l-umam*, 11 vols. in 6. Hyderabad, 1354/1935.
____ *Ṣifat al-ṣafwa*, ed. Maḥmūd al-Fākhūrī. Aleppo, 1389/1969.

Ibn al-Jazarī, Shams al-Dīn Muḥammad. *Ghāyat al-nihāya fī ṭabaqāt al-qurrā'*, ed. Gotthelf Bergstrasser and Otto Pretzl, 3 vols. in 2. Cairo, 1932–35.

Ibn al-Kalbī, Ḥishām b. Muḥammad. *Kitāb al-Asnām*, ed. Ahmed Zeki. Cairo, 1343/1924.

Ibn Khallikān, Abū'l-ʿAbbās Shams al-Dīn. *Wafayāt al-aʿyān wa anbā' abnā' al-zamān*, ed. Iḥsān ʿAbbās. Beirut, 1968–72.

Ibn Kathīr, ʿImād al-Dīn Ismāʿīl b. ʿUmar. *al-Bidāya wa'l-nihāya fī'l-ta'rīkh*. Cairo, n.d.

Ibn Manẓūr, Abū'l-Faḍl Muḥammad b. Mukarram. *Lisān al-ʿarab*. Beirut, 1374/1954–55.

Ibn al-Nadīm, Muḥammad b. Isḥāq. *Fihrist*, ed. and tr. Bayard Dodge as *The Fihrist of al-Nadīm: A Tenth-Century Survey of Muslim Culture*, 2 vols. New York and London, 1390/1970.

Ibn Qayyim al-Jawziyya, Muḥammad b. ʿAlī. *Ighāthat al-lahfān min maṣāyid al-shayṭān*, ed. Muḥammad Ḥāmid al-Faqī. Cairo, 1358/1939.

Ibn Saʿd, Muḥammad al-Zuhrī. *Kitāb al-Ṭabaqāt al-kabīr (Ṭabaqāt al-ṣaḥāba wa'l-tābiʿīn)*, ed. Eduard Sachau *et al.*, 9 vols. Leiden, 1322–59/1905–40.

____ *Kitāb al-Ṭabaqāt al-kabīr*. Cairo, 1377/1957.

Ibn Taghrībirdī, Jamāl al-Dīn Abū'l-Maḥāsin Yūsuf. *al-Nujūm al-zāhira fī mulūk Miṣr wa'l-Qāhira*. Cairo, 1354/1935.

Ibn Ṭāwūs, Raḍī al-Dīn ʿAlī b. Mūsā, al-Ḥusaynī. *Saʿd al-suʿūd*. Najaf, 1369/1950.

al-Iṣfahānī, Abū Nuʿaym Aḥmad b. ʿAbd Allāh. *Ḥilyat al-awliyā' wa ṭabaqāt al-aṣfiyā'*. Cairo, 1351–57/1932–38.

al-Iṣfahānī, Afḍal al-Dīn Ṣadr Turka. *Tanqīḥ al-adilla wa'l-ʿilal fī tarjamat Kitāb al-Milal wa'l-niḥal*, ed. Muḥammad Riḍa Jalālī Nā'īnī, 2nd edn. Tehran, 1335 Sh./1956.

al-Iṣfahānī, al-Rāghib al-Ḥusayn b. Muḥammad. See al-Rāghib.

Jaʿfar b. Manṣūr al-Yaman. *Kitāb al-Kashf*, ed. Rudolf Strothmann. Bombay, 1952.

al-Jawharī, Abū Naṣr Ismāʿīl. *Tāj al-lugha wa ṣiḥāḥ al-ʿarabiyya*, ed. Aḥmad ʿAbd al-Ghafūr ʿAttār. Cairo, n.d.

al-Jawziyya, Ibn Qayyim Muḥammad b. ʿAlī. See Ibn Qayyim.

al-Kashshī, Muḥammad b. ʿUmar b. ʿAbd al-ʿAzīz. *Rijāl al-Kashshī*. See al-Ṭūsī, Abū Jaʿfar Muḥammad b. Ḥasan, *Ikhtiyār maʿrifat al-rijāl*.

al-Khwānsārī, Mīrzā Muḥammad Bāqir al-Mūsawī. *Rawḍāt al-janān fī aḥwāl al-ʿulamā' wa'l-sādāt*. Qum, 1390/1970.

al-Kirmānī, Aḥmad Ḥamīd al-Dīn. *Majmūʿat rasā'il al-Kirmānī*, ed. Muṣṭafā Ghālib. Beirut, 1403/1983.

al-Kulaynī, Abū Jaʿfar Muḥammad b. Yaʿqūb. *Uṣūl al-Kāfī*, ed. and tr. into Persian by Jawād Muṣṭafawī, 4 vols. Tehran, 1386/1966.

____ *al-Furūʿ min al-Kāfī*, ed. ʿAlī Akbar al-Ghaffārī, in vols. 3–8 of Ghaffārī's edition of the *Kāfī*, of which vols. 1–2 comprise *al-Uṣūl min al-Kāfī*. Beirut, 1401/1980.

al-Majlisī, Muḥammad Bāqir. *Biḥār al-anwār fī akhbār al-a'immat al-aṭhār*. Beirut, 1403/1983.

al-Mawṣilī, Abū Ya'lā Aḥmad b. 'Alī. *al-Musnad*, ed. Ḥusayn Salīm Asad. Damascus and Beirut, 1404/1984.

al-Miṣrī, Aḥmad b. Naqīb. *'Umdat al-sālik*, ed. and tr. Nūḥ Hā Mīm Keller as *Reliance of the Traveller*. Beltsville, 1415/1994.

al-Mizzī, Jamāl al-Dīn Abū'l-Ḥajjāj Yūsuf. *Tahdhīb al-kamāl fī asmā' al-rijāl*, ed. Aḥmad 'Alī 'Ubayd and Ḥasan Aḥmad Āghā, 22 vols. Beirut, 1414/1994.

al-Mūsawī, Sayyid 'Abd al-Ḥusayn. *al-Murāja'āt*, tr. Yāsīn al-Jibouri. London, n.d.

Nāṣir-i Khusraw. *Dīwān*, ed. Mujtabā Mīnuwī and Mahdī Muḥaqqiq. Tehran, 1353/1974.

al-Nawawī, Abū Zakariyyā Muḥyī'l-Dīn b. Sharaf al-Dīn. *Tahdhīb al-asmā' wa'l-lughāt*. Tehran, n.d.

al-Naysābūrī. See al-Ḥākim.

Ja'far al-Ṣādiq (attrib.). *Tafsīr*. See Nwyia, Secondary Sources Bibliography.

al-Qāḍī 'Iyāḍ. *al-Shifā' bi-ta'rīf ḥuqūq al-Muṣṭafā*, ed. Qurra 'Alī *et al.*, 2 vols. Damascus, 1392/1972.

al-Qāḍī al-Nu'mān. *Da'ā'im al-islām*, ed. 'Ārif Tāmir, 2 vols. Beirut, 1416/1995.

al-Qifṭī, Abū'l-Ḥasan. *Inbāh al-ruwāt 'alā anbā' al-najāt*, ed. Muḥammad Abū'l-Faḍl Ibrāhīm. Cairo, 1374–5/1955.

al-Qummī, al-Shaykh al-Ṣadūq. See Ibn Bābūya.

al-Qurṭubī, Abū 'Abd Allāh Muḥammad b. Aḥmad al-Anṣārī. *al-Jāmi' li-aḥkām al-Qur'ān*. Cairo, 1387/1967.

al-Rāghib al-Iṣfahānī, al-Ḥusayn b. Muḥammad. *al-Mufradāt fī gharīb al-Qur'ān*, ed. Muḥammad Aḥmad Khalaf Allāh, 2 vols. Cairo, 1390/1970.

al-Rāzī, Abū Ḥātim. *A'lām al-nubuwwa*, eds. Ṣalāḥ al-Ṣāwī and Ghulām-Riḍā' A'wānī. Tehran, 1397/1977.

al-Ṣafadī, Ṣalāḥ al-Dīn Khalīl b. Aybak. *al-Wāfī bi'l-wafayāt*. Damascus, 1373/1953.

al-Ṣaffār al-Qummī, Abū Ja'far Muḥammad b. al-Ḥasan. *Baṣā'ir al-darajāt*, ed. Mīrzā Kūtcha Bāghī. Tabrīz, 1380/1960.

al-Sahmī, Abū'l-Qāsim Ḥamza b. Yūsuf. *Ta'rīkh Jurjān aw Kitāb Ma'rifat 'ulamā' ahl Jurjān*. Hyderabad, 1369/1950.

al-Sam'ānī, Abū Sa'd 'Abd al-Karīm b. Muḥammad. *al-Ansāb*, ed. David Samuel Margoliouth. Baghdad, 1390/1970.

____ *al-Taḥbīr fī'l-Mu'jam al-kabīr*, ed. Maḥmūd al-Tanāḥī and 'Abd al-Fattāḥ al-Ḥalw. Baghdad, 1395/1975.

al-San'ānī, Abū Bakr 'Abd al-Razzāq b. Hammām. *al-Muṣannaf*, 11 vols. Beirut, 1390/1970.

al-Shāfi'ī, Muḥammad b. Idrīs. *Kitāb al-Umm*, 7 vols. Cairo, 1321–26/1903–08.

____ *Risāla*, tr. Majid Khadduri as *al-Shāfi'ī's Risāla*. Cambridge, 1407/1987.

al-Shahrastānī, Muḥammad b. 'Abd al-Karīm. *Kitāb Nihāyat al-iqdām fī 'ilm al-kalām*, ed. and partially tr. Alfred Guillaume as *The Summa Philosophiae of al-Shahrastānī*. Oxford, 1353/1934.

____ *Kitāb al-Milal wa'l-niḥal*, partially tr. A.K. Kazi and J.G. Flynn as *Muslim*

Sects and Divisions: The Section on Muslim Sects in Kitāb al-Milal wa'l-Niḥal. London, Boston, Melbourne and Henley, 1404/1984.

____ *Kitāb al-Milal wa'l-niḥal,* translated into French by Daniel Gimaret, Guy Monnot and Jean Jolivet as *Livre des Religions et des sectes,* 2 vols. Louvain/Paris, 1406–14/1986–93.

____ *Kitāb al-Milal wa'l-niḥal,* tr. into Persian by Muṣṭafā Khāliqdād al-Ḥāshimī as *Tawḍīḥ al-Milal.* Tehran, 1361 Sh./1982.

____ *Mafātīḥ al-asrār wa maṣābīḥ al-abrār,* 2 vols., facsimile of Iranian National Consultative Assembly MS 8086/B78, with an introduction by ʿAbd al-Ḥusayn al-Ḥāʾirī and indices by Parvīz Azkāʾī. Tehran, 1409/1989.

____ *Tafsīr al-Shahrastānī al-musammā Mafātīḥ al-asrār wa maṣābīḥ al-abrār,* vol.1, ed. Ādharshab, Muḥammad ʿAlī. Tehran, 1418/1997.

____ *Majlis-i maktūb-i Shahrastānī-i munʿaqid dar Khwārazm,* ed. Muḥammad Riḍā Jalālī Nāʾīnī, tr. into French by Diane Steigerwald as *Majlis: Discours sur l'ordre et la création.* Saint-Nicolas, 1419/1998.

____ *Kitāb al-Milal wa'l-niḥal,* ed. Muhammad ʿAbd al-Qādir al-Fāḍilī, 2 vols. in 1. Beirut, 1420/2000.

____ *Kitāb al-Muṣāraʿa,* ed. and tr. Wilferd Madelung and Toby Mayer as *Struggling with the Philosopher, A Refutation of Avicenna's Metaphysics: A New Arabic Edition and English Translation of Muḥammad b. ʿAbd al-Karīm al-Shahrastānī's* Kitāb al-Muṣāraʿa. London, 1422/2001.

al-Shīrāzī, al-Muʾayyad fī'l-Dīn. *al-Majālis al-muʾayyadiyya,* ed. Ḥātim Ḥamīd al-Dīn. Bombay, 1422/2002.

al-Sijistānī, Ibn Abī Dāʾūd. *Kitāb al-Maṣāḥif,* ed. and tr. Arthur Jeffery as *Materials for the History of the Text of the Qurʾān.* Leiden, 1356/1937.

al-Subkī, Tāj al-Dīn. *Ṭabaqāt al-shāfiʿiyya al-kubrā,* ed. Maḥmūd Muḥammad al-Ṭanāḥī and ʿAbd al-Fattāḥ al-Ḥalw. Cairo, 1383/1964.

al-Suyūṭī, Jalāl al-Dīn ʿAbd al-Raḥmān. *al-Durr al-manthūr fī'l-tafsīr bi'l-maʾthūr.* Qum, 1404/1983–4.

____ *Bughyat al-wuʿāt,* ed. Muḥammad Abū'l-Faḍl Ibrāhīm. Cairo, 1383/1964.

____ *al-Iṭqān fī ʿulūm al-Qurʾān.* Cairo, 1368/1949.

____ *al-Muzhir fī ʿulūm al-lugha,* ed. Muḥammad Abū'l-Faḍl Ibrāhīm and Muḥammad Aḥmad Jād al-Mawlā. Cairo, n.d.

____ *Ṭabaqāt al-mufassirīn.* Leiden, 1255/1839.

al-Ṭabarī, Abū Jaʿfar Muḥammad b. Jarīr. *Jāmiʿ al-bayān ʿan taʾwīl āy al-Qurʾān.* Cairo, 1373/1954.

____ *Jāmiʿ al-bayān.* Cairo, 1407/1987.

al-Ṭabarsī, al-Faḍl b. al-Ḥasan. *Majmaʿ al-bayān fī tafsīr al-Qurʾān.* Tehran, n.d.

Ṭāshkoprīzādeh, Aḥmad b. Muṣṭafā. *Miftāḥ al-saʿāda wa miṣbāḥ al-siyāda,* ed. Kāmil Kamāl Bakrī and ʿAbd al-Wahhāb Abū'l-Nūr. Cairo, 1387–8/1968.

al-Thaqafī, Abū Manṣūr Ibrāhīm b. Muḥammad al-Kūfī. *al-Ghārāt,* ed. al-Sayyid Jalāl al-Dīn al-Muḥaddith, 2 vols. Tehran, 1354 Sh./1975.

al-Ṭūsī, Abū Jaʿfar Muḥammad b. al-Ḥasan. *al-Fihrist.* Najaf, n.d.

____ *al-Tibyān fī tafsīr al-Qurʾān,* ed. Aḥmad Shawqī Amīn and Aḥmad Ḥabīb

Qaṣr al-ʿĀmilī. Najaf, 1376–83/1956–63.
____ *Ikhtiyār maʿrifat al-rijāl*, known as *Rijāl al-Kashshī*, ed. Ḥasan al-Muṣṭafawī. Mashhad, 1348 Sh./1969.
al-Ṭūsī, Naṣīr al-Dīn. *Sayr wa sulūk*, ed. and tr. Sayyed Jalal Badakhchani as *Contemplation and Action: A New Edition and English Translation of Sayr wa sulūk*. London, 1420/1999.
____ *Maṣāriʿ al-muṣāriʿ*, ed. Wilferd Madelung. Tehran, 1383 Sh./2004.
____ *Rawḍa-yi taslīm*, ed. and tr. Sayyed Jalal Badakhchani as *Paradise of Submission: A Medieval Treatise on Ismaili Thought*. London and New York, 1426/2005.
al-Wāḥidī, ʿAlī b. Aḥmad al-Naysābūrī. *Asbāb al-nuzūl*. Cairo, 1379/1959.
al-Yāfiʿī, ʿAfīf al-Dīn. *Mirʾāt al-janān wa ʿibrat al-yaqẓān fī maʿrifat mā yaʿtabiru min ḥawādith al-zamān*, 4 vols. Hyderabad, 1338/1919–20.
al-Yaʿqūbī, Aḥmad b. Abī Yaʿqūb. *al-Taʾrīkh*, ed. Martijn Theodoor Houtsma. Leiden, 1300/1883.
Yāqūt al-Ḥamawī. *Muʿjam al-buldān*. Beirut, n.d.
____ *Muʿjam al-udabāʾ*. Cairo, 1355–57/1936–38.
____ *Kitāb Muʿjam al-buldān*. Beirut 1374–76/1955–57.
al-Yaman, Jaʿfar b. Manṣūr. See Jaʿfar b. Manṣūr.
al-Zamakhsharī, Maḥmūd b. ʿUmar. *al-Kashshāf ʿan ḥaqāʾiq ghawāmiḍ al-Tanzīl wa ʿuyūn al-aqāwīl fī wujūh al-taʾwīl*. Qum, n.d.
al-Zarkashī, Badr al-Dīn Muḥammad b. ʿAbd Allāh. *al-Burhān fī ʿulūm al-Qurʾān*, ed. Muḥammad Abūʾl-Faḍl Ibrāhīm. Cairo, 1376/1956.
al-Zarqānī, Muḥammad ʿAbd al-ʿAẓīm. *Manāhil al-ʿirfān fī ʿulūm al-Qurʾān*, 2 vols. Cairo, 1373/1954.
al-Zuhrī, Muḥammad Ibn Saʿd. See Ibn Saʿd.

Secondary Sources

Ādharshab, Muḥammad ʿAlī. *Tafsīr al-Shahrastānī*. See al-Shahrastānī, Primary Sources Bibliography.
Amir-Moezzi, Mohammad Ali. *Le Guide divin dans le shiʿisme originel. Aux sources de l'ésotérisme en Islam*. Lagrasse/Paris, 1992, tr. David Streight as *The Divine Guide in Early Shiʿism*. Albany, 1994.
____ *La religion discrète. Croyances et pratiques spirituelles dans l'islam shiʿite*. Paris, 2006.
Asad, Ḥaydar. *al-Imām al-Ṣādiq waʾl-madhāhib al-arbaʿa*. Beirut, 1390/1969.
Bar-Asher, Meir M. *Scripture and Exegesis in Early Imāmī Shīʿism*. Leiden, Boston and Cologne, 1999.
Boullata, Issa J. 'The Rhetorical Interpretation of the Qurʾān: *iʿjāz* and Related Topics' in Andrew Rippin, ed., *Approaches to the History of the Interpretation of the Qurʾān*. Oxford, 1988, pp. 139–57.
Bronkhorst, Johannes. 'Etymology and Magic: Yāska's Nirukta, Plato's Cratylus, and the Riddle of Semantic Etymologies', *Numen*, vol. 48, no. 2, 2001, pp. 147–203.

Campbell, Joseph. *The Hero with a Thousand Faces.* London, 1988.

Daftary, Farhad. *The Ismāʿīlīs: Their History and Doctrines.* Cambridge, 1990.

Dānish-pazhūh, Muḥammad Tāqī. 'Dāʿī al-Duʿāt Tāj al-Dīn-i Shahrastāna' in *Nāma-yi āstān-i Quds*, vol.8, 1347 Sh./1968.

Dodge, Bayard. *The Fihrist of al-Nadīm: A Tenth-Century Survey of Muslim Culture.* See Ibn Nadīm, Primary Sources Bibliography.

Gaiser, Adam R. 'Satan's Seven Specious Arguments: al-Shahrastānī's *Kitāb al-Milal wa-l-Niḥal* in an Ismaʿili Context', *Journal of Islamic Studies*, vol. 19:2, 2008, pp. 178–95.

Gimaret, Daniel. *Livre des Religions et des sectes.* See al-Shahrastānī, Primary Sources Bibliography.

Guillaume, Alfred. *The Summa Philosophiae of al-Shahrastānī.* See al-Shahrastānī.

Gutas, Dimitri. *Greek Thought, Arabic Culture.* London, 1998.

Halm, Heinz. 'The Cosmology of the Pre-Fatimid Ismāʿīliyya' in Farhad Daftary, ed., *Medieval Ismaʿili History and Thought.* Cambridge, 1996, pp. 75–83.

Hartmann, Angelika. 'Ismâʿîlitische Theologie bei sunnitischen ʿUlamâʾ des Mittelalters' in Ludwig Hagemann and Ernst Pulsfort, eds., *"Ihr alle aber seid Brüder": Festschrift für A. Th. Khoury zum 60. Geburtstag.* Würzburg-Altenberge, 1990, pp. 190–206.

Hodgson, Marshal G.S. *The Order of Assassins.* The Hague, 1955.

Izutsu, Toshihiko. *Sufism and Taoism: A Comparative Study of Key Philosophical Concepts.* Berkeley, 1983.

Jeffery, Arthur. *Materials for the History of the Text of the Qurʾān.* Leiden, 1937.

____ ed. *Two Muqaddimas to the Qurʾanic Sciences.* Cairo, 1373/1954.

Jolivet, Jean. *Livre des Religions et des sectes.* See al-Shahrastānī, Primary Sources Bibliography.

Keeler, Annabel. *Sufi Hermeneutics: The Qurʾan Commentary of Rashīd al-Dīn Maybudī.* London, 2006.

Khadduri, Majid, tr. *al-Shāfiʿī's Risāla.* See al-Shāfiʿī, Primary Sources Bibliography.

Kholeif, Fathalla. *A Study on Fakhr al-Dīn al-Rāzī and his Controversies in Transoxiana.* Beirut, 1966.

al-Khūʾī, Abūʾl-Qāsim al-Mūsawī. *al-Bayān fī tafsīr al-Qurʾān.* Najaf, 1401/1981.

Kraus, Paul. 'Les "Controverses" de Fakhr al-Dīn Rāzī', *Bulletin de l'Institut d'Égypte*, vol. 19, 1936–7, pp. 187–214; tr. as 'The controversies of Fakhr al-Dīn al-Rāzī', *Islamic Culture* 12, 1938, pp. 131–53.

Lane, Edward W. *Arabic-English Lexicon.* Cambridge, 1984.

Lecker, Michael. *Jews and Arabs in Pre- and Early Islamic Arabia.* Aldershot, 1998.

Madelung, Wilferd. 'Aspects of Ismāʿīlī Theology: The Prophetic Chain and the God Beyond Being' in Sayyid Hossein Nasr, ed. *Ismāʿīlī Contributions to Islamic Culture*, Tehran, 1977.

Madelung, Wilferd and Toby Mayer. *Struggling with the Philosopher.* See al-Shahrastānī, Primary Sources Bibliography.

Majma' al-Lugha al-'Arabiyya. *Mu'jam alfāẓ al-Qur'ān al-Karīm*. Tehran, 1363 Sh./1984.

Massignon, Louis. *Essai sur les origines du lexique technique de la mystique musulmane*. Paris, 1954.

Michot, Jean R. 'La pandémie Avicennienne au VIe/XIIe siècle', *Arabica* XL, 1993, pp. 287–344.

____ 'L'Avicennisation de la sunna, du Ṣabéisme au leurre de la Ḥanīfiyya: À propos du Livre des religions et des sects, II d'al-Shahrastānī', *Bulletin de Philosophie Médiévale*, 35, 1993, pp. 113–20.

Modarressi, Hossein. *Tradition and Survival: A Bibliographical Survey of Early Shī'ite Literature*, vol. 1. Oxford, 2003.

Monnot, Guy. 'Islam: exégèse coranique', in *Annuaire de l'École Pratique des Hautes Études*, tome 92, 1983–84, pp. 305–16; tome 93, 1984–85, pp. 293–303; tome 94, 1985–86, pp. 347–52; tome 95, 1986–87, pp. 253–9; tome 96, 1987–88, pp. 237–43; tome 101, 1992–93, pp. 197–202.

____ *Livre des Religions et des sectes*. See al-Shahrastānī, Primary Sources Bibliography.

____ 'Les controverses théologiques dans l'œuvre de Shahrastānī' in *La controverse religieuse et ses formes*, ed. Alain Le Boulluec. Paris, 1995, pp. 281–296.

____ 'Opposition et hiérarchie dans la pensée d'al-Shahrastânî', in *Henri Corbin: philosophies et sagesses des religions du Livre* (*Bibliothèque de l'École des Hautes Étude, Sciences religieuses, 126*), ed. M. A. Amir-Moezzi, Christian Jambet and Pierre Lory. Turnhout, 2005, pp. 93–104.

Nā'īnī, Muḥammad Riḍa Jalālī. *Sharḥ-i ḥāl wa āthār-i Ḥujjat al-Ḥaqq Abū'l-Fatḥ Muḥammad b. 'Abd al-Karīm b. Aḥmad Shahrastānī*. Tehran, 1343 Sh./1964.

____ *Du Maktūb*. Tehran 1369 Sh./1990.

Nwyia, Paul. 'Le tafsîr mystique attribué à Ǧa'far Ṣâdiq' in *Mélanges de l'Université Saint-Joseph* 43, no. 4, 1968, pp. 179–230.

Rippin, Andrew ed. *Approaches to the History of the Interpretation of the Qur'ān*. Oxford, 1988.

al-Ṣadr, Sayyid Ḥasan. *Ta'sīs al-shī'a li-'ulūm al-islām*. Tehran, n.d.

Smoor, Pieter. ''Umāra's odes describing the Imām' in *Annales Islamologiques* 35ii, 2001, pp. 549 ff.

Steigerwald, Diane. *La pensée philosophique et théologique de Shahrastānī m. 548/1153*. Saint-Nicolas, 1997.

____ 'Al-Shahrastānī's Contribution to Medieval Islamic Thought' in Todd Lawson, ed. *Reason and Inspiration in Islam: Essays in Honour of Hermann Landolt*. London and New York, 2005, pp. 262–73.

____ *Majlis: Discours sur l'ordre et la* création. See al-Shahrastānī, Primary Sources Bibliography.

Thomas, David W., ed. *Essays and Studies – Presented to Stanley Arthur Cook*. London, 1950.

Trimingham, J. Spencer. *The Sufi Orders in Islam*. Oxford, 1971.

Walker, Paul. *Ḥamīd al-Dīn al-Kirmānī: Ismaili Thought in the Age of al-Ḥākim*. London, 1999.

Wisnovsky, Robert. 'Avicenna' in Peter Adamson and Richard C. Taylor, eds. *The Cambridge Companion to Arabic Philosophy*. Cambridge, 2005, pp. 92–136.

Index of Qur'anic citations

General Index

مفاتيح الأسرار ومصابيح الأبرار

من تصنيف

محمّد بن عبد الكريم الشهرستاني

حققه محمد على آذرشب

وترجمه طوبي ماير إلى الإنكليزية مع تعديلات في النص العربي

دار النشر أكسفورد

بالتعاون مع

معهد الدراسات الإسماعيلية

لندن

٢٠٠٩

مفاتيح الأسرار ومصابيح الأبرار في تفسير القرآن

من تصنيف الإمام المحقّق.. تاج الملة
والدين محمّد بن عبد الكريم الشهرستاني
سقى الله روضته شآبيب الغفران
وأحلّه أعلى فراديس الجنان

مفاتيح الأسرار ومصابيح الأبرار في تفسير القرآن

من تصنيف الإمام المحقّق.. تاج الملة والدين محمّد بن عبد الكريم الشهرستاني

(١ب) بسم الله الرحمن الرحيم وبه نستعين

الحمد لله حمد الشاكرين بجميع محامده كلّها على جميع نعمائه كلّها حمداً كثيراً طيّباً مباركاً كما هو أهله، وصلّى اللّه على محمد المصطفى نبيّ الرحمة [و] خاتم النبيّين وعلى آله الطيبين الطاهرين، صلوة دائمة يزكّيها إلى يوم الدين، كما صلّى على إبراهيم وآل إبراهيم إنه حميد مجيد.

والحمد لله الذي مَنّ [على] عباده بإرسال الأنبياء والرّسل وتأييدهم بتنزيل الكتب، وإيضاح مناهج السبل، منّة عظم وقعها، وعمّ نفعها، وقوّم بأحكامهم حركات بني آدم، وحفظ بشرائعهم نظام العالم، وجعلهم مصادر تكليفه، وموارد تعريفه، ومظاهر أمره، [و] معادن سرّه، فقال تعالى: ﴿يَا بَنِي آدَمَ إِمَّا يَأْتِيَنَّكُمْ رُسُلٌ مِنْكُمْ يَقُصُّونَ عَلَيْكُمْ آيَاتِي، فَمَنِ اتَّقَى وَأَصْلَحَ فَلَا خَوْفٌ عَلَيْهِمْ وَلَا هُمْ يَحْزَنُونَ﴾. والحمد لله الذي منّ على الأمّة الأخيرة بالمصطفى محمّد (صلّى اللّه عليه وآله) دونَ الأمم الماضية، والقرون السالفة، منّةً أعمُّها نفعاً وأعظمها وقعاً، فجعل دينه أكمل الأديان والملل، وشريعته أهمّ الشرائع والنِّحَل؛ ونصبه إمام الأمة، وقائد الخير، ومفتاح البركة؛ وختم النبوّة به ختم النهاية والكمال، لا ختم النقص والزوال؛ وخصّه بالكتاب العزيز الذي ﴿لَا يَأْتِيهِ البَاطِلُ مِنْ بَيْنِ يَدَيْهِ وَلَا مِنْ خَلْفِهِ﴾، فقال عزّ من قائل: ﴿لَقَد

مَنَّ اللّٰهُ عَلَى المُؤمِنِينَ إِذْ بَعَثَ فِيْهِم رَسُولاً مِنْ أَنْفُسِهِم يَتْلُوا عَلَيْهِم آيَاتِهِ وَيُزَكِّيهِمْ ويُعَلِّمُهُمُ الكِتَابَ وَالحِكْمَةَ وَإِنْ كَانُوا مِنْ قَبْلُ لَفِي ضَلَالٍ مُبِينٍ﴾. وسمّى الكتاب قرآناً جمعاً بين المترتبات فيه، وفرقاناً فرقاً بين المتضادات، فقال عزّ ذكره: ﴿وَقُرْءَاناً فَرَقْنَاهُ لِتَقْرَأَهُ عَلَى النَّاسِ عَلَى مُكْثٍ وَنَزَّلْنَاهُ تَنْزِيلاً﴾.

وخصّ الكتاب بحملةٍ من عترته الطاهرة ونقلة من أصحابه الزاكية الزاهرة، ﴿يَتْلُونَهُ حَقَّ تِلَاوَتِهِ﴾، ويدرسونه حقّ دراسته، فالقرآن تركته، وهم ورثته، وهم أحد الثقلين وبهم مجمع البحرين، ولهم قاب قوسين، وعندهم علم الكونين والعالمين.

وكما كانت الملائكة عليهم السلام معقّبات له من بين يديه ومن خلفه، تنزيلاً، كذلك كانت الأئمة الهادية، والعلماء الصادقة معقباتٍ له من بين يديه ومن خلفه تفسيراً وتأويلاً: ﴿إِنَّا نَحْنُ نَزَّلْنَا الذِّكْرَ وإِنَّا لَهُ لَحَافِظُونْ﴾. فتنزيل الذكر بالملائكة المعقّبات؛ وحفظ الذكر بالعلماء، الذين يعرفون تنزيله وتأويله ومحكمه ومتشابهه، وناسخه ومنسوخه، وعامّه وخاصّه، ومجمله ومفصّله، ومطلقه (٢آ) ومقيّده، ونصّه وضامره، وظاهره وباطنه، ويحكمون فيه بحكم اللّه من مفروغه ومستأنفه، وتقديره وتكليفه، وأوامره وزواجره، وواجباته ومحظوراته، وحلاله وحرامه، وحدوده وأحكامه، بالحق واليقين، لا بالظنّ والتخمين، ﴿أولئكَ الَّذِينَ هَدَاهُمُ اللّهُ وَأُولَئِكَ هُمْ أُولُو الأَلْبَابِ﴾ فالقرآن ﴿هُدىً للناسِ﴾ عامة، ﴿وهُدًى وَرَحْمَةً لِقَوْمٍ يُؤْمِنُونَ﴾ خاصةً، وهدىً وذكرٌ للنبي (صلّى اللّه عليه وآله) ولقومه [وهو] أخصّ من الأول والثاني: ﴿وإِنَّهُ لَذِكْرٌ لَكَ ولِقَومِكَ﴾.

ولقد كانت الصحابة (رضي اللّه عنهم) متفقين على أن علم القرآن مخصوص بأهل البيت عليهم السلام إذ كانوا يسألون علي بن أبي طالب (رضي اللّه عنه): هل خُصِصتم أهل البيت دوننا بشيء سوى القرآن؟

وكان يقول: لا والذي فلق الحبة وبرأ النسمة إلا بما في قراب سيفي هذا .. الخبر.

فاستثناء القرآن بالتخصيص دليلٌ على إجماعهم بأنّ القرآن وعلمه: تنزيله وتأويله مخصوص بهم. ولقد كان حبرُ الأمة عبد الله بن عباس (رضي اللّه عنه) مصدر تفسير جمع المفسّرين، وقد دعا له رسول اللّه (صلّى اللّه عليه وآله) بأن قال: «اللهمّ فقّههُ في الدِّين وعلّمه التأويل»، فتلمذ لعليّ (رضي اللّه عنه) حتى فقّهه في الدين وعلّمه التأويل.

ولقد كنت على حداثة سنّي أسمع تفسير القرآن من مشايخي سماعاً مجرّداً حتّى وُفّقت فعلّقته على أستاذي ناصر السنّة أبي القاسم سلمان بن ناصر الأنصاري (رضي اللّه عنهما) تلقّفا، ثم أطلعني، [من] مطالعات كلماتٍ شريفة عن أهل البيت وأوليائهم (رضي اللّه عنهم)، على أسرارٍ دفينةٍ وأصولٍ متينةٍ في علم القرآن، وناداني مَن هو في شاطئ الوادي الأيمن في البقعة المباركة من الشجرة الطيبة: ﴿يا أَيُّها الَّذِينَ آمَنُوا اتّقُوا اللّهَ وكُونُوا مَعَ الصَّادِقِينَ﴾.

فطلبت الصادقين طلب العاشقين، فوجدت عبداً من عباد الله الصالحين كما طلب موسى (عليه السلام) مع فتاه ﴿فوَجَدا عَبْداً مِنْ عِبادِنَا آتَيْنَاهُ رَحْمَةً مِنْ عِندِنا وَعَلَّمْنَاهُ مِنْ لَدُنّا عِلماً﴾، فتعلّمت منه مناهج الخلق والأمر، ومدارج التضاد والترتب، ووجهي العموم والخصوص، وحكمي المفروغ والمستأنف، فشبعت من هذا المِعَا الواحد دون الأمعاء التي هي مآكل الضلال، ومداخل الجهّال ، وارتويت من مشرب التسليم بكأسٍ كان مزاجه من تسنيم، فاهتديت إلى لسان القرآن: نظمه وترتيبه، وبلاغته (٢ب) وجزالته، وفصاحته وبراعته، وهو على رتبة فوق مراتب كلام العرب، كما كان كلام العرب على رتبةٍ فوق سائر لغات الناس، [و] كما كان نطق الإنسان على رتبة فوق منطق الطير وأصوات الحُكْل، وكلّ مرتبةٍ معجزةٌ لما دونها من المراتب.

ثم تطلّعت من العبارة إلى المعنى فوجدته بحراً لا تفنى عجائبه ولا تنفد غرائبه، بحراً بعيداً غوره، مديداً قعره، بحراً من الكلمات القدسية يمدّه سبعة أبحر، بحراً ملآن درّاً والغوّاص واحدٌ، بحراً ملآن غوّاصين والدرّ واحد، فطفقت أرتأي بين أن أخوض سباحةً، واليد جذّاء، والساحل بعيد، وبين أن أطلب سفينةً، وقد غصبها الغاصب، أو خرقها العالم. فأشار إليّ من إشارته حزم وطاعته حتمٌ عليك، بمجمع البحرين أو تمضي حقبا. فهناك ملتقى النهرين، وعين الحياة، والحوت قد اتّخذ سبيله في البحر سربا. فوجدت الحبر العالِم فاتّبعته على أن علّمني مما عُلّم رشدا. وآنست ناراً ووجدت على النار هدى. فنقلت القراءة والنحو واللغة والتفسير والمعاني من أصحابها على ما أوردوه في الكتب نقلاً صريحاً صحيحاً من غير تصرّفٍ فيها بزيادةٍ ونقصانٍ، سوى تفصيل مجملٍ، أو تقصير مطوَّل. وعقّبت كلَّ آيةٍ بما سمعت فيها من الأسرار وتوسّمتها من إشارات الأبرار، وقدّمت على الخوض فيها فصولاً في علم القرآن هي «مفاتيح الفرقان»، وقد بلغت اثني عشر فصلاً، قد أقفرت عنها سائر التفاسير. وسمّيت التفسير بمفاتيح الأسرار ومصابيح الأبرار، وأستعيذ بالله السميع العليم من القول فيها برأي واستبداد، دون روايةٍ وإسناد، والخوض في أسرارها ومعانيها جزافاً وإسرافاً دون العرض على ميزان الحقّ والباطل، وإقامة الوزن بالقسط وتقرير الحقّ، وتزييف الرأي الفايل، إنّه خير معاذ وأكرم [ملاذ].

مفاتيح الفرقان
مقدمة الشهرستاني لتفسيره

الفصل الأوّل
في أوائل نزول القرآن وأواخره وولاء نزوله

روي عن عبد الله بن عباس (رضوان اللّه عليه) قال: أوّل ما أنزل اللّه: ﴿إِقْرَأ باسْمِ ربك..﴾ إلى ﴿علّم الإنسانَ ما لَمْ يَعْلَمْ﴾. وفي رواية مجاهد: أوّل ما نزل من القرآن: ﴿إقرأ﴾، و﴿نون والقلم﴾.

وعن جابر بن عبد الله (رضي اللّه عنه): أوّل شيء نزل من القرآن: ﴿يا أيها المُدَّثِّر﴾. وفي كتاب الكافي عن الكليني عن الصادق أبي عبد الله جعفر بن محمد عليهما السلام قال: «أوّل ما أنزل اللّه تعالى على رسوله (صلّى اللّه عليه وآله): ﴿بسم الله الرحمن الرحيم (٣آ) إقرأ بِاسمِ رَبِّكَ﴾» وفي بعض الروايات: أوّل ما أنزل اللّه تعالى سورة الفاتحة.

وعن عثمان بن عفان (رضوان اللّه عليه) كانت [سورة] براءة آخر ما نزل من القرآن. وعن البراء بن عازب، قال: آخر آية نزلت: ﴿يَسْتَفْتُونَكَ قُلِ اللّهُ يُفْتِيكُمْ في الكَلالَةِ﴾ وعن ابن شهاب قال: آخر القرآن عهداً بالعرش آية الرّبا وآية الدَّين. وعن عطاء بن أبي رباح وابن عباس: آخر آية نزلت: ﴿واتَّقوا يَوْماً تُرجَعُون فيه إلى اللّه﴾. قال ابن عباس: مكث رسول اللّه بعد هذه الآية سبع ليالٍ أُنبئَ به يوم السبت وانتقل يوم الاثنين. وعن الصادق جعفر بن محمد (عليه السلام)، قال: آخر سورةٍ نزلت ﴿إذا جاءَ نَصرُ اللّه والفَتْح﴾.

وعن ابن عباس: أُنزل القرآن جملةً واحدةً إلى السماء الدنيا في ليلة القدر، وفي روايةٍ: نزل القرآن جملةً واحدةً في شهر رمضان إلى البيت المعمور، ثمّ نزل في طول عشرين سنة، وقرأ: ﴿وَقُرآناً فَرقناه لِتَقرأَهُ عَلَى النّاس على مُكْثٍ ونزّلناه تَنزيلاً﴾ وعن واثلة بن الأسقع: نزلت صحف إبراهيم (عليه السلام) أوّل ليلةٍ من شهر رمضان. ونزلت التوراة على موسى (عليه السلام) في ستٍّ من شهر رمضان، ونزل الزبور على داود

(عليه السلام) في اثنتي عشرة من شهر رمضان، ونزل الإنجيل على عيسى (عليه السلام) في ثماني عشرة من شهر رمضان، وأنزل اللّه القرآن على محمد في أربع وعشرين من شهر رمضان. وعن الصادق: «لكل شيء ربيع وربيع القرآن شهر رمضان».

واختلف الرواة في ولاء نزول سور القرآن، مثل مقاتل بن سليمان عن رجاله، ومقاتل أيضاً عن أمير المؤمنين علي (رضي اللّه عنه)، والكلبي عن ابن عباس، وابن واقد بإسناده، وما حكي عن شعبة (كذا) مصحف الصادق، وليس بين مصحفه وبين مصحف ابن واقد كثير اختلافٍ في الترتيب وولاء السور إلا في سورٍ عدّة قد ذُكرت. وقد أثبتها مَن عندَه علمها في جدولٍ، نقلتها على الوجه من غير تصرّفٍ فيها، وسيأتي ذلك بعد ذكر جمع القرآن إن شاء اللّه تعالى.

الفصل الثاني
في ذكر كيفية جمع القرآن

لما فرغ المسلمون من أمر اليمامة واستحرّ القتل هناك بالناس وبقرّاء القرآن، أمر أبو بكر (رضوان اللّه عليه) زيد بن ثابت بجمع القرآن، فقام بنسخه يجمعه من الرقاع والأكتاف ولحاء النخل وصدور الرجال فلم يتّفق في أيامه إلا كتبه على صحف متفرّقة، ثم لما انتهى [الأمر] إلى عمر (رضوان اللّه عليه)، أمر أن يكتب على صحيفة واحدة، وكانت نسخة وصحف أبي بكر (رضي اللّه عنه) عنده مدة طويلة، حتى مات ثم انتقلت إلى بنته حفصة، فلما قام بالخلافة عثمان (رضوان اللّه عليه) (٣ب) اختلف الشاميون والعراقيون في أمر القرآن، وعند كل جماعة صحفٌ تخالف صحف صاحبتها، فبلغ الأمر إلى أن كفّر بعضها بعضاً.

وأنهى الخبر حذيفة بن اليمان إلى عثمان بن عفّان (رضوان اللّه عليه)، وقال: أدرِكْ هذه الأمّة قبل أن يختلفوا كما اختلف اليهود والنصارى. فأرسل عثمان إلى حفصة أن أرسلي إلينا بالصحيفة ننسخها، فأرسلت بها إليه، فأحضر زيد بن ثابت وأبان بن سعيد وأمرهما بجمع القرآن فجمعاه وقابلاه بنسخة عمر، فإذا هما أمرٌ واحد.

وفي روايةٍ أمر عثمان زيد بن ثابت، وعبد الله بن الزبير، وسعيد بن العاص، وعبد الرحمن بن الحارث بن هشام فنسخوها في المصاحف، وقال للرهط القرشيين الثلاثة: إذا اختلفتم أنتم وزيد بن ثابت في شيء من القرآن فاكتبوه بلسان قريش، فإنما نزل بلسانهم، ففعلوا كذلك، حتى إذا نُسخت الصحف، ردّ عثمان إلى حفصة صحيفتها، وأرسل إلى كلّ أفق نسخةً من المصحف، فقال زيد بن ثابت: فُقدت آيةٌ من سورة الأحزاب حين نُسِخت الصحف قد كنت أسمع رسول اللّه (صلّى اللّه عليه وآله) يقرأها، فوجدتها عند خزيمة بن ثابت: ﴿مِنَ المُؤمِنينَ رِجالٌ صَدَقوا ما عَاهَدُوا اللّهَ عَلَيه فَمِنْهُم مَنْ قَضَى نَحْبَهُ وَمِنهُمْ مَن يَنتَظِر وما بَدَّلوا تَبْدِيلاً﴾ فألحقتها بموضعها. وهذا حديث صحيح رواه البخاري في الجامع الصحيح عن موسى بن إسماعيل عن إبراهيم.

قال بعض أهل العلم: كم من آية مثلها قد فقدوها مما كان يتعلّق بمناقب أهل البيت عليهم السلام إذ الآية المقصودة نزلت في شأن أربعة نفرٍ عاهدوا اللّه تعالى على بذل الروح في سبيل اللّه: عبد الله بن الحارث بن عبد المطلب، وحمزة بن عبد المطلب، وجعفر بن أبي طالب (رضي اللّه عنهم). وهؤلاء قضَوا نحبهم، إذ استُشهد عبد الله يوم بدر، وحمزة يوم أحد، وجعفر الطيار يوم مؤتة، والمنتظر عليّ بن أبي طالب (رضي اللّه عنه).

وروى شبابة عن إسرائيل عن أبي إسحاق عن مصعب بن سعد قال: لمّا كثر إختلاف الناس في القرآن، فقرأ بعضهم قراءة عبد الله بن

مسعود، إذ قال النبي (صلّى اللّه عليه وآله) «من أراد أن يقرأ القرآن غضّاً كما أُنزل فليقرأ قراءة إبن أمّ عبد». وقرأ بعضهم قراءة أبيّ بن كعب إذ قرأ النبي (صلّى اللّه عليه وآله) القرآن كلّه عليه، وقرأ بعضٌ قراءة سالم مولى حذيفة. فجمع عثمان أصحاب رسول اللّه (صلّى اللّه عليه وآله) فقال: إني رأيت أن أكتب مصاحف على حرف زيد بن ثابت (٤آ) ثم أبعث بها إلى الأمصار. قالوا: نِعمَ ما رأيت. قال: فأي الناس أعرب؟ قالوا: سعيد بن العاص. قال: وأي الناس أكتب؟ قالوا زيد بن ثابت كاتب الوحي. قال: فَليُملل سعيد وليكتب زيد. ثم كتب مصاحف، فبعث بها إلى الأمصار، قال: فرأيت الناس يقولون أحسن واللّه عثمان، أحسن واللّه عثمان.

وقد خالفه أبيّ بن كعبٍ ومنعه من مصحفه. وكان يقول: سعيد بن العاص أعرب الناس ولم يقرأ قط على رسول اللّه سورة ولا قرأ عليه النبي سورة وخالفه أيضاً عبد الله بن مسعود، وأنكر عليه صنعه بالمصاحف، إذ حرقها. وكان يسمّيه مدة محرّق المصاحف، حتى آل الأمر به إلى أن أمر عثمان غلاماً له، فحمله على عاتقه، وضرب به الأرض، فدقّ أضلاعه ومات من ذلك. وهو له على الخلاف. فمصحفاهما الآن متروكان. وصار الإجماع على ما ألّفه عثمان، ولم يكن له في الجمع كبير تصرف، إذ كان الجامع زيد بن ثابت، وسعيد بن العاص، وهما ينسخان عمّا كان في يد حفصة [من] جمع أبي بكر وعمر، إلّا زياداتٍ قد وجدوها في أيدي الناس، وقد فقدها أبو بكر وعمر (رضوان اللّه عليهما) ثم أمر عثمان (رضي اللّه عنه) بوضع نسخةٍ منها في مسجد المدينة، وسمّوها الإمام، وأنفذ نسخةً إلى مكة ونسخةً إلى الكوفة ونسخةً إلى البصرة ونسخةً إلى الشام ونسخةً إلى اليمن. واتفقوا على أن قالوا لا قرآن إلّا ما تضمنه الإمام.

وروى زِرّ بن حبيش عن أُبيّ بن كعب قال له: كم تَعُدّ آيات سورة

الأحزاب؟ قال: قلت: ثلاثاً وسبعين، أو إثنتين وسبعين. قال: قط؟ قلت: قط. قال: واللّه لقد كانت توازن سورة البقرة، ولقد كانت فيها آية الرجم. قال زر: قلت [يا] أبا المنذر وما آية الرجم؟ قال: إذا زنى الشيخ والشيخة فارجموهما البتة نكالاً من اللّه واللّه عزيزٌ حكيم.

وكذلك روى سعيد بن المسيب أن عمر بن الخطاب (رضي اللّه عنه) قال في قصة طويلة: لا تغفلوا عن آية الرجم، فإنها قد أُنزلت وقرأناها: الشيخ والشيخة إذا زنيا فارجموهما البتة نكالاً من اللّه واللّه عزيزٌ حكيم. ولولا أن يقال زاد عمر في كتاب اللّه لكتبتها بيدي.

وقد روى عطاء عن ابن عباس (رضي اللّه عنه) في قوله تعالى: ﴿يَحْذَرُ الْمُنَافِقُونَ أَنْ تُنَزَّلَ عليهم سُوَرَةً تُنَبِّئُهُمْ بِمَا فِي قُلُوبِهِمْ﴾ أنه كان في هذه السورة أسماء سبعين نفراً من المنافقين بأعيانهم وأسمائهم وأسماء آبائهم، [ثم] نسخ تعطفاً على أولادهم. وفيها: واذكرن ما يُتلى في بيوتِكُنَّ من آيات اللّه [والسنة].

وقد روي عن عبد الله بن مسعود (٤ب) أنه لم يثبت المعوذتين في المصحف. وعن أبي بن كعب أنه أثبت القنوت في المصحف سورتين. وكذلك رُوي عن عبد الله بن مسعود أنّه لم يكتب فاتحة الكتاب في مصحفه. قيل له: لِمَ لَمْ تكتب فاتحة الكتاب؟ قال: لو كتبتها في أوّل سورة البقرة لكتبتها في أوّل كلّ سورة، ظنّاً منه أنها كما هي فاتحة الكتاب فهي فاتحة كلّ سورة.

وعن أبي العالية ومجاهد قالا: كانت سورة الأحزاب ثلاثمائة آيةٍ رفعت كلّها، ومنها كان قوله: اللهمّ عذّب الكفرة وألق في قلوبهم الرعب وخالف بين كلمتهم. وذهب منه كثيرٌ يومَ مسيلمة، ولم يذهب منه حلالٌ وحرام.

وقول عمر بن الخطاب (رضي اللّه عنه): أخاف إن استحرّ القتل بالقراء كما استحرّ يوم مسيلمة أن يذهب من القرآن شيء.

وروى سويد بن علقمة قال: سمعت علي بن أبي طالب (كرم اللّه وجهه) يقول: أيها الناس اللّه اللّه، إياكم والغلوّ في أمر عثمان، وقولكم حرّاق المصاحف، فواللّه ما حرقها إلّا عن ملأ من أصحاب رسول اللّه (صلّى اللّه عليه وآله). جَمَعَنا، وقال: ما تقولون في هذه القراءة التي اختلف الناس فيها، يلقى الرجل الرجل فيقول: قرآني خير من قرآنك. وهذا يجرّ إلى الكفر. فقلنا: ما الرأي؟ قال: أرى أن أجمع الناس على مصحف واحد، فإنكم إن اختلفتم اليوم كان مَن بعدكم أشدّ اختلافا. قلنا: نِعمَ ما رأيت فأرسل إلى زيد بن ثابت وسعيد بن العاص فقال: يكتب أحدهما ويُملي الثاني. فلم يختلفا في شيء إلا في حرف واحد في سورة البقرة، قال أحدهما: التابوت، وقال الآخر التابوه.

وقال عبد الله بن مسعود: أعزل عن المصاحف وقد أخذت من فيّ رسول اللّه سبعين سورة، وزيد بن ثابت ذو ذؤابتين يلعب مع الصبيان؟!

قيل وإنما اختاره عثمان لأنه كان كاتب الوحي، وكان يعرف الاقلام بالعربية والعجمية.

وقد رُوي أن عثمان لما نظر في المصحف الذي كُتِب وفُرِغ منه، قال: أرى فيه لحناً، وستقيمه العرب بألسنتها.

وما رُوي عن ابن عباس أنّه قرأ: أَفَلم يتبيّن الذين آمنوا. فقيل له: ﴿أَفَلَم يَيْأَسِ الذين آمنوا﴾. قال: أظنّ أنّ الكاتب كتبها وهو ناعس.

وقد كانت عائشة تقول في بعض الحروف: إنها خطأ من الكاتب. فكيف تظنّ بالصحابة أنهم يرون (٥آ) اللحن والخطأ في المصحف فلا يصلحونه، ويقولون: ستقيمها العرب بألسنتها، والاختلافات في الحروف مما لا يعدّ ولا يحصى، فمنها ما هو واقع في الكتابة، ومنها ما هو واقعٌ في اللّفظ، وكيف يصحّ الإجماع مع هذا الاختلاف على أنّ ما بين الدّفتين كلام اللّه؟!

ودع هذا كلّه، كيف لم يطلبوا جمع عليّ بن أبي طالب؟! أوَما كان

أكتبَ من زيد بن ثابت؟! أوَما كان أعرب من سعيد بن العاص؟! أوَما كان أقرب إلى رسول اللّه (صلّى اللّه عليه وآله) من الجماعة؟! بل تركوا بأجمعهم جمعه واتّخذوه مهجورا، ونبذوه ظهريّا، وجعلوه نَسْيا منسِيّا، وهو (عليه السلام) لما فرغ من تجهيز رسول اللّه (صلّى اللّه عليه وآله) وغسله وتكفينه والصلاة عليه ودفنه آلى أن لا يرتدي بُرداً إلّا لجمعة حتّى يجمع القرآن، إذ كان مأموراً بذلك أمراً جَزْما، فجمعه كما أُنزل من غير تحريف وتبديلٍ وزيادةٍ ونقصان. وقد كان أشار النبي (صلّى اللّه عليه وآله) إلى مواضع الترتيب والوضع والتقديم والتأخير.

قال أبو حاتم: إنّه وضَع كلّ آيةٍ إلى جنب ما يشبهها.

ويروى عن محمد بن سيرين أنّه كان كثيراً ما يتمنّاه، ويقول: لو صادفنا ذلك التأليف، لصادفنا فيه علماً كثيرا.

وقد قيل إنه كان في مصحفه المتن والحواشي؛ وما يعترض من الكلامين المقصودين، كان يكتبه على العرض والحواشي ويروى أنّه لما فرغ عن جمعه أخرجه هو وغلامه قنبر إلى الناس، وهم في المسجد يحملانه ولا يقلّانه وقيل إنه كان حمل بعير، وقال لهم: هذا كتاب اللّه كما أنزله على محمدٍ جمعته بين اللوحين. فقالوا: ارفع مصحفك لا حاجة بنا إليه. فقال: واللّه لا ترونه بعد هذا أبداً، إنّما كان عليّ أن أخبركم حين جمعته. فرجع إلى بيته قائلاً: ﴿يَا رَبِّ إِنَّ قَوْمِي اتَّخَذُوا هَذَا القُرْآنَ مَهْجُوراً﴾ وتركهم على ما هم عليه كما ترك هارون (عليه السلام) قوم أخيه موسى بعد إلقاء الحجّة عليهم، واعتذر عن أخيه بقوله: ﴿إِنِّي خَشِيتُ أَنْ تَقُولَ فَرَّقْتَ بَيْنَ بَنِي إِسْرَائِيلَ وَلَمْ تَرْقُبْ قَوْلِي﴾، وبقوله: ﴿يَا ابنَ أُمَّ إِنَّ القَوْمَ اسْتَضْعَفُونِي وَكَادُوا يَقْتُلُونَنِي فَلَا تُشْمِتْ بِيَ الأَعْدَاءَ وَلَا تَجْعَلْنِي مَعَ القَوْمِ الظَّالِمِينَ﴾.

أفترى يا أخي لو أنصفتني أنّ النبي (صلّى اللّه عليه وآله) يوحى إليه مثل هذا القرآن فيتركه متفرّقاً في الأكتاف والأوراق ولحاء الشجر

وصدور الرجال فلا يشير (٥ب) إلى من يثق به إشارةً، وهو يعلم أنّ مثل ذلك المتفرّق، لو لم يجمع، ذهب هملاً وتفرّق الناس به بعد أن أُنزل سبباً لجمع الناس به واتّباع ما فيه. وقد قال تعالى: ﴿اتَّبِعُوا مَا أُنْزِلَ إِلَيْكُم مِن رَبِّكُمْ وَلا تَتَّبِعُوا مِن دُونِهِ أَولياءَ قَلِيلاً مَا تَذَكَّرُونَ﴾. أو أشار وأمر وعرّف كيفية الترتيب من التقديم والتأخير؟! فمن الذي تولّى ذلك على منهاج النصّ والإشارة؟

ومن المعلوم انّ الذين تولّوا جمعه كيف خاضوا فيه، ولم يراجعوا أهل البيت عليهم السلام في حرف بعد اتّفاقهم على أنّ القرآن مخصوص بهم وأنّهم أحد الثّقلين في قول النبي (صلّى اللّه عليه وآله) «إنّي تاركٌ فيكم الثّقلين: كتاب اللّه وعترتي - وفي رواية - أهل بيتي، ما إن تمسكتم بهما لن تضلّوا، وإنّهما لم يفترقا حتى يردا عليّ الحوض». بلى واللّه، إنّ القرآن محفوظٌ لقوله تعالى: ﴿إنَّا نَحْنُ نَزَّلْنا الذِّكْرَ وإنّا لَهُ لَحافِظون﴾ وإنما حفظه بحفظ أهل البيت. فإنهما لا يفترقان قط، فلا وصل القول ينقطع لقوله تعالى: ﴿وَلَقَدْ وَصَّلْنَا لَهُمْ القَوْلَ﴾ ولا جمع الثقلين يفترق لقوله تعالى: ﴿إِنَّ عَلَيْنَا جَمْعَهُ وَقُرآنَهُ﴾ فنسخته إن كانت عند قومٍ مهجورةً، فهي - بحمد اللّه- عند قومٍ محفوظةٌ مستورةٌ، ﴿بَلْ هُوَ قُرآنٌ مجيدٌ في لَوحٍ مَحْفُوظٍ﴾.

ولم يُنقل عنه (عليه السلام) إنكارٌ على ما جمعه الصحابة (رضوان اللّه عليهم) لا كما قال عثمان: أرى فيه لحناً وستقيمه العرب؛ ولا كما قال ابن عباس: إن الكاتب كتبه وهو ناعسٌ. بل كان يقرأ من المصحف ويكتب بخطّه من الإمام. وكذلك الأئمّة من ولده عليهم السلام يتلون الكتاب على ما يتلوه، ويعلّمون أولادهم كذلك.

واللّه تعالى أكرم وأمجد من أن يدع كتابه الكريم المجيد على لحنٍ حتّى تقيمه العرب ﴿بَلْ لَهُ عِبادٌ مُكْرَمُونَ لا يَسْبِقُونَهُ بالقولِ وهُم بأمرِهِ يَعْمَلُونَ﴾.

ولا يُستبعد أن يكون لكتابه المنزل نسختان، لا تختلفان اختلاف التضاد، وكلاهما كلام اللّه (عزّ وجلّ) أليس التوراة كَتبها بيده -كما ورد به الخبر - وعنها نسخةٌ خاصةٌ في الألواح وهي عند الخاصة من أولاد هارون (عليه السلام)؟! ومع أن اليهود حرّفوا الكلم عن مواضعه، لم تخرج التوراة عن شرف كلام اللّه، وأنت تقرأ من القرآن كيف عظّمها وأخبر أنها ﴿هُدىً وَنُورٌ يَحْكُمُ بِها النَبِيُّون﴾.

وكذلك الإنجيل كتاب اللّه، وهو أربع نسخ جمعها أربعة رجال من الحواريين، وفيها من الاختلافات ما لا يُحصى. فليست بكلّيتها كلام اللّه تعالى وحياً، بل هي كبعض القرآن من تفسير المفسرين (٦ آ) أوردها يوحنّا ومارقُس ولوقا ومتّى، بل فيها فصول هي وحي من اللّه تعالى ومع ذلك ذكرها اللّه تعالى في القرآن على تبجيل وتعظيم قال: «ومصدّقاً لما بين يديه من الإنجيل» (كذا).

فالقرآن الذي بين أظهرنا كلام اللّه بين الدفّتين محفوظ بحفظ اللّه عن التغيير والتبديل واللحن والخطأ. فلا كاتبه ناعسٌ، ولا تاليه لاحنٌ، وله قومٌ يتلونه حقّ تلاوته، ويعرفونه بتأويله وتنزيله، وينفون عنه زيغ الزائغين وانتحال المبطلين: ﴿والرَّاسِخُونَ في العِلْمِ يَقُولُونَ آمَنَّا بِهِ كُلٌّ مِنْ عِنْدِ رَبِّنا، وَما يَذَّكَّرُ إلَّا أُولوا الألْبَاب﴾.

الفصل الثالث

في ذكر اختلاف الرواة في ترتيب نزول سور القرآن مثل مقاتل عن رجاله، ومقاتل عن علي، والكلبي عن ابن عباس، وابن واقد بإسناده، وجعفر بن محمد الصادق

إن الصدر الأوّل من الصحابة والتابعين بإحسانٍ (رضي اللّه عنهم) إختلفوا في ترتيب نزول سور القرآن وترتيب كتابتها في المصاحف.

والصدر الثاني وجدوا مصاحف بالحجاز والعراق والشام مختلفة السور والآيات والكلمات، فهجروها واتفقوا على الرجوع إلى المصحف الذي هو الإمام وفيه قليل تفاوتٍ في الكتابة مثل قوله تعالى: ﴿وَقَالُوا اتَّخَذَ اللّهُ وَلَداً﴾، كُتِبَ في مصاحف أهل الشام بغير الواو، وكُتِب في مصاحف المدينة بالواو، وكذلك ﴿وأَوْصَى بِهَا إِبْرَاهِيم﴾ بألفٍ، وفي غيرها بغير ألف، وكُتِبَ فيها ﴿سارِعُوا﴾ بغير واو، وكُتِبَ فيها ﴿فإنَّ اللّهَ الغَنِي الحَمِيد﴾ وفي غيرها ﴿هُوَ الغَنِي﴾، ومثله ﴿تَجْرِي تَحْتِها الأَنْهَار﴾ بغير من، ومثله ﴿وَالزُّبُر﴾، و﴿بِالزُّبُر﴾.

وقد قيل إن المصحف لمّا عُرِض على أبيّ بن كعب غيّر منها ثلاثة أحرف كان فيه: لَمْ يَتَسَنَّ، فكتبه ﴿لَمْ يَتَسَنَّهْ﴾، وكان فيه: فإمْهِلِ الكافرين، فكتبه ﴿فَمَهِّلْ﴾، وكان فيه: ﴿لا تَبْدِيلَ لِخَلْقِ اللّهِ﴾ بلامين فمحى إحدى اللامين.

ومما جاء في كتابة القرآن على غير المعتاد ﴿يَوْمَ يَأْتِ﴾، ﴿وَمَا كُنَّا نَبْغِ﴾، و﴿سَنَدْعُ﴾ و﴿يَدْعُ الإنْسَان﴾. و﴿مَالِ هؤُلَاءِ﴾، و﴿مَالِ هذا الكِتَابِ﴾ و﴿مَالِ هذا الرَسُولِ﴾، و﴿فَمَالِ الَّذِينَ كَفَرُوا﴾، أربع مواضع في القرآن كُتِبَت اللام فيها مفصولة.

وكذلك ﴿الملأ﴾ كُتِب في بعضها بالواو والألف، وكذلك ﴿مِنْ نَبَأِ المُرْسَلِين﴾ بياء بعد الهمزة، و﴿مِن وَرَاء حِجَابٍ﴾ بياء بعد الهمزة، ﴿مِن

تِلْقَاءِ نَفْسِي﴾، ﴿بَنَينَاهَا بأَيْيْدٍ وإنّا﴾.

وفي النمل: ﴿أو لَأَذْبَحَنَّهُ﴾ بألفٍ وفي التوبة ﴿وَلَأَوْضَعُوا﴾ وفي آل عمران: ﴿ولَا اتَّبَعْنَاكُمْ﴾.

فقيل فيها وأمثالها إنّ بعضها على لغة قريش وكتابتها، وبعضها (٦ب) على لغة هذيل والحارث بن كعب، ولعل الكاتب كان يجمع بين عادات القبائل تزيينا للمصحف بالكتابة. وهو مثل ما في بعض الألسن من الامالة والغُنّة والإدغام والتفخيم والترقيق.

وقد قيل في معنى قول النبي: «أُنزل القرآن على سبعة أحرف» إنها هي الجهات التي تحتملها الكلمات، وهي ما اختلف فيها القراء السبعة من الإمالة والإشمام والإدغام. وقيل هو محمول على اختلاف اللغات السبع توسعةً من اللّه تعالى على العباد، إذ كان لسان كلّ قوم جارياً على ما اعتاده متقلّصاً عن غير المعتاد، فوسّع اللّه عليهم قراءة القرآن رحمةً وعطفاً. وقد قيل إنه محمولٌ على سبعة أبطُنٍ من التأويل، إذ قال لكلّ آيةٍ منها ظهرٌ وبطنٌ وسماها حروفا، إذ حرف كلّ شيء حدّه وطرفه الذي ينتهي به، فحروف المعاني حدودها التي تنتهي إليها، وتلك الحروف ظروف المعاني والأسرار، من غير أن تترك الظواهر ويُصار إلى ما لا يُشعِر به اللفظ، ولم توضع له العبارة والكلمة. وسنذكر ذلك إن شاء اللّه.

ثم إن ترتيب نزول القرآن بحكم الوحي سورةً فسورةً، وآية فآية، فممّا لا يقف عليه إلاّ الخواصّ من العلماء الذين عندهم الروايات الصحيحة، والنصوص الصريحة. وأما السور فقد نُقلت كيف نزلت على اختلاف الروايات، وأنها مكية، وأنها مدنية، وكيف كُتبت في المصاحف الخمسة. وقد رأيناها جمعت في جداول على اختلافاتٍ فيها بين الرواة، فنقلناها كما وجدنا، ولا عُهدة على الناقل، وألحقنا بها ذكر السور الطوال والمثاني والمفصّل القصار.

والنقل عن رجالٍ هم ثقات، ومن كتب هي معتبرةٌ، لا يطور بجنابها شبهاتٌ، ولعلك لا تجدها مسطورةً في سائر التفاسير، فإنها أقفرت عن أمثالها، لا لأنّ المفسرين خلوا عن الإحاطة بها، والاعتماد عليها، ولكن لقلّة الفائدة فيها، وكثرة المهمّات الشاغلة عنها، وقد أوردتُها في جداولها كما وجدت. واللّه أعلم بالصواب فيها والخير أردت.

[ترتيب نزول القرآن]

(آ٧)	العدد	مقاتل عن رجاله		مقاتل عن أمير المؤمنين كرم الله وجهه		ابن عباس رضي الله عنه		ابن واقد		الصادق رضي الله عنه	
أ	١	إقرأ	٩٦	إقرأ	٩٦	إقرأ	٩٦	إقرأ	٩٦	إقرأ	٩٦
ب	٢	ن	٦٨	ن	٦٨	ن	٦٨	ن	٦٨	ن	٦٨
ج	٣	والضحى	٩٣	المزمل	٧٣	والضحى	٩٣	المزمل	٧٣	المزمل	٧٣
د	٤	المزمّل	٧٣	المدثر	٧٤	المزمل	٧٣	المدثر	٧٤	المدثر	٧٤
هـ	٥	المدثر	٧٤	تبت	١١١	المدثر	٧٤	تبت	١١١	تبت	١١١
و	٦	تبت	١١١	كورت	٨١	الفاتحة	١	كورت	٨١	كورت	٨١
ز	٧	كوّرت	٨١	الأعلى	٨٧	تبت	١١١	الأعلى	٨٧	الأعلى	٨٧
ح	٨	الأعلى	٨٧	والليل	٩٢	كورت	٨١	والليل	٩٢	والليل	٩٢
ط	٩	والليل	٩٢	والفجر	٨٩	الأعلى	٨٧	والفجر	٨٩	والفجر	٨٩
ي	١٠	والفجر	٨٩	والضحى	٩٣	والليل	٩٢	والضحى	٩٣	والضحى	٩٣
يا	١١	الم نشرح	٩٤	الم نشرح	٩٤	والفجر	٨٩	الم نشرح	٩٤	الم نشرح	٩٤
يب	١٢	الرحمن	٥٥	والعصر	١٠٢	ألم نشرح	٩٤	والعصر	١٠٣	والعصر	١٠٣
يج	١٣	الكوثر	١٠٨	الكوثر	١٠٨	الرحمن	٥٥	والعاديات	١٠٠	والعاديات	١٠٠
يد	١٤	التكاثر	١٠٢	الدين	١٠٧	والعصر	١٠٣	الكوثر	١٠٨	الكوثر	١٠٨
يه	١٥	الدين	١٠٧	الكافرون	١٠٩	الكوثر	١٠٨	التكاثر	١٠٢	التكاثر	١٠٢
يو	١٦	الفيل	١٠٥	الفيل	١٠٥	التكاثر	١٠٢	الدين	١٠٧	الدين	١٠٧

يز	١٧	الكافرون	١٠٩	الإخلاص	١١٢	الدين	١٠٧	الكافرون	١٠٩	الكافرون	١٠٩
يح	١٨	الإخلاص	١١٢	التكاثر	١٠٢	الفيل	١٠٥	الفيل	١٠٥	الفيل	١٠٥
يط	١٩	والنجم	٥٣	والنجم	٥٣	الكافرون	١٠٩	العلق	٩٦	الفلق	١١٣
ك	٢٠	الأعمى	٨٠	الأعمى	٨٠	الإخلاص	١١٢	الناس	١١٤	الناس	١١٤
كا	٢١	والشمس	٩١	قريش	١٠٦	والنجم	٥٣	الإخلاص	١١٢	الإخلاص	١١٢
كب	٢٢	البروج	٨٥	القارعة	١٠١	الأعمى	٨٠	والنجم	٥٣	والنجم	٥٣
كج	٢٣	التين	٩٥	القيامة	٧٥	القدر	٩٧	الأعمى	٨٠	الأعمى	٨٠
كد	٢٤	قريش	١٠٦	الهمزة	١٠٤	والشمس	٩١	القدر	٩٧	القدر	٩٧
(٧ب)كه	٢٥	القارعة	١٠١	والمرسلات	٧٧	البروج	٨٥	والشمس	٩١	والشمس	٩١
كو	٢٦	القيامة	٧٥	ق	٥٠	والتين	٩٥	البروج	٨٥	البروج	٨٥
كز	٢٧	الهمزة	١٠٤	الطارق	٨٦	قريش	١٠٦	والتين	٩٥	والتين	٩٥
كح	٢٨	والمرسلات	٧٧	القمر	٥٤	القارعة	١٠١	قريش	١٠٦	قريش	١٠٦
كط	٢٩	ق	٥٠	ص	٣٨	القيامة	٧٥	القارعة	١٠١	القارعة	١٠١
ل	٣٠	البلد	٩٠	الجن	٧٢	الهمزة	١٠٤	القيامة	٧٥	القيامة	٧٥
لا	٣١	الطارق	٨٦	يس	٣٦	والمرسلات	٧٧	الهمزة	١٠٤	الهمزة	١٠٤
لب	٣٢	القمر	٥٤	الفرقان	٢٥	ق	٥٠	والمرسلات	٧٧	والمرسلات	٧٧
لج	٣٣	ص	٣٨	الملائكة	٣٥	البلد	٩٠	ق	٥٠	ق	٥٠
لد	٣٤	الأعراف	٧	مريم	١٩	الطارق	٨٦	البلد	٩٠	البلد	٩٠
له	٣٥	الجن	٧٢	طه	٢٠	القمر	٥٤	الطارق	٨٦	الطارق	٨٦
لو	٣٦	يس	٣٦	الواقعة	٥٦	ص	٣٨	القمر	٥٤	القمر	٥٤
لز	٣٧	الفرقان	٢٥	الشعراء	٢٦	الأعراف	٧	ص	٣٨	ص	٣٨

العدد		مقاتل عن رجاله		مقاتل عن أمير المؤمنين		ابن عباس (ر)		ابن واقد		الصادق (ر)	
لح	٣٨	الملائكة	٣٥	النمل	٢٧	الجن	٧٢	الأعراف	٧	الأعراف	٧
لط	٣٩	مريم	١٩	القصص	٢٨	يس	٣٦	الجن	٧٢	الجن	٧٢
م	٤٠	طه	٢٠	هود	١١	الفرقان	٢٥	يس	٣٦	يس	٣٦
ما	٤١	الشعراء	٢٦	يوسف	١٢	الملائكة	٣٥	الفرقان	٢٥	الفرقان	٢٥
مب	٤٢	النمل	٢٧	الحج	٢٢	مريم	١٩	الملائكة	٣٥	الملائكة	٣٥
مج	٤٣	القصص	٢٨	الأنعام	٦	طه	٢٠	مريم	١٩	مريم	١٩
مد	٤٤	بنو إسرائيل	١٧	والصافات	٣٧	الشعراء	٢٦	طه	٢٠	طه	٢٠
مه	٤٥	يونس	١٠	لقمان	٣١	النمل	٢٧	الواقعة	٥٦	الواقعة	٥٦
مو	٤٦	هود	١١	سبأ	٣٤	القصص	٢٨	الشعراء	٢٦	الشعراء	٢٦
مز	٤٧	يوسف	١٢	الروم	٣٠	بنو إسرائيل	١٧	النمل	٢٧	النمل	٢٧
مح	٤٨	الحجر	١٥	القدر	٩٧	يونس	١٠	الشعراء	٢٨	القصص	٢٨
مط (آ٨)	٤٩	الأنعام	٦	والشمس	٩١	هود	١١	بنو إسرائيل	١٧	بنو إسرائيل	١٧
ن	٥٠	والصافات	٣٧	البروج	٨٥	يوسف	١٢	يونس	١٠	يونس	١٠
نا	٥١	لقمان	٣١	التين	٩٥	الحجر	١٥	هود	١١	هود	١١
نب	٥٢	سبأ	٣٤	المؤمن	٢٠	الأنعام	٦	يوسف	١٢	يوسف	١٢
نج	٥٣	الم السجدة	٣٢	حم السجدة	٤١	والصافات	٣٧	الحجر	١٥	الحجر	١٥
ند	٥٤	حم المؤمن	٤٠	الدخان	٤٤	لقمان	٣١	الأنعام	٦	الأنعام	٦
نه	٥٥	حم السجدة	٤١	حم عسق	٤٢	سبأ	٣٤	والصافات	٣٧	والصافات	٣٧
نو	٥٦	حم عسق	٤٢	الجاثية	٤٥	الزمر	٣٩	لقمان	٣١	لقمان	٣١
نز	٥٧	الزخرف	٤٣	الأحقاف	٤٦	المؤمن	٤٠	سبأ	٣٤	سبأ	٣٤

نح	٥٨	الدخان	٤٤	الكهف	١٨	حم السجدة	٤١	الزمر	٣٩	الزمر	٣٩
نط	٥٩	الجاثية	٤٥	الم السجدة	٣٢	حم عسق	٤٢	المؤمن	٤٠	المؤمن	٤٠
س	٦٠	الأحقاف	٤٦	الأنبياء	٢١	الزخرف	٤٣	حم السجدة	٤١	حم السجدة	٤١
سا	٦١	والذاريات	٥١	النحل	١٦	الدخان	٤٤	حم عسق	٤٢	حم عسق	٤٢
سب	٦٢	الغاشية	٨٨	نوح	٧١	الجاثية	٤٥	الزخرف	٤٣	الزخرف	٤٣
سج	٦٣	الكهف	١٨	إبراهيم	١٤	الأحقاف	٤٦	الدخان	٤٤	الدخان	٤٤
سد	٦٤	النحل	١٦	الطور	٥٢	والذاريات	٥١	الجاثية	٤٥	الجاثية	٤٥
سه	٦٥	نوح	٧١	الملك	٦٧	الغاشية	٨٨	الأحقاف	٤٦	الأحقاف	٤٦
سو	٦٦	إبراهيم	١٤	الحاقة	٦٩	الكهف	١٨	والذاريات	٥١	والذاريات	٥١
سز	٦٧	الأنبياء	٢١	المعارج	٧٠	النحل	١٦	الغاشية	٨٨	الغاشية	٨٨
سح	٦٨	المؤمن	٤٠	النبأ	٧٨	نوح	٧١	الكهف	١٨	الكهف	١٨
سط	٦٩	الرعد	١٣	والنازعات	٧٩	إبراهيم	١٤	النحل	١٦	النحل	١٦
ع	٧٠	الطور	٥٢	والذاريات	٥١	الأنبياء	٢١	نوح	٧١	نوح	٧١
عا	٧١	الملك	٦٧	انشقت	٨٤	المؤمنون	٢٣	إبراهيم	١٤	إبراهيم	١٤
عب	٧٢	الحاقة	٦٩	انفطرت	٨٢	الرعد	١٣	الأنبياء	٢١	الأنبياء	٢١
(٨ب) عج	٧٣	المعارج	٧٠	الزمر	٣٩	الطور	٥٢	المؤمنون	٢٣	المؤمنون	٢٣
عد	٧٤	النبأ	٧٨	العنكبوت	٢٩	الملك	٦٧	الم السجدة	٣٢	الم السجدة	٣٢
عه	٧٥	والنازعات	٧٩	يونس	١٠	الحاقة	٦٩	الطور	٥٢	الطور	٥٢
عو	٧٦	انفطرت	٨٢	الحجر	١٥	المعارج	٧٠	الملك	٦٧	الملك	٦٧
عز	٧٧	انشقت	٨٤	المؤمنون	٢٣	النبأ	٧٨	الحاقة	٦٩	الحاقة	٦٩
عح	٧٨	الروم	٣٠	المطففون	٨٣	النازعات	٧٩	المعارج	٧٠	المعارج	٧٠

العدد		مقاتل عن رجاله		مقاتل عن أمير المؤمنين		ابن عباس (ر)		ابن واقد		الصادق (ر)	
عط	٧٩	العنكبوت	٢٩	الأنفال	٨	انفطرت	٨٢	النبأ	٧٨	النبأ	٧٨
ف	٨٠	الإنسان	٧٦	البقرة	٢	انشقت	٨٤	النازعات	٧٩	النازعات	٧٩
فا	٨١	الزمر	٣٩	آل عمران	٣	الروم	٣٠	انفطرت	٨٢	انفطرت	٨٢
فب	٨٢	الواقعة	٥٦	النساء	٤	العنكبوت	٢٩	انشقت	٨٤	انشقت	٨٤
فج	٨٣	المطففون	٨٣	المائدة	٥	المطففون	٨٣	الروم	٣٠	الروم	٣٠
فد	٨٤	الفاتحة	١	الأحزاب	٣٣	البقرة	٢	العنكبوت	٢٩	العنكبوت	٢٩
فه	٨٥	البقرة	٢	الممتحنة	٦٠	الأنفال	٨	المطففون	٨٣	المطففون	٨٣
فو	٨٦	الأنفال	٨	الحديد	٥٧	آل عمران	٣	البقرة	٢	البقرة	٢
فز	٨٧	آل عمران	٣	سورة محمد	٤٧	الحشر	٥٩	الأنفال	٨	الأنفال	٨
فح	٨٨	الحشر	٥٩	الرعد	١٣	الأحزاب	٣٣	آل عمران	٣	آل عمران	٣
فط	٨٩	الأحزاب	٣٣	الرحمن	٥٥	النور	٢٤	الأحزاب	٣٣	الأحزاب	٣٣
ص	٩٠	النور	٢٤	الإنسان	٧٦	الممتحنة	٦٠	الممتحنة	٦٠	الممتحنة	٦٠
صا	٩١	الصمد	١١٢	الطلاق	٦٥	الفتح	٤٨	النساء	٤	النساء	٤
صب	٩٢	الفتح	٤٨	لم يكن	٩٨	النساء	٤	إذا زلزلت	٩٩	إذا زلزلت	٩٩
صج	٩٣	النساء	٤	الشمس	٩١	إذا زلزلت	٩٩	الحديد	٥٧	الحديد	٥٧
صد	٩٤	إذا زلزلت	٩٩	إذا زلزلت	٩٩	الحج	٢٢	سورة محمد	٤٧	سورة محمد	٤٧
صه	٩٥	والعصر	١٠٣	النصر	١١٠	الحديد	٥٧	الرعد	١٣	الرعد	١٣
صو	٩٦	الحج	٢٢	النور	٢٤	سورة محمد	٤٧	الرحمن	٥٥	الرحمن	٥٥
(٩آ) صز	٩٧	الحديد	٥٧	المنافقون	٦٣	الإنسان	٧٦	الإنسان	٧٦	الإنسان	٧٦
صح	٩٨	سورة محمد	٤٧	المجادلة	٥٨	الطلاق	٦٥	الطلاق	٦٥	الطلاق	٦٥

صط	٩٩	الطلاق	٦٥	الحجرات	٤٩	لم يكن	٩٨	لم يكن	٩٨	لم يكن	٩٨
ق	١٠٠	القدر	٩٧	لم تحرّم	٦٦	الجمعة	٦٢	الحشر	٥٩	الحشر	٥٩
قا	١٠١	لم يكن	٩٨	الجمعة	٦٢	الم السجدة	٣٢	النصر	١١٠	النصر	١١٠
قب	١٠٢	الجمعة	٦٢	الصف	٦١	المنافقون	٦٣	النور	٢٤	النور	٢٤
قج	١٠٣	المنافقون	٦٣	التوبة	٩	المجادلة	٥٨	الحج	٢٢	الحج	٢٢
قد	١٠٤	المجادلة	٥٨	الفلق	١١٣	الحجرات	٤٩	المنافقون	٦٣	المنافقون	٦٣
قه	١٠٥	الحجرات	٤٩	الناس	١١٤	لم تحرّم	٦٦	المجادلة	٥٨	المجادلة	٥٨
قو	١٠٦	لم تحرم	٦٦	الفتح	٤٨	التغابن	٦٤	الحجرات	٤٩	الحجرات	٤٩
قز	١٠٧	التغابن	٦٤	القارعة	١٠١	الصف	٦١	لم تحرم	٦٦	لم تحرم	٦٦
قح	١٠٨	الصف	٦١	والعاديات	١٠٠	المائدة	٥	الصف	٦١	الصف	٦١
قط	١٠٩	المائدة	٥	الأعراف	٧	التوبة	٩	الجمعة	٦٢	الجمعة	٦٢
قي	١١٠	التوبة	٩	بنو إسرائيل	١٧	النصر	١١٠	التغابن	٦٤	التغابن	٦٤
قيا	١١١	النصر	١١٠	الغاشية	٨٨	الواقعة	٥٦	الفتح	٤٨	الفتح	٤٨
قيب	١١٢	والعاديات	١٠٠			والعاديات	١٠٠	التوبة	٩	التوبة	٩
قيج	١١٣	الفلق	١١٣			الفلق	١١٣	المائدة	٥	المائدة	٥
قيد	١١٤	الناس	١١٤			الناس	١١٤				
				سقط منه المائدة والزخرف والتغابن والبلد				سقط منه الفاتحة لا اختلاف بينهما إلا في هذه السورة		لم يذكر الفاتحة قال: هي والبقرة في كراسة مفردة والجملة [] حرفا والمعوذتان على الحاشية	

(٩ب) ذكر ولاء السُّوَر في المصاحف

العدد		مصحف أميرالمؤمنين عثمان رضي الله عنه		عبد الله بن مسعود		أبي بن كعب		رواية محمد بن خالد البرقي		من تاريخ ابن واضح	
أ	١	الفاتحة	١	الفاتحة	١	الفاتحة	١	أم الكتاب	١	الفاتحة	١
ب	٢	البقرة	٢	البقرة	٢	البقرة	٢	البقرة	٢	البقرة	٢
ج	٣	آل عمران	٣	النساء	٤	النساء	٤	مريم	١٩	يوسف	١٢
د	٤	النساء	٤	آل عمران	٣	آل عمران	٣	الزخرف	٤٣	العنكبوت	٢٩
هـ	٥	المائدة	٥	الأعراف	٧	الأنعام	٦	الدخان	٤٤	الروم	٣٠
و	٦	الأنعام	٦	الأنعام	٦	الأعراف	٧	الجاثية	٤٥	لقمان	٣١
ز	٧	الأعراف	٧	المائدة	٥	المائدة	٥	الأحقاف	٤٦	الم السجدة	٣٢
ح	٨	الأنفال	٨	يونس	١٠	يونس	١٠	سورة محمد	٤٧	حم السجدة	٤١
ط	٩	التوبة	٩	التوبة	٩	الأنفال	٨	الفتح	٤٨	والذاريات	٥١
ي	١٠	يونس	١٠	النحل	١٦	التوبة	٩	الفجر	٨٩	الإنسان	٧٦
يا	١١	هود	١١	هود	١١	هود	١١	البلد	٩٠	والنازعات	٧٩
يب	١٢	يوسف	١٢	يوسف	١٢	مريم	١٩	الشمس	٩١	كورت	٨١
يج	١٣	الرعد	١٣	الكهف	١٨	الشعراء	٢٦	والليل	٩٢	انفطرت	٨٢
يد	١٤	إبراهيم	١٤	بنو إسرائيل	١٧	الحج	٢٢	والضحى	٩٣	انشقت	٨٤
يه	١٥	الحجر	١٥	الأنبياء	٢١	يوسف	١٢	الم نشرح	٩٤	الأعلى	٨٧
يو	١٦	النحل	١٦	طه	٢٠	الكهف	١٨	والتين	٩٥	إقرأ	٩٦
يز	١٧	بنو إسرائيل	١٧	المؤمنون	٢٣	النحل	١٦	إقرأ	٩٦	لم يكن	٩٨

يح	١٨	الكهف	١٨	الشعراء	٢٦	الزخرف	٤٣	آل عمران	٣	آل عمران	٣
يط	١٩	مريم	١٩	والصافات	٣٧	بنو إسرائيل	٣٧	والصافات	٣٧	هود	١١
ك	٢٠	طه	٢٠	الأحزاب	٣٣	الزمر	٣٩	ص	٣٨	الحجر	١٥
كا	٢١	الأنبياء	٢١	الحج	٢٢	طه	٢٠	الزمر	٣٩	الحج	٢٢
كب	٢٢	الحج	٢٢	القصص	٢٨	الأنبياء	٢١	الدخان	٤٤	الأعراف	٧
(١٠آ) كج	٢٣	المؤمنون	٢٣	النحل	٢٧	القصص	٢٨	حم السجدة	٤١	الدخان	٤٤
كد	٢٤	النور	٢٤	النور	٢٤	المؤمنون	٢٣	حم عسق	٤٢	الرحمن	٥٥
كه	٢٥	الفرقان	٢٥	الأنفال	٨	سبأ	٣٤	الحجرات	٤٩	الحاقة	٦٩
كو	٢٦	الشعراء	٢٦	مريم	١٩	العنكبوت	٢٩	ق	٥٠	المعارج	٧٠
كز	٢٧	النمل	٢٧	العنكبوت	٢٩	الفرقان	٢٥	والذاريات	٥١	الأعمى	٨٠
كح	٢٨	القصص	٢٨	الروم	٣٠	المؤمن	٤٠	والطور	٥٢	والشمس	٩١
كط	٢٩	العنكبوت	٢٩	يس	٣٦	الرعد	١٣	عم يتساءلون	٧٨	القدر	٩٧
ل	٣٠	الروم	٣٠	الفرقان	٢٥	القصص	٢٨	والنازعات	٧٩	زلزلت	٩٩
لا	٣١	لقمان	٣١	الحجر	١٥	النمل	٢٧	عبس	٨٠	الهمزة	١٠٤
لب	٣٢	الم السجدة	٣٢	الرعد	١٣	الصافات	٣٧	إنا أنزلناه	٩٧	الفيل	١٠٥
لج	٣٣	الأحزاب	٣٣	سبأ	٣٤	ص	٣٨	لم يكن	٩٨	يونس	١٠
لد	٣٤	سبأ	٣٤	الملائكة	٣٥	يس	٣٦	النساء	٤	النساء	٤
له	٣٥	الملائكة	٣٥	إبراهيم	١٤	الحجر	١٥	الروم	٣٠	النحل	١٦
لو	٣٦	يس	٣٦	ص	٣٨	حم عسق	٤٢	لقمان	٣١	المؤمنون	٢٣
لز	٣٧	الصافات	٣٧	سورة محمد	٤٧	الروم	٣٠	الم السجدة	٤١	يس	٣٦
لح	٣٨	ص	٣٨	لقمان	٣١	الزخرف	٤٣	الأحزاب	٣٣	حم عسق	٤٢

العدد		مصحف أميرالمؤمنين عثمان رضي الله عنه		عبد الله بن مسعود		أبي بن كعب		رواية محمد بن خالد البرقي		من تاريخ ابن واضح	
لط	٣٩	الزمر	٣٩	الزمر	٣٩	حم السجدة	٤١	السبأ	٣٤	الواقعة	٥٦
م	٤٠	المؤمن	٤٠	المؤمن	٤٠	ابراهيم	١٤	الملائكة	٣٥	الملائكة	٣٥
ما	٤١	حم السجدة	٤١	الزخرف	٤٣	الملائكة	٣٥	يس	٣٦	المدثر	٧٤
مب	٤٢	حم عسق	٤٢	السجدة	٣٢	الفتح	٤٨	والنجم	٥٣	الدين	١٠٧
مج	٤٣	الزخرف	٤٣	حم عسق	٤٢	سورة محمد	٤٧	القمر	٥٤	تبت	١١١
مد	٤٤	الدخان	٤٤	الأحقاف	٤٦	الحديد	٥٧	الحاقّة	٦٩	الإخلاص	١١٢
مه	٤٥	الجاثية	٤٥	الجاثية	٤٥	نوح	٧١	المعارج	٧٠	النصر	١١٠
مو	٤٦	الأحقاف	٤٦	الدخان	٤٤	الأحقاف	٤٦	نوح	٧١	القارعة	١٠١
(١٠ب) مز	٤٧	سورة محمد	٤٧	الفتح	٤٨	ق	٥٠	الجن	٧٢	البروج	٨٥
مح	٤٨	الفتح	٤٨	الحديد	٥٧	الدخان	٤٤	الأعلى	٨٧	التين	٩٥
مط	٤٩	الحجرات	٤٩	الحشر	٥٩	لقمان	٣١	الغاشية	٨٨	النحل	١٦
ن	٥٠	ق	٥٠	الم السجدة	٣٢	الجاثية	٤٥	المائدة	٥	المائدة	٥
نا	٥١	والذاريات	٥١	ق	٥٠	المجادلة	٥٨	الفرقان	٢٥	يونس	١٠
نب	٥٢	الطور	٥٢	الطلاق	٦٥	الملك	٦٧	الشعراء	٢٦	الرعد	١٣
نج	٥٣	والنجم	٥٣	الحجرات	٤٩	الم السجدة	٣٢	النمل	٢٧	مريم	١٩
ند	٥٤	القمر	٥٤	الملك	٦٧	الرحمن	٥٥	القصص	٢٨	الشعراء	٢٦
نه	٥٥	الرحمن	٥٥	التغابن	٦٤	الواقعة	٥٦	العنكبوت	٢٩	الزخرف	٤٣
نو	٥٦	الواقعة	٥٦	المنافقون	٦٣	الجنّ	٧٢	الرحمن	٥٥	الحجرات	٤٩

نز	٥٧	الحديد	٥٧	الجمعة	٦٢	النجم	٥٣	الواقعة	٥٦	ق	٥٠
نح	٥٨	المجادلة	٥٨	الصف	٦١	المعارج	٧٠	الطلاق	٦٥	القمر	٥٤
نط	٥٩	الحشر	٥٩	الجن	٧٢	المزمل	٧٣	لم تحرّم	٦٦	الممتحنة	٦٠
س	٦٠	الممتحنة	٦٠	نوح	٧١	المدثر	٧٤	الملك	٦٧	الطلاق	٦٥
سا	٦١	الصف	٦١	المجادلة	٥٨	القمر	٥٤	ن	٦٨	البلد	٩٠
سب	٦٢	الجمعة	٦٢	الممتحنة	٦٠	الطور	٥٢	الإنسان	٧٦	الم نشرح	٩٤
سج	٦٣	المنافقون	٦٣	لم تحرّم	٦٦	والذاريات	٥١	والمرسلات	٧٧	العاديات	١٠٠
سد	٦٤	التغابن	٦٤	الرحمن	٥٥	ن	٦٨	إذا زلزلت	٩٩	الكوثر	١٠٨
سه	٦٥	الطلاق	٦٥	النجم	٥٣	الحاقة	٦٩	العاديات	١٠٠	الكافرون	١٠٩
سو	٦٦	لم تحرم	٦٦	الذاريات	٥١	الحشر	٥٩	الأنعام	٦	الأنعام	٦
سز	٦٧	الملك	٦٧	الطور	٥٢	الممتحنة	٦٠	طه	٢٠	بنو إسرائيل	١٧
سح	٦٨	ن	٦٨	القمر	٥٤	والمرسلات	٧٧	الأنبياء	٢١	الأنبياء	٢١
سط	٦٩	الحاقة	٦٩	الحاقة	٦٩	النساء	٤	الحج	٢٢	الفرقان	٢٥
ع	٧٠	المعارج	٧٠	الواقعة	٥٦	الإنسان	٧٦	المؤمنون	٢٣	القصص	٢٨
(١١آ) عا	٧١	نوح	٧١	ن	٦٨	القيامة	٧٥	النور	٢٤	المؤمن	٤٠
عب	٧٢	الجن	٧٢	والنازعات	٧٩	كورت	٨١	الحديد	٥٧	المجادلة	٥٨
عج	٧٣	المزمّل	٧٣	المعارج	٧٠	والنازعات	٧٩	المجادلة	٥٨	الحشر	٥٩
عد	٧٤	المدثّر	٧٤	المدثر	٧٤	الطلاق	٦٥	الحشر	٥٩	الجمعة	٦٢
عه	٧٥	القيامة	٧٥	المزمّل	٧٣	التغابن	٦٤	الممتحنة	٦٠	المنافقون	٦٣
عو	٧٦	الإنسان	٧٦	المطففون	٨٣	الأعمى	٨٠	القارعة	١٠١	ن	٦٨
عز	٧٧	والمرسلات	٧٧	الأعمى	٨٠	المطففون	٨٣	إلهاكم	١٠٢	الجن	٧٢

العدد		مصحف أميرالمؤمنين عثمان رضي الله عنه		عبد الله بن مسعود		أبي بن كعب		رواية محمد بن خالد البرقي		من تاريخ ابن واضح	
عح	٧٨	النبأ	٧٨	الإنسان	٧٦	انشقت	٨٤	والعصر	١٠٣	والمرسلات	٧٧
عط	٧٩	والنازعات	٧٩	القيامة	٧٥	التين	٩٥	الهمزة	١٠٤	الضحى	٩٣
ف	٨٠	الأعمى	٨٠	والمرسلات	٧٧	إقرأ	٩٦	الفيل	١٠٥	نوح	٧١
فا	٨١	كورت	٨١	النبأ	٧٨	الحجرات	٤٩	قريش	١٠٦	التكاثر	١٠٢
فب	٨٢	انفطرت	٨٢	كورت	٨١	المنافقون	٦٣	الأعراف	٧	الأعراف	٧
فج	٨٣	المطففون	٨٣	انفطرت	٨٢	الجمعة	٦٢	ابراهيم	١٤	ابراهيم	١٤
فد	٨٤	انشقت	٨٤	الغاشية	٨٨	لم تحرم	٦٦	الحجر	١٥	الكهف	١٨
فه	٨٥	البروج	٨٥	الأعلى	٨٧	الفجر	٨٩	النحل	١٦	النور	٢٤
فو	٨٦	الطارق	٨٦	والليل	٩٢	البلد	٩٠	بنو إسرائيل	١٧	ص	٣٨
فز	٨٧	الأعلى	٨٧	والفجر	٨٩	والليل	٩٢	الكهف	١٨	الزمر	٣٩
فح	٨٨	الغاشية	٨٨	البروج	٨٥	انفطرت	٨٢	الصف	٦١	الجاثية	٤٥
فط	٨٩	والفجر	٨٩	انشقت	٨٤	والشمس	٩١	الجمعة	٦٢	محمد	٤٧
ص	٩٠	البلد	٩٠	إقرأ	٩٦	البروج	٨٥	المنافقون	٦٣	الحديد	٥٧
صا	٩١	والشمس	٩١	البلد	٩٠	الطارق	٨٦	التغابن	٦٤	المزمل	٧٣
صب	٩٢	والليل	٩٢	والضحى	٩٣	الأعلى	٨٧	المزمل	٧٣	القيامة	٧٥
صج	٩٣	والضحى	٩٣	الطارق	٨٦	الغاشية	٨٨	كورت	٨١	النبأ	٧٨
صد	٩٤	ألم نشرح	٩٤	والعاديات	١٠٠	الصفّ	٦١	أرأيت	١٠٧	الغاشية	٨٨
(١١ب)صه	٩٥	والتين	٩٥	الدين	١٠٧	لم يكن	٩٨	الكوثر	١٠٨	والفجر	٨٩

صو	٩٦	إقرأ	٩٦	القارعة	١٠١	والضحى	٩٣	الكافرون	١٠٩	والليل	٩٢
صز	٩٧	القدر	٩٧	لم يكن	٩٨	الم نشرح	٩٤	النصر	١١٠	النصر	١١٠
صح	٩٨	لم يكن	٩٨	والشمس	٩١	القارعة	١٠١	الأنفال	٨	الأنفال	٨
صط	٩٩	إذا زلزلت	٩٩	والتين	٩٥	التكاثر	١٠٢	التوبة	٩	التوبة	٩
ق	١٠٠	والعاديات	١٠٠	الهمزة	١٠٤	والعصر	١٠٣	يونس	١٠	طه	١٠
قا	١٠١	القارعة	١٠١	الليل	٩٢	الهمزة	١٠٤	هود	١١	سبأ	٣٤
قب	١٠٢	التكاثر	١٠٢	قريش	١٠٦	إذا زلزلت	٩٩	يوسف	١٢	الملائكة	٣٥
قج	١٠٣	العصر	١٠٣	التكاثر	١٠٢	والعاديات	١٠٠	الرعد	١٣	الصافات	٣٧
قد	١٠٤	الهمزة	١٠٤	القدر	٩٧	الفيل	١٠٥	المدثر	٧٤	الأحقاف	٤٦
قه	١٠٥	الفيل	١٠٥	إذا زلزلت	٩٩	القدر	٩٧	القيامة	٧٥	الفتح	٤٨
قو	١٠٦	قريش	١٠٦	والعصر	١٠٣	الكافرون	١٠٩	انفطرت	٨٢	الطور	٥٢
قز	١٠٧	الدين	١٠٧	النصر	١١٠	النصر	١١٠	المطففون	٨٣	النجم	٥٣
قح	١٠٨	الكوثر	١٠٨	الكوثر	١٠٨	تبت	١١١	انشقت	٨٤	الصف	٦١
قط	١٠٩	الكافرون	١٠٩	الكافرون	١٠٩	قريش	١٠٦	البروج	٨٥	التغابن	٦٤
قى	١١٠	النصر	١١٠	تبت	١١١	الدين	١٠٧	الطارق	٨٦	الطلاق	٦٥
قيا	١١١	تبت	١١١	الإخلاص	١١٢	الكوثر	١٠٨	تبت	١١١	لم تحرم	٦٦
قيب	١١٢	الإخلاص	١١٢			الإخلاص	١١٢	الإخلاص	١١٢	المطففون	٨٣
قيج	١١٣	العلق	١١٣			العلق	١١٣	العلق	١١٣	الناس	١١٤
قيد	١١٤	الناس	١١٤			الناس	١١٤	الناس	١١٤	العلق	١١٣

بسم الله الرحمن الرحيم، اللهم إنا نستعينك و نثني عليك وبخير ونخلع ونترك من يفجرك.

بسم الله الرحمن الرحيم، اللهم إياك نعبد ولك نصلي ونسجد، واليك نسعى ونحفد، نخشى عذابك ونرجو رحمتك إن عذابك بالكفار ملحق.

(١٢آ) من كتاب الإستغناء في سور القرآن عن أبي عبد الله الحسين بن أحمد الرازي:

السبع الطول: البقرة، آل عمران، النساء، المائدة، الأنعام، الأعراف وسابعها الأنفال فالتوبة. والسبع المثاني: وهي سبع سور أولها سورة يونس، وآخرها النحل: يونس، هود، يوسف، الرعد، إبراهيم، الحجر، النحل، وكأنّ السبع الطول هي المبادي في القرآن العظيم، والسبع المثاني هي التي تتلوها في الطول والمعاني.

وقيل السبع المثاني هي فاتحة الكتاب، لأنها تثنّى في كل صلاة، ولأن المثاني من حيث المعاني في طيّها وضمنها كما سيأتي.

السبع المئون، أولها سورة بني إسرائيل، وآخرها سورة المؤمنين: بنو إسرائيل، الكهف، مريم، طه، الأنبياء، الحج، المؤمنون.

يقال لها المئون لأن كل سورة منها مائة آية أو نحوها، وهي تتلو المثاني.

المفصّل، سمّي مفصلاً لأنها سور قصار لقرب تفصيل سورة عن سورة، وهو معروف. وقيل سمي مفصلاً لما فيها من البيان والتفصيل، والأول أصح، لأن المفصل ليس بأكثر بياناً وتفصيلاً من الآخر.

من كتاب المختار في القراءات عن أبي بكر محمد بن موسى الصيدلاني

السبع الطُّوَل سبع سور: البقرة، آل عمران، النساء، الأعراف، الأنعام، المائدة، يونس. قال أبو عبيدة: والأنفال من المثاني، وهي من أوائل ما نزل بالمدينة، ويونس نزلت بمكة. والمئون إحدى عشرة سورة: براءة، النحل، هود، يوسف، الكهف، بنو إسرائيل، الأنبياء، طه، قد أفلح، الشعراء، الصافات.

والمثاني عشرون سورة: الأحزاب، الحج، النمل، القصص، النور، الأنفال، مريم، العنكبوت، الروم، يس، الحجر، الرعد، الفرقان، سبأ، الملائكة، إبراهيم، ص، سورة محمد، لقمان، الزمر.

(١٢ب) والحواميم سبع سور: المؤمن، الزخرف، حم السجدة، حم عسق، الدخان، الأحقاف، الجاثية.

والممتحنة أربع عشرة سورة: الفتح، الحديد، الحشر، الم السجدة، ق، الطلاق، الحجرات، تبارك، التغابن، المنافقون، الصف، الجن، نوح، المجادلة.

والمفصّل هي ما في السور تسع وأربعون سورة، قد عدّها.

وفي كتاب الاستغناء عن رسول اللّه: «أُعطيت السبعَ الطُّوَلَ مكان التوراة، وأُعطيتُ المئينَ مكانَ الإنجيل، وأعطيتُ المثانيَ مكانَ الزبور، وفضلت بالمفصل».

وعن سعيد بن جبير في قوله تعالى: ﴿ولقد آتيناك سبعاً من المثاني﴾ قال: هي السبع الطوال: البقرة، وآل عمران، والنساء، والمائدة، والأنعام، والأعراف، ويونس تمسى السابعة.

وعن يحيى بن الحارث الديناري مثل ذلك، وزاد: ليست تعدّ الأنفال ولا براءة من السبع الطوال.

الفصل الرابع
في القراءات

إعلم أنّ القراءات بعد جمع الصحابة (رضي اللّه عنهم) المصحف والاتفاق عليه منسوبةٌ إليهم. والمهاجرون والأنصار والتابعون لهم بإحسان على طبقاتهم ودرجاتهم في العلم كانوا يقرؤون القرآن على طرائق شتّى من لغةٍ لغةٍ، ولا يختلفون كثير اختلافٍ يختلف به المعنى، إلى أن انتهى علمها إلى جماعةٍ من أهل العلم تجرّدوا لها، وقاموا بضبطها، فصاروا بذلك أئمةً يأخذها الناس عنهم، ويهتدون فيها بهم.

وهم عشرة نفرٍ سبعةٌ منها هم المشاهير الذين إليهم المرجع في علمها، وعليهم الاعتماد في معرفتها؛ وثلاثةٌ منها هم الذين اختارهم الناس، وألحقوهم بهم في القراءة والفضل؛ فهذه عشرة أنفسٍ هم قرّاء الأمصار الثلاثة، حجازها، وعراقها، وشامها، ونحن أوردنا أساميهم وأنسابهم ومَنْ تلقّى العلم منهم، ونسب الرواية إليهم.

الحجازيّون
وهم أهل مكة، والمدينة

(١٣آ) فمن أهل مكة:

ابن كثير:

أبو محمد [أو] أبو معبد [أو] أبو عبّاد، عبد الله بن كثير الدارمي الكناني، مولى عمرو بن علقمة، مات بمكة سنة عشرين ومائة. فالمشهور منه [رواية]:

القوّاس: وهو أبو الحسن أحمد بن عون النبّال وهو القوّاس قرأ على وهب بن واضح، وهو قرأ على إسماعيل بن عبد الله القسط، قال: قرأت على شبل بن عباد، ومعروف بن مشكان، قرأ على ابن كثير.

البرقي: أبو الحسن أحمد بن محمد بن عبد الله بن أبي بزه البرقي، وقرأ هو على عكرمة بن سليمان، وعكرمة قرأ على شبل والقسط، قرآ على ابن كثير، وبطريق أبي عمرو محمد بن عبد الرحمن البرقي المكي الملقب بقنبل عن القواس، وبطريق أبي بكر محمد بن موسى الهاشمي عن قنبل.

ابن فليح: أبو اسحق عبد الوهاب بن فليح المكّي قرأ على داود بن شبل، قرأ داود على أبيه وعلى القسط، قرأ على ابن كثير باسناده. ويروى عن ابن كثير أيضاً بطريق أبي عبد الرحمن الليثي عن أبي بدره باسناده عن ابن كثير.

وابن كثير قرأ على مجاهد بن جبر ودرباس مولى ابن عباس، قرأ على ابن عباس وابن عباس قرأ على أُبيّ بن كعب، وأُبيّ قرأ على رسول اللّه.

ومن المدنية:

نافع:

أبو رويم [أو] أبو الحسين [أو] أبو عبد الرحمن نافع بن عبد الرحمن بن أبي نعيم مولى جعونة بن شعوب الليثي، أصله من اصفهان مات بالمدينة سنة سبع وسبعين ومائةٍ وقيل سنة ستٍّ وستين. والمذكور منه [رواية]:

قالون: وهو أبو موسى عيسى بن مينا قالون من طريق أبي النشيط محمد بن هارون المروزي عن قالون عن نافع.

وورش: أبو القاسم، عثمان بن سعيد الملقب بورش، أبو عمرو، أبو سعيد، من طريق أبي الأزهر، عبد الصّمد بن عبد الرحمن العتيقي عن ورش عن نافع.

والمدني: أبو بشر إسماعيل بن جعفر المدني من طريق أبي الزعراء عبد الرحمن بن عبدوس عن أبي عمر حفص بن عمر الأزدي عن أبي بشر عن نافع. (١٣ب) قرأوا جملتهم على نافع.

وقال نافع: أدركت بالمدينة أئمةً يُقتدى بهم، فنظرت إلى ما اجتمع إثنان منهم فأخذته، وما شذّ فيه واحدٌ تركته حتى ألّفت قراءتي هذه.

والعراقيون

أهل البصرة والكوفة

فمن البصرة:

أبو عمرو:

أبو عمرو بن العلاء بن عمار بن عبد الله بن الحصين بن الحارث بن جلهم بن خزاعة بن مازن بن مالك بن عمرو بن تميم، وقيل اسمه عربان، وقيل زبّان، وقيل يحيى، وقيل عيينة، وقيل كنيته اسمه. كان ورعا ديّناً عالماً بالقرآن واللغة، مات بالكوفة عند محمّد بن سليمان سنة أربعٍ وخمسين ومائة، وله ستّ وثمانون سنة. ويقال: إنه كان مسدول الأسنان بالذهب. والمشهور عنه رواية:

اليزيدي: أبو عمرو بن يحيى مبارك اليزيدي من طريق السوسي وأبي عمر الدوري، قرآ على اليزيدي وهو على أبي عمرو، وأبو عمرو على سعيد بن جبير ومجاهد بن جبر وغيرهما، قرآ على ابن عباس، وابن عباس على أبيّ بن كعب.

وشجاع: أبو نعيم شجاع بن أبي نصر البلخي من طريق أبي جعفر محمد بن غالب، قرأ على شجاع، وشجاع على أبي عمرو بإسناده.

ومن الكوفة:

عاصم:

وهو أبو بكر عاصم بن أبي النجود الكوفي، وهو مولى بني حنيفة بن مالك قيل اسم أبي النجود بهدله، وقيل هو اسم أمه، مات سنة ثمان وعشرين ومائة. والمذكور منه رواية:

(١٤آ) ابن عياش: أبو بكر بن عيّاش بن سالم الأسدي الحنّاط من طريق أبي يوسف يعقوب بن خلف الأعشى ويحيى بن آدم الكوفي، كلاهما عن أبي بكر برواية الشموني عن الأعشى عن أبي بكر عن عاصم ورواية شعيب بن أيوب عن يحيى عن أبي بكر عن عاصم.

وحفص: أبو عمر وحفص بن سليمان بن مغيرة البزاز الأسدي من طريق عمرو وعبيد إبني الصباح عن حفص برواية أبي الحسن روعان بن أحمد الدقاق عن عمرو وحفص عن عاصم. ورواية أبي لعيان أحمد بن سهل بن فيروز عن عبيد عن حفص عن عاصم. وقرأ عاصم على زِرّ بن حُبَيْش، وقرأ زرّ على عبد الله بن مسعود، وقرأ عاصم أيضاً على أبي عبد الرحمن السلمي، وقرأ السلمي على أمير المؤمنين علي بن أبي طالب (رضي اللّه عنه).

حمزة:

أبو عمارة حمزة بن حبيب بن عمارة الزيّات مولى بني عجل، من أولاد أكثم بن صيفي، كان وَرِعاً ديّناً، وكان يحمل الزيت من العراق إلى حلوان، ويحمل الجوز والجبن من حلوان إلى الكوفة، مات بحلوان سنة ستٍّ وخمسين ومائة. والمشهور عنه رواية:

أبو محمّد [أو] أبو عيسى سليم بن عيسى من طريق أبي محمد خلف بن هشام البزّاز، وخلاّد بن خالد الأحول، قرآ على سليم، وسليم قرأ

على حمزة عشر مرات، وقرأ حمزة على عبد الرحمن بن أبي ليلى وسليمان بن مهران الأعمش؛ وأبي عمرو حفص بن عمر الدوري عن سليم عن حمزة. فما كان من طريق [ابن أبي] ليلى فهو إلى علي بن أبي طالب، وما كان عن طريق الأعمش فهو عن عبد الله بن مسعود.

(١٤ب) الكسائي:

أبو الحسن علي بن حمزة، كان من العلماء بالعربية واللغة، مات هو ومحمد بن الحسن الفقيه والأحنف وإبراهيم الموصلي في يوم واحد، وأمر هارون الرشيد ابنه المأمون أن صلى عليهم بقرية من قرى الريّ يقال لها (الزنبويه) سنة تسع وثمانين ومائة، وقيل واحد وثمانين وقيل اثنتين وثمانين. والمعروف عنه رواية:

أبي عمر حفص بن عمر الدوري، وأبي الحارث ليث بن خالد. قرآ على الكسائي، وقرأ هو على حمزة أربع مرات. وكان الكسائي يتخير القراءات وأدرك أشياخاً بالكوفة من القراء والفقهاء واعتمد فيما يختاره على حروفٍ رُفِعَت إلى النبي (صلّى اللّه عليه وآله)، وحروفٍ رُويت عن عليّ بن أبي طالب والحسن بن عليّ، وابن عباس، وقرأ حرفاً بغير قراءة ابن مسعود وهو قوله تعالى: ﴿وَأَنَّ اللَّهَ لَا يُضِيعُ أَجرَ المُؤْمِنِين﴾ وفي مصحف عبد الله بن مسعود: ﴿واللّه لا يُضيع أجرَ المؤمنين﴾

والشاميون:

ابن عامر

أبو عمران [أو] أبو عثمان [أو] أبو هشيم عبد الله بن عامر اليحصبي مات بدمشق سنة ثمان عشرة ومائة. والمذكور منه رواية:

ابن ذكوان: أبو عمرو عبد الله بن محمد بن ذكوان، ويقال عبد الله بن أحمد بن بشير بن ذكوان، قارئ أهل دمشق، قرأ على ابن ذكوان أبو

عبد الله بن موسى بن شريك الأخفش الدمشقي.

وهشام: أبو الوليد هشام بن عمار الدمشقي؛ وهما قرآ على أيوب بن تميم النخعي القاري، وأيوب على يحيى بن الحارث الذماري، ويحيى على ابن عامر. وقرأ على أيوب أيضاً أبو عمرو بن أحمد بن يوسف التغلبي أحد رواة ابن عامر.

قال ابن ذكوان: قرأ ابن عامر على رجل، قرأ ذلك الرجل على عثمان بن عفان. (١٥آ) قال الأخفش: لم يسمّ لنا ابن ذكوان الرجل الذي قرأ عليه ابن عامر وسمّاه لنا هشام فقال: هو المغيرة بن أبي شهاب المخزومي، قرأ عليه ابن عامر، وقرأ المغيرة على عثمان ليس بينهما أحد، وقرأ عثمان على النبي.

فهؤلاء السبعة هم الذين تؤثر عنهم القراءات المشهورة، أما الثلاثة الذين اختارهم الناس وألحقوهم بدرجاتهم في علمها، أحدهم:

[ابن القعقاع]:

أبو جعفر يزيد بن القعقاع المدني، مولى عبد الله بن عباس، بن أبي ربيعة المخزومي. كان أستاذ نافع، وكان يقرأ القرآن في مسجد النبي (صلّى اللّه عليه وآله)، قُتل بالحرّة، وكانت الحرّة على رأس ثلاث وستين من مقدم النبي (صلّى اللّه عليه وآله) المدينة. لم يعدّوه من السبعة لأنه كان يقرأ القراءات الشاذة الغريبة.

راوياه: عيسى بن وردان الحذاء، وسليمان بن مسلم الجمّاز. قال سليمان: أخبرني أبو جعفر أنه أخذ القراءة عن مولاه عبد الله بن عباس وأبي هريرة، وقد ذكرنا إسناد ابن عباس.

[يعقوب بن اسحق]:

والثاني، وهو أبو محمد يعقوب بن اسحق بن زيد بن عبد الله

الحضرمي، البصريّ مات يوم الأحد سنة خمس وثمانين، اختار في القراءة اختياراً حسناً عن خارج عن الأثر. قرأ القراءات على سلام بن سليمان، وقرأ سلام على عاصم بإسناده.

راوياه: أبو عبد الله محمد بن المتوكل اللؤلؤي المعروف برويس، وروح بن عبد المؤمن المقرئ، من طريق محمد بن [وهب بن] يحيى بن العلاء الثقفي، عن روح، عن يعقوب. وكذلك يروي محمد بن الجهم بن هارون، عن الوليد بن حسان الثوري عن يعقوب.

[خلف بن هشام]:

والثالث، أبو محمد خلف بن هشام بن طالب بن غراب البزار الكوفي، كان مقدّماً في الحديث والقرآن، عالماً بوجوه القراءات، مات سنة تسع وعشرين ومائتين. يروى عنه من طريق أبي اسحاق إبراهيم المروزي أخي أبي العباس ورّاق خلف، قال قرأت على خلف، وقرأ خلف على سليم، وسليم على حمزة الزيات، وقد ذكرنا إسناد حمزة.

فهذه جملةٌ يُكتفى بها من أسانيد القرّاء العشرة وأساميهم وإسناد رواتهم الذين إليهم المرجع في علم القراءة.

وبعد، فلا يظُننّ ظانّ أنّ القراءات المنسوبة إلى هؤلاء القرّاء هي من اختراعاتهم، بل هي اختياراتهم، مما سمعوها من أوائلهم، خلفاً عن سلف، حتى ينتهي إلى النبي (صلّى اللّه عليه وآله)، فقراءات أهل الكوفة (١٥ب) والبصرة وكور العراق تنتهي إلى أمير المؤمنين عليّ (رضي اللّه عنه) وعبد اللّه بن مسعود؛ وقراءات أهل الحجاز وتهامة ونواحيها تنتهي إلى عثمان بن عفّان وأبيّ بن كعب وزيد بن ثابت (رضوان اللّه عليهم)؛ وقراءات أهل الشام وكورها تنتهي إلى عثمان بن عفّان (رضي اللّه عنه) ومخرج قراءات هؤلاء من قراءة النبي (صلّى اللّه عليه وآله)، فليس لأحدٍ من الصحابة والتابعين وغيرهم أن يقرأ بحرف

من اختراعه لم يُسبق إليه، كما ليس لأحدٍ منهم أن يفسّر القرآن برأيه.

وقد قال النبي (صلّى اللّه عليه وآله): «من فَسَّر القرآن برأيه، فإن أصاب فقد أخطأ، وإن أخطأ فليتبوّأ مقعده من النار».

وقد قيل: «ليس شيء بأبعد من عقول الرجال من تفسير القرآن»، اللهمّ إلّا رجالاً يؤتيهم اللّه فهماً في القرآن، هم أوتاد الأرض؛ وأمان أهلها، وورثة الأنبياء، وأحد الثقلين، وصفوة الكونين والعالمين، أولئك آل اللّه، وخاصّته، وحزبه [ومستودع] سرّه، ومعادن حكمته، والحكّام على خليقته.

نسأل اللّه تعالى أن يجعلنا بهم متمسكين، ولهم سامعين مطيعين، وفي رضاهم ساعين مجتهدين، وعندهم بالخير مذكورين وعلى ولايتهم مقيمين أبد الآبدين. آمين ربّ العالمين.

الفصل الخامس

فيما يستحبّ لقارئ القرآن ويكره له في الاستعاذة

مما يستحبّ للقارئ أن يتمسّك بالقراءات المشهورة المأثورة عن الصحابة والتابعين والقراء المعروفين، ولا يجاوزها البتة إلى شيء من اختراعاته أو الشواذ من قراءات المتكلّفين، وإن احتملت المعاني وصحّت في وجوه الإعراب.

ويُستحبّ له أن يتخيّر منها أفصحها لفظاً، وأجمعها معنىً، وأحسنها نظماً واتساقاً، وأجودها لغةً وإعراباً، دون المستبشع الوحشي الذي لا يعرفه بعض فحول القراء فضلاً عن العوام، كعنعنة تميم، وكسكسة ربيعة وغيرها من غريب الروايات، فلا يبدل الهمزة عينا في قوله تعالى: ﴿فَعَسَى اللَّهُ أَنْ يَأْتِيَ بِالْفَتْحِ﴾ فيقرأ «عن يأتي» وهذه عنعنة تميم، ولا

يجعل كاف المؤنث سينا في قوله تعالى: ﴿قَدْ جَعَلَ رَبُّكِ تَحْتَكِ سَرِيًّا﴾ فيقرأ ﴿قد جعل ربُّسِ تحتَسِ سريّا﴾ وهذه كسكسة ربيعة، وكذلك لا يقرأ بالشواذ من القراءات التي لا تصحّ طرقها، ولا تؤثر روايتها، إلا أن يريد الوقوف عليها علماً، دون الأخذ بها قراءة. بل ينبغي أن يلزم الواضح الشهير من القراءات والمأمون المعتمد من الروايات، والنمط الأوسط في الترتيل (١٦آ)، والحدّ الأقرب من الخفض والجهر، لا يهذّه هذّ الشّعر، ولا ينثره نثر الدّقل، ولا يجهر جهراً مجهداً يقشعرّ منه جلد المستمع، وينفر قلبه عنه، ولا يخفض خفضاً يخفي قراءته على من يقرب منه، ولكن يحافظ على خير الأمور، وهي أوساطها، متمثّلاً ما أمر الله به ونهى عنه نبيّه (صلّى الله عليه وآله): ﴿وَلَا تَجْهَرْ بِصَلَاتِكَ وَلَا تُخَافِتْ بِهَا وَابْتَغِ بَيْنَ ذَلِكَ سَبِيلاً﴾. ويروى عنه (عليه السلام) أنه مرّ بأبي بكر، وهو يخافت، فقال: «إرفع شيئاً»، ومرّ بعمر وهو يجهر فقال: «اخفض شيئاً». ويُروى عن سعيد بن جبير أنه قال إقرأوا القرآن ضياء منه ولا تنطّعوا.

ويُستحبّ له إذا حقّق القرآن أن لا يجهد نفسه في التحقيق حتى يجاوزه إلى الإفراط والتعمّق فيه، كما يُحكى عن حمزة الزيات؛ على أنّ حمزة لم يكن مختاراً لها بل كان يفعل ذلك بالمتعلّم الذي قلّت معرفته، وخفّ لسانه ليقف بالإبلاغ في التحقيق على القدر الذي هو حدّه.

وإنّ التحقيق أن يشدّد المشدّد، ويخفّف المخفّف، ويمدّ الممدود، ويقصر المقصور، ويسكّن الساكن، ويحرّك المتحرّك، ويهمز المهموز، ويقطع المقطوع ويصل الموصول، ويخرج الحروف عن مخارجها، صافيةً دون الاختلاط بغيرها؛ فيشدّد المشدود تشديداً يزيله عن التخفيف، ويحرّك المتحرّك تحريكاً يزيله عن الساكن، ويسكّن الساكن تسكيناً يزيله عن المتحرّك؛ لا يرينّ يفرط أو يفرّط حتى يكون تحريكه

تشديداً، أو يكون تسكينه وقفاً وسكنةً؛ ويقصّر المقصور قصراً يزيله عن الممدود؛ ويمدّ الممدود مداً يزيله عن المقصور، لا أن تكون المدّة الواحدة كالمدتين والثلاث؛ ويهمز المهموز همزاً مختلساً يزيله عن غير المهموز، لا أن يتّكأ عليه فيشدّده تشديداً؛ على أنّ تخفيف الهمز جائزٌ في جميع القرآن، إلا أنْ تكون همزةً مبتدأةً، فلا يمكن تخفيفها لأنّ التخفيف قريبٌ من الساكن، ولا يمكن الابتداء بالساكن.

فأما الذي أحدثه المتأخرون وسمّوها قراءة الوزن فمن التكلّف والتعسّف والتعيّب. ولم يُرْوَ من العرب التي أُنزل القرآن بلسانهم؛ وقد قال رسول الله: «إقرأوا القرآن بلحون العرب وأصواتها».

ويُستحبّ أن يرتّل القرآن ترتيلاً، فيقف على الوقوف التامّة والحسنة والكافية بحيث يميّز المعنى عن المعنى بالختم والابتداء، ويراعي في الترتيل الغنّة في مواضعها من الحروف التي هي حروف العلل قبلها تنوينٌ، فإنّ ذلك يزيّن الصوت (١٦ب). ويراعي التفخيم في اسم الله وقبله مرفوعٌ أو مفتوحٌ؛ والترقيق فيه وقبله مخفوضٌ. ويشير إلى أقوى حرفٍ في الكلمة، فيخرج أضعفه صافياً من مخرجه، ويشير إلى «ما» آت القرآن بالنفي إشارة النفي، وبالإثبات إشارة الإثبات. وإذا أنهى قصةً نهايتها وقف، فيبيّن الابتداء بالقصّة والكلام الذي بعدها، وإذا انتهى إلى موضع الاعتبار اعتبر وكرّر، وموضع الاعتراف اعترف وتذكّر، وموضع التعجّب تعجّب وتفكّر، إن ﴿الذين [آتيناهم الكتاب] يتلونَهُ حَقَّ تِلاوتِهِ أولئكَ يُؤمِنُونَ بِهِ﴾.

وأما الاستعاذة عند افتتاح القراءة فمندوبٌ إليه ندبا مؤكداً. قال الله تعالى: ﴿فإذا قَرَأْتَ القرآنَ فاسْتَعِذْ بِالله﴾ قرأ أهل البصرة وابن كثير: أعوذ بالله من الشيطان الرجيم، وفي رواية قنبل عن ابن كثير: أعوذ بالله العظيم السميع. وحفص عن عاصم: أعوذ بالله العظيم السميع العليم. وعن نافع وابن عامر والكسائي: أعوذ بالله من الشيطان الرجيم إنّ الله

هو السميع العليم. وعن حمزة: نستعيذ بالله السميع العليم من الشيطان الرجيم.

وفي حديث ابن مسعود قال: قرأت على رسول الله (صلّى الله عليه وسلّم) فقلت: أعوذ بالله السميع العليم. فقال لي: «أعوذ بالله من الشيطان الرجيم، لأني جلست بين يدي جبريل (عليه السلام) فقلت: أعوذ بالسّميع العليم، فقال لي جبريل: أعوذ بالله من الشيطان الرجيم، قال جبريل: هكذا أخذته من ميكائيل وميكائيل عن إسرافيل، وإسرافيل هكذا أخذه من اللوح المحفوظ». وهو يوافق ما في كتاب الله: ﴿فإذا قَرَأْتَ الْقُرْآنَ فَاسْتَعِذْ باللَّهِ مِنَ الشَّيطَانِ الرَّجِيمِ﴾.

وفي بعض الأخبار: «من قال حين يصبح ثلاث مراتٍ: أعوذ بالله السميع العليم من الشيطان الرجيم، وقرأ ثلاث آياتٍ من آخر سورة الحشر، وَكّلَ اللهُ به سبعين ألف مَلَكٍ يُصلّون عليه [حتى] يمسي، وإنْ مات في ذلك اليوم مات شهيداً». وعن الصادق (عليه السلام) أنه كان يتعوذ بعد التوجه، من الشيطان، يقول: أعوذ باللّه السميع العليم من الشيطان الرجيم.

ومما يستحب لقارئ القرآن أن يكون على طهارةٍ، فالجُنُبُ والحائض لا يقرآن القرآن، والمحدث يقرأ لا بأس به، والأولى أن يكون متطهّراً متوجّهاً إلى القبلة يقرأه على تعظيمٍ وتوقيرٍ، بأحزن صوتٍ، وأصفى وقتٍ وحالٍ، وأحضر قلبٍ وبالٍ. يقشعرّ منه جلده إذا مرّ بآية عذابٍ وعقوبةٍ، ويلين منه جلده إذا مرّ بآية رحمةٍ وكرامة (١٧آ). وإنّ اللّه تعالى يستمع إلى كل قارئ حسن الصوت بالقرآن.

الفصل السادس
في أعداد سور القرآن وآياته وكلماته وحروفه على ما اختلفوا فيه واتفقوا عليه

عدد سور القرآن على ما وجد عليه مصحف عثمان، وهو أيضاً مرويّ عن علي بن أبي طالب (رضي الله عنه) ١١٤؛ وعلى ما وجد في مصحف عبد الله بن مسعود، لأنه لم يعدّ المعوّذتين وعدّ «الضحى» و«الم نشرح» سورة واحدة، ١١١؛ وعلى ما وجد في مصحف أُبيّ بن كعب لأنه عدّ القنوت سورتين: ١١٦؛ وعلى قول من عدّ الأنفال وبراءة سورة واحدة، ١١٣.

وآياته في عدد الكوفيين، وهو العدد الذي رواه الكسائي عن حمزة، ورفعه حمزة إلى علي بن أبي طالب (رضي الله عنه) ٦٢٣٦؛ وفي عدّ البصريين، وهو العدد الذي عليه مصاحفهم ٦٢٠٤؛ وفي عدد المدني الأول عن الحسين بن علي وعبد الله بن عمر ٦٢١٧؛ وفي عدد المدني الآخر عن أبي جعفر وشيبة وإسماعيل ٦٢١٤؛ وفي عدد المكيين ٦٢١٩؛ وفي عدد أهل الشام ٦٢٢٦.

وكلماته: ٧٧٤٣٩، وقيل: ٧٧٤٣٦. وحروفه ٣٢٣٥١٤، وقيل: ٣٢٢٦١٧، وقيل: ٣٢٥١٨٨، وقيل ٣٢١٦٧٥. وقد قيل: علة الاختلاف في عدد الحروف والكلمات أن بعضهم كان يعدّ كل حرف مشدّد حرفين، فصارت حروفه عنده أكثر من حروف مَن عَدّه حرفاً واحداً، وعدّ بعضُهم مثلاً «في خلق..» كلمتين، كان يعدّ «في» كلمة و«خلق» كلمة، فصار عدد كلماته أكثر من عدد مَن عدّهما كلمة واحدة.

وفي نسخة عن بعض العادّين المتأخرين نقلت هو عبد الله بن عبد العزيز:

عدد آي القرآن: ٦٢٤٦، وكلماتها: ٧٧٤٣٦، وحروفها: ٣٢٥٢١١، وعدد ما في القرآن من: الألف: ٤٨٩٥٥، والباء: ١٢٥٥، والتاء: ١٥١٩٩، والثاء: ١٢٥٥، (١٧ب) والجيم: ٣٢٧٣، والحاء: ٣٩٩٣، والخاء: ٢٤١٦، والدال: ٢٤١٢، والذال: ٤٦٤٢، والراء: ١١٧٩٣، والزاء: ١٤٥٥، والسين ٤٩٩١، والشين: ٢٢٤٣، والصاد: ٢٥٨١، والضاد: ٢٦٥٧، والطاء: ١٢٧٤، والظاء: ٨٤٢، والعين: ٩٥٢٥.، والغين: ٢٢٥٨، والفاء: ٨٤٧٧، والقاف: ٦٨١٣، والكاف: ١٥٣٤٤، واللام: ٣٣٤٢٢، والميم: ٢٦١٣٤، والنون: ٢٦٤٦٤، والواو: ٢٤٤٣٦، والهاء: ١٧٥٧٥، والياء: ٢٤٩١٩. وقد عدّوا آيات سورة الفاتحة ٧ وكلماتها ٢٨ وقيل ٢٩ وحروفها ١٤٤ وكلماتها التامات ١٢، وتحت كلّ عدد سرّ، ﴿وفَوْق كُلِّ ذِي عِلْمٍ عَلِيمٌ﴾.

الفصل السابع

في تعديد المفسرين من الصحابة وغيرهم وتعديد التفاسير المصنّفة والمعاني وأصحابها

فمن الصحابة من تكلم في تفسير القرآن: أمير المؤمنين علي؛ وعبد الله بن عباس؛ وعبد الله بن مسعود؛ وأُبيّ بن كعب؛ وسعيد بن المسيّب؛ وعمر بن الخطاب؛ ومعاذ بن جبل (رضى الله عنهم).

ومن الرواة عنهم والمصنفين في التفسير: علي بن أبي طلحة الوالبي، عن ابن عباس؛ عطية بن سعد العوفي عن ابن عباس وله تفسير؛ عكرمة

مولى ابن عباس عن ابن عباس، وله تفسير؛ الضحاك بن مزاحم الهلالي عن ابن عباس، وله تفسير؛ ومجاهد بن جبر وسعيد بن جبير عن ابن عباس؛ الكلبي، محمد بن السائب عن أبي صالح باذان مولى أم هانئ عن ابن عباس، وله تفسير؛ عطاء بن أبي رباح؛ عطاء بن أبي مسلم الخراساني؛ عطاء بن دينار؛ أبو بكر محمد بن مسلم بن شهاب الزهري؛ أبو سعيد بن أبي الحسن البصري، وله تفسير؛ قتادة بن دِعامة السَّدوسي وله تفسير؛ أبو العالية الرياحي، وله تفسير؛ مقاتل بن حيان، وله تفسير؛ مقاتل بن سليمان، وله تفسير؛ الحسن بن واقد الواقدي، وله تفسير؛ إسماعيل بن [عبد الرحمن] السدي، وله تفسير؛ عبد الله بن أبي جعفر الرازي (١٨آ)، وله تفسير؛ محمد بن جُريج، وله تفسير؛ سفيان بن [سعيد] الثوري وله تفسير؛ سفيان بن عيينة، وله تفسير؛ وكيع بن الجراح، وله تفسير؛ هُشَيم بن بشير، وله تفسير؛ شِبْل بن عبّاد المكي، وله تفسير؛ ورقاء بن عمر، وله تفسير؛ زيد بن أسلم، وله تفسير؛ رَوْح بن عُبادة القيسي، وله تفسير؛ محمد بن يوسف الفِرْيابي، وله تفسير؛ قُبيصة بن عُقبة السوائي، وله تفسير؛ أبو عبد الله موسى بن مسعود النّهديّ، وله تفسير؛ سعيد بن منصور، وله تفسير؛ عبد الله بن وهب الفهري، وله تفسير؛ عبد الحميد بن حميد، وله تفسير؛ محمد بن أيوب، وله تفسير؛ أبو بكر الأصم، وله تفسير؛ أبو سعيد عبد الله بن سعيد الأشجّ، وله تفسير؛ أبو حمزة الثمالي، وله تفسير؛ المسيّب بن شريك، وله تفسير؛ عبد الله بن حامد، وله تفسير؛ أبو بكر بن عبدوس، وله تفسير؛ أبو عمرو أحمد بن محمد الفراتي (كذا)، وله تفسير؛ أبو بكر بن فورك، وله تفسير؛ أبو القاسم بن حبيب، وله تفسير؛ أبو علي عبد الوهاب لحياي (كذا)، وله تفسير؛ القاضي عبد الجبار، وله تفسير؛ محمد بن عثمان، وله تفسير؛ أبو الحسن محمد بن القاسم الفقيه؛ أبو إسحق أحمد بن محمد الثعلبي وله تفسير ؛ أبو بكر عبد الله بن محمد

النقاش، وله تصنيف، فيه تفسير جبرئيل، وتفسير النبي، وتفسير الصحابة؛ علي بن محمد الواحدي.

وعلى كل مذهب من مذاهب المتكلمين تفسير فسّره صاحب المقالة على موجب مذهبه؛ فللمعتزلة تفاسير، وللأشعرية تفاسير، وللكرامية تفاسير، وللخوارج تفاسير، وللشيعة تفاسير.

والمصنفون في المعاني

أبو زكريا يحيى بن زياد الفرّاء، وأبو اسحاق إبراهيم بن السّريّ الزجاج، وعلي بن حمزة الكسائي، وأبو عبيد القاسم بن سلّام، وأبو الحسن سعيد بن مسعدة الأخفش، وأبو عبيدة مَعْمَر بن المثنّى التّميمي، وأبو علي الحسن بن يحيى بن نصر الجرجاني، صاحب النظم؛ والمؤرّج بن عمرو بن أبي فايد السدوسي، والنضر بن شميل، وغريب القرآن عن عبد الله بن مسلم بن قُتيبة الدينوري القتيبي، ومشكل قُطرُب أبي علي محمد بن المستنير، وأبو بكر محمد بن القفّال الشاشي، وأبو مسلم محمد بن بحر وأمثالهم يُعدّون من أصحاب المعاني (١٨ب). وجماعة صنّفوا في التفسير وهم يُعدّون من أصحاب المعاني لا من أهل التفسير.

فنحن نخرج على الحواشي بالهمزة (كذا): اللغة، والنحو، والقراءات، والتفسير، والمعاني، ثم نشير إلى الأسرار التي هي مصابيح الأبرار، وقد سمّينا الكتاب بذلك، والله تعالى نسأل أن يعصمنا من التفسير بالرأي وتسويل النفس ووسواس الشيطان، وأن يهدينا صراطه المستقيم صراط الذين أنعم عليهم من النبيّين والصدّيقين والشهداء والصالحين وحَسُن أولئك رفيقاً. وإذا قلت: قال أهل القرآن، أو أصحاب الأسرار، أو الذي شققت له اسماً من معنى الآية، فلا أريد به نفسي عياذاً بالله، وإنّما أريد الصدّيقين من أهل بيت النبي، فهم الواقفون على الأسرار، وهم من المصطفين الأخيار.

الفصل الثامن
في معنى التفسير والتأويل

قال أهل اللغة: التفسير تفعيل من الفَسر وهو إظهار الشيء وإبانته، يقال: فسرت الشيء أفسره بالكسر فسراً إذا بيّنته، ثم إذا بولغ في التّعب قيل: فسّر به تفسيراً.

وقال بعضهم: ليس يبعد أن يكون معنى الفَسر راجعاً إلى معنى السِّفر؛ يقال: سفرت المرأة إذا كشفت عن وجهها، ثم يكون سفر وفسر من باب المقلوب مثل جذب وجبذ؛ ثم لا يكون التفسير إلا ما دلّ عليه ظاهر اللفظ من حيث اللغة، فتُفسَّر العربية بالعربية، أو بالعجمية؛ وكذلك تفسر العجمية بالعربية وكلا الأمرين يسمّى تفسيراً.

ومبنى التفسير على أمرين: أحدهما ما دلّ عليه اللفظ من حيث اللغة على الشيوع من أهل اللغة؛ والثاني ما وَرَّدَ به السمعُ إما الخبر وإما الأثر، فيكون اللفظ محتملاً، ومع احتماله فيرد به نصّ، فيجب حمل اللفظ عليه، وربّما يكون اللفظ مشتركاً، فتُعيَّن جهته بالسّمع، وربما يكون عاماً، فيخصّص بالسمع. ومن حقّ المتصرّف فيه أن يكون عالماً بوجوه اللغة، عارفاً باختلاف أحوال المفسّرين فيه، والمخبرين عنه؛ فانّ كثيراً من ألفاظ التنزيل دلّ على معنى، وقد ورد في الأخبار صرف ذلك المعنى إلى جهةٍ من الجهات أو شخصٍ من الأشخاص مثل: ﴿والنَازِعَاتِ غَرْقاً﴾، ومثل: ﴿والذَارِيات﴾، ﴿والصَّافَّاتِ﴾، ﴿والعَادِيات﴾ فإن اللفظ لا يدل من ذلك إلّا على معنى النزع والذّرو والصفّ والعَدْو؛ ثم قد ورد السمع بتفسير ذلك تارة بالملائكة، وتارة بالغزاة (١٩ آ)، فيجب صرف المعنى إلى جهة السمع، و لا يمكن أن يتصرّف فيه بالرأي والقياس، وعليه حُمِل قول النبي (صلّى الله عليه وآله) «من فسّر القرآن برأيه فليتبوّأ مقعده من النار».

ثم المفسرون معروفون بأساميهم التي ذكرناها، فما نُقل عنهم بروايةٍ صحيحةٍ قيل هو تفسير.

وأما التأويل، فقد قال أهل اللغة إنه من الأَوْل، وهو الرجوع. يقال: آل الشيء يؤول إذا رجع، وهو تفسير ما يؤول إليه الشيء، وعلى هذا: التفسير أعمّ من التأويل. فكلّ تأويلٍ تفسيرٌ، وليس كلُّ تفسيرٍ تأويلاً.

وصار أكثر العلماء إلى الفرق بين اللفظين على وجهين مختلفين. فقال بعضهم: إنّ التفسير يوضع بإزاء الألفاظ، والتأويل يوضع بإزاء المعاني. يقال: فسّر القرآن إذا أوضح ما انغلق من ألفاظه، وأوّله إذا أوضح ما استَبْهَمَ من معانيه. قال الله تعالى: ﴿ذلكَ الكِتَابُ لا رَيْبَ فِيهِ﴾ تفسيره: لا شك فيه؛ وتأويله لا يرتابوا فيه؛ فهو خبرٌ بمعنى النهي.

وقال قائلون: إن لفظ التفسير يستعمل في إيضاح معاني القرآن ومعاني الأحاديث والأشعار، ولفظ التأويل يُستعمل فيما يتعلّق بالدين. ولذلك صارت التأويلات المختلفة أصولاً للمذاهب المختلفة؛ والتفسير بخلافه.

وقال بعضهم: التفسير هو العلم بسبب نزول السور والآيات وقصصها، وحمل العمومات منها على أقوامٍ وأشخاصٍ مخصوصين، نحو قوله تعالى: ﴿وإنْ طَائِفَتَانِ مِنَ المُؤْمِنِينَ اقْتَتَلُوا﴾ قالوا: هم الأوس والخزرج. وقوله: ﴿ألَمْ تَرَ إلى الَّذينَ بَدَّلُوا نِعْمَةَ اللهِ كُفْرًا﴾ قالوا: هم بنو أمية وبنو مخزوم. وقوله: ﴿قُلْ لِلمخلّفِينَ مِنَ الأَعراب﴾ قيل: هم بنو حنيفة؛ وأمثال ذلك لا يثبت إلّا بالسماع.

قالوا: والتأويل يتعلّق بدراية العقل. قال الحسين بن الفضل البجليّ: التأويل صرف الآية إلى معنى يحتمله اللفظ، موافق لما قبل الآية وما بعدها.

وقيل: التأويل هو البحث عن مراد اللافظ، وما يؤول إليه معناه.

وقيل: إنّ علوم القرآن تنقسم إلى معرفة ألفاظه وإلى معرفة معانيه.

ومعرفة الألفاظ تنقسم أربعة أقسامٍ: علم المقاطع والمبادي وهو: علم الوقوف والابتداءات؛ وعلم اختلاف القراءات، وعلم تفسير اللغة، وعلم الإعراب. وأما معرفة المعاني فثلاثة أقسامٍ: علم النزول وأسبابه، وذلك إلى أصحاب الحديث، وعلم ما يختلف فيه من المتشابهات مما يتعلق بأصول الدين، وذلك إلى أهل النظر والعقل، وعلم ما يتعلق بالشرائع والأحكام (١٩ب) وذلك إلى أهل الاجتهاد والقياس فعلى هذه القاعدة لم يتعلق من القرآن بالسمع والحديث إلا أسباب النزول فقط، والباقون قد فسّروا القرآن برأيهم إما نظراً في الأصول، وإما اجتهاداً في الفروع.

ولو تدبّر متدبّر آيات القرآن لم يجد فيها آيةً واحدةً يُستغنى فيها عن خبرٍ وتوقيف، وإلا فيكون التفسير والتأويل فيها على ظنٍّ وحسبان.

وإن الفارقين بين التفسير والتأويل لمّا لم يذكروا أقسام التفسير وأقسام التأويل لم يتحقّق ببيانهم الفرق بينهما، فلربّما لا يتقابل قسمان منهما فلا يكون الفرق بينهما صحيحاً؛ وقد وضع بعضهم التنزيل والتأويل متقابلين، ووضع بعضهم الظاهر والتأويل متقابلين، ووضع بعضهم الظاهر والباطن متقابلين، والتفسير والتأويل متقابلين. وقد يتّفق اللفظان في المعنى، فيكون التفسير تأويلاً، والتأويل تفسيراً، والظاهر باطناً، والباطن ظاهراً.

وقد يختلف اللفظان في المعنى، فيكون التفسير غير التأويل، مثل قوله تعالى: ﴿هَلْ يَنظُرونَ إلّا أَنْ يأْتِيَهُمُ اللهُ في ظُلَلٍ منَ الغَمامِ﴾. ولنذكر هاهنا أقسام التأويل بعد تحقيق معناه. فما قيل فيه إنه مشتق من الأول وهو الرجوع، فهو صحيح؛ وعليه العامة. وقد قيل فيه إنه مشتق من الأوّل المقابل للآخر. فقال بعض كبار الأئمة (رضي الله عنهم): التأويل ردّ الشيء إلى أوّله، كما إن التأخير دفعه إلى آخره، وهذا كلام متين، أُسلوبه كلام النبوّة. ولمّا كان مآل كلّ شيء إلى أوّله، قيل فيه إنّه تأويله، وإنه مشتقٌ من الأول وهو الرجوع.

ثم التأويل المذكور في القرآن على أقسام: منها تأويل الرؤيا بمعنى التعبير: ﴿هذا تَأْوِيلُ رُؤْيَايَ مِن قَبْلُ﴾؛ ومنها تأويل الأحاديث: ﴿وَيُعَلِّمُكَ مِن تَأْوِيلِ الأَحاديث﴾؛ ومنها تأويل الأفعال: ﴿ذلك تَأْوِيلُ مَا لَمْ تَسْطِعْ عَلَيْهِ صَبْراً﴾؛ ومنها الردّ إلى العاقبة والمآل: ﴿هَلْ يَنْظُرُونَ إلّا تَأْوِيلَهُ﴾؛ ومنها الردّ إلى الله والرّسول: ﴿وإِنْ تَنَازَعْتُم في شَيءٍ فرُدُّوهُ إلى اللهِ والرّسُولِ إِنْ كُنْتُم تُؤْمِنُونَ باللهِ واليوم الآخر، ذَلِكَ خيرٌ وأحسنُ تَأْوِيلا﴾؛ ﴿أَنا أُنبِّئُكُم بتأْوِيلِه فأَرْسِلُونَ﴾ ومنها تأويل المتشابهات: ﴿فأَمّا الَّذِينَ في قُلُوبِهم زَيغٌ فيتَّبِعُونَ ما تشابَه مِنهُ ابتِغاءَ الفتنةِ وابتِغاءَ تأْويله﴾.

وفي القرآن أحكام المفروغ وأحكام المستأنف، وأحكام متقابلات (٢٠آ) على التضاد، وأحكام متفاضلات على الترتب. فرؤية المستأنف هو الظاهر والتنزيل والتفسير؛ ورؤية حكم المفروغ هو الباطن والتأويل والمعنى والحقيقة؛ ﴿والرّاسِخُونَ في العِلْمِ يَقُولُونَ آمنّا بِه كلٌّ من عِنْدِ رَبِّنَا، ومَا يَذَّكَّرُ إلّا أُولُوا الألْبَابِ﴾.

الفصل التاسع
في العموم والخصوص والمحكم
والمتشابه والناسخ والمنسوخ

إنّ العموم والخصوص لا يرجعان إلى الألفاظ من حيث هي حروفٌ وأصواتٌ، بل من حيث إنها دالّةٌ على معانيها بالوضع أو الاصطلاح في الأذهان والأعيان. فالعموم والخصوص إذاً في الأذهان والأعيان؛ والعموم بالأذهان أولى، والخصوص بالأعيان أولى.

وما من لفظٍ عامٍّ في القرآن إلّا وقد دخله التّخصيص وما من تخصيصٍ إلّا وقد قارنه التشخيص. فأما تخصيص العمومات، فمثل قوله

تعالى: ﴿يا أَيُّها النّاسُ اعبُدُوا ربَّكم﴾. وهو خطابٌ عامٌّ لجميع الناس، ومن ينطلق عليه اسم الإنسانية. ثم لم يمكن إجراءه على عمومه، لأنّ المجنون والصبيّ إنسان، ولم يتناوله الخطاب، فوجب تخصيص اللفظ العامّ بمن له عقلٌ كاملٌ، والمجنون ليس بعاقلٍ، والصبيّ ليس بكاملٍ.

وأما تشخيص المخصوصات فممّا أغفلها كثيرٌ من أهل العلم؛ فإن «الناس» قد خصّص بالمكلفين، وقد يشخّص بجماعةٍ مخصوصين: ﴿ثُمَّ أفِيْضُوا مِنْ حَيثُ أَفاضَ الناس﴾، والتكليف بالإفاضة على ناسٍ مخصوصين، و ﴿من حيثُ أَفاضَ الناسُ﴾ هم قومٌ غير أولئك المكلّفين، هم الهداة المهديّون؛ فتخصّص منهم أيضاً شخص واحد، هو الناس: ﴿أمْ يَحْسُدونَ الناسَ على ما آتاهُم اللهُ مِنْ فضلِهِ﴾ قيل في التفسير هو محمد (صلّى الله عليه وآله)؛ وذلك هو تشخيص الخاص؛ ونسبته إلى الأشخاص نسبة الخصوص إلى العموم.

ومن ذلك القبيل قوله تعالى: ﴿وَرَحْمَتِي وَسِعَت كلَّ شيء﴾، وذلك عام لا عموم فوقه، ثم خصّ الرحمة بقومٍ، فقال: ﴿فَسأَكتُبُهَا للذيْنَ يتَّقُونَ ويُؤتُونَ الزكاةَ والذينَ هُم بآياتِنا يُؤمِنُون﴾ ثم خصها بقوم فقال: ﴿الذينَ يتّبِعُونَ الرسولَ النبيَّ الأُميَّ﴾ ثم تشخصها بشخص مخصوص هو الرحمة: ﴿وما أرْسَلْنَاكَ إلّا رحمةً للعَالَمين﴾. ومن ذلك القبيل قوله تعالى: ﴿آمَنّا بِرَبِّ العَالَمِينَ﴾، وهو إشارةٌ إلى عموم الربوبية لجميع العالمين. ثم قال بعده: ﴿رَبِّ موسى وهارون﴾ وذلك تخصيص الربوبية (٢٠ب) لشخصين.

وكما عمّت الربوبية وخُصّت، كذلك عمّت العبودية وخُصّت في قوله: ﴿إنْ كُلُّ مَن في السَّمَاوَاتِ وَالأَرْضِ إلّا آتي الرَّحْمَنِ عَبْداً﴾، وذلك عمومٌ في العبوديّة وفي قوله: ﴿وَعِبَادُ الرَّحْمَنِ﴾ وذلك خصوص في العبودية، وفي قوله: ﴿عَيْناً يَشْرَبُ بِهَا عبادُ اللَّهِ﴾ وذلك تشخيص ذلك الخاص. فعلى وجهي الربوبية والعبودية خصوصٌ وعمومٌ؛ سواءٌ

نسبت الربوبية إلى الخلق أو أُضيفت العبودية إلى الربّ تعالى.

ولقد كان واحدٌ من أهل العلم يدّعي العلم بالتفسير، فقال أمير المؤمنين علي (رضى الله عنه): مَن إله المؤمن والكافر؟ قال: الله. قال: صدقت ثم قال له: مَنْ مولى المؤمن والكافر؟ قال: الله، قال: كذبت، ﴿ذلِكَ بأَنَّ اللهَ مَولَى الذينَ آمَنُوا وأنَّ الكافرين لا مَوْلَى لهم﴾ فامتحنه بالعموم والخصوص، فلما لم يهتد إلى ذلك أفحمه وأعلمه أن لا علم له بالقرآن وسيأتي في التفسير إشارات إلى أسرار العموم والخصوص؛ وكيفية إضافة الخير والشرّ إلى القدر إضافة العموم والخصوص. وذلك هو العلم المكنون والسرّ المدفون لا يعلمها إلا العالمون.

وأما المحكم والمتشابه، فاعلم أن القسمة الأولى على الآيات في القرآن هي قسمة المحكم والمتشابه. قال الله تعالى: ﴿هُوَ الذي أَنْزَلَ عليكَ الكِتَابَ مِنهُ آياتٌ مُحكماتٌ هُنَّ أمُّ الكتابِ وأُخَرُ مُتَشَابِهَات﴾ واختلف المفسرون في المحكمات ما هي، والمتشابهات ما هي كما يأتي في التفسير.

ومن العجب أنّ المحكمات والمتشابهات عندهم قد صارت من المتشابهات، حيث لم يتبيّن تفسيرها على اليقين! ثم التأويل إنما يطرق إلى المتشابه منها لا إلى المحكم؛ لأنه قال: ﴿فأمّا الذِيْنَ في قلُوبِهم زيغٌ فيتّبِعونَ ما تَشَابَه مِنهُ ابتغاءَ الفِتنةِ وابتغاءَ تَأوِيلِهِ﴾. والذي عليه أهل التحقيق من العلماء - كثّرهم الله - أنّ الآيات قد انقسمت إلى آياتٍ خلقية وآيات أمرية، ثم الآيات الخلقية انقسمت إلى آيات مُحكمةٍ مفروغةٍ لا تتبدّل ولا تتغيّر، وهي في ذواتها كاملةٌ لا نقص فيها، مقدسة لا عائبة عليها؛ وإلى آيات متشابهة مستأنفة يتطرق إليها التغيير والتبديل، وهي ناقصة متوجّهة إلى الكمال، فكذلك الآيات الأمرية انقسمت إلى محكمات مفروغات، وإلى متشابهاتٍ مستأنفات. فكل ما يتعلق بأحكام القدر المفروغ عنه، والحكم السابق المعلوم فهو من

المحكمات؛ وكل ما يتعلق (٢١آ) بأحكام القضاء المستأنف والحكم المتأخّر المشروع فهو من المتشابهات.

وقد يرد في القرآن المحكم بإزاء المفصّل، كما قال تعالى: ﴿الر، كِتَابٌ أُحْكِمَتْ آياتُهُ ثَمَّ فُصِّلَتْ﴾ أي أحكمت بالتنزيل وفُصّلت بالتأويل؛ فيكون التفصيل في مقابلة الإحكام. وقد قيل إنّ المحكمات هي التي لم يتطرّق إليها نَسخٌ البتة، وهي عشر آياتٍ في آخر سورة الأنعام وفي سورة السبحان وقد قيل إن المحكمات هي جميع آيات القرآن، والمتشابهات الحروف التي هي على مبادئ السور، يقال لها: مفاتيح السور.

وقد قيل إن المتشابهات هي التي أشعرت بالتشبيه الذي يحتُّ تنزيه الباري تعالى عنها، والمحكمات هي التي أشعرت بالتوحيد والتقديس.

وأما الناسخ والمنسوخ فقد قيل في حدّ النسخ إنه رفع الحكم الثابت، وقيل إنه انتهاء مدّة الحكم؛ وقد قيل إنه تكميلٌ، بمعنى أنّ مقاصد الأحكام إذا انتهت نهايتها وبلغت غايتها فقد كملت بأحكام أُخَر لها مقاصد أشرف وأكمل من الأولى؛ وهكذا كلامنا في الخلقيات، مثل انتساخ النطفة بالعلقة والعلقة بالمضغة إلى المرتبة السابعة التي هي خلقٌ آخر.

فالشرائع ابتدأت من آدم (عليه السلام)، وانتهت بالقيامة التي هي النشأة الأخرى. وكلّ شريعةٍ ناسخةٌ لما قبلها، أي مكمّلة لها إلى ما بعدها من كمالٍ آخر. قال الله تعالى: ﴿ما نَنْسَخْ مِنْ آيةٍ أو نُنسِها نأتِ بِخَيرٍ مِنْهَا أَو مِثْلِهَا﴾، فافهم هذه الدقيقة، و لا تظنّن أنّ شريعةً من الشرائع تبطل بشريعة أخرى أو ترتفع أحكامها [و] توضع أخرى، فإنّ النطفة في الخلقيّات لو بطلت أو ارتفعت لم تصل إلى المرتبة الثانية والثالثة، بل انتهت نهايتها من التمام، وليست صورةً أخرى من الكمال مع استيفاء ذاتها كذلك الشريعة الأولى لو بطلت أو ارتفعت لم تصل

إلى الثانية والثالثة، بل انتهت نهايتها من التمام، وليست صورة الكمال مع استحكام ذاتها. وكذلك الشريعة الأخيرة التي هي أشرف الشرائع قد اشتملت على أحكام لم تتبدّل، وهي أصول الديانة، نازلةٌ منزلة الأساس للبيت، والذات للصورة؛ وهي المحكمات من الآيات التي هي أمّ الكتاب. وقد اشتملت على أحكام تتبدّل وهي فروع الديانة، نازلةٌ منزلة الأغصان للشجرة والصور للذات، وهي المتشابهات من الآيات التي ﴿يَمْحُوا اللَّهُ مَا يَشَاءُ (٢١ب) وَيُثْبِتُ﴾، ولا يمحو إلا لكمالٍ قد انتهى إليه، ولا يُثبت إلا لمبدأ متوجهٍ إلى كمال.

فتقرير الدعوة إلى التوحيد من حيث القول لما انتهى إلى كمالٍ، تميّز الحقّ به عن الباطل كلّ التميّز، وتبرّأ التفريق عن الفريق (كذا) كلّ التبرّؤ، حتى قال في سورة التبرّؤ عن أديان الكافرين: ﴿لكُمْ دِينُكُمْ وَلِيَ دِينِ﴾. ابتدأ الدعوة إلى التوحيد من حيث الفعل بالسيف ليتميّز المحقّ عن المبطل، ﴿وَلِيُمَحِّصَ اللهُ الَّذِينَ آمَنوا وَيمْحَقَ الكافِرِينَ﴾؛ فظنّ قومٌ أنّ آية التبرّي: ﴿لكُم دينُكُم وليَ دينِ﴾ منسوخةٌ بآية السيف: ﴿كُتِبَ عليكُم القِتَالُ﴾، ﴿قَاتِلُوهُمْ يُعَذِّبْهُمُ اللهُ بِأَيْدِيكُمْ﴾، ولم يعلموا أنّ قوله: ﴿لكُمْ دِينُكُم وليَ دين﴾ نهايةٌ في التبرّي بالقول، وتقرير التوحيد باللسان والاعتقاد، وإنما يتمّ كلّ التمام إذا أُقرّت بداية التبرّي بالفعل، وتقرير التوحيد بالسيف والإزهاق؛ وكذلك كلّ آيةٍ من القرآن قيل إنها منسوخةٌ بآيةٍ أخرى وجدت الآية الناسخة مقررةً للآية المنسوخة لا رافعةً ولا مبطلةً ﴿يَمْحُوا اللَّهُ ما يَشاءُ وَيُثْبِتُ وَعِنْدَهُ أُمُّ الكِتَابِ﴾.

الفصل العاشر
في حكمي المفروغ والمستأنف وطرفي التضاد والترتب على قاعدتي الخلق والأمر

إعلم أنّ لفظ المفروغ والمستأنف إنما أُخذ من الشيخين العمرين أبي بكر وعمر (رضوان الله عليهما)، حيث تكلّما في القدر، وارتفعت أصواتهما حتى بلغ النبي (صلّى الله عليه وآله) صوتهما وهو في الحجرة، فخرج إليهما، ووجنتاه كأنّهما رمّانةٌ شقت بنصفين فقال (عليه وآله السلام): «فيم أنتم؟» قالوا: نتكلم في القدر. فقال: «هل اتكلمتم في مَلَكٍ خلقه الله تعالى نصفه من نارٍ ونصفه من ثلج، فلا النار تذيب الثلج، ولا الثلج يطفئ النار، تسبيحه سبحان من جمع بين النار والثلج». فقام إليه عمر حتى جلس عنده، وقال: يا رسول الله أنحن في أمرٍ مبتدأ أم نحن في أمرٍ مفروغ؟ وفي رواية قال الأمر أنف؟ فقال (عليه السلام): «نحن في أمر مفروغٍ عنه». فقال عمر: إن كان الأمر قد فرغ منه ففيم العمل إذاً؟ فقال (عليه وآله السلام): «يا عمر اعمَلوا وكلٌّ ميسَّرٌ لما خُلِقَ لَه».

فأُخذ لفظ المفروغ والمستأنف من ذلك المجلس. وذهب قوم إلى أن الأحكام كلّها مفروغةٌ مقدّرةٌ في الأزل؛ والخلق مجبورون تحت مجاري الأقدار، لا يملكون تأخّراً عمّا قدّمهم إليه ولا يستطيعون (٢٢آ) تقدّماً إلى ما أخّرهم عنه، حتى بلغوا إلى حدّ التفريط في نفي الاستطاعة وإثبات تكليف ما لا يُطاق.

وذهب قومٌ إلى أنّ الأحكام كلّها مستأنفة مقدّرةٌ على اختيار العبد؛ والمكلَّفون كلّهم مُختارون في مجاري التكليف بما يكون النفع والضرّ؛ ويحدثون الإيمان والكفر، حتى بلغوا في حدّ الإفراط إلى إثبات الاستقلال ونفي الاستعانة في جميع الأفعال.

والمذهبان محمولان على طرفي الإفراط والتفريط. ومصدرهما اختلاف الشيخين في الحكمين؛ ولو عرفوا أنّ القول فيه أمرٌ بين أمرين، لا جبر ولا تفويض، وأن المفروغ والمستأنف على مثال ملكٍ نصفه من نارٍ ونصفه من ثلج، والنار جانب المفروغ، والثلج جانب المستأنف؛ وكما لا يذيب النار الثلج ولا يطفئ الثلج النار، كذلك لا يُبطل حكم المفروغ حكم المستأنف، ولا يُبطل حكم المستأنف حكم المفروغ. ولذلك أحال النبي (صلّى الله عليه وآله) نظرهما إلى ذلك المَلَك؛ ولما عاودوه على إقامة الحجّة بعد الحكم: إن كان الأمر قد فرغ منه ففيم العمل إذاً؟! قال: «اعمَلُوا وكلٌّ ميسَّرٌ لما خُلِقَ لَه» فقد أفتى بالحكمين: فإنّ قوله «اعملوا» إشارةٌ إلى حكم المستأنف؛ وقوله: «وكلٌّ مُيَسّر لِمَا خُلِقَ له» إشارة إلى حكم المفروغ.

وأنت إذا لاحظت الخلقيات وجدتها على قسمين: أحدهما موجوداتٌ حاصلةٌ بالفعل، كاملةٌ في الذات، منزهةٌ عن المادة والزمان والمكان، كالقدسيّات من الملائكة، والمقرّبين من الروحانيات. والثاني: موجوداتٌ حاصلةٌ بالقوّة متوجّهةٌ إلى الكمال، مخلوقةٌ من مادةٍ وفي زمانٍ ومكان. كذلك إذا لاحظت الأمريّات وجدتها على قسمين: أحدهما أحكامٌ مفروغةٌ قد تمّت وكلماتٌ تامّةٌ قد كملت، كما قال تعالى: ﴿وَتَمَّتْ كَلِمَةُ رَبِّكَ صِدْقاً وعَدْلاً لا مُبَدِّلَ لِكَلِمَاتِهِ﴾؛ والثاني: أحكامٌ مستأنفةٌ قد توجّهت إلى التمام والكمال. فمن حكم المفروغ قيل: «جرى القلم بما هو كائن»، وقيل: «فرغ ربّكم عن الخَلق والخُلق والرزق والأجل». وصدق الخبر: «السّعيد من سعد في بطن أمّه، والشّقيّ من شقي في بطن أمّه». ودلّت عليه آيات الختم والطّبع والإقفال وحُمِلت عليه آيات اليأس من إيمان الكفار: ﴿سَوَاءٌ عَلَيْهِمْ أَأَنذَرتَهُم أَمْ لَمْ تُنْذِرْهُم لا يُؤمِنُون﴾، (٢٢ب) ﴿سَوَاءٌ عَلَيْكُم أَدَعَوْتُمُوهُمْ أَمْ أَنْتُمْ صَامِتُونَ﴾، ﴿فَلَعَلَّكَ باخعٌ نَفْسَكَ على آثارِهم إنْ لم يُؤمنوا بهذا

الحديثِ أَسَفاً﴾ إلى أمثال ذلك.

ومن حكم المستأنف «جرى قلم التكليف بما سيكون». وتوجُّه الخطاب إلى المختارين بفعل الخير، واعتقاد الحق، وقول الصدق؛ وتقدُّر الجزاء على الأفعال خيرها وشرّها، وإيمانها وكفرها، وطاعتها وعصيانها؛ ودلّت عليه آيات التكليف والتعريف والإنذار والتحذير، وحملت عليه آيات الامتحان والافتتان والتّرجية والأطماع، مثل قوله تعالى: ﴿قُمْ فأَنْذِرْ﴾، و ﴿وَأَنْذِرْهُمْ﴾، ﴿وَلِتُنْذِرَ قَوْماً﴾، ﴿لِتُنْذِرَ بِهِ وذِكْرَى للمُؤْمِنِين﴾، ﴿فَقُولا لَهُ قَوْلاً لَيِّناً لَعَلَّهُ يَتَذَكَّرُ أَوْ يَخْشَى﴾، ﴿فَذَكِّرِ إنْ نَفَعَتِ الذِّكْرَى سَيَذَّكَّرُ مَنْ يَخْشَى﴾ إلى أمثال ذلك.

ومن لم يعرف الحكمين تعذر عليه الجمع بين آيات الثابتين على الإنذار وبين آيات الأمر بالإنذار، وذلك هو سرّ الأسرار.

وأما التضاد والترتب في آيات القرآن فهو مبنيٌّ على فطرة الخلائق من الأخيار والأشرار، والأولياء والأعداء، والمؤمنين والكفار، والأبرار والفجّار. فما من قصّةٍ إلا وفيها ذكر الفريقين وحكم الخصمين. وقد قال الصادق (عليه السلام): «القرآن نصفه فينا ونصفه في عدوّنا، والذي في عدوّنا فهو فينا» وما دام التخاصم بين الحق والباطل، والمحقّ والمبطل موجوداً، وكان أحكم الحاكمين حاكماً بينهما، وكان الرّسل والأنبياء عليهم السلام متوسّطين في هذا الحكم، كان ذكر التضادّ جارياً على لسان النبوّة، مكتوباً في صحف الرسالة حتى يفصل بينهم يوم الفصل فيما كانوا فيه يختلفون.

وكما تجد التضادّ في الموجودات بين المتعاندين على وجهين مختلفين، كما بين موجود ومعدومٍ، أو كما بين موجود وموجودٍ، كذلك تجد التضادّ في الأمريات بين المتعاندين على وجهين مختلفين، كما بين إيمان وكفر، أو كما بين إيمانٍ وإيمان، وإسلام وإسلام، ودينٍ ودين؛ حتى لو تفحّصت كلمات القرآن وجدت هذا التضاد في كلّ

كلمةٍ إلّا ما شاء الله. وما من آية في حقّ المؤمنين إلّا وتعقبها آيةٌ في حقّ الكافرين، وما من خصلةٍ من خصال الخير إلا وتُذكر عقيبها خصلةٌ من خصال الشرّ، وكذلك الترتّب والتفاضل بين شخصٍ وشخص، وفعلٍ وفعل، ثم كيف يشترك الفريقان في قضيةٍ، وكيف يفترقان في قضيّة، وحكم الشريعة مبنيٌّ على موضع الاشتراك (٢٣آ)، وحكم القيامة مبنيٌّ على موضع الافتراق، فإنما يتبين لك من ميزان الحق والباطل؛ فإنهما يشتركان في قضية الوجود ويفترقان في أنّ الحقّ حقٌ والباطل باطلٌ. وكذلك الصدق والكذب ، فإنهما يشتركان في السمع ويفترقان في البصر؛ وكذلك الخير والشرّ فإنهما يشتركان في الصورة ويفترقان في المعنى. ولكلّ مثالٍ شرحٌ يُطلب من موضعه.

وليس التضادّ بين الأشياء مقصوراً على تضادّ الحركة والسكون، والاجتماع والافتراق، والحرارة والبرودة، والرطوبة واليبوسة، والسواد والبياض، والحلاوة والمرارة، واللّين والخشونة، ولا مقصوراً أيضاً على مثل العلم والجهل، والقدرة والعجز، والإرادة والكراهة، والكلام والسكوت، والعمى والإبصار، والصمم والسمع؛ ولا أيضاً مقصوراً على مثل الحياة والموت، والحيوان والجماد، والملائكة والشياطين؛ ولكنّ أكثر التضادّ في القرآن المجيد وعلى لسان الأنبياء عليهم السلام: التضاد بين مثلٍ ومثل، كأمرٍ وأمر، وكلمةٍ وكلمة، وعقلٍ وعقل، ونفسٍ ونفس، وطبيعةٍ وطبيعة، وفطرةٍ وفطرة؛ إلى غيرها من المتماثلات من حيث الصورة والشكل والاسم، والمتباينات من حيث المعنى، وبالجوهر والحقيقة؛ وعلى كلّ مثالٍ ومثلٍ مثالٌ، ونصٌّ في القرآن والأخبار، وسيأتي ذلك في مواضعها.

وأما الترتّب والتفاضل بين الكلمات، وأصحاب المراتب والدرجات فيُعلم أيضاً من الآيات؛ وكلُّ الخلائق معترفون بذلك فطرةً وضرورةً؛ فالملائكة تقول: ﴿وما مِنّا إلّا لَهُ مقامٌ مَعلومٌ﴾؛ ويعترفون بفضل آدم

(عليه السلام) على من قال منهم: ﴿أَتَجْعَلُ فيها مَن يُفسِدُ فيها﴾ إذ أنبأهم بأسمائهم بعد قولهم: ﴿سُبْحَانَكَ لا عِلْمَ لَنا إلّا ما عَلَّمْتَنا﴾ وكذلك الأنبياء عليهم السلام: ﴿ولقد فَضَّلنا بَعْضَ النَّبِيِّينَ عَلَى بَعْضٍ﴾؛ وكذلك العلماء بعدهم: ﴿والذين أوتوا العِلمَ دَرَجاتٍ﴾؛ وكذلك العاملون بعدهم: ﴿ولكلٍّ دَرَجاتٌ مِمَّا عَمِلُوا﴾؛ وكذلك الناس على العموم، فعالِمٌ ومتعلّم، وهو الترتّب، وسائر الناس همجٌ لا خير فيهم، وذلك هو التضاد.

وفي الأخبار: «لا يزال الناس بخير ما تفاوتوا فإذا استووا هلكوا» فلا يكون التساوي إلا حيث الظُّلمة، ظلمة العدم. و لا يكون الترتب والتفاضل إلّا حيث النور، نور الوجود. قال الله تعالى: ﴿وَالسَّمَاءَ بَنَيْنَاهَا بِأَيْيْدٍ وإِنَّا لَمُوسِعونَ، وَالأَرْضَ فَرَشْنَاهَا فَنِعْمَ المَاهِدُونَ (٢٣ب) وَمِنْ كُلِّ شَيْءٍ خَلَقنَا زَوْجَينِ لَعَلَّكُمْ تَذَكَّرُونَ﴾.

هذا هو الفطرة، وما سوى ذلك فخروجٌ عن الفطرة. فلو طلبت التضادّ والترتّب في الخلق والخلقيات وجدتهما على هذه القاعدة، ولو طلبتهما في الأمر والأمريات وجدتهما على مثل ذلك، حذو النعل بالنعل.

وأما قاعدة الخلق والأمر في علم القرآن فهو الأساس الذي تبنى عليه جميع أحكام المفروغ والمستأنف، والتضاد والترتب، والمبدأ والمعاد، وهو الميزان الذي توزن به أحكام العالمين؛ إحدى كفتيه الخلق وما في بابه، والثانية الأمر وما في بابه؛ قال الله تعالى: ﴿وَالسَّمَاءَ رَفَعَهَا وَوَضَعَ المِيزَانَ﴾.

وقال تعالى: ﴿اللهُ الَّذِي أَنْزَلَ الكِتَابَ بِالحَقِّ وَالمِيزَانَ﴾: ومن له مسكةٌ من العقل يعرف أنّ ميزان الثقلين لا يكون قرين السماء، ولا قرين الكتاب؛ بل الميزان الموضوع في اقتران السماء المرفوعة، هو كالأمر في إقران الخلق، وكالكلمة الطيبة في اقتران الشجرة الطيبة، وكقول:

«لا إله إلا الله» في اقتران قول «محمد رسول الله». وكذلك الميزان الموضوع في اقتران تنزيل الكتاب بالحق، هو كإقران ﴿الرَّحْمنُ عَلَّمَ القُرْآنَ خَلَقَ الإِنْسَانَ عَلَّمَهُ البَيَانَ﴾؛ حتى إذا كان الموزون من الأمريات والشرعيات كان ميزانه الخلق والخلقيات؛ وإذا كان الموزون من الخلقيات كان ميزانه من الأمريات. والمخاطَب بقوله: ﴿وأَقِيمُوا الوَزْنَ بِالقِسْطِ وَلَا تُخْسِرُوا المِيزَانَ﴾ هم قوم مخصوصون قائمون بالقسط، وبيدهم موازين القسط ليوم القيامة: ﴿وَنَضَعُ المَوَازِينَ القِسْطَ لِيَوْمِ القِيَامَةِ، فَلَا تُظْلَمُ نَفْسٌ شَيْئاً وَإِنْ كَانَ مِثْقَالَ حَبَّةٍ مِنْ خَرْدَلٍ أَتَيْنَا بِهَا وَكَفَى بِنَا حَاسِبِينَ﴾.

الفصل الحادي عشر
في إعجاز القرآن نظماً وفصاحة وجزالة وبلاغة وهداية

النظم

قد يراعى كماله وشرفه في تناسب الحروف، وتوافق مخارجها فلا ينظم بين الحاء والعين، والقاف والغين، والضاد والطاء، إلى غيرها مما يثقل على اللسان التفوّه به؛ فجميع ما في القرآن من الحروف المنتظمة كلماتٌ على تناسبٍ وتناصفٍ لا يوجد مثله في كلام العرب وسائر اللغات.

وقد يراعى كماله وشرفه في تأليف الكلمات على تناسبٍ بين الثلاثي والرباعي والخماسي والسداسي، وعلى ازدواجٍ بين لفظين متقاربين في الحروف، متناسبين في المعنى.

وكذلك نظم آيةٍ بآيةٍ، فالشرف فيها اتّساق المعاني (٢٤آ)، واتفاق المقاطع والمباني، وتناسب الصدور والأعجاز، والمبادئ والغايات.

وكلّ الشرف في نظم الحروف بعضها ببعضٍ إنّما يكون في اللفظ المجرّد دون المعنى وكلّ الشرف في نظم الآيات بعضها ببعضٍ فانّما يكون في المعنى المجرّد دون اللفظ؛ والشرف في نظم الكلمات بعضها ببعضٍ فإنما يكون من الجهتين: اللفظ والمعنى.

[وأما الفصاحة]

فإنما تتحقّق على وجهين: أحدهما إفصاح اللفظ عن مخارجه بالصحّة والصّفوة؛ والثاني إفصاح المعنى عن الالتباس بغيره باللفظ المطابق له، المعبّر عن حقيقته المساوي له في عمومه وخصوصه. ثم قد تكون الفصاحة في لفظٍ واحد، وقد تكون في لفظين فصاعداً؛ وقد يعبّر عن شيء واحد بألفاظ مختلفة، فيكون أحدها أدلّ على المقصود، وأعرب عمّا في الضمير، فيُسمّى ذلك اللفظ أفصح الألفاظ.

[وأما الجزالة]

فقد تكون من وجهين: أحدهما، في مفردات الألفاظ، وهو اختيار الثلاثي على الرباعي والخماسي، إلّا فيما تؤدي إليه الضرورة؛ والثاني، في مركّبات الألفاظ، وهو أن يؤدّى المعنى بأقصر عبارةٍ، وأوجز لفظ، فيفلّ الحزّ ويصيب المفصل.

[وأمّا البلاغة]

فأكثرها في المعنى، وهو أن يكون المتصوّر في الذّهن من المعنى فصيحاً صحيحاً متيناً يعبّر عنه بأصحّ العبارات دلالةً، وأفصحها بياناً، وأجزلها لفظاً. ومن المعلوم الذي لا مرية فيه أنّ الإنسان كما تميّز عن الحيوان والمَلَك بالنطق، قبولاً من الغير، وأداءً إلى الغير؛ فلم يكن لحيوانٍ ما قبول ما في ضمير الغير بواسطة النطق، وأداؤه إلى الغير كذلك؛ ولم يكن لملك ما القبول والأداء إلّا من جهة الفعل والانفعال؛

والتفهّم والإفهام بينهم جاريان على نمط غير النطق واللفظ؛ فاختص الإنسان بالنطق الذي هو فضله الذاتي عمّا فوقه من الملائكة، وعمّا تحته من الحيوانات. ولما كان النطق مطلقاً على معنيين: أحدهما التفكير والتمييز، والثاني التعبير عمّا يفكّر ويميّز؛ وكان الناطقون على ترتب وتفاضلٍ فيهما جميعاً، وينتهي في الارتقاء إلى درجة الاستغناء عن التفكير في قسم التمييز، حتى يصير الغيب له شهادة؛ وما يحصل لغيره بالفكرة حصل له بالفطرة؛ وكذلك في قسم التعبير حتى يصير نطقه كلّه وحياً وما يحصل لغيره بالتعليم حصل له بالبديهة؛ فامتاز نطقه من الوجهين جميعاً (٢٤ب) عن نطق سائر الناطقين كمالاً وشرفاً. وكما صار النطق معجز الإنسان على الحيوان كذلك صار ذلك الكمال فيه معجز النبيّ على الإنسان. وكما اختلفت وجوه الإعجاز في أصل النطق، وإن كان جنسه معجزاً، فالعربية معجزة والعجمية معجزة، كذلك اختلفت وجوه الإعجاز في كمال النطق، وإن كان نوعه معجزاً، فالفصاحة معجزةٌ، والبلاغة معجزة، وكذلك النظم والجزالة، وكذلك الحكم والأمثال والمواعظ والزواجر. فالأَولى أن يقال: القرآن بكليّته معجِزٌ بعبارته ومعناه؛ ولم تقدر العرب على معارضته: ﴿قُلْ لئِنِ اجتَمَعَتِ الإنْسُ وَالجِنُّ على أن يَأْتُوا بِمِثْلِ هذَا القُرْآنِ لَا يَأْتُونَ بِمِثْلِهِ، وَلَو كانَ بَعْضُهُمْ لِبَعْضٍ ظَهِيراً﴾.

ومن تكلّف في طلب الأفصح من كلماته وآياته فقد أزرى بالقرآن، حيث اختار منه كلماتٍ معدودةً، وقصر كمال الفصاحة عليها، وعرّض بأنّ الباقي ليس على رونق ذلك الكمال. وما يدريه لعلّ ما اعتقده فصيحاً هو دون ما زيّفه مردوداً؛ ومن تصدّى للانتقاد فيجب أن يكون له كلامٌ فوق المنقود حتى يصحّ منه الانتقاد.

وإنّ الفصحاء من العرب أخرجوا كلمات القرآن عن جنس كلام البشر، فتارةً وصفوه بالسحر المبين، وتارةً نسبوه إلى الله تعالى. وكذلك

الجنّ حين استمعوا قالوا: ﴿إِنَّا سَمِعْنا قُرآناً عجباً، يَهدي إلى الرُّشْدِ﴾، فوصفوه من حيث اللفظ بالعجب، ووصفوه من حيث المعنى بالهداية والرشد جمعاً بين العبارة والمعنى في الكمال؛ ولأنّ الكمال في الصوت أن يكون كلاماً مفهوماً، والكمال في الكلام أن يكون بالهداية مشعراً، ﴿أَلَمْ يَرَوا أَنَّهُ لا يُكَلِّمُهُمْ وَلَا يَهْدِيهِم سَبِيلاً﴾؛ فلما تعرّى صوت العجل عن الكمالين كان خواراً؛ فمن اعتبر الفصاحة والجزالة والنظم والبلاغة من حيث اللفظ فقد أثبت الكمال الأوّل دون الكمال الثاني؛ ومن اعتبر الهداية والإرشاد والتنبيه على الحقائق والحكم من حيث المعنى مع الكمال الأوّل، فقد استوفى حدّ البلاغ والكمال المعجز: ﴿قُلْ فَأْتُوا بِكِتابٍ مِنْ عِندِ اللهِ هُوَ أَهْدَى مِنْهُمَا﴾.

وقَلَّ ما نجد في القرآن ذكر الشرف والكمال فيه إلّا ويشير إلى الهداية والروح والرّحمة والإنذار والتذكير، قال الله تعالى: ﴿شَهْرُ رَمَضَانَ الَّذِيْ أُنْزِلَ فِيهِ القُرآنُ هُدىً لِلنَّاسِ وَبَيِّنَاتٍ مِن الهُدى وَالفُرْقَان﴾؛ وقال: ﴿وَكَذَلِكَ أَوحَيْنَا إِلَيْكَ رُوحاً من أَمْرِنَا﴾؛ وقال: ﴿وَلَقَد جِئْنَاكُم بِكِتَابٍ فَصَّلْنَاهُ عَلَى عِلْمٍ (٢٥آ) هُدىً وَرَحْمَةً لِقَومٍ يُؤْمِنُونَ﴾؛ وقال: ﴿لِتُنْذِرَ بِهِ وَذِكْرَى لِلمُؤمِنِينَ﴾؛ وقال: ﴿وأَنْذِرْ بِهِ الَّذِينَ يَخَافُونَ﴾.

فكما لاحظنا جانب اللفظ حتى عرفنا بلاغته فوق سائر البلاغات، وجب أن نلاحظ جانب المعنى حتى نعرف هدايته فوق سائر الهدايات.

وكما أنّ النبيّ إنّما تميّز عن البشر بأنّه يوحى إليه أن لا إله إلا الله، وكان نفس دعواه معجزاً، إذ لم ينازعه في تلك الدعوى منازع؛ وإن جحده منكر فالمنكر ليس بمنازع، كذلك القرآن إنما تميّز عن سائر الكلام بأنّه مشتمل على ذلك التوحيد ونفي الأنداد، فلا يعارضه في تلك الخاصيّة معارضٌ؛ وإن أنكره جاحد، فالجاحد ليس بمعارض.

فالنبي والقرآن متصادقان في الشهادة تصادق الحقّ والمحقّ، فيُعرف المحقّ بالحقّ معرفةً مجملةً؛ ويعرف الحقّ بالمحقّ معرفةً مفصّلةً،

كذلك النبيّ يُعرف صدقه بالقرآن، والقرآن يُعرف صدقه بالنبي، فهما يتصادقان ويتشاهدان، فالنبي يشهد للقرآن، والقرآن يشهد للنبيّ صلوات الله عليه وآله.

الفصل الثاني عشر
في شرائط تفسير القرآن

قال الله تعالى: ﴿وأَنْزَلْنَا إِلَيْكَ الذِّكْرَ لِتُبَيِّنَ لِلنَّاسِ ما نُزِّلَ إِلَيْهِم﴾ دلّ الخطاب بنصّه وصريح لفظه على أنه يحتاج إلى مبيّن، إذ لم يقل «لِيَتَبَيَّنَ لِلنَّاسِ»، فليس كل من عرف اللغة ساغ له تفسير القرآن؛ فإنّ العرب كانوا يعرفون لغتهم، فلم يكتف بمعرفتهم لسان العرب، حتى قال: ﴿لِتُبَيِّنَ لِلنَّاسِ مَانُزِّلَ إِلَيْهِمْ وَلَعَلَّهُمْ يَتَفَكَّرُونَ﴾.

ولعمري وجب للمفسّر معرفة صدر صالح من اللغة والنحو والوقوف على مناهج استعاراتهم ومجاري عباراتهم خصوصاً إذا كان أعجمياً. ثم يجب له تتبّع أقوال المفسّرين من الصحابة والتابعين، وأخذها من الرواة المعتبرين، ثم ينبغي له سماع الأخبار، وتعقّب أحوال المحدّثين، خصوصاً ما يتعلق منها بتفسير القرآن، فلا يأخذها إلّا من السُّنن والصحاح المتّفق عليها عند أصحاب الحديث، حتى يبني كلّ ما يفسّره من الكلمات والآيات على روايةٍ صحيحة، وخبر وأثر صحيح، دون أن يتصرّف فيه بالرأي المحض. وقد قال النبي(صلّى الله عليه وآله): «من فسّر القرآن برأيه فإن أصاب فقد أخطأ وإن أخطأ فليبوّأ مقعده من النار».

ومن المفسرين من قال: إنّ كلمات القرآن على أقسام، منها ما لا يمكن تفسيره إلّا بنصّ خبر (٢٥ب) وسماع أثر، مثل بيان المبهمات وتفصيل المجملات، كقوله تعالى: ﴿وأَقِيمُوا الصَّلاةَ وآتُوا الزَّكَوة﴾ فليس

يعرف من حيث اللغة إلّا الدعاء من لفظ الصلاة، والتطهير والتنمية من لفظ الزكاة، وذلك قبل الاتّفاق على أنها صُرّفت عن وضعها الأصلي إلى الوضع الشرعي؛ فحمل اللفظ على الأركان المخصوصة لا يكون إلّا بعد بيان المجمل من شارع الأحكام، وذلك لا يتحقّق إلّا بعد السماع؛ ومن ذلك القبيل الأقسام المذكورة في أوائل السور، مثل: والصافات، والذاريات، والعاديات، إلى أمثالها، لا يجوز حملها على مجرّد ما دلّ اللفظ عليها من معانيها، ولا يجوز حملها على الملائكة أو على أشخاص موصوفين بها إلّا بنصٍ وتوقيف. ومن ذلك القبيل الحروف في أوائل السور على مذهب من فسّرها، فلا يجوز تفسيرها إلّا بخبر أو أثر. وكذلك أسباب النزول، وتخصيص العمومات، وتعميم الخصوصات، وحمل المجملات على المقيّدات، وصرف الألفاظ المشتركة إلى إحدى الجهات، فلا يثبت ذلك كلّه إلّا بالأخبار الصحيحة.

وأما ما يمكن تفسيره فهو ظواهر الكتاب ونصوصه، وما لا يحتمل اللفظ غيره؛ فلو استعمل المفسّر عقله ونظر فيه، علم أنّه ما أخلّ بمعنى اللفظ لغةً، ولا خالف الحسّ والعقل حقيقةً؛ فليس ذلك من جملة تفسير القرآن بالرأي والقياس.

وكذلك تأويل ما يوهم ظاهره التشبيه أو التعطيل أو الجبر أو القدر، فذلك بنظر العقل وقياس اللغة جائز؛ فإنّه يُعْلَمُ قطعاً أنّ التشبيه والتعطيل باطلٌ، ولا يجوز حمل كلمات القرآن على باطلٍ فلا بدّ إذاً من تأويلٍ؛ وشرطه أن لا يعدل عن مقتضى اللغة والعرف فيها، ولا يميل إلى مذهبٍ ومقالة، والتعصب لها، بل يجري على الجادة، ويراعي الوسط، ويتجنّب بنيّات الطرق، ولا يركن إلى تقليد الآباء، ويألف مذاهب تربية الأبناء، ولا يقول ﴿إِنَّا وَجَدْنَا آباءَنَا عَلَى أُمَّةٍ وإِنَّا عَلَى آثَارِهِم مُهْتَدُونَ﴾ أو ﴿مُقْتَدُونَ﴾.

ورعاية هذه الشروط في تفسير الآيات المتشابهة وتأويلها عسرٌ جداً، ولا يكاد يفي بذلك أكثر المفسّرين؛ فإنّك تجد التفاسير كلّها مبنيةً على المذاهب المحلّلة؛ فالقدري يفسّر آيات القدر على ما يوافق مذهبه؛ والأشعري على ما يوافق مذهبه، والمُشَبهي يتمسّك بالظاهر، ويقول: الظاهر معي، والتأويل مظنون، وإني لا أترك ظاهر اللفظ بأمر مظنون، وغايتي أن أقول: لا أعدل عن الظاهر، ولا أعوّل (٢٦آ) على التأويل؛ والمعطِّل يترك الظاهر، ويتأوّل العبادات كلّها على رجالٍ، والمحظورات على رجالٍ، والدين معرفة ذلك الرجل؛ وقد تبرّأ منهم الصادق جعفر بن محمد (عليه السلام). ومن الواقفة من يقول: إني أقف وأُكِل علمه إلى الله، فأقول: كلٌّ من عند الله، وذلك هو طريق السلامة، وهو كما قال بعض السلف في الاستواء على العرش: الاستواء معلومٌ، والكيفية مجهولةٌ، والإيمان به واجبٌ، والسؤال عنه بدعة.

وإنما وقع لهم هذا التحيّر لأنهم لم يأتوا العلم من بابه، ولم يتعلّقوا بذيل أسبابه، فانغلق عليهم الباب، وتقطّعت بهم الأسباب، وذهبت بهم المذاهب حيارى ضالّين؛ ﴿ذلك بِأَنَّهُمْ كَذَّبُوا بِآيَاتِنَا وَكَانُوا عَنْهَا غَافِلِينَ﴾؛ وآيات الله أولياؤه، كما قال الله تعالى: ﴿وجَعَلْنَا ابْنَ مَرْيَمَ وَأُمَّهُ آيَةً﴾؛ وقد قال عزّ من قائل: ﴿وَلَوْ رَدُّوهُ إِلَى الرَّسُولِ وَإِلَى أُولِي الأَمْرِ مِنْهُمْ لَعَلِمَهُ الَّذِينَ يَسْتَنْبِطُونَهُ مِنْهُمْ﴾؛ ولا كلّ مستنبِطٍ مصيب، وإلّا لبطل فائدة «منهم» و«منهم».

وأذكر الخبر عن النبي(صلّى الله عليه وآله): «عليٌّ منّي وأنا مِنه».
وقال حين نزلت سورة براءة: «يُبَلِّغُها رَجُلٌ مِنْك».
وعن عبد الله بن مسعود (رضي الله عنه): «إن القرآن أُنزِل على سبعة أحرف، ما منها حرفٌ إلا له ظهرٌ وبطنٌ، فإنّ عليّاً عنده منه علم الظاهر والباطنّ».
وقد قال علي (رضي الله عنه): «والله ما نزلت آيةٌ إلّا وقد علمتُ

فيم أنزلت وأين أنزلت، إنّ ربّي وهب لي قلباً عقولاً، ولساناً سؤولاً».

وروي أنّ سدير الصيرفي سأل جعفر بن محمد الصادق (عليه السلام) فقال: جعلت فداك، إنّ شيعتكم اختلفت فيكم، فأكثرت حتى قال بعضهم: إن الإمام يُنكت في أذنه، وقال آخرون يوحى إليه، وقال آخرون: يقذف في قلبه، وقال آخرون يُرى في منامه، وقال آخرون إنما يفتي بكتب آبائه؛ فبأيّ جوابهم آخذ جعلني الله فداك؟ قال: «لا تأخذ بشيءٍ مما يقولون يا سُدير، نحن حجة الله وأمناؤه على خلقه، حلالنا من كتاب الله، وحرامنا منه».

وروي أن الفيض بن المختار دخل على جعفر بن محمد (عليه السلام) فقال: جعلت فداك، ما هذا الاختلاف الذي بين شيعتك، فإني ربما أجلس في حلقتهم بالكوفة فأكاد أن أشك، فأرجع إلى المفضَّل فأجد عنده ما أسكن إليه. فقال أبو عبد الله: (٢٦ب) «أجل إنّ الناس أُغروا بالكذب علينا حتى كأن الله عزّ وجلّ فرضه عليهم، لا يريد منهم غيره، وإني لأُحدّث أحدهم الحديث فلا يخرج من عندي حتّى يناوله على غير تأويله».

وقد كُتِبَ إليه أن قوماً من شيعته قالوا: إنّ الصلاة رجلٌ، والصوم رجلٌ، والزكاة رجلٌ، والحج رجلٌ، فمن عرف ذلك الرجل فقد صلّى وصام وزكّى وحجّ، وكذلك تأوّلوا المحارم على أشخاص، فقال: «من كان يدين الله بهذه الصِّفة التي سألت عنها فهو عندي مشركٌ بيّن الشّرك. واعلم أن هؤلاء القوم قومٌ سمعوا ما لم يقفوا على حقيقته، ولم يعرفوا حدوده فوضعوا حدود تلك الأشياء مقايسةً برأيهم، ومنتهى عقولهم، لم يضعوها على حدود ما أُمروا به تكذيباً وافتراءً على الله وعلى رسوله، وجرأة على المعاصي، والله تعالى لم يبعث نبياً يدعو إلى معرفةٍ ليس فيها طاعة، وإنما يقبل الله عزّ وجلّ العمل من العباد بالفرائض التي فرضها عليهم بعد معرفة من جاء بها من عنده. فأوّل

ذلك معرفة من دعا إليه، وهو الله الذي لا إله إلّا هو، وتوحيده، والإقرار بربوبيّته ومعرفة الرسول الذي بلّغ عنه، وقبول ما جاء به، ثم معرفة الأئمة بعد الرسل الذين افترض طاعتهم في كلّ عصر وزمانٍ على أهله، ثم العمل بما افترض الله عزّ وجلّ على العباد من الطاعات ظاهراً وباطناً، واجتناب ما حرّم الله عزّ وجلّ عليهم تحريماً ظاهراً وباطناً، وإنما حرّم الظاهر بالباطن، والباطن بالظاهر معاً جميعاً، والأصل والفرع كذلك».

ورُوي عن عليّ (رضي الله عنه) أنه ذُكِرَ القرآنُ فقال: «ظاهره عملٌ موجوبٌ، وباطنه علم مكتومٌ محجوب».

وعن جعفر بن محمد (عليه السلام): أن رجلاً سأله فقال: من عندنا يقولون في قوله تعالى: ﴿فاسْأَلُوا أَهْلَ الذِّكْرِ إنْ كُنْتُمْ لَا تَعْلَمُونَ﴾: إنّ الذكر هو التوراة، وأهل الذكر هم: علماء اليهود: فقال: «إذاً واللهِ يَدعُوننا إلى دينِهِم، بل نَحنُ واللهِ أهلُ الذكر الذين أمر الله تعالى بردّ المسألةِ إلَيْنا»، وكذلك نُقِلَ عن عليّ (رضي الله عنه) أنه قال: «نحن أهل الذّكر».

وروي أنّ أبا ذرّ الغفاري (رضي الله عنه) شهد الموسم بعد وفاة رسول الله فلمّا احتفل الناس في الطواف وقف بباب الكعبة وأخذ بحلقة الباب ونادى: أيّها الناس ثلاثاً. فاجتمعوا وأنصتوا، ثم قال: «مَن عرفني فقد عرفني (٢٦آ)، ومن لم يعرفني فأنا أبو ذرّ الغفاريّ أحدّثكم بما سمعته من رسول الله سمعته حين احتضر يقول: إنِّي تارِكٌ فِيكُم الثَّقلَين كتاب الله وعترتي، وإنهما لم يفترقا حتى يردا عليّ الحوض كهاتين، وجمع بين إصبعيه المسبّحتين من يديه، وقرنهما وساوى بينهما، ولا أقول كهاتين، وقرن بين إصبعه الوسطى والمسبّحة من يده اليمنى، لأنّ إحداهما تسبق الأخرى. ألا وإنّ مثلهما فيكم مثل سفينة نوحٍ. من ركبها نجا ومن تركها غرق».

وقد قال علي (رضي الله عنه): «سلوني قبل أن تفقدوني، فما أحدٌ

أعرف بما في اللوحين منّي». وقال: «لو ثنيت لي وسادة وجلست عليها لحكمت لأهل التوراة بتوراتهم، ولأهل الإنجيل بإنجيلهم، ولأهل القرآن بقرآنهم». وقال (عليه السلام): «ما من آيةٍ إلّا ولها أربعة معانٍ ظاهرٌ وباطنٌ وحدٌّ ومطلعٌ. فالظاهر للتلاوة، والباطن للفهم. والحدّ هو أحكام الحلال والحرام، والمطلع مراد الله من العبيد بها».

وقال جعفر بن محمد (عليه السلام): «كتاب الله على أربعة أشياء: العبارة والإشارة واللطائف والحقائق».

وقال عبد الله بن مسعود: «أُنزل القرآن على سبعة أحرفٍ، لكلِّ آيةٍ منها ظهرٌ وبطنٌ ولكلّ حرفٍ منها حدٌّ ومطلع».

تفسير سورة الفاتحة

ذكر فضائل سورة الفاتحة

بسم الله الرحمن الرحيم

ذكر الإمام أبو عبد الله محمد بن إسماعيل البخاري في الجامع الصحيح بإسناده عن أبي سعيد بن المعلّى قال:

كنت أصلّي في المسجد فدعاني النبيّ فلم أجبه، فقلت: يا رسول الله كنت أصلّي. قال: «ألم يقل الله عزّ وجلّ: ﴿اسْتَجِيبُوا لِلّهِ وِللرَّسُولِ إِذَا دَعَاكُمْ لِمَا يُحْيِيكُمْ﴾؟!» ثمّ قال لي: «لأُعلمنّك سورةً هي أعظم السور في القرآن قبل أن تخرج من المسجد». ثم أخذ بيدي، فلما أراد الخروج، قلت: ألم تقل يا رسول الله لأُعلمنّك سورةً هي أعظم سور القرآن؟! قال: «الحمد لله رب العالمين هي السبع المثاني والقرآن العظيم الذي أوتيته».

وروى أُبيّ بن كعب عن النبي أنه قال:

«ألا أعلّمك سورةً ما نزلت في التوراة ولا في الإنجيل ولا في الزّبور ولا في الفرقان مثلها؟» قلت: بلى يا رسول الله. قال: «ما تقرأ في الصلاة إذا قمت لها؟» قلت: فاتحة الكتاب. فقال: «هي هي، وهي السبع المثاني التي قال الله عزّ وجلّ: ﴿ولَقَدْ آتَيْنَاكَ سَبْعاً مِنَ المَثَانِيْ والقُرآنَ العَظِيمَ﴾».

وعن أبي هريرة (رضي الله عنه) عن النبيّ قال الحمد لله ربّ العالمين سبع آياتٍ إحداهنّ ﴿بسم الله الرحمن الرحيم﴾ هي السبع المثاني، وهي أمّ القرآن وهي فاتحة الكتاب.

وروى عبد خيرٍ عن علي وسعيد بن جبير عن ابن عباس (رضي الله

عنه) والربيع بن أنس عن أبي العالية أنهم قالوا في قوله تعالى: ﴿آتَيْنَاكَ سَبْعاً مِنَ المَثَانِي﴾ هو فاتحةُ الكتاب. وهم عن أبي هريرة عن النبي قال:

«قال الله عزَّ وجلَّ: قسمتُ الصلاةَ بيني وبين عبدي نصفين: فنصفها له، يقول عبدي إذا افتتح الصلاة ﴿بِسْمِ اللّٰهِ الرَّحْمَنِ الرَّحِيمِ﴾، فيذكرني عبدي. ثم يقول ﴿الحَمْدُ لِلّٰهِ رَبِّ العَالَمِينَ﴾ فأقول: حمدني عبدي، ثم يقول: ﴿الرَّحْمٰنِ الرَّحِيمِ﴾ فأقول: أثنى عَلَيَّ عبدي، ثم يقول ﴿مَالِكِ يَوْمِ الدِّينِ﴾، فأقول: مَجَّدني عبدي. ثم يقول ﴿إِيَّاكَ نَعْبُدُ وَإِيَّاكَ نَسْتَعِينُ﴾. فهذه الآية بيني وبين عبدي نصفين. وآخر السورة لعبدي، ولعبدي ما سأل».

وعن أبي سعيد الخدري قال:

نزلنا منزلاً فجاءتنا جاريةٌ وقالت: إنَّ نفرنا غُيِّب وإن سيِّد الحيّ سليمٌ، فهل في القوم من راقٍ؟ فقام رجل فقال: نعم، وما كنا نأْبُنُه لِرُقْيَةٍ، ولا نراه يحسنها فذهب فرقاه، فأمر له بثلاثين شاةً (٢٨آ)، وأحسب أنه قال وسقانا لبناً قال فلما جاء قلنا: ما كنّا نراك تحسن رقيةً! قال: ولا أحسنها، إنما رقيته بفاتحة الكتاب. قال: فلما قدمنا المدينة قلت: لا تحدّثوا شيئاً، حتى آتي رسول الله فأذكر ذلك له، فأتيته فذكرت ذلك له، فقال: «ما كان يدريك أنّها رقيةٌ؟! اقتسموها واضربوا بسهمي معكم».

ذكر أسماء سورة الفاتحة

تسمّى السورة: فاتحة الكتاب، وأمّ الكتاب والسبع المثاني. قال أهل التفسير: إنّما سمّيت فاتحة الكتاب لأنّه يفتتح بها القرآن والصلاة، وسمّيت أمّ القرآن لأنها تؤمّ القرآن وتتقدّمه، أو لأنّها أصل القرآن. وأمّ

الشيء أصله. ولما كانت الفاتحة مشتملةً على معانٍ هي أصول الكتاب سمّيت أمّ القرآن. وقالوا: إنّما سمّيت السبع المثاني لأنّها سبع آياتٍ نزلت مرّتين: مرّة بمكة، ومرّة بالمدينة. أو لأنها تثنّى في الصلاة قراءةً، والمكرّرات فيها مثاني، مثل:«الرحمن الرحيم» و«إياك وإياك»، و«الصراط والصراط». وقيل: إنّما سميت مثاني لأنها استُثْنِيَت لهذه الأمة، فلم تخرج لأحدٍ من الأمم إلّا لهذه الأمّة. وقال أبو معاذ: ثنيت لك من المال بمعنى: استَثْنَيتُ. وروى سعيد بن جبير عن ابن عباس أنه قال: استثناها لهذه الأمّة حتّى أخرجها لهم. وقيل إنّ المثاني هي القرآن لأنه ثُنيت فيه القصص والأخبار والأمر والنهي وكُرِّرَ فيه الأمثال والمواعظ. ويقال: ثني الشيء: عطفه، ومثانيه: معاطفه. وفي السورة مثاني ومعاطف وأزواجٌ من الألفاظ والكلمات، كما سيأتي من أسرار الآيات.

ذكر نزول سورة الفاتحة

قال الأكثرون من أهل التفسير: إنها نزلت بمكة. وهو قول عليّ وقتادة والواقديّ، ورواية أبي صالح عن ابن عباس، وقول أُبيّ بن كعب. ويدلّ على ذلك إجماع الأمّة على أنّ سورة الحجر مكيّة، وفيها قوله تعالى: ﴿وَلَقَدْ آتَينَاكَ سَبْعاً مِنَ المَثَانِي﴾ وقال أبو ميسرة: إن أول ما أقرأ (٢٨ب) جبريل النبيّ (صلّى الله عليهما) سورة فاتحة الكتاب. وقال قائلون: إنها نزلت بالمدينة، وهو رواية منصور عن مجاهد، وقول الزهري ومقاتل وعطاء الخراساني وغيرهم. والأَولى أن يجمع بين الروايتين فيقال: إنها نزلت مرّتين: مرّة بمكة ومرّة بالمدينة.

ذكر عدد آياتها والتسمية

روى أبو سعيد المقبري عن أبي هريرة (رضي الله عنه) عن النبي أنه قال: «الحمد لله ربّ العالمين» سبع آياتٍ، إحداهنّ: ﴿بِسْمِ اللّهِ الرَّحْمَنِ الرَّحِيمِ﴾. وروى ابن أبي مليكة عن أمّ سلمة قالت: كان رسول الله يقول: ﴿بِسْمِ اللّهِ الرَّحْمَنِ الرَّحِيمِ، الحَمْدُ لِلّهِ رَبِّ العَالَمِينَ﴾ إلى آخره. قطّعها آية آية وعدّها سبع آياتٍ فعدّ ﴿بِسْمِ اللّهِ الرَّحْمَنِ الرَّحِيمِ﴾ آيةً ولم يَعُدَّ ﴿عَلَيْهِمْ﴾.

وروى أبو روق عن الضحاك عن ابن عباس (رضي الله عنه) قال: أول ما نزل جبريل على محمد (صلوات الله عليهما)، قال: يا محمد! استعذ بالسميع العليم من الشيطان الرجيم. ثم قال: قل بسم الله الرحمن الرحيم.

وفي حديث أبي اسحق السبيعي عن عمرو بن شرحبيل قال: إن رسول الله في بدءِ الوحي أسرّ إلى خديجة وقال: لقد خشيت أن يكون خالطني شيء، فقالت: وما ذاك؟ قال: إنّي إذا خلوت سمعت النداء، فأفرّ. فأخبرتْ أبا بكر، فانطلق به أبو بكر إلى ورقة بن نوفل، وقصّ له القصة، فقال له ورقة: إذا أتاك فاثبت له. فأتاه جبريل فقال له: قل ﴿بِسْمِ اللَّهِ الرَّحْمَنِ الرَّحِيمِ، الحَمْدُ لِلَّهِ رَبِّ العَالَمِينَ﴾.

وقال قائلون: إنّ أوّل ما نزل صدر سورة ﴿إقْرَأْ بِاسْمِ رَبِّكَ﴾ ثم نزل بعد ذلك أمّ القرآن.

وروى سعيد بن جبير عن ابن عباس: ﴿ولقد آتَيْنَاكَ سَبْعاً مِنَ المَثَانِي﴾، قال: فاتحة الكتاب. ثم قال: ﴿بِسْمِ اللّهِ الرَّحْمَنِ الرَّحِيمِ﴾ الآية السابعة.

واتّفقت الأمّة على أنّ الفاتحة سبع آياتٍ، إلّا أنّهم اختلفوا في أنّ التسمية هي الآية الأولى منها أم ﴿أَنْعَمْتَ عَلَيْهِمْ﴾ هي السادسة منها.

فقال علماء المدينة والبصرة والكوفة مثل مالك بن أنس، والأوزاعي، وأبي حنيفة وأصحابه: إنها ليست من الفاتحة آيةً، ولا من كلّ سورةٍ إلّا في سورة النّمل. وإنما هي فاصلةٌ بين سورةٍ وسورة، يُبتدأ بها تيمّناً وتبرّكاً باسم الله عزّ وجلّ.

وقال علماء الحجاز وغيرهم مثل: الشافعي وسفيان الثوري وعبد الله بن المبارك (رضي الله عنهم) إنها هي الآية الأولى من فاتحة الكتاب (٢٩آ) قطعاً، وأكثرهم على أنّها آية من كل سورة إلّا التوبة، ولكنّ العدّادين قد عدّوها آيةً من الفاتحة، ولم يعدّوها آيةً من كلّ سورة لما روي عن النبي أنه قال: «في القرآن سورةٌ تُجادِل عن ربّها، وهي ثلاثون آيةً، وهي سورة الملك»، قالوا: فهي ثلاثون آيةً دون التسمية.

وقد أورد مسلم بن الحجاج في صحيحه بإسناده عن النبي أنه قال: «قد أنزلت عليّ سورة من شأنها كذا وكذا وهي: ﴿بِسْمِ اللّٰهِ الرَّحْمَنِ الرَّحِيمِ، إنَّا أَعْطَيْنَاكَ الكَوْثَر﴾ إلى آخرها».

ورُوي عن عليّ بن أبي طالب (رضي الله عنه) أنه كان إذا افتتح السورة في الصلاة يقرأ: بِسْمِ اللّٰهِ الرَّحْمَنِ الرَّحِيمِ. وروي أنه كان يجهر بها في الفاتحة حتى في الظهر والعصر.

وروى ابن بُريدة عن أبيه قال: قال رسول الله: «ألا أخبرك بآيةٍ لم تنزل على أحدٍ بعد سليمان غيري؟» فقلت: بلى. قال: «بأيّ شيٍ تفتتح القرآن إذا افتتحت الصلاة؟» قلت: ببسم الله الرحمن الرحيم. قال: «هي هي».

وروى جابر بن عبد الله عن رسول الله قال له: «كيف تقول إذا قمت إلى الصلاة؟» قال: أقول: ﴿الحَمْدُ لِلّٰهِ رَبِّ العَالَمِينَ﴾. قال: «قل: ﴿بِسْمِ اللّٰهِ الرَّحْمَنِ الرَّحِيمِ﴾».

وعن أبي هريرة (رضي الله عنه) أنّ رجلاً افتتح الصلاة بالحمد لله. فقال رسول الله (صلّى الله عليه وآله): «يا رجل! أما علمت أنّ ﴿بِسْمِ

اللَّهِ الرَّحْمَنِ الرَّحِيمِ﴾ من الحمد، فمن تركها فقد ترك آيةً من الحمد؟!»

ونحوه قال طلحة بن عبيد الله أنّ رسول الله قال: «من ترك ﴿بِسْمِ اللَّهِ الرَّحْمَنِ الرَّحِيمِ﴾ فقد ترك آيةً من كتاب الله».

وقال علي بن الحسين بن شقيق: سمعت عبد الله بن المبارك (رضي الله عنهما) يقول: مَنْ ترك قراءة التسمية فقد ترك مائةً وثلاث عشرة آية من القرآن.

وعن سعيد بن جبير عن ابن عباس (رضي الله عنه) قال: كان رسول الله (صلّى الله عليه وآله) لا يعرف ختم السورة حتى تنزل عليه ﴿بِسْمِ اللَّهِ الرَّحْمَنِ الرَّحِيمِ﴾.

وعن عبد الله بن مسعود قال: ما كنا نعلم فصل ما بين السورتين حتى تنزل ﴿بِسْمِ اللَّهِ الرَّحْمَنِ الرَّحِيمِ﴾.

وكان سعيد بن جبير وابن عباس يجهران بالتسمية في كلّ ركعة.

وقال الأزرق بن قيس: صلّيت مع ابن الزبير فقرأ: ﴿بِسْمِ اللَّهِ الرَّحْمَنِ الرَّحِيمِ﴾. وقال: ﴿غَيْرِ المَغْضُوبِ عَلَيْهِمْ وَلَا الضَّالِّينَ﴾. ثم قال: ﴿بِسْمِ اللَّهِ الرَّحْمَنِ الرَّحِيمِ﴾.

وأهل الحرمين يفصلون بين كل سورتين (٢٩ب) ببسم الله الرحمن الرحيم. وعن الحسن بن مجاهد عن أهل المدينة ما كنّا نجهر الاستعاذة ولا نخفي البتة، بل كنّا نقرأ بسم الله الرحمن الرحيم في أوّل الفاتحة وأوّل سورة البقرة، وبين السورتين وإذا افتتحنا من بعض السورة. وكان عاصم يوافق أهل المدينة.

وأما أهل البصرة وحمزة فيصلون آخر السورة بالسورة التي تليها ويتركون التسمية، وهي رواية الفراء عن الكسائي، إلّا في أوّل فاتحة الكتاب فإنّه جهر بها. وظاهر مذهب الكسائي أنه كان يفصل بين السورتين بالتسمية، وكذلك إذا ابتدأ من بعض السورة. وعن أبي عمرو مثل ذلك، ولم يأت عن ابن عامر في ذلك شيء.

وقال خلف: كنّا نقرأ على سليم فنخفي التعوّذ والتسمية في سائر القرآن. وقال: هكذا كان يقرأ على حمزة.

وعن سعيد بن جبير: أن الصحابة لا يعرفون انتهاء السورة حتى تنزل بسم الله الرحمن الرحيم. فإذا نزلت علموا أنّ السورة انقضت ونزلت سورة أخرى.

وعن الصادق (عليه السلام): من دعا ببسم الله الرحمن الرحيم كان أقرب إلى اسم الله الأعظم من سواد العين إلى بياضها. وعنه في تفسير العياشي: بسم الله الرحمن الرحيم اسم الله الأكبر الأعظم. وعنه في كتاب الكليني، قال: «يا مُفضّل! إحتجز من الناس كلهم ببسم الله الرحمن الرحيم، وبقل هو الله أحد، إقرأها عن يمينك وشمالك، ومن بين يديك ومن خلفك، ومن فوقك ومن تحتك، وإذا دخلتَ على سلطانٍ جائرٍ فاقرأها حين تنظر إليه ثلاث مراتٍ، واعقد بيدك اليسرى ثمّ لا تفارقها حتى تخرج من عنده».

وعن جابر بن عبد الله قال: قال رسول الله: «كيف تقرأ إذا قمت في الصلاة؟» قال: قلت ﴿الحَمْدُ لِلَّهِ رَبِّ العَالَمِينَ﴾ قال: «قل ﴿بِسْمِ اللَّهِ الرَّحْمَنِ الرَّحِيمِ، الحَمْدُ لِلَّهِ رَبِّ العَالَمِينَ﴾».

وفي الصحيح من أخبار أهل البيت عليهم السلام أن رسول الله والأئمة من ولده عليهم السلام كانوا يجهرون ببسم الله فيما يُجهر به من الصلوات في أوّل فاتحة الكتاب وأوّل السور في كلّ ركعةٍ ويخافتون فيها فيما يُخَافَت من السور. وقالوا: اجتمعنا ولد فاطمة على ذلك.

وعن الصادق (عليه السلام): التقية ديني ودين آبائي إلّا في ثلاثٍ: شرب المسكر والمسح على الخفين وترك الجهر ببسم الله الرحمن الرحيم. (٣٠آ) وعن سعيد بن جبير أنه كان يفعل كذلك يفتتح بها ويختتم بها.

وروي أنّ معاوية بن أبي سفيان قدم المدينة فصلّى بالناس صلاة

يجهر فيها، وقرأ فاتحة الكتاب وترك التسمية. فلما قضى صلاته ناداه كلّ من في المسجد من المهاجرين والأنصار من كلّ ناحيةٍ: يا معاوية أسرقت الصلاة أم نسيت؟ فصلّى بهم صلاة أخرى فقرأ فيها للسورة التي بعدها يعني في آخرها لا في أوّلها.

وفي بعض الروايات أن بسم الله الرحمن الرحيم كانت آية من القرآن سرقها الشيطان.

فمن قال إنها آية من كل سورةٍ قد أُنزلت معها استدل بأنها لو كانت فاصلةً بين سورةٍ وسورة لكُتِبَت بين سورتي الأنفال والتوبة. ولو كانت للافتتاح في كلّ سورة لكُتِبت في أوّل سورة التوبة، ولو كانت للاغتنام لكتبت بغير السواد كأسامي السور وعدد الآيات، لا على منهاج كتبة الآيات، فَعُلِم أنّها منزّلة في كلّ سورة، ويقطع يقيناً أنها من الفاتحة باستفاضة الأخبار، وبما نذكره عند ذكر الأسرار.

تفسير آية التسمية

قوله تعالى: بِسْمِ اللّٰهِ الرَّحْمَنِ الرَّحِيمِ

[الباء]

اللغة

تكلّم أهل التفسير في باء «بسم الله»: ما وجه الافتتاح بها، ولِمَ كُتِبَت طويلة، ولِمَ حُذِفت الألف عنها. فقالوا: فيه إضمار واختصار، فتقديره: أفتتح القراءة باسم الله، أو افتتحت، أو افتتحوا القراءة، أو بدأت، والحال تبين أنك مبتدئ فاستُغني عن ذكره. وقد يكون المُضمَر متأخّراً عن الكلمة وتقديره بسم الله أفتَتِحُ القراءة، وهو قول ثعلب. وكذلك المعنى في كلّ ما افتتح الناس فعلهم من قيام وقعود وأكل وشرب. وربّما يظهر خبر المضمر، كما قال جلّ وعزّ: ﴿بِسْمِ اللَّهِ مَجْرِيهَا وَمَرْسِيهَا﴾، وقال: ﴿إِقْرَأْ بِاسْمِ رَبِّكَ﴾ ففي ذلك دليل على أنّ خبرها مضمرٌ، إذا لم

يُذكر، إما مقدّماً عليه، وإما مؤخراً (٣٠ب) عنه، وإنّ معناه أبتدئ بهذا الأمر بسم الله تيمناً وتبرّكاً.

النحو

وأهل النحو من البصريين يسمّونها حرف الإلصاق، كما يقال: كتبتُ بالقلم، وقطعتُ بالسكين ومعناه أن الباء تلصق الأفعال بالأسماء. وهي من الحروف الجارّة.

التفسير

ولقول القائل افتتحت هذا باسم الله وجهان: أحدهما، أنّ معناه: أفتَتِحه باسم الله تبرّكاً به، وتيمناً بذكره، واستنجاحاً للطلبة، وتيسيراً للخير، وتوجّهاً إلى حسن العاقبة، وكأنه قال: افتَتِحته بذكره تبرّكاً باسمه حتّى يتمّ الأمر ولا يتبتّر.

والوجه الثاني: أنّ معناه: بالله أفتتح، وبالله أفعل ما عزمت عليه، والاسم صلةٌ على هذا الوجه. وقد أجاز أهل اللغة هذا المعنى فيقال: فعلت هذا لوجهك. ولولا مكانك ما أقمت هاهنا، ولولا ظلّ فلانٍ أصابني كذا. فالوجه والمكان والظلّ زيادات في الكلام للتفخيم. وهو قول أبي عبيدة، واحتج بقول لبيد:

إلى الحول ثمّ اسم السلام عليكما
ومن يبك حولاً كاملاً فقد اعتذر

أي: ثم السلام عليكما.

وقيل على هذا الوجه إنما دخل الاسم فيه ليكون فرقاً بين اليمين والتيمّن.

وإذا قلنا إنّ الاسم صلةٌ فهو بمعنى المسمّى، وعلى الوجه الأوّل هو بمعنى التسمية. ويجوز أن يكون بمعنى المسمّى أيضاً بإضمار فعلٍ، والمعنى: بحول الله وقوّته وتيسيره أبتدئ.

الكتابة

وأما تطويل الباء، وقد شبّهت بالألف لأمرين: أحدهما – إنهم لم يريدوا افتتاح كلام الله وكتابه إلا بحرف مفخّم ومطوّل للعينين. والثاني - إنهم لما أسقطوا الألف من الكلمة ردّوا طول الألف إلى الباء، وإنما حذفوا الألف من الاسم لكثرة استعمالها طلباً للخفّة، ولمّا لم يكن أمثالها كثيرة الاستعمال أثبتوا الألف فيها. وقيل إنّما طوّلت الباء لئلّا تشتبه بالسين.

[الاسم]

الاشتقاق

وفي اشتقاق الاسم قولان: أحدهما، وهو قول البصريّين، أنه من السموّ، ومعناه أنه يسمو على المعنى، ويُظهر المعنى. وتصغيره سمّي. والثاني، أنه من السمة وهي العلامة، لأنه ينزل على المسمّى. والقول الأول أصحّ، لأنه لو كان مشتقاً من الوسم لقيل في تصغيره وُسَيم، كما قالوا: وعدٌ ووُعَيد ووصلٌ ووُصَيل.

وروى أبو سعيد الخدري عن النبي (٣١آ): «إن عيسى بن مريم (عليهما السلام) أسلمته أمّه إلى المعلّم، فقال له المعلّم: قل بسم الله. قال له عيسى: وما اسم؟ (أي وما: باء، سين، ميم) قال: لا أدري، قال عيسى (عليه السلام): الباء بهاء الله، والسين سناه، والميم ملكه».

والقول في أسرار الحروف ومعانيها إنما [هو] تسليمٌ للأنبياء والأصفياء عليهم السلام، وتقصر عن الوقوف عليها عقول غيرهم.

القول في اسم الله وتفسيره

قال جماعة من علماء البصرة وغيرهم: إن أصل الكلمة إله، فأُدخِلت اللام، وفُتِحت الألف تفخيماً وتعظيماً، فصار الألاه، فحذفت الهمزة الأصلية تخفيفاً لكثرته في الكلام فصار ألّلاه؛ فأدغمت إحدى اللامين

في الأخرى وقالوا: الله. وهذا أحد قولي سيبويه، وقد حكاه أبو العباس أحمد بن يحيى عن الخليل.

وقال علماء الكوفة: أصلها لاه، فزيد في الكلمة الألف واللام فقالوا: الله، وهذا اختيار المبرّد والزجّاج. والقولان ذكرهما سيبويه.

قال أبو نصر إسماعيل بن حماد الجوهري صاحب كتاب الصحاح: أصل الكلمة: إلاهٌ على فعالٍ بمعنى مفعول، لأنه مألوهٌ بمعنى معبود، كقولنا: إمام بمعنى مفعول لأنه مؤتمّ به. قال: وهو مشتق من قولهم: أله بالفتح، إلاهة، أي عبد عبادة. ومنه قول ابن عباس: ﴿وَيَذَرَكَ وإلهَتَكَ﴾، أي عبادتك. قال: وجوّز سيبويه أن يكون أصلها لاه أُدخلت عليه الألف واللام فجرى مجرى اسم العلم كالعباس والحسن إلّا أنّه يخالف الأعلام من حيث كان صفة.

الأسرار

قال المعظّمون لأسماء الله: إن جعلت اسم الله من أسماء الأعلام، ولم تذهب إلى أنه مشتقٌ، وكيف اشتقاقه، فلا تغفل من سرٍّ في تركيب حروفه، وأنّ أصل الكلمة وبناءها من الألف واللام والهاء. وقد قيل في وضع اللغة: الألف للتعريف، واللام للتمليك، والهاء للشيئية. وقيل في وضع الحكمة: إنه لا يدرك من جلال الله تعالى إلا هويته فقط. فهو هو، وفي الدعوات: «يا مَنْ هُوَ هُوَ». والأصل فيه الهاء فقط، إلا أنها إذا حُرّكت بأقوى الحركات، وهو الرفع، حركت بقرينتها وهي الواو، ثم وصل بالهاء لام التمليك حتى صار له كلّ شيءٍ خلقاً وأمراً، ومِلكاً ومُلكاً. فهو من حيث هُوَ هُوَ لا يُدرَك، وهو من حيث له كلّ شيء لا ينكر. فذاك جلاله وهذا إكرامه.

ثم وصل باللام الألف تعريفاً فهو أعرف من كلّ شيء، وأظهر من كلّ ظاهر، وأخفى من كلّ باطن. كما قال عليّ (رضي الله عنه): «إن

الله تعالى أعزّ من أن يُرى، وأظهر من أن يخفى» (٣١ب) فدلّت الحروف التي هي بناء الكلمة على ما كُلِّف بمعرفته وعُرِّف بتكليفه، وليس ولا واحدٌ من أسماء الموجودات ما يدلّ حرفٌ منه على جزءٍ من المسمّى وعلى صفته سوى هذا الاسم الأعلى. فإنّ كلّ حرفٍ منه يدلّ على مدلولٍ خاص، ومجموعها يدلّ على كلّ المعرفة.

ولا مخطى لعقول العقلاء دون هذه المعاني، فإنّ من تخطّى عنه وقع في دُرْدُورِ الحيرة، ولم يرجع عنه إلّا بالحسرة. ولذلك لمّا تخطّى قومٌ من لفظ «هو» قرنوا به «ما هو» فطلبوا الماهية، ثم تخطّوا إلى الكمية فقالوا: «كم هو» ثم تخطّوا إلى الكيفيّة فقالوا: «كيف هو»، فوقعوا في الشرك والإثنينيّة والتثليث والتشبيه والتعطيل، وضلّوا عن قصد السبيل.

والأنبياء (عليهم السلام) قرّروا التوجيه في مثل معاني أسماء سورة الإخلاص، حيث ابتدأ التوحيد بهو وزاد عليه: «اللّه» الأحد الصمد. فاسم الله يعطي معنى أُلوهِيَّتِهِ بنفي الماهية. والأحد يعطي معنى التوحيد بنفي الكمية، والصمد يعطي معنى التمجيد بنفي الكيفية. وكل ما يقترن بهو من «ما» و«كم» و«كيف» فهو منزّه عن ذلك. وكلّ ما يقترن بالهاء من الله من لام المُلك والمِلك وألف الأمر والكلمة فهو منعوتٌ بذلك.

ومن العجب أنّ اللام في الكتابة مكرّرة والألف القول مكررةٌ وليس يخرج الاسم عن الحروف الأربعة في اللسان والقلم.

وقد قيل إنه يُستدل بالحروف الأربعة على المبادئ الأربعة التي هي أصول الموجودات، وبها حصلت الكائنات، وكأنّ تلك المبادئ حصلت بهذه الحروف العلوية. والموجودات حصلت بتلك المبادئ العقلية، فيكون سبب وجود الموجودات اسمه تعالى «اللّه»، ولا يسمّى به غيره.

وعلى الحروف الأربعة ترتيب المراتب الأربعة في قوله تعالى: ﴿سَبِّحْ

اسْمَ رَبِّكَ الأَعْلَى، الَّذِيْ خَلَقَ فَسَوَّى، وَالَّذِيْ قَدَّرَ فَهَدَى﴾ ونسبة التسوية إلى الخلق كنسبة الهداية إلى التقدير، وحيثما كان خلقٌ فتعقبه تسوية، حتى يحصل الاعتدال؛ وحيثما كان تقدير فيعقبه بهدايةٍ حتى يحصل الكمال. فالخلق حصل بألف الأمر، والتسوية حصلت باللام الأولى، والتقدير حصل باللام الأخرى، والهداية حصلت بالهاء الخاتمة. وهو الاسم الأعلى، وجب تسبيحه وتحميده وتكبيره. وهو أوّل اسم جرى به القلم. وفي الخبر: أوّل ما كتب الله تعالى بالقلم «إني أنا اللّه لا إله إلّا أنا».

وهو المكتوب (٣٢آ) على ساق العرش. ومن حروفه الثلاثة حصل الجسم الأول ذو الطول كالألف، والعرض كاللام والعمق كالهاء. ومنها تركيب كلمة الشهادة: لا إله إلّا اللَّه.

الوضع

وقال بعض العلماء: إنّ هذا الاسم ليس بمشتقٍ، وإنه تفرّد به الباري تعالى، يجري في وصفه مجرى الأسماء الأعلام، لا يشركه فيه أحد. قال تعالى: ﴿هَلْ تَعلَمُ لَهُ سَمِيّاً﴾ أي هل تعلم أحداً يسمّى الله غيره. ويحكى هذا القول عن الخليل بن أحمد وابن كيسان، وهو اختيار أبي بكر القفال الشاشي. وهو اسم موضوع للتعظيم، وكانت عادة العرب تسمية ما يعظّمونه إلهاً، ولذلك كانوا يسمّون الأصنام التي كانوا يعبدونها آلهة.

وكذلك عادة العجم يسمّون المعظَّم من ملوكهم بالاسم الذي هو ترجمة اسم «الإله» فيقولون: «خداوند» و«خدايكان». فهذا الاسم يدلّ على مسمّى موصوفٍ بصفات الجلال والعظمة. وهو له (جلّ ثناؤه) اسم علم يبتدأ بذكره، ثم يتبع بذكر صفاته، فيقال: الله قادِرٌ عالِمٌ، وَاللهُ خالِقٌ آمِر.

قال المفضّل: والأسماء التي هي صفاتٌ لا تكون إلا مشتقّة، كالرّحمن الرحيم من رَحِم، والعزيز من عَزَّ ونحوهما. كما يقال: من الإله، أله، يأله، وتألّه يتألّه. قال: ومن الدليل على أنّه ليس مشتقاً من فعل أنه لا يُثنّى ولا يُجمع والاله يُجمع بالآلهة، فثبت أنّه اسمٌ خاصٌّ للمعبود. وقال بعض من ذهب إلى هذا المعنى: إن كلمة الشهادة تشتمل على نفيٍ وإثبات. ولو كان المثبت المستثنى مشاركاً للمنفي في المعنى المستفاد منه لما تحقّق التمييز بينهما، ويكون بمثابة قولك: لا زيد إلاّ زيدٌ.

وقال الأكثرون: إنّه مشتقٌ، ثم اختلفوا في اشتقاقه. فقال النّضر بن شميل: هو من التألّه. ويقال: ألَهَ إلاهةً: أي عبد عبادةً فسُمّيَ إلهاً، لأنه لا تحقّ العبادة إلاّ له. قال مجاهد: الله الذي يألهه كلّ شيءٍ أي يعبده. وروى مقاتل بن سليمان عن الضحاك عن ابن عباس في قوله «اللّه» قال: يريد نفسه لأنّه «المعبود»، ولا معبود سواه. قال الأعشى: وأعجلنا الإلهة أن تؤوبا. والإلهة الشمس سمّوها إلهة للتعظيم. وقال رؤبة: سبَّحن واسترجعن من تألّهي.

والتأله: التنسّك والتعبّد. وقال قائلون: إن هذا الاسم مشتقٌ من وله العباد إليه، تولّهوا، أي تعلّقت قلوبهم به، وفزعوا إليه. وتوقّعوا الغياث والنصر منه. فقال: أَلَهَ يَأْلَهُ أَلَهاً، أي تحيّر. واصله وَلَهَ يَوْلَهُ وَلَهاً، وقد أَلِهتُ على فلان: أي اشتدّ جزعي عليه، مثل (٣٢ب): وَلِهتُ.

قال الحسن بن يحيى الجرجاني: إن الله أصله إله، وإله اسمٌ موضوع من قولهم: أَلِهَ الرجل إلى فلان، إذا فزغ من أمرٍ نزل به، فآلهه أي أجاره وآمنه. فسمّي إلهاً لأنه يوله إليه، كالإمام الذي يؤتمّ به. ثم أرادوا تفخيمه بالتعريف الذي هو الألف واللام، لأنهم أفردوه لهذا الاسم دون غيره فقالوا: الإله، فاجتمعت الهمزتان في كلمةٍ كثر استعمالهم لها، فحذفوا الهمزة الأصلية فقالوا: «اللّه»، لأنّ فيما بقي دلالةً عليها.

التفسير

روى أبو صالح والضحاك عن ابن عباس (رضي الله عنه) قال: هو الذي يألهون إليه، وقوله: ﴿أَإِلٰهٌ مَعَ اللّٰهِ﴾ معناه: أيؤله إلى غيره في المهمات؟ قال المبرّد: هو من قولهم: ألهت إليه: أي سكنت.

قال الشاعر:

أَلِهْتُ إليها والحوادث جمّةٌ.

وقال قائل:

أَلِهْتُ إليها والركائب وقّف.

فيحتمل أن يكون المعنى فزعت إليه والتجأت إليه، ويحتمل سكنت إليه. وقال شاعر:

لاهَت فما عُرِفَت يوماً بجارحةٍ
يا ليتها خرجت حتى رأيناها

أي: احتجبت.

وقال آخر:

لَاهَ ربّي عن الخلائق طُرّاً
خالق الخلق لا يُرَى ويَرانا

اي: احتجب عن الخلائق.

المعاني

وقال أبو عمرو بن العلاء: هو من ألهت في الشيء إذا تحيّرت فيه. فسمّي إلهاً لأنّ العقول تتحيّر في عظمته. وقيل معناه: المتعالي من قولهم: لاه إذا علا. ومنه قيل للشمس: إلاهةً. وقيل: معناه المستحقّ لأوصاف الجلال، وقيل: معناه القادر على الاختراع. وقال شهر بن

حوشب: معناه خالق كل شيء، وكذلك نقل عن سلف الأئمة في معنى: لا إله إلّا الله، أي لا خالق إلّا الله.

القول في اسم الرحمن الرحيم وتفسيرهما

اللغة

قال علماء الأمة: هما اسمان مشتقان من الرحمة موضوعان للمبالغة جمع بينهما للتأكيد، وكُرِّر بلفظين مختلفين، وإن اتفقا في المعنى. وكان ذلك أحسن من تكريرهم إيّاه بلفظةٍ واحدة، كما قالوا: جادٌّ مجدٌّ، وحطومٌ محطِّمٌ. قال الله تعالى: ﴿إِنَّهَا سَاءَتْ مُسْتَقَرّاً ومُقَاماً﴾؛ وقال عديّ بن زيد: وألفى قولها كذباً ومنّا.

وحقيقة المعنى في هذا التكرير أنّه ذو الرحمة الواسعة، الذي تتابعت رحمته، وتواصلت على عباده نعمته، فكأنه قال: بسم الله الذي تتابعت رحمته، والذي له النّعم بعد النّعم. ومن ذهب إلى هذا قال: هما اسمان موضوعان للمبالغة، مثل: ندمانٍ ونديم، ولهفانٍ ولهيف. ومعناهما: ذو الرحمة. وهذا قول أبي عمرو بن العلاء وأبي الهيثم وقطرب.

(٣٣آ) ومن العلماء من فرّق بين الاسمين. فقال قوم: الرّحمن أشدّ مبالغةً من الرّحيم لأنّه مبنيٌّ على فعلان. وهو لا يقع إلّا على مبالغة الفعل نحو غضبان للممتلئ غضباً، وسكران لمن غلبه السُّكر.

التفسير والمعاني

قال أبو عبيدة: الرحمن ذو الرحمة، والرحيم هو الراحم. وقال ابن عباس في رواية عطاء: الرّحمن: اللطيف العطوف والرحيم بأوليائه وأهل طاعته. وقال في روايةٍ الرّحمن: الرفيق والرحيم العطوف. وهما اسمان رفيقان وقال في رواية أبي صالح اسمان رفيقان، أحدهما أرقّ من الآخر. قال الحسين بن الفضل: لعلّه قال اسمان رفيقان أحدهما أرفق من الآخر. وروي عنه أنه قال: الرحمن: العاطف على البرّ والفاجر في الرزق

لهم، وليس في السماوات والأرض رحمنٌ غيره. والرحيم بالمؤمنين خاصةً وروي عنه أيضاً قال: الرحمن بجميع خلقه والرحيم بالمؤمنين خاصةً. وقال سعيد بن جبير: هو الرحمن لأنه يعمّ المؤمن والكافر بالرحمة. قال الله تعالى: ﴿وَرَحْمَتِيْ وَسِعَتْ كُلَّ شَيْءٍ﴾ والرحيم هو الذي يختصّ المؤمنين بالرحمة. قال تعالى: ﴿فَسَأَكْتُبُهَا لِلَّذِيْنَ يَتَّقُون﴾ وهو قول مقاتل.

وروى منصور عن مجاهد قال: الرّحمن بأهل الدنيا، الرحيم بأهل الآخرة. وجاء في الخبر: يا رحمن الدنيا ورحيم الآخرة. ومن صار إلى هذا المذهب قال: الرحمن: خاصّ الاسم عامّ المعنى، والرحيم عامّ الاسم خاصّ المعنى. ومعنى ذلك أنّه لا يجوز أن يسمّى أحدٌ باسم الرّحمن غير الله تعالى. وهو عامّ المعنى من حيث أنه العاطف على جميع خلقه بالرزق لهم، ودفع البلاء عنهم، وهو لا يقع إلّا على مبالغة الفعل. وقولنا: الرحيم عامّ اللفظ خاصّ المعنى أنّه قد يسمّى بهذا الاسم غير الله تعالى، كما قال تعالى: ﴿بِالْمُؤْمِنِيْنَ رَؤُوْفٌ رَحِيْمٌ﴾ وقال في صفة أصحابه: ﴿رُحَمَاءُ بَيْنَهُمْ﴾ وقال: ﴿وَكَانَ بِالْمُؤْمِنِيْنَ رَحِيْمًا﴾. فالرحيم يختصّ بالمؤمنين.

ومن العلماء من صار إلى أنّ الرحيم أبلغ من الرّحمن من حيث أن رحمته تخصّص بالمؤمنين حقيقةً. قال الله تعالى: ﴿قُلْ مَنْ حَرَّمَ زِيْنَةَ اللَّهِ الَّتِيْ أَخْرَجَ لِعِبَادِهِ وَالطَّيِّبَاتِ مِنَ الرِّزْقِ قُلْ هِيَ لِلَّذِيْنَ آمَنُوا فِي الحَيَوةِ الدُّنْيَا خَالِصَةً يَوْمَ القِيَامَةِ﴾. وقال تعالى خبراً عن إبراهيم (عليه السلام): ﴿وارْزُقْ أَهْلَهُ مِنَ الثَمرَاتِ مَنْ آمَنَ مِنْهُمْ بِاللَّهِ واليَوْمِ الآخِرِ قال: وَمَنْ كَفَرَ فَأُمتِّعُهُ قَلِيْلاً ثُمَّ أَضْطرُّهُ إِلَى عَذَابِ النَّارِ﴾.

وقد حكينا عن جماعةٍ من المفسّرين أنّ الرحيم يختصّ بالمؤمنين، وهو قول (٣٣ب) وكيع بن الجراح، ومرويّ عن ثعلب وروي عن عكرمة أنّه قال: الرّحمن برحمةٍ واحدةٍ والرحيم بمائة رحمة. وإنما أخذ

هذا من قوله (صلّى الله عليه وآله): «إنّ لله تعالى مائة رحمةٍ، وإنّه أنزل منها واحدةً إلى الأرض فقسّمها بين خلقه، فيها يتعاطفون ويتراحمون، وأخّر تسعاً وتسعين لنفسه يرحم بها عباده يوم القيامة».

ومن العلماء من قال: إنما جمع بين الكلمتين: الرحمن الرحيم من حيث إنّ الرحمن اسمٌ يشترك فيه ألسنة أهل الكتابين، وكانوا يقولون، رحمانا. وكان مشركو مكة ينكرون هذا الاسم كما أخبر عنهم، فقال تعالى: ﴿وَإِذَا قِيلَ لَهُم اسْجُدُوْا لِلرَّحْمَنِ قَالُوا: وَمَا الرَّحْمَنُ﴾ وقال: ﴿وَهُمْ يَكْفُرُونَ بِالرَّحْمَنِ﴾ وكانوا يعرفون الرحيم فجمع بينهما. وقال قوم: الرحمن عبرانيّ، ولهذا أنكرته العرب فجمع بين الاسمين لذلك. وهذا لا يصحّ فإن القرآن إنّما أُنزل بلغة العرب، وليس فيه غير لغتهم. وقد وُجد الرحمن في كلام العرب كاللّهفان والغضبان والندمان. وقال الشنفرى:

ألا ضَرَبَتْ تلك الفتاة هجينها
ألا قَطَعَ الرحمن ربّي يمينها

وكانت العرب تقول: لا رحمن إلّا رحمن اليمامة، يعنون مسيلمة الكذاب. فقال تعالى: ﴿وَهُمْ يَكْفُرُونَ بِالرَّحْمَنِ﴾، ثم الرحمة على معنيين: أحدهما، إرادة النعمة والثاني، هي النعمة نفسها. فإذا قيل لم يزل رحيماً ورحماناً، فمعناه مزيد الأنعام. وإذا قيل: رحم الله فلاناً، فمعناه: أنعم الله عليه. وقد قال تعالى: ﴿أَهُمْ يَقْسِمُونَ رَحْمَةَ رَبِّكَ﴾ أي نعمة ربّك. والرّحمن هو الذي يتولّى عباده بالكفاية والرزق والحفظ. فبرحمته قوامهم، وبها بقاؤهم. والرحيم هو الذي يتولّى عبادَهُ المخلصين بالرعاية واللّطف والكرامة، فبرحمته قوامهم وبها بقاؤهم، وقد يقال: يا رحمن الدنيا والآخرة ورحيمهما.

والرحمة في اللغة راجعةٌ إلى رقة القلب والشفقة واللين والرفق، وضدّها الفظاظة وغلظة القلب. وكمالها من حيث الفعل: العفو والصفح والإنعام والإكرام، تطلق على الباري تعالى، لا بحسب المعنى الأوّل بل بحسب المعنى الثاني. وعلى هذا النحو يجري في تأويل ما ورد من الصفات المضافة إلى الله عزّ وجلّ مثل: التحية والرضا والسخط والغضب والأسف والفرح والشوق والضحك، وما أشبه ذلك.

قال ابن المبارك: الرّحمن هو الذي إذا سُئل أعطى، وإذا لم يُسأل غضب، وأنشد:

(٣٤آ) الله يغضب إن تركت سؤاله
وبُني آدم حين يسأل يغضب

وقد قيل اسم الله يدلّ على أنه تعالى مفزع الخلائق، يضطرون إليه في قوام وجودهم. واسم الرّحمن يدلّ على أنّه تعالى ملجأ الخلائق يضطرون إليه في بقاء وجودهم، واسم الرحيم يدل على أنه تعالى معاذ الخواصّ من عباده، يعوذون به في الشدائد ويتوكّلون عليه في الأحوال كلّها، وسيأتي عند ذكر الأسرار نظم الأسامي الثلاثة.

القول في أسرار نظم الكلمات في التسمية

إنّ المفسرين تكلّموا في معاني الكلمات والأسامي لغةً وروايةً، ولم يتكلموا في أسرارها نظماً وترتيباً، ولأيّ معنى خصّت بهذه الأسامي آية التسمية دون سائر الأسماء. وما السر في تقديم اسم الله على اسم الرحمن، وتقديم اسم الرحمن على اسم الرحيم، ومن ذا الذي يقدر على الوقوف على هذه الأسرار دون هدايةٍ من أهل القرآن الذين هم أهل الله وخاصته عليهم السلام، أو يجسر على إيرادها في الكتب دون إجازةٍ وإذن منهم، لكنّي لما خُصِصْتُ بالدعاء المأثور: «اللّهم انفعنا بما

علّمتنا وعلّمنا ما تنفعنا به بحقّ المصطفين من عبادك».، وجدت من نفسي قوة الهداية إلى كلام النبوّة وعرفت لسان الرسالة، فاهتديت منها إلى أسرار كلماتٍ في القرآن المجيد دون أن أُفسّر القرآن برأي. واستعذت بالله السميع العليم من الشيطان الرجيم حتى لا يقع في خاطري ولا يجري على قلمي ما أتبوّأ مقعدي من النار، أعاذنا الله عزّ وجلّ من النار وسعيرها، وحفظنا عن الزيغ والزّلل في تأويل آيات القرآن وتفسيرها.

قال أهل القرآن: إن «بسم الله الرحمن الرحيم» آية منزلة كسائر الآيات، وهي من الفاتحة قطعاً، وهي أول آيةٍ جرى بها القلم الأوّل. وأول آيةٍ نزل بها جبرئيل على المصطفى محمد (صلوات الله عليهما) في سورة: إِقْرَأْ بِاسْمِ رَبِّكَ أو المدثر أو الفاتحة على اختلاف الروايات، وأوّل آية علّمها خديجة وأهل بيته عليهم السلام، وأول آيةٍ قرأها في الصلاة وجهر بها. والدليل على ذلك الأخبار الصحيحة التي رويناها، والأسرار المتينة التي نحن بصدد تقريرها، وقد أجمعت الأمة على أن الفاتحة سبع آيات، وأكثرهم على أنها هي السبع المثاني. ومن قال إنها ليست من الفاتحة وقد عدّ (٣٤ب) ﴿أَنْعَمْتَ عَلَيْهِمْ﴾ آخر الآية السادسة، فانظر إلى أواخر الآيات، كيف تجد انسياقها من حيث اللفظ، ولا تشك أنّها كسرة وبعدها ياء ساكنة، وبعدها وقفة، وهي: حِيم ومِين ودِين وعِين وقِيم ولِين. فلو قلت ﴿أَنْعَمْتَ عَلَيْهِمْ﴾ آخر آية، أخرجت النسق المطّرد في أواخر الآيات وأدخلت فيها ما لا يناسبها لفظاً. على أنّ الوقف على :«عَلَيْهِمْ» ليس يصحّ، فإن الوقوف في الفاتحة باتفاق القراء أربعة، ولم يجوّزوا الوقفة على «عَلَيْهِمْ». فاختلاف النسق ومنع الوقف يدلّان على أنّ «عَلَيْهِمْ» ليس آخر الآية السادسة. وهذه من الأمارات المغلبة على الظنّ، الموجّهة إلى اليقين. وأما اليقين فيها إنما يُقتنص من معانيها.

قال أهل القرآن الذين يتلونه حقّ تلاوته: إنّ الأمور التي لها بال، فلها مبدأ ووسط وكمال. وكلّ ما لا مبدأ له فلا كمال له. وكلّ ما لا كمال له فلا مبدأ له. وإنّ المبادئ كلّها تُقرأ عليها بسم الله. قال النبي (ص): «كلّ أمرٍ ذي بالٍ لم يُبدأ فيه باسم الله فهو أبتر». وإنّ الكمالات كلّها يُقرأ عليها: الحمد لله. قال تعالى: ﴿وَآخِرُ دَعْوَاهُمْ أَنِ الحَمْدُ لِلَّهِ رَبِّ العَالَمِينَ﴾.

وإنما تساق المبادئ إلى الكمالات برحمتي العامة والخاصة فيها على الأوساط. ثم الرحمانية العامة تجاور ﴿بِسْمِ اللَّهِ﴾ وهو على المبادئ. والرحيمية الخاصة تجاور ﴿الحَمدُ للهِ رَبِّ العَالَمِيْن﴾، وهو على الكمالات. والعموم بالمبادئ أولى، والخصوص بالكمالات أحرى. فلو لم يكن ﴿بِسْمِ اللَّهِ الرَّحْمَنِ الرَّحِيمِ﴾ آيةً من الفاتحة لما كانت الفاتحة كاملة، بل كانت سورة بتراء. وإنها من الأمور التي لها بال، وأيّ بال؟! وكمالٌ، وأيّ كمال؟!

وما رُوي: «كل أمرٍ ذي بالٍ لم يبدأ فيه بحمد الله فهو أبتر» رواية غير صحيحة؛ وإنّ الحمد تُقرأ على تمام النعمة، كما إنّ اسم الله يُقرأ على ما به النعمة. ألا تبتدئ الحركات والصناعات كلّ ببسم الله، وتختمها بالحمد لله؟

وسرّ آخر في المثاني ما يتبيّن لك في آخر التفسير للسورة، أنّ المثاني في نفس الفاتحة وأنها سبع مردوداتٍ من المعاني لفظاً ومعنى.

المثنى الأول منها: بسم الله، والحمد لله وهما في اللفظ متساوقان، وفي المعنى – كما بيّنّا متوازيان. فإن بسم الله (٣٥آ) على المبادئ والحمد لله على الكمالات.

والمثنى الثاني: رحمتان بين المبادئ والكمالات، رحمة عامة تشمل الموجودات كلّها من غير فرق بين موجود وموجود، وذلك لأنه جوادٌ. ورحمةٌ خاصةٌ تخصّ بعض الموجودات على فرقٍ بين موجودٍ وموجود،

وذلك لأنه كريم. فلولا عموم رحمته لم تتحرّك المبادئ متوجهةً إلى الكمالات. ولولا خصوص رحمته لم تنعطف الكمالات على المبادئ. قال الله تعالى: ﴿وَرَحْمَتِيْ وَسِعَتْ كُلَّ شَيْءٍ﴾، وهو إشارةٌ إلى عموم الرحمة للخلائق برّها وفاجرها. وقال: ﴿فَسَأكْتُبها للذِينَ يَتَّقُون ويُؤتُونَ الزَّكاةَ والذِينَ هُمْ بآياتِنَا يُؤمِنُون﴾ وهو إشارة إلى خصوص الرحمة برّها دون فاجرها، ومؤمنها دون كافرها. وأنت عرفت قاعدة العموم والخصوص في مقدّمات علم القرآن. فالعامّ والخاصّ إذاً مثنى آخر، وستأتي باقيات المثاني إن شاء الله.

وسرٌّ آخر، أنّ العوالم قد تعدّ على ولاء النسبة إلى الباري تعالى ثلاثة: عالم الخلق، وعالم الأمر، وعالم الثواب. فتقدّرت العوالم الثلاثة على الأسامي الثلاثة. فالإلهية تعطي معنى الخلق، قال الله تعالى: ﴿ولَئِنْ سَألتَهم مَنْ خَلَقَهُم لَيَقُولُنَّ اللَّهُ﴾، والرحمانية تعطي معنى الأمر. قال الله تعالى: ﴿وإذَا قِيلَ لَهُمُ اسجُدُوا للرَّحْمن قَالُوا: وَمَا الرَّحْمَنُ أَنَسْجُدُ لِمَا تَأْمُرُنَا﴾. فلم ينكروا اسم الله، إذ لم ينازعوه في الخلق. وأنكَروا اسم الرّحْمن إذ نازعوه في الأمر: قالوا: ﴿أنَسْجُدُ لِمَا تَأْمُرُنا وَزَادَهُم نُفُوراً﴾. والرحيمية تُعطي معنى الثواب. قال الله تعالى ﴿وَكَانَ بِالمُؤْمِنينَ رَحِيماً، تَحِيَّتُهُم يَومَ يَلقَوْنَه سَلامٌ وأَعَدَّ لَهُمْ أجْراً كَرِيماً﴾.

ثم الأول خلق وإبداع، ثم تكليف وأمر، ثم جزاء وثواب. كذلك الترتيب في الأسامي الثلاثة، الأول: الله، الثاني: الرحمن، الثالث: الرحيم. وما لم تسبق النعمة لم يجب الشكر. فقدّم ذكر النعمة والرحمة، وعقبها بالحمد والشكر، وهو دليلٌ على أنّ التسمية من السورة يقيناً ولا يجوز الفصل بينهما أصلاً.

وسرٌّ آخر، «إنّ الله تعالى تجلّى لعباده بكتابه» من كلمات الصادق جعفر بن محمد (رضوان الله وسلامه عليهما) وكما تجلّى بكتابه تجلّى بأساميه العالية للمخصوصين من أوليائه (٣٥ب) حتى كانت الإلهية في

التجلّي لواحدٍ من أوليائه، والرحمانية لواحدٍ، والرحيمية لواحدٍ، وقد يجتمع الثلاثة لواحدٍ. وحيثما وجدْتَ في القرآن لفظ الذي مقروناً باسم من الأسامي فهو للتعريف وكلّ تعريفٍ فهو تعرّفٌ إلى شيء، وكلّ تعرّفٍ فهو تجلٍّ له، وقد يكون التجلّي عاماً، وقد يكون خاصّاً.

قوله تعالى: ﴿إِنَّ رَبَّكُمُ اللَّهُ الَّذِي خَلَقَ السَّمَاوَاتِ وَالأَرْضَ﴾، تعرّف عام. وقوله تعالى: ﴿إِنَّ وَلِيِيَ اللَّهُ الَّذِي نَزَّلَ الكِتَابَ وَهُوَ يَتَوَلَّى الصَّالِحِينَ﴾ تعرّف خاص. فحصل التجلّي بهذه الأسماء الثلاثة للعوالم الثلاثة حتى وُجِدَتْ وحصلت، وللأشخاص الثلاثة من النبيّين والصدّيقين والشهداء حتى قاموا بها واستقاموا عليها والتجأوا إليها. وأما نظم الكلمات والحروف من حيث اللفظ وترتيب بعضها على البعض، وظاهر الإعجاز من وجه تناسب الصدور والأعجاز، والحكمة في أعداد الكلمات لم كانت أربعة؟ وأعداد الحروف لم كانت تسعة عشر؟ فليس بِعُشِّنا فلندرج إذ هو من العلوم الخاصّة بالأنبياء والأولياء عليهم السلام، لكنّا نعلم إنّا إذا نظرنا بإرشادهم إلى الآيات فرأينا نظمها مشتملاً على معانٍ خفيةٍ. وإذا لحظنا بإشاراتهم إلى الكلمات رأينا نظمها مشتملاً على أسرارٍ دفينةٍ تطلّعنا منها إلى الحروف، فعرفنا أنها لا تخلو من أسرارٍ أُخر، وأنها توازن من حيث العدد أضرابها من الموجودات، وأنها إذا كانت أوّل ما كتب بالقلم الأول في اللوح المحفوظ فهي مبادئ الموجودات، ومن نور كل حرف منها حصل موجودٌ في العالم العلويّ والسفليّ؛ وهي مفاتيح الغيب ومقاليد السماوات والأرض، وهي الحروف العلويّة، والحدود العقلية لا يعلمها إلا هو تبارك الله ربّ العالمين.

القول في تفسير: الحمد لله

التفسير واللغة

قال بعض المفسرين هو ابتداء ثناءٍ وحمدٍ أثنى الله تعالى على نفسه تعظيماً لجلاله، وتعليماً لعباده، حتى إذا حمدوه قالوا: الحمد لله. وقال بعضهم فيه إضمار فعلٍ، فمعناه قولوا الحمد لله. فلفظه خبرٌ ومعناه أمرٌ. وهو قول الكسائي. ويروى عن ابن عباس كذلك. وقيل القول المضمر في أوّل السورة يتجزّأ إلى ﴿الحَمْدُ لِلَّه﴾.

وأما الألف واللام فيه لاستغراق الجنس، ويجوز أن يكون للعهد. واللام في قوله ﴿لِلَّهِ﴾ لأمر الإضافة، فيجوز أن يكون (٣٦آ) للتمليك على أنه مالك الحمد. ويجوز أن يكون للاختصاص والاستحقاق كما يُقال الباب للدار.

ثم الحمد له معنيان: أحدهما: الشكر، والثاني: الثناء والمدح. فإذا كان في مقابلة النعمة كان معناه الشكر، وإذا كان على فضيلةٍ ومنقبة كان بمعنى الثناء. يُقال: حمدت فلاناً على نعمته، أي شكرته؛ وحمدته على شجاعته أي مدحته.

وفي كتاب الخليل: الحمد نقيض الهجاء، وهو حسن الثناء. والمدح نقيض الذمّ. قال الأخفش: حمد الله: الثناء عليه والشكر لنعمه. ويقال فلان يشتري الحمد بماله: أي المدح. ويقال للرجل: لا تحمدنّ امرءاً حتى تجرّبه، أي: لا تمدحنّه.

قال تعالى: ﴿وَقُلِ الحَمْدُ لِلَّهِ الَّذِي لَمْ يَتَّخِذْ وَلَداً﴾ أي الثناء على الله بذلك. وفي الحديث: «ليس شيءٌ أحب إلى الله من الحمد، ولذلك أثنى على نفسه فقال: ﴿الحمد لله﴾». وفي الصلاة نقول: ربّنا لك الحمد أهل الثناء والمجد. فالحمد يؤدّي معنى الشكر كلّه. والشكر لا يؤدي معنى الحمد كلّه. فالحمد اسمٌ عامٌّ لجنس الثناء، والشكر على مقابلة نعمة وعلى غيرها.

قال ابن عباس في رواية عطاء وأبي صالح والضحّاك ويوسف بن مهران وهو قول مقاتل أيضاً: إنّ الحمد لله معناه الشكر لله أن صنع إلى خلقه فحمدوه، وأنعم عليهم فشكروه.

وروى الحكم عن السُدّي قال: أوّل هذه السورة الحمد لله وهو الثناء على الله، ووسطها الإخلاص وآخرها مسألة الله. وقال الحسن: الحمد بمعنى الثناء.

النّحو

وحظّ النحو فيه أنّ الحمد رفع بالابتداء والله كسر باللام الجارّة.

الأسرار

قال أهل القرآن إن الله تعالى ذو الجلال والإكرام. فبجلاله استحقّ الثناء، وبإكرامه استحقّ الشكر. والألف واللام لاستغراق جنس الثناء وجنس الشكر لله ذي الجلال والإكرام. احتجب عنهم بجلاله فلم يدركوه، وتجلّى لهم بإكرامه فلم ينكروه.

قوله عزّ وجلّ: رب العالمين

النّظم [والإعراب]

ولما ذكر الشكر ذكر بعده موجبات الحمد والشكر، فقال: ﴿رَبُّ العَالَمِينَ﴾، وهو وجه النظم بينه وبين ما قبله، وكسر ربّ لأنّه صفةٌ لله، والعالمين في محلّ بالكسر بالإضافة.

اللغة

والربّ له معنيان: أحدهما من ربّ الشيء إذا ربّاه وأصلحه وأتمّه. وربّ ضيعته: إذا أقام عليها، قاله الأصمعي؛ والثاني، من ربّ الشيء إذا ملكه فهو ربّه، أي مالكه. قال الجوهري: فقال رببت القوم أي سستهم، وكنت فوقهم. قال: وهو من الربوبيّة؛ وربّ فلانٌ ولده يربّه ربّا وربّبه

بمعنى ربّاه، والمربوب بمعنى المربّى.

(٣٦ب) وقال غيره: ربّيت الغلام، أربّيه تربيتاً إذا أصلحت أموره وقمت عليه، وربّيته تربيةً مثله.

ويقال: ربّ فلانٌ بالمكان وأربّ أي أقام به، فهو رابٌّ ومُرِبٌّ. والربُّ من أسماء الله تعالى المعرب عن جملة هذه المعاني. فهو المربّي والخالق والسيد والمالك والقائم بأمورهم. ولا يقال لأحدٍ الربّ على الإطلاق، إلّا أن يضاف إلى شيء. يقال: ربّ الغلام، وربّ الدار. وقد جاء في لغة العرب تسمية السيد المطاع ربّاً. قال الأعشى:

وأهلَكْنَ يَوماً رَبَّ كندةَ وابنَهُ
ورَبَّ مَعَدٍّ بينَ خَبْتٍ وعَرعَرِ

وفي قصة حنين حين انهزم أصحاب رسول الله قال رجل: الآن بطل السحر. قال صفوان بن أميّة: بفيك التراب لربٌّ من قريشٍ أحبّ إليّ من ربٍّ من هوازن.

وأما تفسير «العالمين» فهو جمع عالم. ولا واحد للعالم من لفظه كالرهط والجيش والقوم ونحوها. واشتقاقه على وجهين: أحدهما: أنه من العِلْم، فهو اسم لما يُحسّ ويُعلم. والثاني: أنه من العَلَم والعلامة وهي الدلالة. فإنها دلالة على الخالق.

والوجه الأول قول الفراء وأبي عبيدة وأبي معاذ النحوي والنضر بن شميل وأبي الهيثم، قال النضر: هو اسم للجمع الكثير، وقال أبو معاذ النحوي: هو بنو آدم. وقال أبو الهيثم: هو اسم الجنّ والإنس. وقال الفراء وأبو عبيدة: هو اسمٌ لما يَعقل وهم أربعة: الملائكة والإنس والجن والشياطين.

والوجه الثاني: قول ابن فارس صاحب المجمل، قال: كلّ جنسٍ من الخلق، فهو في نفسه مَعْلَم وعَلَمٌ. ذكره في كتاب المقاييس. قال:

وقال قومٌ سمّي العالم عالماً لاجتماعهم، فهو ربّ العالمين، معناه ربّ الخلائق أجمعين.

وقال الجوهري في الصحاح: العالم الخلق، والجمع العوالِم، والعالَمون أصناف الخلق.

التفسير

وكلام المفسرين يؤول إلى هذين الوجهين، روى الربيع بن أنس عن شهر بن حوشب عن أُبيّ بن كعب، قال: العالمون هم الملائكة وهم ثمانية عشر ألف مَلَك في أكناف الدنيا، مع كل مَلَك من الأعوان ما لا يعلم عددهم إلّا الله، ومن ورائهم أرضٌ بيضاء كالرّخام، عرضها مسيرة الشمس أربعين يوماً، لا يعلم طولها إلّا الله، مملوءة ملائكةً. وقال: إنهم الروحانيون وهم العالمون منتهاهم إلى حملة العرش.

وقال ابن عبّاس في رواية سعيد بن جُبير وعكرمة وعطية في قوله: ﴿رَبِّ العَالَمِينَ﴾، هم الجنّ والأنس.

وقال أبو عمرو بن العلاء: هم الروحانيون، وهو رواية الكلبي عن ابن عباس. وقال قتادة ومجاهد والحسن في إحدى الروايتين: العالمون جميع الخلائق، وهذا قول أبي روق (٣٧آ) والضحاك، ورواية عطاء والضحاك عن ابن عباس، واختيار أبي اسحاق وأبي عبيد. واحتجّوا بقوله تعالى: ﴿وَقَالَ فِرْعَوْنُ وَمَا رَبُّ العَالَمِينَ؟ قَالَ: رَبُّ السَمَاوَاتِ والأَرْضِ وَمَا بَيْنَهُمَا﴾. وهذا هو الأشبه، لأنه تفسير موسى (عليه السلام).

وروى عمرو عن الحسن يعني بذلك العالم من كلّ زمان لأنّ لكلّ زمان عالَماً. وهذا اختيار القفّال. فقال المراد بالعالمين هاهنا طبقات المخلوقين، وما يجمعه كلّ زمانٍ منهم من الإنس والجنّ مَنْ مضى منهم ومَن بقي، ومن هو كائن إلى يوم القيامة. قال العجاج: «وخِنْدِفٌ هامة هذا العالم». إنّما عنى من كان في دهرهم من الناس.

وقال ابن عباس: ربّ العالمين، سيّد ما خلق وإلهه. وقال سعيد بن المسيّب: لله تعالى ألف عالم، ستمائةٍ في البحر وأربعمائة في البرّ. وقال الضحاك: منهم ثلاثمائةٍ وستون عالماً حفاةٌ عراةٌ لا يعرفون مَن خالقُهم، وأربعون يلبسون الثياب. وقال وهب بن منبه: لله تعالى ثمانية عشر ألف عالم، الدنيا عالم واحدٌ منها. وقال أبو العالية: الجنّ والإنس عالم من العالمين. وقال أبو سعيد الخُدريّ: لله عزّ وجلّ أربعون ألف عالم. الدنيا عالم واحدٌ من ذلك. وقال مقاتل بن حيّان: لله تعالى ثمانون ألف عالم، أربعون ألفاً في البحر، وأربعون ألفاً في البرّ. وقال كعب: لا يحصي أحدٌ عدد العالمين إلّا الله عزّ وجلّ.

الأسرار

قال أهل القرآن، أهل الله وخاصّته: لا تغفلوا عن عمومات القرآن وخصوصاته، ففي كلّ ما يضاف إلى الربّ – تعالى- فعلاً وقولاً وخَلقاً وأمراً، خصوصٌ وعموم. وفي كلّ اسمٍ من أسماء الله – تعالى – يُضاف إلى كلّ شيء من خلقه عموماً، خصوص إضافةٍ إلى واحدٍ من خلقه. وتعرّفوا السرّ في قوله – تعالى – خبراً عن سحرة فرعون: ﴿آمَنَّا بِرَبِّ العَالَمِيْنَ رَبِّ مُوسَى وَهرُون﴾. وفي قوله تعالى: ﴿وَرَحْمَتِيْ وَسِعَتْ كَلَّ شَيءٍ، فَسَأَكْتُبُها لِلَّذِينَ يتَّقُون﴾ الآية. فإضافة الربوبية إلى العالمين بأسرهم مشروطة بإضافتها إلى قوم مخصوصين، أو إلى واحدٍ مخصوص، فيكون العالم كلّه فيه وله وهو.

ثم وجه النظر بين ﴿الحَمْدُ لِلَّهِ﴾ و ﴿رَبِّ العَالَمِينَ الرَّحْمَنِ الرَّحِيمِ. مَالِكِ يَومِ الدِّينِ﴾ أنّه تعالى لمّا ذكر الحمد بمعنى الثناء والشكر لله ذكر بعده ما يستوجب به الثناء والشكر من تربية العالمين، والرحمة عليهم عموماً وخصوصاً، وملك يوم الدين مِلكًا ومُلكًا.

وكما إن ﴿بِسْمِ اللَّهِ الرَّحْمَنِ الرَّحِيمِ﴾ و ﴿الحَمْدُ لِلَّهِ رَبِّ العَالَمِينَ﴾ متناسبان في التلفّظ، متوافقان في المبادئ والكمالات، والبدايات

والعواقب (٣٧ب) وهما: المثنى الأوّل وبينهما رحمتان واصلتان للمبادئ بالكمالات: رحمةٌ عامةٌ ورحمةٌ خاصة، وهما المثنى الثاني كذلك ﴿رَبِّ العَالَمِينَ﴾ و﴿مَالِك يَوْمِ الدِّينِ﴾ متناسبان في التلفّظ، متوافقان في المبدأ والكمال، والخلق والأمر، والمُلك والمِلك والجسمانيّ والروحانيّ، والأولى والآخرة، وهما: المثنى الثالث. وبينهما رحمتان واصلتان للمبادئ بالكمالات، جامعتان بين الخلق والأمر، متصرّفتان في المُلك والمِلك، مستوليتان على الجسمانيّ والروحاني، مشعرتان بالأولى والآخرة، وهما المثنى الرابع.

له الحمد في الأولى والآخرة، فالرحمتان في التسمية مقرّرتان على مبادئ الأشياء وكمالاتها، سابقتان للمصادر إلى المظاهر، والرحمتان في التحميد بين ﴿رَبِّ العَالَمِينَ﴾ و ﴿مَالِكِ يَومِ الدِّينِ﴾ مقرّرتان على الخلق والأمر، سابقتان للجسمانيات إلى الروحانيات واصلتان بين الدنيا والآخرة، وهما يؤدّيان معنى آخر غير المعنى في التسمية، وهذا فائدة التكرار.

قوله جلّ وعزّ: مالك يوم الدين

قرأ جماعةٌ من القراء بالألف، وقالوا: هي قراءة النبي (صلّى الله عليه وآله) والخلفاء الراشدين وطلحة والزبير وسعدٍ وعبد الرحمن بن عوف وابن مسعود وابن عباس ومعاذٍ وأُبيّ بن كعب وأبي ذرّ وأنسٍ وأبي هريرة، ومن التابعين وأتباعهم جماعةٌ كبيرة، وعاصم وعيسى بن عمر والكسائي وخلف والحسن ويعقوب وأبي عبيدة والأخفش. وقرأ جماعةٌ بغير الألف وكسر اللام وكسر الكاف على النعت، وهي قراءة النبي (صلّى الله عليه وآله) وعثمان وعليّ وزيد بن ثابت وابن عمر وشيبة ونافع ومجاهد وابن كثير وابن محيصن وحميد ويحيى بن وثّاب وحمزة وأبي عمرو وابن عامر. وروت أمّ سلمة عن رسول الله (صلّى الله عليه وآله) كذلك.

وقُرِئَ ﴿مَالِكَ يَوْمِ الدِّين﴾ و﴿ملكَ﴾ بنصب الكاف على النداء وهي قراءة الأعمش وعطية بن قيس. وقد قرأ برفع الكاف على الابتداء.

اللغة

وأما الفرق بين مالك ومَلِك فقيل لا فرق بينهما، وهما لغتان مثل: فارِه وفَرِه، وفاكه وفكه، ونحوها، وقال أبو عبيدة والأخفش والأصمعي وأبو حاتم وأبو الهيثم: مالك أوسع وأبلغ في المدح، يقال: الله مالك كلّ شيء، ولا يقال ملك كلّ شيء. إنما يقال: ملك الناس، ملك يوم الدين. ولا يكون مالكاً للشيء إلّا وهو يملكه، وقد يكون ملك الشيء وهو لا يملكه، كما يقال: ملك العرب والعجم.

وقد قيل إنّ مالك أبلغ في مدح الخالق من ملك، وملك أبلغ في مدح المخلوقين (٣٨آ) من مالك، لأنّ المخلوق قد يكون مالكاً وهو غير ملك. قال أبو عبيد: والذي أختاره ملك يوم الدين لأنّ الإسناد عن النبي فيه أثبت، ومن قرّائها من أهل العلم أكثر. وقد قال تعالى: ﴿فَتَعَالَى اللَّهُ المَلِكُ الحَقُّ﴾، و ﴿المَلِكُ القُدُّوسُ﴾، و ﴿المُلْكُ يَومَئِذٍ لِلَّهِ﴾ و«المُلك» مصدر «المَلِك» لا غير. والمُلك يصحّ للمالك والمَلِك ثم هما لغتان فصيحتان ومعناهما الربّ. يقال: مَلَك الشيء يملِكُه مِلكاً فهو مالكٌ؛ ومَلكه يَمْلِكه مُلكاً فهو ملكٌ.

التفسير

وفيما أعبّرها عنه وجهان، أحدهما: أنّ معناه القدرة؛ والثاني: أنّه من الربط والشدّ. قال المفضّل: من قرأ بالألف فمعناه القادر على يوم الدين بالمِلكة والمُلك، ومن قرأ «مَلِك» فمعناه أنّ له السلطان العالي على يوم الدين. وعلى الوجه الثاني، مالك الشيء من ربطه لنفسه، ومَلِك القوم من تصدّى لهم وضبط أمرهم، ومنه ملكت العجين. فمن قرأ «مالك» قال أبو العباس: معناه مالك يوم الدين بالإحكام، أي يملك الحكم يوم

الدين، ويملك إقامته. ومن قرأ «ملك» فمعناه أنه المَلِك في هذا اليوم الذي هو يوم الحساب والجزاء، لقوله: ﴿المُلْكُ يَومَئِذٍ لِلَّهِ﴾. على معنى أنه لا يجري لأحد سلطانٌ على أحدٍ يتغلّب كما يكون ذلك في الدنيا، ولا يشفع أحد لأحد إلا بإذنه، ولا يملك الأحكام والقضاء بين العباد فيه إلّا الله. ومجاز هذه الإضافة قول القائل: فلانٌ أمير هذا البلد. أي هو الأمير فيه، كذلك والتقدير: هو المَلِك في يوم الدين.

وقيل: إنّ في قوله تعالى: ﴿رَبُّ العَالَمِينَ﴾ إشارةً إلى مُلك الدنيا وما فيها، وفي قوله: ﴿مَلِكِ يَوْمِ الدِّينِ﴾ إشارة إلى أنّه الملك في الآخرة. فلهذا خُصَّ يوم الدين بالمِلك والمُلك. والمراد باليوم الوقت الذي يقع فيه الحساب والجزاء. ويوم الدين: يوم القيامة. قال الله تعالى: ﴿يَصْلَوْنَهَا يَوْمَ الدِّينِ﴾ والدين: الحساب والجزاء. قال الله تعالى: ﴿وَإِنَّ الدِّينَ لَوَاقِعٌ﴾ وقال: ﴿ذَلِكَ الدِّينُ القَيِّمُ﴾ أي الحساب المستقيم. وفي المثل: «كما تدينُ تُدان» أي كما تفعل تُجازى وكما تُجازي تُجازى. قال خالد بن نوفل:

واعلم وأيقن أنّ ملكك زائل
واعلم بأنّ كما تدين تدان

قال قتادة يعني يوم يدين الله العباد بأعمالهم. وروى أبو روق عن الضحاك عن ابن عباس (رضي الله عنه) قال: لا يملك أحدٌ في ذلك اليوم حكماً كملكهم في الدنيا. قال: ويوم الدين: يوم حساب (٣٨ب) الخلائق، وهو يوم القيامة، يدينهم بأعمالهم. وهذا قول عطاء عن ابن عباس (رضي الله عنه) وقول سعيد بن جُبير، والحسن واختيار أبي عبيد: وقال ابن عباس والسدّي ومقاتل معناه قاضي يوم الحساب، ونحوه قال مجاهد.

وقال الكلبي عن ابن عباس: الدين القضاء والحكم. قال الله تعالى: ﴿وَلَا تَأْخُذْكُم بِهِمَا رَأفَةٌ فِي دِينِ اللَّهِ﴾ أي في حكم الله. وقال تعالى:

﴿مَا كَانَ لِيَأْخُذَ أَخَاهُ فِيْ دِينِ المَلِكِ﴾ أي في حكمه. ويقال للحاكم «ديّان». المعنى: لا يملك الحكم والقضاء في ذلك اليوم غيره.

المعاني

قال الفراء: يقال دان بنو فلانٍ لفلانٍ أي أطاعوه، ودِنت القوم أدينهم: أي قهرتهم. فدانوا أي أطاعوا وذلّوا له. ﴿وَالدِّينُ لِلَّهِ﴾ إنما هو من هذا. ودين الرجل خلقه وعمله وطاعته وعادته. قال القرظي مالك يوم لا ينفع فيه إلا الدين: أي الطاعة والعمل والإنقياد.

الأسرار

قال أهل القرآن الذين أُحكمت آياته بهم وفُصّلت لديهم: إنّ لله تعالى الخلق والأمر، والإبداء والإعادة له، والمِلك والمُلك له. والمَلِك اسمٌ جامعٌ لجميع أوصاف الجلال والكمال، متضمّن لمعنى الأمر والحكم والقضاء. ولمّا كان الدين اسماً جامعاً للطاعة والعمل بأمره والإنقياد لحكمه والتسليم لقضائه أُضيف اسم ﴿المَلِك﴾ إلى ﴿يوم الدين﴾.

قال الله تعالى: ﴿وَمَا أَدْرَاكَ مَا يَوْمُ الدِّينِ، ثُمَّ مَا أَدْرَاكَ مَا يَوْمُ الدِّينِ. يَوْمَ لَا تَمْلِكُ نَفْسٌ لِنَفْسٍ شَيْئاً، وَالأَمْرُ يَوْمَئِذٍ لِلّهِ﴾ وقال: ﴿المُلْكُ يَومَئِذٍ الحَقُّ للرَّحْمَنِ﴾. فأدّى اسم ﴿رَبِّ العَالَمِينَ﴾ معنى الخلق، وأدّى اسم ﴿مَلِكِ يَوْمِ الدِّيْنِ﴾ معنى الأمر، فالخلقيات كلّها جبروته، وهي بالأبدان أولى. والأمريات كلها ملكوته وهي بالأرواح أولى. وكذلك الخلقيات كلّها مُلكه، والأمريات كلّها مِلكه.

قال الصادق، أبو عبد الله، جعفر بن محمد (رضوان الله وسلامه عليهما): «الأرواح مِلكه، والأجساد مُلكه فأحلّ مِلكه في مُلكه، وله عليها شُرط ولها قِبَلَه وعدٌ فإن وفوا بشرطه وفى لهم بوعده».

وقال(عليه السلام): «إنّ الله تعالى أسّس دينه على مثال خلقه ليستدلّ بخلقه على دينه، وبدينه على وَحدانيّته».

فما من موجودٍ من موجودات العالم خلقه من شيء أو أبدعه لا من شيء إلا ومعه من ملكوته مَلَكٌ يدبّره، وكلمةٌ فعالة تقدّره، حتى القطرة من السماء تنزل ومعها مَلَك، والذرّة من الأرض تصعد ومعها مَلَك. والعالَمان ليسا يتجاوران تجاور الأجرام، ولا يختلطان اختلاط الأجسام بالشكل والصورة، بل هما يتمايزان بالمعنى والحقيقة. وكما أُجري عموم وخصوص (٣٩آ) في اسم الربّ وإضافته إلى العالمين، يجب أن يجري عمومٌ وخصوصٌ في اسم المَلِكِ، وإضافته إلى يوم الدين.

وكما كان كلّ خصوصٍ من عمومٍ ينتهي بشخصٍ معيّن في الخلقيات، كذلك كلّ خصوصٍ من عموم ينتهي بشخص معيّن في الأمريّات. وكما تجلّى الربّ تعالى باسم الربوبية لشخص معيّن أو لشخصين: ﴿رَبِّ مُوْسَى وَهَرُونَ﴾، وتجلّى باسم الإلهية لأشخاصٍ مخصوصين أو لشخص معيّن: ﴿نَعْبُدُ إِلَهَكَ وَإِلَهَ آبَائِكَ إِبْرَاهِيمَ وَإِسْمَاعِيلَ وَإِسْحَقَ إِلهاً واحِداً﴾، وتحقّقت الوحدانية بهذا التخصيص والتعريف، كذلك تجلّى الربّ تعالى باسم المالكية والملكية لشخصٍ معيّن أو أشخاص مخصوصين، فقال: ﴿أَعُوذُ بِرَبِّ النَّاسِ مَلِكِ النَّاسِ إِلَهِ النَّاسِ﴾ وهم ناسٌ مخصوصون: ﴿أَمْ يَحْسِدُوْنَ النَّاسَ عَلَى مَا آتَاهُمُ اللهُ مِنْ فَضْلِهِ﴾.

وقال أبو جعفر محمد بن علي الباقر (رضوان الله وسلامه عليهما): «نحن الناس، وشيعتنا أشباه الناس، وسائر الناس نسناس».

وقد قال الله (عزّ وجلّ): ﴿ثُمَّ أَفِيضُوا مِنْ حَيْثُ أَفَاضَ النَّاسُ﴾.

وقال النبي: «الناس اثنان عالِمٌ ومتعلّمٌ وسائر الناس هَمَجٌ لا خير فيهم».

وليس في جميع القرآن اسمٌ من أسماء الله تعالى يضاف إلى أشخاصٍ مخصوصين من الناس إلّا بهذه الأسامي الثلاثة: الله، الربّ، المَلِك. وهي كما تضاف إلى الخلائق عموماً تضاف إلى الناس

خصوصاً.

وقد ورد في الأخبار أنّ داود (عليه السلام) سأل الله (عزّ وجلّ) أن يقال في الدعاء: يا إله داود، كما يقال: يا إله إبراهيم وإسماعيل واسحق، فلم يُجِب إلى ذلك. فلولا أنّ فيه سرّاً خفيّاً من اللطف والكرامة لما ميّز فيه بين شخصٍ وشخص.

ثم كما تجلّى تعالى باسم الربوبيّة للذريّة المأخوذة من بني آدم فقال: ﴿أَلَسْتُ بِرَبِّكُمْ﴾، فأقرّوا وقالوا: بلى، بلسان الحال أو لسان المقال كذلك تجلّى تعالى باسم المَلَكِيّة للخليقة المحشورة يوم الدين في الآخرة فقال: ﴿لِمَنِ المُلْكُ اليَوْمَ﴾، حتّى أقرّوا وقالوا: ﴿لِلَّهِ الوَاحِدِ القَهَّارِ﴾ بلسان الحال أو لسان المقال.

قوله جلّ وعزّ: إيّاك نعبُدُ وإيّاكَ نستعين

اللغة والنحو

قال أهل اللغة «إيّا» اسمٌ مفرد مضمر يتغيّر آخره كما يتغيّر أواخر المضمرات، وهو موضوعٌ للتخصيص، قال الأخفش: إنّ الكاف فيه ليست باسم، وإنّما هي لدلالة الخطاب عليه، بمنزلة كاف «ذلك» والهاء والياء في «إيّاه» و«إيّاي». وهو اختيار أبي علي الفسويّ، وقال: هو اسم مضاف إلى المخاطب، والكاف في محلّ الخفض بإضافة «إيّا» إليه. وجملته (٣٩ب) في محلّ النصب بوقوع الفعل عليه وهو العبادة والاستعانة.

قال صاحب النّظم: معنى إيّاك التخصيص. تقول: إيّاك أقول، أي: القول اختصّ بك، ومعناه: أخصّك بالعبادة، وأخصّك بالاستعانة. وقال الزجّاج: العبادة في اللغة: الطاعة مع الخضوع. يقال: طريق معبّد أي مذلّل وطئته السابلة فصار الجادّة البيضاء.

التفسير والمعاني

وقال ابن عبّاس: ﴿إِيَّاكَ نَعْبُدُ﴾: نوحّد ونخاف ونرجوك يا ربّنا لا غيرك. ﴿وَإِيَّاكَ نَسْتَعِينُ﴾ على طاعتنا وعلى أمورنا كلّها؛ وهو رواية أبي روق والضحاك عنه. وقال في روايةٍ أخرى، ﴿نَعْبُدُ﴾: نوحّد، و﴿نَسْتَعِينُ﴾ على عبادتك.

وقال مجاهد: ﴿نَسْتَعِينُ﴾: نستوفق لأداء العبادة. وقال الأخفش: العابد، الموحّد المجتهد.

وقال أهل المعاني: لك نَذِلُّ ونخضع بالطاعة والتعظيم، ومنك نسأل القوّة والتوفيق لهذه العبادة والدوام عليها. والاستعانة: طلب المعونة والتيسير يقال: استعنته واستعنت به. وقال محمد بن جرير: معناه ﴿إِيَّاكَ نَعْبُدُ﴾، لا سواك. ﴿وَإِيَّاكَ نَسْتَعِينُ﴾: أي نطلب المعونة لا سواك، وقيل: إنما كرر إياك لتكون أدلّ على الإخلاص والاختصاص، كما قال عزّ وجلّ، خبرا عن موسى (عليه السلام) ﴿كَيْ نُسَبِّحَكَ كَثِيْراً وَنَذْكُرَكَ كَثِيْراً﴾، وقيل: إنّما قدّم العبادة على الاستعانة لتكون أدلّ على الخضوع والواو تقتضي التشريك والجمع، فالمعنى: ﴿وَإِيَّاكَ نَسْتَعِينُ﴾ على أداء عبادتك. وقيل: ﴿وَإِيَّاكَ نَسْتَعِينُ﴾ على مثلها في المستأنف وعلى الثبات والدوام عليها.

الأسرار [والنظم]

ووجه النظم بين ما قبل الكلمتين وبينهما أنّ الربّ – تعالى – كما علّمنا كيف نذكره بالأسامي العُلى، وعرّفنا كيف نحمده بالمحامد الكبرى، عقّب ذلك بذكر الإخلاص في العبادة والاستعانة، كيف نخصّه بالتوحيد والتحميد والثناء والتمجيد والطاعة والتسليم، وكيف نخصّه بالاستعانة به وطلب التوفيق منه؛ فإنّ الأسامي السابقة تستدعي الثناء عليه والشكر له والعبادة إيّاه والاستعانة به. وهي أسامي الجلال والإكرام

والرحمة والإنعام والمِلك والمُلك في الدارين والقدرة والقهر في المنزلتين.

والكلمتان متطابقتان متوازيتان لفظاً ومعنىً وهما المثنى الخامس في المثاني السبعة. وأشعرت الكلمة الأولى بقبول التكليف والاعتراف بالاستطاعة والاكتساب وفيها نفي الجبر المحض. وأشعرت الكلمة الثانية بتحقيق التقدير وطلب المعونة والتيسير، وفيها نفي القدر المحض؛ وفي العبادة والاستقلال بها حكم المبتدأ والمستأنف، وفي الاستعانة والاحتياج إليها (٤٠آ) حكم المفروغ والسابقة.

وقد تُقدّم الاستعانة على العبادة وذلك في القنوت والدعاء: «اللهم إنّا نستعينك» أوّلاً، «اللهمّ إيّاك نعبد» آخراً وقد تقدّم العبادة على الاستعانة، وذلك في العبادة والصلاة: ﴿إِيَّاكَ نَعْبُدُ وإِيَّاكَ نَسْتَعِينُ﴾ لأنّ الدعاء عرض الحاجة وطلب الإجابة، والعبادة عرض العبودية وبذل المجهود في الطاعة. ثم كما أشار بإيّاك الأوّل إلى أنّ العبادة له تعالى، وخاصةٌ به، فلا معبود سواه، كذلك أشار بإيّاك الثاني إلى أنّ طلب التوفيق والمعونة منه، فلا مستعان سواه.

فمن ابتداء السورة إلى ﴿إِيَّاكَ نَعْبُدُ﴾ كلّها تعريفاتٌ؛ ومنه إلى آخر السورة كلُّها تكليفات. وفي الخبر المعروف: «قَسَمْتُ الصلاةَ بيني وبين عبدي نصفين». وفيه: إذا قال العبد: ﴿إِيَّاكَ نَعْبُدُ وَإِيَّاكَ نَسْتَعِينُ﴾ يقول الربّ تعالى: «هذا بيني وبين عبدي» الخبر بتمامه.

وقال بعض أهل الإشارة إنّ الكاف والنون تواصلتا في الكلمتين. والكاف تقتضي المشاهدة إذ هي خطاب للحاضر؛ والنون تقتضي المجاهدة إذ هي حكايةٌ عن المستطيع القادر، وكما استنارت الكائنات باتّصال الكاف والنون عند الإبداع والتكوين، كذلك استنارت القلوب باتّصال الكاف والنون عند الطاعة والتسليم.

وقال بعضهم إنّ اسم الله يعطي معنى استحقاق العبادة. قال الله

تعالى: ﴿اِعْبُدُوا اللَّهَ﴾، وإن اسم الرحمن يعطي معنى استحقاق الاستعانة، قال الله تعالى: ﴿وَرَبُّنَا الرَّحْمَنُ المُسْتَعَانُ﴾. وإنّ اسم الرحيم يعطي معنى استحقاق الهداية. قال الله تعالى: ﴿هُدىً وَرَحْمَةً لِقَوْمٍ يُؤْمِنُونَ﴾. فكما كان ابتداء التعريف بهذه الأسامي الثلاثة، كذلك كان ابتداء التكليف بهذه المعاني الثلاثة. والله أعلم.

قوله جلّ وعزّ: إهدنا الصراط المستقيم

اللغة

قال أهل اللغة هديت فلاناً الطريق هدايةً، وهديته في الدين هدىً وهدايةً؛ والهادي الراشد الذي يدلّ على الطريق. والهادي: العنق، سمّي بذلك لأنّه يتقدّم الجسد. وهوادي الخيل والوحش هي التي تتقدّم للدلالة، ثمّ سمّي كلّ متقدّم هادياً، وإن لم يتقدم للدلالة ولذلك سمّي العنق هادياً. واهتدى افتعل من الهدى. ومنه قوله تعالى: ﴿فَإِنْ آمَنُوا بِمِثْلِ مَا آمَنْتُمْ بِهِ فَقَدِ اهتَدَوا﴾ أي أبصَروا رُشدهُم. وهَدَيتُ لَكَ: بمعنى بيّنْتُ لك. ومنه قوله تعالى: ﴿أوَلَمْ يَهدِ لَهُم﴾ أي لم يتبيّن لَهُم وقوله تعالى: ﴿وأمّا ثَمُودُ فَهَدَيْنَاهُم﴾ أي بيّنّا لَهُم.

وقال قوم: أصل الهداية الإحالة، يقال: هدَيتُ العروس إلى بيت زوجها (٤٠ب) هدياً، وأهديتها إهداءً، وأهديت الهديّة، أهديها إهداءً والهدية مصدرٌ أيضاً، ومن ذلك الهدي.

وفي الحديث: أنّ النبي (صلّى الله عليه وآله) خرج في مرضه الذي مات فيه يهادي بين اثنين، أي إنه كان يعتمد عليهما لضعفه وتمايله. والفعل منه يتعدّى إلى مفعولين. وإنما يتعدّى إلى الثاني بأحد حرفي الجرّ: إلى واللام. وقد يُحذَف حرف الجرّ، فيقال: هديته الطريق، وهو أفصح. ويقال: هديت هدي فلانٍ: إذا سرت سيرته.

قال المفضّل بن سلمة، قوله إهدنا أي زدنا هدىً وإرشاداً ولا تزغ

قلوبنا عنه بعد إذ هديتنا له.

وقال غيره: الهدى في القرآن على وجهين: هدى دعاء وبيان، كقوله تعالى: ﴿أَوَلَمْ يَهدِ لَهُم﴾، وقوله: ﴿وإنَّكَ لتَهْدِي إلَى صِرَاطٍ مُسْتَقِيْم﴾ وقال في صفة الشيطان: ﴿كُتِبَ عَلِيهِ أَنَّهُ مَنْ تَوَلَّاه فَإِنَّهُ يُضِلُّهُ ويَهْدِيْهِ إِلَى عَذَابِ السَّعِيرِ﴾ أي يدعوه، والثاني: هدى توفيق وبنيان، كقوله تعالى: ﴿يُضِلُّ مَنْ يَشَاءُ ويَهْدِيْ مَنْ يَشَاء﴾ وكقوله: ﴿واللهُ يَدْعُو إِلَى دَارِ السَّلَامِ ويَهْدِيْ مَنْ يَشَاءُ﴾ وقوله: ﴿لَوْ يَشَاءُ اللهُ لَهَدَى النَّاسَ جَمِيعاً﴾ وقوله: ﴿إنَّكَ لَا تَهْدِيْ مَنْ أَحْبَبْتَ ولَكِنَّ اللَّهَ يَهدِي مَن يَشَاءُ﴾ فالذي نُفِيَ عَنه هَدى التوفيق وخلق الإيمان، والذي أُثبِتَ لَهُ هُدى الدعوة والبيان. فقوله ﴿إهْدِنَا الصِّرَاطَ المُسْتَقِيْم﴾ أي وفّقنا وألهمنا وأرشدنا وثبّتنا. وقال بعض المتكلّمين: معناه اسلك بنا طريق الجنّة وقدّمنا إليه، كقوله تعالى: ﴿سَيَهدِيهِم ويُصلِحُ بَالَهم﴾.

التفسير والمعاني

وإنّما قاموا وقعدوا في تفسير «إهدِنَا» لإشكالٍ فيه من وجهين: أحدهما، أن السؤال إنّما يكون لشيءٍ مفقودٍ عند السائل، والموجود لا يُطلب بالسؤال. والثاني أنّ السؤال إنّما يكون إذا لم يعطه المسؤول، وإذا أزاح الله تعالى العلل بنصب الأدلة في الأفعال فقد هداهم وأغناهم عن السؤال. أمّا الأوّل فقد أجابوا عنه بأنّ معناه: ثبّتنا على صراطك المستقيم، وأما الثاني فقد أجابوا عنه بأحد وجهين: إمّا بالتوفيق وخلق الهداية، وذلك طريق الأشعريّة؛ وإما بالهداية إلى طريق الجنّة وذلك طريق المعتزلة. ولو عرفوا عمومات القرآن وخصوصاته في محكماته ومتشابهاته لما خبطوا خبط العشواء في ظلماته. ونعود إليه إن شاء الله.

قال المفسرون: الصراط المستقيم هو الطريق الواضح المستوي الذي لا عوج فيه ولا أَمْت، ولا اختلاف فيه في القول والعمل، ولا تناقض فيه في النفي والإثبات (١٤١آ). ثم قال بعضهم: هو كتاب الله، وهو قول

عليّ وعبد الله بن مسعود وأبي العالية. وقال جابر بن عبد الله والكلبيّ ومقاتل وعطاء عن ابن عباس: إنه الإسلام. وقال سعيد بن جبير والسُّدي: هو طريق الجنة. وروى عاصم الأحول عن أبي العالية الرياحي: أنه طريق رسول الله وصاحبيه من بعده أبي بكر وعمر (رضي الله عنهما)؛ قال عاصم: وذكرنا ذلك للحسن، فقال: صدق أبو العالية. وقال محمّد بن الحنفية: هو دين الله الذي لا يقبل غيره.

المعاني

وقال القفّال: المعنى هو السؤال من الله تعالى حتى يهديهم ويرشدهم الطريق الذي لا اعوجاج فيه ولا اختلاف ولا تناقض كتناقض أحوال أهل الكتابين واختلاف لواء المشركين؛ وتشبيه الحق بالصراط من جهة أنّ الحقّ كالطريق الواضح المسلوك المنصوب عليه الأعلام والمنار، وهو يفضي بصاحبه إلى حيث يقصده، وكذا الحق، أعلامه واضحة، ودلائله بيّنة لمن تدبرها، وهو يفضي بصاحبه إلى الصواب ونيل الثواب.

ثم بيّن الصراط المستقيم فقال عزّ من قائل:

صراط الذين أنعمت عليهم

التفسير

يعني مننت عليهم بالتوفيق والهداية والصواب في القول والعمل، وهم الأنبياء والأولياء (عليهم السلام)، وهم المذكورون في قوله تعالى: ﴿وَمَنْ يُطِعِ اللهَ وَالرَّسُولَ فَأُولَئِكَ مَعَ الَّذِينَ أَنْعَمَ اللَّهُ عَلَيْهِمْ مِنَ النَّبِيِّينَ وَالصِّدِّيقِينَ وَالشُّهَدَاءِ وَالصَّالِحِينَ﴾ وهو رواية عطاء وأبي روق عن الضحاك عن ابن عباس (رضي الله عنه).

وقال ابن عباس أيضاً: هم قوم موسى وعيسى (عليهما السلام) قبل التحريف. وقال عبد الرحمن بن زيد: هم النبيّ والمؤمنون. قال عكرمة: ﴿أَنْعَمْتَ عَلَيْهِمْ﴾ بالبيّنات على الإيمان والاستقامة. ونحوه قال أُبيّ بن

كعب والواقدي والحسن بن الفضل. وقال محمّد بن جرير: ﴿أَنْعَمْتَ عَلَيْهِمْ﴾ بالهداية إلى الصراط الحقّ، ووفّقتهم للسداد.

اللغة والمعاني

والنّعمة بكسر النون ما أنعم الله به على العبد من الملاذّ الدنيوية والمعارف الدينيّة. وبفتح النون هي التنعّم وسعة العيش، وقد نَعِمَ يَنْعَم نَعمةً فهو ناعم. وأنعمت عليه إنعاماً ونِعمةً.

واختلف أرباب الأصول في حقيقة النّعمة شرعاً وعقلاً. وقال قوم: هي اللّذة المطلقة. وقال قوم هي اللّذة الخالصة من شوائب الضّرر في العاجل والآجل، وعلى هذا القول ليس لله تعالى على الكافر نعمةٌ أصلاً لا دينية ولا دنيوية، وما يتنعّمون به مكرٌ واستدراج. وقال علي بن الحسين الواقدي: ﴿أَنْعَمْتَ عَلَيْهِمْ﴾ بالشكر على السرّاء والصبر على الضرّاء، وهذا مخصوص بالمؤمنين. وقال بعض أهل العلم: إنّ الصراط المستقيم (٤١ب) هو ما ذكره من ابتداء السورة إلى آخرها، من ذكر الأسامي والمحامد، والإخلاص في العبادة والاستعانة، وطلب الهداية على صراط الأنبياء والأولياء، والاستعاذة من طريق المغضوب عليهم والضالين.

[الأسرار]

قال الذين أنعم الله عليهم بالهداية: إن الله تعالى، كما عرّفنا كيف نحمده ونعبده وكيف نستعين به ونتوكّل عليه، كذلك عرّفنا كيف نسأل عند الحاجة، وأي الحاجات أهم، وأي السؤالات أتم. ولما كانت الهداية أهمّ المهمات للعبد، وأعمّ الحوائج في الدين والدنيا، والآخرة والأولى قرن الأهم والأعم بالعبادة والاستعانة وذلك وجه النّظم بين الآية السابقة وبين الآية اللاحقة.

وسرٌّ آخر أنّ المحامد والأثنية على الكمال قد سبقت. ومن إلتمسَ

حاجةً فيجب أن يقدّم ثناءً وحمداً للمحتاج إليه. كما أنّ من ذكر حمداً وثناءً لمستحقّ الحمد فيجب أن يعرض عليه حاجةً حتى يتبيّن أن المحمود منتهى مطلب الحاجات ومَن عنده نيل الطلبات، وأنه يُستغنى به ولا يُستغنى عنه، وأنه يُرغب إليه ولا يرغب عنه. فقرن أهمّ الحاجات وأعمّ المهمّات بأتمّ التحميدات وأكمل التمجيدات.

وأما السرّ في ﴿إِهْدِنَا الصِّرَاطَ المُسْتَقِيْم﴾ كيف قرن الصراط بإهدنا، مع أن الهداية تُعطي معنى الصراط، وكان من الواجب أن يُكتفى بذكرها، وكذلك الصراط يعطي معنى الاستقامة وقد وصفه بها، وعرّف الصراط المستقيم بقومٍ مخصوصين، وهم الذين أنعم عليهم من النبيين وأكّد ذلك بنفي طريق الأضداد الضالين المُضلّين أن الهداية يجري فيها التضادّ والترتّب.

أما التضادّ فمثل ما ورد في قوله تعالى: ﴿يَهْدِيْهِمْ إِلَى عَذَابِ السَّعِيْرِ﴾. فقد أثبت هدايةً إلى العذاب كما أثبت هدايةً إلى الثواب. وذلك هو التضاد. وأما الترتّب فمثل ما ورد في قوله تعالى: ﴿أَفَمَنْ يَهْدِي إِلَى الحَقِّ أَحَقُّ أَنْ يُتَّبَعَ أَمَّنْ لا يَهْدِيْ إلّا أَنْ يُهدَى﴾. فقد أثبت هادياً ومهتدياً، وذلك هو الترتّب. قوله: ﴿إِهْدِنَا الصِّرَاطَ المُسْتَقِيم﴾ لنفي ذلك الضدّ، وقوله: ﴿صِرَاطَ الَّذِينَ أَنْعَمْتَ عَلَيْهِم﴾ لإثبات هذا الترتّب.

وسرٌّ آخر: ﴿إِهْدِنَا﴾ طلب الهداية، وهو على الإطلاق، وقوله: ﴿الصِّرَاطَ المَسْتَقِيمَ﴾ تخصيصٌ لذلك المطلق. وقوله: ﴿صِرَاطَ الَّذِيْنَ أَنْعَمْتَ عَلَيْهِم﴾ تعيينٌ لذلك الخاص، وقوله: ﴿غَيْرِ المَغْضُوبِ عَلَيْهِمْ وَلَا الضَّالِّينَ﴾ تلخيصٌ لذلك المعيّن حتّى لا يبقى في السؤال شوب الإجمال.

وسرٌّ آخر أنّ طالب الهداية لا بدّ له من هادٍ يُسْعِفُهُ إلى طلبته. والهادي في الحقيقة هو الله عزّ وجلّ، لكنّه أضاف هدايته إلى قومٍ مخصوصين قد عرّف الصراط بهم، فقال: ﴿صِرَاطَ الَّذِيْنَ (٤٢آ) أَنْعَمْتَ

عَلَيْهِم﴾ لتعرف أنّ في العالم قوماً قد أنعم الله عليهم بالهداية وقوماً قد وفّقهم الله لطلب الهداية، فيكون أحدهما عالماً، والثاني متعلّماً. وأحدهما هادياً والثاني مهتدياً، وهما مزدوجان، فصارا المثنى السادس من المثاني السبعة.

وسرٌّ آخر أنّ طالب الهداية مبتدئٌ وله حكم المبتدأ والمستأنف؛ والهادي للطالب منتهٍ، وله حكم الكامل والمفروغ، فيتبيّن في ذكر الفريقين حكم الكونين، ويتحقق كون الحكمين، وأنّ العالم ليس يخلو عن الذين أنعم الله عليهم بالهداية، وهم المفروغون البالغون الكاملون، كما ليس يخلو عن الذين وفّقهم الله لطلب الهداية وهم المبتدئون المتوجّهون إلى الكمال.

وسرٌّ آخر أنّ العموم والخصوص جاريان في الهداية جريانهما في سائر الألفاظ والمعاني، ولله عزّ وجلّ هدايةٌ عامة سارية في جميع الموجودات على حسب أوضاعها وطباعها وخصوصاً في الحيوانات، فإنّ كلّ حيوانٍ مخصوصٌ بهدايةٍ إلى مصالح وجوده وبقائه باستحفاظ نوعه وشخصه، وذلك بالطبع والفطرة دون التعليم والفكرة؛ وأخصّ منه هداية الإنسان، فإنّه مخصوصٌ بهدايةٍ إلى مصالح وجوده وبقائه باستحفاظ نوعه وشخصه واستصلاح غير نوعه، وذلك بالتعليم والفكرة، وأخصّ منه هداية الأنبياء والأولياء (عليهم السلام)، فإنّهم مخصوصون بهدايةٍ إلى مصالح وجودهم وبقائهم باستحفاظ نوعهم وشخصهم واستصلاح غير نوعهم من الإنسان في معاشهم ومعادهم، وذلك بالوحي والإلهام، وكما صار الإنسان مَلِكاً على أنواع الحيوانات بالهداية الخاصة له كذلك صار النبي (عليه السلام) مَلِكاً على أصناف الإنسان بالهداية الخاصة به. وكما صارت حركات الإنسان معجزات الحيوان، أعني حركاته الفكرية والقولية والعملية، كذلك صارت حركات الأنبياء (عليهم السلام) معجزات الإنسان، أعني حركاتهم الفطرية والوحيية

والخلقية، فهم الذين أنعم الله (عزّ وجلّ) عليهم بالهداية العلوية القدسية؛ وصراطهم صراط الله؛ ودينهم صبغة الله؛ وشريعتهم شرعة الله؛ فمن اقتدى بهم فهو المهتدي إلى الصراط المستقيم، ومن اعتدى عليهم فهو الهاوي إلى سواء الجحيم.

وإذا عَرَفت مراتب العموم والخصوص في الهداية، اطلعت على مزلّة أقدام الضالين فيها؛ وإنّ الذين قالوا من القدريّة إنّ الله تعالى قد يهدي المؤمن والكافر بنصب الآيات والأدلّة، وإنما يهتدي من نظر فيها واعتبر، وإنما ضلّ من نَازَلَ واستكبر، وحملوا عليه قوله تعالى: ﴿وأَمَّا ثَمُودُ فَهَدَيْنَاهُم (٤٢ب) فَاسْتَحَبُّوْا العَمَى عَلَى الهُدَى﴾ فقد ضلّوا إذ حكموا بعموم الهداية دون الخصوص. وإن الذين قالوا من الجبريّة: إنّ الله تعالى قد هدى المؤمن دون الكافر بالتوفيق وخلق الإيمان فمن اهتدى فبهداية الله، ومن ضلّ فإضلال الله، وحملوا عليه قوله عزّ وجلّ ﴿مَنْ يَهْدِ اللهُ فَهُو المُهْتَدِي وَمَنْ يُضْلِلْ فَأُولئِكَ هُمُ الخَاسِرُونَ﴾ فَقَد ضَلُّوا إذ حكموا بخصوص الهداية دون العموم.

وأين الفريقان المختصمان من معرفة أسرار القرآن في العموم والخصوص، والتضادّ والترتّب، والمفروغ والمستأنف، وإثبات الكونين وتقرير الحكمين؟ ﴿أَفَلَا يَتَدَبَّرُونَ القُرْآنَ أَمْ عَلَى قُلُوبٍ أَقْفَالُهَا﴾.

وسرٌّ آخر، ظهور المعاني بالكلمات والأسامي أمرٌ معلوم، وذلك هو التفسير، لكنّ تشخيص الأسامي والمعاني بالأشخاص والأعيان أمرٌ مشكل، وذلك هو التأويل. وكما إنّ رحمة الله عزّ وجلّ مشخّصة بشخص هو النبي (صلّى الله عليه وآله) بعينه وشخصه بدليل قوله تعالى: ﴿وَمَا أَرْسَلْنَاكَ إلّا رَحْمَةً لِلْعَالَمِينَ﴾ كذلك نعمة الله (عزّ وجلّ) متشخّصة بشخصه (عليه وآله السلام)، بدليل قوله: ﴿يَعْرِفُونَ نِعْمَةَ اللهِ ثُمّ يُنْكِرُونَهَا﴾، فالرّحمة والنّعمة في التنزيل على الإطلاق يعمّان الموجودات عموم الوجود والكرم في وجودها وبقائها ودفع الآفات

عنها؛ وهما في التأويل على التعيين يخصّان شخصاً أو شخصين خصوص اللّطف والقربة في أحوال وجودهما وبقاء نوعهما ودفع الآفات عنهما.

وكما أنّ الحمد والمُلك موضوعان للثناء والمجد لغةً وتنزيلاً، كذلك هما موضوعان على شخصين معيّنين معنىً وتأويلاً. فرحمة الله رجلٌ من الرجال، ونعمة الله شخصٌ على الكمال. والحمد لله حامدٌ له على كلّ حال، والمُلك لله مُلكٌ شديد المحال. وفي القرآن: ﴿لَهُ الْمُلْكُ وَلَهُ الْحَمْدُ﴾ وفيه: «لَهُ الْحَمْدُ وَلَهُ الْمُلْك». واللام قد تكون لام التمليك وقد تكون لام التخصيص، وعلى هذا المنهاج: الصراط في التنزيل طريقٌ مستقيمٌ، وفي التأويل شخصٌ مستقيم.

قوله عزّ وجلّ: غير المغضوب عليهم ولا الضالين

النحو [والقراءة]

قال أهل النحو في انخفاض «غير» أربعة أوجهٍ: أحدها – لأنّه بدلٌ عن الذين. والثاني – لأنه نعت الذين. والثالث – لأنّه بدلٌ أو صفةٌ لضمير عليهم. والرابع – أنّه على نيّة تكرير الصراط.

وتوجيه الأقوال

قال الفرّاء: «الذين» معرفةٌ ولا توصف المعارف بالنكرات، ولا النكرات بالمعارف، إلا أن «الذين» (٤٣آ) ليس معرفةً موقّتة كزيد وعمرو، وإنما هي كالنكرات المجملات مثل «الرجل» و«البعير»، فإذا كان «غير» مضافاً إلى مجهول من الأسماء كان نظير اسم هو معرفةٌ غير مؤقتةٍ فجاز أن يُنعت به، كما يقول: صراطُ القاصد غيرُ الجائر. ولو كان اسماً مؤقّتاً محدوداً كعبد الله وزيدٍ لم يجز أن ينعت بنكرةٍ.

وقال أبو علي: لو قلت إن غير تنخفض على البدل من «الذين» كان صحيحا؛ والفرق بين البدل والصفة، في قول سيبويه أنّ البدل على

تقدير تكرير العامل بدلالة جواز تكرير حرف الجرّ صريحاً، مثل قوله تعالى: ﴿قَالَ المَلأُ الَّذِينَ اسْتَكْبَرُوا مِنْ قَوْمِهِ لِلَّذِينَ اسْتُضْعِفُوا لِمَن آمَنَ مِنْهُمْ﴾، وأما الصفة فلا تستدعي تكرير العامل.

وأما صرف الخفض إلى ضمير «عليهم» إمّا بدلاً وإمّا صفةً كصرفه إلى «الذين».

وأما الوجه الرابع وهو بنيّة تكرير «الصراط» فتقديره: صراطَ غيرِ المغضوب عليهم. وقال أبو بكر السرّاج: إنّ «غير» مع ما أضيف إليه معرفة؛ وهو صفة الذين أُنعِم عليهم بالإيمان، ومن أُنعِم عليه فهو غير مغضوبٍ عليه.

وروى الخليل عن ابن كثير: ﴿غَيْرَ المَغْضُوبِ عَلَيْهِمْ﴾ بالنصب وله وجهان: أحدهما: الحال من الذين، أو الهاء والميم من عليهم، أي لا مغضوباً عليهم. والثاني: الاستثناء، وتقديره إلّا المغضوب عليهم.

وروي عن عمر وعليّ أنهما قرآ ﴿وغيرَ الضَّالِّينَ﴾.

وأما إعادة «لا» على قراءة العامة في قوله ﴿وَلَا الضَّالِّينَ﴾ قال أبو عبيدة: إنها من حروف الزوائد لتتميم الكلام يستحسن إيرادها، والمعنى إلغاؤها. كما قال العجاج: «في بئر لا حُورٍ سرى وما شعر» أي في بئر حور. فمعناه إذاً: والضالين، كقوله تعالى: ﴿وَمَا يَسْتَوِيْ الأَحْيَاءُ وَلَا الأَمْوَاتُ﴾.

وقال الفراء: معنى «غير» هاهنا معنى «لا»، وهو كقولك: فلانٌ غير محسنٍ ولا مجمل. وقال الزجاج: إنما جاز أن يُعطف بلا على «غير» لأن «غير» يتضمّن معنى النفي فهو بمعنى «غير المغضوب عليهم وغير الضالين» وكذلك قال المبرد. وقال صاحب النظم: إنما زيدت «لا» تأكيداً للنفي، وتبييناً أنّ الضالين هم غير المغضوب عليهم، ولو عُطِف عليه من غير ذكر لا احتمل أن يكون «والضالين» نعتاً للمغضوب عليهم.

التفسير

وأما التفسير فقد روى عديّ بن حاتم عن النبي أنه قال: ﴿غَيْرِ المَغْضُوبِ عَلَيْهِمْ﴾ اليهود، ﴿وَلَا الضَّالِّينَ﴾ النصارى؛ وهذا قول ابن عباس (٤٣ ب) وابن مسعود ومجاهد والكلبي والسدّي ومقاتل، وتصديق ذلك قوله تعالى في اليهود: ﴿مَنْ لَعَنَهُ اللهُ وغَضِبَ عَلَيْهِ﴾ وقوله في النصارى: ﴿لَا تَتَّبِعُوا أَهْوَاءَ قَوْمٍ قَدْ ضَلُّوا مِنْ قَبلُ﴾.

وروى الضحّاك عن ابن عباس (رضي الله عنه) أنه كان يقول: «اللهم ألهمنا دينك الحقّ، وهو: لا إله إلّا الله وحده لا شريكَ له، حتّى لا تغضب علينا كما غضب على اليهود، ولا تُضلّنا كما أضللت النصارى، فتعذّبنا كما عذّبتهم».

وقال الفراء ليس ينكر أن يكون اليهود ضالّين والنصارى مغضوباً عليهم، وكذلك المشركون. ثم تفرّد كلّ فريق منهم باسمٍ يعرف به، كما إن الضالين كلّهم مشركون. ثم يختصّ اسم الشرك بمن لا كتاب له.

المعاني

وقد قيل في التفسير إنّ الغضب من الله تعالى يُذكر بمعنيين: أحدهما إرادة العقوبة، والثاني العقوبة نفسها. وقيل إنّ المغضوب عليه من لا يرجى عوده إلى الصراط المستقيم، والضالين من لا ينقطع الرجاء عنهم؛ فإنّ من غضب الله عليه ولعنه فقد سبق علمه فيه أنه الكافر الذي يموت على كفره؛ ومن ضلّ عن الطريق فربما يهتدي بعد الضلال.

والمعنى في قوله ﴿غَيْرِ المَغْضُوبِ عَلَيْهِمْ﴾ أي غير الذين غضبت عليهم.

قال الأخفش: كلّ فعلٍ تعدّى إلى مفعوله بحرف الجرّ كان جمعه وتثنيته في المكنّى المتصل بحرف الجر، كقولك: المأخوذ منه ومنهم

ومنها، والممرور به وبهما وبهم. فعلامة الجمع والتثنية والتذكير والتأنيث تلحق بأواخر الأسماء عند تمامها.

اللغة

والضّلال في اللغة الغيبوبة. يقال ضلّ الماء في اللبن إذا غاب. وضلّ الكافر إذا غاب عن المحجّة، وعدل عن قصد السبيل؛ والضلال الهلاك وهو راجعٌ إلى الغيبوبة. وقد يطلق الضلال على الإفراط في المحبة، وهو أيضاً راجعٌ إلى الغيبوبة، وعليه يحمل قوله تعالى: ﴿إِنَّكَ لَفِي ضَلالِكَ القَدِيمِ﴾.

الأسرار

قال الذين أوتوا العلم والإيمان واطّلعوا على أسرار القرآن: إن الناس اثنان عالمٌ ومتعلّم، وهادٍ وطالبٌ، وسائر الناس همج، وهم أيضاً اثنان: واحدٌ في مقابلة العالم الهادي بالضدّ، وواحدٌ في مقابلة المتعلّم الطالب بالضدّ. فالمغضوب عليهم هم خصماء العلماء من الأنبياء والأولياء (عليهم السلام). والضالون هم خصماء المتعلمين الطالبين من المؤمنين، لينطبق القسمان في جانب الباطل على القسمين في جانب الحقّ؛ وهما مزدوجان، وذلك هو المثنى السابع.

وسرٌّ آخر أنّ الأنبياء والأولياء عليهم السلام لما كانوا عالمين بالفطرة ولهم حكم المفروغ عنهم (٤٤آ) إذ بلغوا النهاية والكمال، ولذلك عرّف الصراط بهم، وأفاض نعمة الهداية عليهم. كذلك الذين خاصموهم بالتضاد، لهم حكم المغضوب عليهم باللعنة، المفروغ عنهم بتمام الضلالة المأيوس منهم في الرشاد والهداية.

وكما إن المتعلمين هم على حدّ البداية ولهم حكم المستأنف والمبتدأ، كذلك الذين قابلوهم بالتضاد من الضالين ليس لهم حكم الذين غضب الله عليهم، ولا فرغ عنهم بتمام الضّلالة، ولم يتحقّق

اليأس عنهم في الرشد والهداية بل هم على حدّ الإمكان من الخروج عن الضّلال إلى الهدى والإيمان. فتقابل الفريقان مفروغاً ومستأنفاً وتعارض القسمان حقاً وباطلاً ونعمةً وغضباً وهدايةً وضلالةً. والترتّب، وإن كان بجانب الحقّ أولى، إلّا إنّ التفاوت في جانب الباطل كالترتّب في جانب الحق.

ولقد آتيناك سبعاً من المثاني
مجموع ما ذكرناه من الأسرار

بسـم اللـه | **الرحمـن** | **الرحيـم**

مثنى (أ)

على المبادئ — عموم الرحمة — خصوص الرحمة

الكلمـات التامـات — على الأوساط

المقدسات — **مثنى (ب)** — فسأكتبها للذين

الحمد لله — ورحمتي [وسعت] كل شيء — يتقون

على الكمالات — رحمن الدنيا — رحيم الآخرة

الكلمـات الكاملـات — النعمة الظاهرة — النعمة الباطنة

المشخصات

مثنى (ج)

رب العالمين — **الرحمـن** — **الرحيـم**

الخلق الدنيا — رحمة الخلق — رحمة الأجر

المبدأ — والأمر — والثواب

المعاد — **مثنـى(د)**

ملك يوم الديـن

الأمر الآخرة

مثنى (هـ)

إياك نعبد — لا جبر

التزام التكليف — حكم المستأنف على الاستطاعة

(اعملوا) ولا إهمال

وإياك نستعين — ولا تفويض

طلب التوفيق — حكم المفروغ على الاستعانة والاستقلال،

وكل ميسّر لما خُلق له.

مثنى (و)

اهدنا الصراط المستقيم — المتوجه إلى الكمال (المتعلم)

طلب الهداية

[illegible]

صراط الذين أنعمت عليهم — الكامل المفروغ (العالم).

هداية الطالب

التضاد

غير المغضوب عليهم — التفاوت

المُضِل

ولا الضالّين

المَضْلول

مثنى (ز)

(٤٤ب) ومن أسرار الفاتحة الكلام على أعداد الآيات والكلمات والحروف، وتقدير العدد فيها على المعدود. وأنت تعرف أنّ الفاتحة سورةٌ واحدة، ثم قسّمت نصفين كما ورد: «قسمتُ الصلاةَ بيني وبين عبدي..» وعرفت أنّ النصف الأوّل تعريفٌ والنصف الثاني تكليف.

ثم قسّمت أثلاثاً، فثلث محامد الله تعالى خاصةً، وثلثٌ محاوج العبد خاصةً، وثلثٌ بينهما. كما قال (عزّ وجلّ) في ﴿إِيَّاكَ نَعْبُدُ وَإِيَّاكَ نَسْتَعِيْن﴾: «هذا بيني وبين عبدي».

ثم قسّمت أرباعاً، وهي الوقوف الأربعة فيها: «الرحيم»، «الدين»، «نستعين»، «الضالين». وفي المعنى: التسمية، والتحميد، والتعبّد، والهداية.

ثم قسّمت أخماساً وهي: الأسامي، والمحامد، والتعبّد، والحاجة إلى التوفيق، وطلب الهداية.

ثم قُسّمت أسداساً وهي الأسامي على المبادئ، والمحامد على الكمالات، وإفاضة الرحمة على عالمي الخلق والأمر، وإقامة الطاعة في حالتي الاستطاعة والاستعانة، والتولي لأولياء الله والتبرّي من أعداء الله.

ثم قسّمت أسباعاً وهي سبع آياتٍ متناسبة المبادئ والمقاطع، وهي السّبع المثاني متوازية الألفاظ والمعاني.

ثم كلماتها التامّات، التي يفهم من كلّ واحدةٍ منها معنى تامٌّ، اثنتا عشرة كلمةً. ثم كلماتها المفردات ثمان وعشرون كلمةً، ثم حروفها إن عدّت على ولاء المكتوب فمائة واثنان وأربعون، وإن عدّت على ولاء الملفوظ فمائةٌ وأربعة وأربعون، وهي من ضرب اثني عشر في اثني عشر.

ومن الذي يعرف أسرار هذه الأعداد وتركيبها على المعدودات، وأن الوحدة فيها تقابل وحدة الأمر، وأن الاثنين فيها تقابل العالمين: عالمي الخلق والأمر، والجسماني والروحاني، وأن الثلاثة فيها تقابل المبادئ

الأولى: الأمر والقلم واللوح، وأن الأربعة فيها تقابل كلّ ما هو أربعةٌ، وأنّ الخمسة فيها تقابل كلّ ما هو خمسةٌ، وكذلك الستة والسبعة والاثنا عشر والثمانية والعشرون حتى يتقرّر أن العالم كلّه فيها، وهي مفاتيح الغيب ومقاليد السماوات والأرض، وفاتحة كلّ كمالٍ، وخاتمة كلّ مقالٍ، فتحت بالثناء، وختمت بالدعاء، وهي شفاء من كلّ داءٍ.

وفي الخبر عن النبي: «كل ما لا يشفيه الحمد لا يشفيه شيءٌ» وعن عبد الله بن عباس: «إن علياً (رضي الله عنه) ابتدأ معي شرح الفاتحة من العتمة (٤٥آ) فأصبحنا وما فرغ عن شرح باء ﴿بِسْمِ اللَّهِ﴾».

وعن بعض العلماء أن كلّ ما هو مذكورٌ في الكتب المنزلة فهو مذكورٌ في القرآن، وكلّ ما هو مذكورٌ في القرآن فهو مذكورٌ في الفاتحة، وكل ما هو مذكور في الفاتحة فهو مذكور في ﴿بِسْمِ اللَّهِ الرَّحْمَنِ الرَّحِيمِ﴾، وكلّ ما هو مذكورٌ في ذلك فهو مذكور في باء ﴿بِسْمِ اللَّهِ﴾. ولا تعجب من ذلك ومِن قولهم؛ إن الأحكام الشرعية كلّها مذكورةٌ في كلمة «لا إله إلا الله» وأنت تعرف أن أعضاء الإنسان كلّها مخفيةٌ في نطفته، وأنّ أجزاء الشجرة كلّها مستبطنة في نواتها، وإنما تبصرها عين البالغين من الرجال.

III

The Arabic text

Mafātīḥ al-asrār maṣābīḥ al-abrār